The 2005-
Arriv
Bus Hand

CW00519008

British Bus Publishing

Body codes used in the Bus Handbook series:

Type:
A	Articulated vehicle
B	Bus, either single-deck or double-deck
BC	Interurban - high-back seated bus
C	Coach
M	Minibus with design capacity of 16 seats or less
N	Low-floor bus (*Niederflur*), either single-deck or double-deck
O	Open-top bus (CO = convertible - PO = partial open-top)

Seating capacity is then shown. For double-decks the upper deck quantity is followed by the lower deck.

Door position:-
C	Centre entrance/exit
D	Dual doorway.
F	Front entrance/exit
R	Rear entrance/exit (no distinction between doored and open)
T	Three or more access points

Equipment:-
L	Lift for wheelchair	TV	Training vehicle.
M	Mail compartment	RV	Used as tow bus or engineers vehicle.
T	Toilet	w	Vehicle is withdrawn and awaiting disposal.

e.g. - B32/28F is a double-deck bus with thirty-two seats upstairs, twenty-eight down and a front entrance/exit.
N43D is a low-floor bus with two or more doorways.

Re-registrations:-
Where a vehicle has gained new index marks the details are listed at the end of each fleet showing the current mark, followed in sequence by those previously carried starting with the original mark.

Regional books in the series:
The Scottish Bus Handbook
The Ireland & Islands Bus Handbook
The North East Bus Handbook
The Yorkshire Bus Handbook
The North West Bus Handbook
The East Midlands Bus Handbook
The West Midlands Bus Handbook
The Welsh Bus Handbook
The Eastern Bus Handbook
The London Bus Handbook
The South East Bus Handbook
The South West Bus Handbook

Annual books are produced for the major groups:
The Stagecoach Bus Handbook
The Go-Ahead Bus Handbook
The First Bus Handbook
The Arriva Bus Handbook
The National Express Handbook (bi-annual)
Most editions for earlier years are available direct from the publisher .

Associated series:
The Hong Kong Bus Handbook
The Malta Bus Handbook
The Leyland Lynx Handbook
The Model Bus Handbook
The Postbus Handbook
The Overall Advertisment Bus Handbook - Volume 1
The Toy & Model Bus Handbook - Volume 1 - Early Diecasts
The Fire Brigade Handbook (fleet list of each local authority fire brigade)
The Police Range Rover Handbook

2005-2006 Arriva Bus Handbook

The Arriva Bus Handbook is a special edition of the *Bus Handbook* series which contains the various fleets of Arriva plc, one of the major operators across Europe. The *Bus Handbook* series is published by British Bus Publishing, an independent publisher of quality books for the industry and bus enthusiasts. Further information on these may be obtained from the address below.

Although this book has been produced with the encouragement of, and in co-operation with, Arriva plc management, it is not an official group fleet list and the vehicles included are subject to variation, particularly as the vehicle investment programme continues. Some vehicles listed are no longer in regular use on services but are retained for special purposes. Also, out of use vehicles awaiting disposal are not all listed. The services operated and the allocation of vehicles to subsidiary companies are subject to variation at any time, although accurate at the time of going to print.

To keep the fleet information up to date we recommend the Ian Allan publication *Buses*, published monthly or, for more detailed information, the PSV Circle monthly news sheets.

Edited by Bill Potter, Stuart Martin and David Donati

Acknowledgments:
We are most grateful to Keith Grimes, Mark Jameson, Tom Johnson, Harry Laming, Colin Lloyd, Colin Martin, Kevin O'Leary, the PSV Circle and the management and officials of Arriva Group plc, and their operating companies, for their kind assistance and co-operation in the compilation of this book.

ISBN 1 904875 25 4

Published by *British Bus Publishing Ltd*
16 St Margaret's Drive, Telford, TF1 3PH

© British Bus Publishing Ltd, September 2005
Telephone 01952 255669 - Facsimile 01952 222397 - www.britishbuspublishing.co.uk

Contents

ARRIVA plc

The Arriva Group: A Company Profile

Arriva plc is firmly established as one of Britain's top 250 companies quoted on the London Stock Exchange and is one of the largest transport services organisations in Europe, providing more than one billion passenger journeys a year. Its operations include an extensive range of services including buses, trains, commuter coaches and water buses. It operates a national vehicle rental business in the UK and is engaged in bus and coach distribution. In 2003, Arriva bus Group turnover was £1.751 billion, and it employed around 30,000 staff.

Arriva is one of the UK's largest bus operators, with over 6,000 vehicles serving customers in the North East, North West, London and the South East of England, Yorkshire, the Midlands, Wales and Scotland. Many of Arriva's UK Bus division's operating companies are long established but the grouping emerged out of the privatisation of public sector transport companies, pursuant to the Transport Act 1985, and the subsequent consolidation of the sector. The division is organised into autonomous operating subsidiaries in order that management teams and staff can focus upon the discrete local and regional markets that they serve.

The core activity is the operation of urban, interurban and rural local bus services, demand-responsive transit, commuter and express coach services within England, Scotland and Wales. Arriva is the second largest bus operator in the UK, and is the largest operator in London covering 18.5 per cent of the scheduled network.

Additionally, Arriva operates bus, train, coach, demand responsive and disabled persons travel in Denmark, Germany, Italy, the Netherlands, Portugal, Spain and Sweden. Arriva offers local and regional rail passenger services in the UK, Denmark, Germany and the Netherlands. The Group makes significant capital investment in the replacement and improvement of assets. Over the last five years, £250 million was spent on capital investment in equipment and facilities for Arriva's UK Bus division alone. As a result of recent investment, the bus fleet has been substantially modernised.

Recent years have witnessed a renewed interest in rapid transit systems and the development of intermediate technologies. Arriva has been actively positioning itself within this broadened public transport market. It has been a leading member of a number of consortia bidding to fund, design, build and operate tram and guided bus systems. With FirstGroup, Arriva is one of the operators of the East Leeds guided bus system, Elite. In addition, Arriva is working with Luton Borough Council on the proposed Luton-Dunstable Translink system.

After the original South Leeds scheme fell, West Yorkshire PTE continued to press the case for its tramway scheme and received initial approval in 2001. The Leeds Supertram project, based on the South Leeds route plus a northern and an eastern route was agreed by Government and new bids for the concession were invited. To bid for this concession, Arriva formed a new consortium, named Airelink. The other partners in the consortium are Transdev, AMEC and Siemens. The two consortia listed for the project submitted bids in 2002. West Yorkshire PTE and the Government have been involved since that date in a continuing dialogue about the costs and benefits of the scheme, which should be resolved in 2004. In the UK, Arriva's UK Trains division operates two rail passenger operating companies. Arriva Trains Wales/Trenau Arriva Cymru operates interurban, commuter and rural passenger services throughout Wales and the border counties. Northern operates extensively across the north of England. Arriva continues to pursue a European strategy, which has resulted in acquisitions in Denmark, Germany, Italy, the Netherlands, Portugal, Spain and Sweden recently, with opportunities being actively pursued in other countries and geographical regions in Europe. A fundamental aspect of the European strategy is to invest both in companies and in management teams in order to ensure local market knowledge and expertise.

Arriva Bus and Coach is the group's bus and coach distribution business with exclusive import rights for all VDL chassis supported by a wide range of bus and coach bodywork options, from Van Hool of Belgium, Ikarus from Hungary and Plaxton from the UK, to meet new market demands.

In 2001, Arriva took the first double-deck buses built by Wrights of Ballymena. Many similar buses are now in service with London operators, mostly on Volvo chassis but Arriva London is currently taking delivery of its second batch on DAF chassis, which will bring its fleet of Wright's double-decks to 199 on Volvo and 93 on DAF chassis. Arriva has also made its first purchases of East Lancs bodywork for some years.

In 2004, Arriva invested in excess of £10 million in Project Overdrive – an investment programme in the Medway Towns which saw 61 new vehicles together with a further 40 refurbished modern vehicles introduced in a single day. The investment was complemented by improvements to service levels and infrastructure.

Now to some historical background to a group with a complex pedigree.

COWIE

The Cowie name - early years

In 1931, the Cowie family started a motorcycle repair business in Sunderland. In 1934 the first sales outlet opened on what became the location of the Group Head Offices. Business came to a halt in 1942 because of the effects of the war, but reopened in 1948 and benefited from the boom in personal mobility offered by the motorcycle. A second motorcycle shop was opened in Newcastle in 1952. Further expansion occurred in 1955 with another branch in Newcastle, and new branches in Durham and Stockton-on-Tees. A move into the Scottish market was taken with the acquisition of the J R Alexander motorcycle dealerships in Edinburgh and Glasgow in 1960. However, there were signs that the market was moving against the motorcycle, and in favour of the motor car which was becoming a more mass market item in availability and price.

In 1962, Cowie acquired its first car dealership in Sunderland, and such was the pace of change that, by 1963, motor car sales constituted 80% of revenue. On the back of this change, a public company, T Cowie plc, was formed in 1965 and, in that year, a further two car dealerships were acquired, one in Redcar and a second in Sunderland. In 1967, there was investment in new car showrooms for the Ford franchise in Sunderland; there has been a long association with Ford over the years. In 1971, this was strengthened with the acquisition of Ford Blackburn and a further Ford dealership, this time in Middlesbrough. By 1971, the group turnover reached £8m per annum.

Growing on the motor business

In 1972 a new business was set up in the form of Cowie Contract Hire. This and its successors grew to be a large element of the present group.

The first exposure to the bus and coach industry came in 1980. In that year, Cowie took over The George Ewer Group which had various motor interests including Eastern Tractors and these assets were bought with the business. It also included the long established Grey Green coach operation and this was to lead to a sea change in the make-up of the business.

In 1984 Cowie acquired the Hanger Group and this brought Ford dealerships in Nottingham and Birmingham and, significantly, Interleasing, the contract hire business. Expansion continued in 1987 when seven main dealerships were acquired from the Heron Group. On the leasing side, Marley Leasing was acquired. Further growth in this business area came in 1991 when RoyScot Drive and Ringway Leasing were also acquired, adding to the prominence of this activity for the group.

1992 was the year that Cowie very nearly took another step into the bus and coach market, narrowly failing to purchase Henlys which, by that time, had ownership of Plaxtons along with several car franchises. Consolation came with the addition of a Ford dealership in Swindon, a Peugeot dealership in Middlesbrough, and a Toyota dealership in Wakefield. In 1993, the Keep Trust Group was acquired, the dealership network being boosted by 70%.

Another notable event in 1993 was the retirement of Sir Tom Cowie, the Chairmanship of the business being taken up by Sir James McKinnon in 1994 and continuing until he retired at the end of 1999, when Gareth Cooper took over the role.

Explosion into Buses!

The Cowie group's first involvement with the bus and coach sector came with the purchase of the Ewer Group in 1980. Its subsidiary, Grey Green, was a most distinguished name in coaching but, under the Ewer Group, had already started to operate bus services for London Transport.

Grey Green, which had operating bases in Stamford Hill and Dagenham in London, and in Ipswich in East Anglia, participated in historic operations such as East Anglian Express, the Eastlander Pool, and joint services to Scotland in association with Scottish Bus Group. Private Hire coaching also played a large part in the business.

Great opportunities were perceived in the 1980s in commuter coaching after the deregulation of coach services under the 1980 Act. Commuter coach services thrived for a while, but the involvement in British Coachways was not successful. In the mid 1980s, Grey Green's involvement in the East Anglian Express Pool was taken into the National Express operation.

Early success in London Bus tendering brought Grey Green operation into to the very heart of London, notably on route 24 which passes the Palace of Westminster. After that, Grey Green gradually ceased all coach activities and concentrated entirely on tendered bus services in London.

The privatisation of the newly created subsidiaries of London Buses offered the opportunity to build on the favourable experience of Grey Green in the London bus market. Leaside was acquired in 1994 and was renamed Cowie Leaside. Later in 1995, the South London company was purchased, becoming Cowie South London. These two acquisitions made Cowie the largest single operator in the London Buses area. As the London operations were tidied up, the former Kentish Bus/Londonlinks operations at Cambridge Heath, Battersea, Croydon (Beddington Farm) and Walworth, and the East Herts & Essex operations from Edmonton were gradually incorporated into the London operation.

In 1996, Cowie purchased County Bus from the National Express Group, adding to the group's presence in the south-east of England. Then, in August 1996, Cowie completed the acquisition of British Bus plc and, at a stroke, became the second largest bus operating group in the United Kingdom. The acquisition of British Bus plc added a whole raft of bus companies across the country and very nearly brought all the disparate elements of the former London Country company, including Green Line Travel, under one ownership. There was a Monopolies and Mergers Commission inquiry into the acquisition of British Bus, with particular focus on the situation in London and the South East, but the report did not require any divestment.

The final acquisition of 1996, also in August, brought another previously divided company back under common ownership. In 1986, United Automobile Services had been split into two separate companies for privatisation: North East Bus and Northumbria. Northumbria was sold to Proudmutual, a company which had been set up to facilitate the management buyout and was acquired by Cowie in 1994. United Auto was sold in December 1987 to Caldaire who sold it on, as North East Bus, to West Midlands Travel. West Midlands Travel itself then merged with the National Express Group which decided to concentrate on its core operations and, in 1996, sold first County Bus then North East Bus to Cowie/Arriva.

The former British Bus headquarters at Salisbury, which dated back to Drawlane days, was wound down and closed at the end of 1996, with the group administration being moved to Sunderland.

BRITISH BUS

The growth of British Bus plc

With the acquisition of British Bus plc, Cowie became the second largest bus operating group in the United Kingdom. This move led to the reclassification of the enlarged group from being motor trade to transport.

Drawlane Ltd

The privatisation of the National Bus Company followed the 1985 Transport Act with the National Bus Company becoming a vendor unit selling its subsidiaries to pre-qualified parties. Endless Holdings Ltd was one of those interested parties, being a group of companies based in the cleaning and building management sector with a head office on Endless Street in Salisbury. The prime mover in Endless was Ray McEnhill. Endless set up a subsidiary called Drawlane Ltd to bid for NBC companies as they were made ready for sale.

The first company bought by Drawlane was Shamrock & Rambler in July 1987. This was the major part of the coaching activities of Hants and Dorset and was based at a modern depot in Bournemouth. The business was heavily dependent on National Express contracts, although a minibus operation was set up to compete with Yellow Buses in the Bournemouth area. Shamrock & Rambler did not survive for long: their bus operations were quickly reduced in scale, and difficulties with the National Express contracts led to notice of termination being given to Shamrock & Rambler which sealed its fate. National Express set up a local joint venture company called Dorset Travel Services Ltd to take over the workings of Shamrock & Rambler using other vehicles and based as a tenant of Yellow Buses at Mallard Road. Yellow Buses eventually purchased Dorset Travel Services. The Shamrock & Rambler vehicles were dispersed around the then Drawlane Group fleets and Shamrock & Rambler was wound up.

Drawlane was preferred bidder for three more companies: Southern National, North Devon, and London Country (South West). Each purchaser was limited to three NBC companies in the first instance. However there was concern that Drawlane might be related to another bidder called Allied Bus which had been selected as preferred bidder for another three companies: Lincolnshire Road Car, East Midland Motor Services and Midland Red North. The concern was sufficient for the preferred bidder status to be withdrawn from both and offers were re-invited.

Drawlane was successful in acquiring Midland Red (North) in January 1988 which, at the time of purchase, had 248 vehicles and 491 employees. The following month, London Country (South West) Ltd was purchased with 415 vehicles and 1250 employees, although the garages were purchased separately by Speyhawk Properties, who then leased them to the bus company with varying securities of tenure, reflecting the premium value of property in London and the South East. Finally, in March 1988, Drawlane acquired the 'new' North Western Road Car Company Ltd based in Bootle, with 340 vehicles and 870 staff.

Drawlane had also bought East Lancashire Coachbuilders from the industrial conglomerate John Brown. East Lancs was based in Blackburn and had a strong customer base in the local authority sector.

Further expansion for Drawlane would now come from acquiring bus operations from other sources. ATL (Western) Ltd had purchased Crosville Motor Services from NBC in March 1988 and in early 1989 was ready to sell. Drawlane purchased the company adding a further 470 vehicles. A quick overview of the future of Crosville is appropriate here. In an exercise to realise value from the company, the South Cheshire operations at Crewe and Etruria were transferred to Midland Red North, the Runcorn and Warrington depots were transferred to North Western, and the Macclesfield and Congleton depots were merged into Bee Line Buzz, of which more later. The remaining operations at Rock Ferry and Chester, together with the vehicles, were sold to PMT Ltd along with the 'Crosville' trading name. The original Crosville Motor Services Company was renamed North British Bus Ltd, and, though it existed for some time thereafter, it did not trade as a bus company.

Midland Fox was bought from its management team in September 1989 along with a minority share holding in the company from Stevensons of Uttoxeter. Bee Line Buzz operations in Manchester had been started up by BET, which had sold its bus operations in 1968, venturing back into bus operation in the UK. A similar operation was started in Preston. Both were sold to Ribble's management buyout team who, in turn, sold Ribble Buses to the Stagecoach Group. As part of an exchange of assets with Stagecoach in the Manchester area, Drawlane bought Bee Line Buzz from Stagecoach along with Hulme Hall Road depot in Manchester and added into the company the former Crosville operations at Macclesfield and Congleton. Bee Line had an independent existence within the group until 1993 when its operations were merged into North Western, with Macclesfield depot going to Midland Red North.

Drawlane in Transition

In 1991, Drawlane became a partner in a consortium with several banks setting up a company called Speedtheme Ltd in a bid to buy National Express Holdings from its management team. As well as the main National Express business, National Express Holdings owned Crosville Wales Ltd and its Liverpool subsidiary Amberline Ltd, Express Travel in Perth, and Carlton PSV the Neoplan coach dealer in Rotherham. Speedtheme Ltd did not want Crosville Wales and Amberline/Express Travel, and these were immediately sold to a company, called Catchdeluxe Ltd, set up by two of the main shareholders of Drawlane, Ray McEnhill and Adam Mills. Although not part of Drawlane at this time, these two companies were under common management, and it was not long before they became part of the Drawlane Group.

Ray McEnhill became the Chairman and Chief Executive of National Express Group and, as this group prepared for its floatation on the Stock Exchange, Ray McEnhill and Adam Mills severed their involvement with Drawlane. The London & Country business called Speedlink Airport Services was sold by Drawlane to National Express at this time, though Drawlane retained the Green Line Travel Company, along with the Green Line trading name.

There was, in effect, a management buyout of Drawlane in the autumn of 1992 to coincide with the successful floatation of National Express and shortly thereafter Drawlane was renamed British Bus plc. (British Bus Ltd had been a dormant subsidiary of National Express Holdings, originally set up by NBC to market the Britexpress card overseas.)

British Bus grows

Throughout this period, there were various smaller acquisitions by the group companies but these are dealt with in the short histories of these companies that follow.

In 1993, British Bus purchased Southend Transport and Colchester Transport, both former municipal operations which had been offered for sale after being weakened by competition from Badgerline subsidiaries, Thamesway in Southend and Eastern National in Colchester. After acquisition, the two companies were put under common management and the supervision of London & Country. A programme of rationalisation put both back onto a firm footing, though down-sized.

In 1993, North Western acquired Liverline of Liverpool which, by then, had grown to a fifty-one vehicle company. It was run as a separate subsidiary until 1997. North Western had by this time absorbed the bus operations of Amberline.

Also in 1993, Tellings Golden Miller was sold back to its original owners. Tellings had been taken over by Midland Fox and came into the group. At the time of its sale, it had bases in Surrey and Cardiff. In the latter location, Tellings had become the joint operator of the Trawscambria service with Crosville Cymru! That role then passed to Rhondda Bus in which British Bus had a share holding for a while.

At the end of 1993, British Bus became the preferred bidder for the purchase of GM Buses North, but the position was overturned by the vendors and new bids invited. The outcome of this exercise was a winning bid from an employee-based team which was eventually completed in the spring of 1994. They subsequently sold out to First.

Further growth was funded by expanding the capital base of the group through investment by two merchant banks who took a share of the increased equity in a new parent company British Bus Group, though operational control remained with British Bus plc.

During 1994, ownership of both East Lancashire Coachbuilders Ltd and Express Travel was transferred out of the group, though they were still associated companies. East Lancs in particular was still a preferred supplier to the group for bus bodywork.

The National Greenway programme was coming to an end at this point. This programme involved the stripping down and re-engineering of Leyland National shells with new a Gardner or Volvo engine, new gearbox and new body panels mounted on the shell framework. The stripping down and mechanical overhaul work was carried out at London and Country's Reigate garage, though later some of this work was carried out by Blackburn Transport, as this was closer to East Lancs. East Lancs then did the body work with customer options as to the front design. Notable numbers were carried out both for Group companies and other operators.

Luton, Derby, Clydeside and Stevensons

In July 1994, British Bus acquired Luton and District Transport from its employees. By this time, the business included the former London Country Bus North West and a large part of the Stevenage operations bought from Sovereign Bus. This meant that a sizeable part of the former London Country company was now back in common ownership.

Luton and District had also assisted other employee buyouts such as Derby City Transport in which it had a 25% share holding, and Clydeside 2000 plc, where there was a 19% share holding. In both companies, the shareholders voted to accept offers from British Bus for the balance of the shares and they became fully owned members of the British Bus group. A third company, Lincoln City Transport, had not met with success and the employees had already agreed its sale to Yorkshire Traction-owned Lincolnshire Road Car Company Ltd before the British Bus take-over.

At the same time, there were discussions about the acquisition of Stevensons of Uttoxeter. Stevensons had grown dramatically after deregulation and operated well away from its traditional area. A strong expansion in the West Midlands was initially successful but West Midlands Travel responded to the competition and used its Your Bus acquisition to start up operations in Burton on Trent which was by then the heartland of Stevensons. A long struggle looked in prospect and a sale to British Bus was agreed. Operations in the West Midlands were scaled down and surplus vehicles were distributed around the group. After this process was complete, the geographically separated Macclesfield depot of Midland Red North was transferred to Stevensons control in January 1995.

Proudmutual and Caldaire Holdings

In the summer of 1994, British Bus also acquired the Proudmutual group. Proudmutual had been the buyout vehicle for the management team of Northumbria Motor Services to buy their business from NBC. It had also acquired some smaller businesses in the North East, including Moor-Dale.

Proudmutual had previously purchased Kentish Bus, the former London Country South East from NBC in March 1988. They had considerable success in the London Transport tendering process and further LT work was added when the LT contracts of Boro'line were purchased in February 1992. The Proudmutual acquisition thus gave British Bus a very strong position in LT tendering when the activities of London and Country and the LDT group were taken into account. It also brought another part of the former London and Country into common ownership.

The privatisation of the London Transport Bus companies brought no success for British Bus but, as we have seen earlier, the Cowie Group was successful in acquiring two of the subsidiaries.

In March of 1995, the Caldaire group was acquired. Caldaire was the buyout vehicle with which the management of West Riding Group had purchased their business from NBC in January 1987. In the December of that year they also bought United Auto from NBC. A demerger later on saw the United business being separated off again into North East Bus. The long established independent South Yorkshire Road Transport was acquired and formed one of the trading identities of the Caldaire Group, the others being West Riding, Yorkshire Woollen, and Selby & District. After acquisition, the group of companies was renamed Yorkshire Bus Group by British Bus.

Maidstone & District

What turned out to be the last major acquisition by British Bus was made in April 1995. Maidstone and District had been one of the earliest of NBC sales in late 1986. It had purchased New Enterprise of Tonbridge in 1988, and the assets of Boro'line Maidstone in 1992. Under British Bus ownership, the company was put under common management with Kentish Bus and Londonlinks as the Invictaway Group with its head office at Maidstone.

Floatation or Trade Sale?

Throughout 1995, preparations for floatation had been underway with the appointment of advisors. However, in the summer of 1995, these plans were thrown off course by reports of alleged irregularities involving support from the Bank of Boston for British Bus at an earlier point in the group's history. The timing of these allegations led to the postponement of the floatation. The alternative route for shareholders and the investing banks to realise their investment was a trade sale of the group and discussions were held with various interested parties.

Concurrently, the group was also looking to expand its interests into other modes of transport as the opportunities in the bus industry were becoming scarce due to the growth of the major players. The subsequent sales of the two former GM Buses companies by their employee owners and that of Strathclyde Buses were opportunities for growth, but British Bus was not successful.

In June 1996 the Cowie Group made an offer to acquire British Bus, (which has already been covered). There was a Monopolies and Mergers Commission investigation into the take-over in view of the concentration of operation in London and the South East in the combined business. However, the resulting report made no recommendation about disinvestment, recognising the considerable presence of the other groups in the area. The acquisition by Cowie was completed in August 1996

Trams and trains

As part of its drive to expand its business, British Bus pursued tramway operations and had become a partner in the Eurotrans consortium which bid for both the Leeds Supertram and Manchester Metrolink concessions. British Bus was also part of a consortium bid for the Croydon Tramlink project

Eurotrans was selected as the preferred bidder for the South Leeds Supertram Project which was being promoted by West Yorkshire PTE. This was a PFI project where bidders were fighting for the concession to design, build, operate, and maintain the tramway for a period of thirty years. The Eurotrans consortium included big construction companies such as Taylor Woodrow, Morrison Construction, and Christiani & Neilsen. The tram supplier was Vevey Technologies of Switzerland, now part of the Bombardier Group. The intention was for Arriva Yorkshire to set up a tram operating subsidiary to operate the tramway for the concession life on behalf of Eurotrans. The project stalled waiting for UK Government funding commitment, but was revived, in expanded form, in 2001 when funding was secured.

British Bus was also active in the process of franchising of the Train Operating Companies by OPRAF although none of their bids were successful. However, the exposure to the process paid off in arranging through ticketing deals with the successful bidders later on.

ARRIVA

In 1997 the group started a rebranding of all its business interests under the new trading identity of 'Arriva'. The bus division became a separate legal identity on 1 January 1998, becoming Arriva Passenger Services (APS). The group livery and identity started to replace the former colours and names progressively from 1999.

A link with the past was broken when the Group Headquarters relocated in the latter part of 1998 from Hylton Road in Sunderland to new purpose built premises on the Doxford International Business Park on the outskirts of Sunderland near the A19.

Arriva Passenger Services shared the head office premises of Arriva Fox, first at Millstone Lane and then, from September 1997, at Thurmaston, although several staff were quartered at offices in bus depots around the country. Then, in August 1999, APS moved to purpose-built offices in the Meridian Business Park on the other side of Leicester.

In September 1997, Arriva made its first acquisition outside Britain with the purchase of Unibus Holdings in Denmark. Arriva continues to expand within Europe, and now has operations in Denmark, Germany, Italy, the Netherlands, Portugal, Spain and Sweden.

In 2000, Arriva purchased MTL, the Liverpool-based transport group, which included the major bus operator in Merseyside plus the two rail franchises. A subsidiary operation at Heysham was soon sold on and the MTL bus operation was absorbed into Arriva North West. Gilmoss depot and its operations were sold on to meet the terms required by the Office of Fair Trading for its approval of the purchase of MTL.

Arriva in London

When the Arriva name was introduced, Grey Green was renamed Arriva London North East. Cowie Leaside became Arriva London North, and Cowie South London became Arriva London South. The three companies have moved gradually closer to functioning as one unit, and the London North East operations were absorbed into London North in 2003. The head office for both London companies is at Wood Green. The Beddington Farm depot of Londonlinks transferred from Southern Counties to London South in October 1999. The Leaside Travel coach and bus contract hire fleet still retains a separate livery.

Arriva provided the first low-floor double-deck buses in London and deliveries continue apace. The first buses were DAF with Alexander bodies but Volvo chassis and Plaxton bodies are now in fleet service. In 2001, Arriva London took the first Wrightbus double-deck bodies, on Volvo chassis. More recent orders for Wright double-decks have been on DAF chassis, while Alexander bodies have also switched from Volvo to DAF chassis.

In line with the Mayor's strategy for transport in London, which includes the introduction of Congestion Charging, the Arriva London fleet has seen growth of over 200 extra buses together with rapid fleet renewal. The fleet is now close to being entirely low-floor. To accommodate this growth, Stamford Hill garage has been reopened, the former tram shed at Brixton was brought back into use in February 2003, and facilities elsewhere are being expanded. Premises at Tottenham Hale have been leased for storing vehicles to make room at operational depots, and further new depot sites are being sought.

County Bus and Coach into Arriva East Herts and Essex

County Bus & Coach came into being at the beginning of 1989 to carry on the eastern operations of the former London Country North East, which in itself was one of the four parts into which London Country was divided. Operations were based at Harlow, Hertford and Grays. Ownership had progressed through the AJS group in 1988, the South of England Travel group in 1989 and the Lynton Travel group in 1990. The company was then purchased by the West Midlands Travel holding company, becoming part of the National Express Group when WMT merged into NEG. A retraction into core business led NEG to sell County to Cowie in 1996. A significant acquisition in 1989 was the bus interests and depot of Sampsons of Hoddesdon.

A restructuring of responsibilities saw County Bus take over the controlling supervision of Southend Transport and Colchester Borough Transport from London & Country and, during 1998, this responsibility passed to Arriva The Shires, along with overall control of what was now Arriva East Herts and Essex. The Edmonton operation passed to the Arriva London group in a rationalisation of responsibilities within London. During 1999 the fleets of these various component operations were renumbered into a single series.

In a further restructuring in 2001, responsibility for Colchester, Grays and Southend passed to Arriva Southern Counties.

The Shires becomes Arriva the Shires and Essex Ltd

In 1986, United Counties Omnibus Company Ltd was divided into three parts, the southern most of these being Luton and District Transport Ltd which took over operations in Aylesbury, Dunstable, Hitchin and Luton. The new head office of the company was in Luton.

In August 1987 Luton and District became the first employee owned bus operator in the UK when its employees bought it from NBC. In the period from January 1988 to October 1990, LDT expanded the size and the area of its operations through a number of acquisitions. The assets and business of Red Rover Omnibus Ltd, operating bus services from a depot in Aylesbury, were acquired in January 1988. In June 1988, Milton Keynes Coaches was acquired, joined in May 1990 by two thirds of the bus services operated in the Stevenage area latterly Sovereign Bus Ltd.

In October 1990, LDT acquired London Country North West Ltd. LCNW operated a vehicle fleet of a similar size to LDT from a head office and depot in Garston and other depots in Hemel Hempstead, High Wycombe, Amersham, and Slough. LDT assisted in the employee buyouts of two other companies and acquired a share holding in both, Derby City Transport in 1989, and Clydeside 2000 plc in 1991.

In July 1994 LDT became part of British Bus. In October 1994, the bus operations of Stuart Palmer Travel based in Dunstable was taken over, followed in May 1995 by Buffalo Travel of Flitwick, and Motts Travel of Aylesbury in July 1995.

April 1995 saw the launch of a brand new blue and yellow company livery with local trading names replacing the previous red and cream of LDT and green and grey of LCNW. The legal name was changed to LDT Ltd in May and the corporate operating name became The Shires.

In late 1997, Lucketts Garages (Watford) Ltd was acquired. In addition to local bus services in Watford there were substantial dial-a-ride operations and a commercial workshop.

Lutonian Buses was acquired in March. Since then, there has been a ruling that the business should be sold under Competition regulations. The Group's challenge was unsuccessful and Lutonian was sold during 2000.

The Arriva branding saw vehicles carrying the name 'Arriva serving the Shires', except at Garston garage which carries 'Arriva serving Watford'. Management responsibility for Arriva East Herts & Essex now falls to Arriva the Shires and Essex Ltd. Responsibility for Colchester, Grays and Southend passed to Arriva Southern Counties in 2001.

Kentish Bus part of Arriva Southern Counties

Kentish Bus started as London Country South East on the division of London Country Bus Services in 1986. It had its Head Office at Northfleet and in April 1987 was relaunched as Kentish Bus and Coach Ltd with a new livery of cream and maroon.

In March 1988 Kentish Bus was sold to Proudmutual on privatisation. There was considerable expansion into the LT tender market for which new buses were added, many with registration indices originating in the North East. In February 1992 there was further expansion in this area when Kentish acquired the LT tendered work of the troubled Boro'line Maidstone operation, along with some 57 vehicles.

After the acquisition of the Proudmutual group by British Bus in 1994, Kentish Bus and Londonlinks were jointly managed from Northfleet. However, on the acquisition of Maidstone and District by British Bus, the management was relocated to Armstrong Road, Maidstone under the Invictaway grouping. The balance of the operation continued to be controlled from Maidstone after the reallocation of the two London depots to South London and Leaside.

Its size was significantly reduced by the transfer of operations at Battersea to the control of South London and the operations at Cambridge Heath to Leaside.

However the local Kent Thameside network was expanded and upgraded with low floor vehicles upon the opening or the Bluewater shopping centre in 1999.

The Arriva identity was applied as 'Arriva serving Kent Thameside' to the operations at Dartford and Northfleet.

London & Country into Arriva Surrey and West Sussex

London & Country was the trading name of London Country Bus (South West) Ltd, which was one of the four operations that London Country Bus Services Ltd was divided into prior to the privatisation of NBC. The former head office of LCBS at Reigate became that of L&C. The company was bought by Drawlane, as outlined above, in February 1988. However, the properties were leased back having been sold separately. The company was relaunched with a new livery and trading name in April 1989.

London & Country was successful in winning LT tenders and this led to the addition of new vehicles and the high profile opening of an impressive new garage at Beddington Farm in Croydon. Responsibility for this operation passed to Arriva London in 1999.

In 1990 the Woking, Guildford, and Cranleigh operations of the former Alder Valley business were purchased, and though kept as a separate operating company - Guildford and West Surrey - they were put under the same management as L&C. Also in 1990, a separate company called Horsham Buses was established for operations in the Horsham area.

Spare capacity at the Reigate garage allowed the development of the National Greenway concept in conjunction with East Lancs and many vehicles were prepared at Reigate.

Briefly, London & Country had two subsidiaries in Dorset: Stanbridge and Crichel and Oakfield Travel. Both of these were later sold to Damory Coaches. Another subsidiary was Linkline Coaches of Harlesden in London, which specialised in coaching and corporate work. This was later sold to its management.

1993 saw the acquisition of Southend Transport and Colchester Transport and many L&C influences followed. These companies transferred to the supervision of County Bus but returned to Southern Counties in 2001.

The Croydon based operations and other LT tender operations at Walworth were transferred into a new company called Londonlinks. In 1995 Londonlinks was put under common management with Kentish Bus and Maidstone and District as part of the Invictaway Group. Reallocation of responsibilities in the enlarged group later saw the Croydon depot of Londonlinks return to L&C control before finally passing to London South.

A consequence of the property sales was the vacation of Reigate garage and its replacement by a facility at Merstham. The Head Office functions were consolidated in 1997 when the Reigate office closed as the functions moved to other premises including Crawley garage.

The three companies were renamed as Arriva Croydon and North Surrey, Arriva West Sussex, and Arriva Guildford and West Surrey. However the trading identity used is Arriva Surrey & West Sussex. In August 1998 the Countryliner coaching operation was sold to its manager. In 2001, the Crawley operation and depot was sold to Metrobus and the Merstham depot was closed.

In Guildford, significant investment has taken place with the depot completely rebuilt in 2002 and the fleet updated.

Maidstone and District becomes Arriva Kent & Sussex

This is the original Maidstone and District Motor Services Ltd which was founded in 1911. Under NBC, it shared common management with East Kent from 1972 to 1983. In 1983 the Hastings and Rye area services were hived off as Hastings and District.

Maidstone and District was one of the first NBC companies to be privatised, being bought by its management team in November 1986. In 1988 New Enterprise of Tonbridge was purchased and is still kept as a separate entity. In June 1992 the assets of Maidstone Boro'line Maidstone including the premises at Armstrong Road were purchased.

In April 1995 the company was sold to British Bus, and in November the Head Office at Chatham was closed and staff moved along with Kentish Bus head office staff from Northfleet to the former Maidstone Boro'line premises at Maidstone under the Invictaway banner.

Under British Bus Cowie control, the group acquired a number of additional operatorions including Mercury Passenger Services of Hoo, Wealden Beeline of Five Oak Green, and the Grey Green (Medway) bus operation. In May of 1997 the Green Line operations in Gravesend and the Medway Towns were sold to the Pullman Group (London Coaches).

The Arriva branding used three identities, 'Arriva serving the Medway Towns', 'Arriva serving Kent and East Sussex', and 'Arriva serving Maidstone'.

Midland Fox turns into Arriva Fox County Ltd

Midland Red East Ltd was formed in 1981 to take over the Leicestershire operations of Midland Red. In 1984 the company name was changed to Midland Fox Ltd, and there was a major relaunch of the company with a new livery and fox logo. There was also the launch of a new minibus network in Leicester under the, now discontinued, Fox Cub brand.

In 1987 the company was bought from NBC by its management with the help of the directors of Stevensons of Uttoxeter who, separately, bought the Swadlincote depot. Several smaller operators were also taken over. These included Wreake Valley of Thurmaston, Fairtax of Melton Mowbray, Astill and Jordan of Ratby, Shelton Orsborn of Wollaston, Blands of Stamford, and Loughborough Coach and Bus.

In 1989 Midland Fox was acquired by Drawlane. The following year it acquired Tellings-Golden Miller in Byfleet and this business, in turn, acquired the Coach Travel Centre in Cardiff, amongst others. Tellings bus operations eventually became part of London and Country, while Tellings was sold back to its management in 1994 before its expansion into bus operation in Cardiff.

In 1994 Pickering Transport was purchased by British Bus. Pickering build lorry bodies at their extensive site at Thurmaston, and now offer body repair and painting services which has resulted in many group vehicles appearing there. The site also houses one of Fox's three Leicester area depots. 1996 saw a launch of high quality services under the Urban Fox brand in a striking new blue livery.

Derby City Transport Ltd was a long established municipally owned bus company. In August 1989 it was sold to its employees who were assisted by Luton and District Transport. Luton and District took a 25% share holding in the business. There was a competitive interlude in Derby where Midland Red North started operations, but this ended with Derby buying out the competition in February 1990.

In 1994, after the acquisition of Luton and District by British Bus, the shareholders in Derby decided to accept an offer from British Bus for the rest of the share capital of the company. After a period of autonomy, the business was relaunched under the City Rider brand name and a yellow, red and blue livery. In January 1996, Derby City Transport was incorporated into the Midland Fox group; full integration and renumbering of the fleet took place at the start of 2000.

In 1990, "75" Taxis started as a division of Derby City Transport, building up a fleet of London style taxis. In September 1994, Midland Fox launched a new taxi service in Leicester marketed as Fox Cabs, but this operation was sold in 2001.

In September 1996, the Head Office of Midland Fox moved to the Pickering of Thurmaston premises along with a depot facility. It was later joined by the British Bus head office, now Arriva Passenger Services Ltd, which has since moved to new premises on the other side of Leicester.

The Arriva branding had vehicles carrying the 'Arriva serving the Fox County', or 'Arriva serving Derby' identities as appropriate. The taxi business remains under its previous brand. Special liveries include four vehicles in Quick Silver Shuttle for Leicester Park and Ride, Airport Car Park Shuttle and Airport Rail Link, three vehicles in a blue livery for East Midland Airport, two buses in a Corby to Kettering Rail Link for Midland Main Line, and two vehicles in a green livery for a Marks and Spencer shuttle service.

In 2003 Arriva Fox County and Arriva Midlands North merged to become Arriva Midlands.

Midland Red North & Stevensons become Arriva Midlands North

Midland Red North Ltd was founded in 1981 when the Midland Red company was divided into four operating parts by NBC. The company traded with local network names such as Chaserider for a considerable time. These were based upon the networks generated from the Viable Network Project later carried out across NBC as Market Analysis Project (MAP). The area included the then new town of Telford where a network of new services was introduced displacing many of the long-traditional operators.

The company was sold to Drawlane in January 1988 after a false start as described earlier. In 1989, it took over the Crewe and Etruria depots of fellow Drawlane subsidiary Crosville Motor Services Ltd. In 1992, Midland Red North purchased the Oswestry and Abermule operations of Crosville Wales Ltd, then an associated company. In 1993, with the dispersion of the Bee Line Buzz Company, the Macclesfield depot of that company which had traded as C-Line was taken over, having been part of Crosville for some time.

Stevensons of Uttoxeter commenced services in that part of Staffordshire in 1926 and continued as a small but successful family owned business. During the 1980s, and particularly after deregulation, significant growth occurred. In 1985 a controlling interest was acquired in the East Staffordshire Borough Council's bus operations in Burton-on-Trent. In 1987, the Swadlincote depot of Midland Fox and the Lichfield out station were purchased from NBC.

Growth in the West Midlands and the acquisition of a number of small companies including Crystal Coaches in Burslem and Viking Tours and Travel saw the company become a major independent operator in the early 1990s.

In April 1994, however, West Midlands Travel used its Your Bus subsidiary to retaliate in the Burton area against the significant level of operation Stevensons then had in the West Midlands area. This led to the sale of the company to British Bus in August 1994 and a significant scaling down of Stevensons operations in the West Midlands.

Macclesfield depot was transferred from Midland Red North into Stevensons in January 1995. From April 1995, Midland Red North and Stevensons were jointly managed. The closure of the Stevensons Head Office at Spath with the provision of central administration services from the Cannock head office became effective in 1996. A common livery was established between the two fleets though the Stevensons fleet name was retained on vehicles allocated to former Stevensons depots. Viking coaches retained a separate livery of two shades of grey until the operation was sold.

The application of Arriva livery and branding saw the trading identity 'Arriva serving the North Midlands' applied to all buses.

In May 1998, the Shifnal depot of Timeline was acquired along with nineteen vehicles. The bus operations of Matthews Handybus in the Newcastle under Lyme area were acquired in February 1998, but no buses were involved. In August of the same year, the local bus operations of Williamsons of Knockin Heath were taken over and four vehicles came with the work.

1999 saw many SLF Dennis Darts arrive and these were followed by thirty Volvo B6BLE buses fitted with Wright Crusader 2 bodywork. All private hire coaching operations along with the vehicles were disposed of during the year.

Arriva Midlands

In February 2003, Macclesfield, Crewe and Winsford depots were transferred from Arriva Midlands North to Arriva North West. The remaining depots of Midlands North were combined with Arriva Fox County to become Arriva Midlands.

North Western Road Car Co Ltd becomes Arriva North West

Ribble Motor Services was another NBC company divided in preparation for privatisation. The dormant Mexborough & Swinton Traction Company was renamed as above to take over the Merseyside, West Lancashire and Wigan operations of Ribble in September 1986. The head office of the new company was sited at Hawthorne Road, the Bootle area office north of Liverpool.

The company was acquired by Drawlane in March 1988. In 1989, the Runcorn and Warrington depots of Crosville were acquired. Expansion saw North Western open a depot in Altrincham, though eventually rationalisation saw the operations assumed by the Bee Line Buzz Company during its independent existence as a Drawlane subsidiary.

In 1993 Bee Line was put under the same management as North Western and a few weeks later, Liverline of Bootle was acquired along with 51 vehicles. Both were maintained as separate identities under the same management. Also acquired in 1993 were the bus operations of Express Travel, which at the time were still branded as Amberline, though this identity was not maintained.

The head office of the company later moved to Aintree depot, though a subsequent move saw the depot sold and redeveloped leaving the head office building free standing.

1995 was a busy year with two operations in the Wigan area acquired; Little White Bus and Wigan Bus Company. Also acquired in 1995 was Arrowline Travel based in Knutsford, which traded as Star Line. This brought luxury coaches on Airport related work as well as a modern fleet of mini and midi buses. The Star Line operation was later relocated to Wythenshaw, while the coaching operation was sold to Selwyns of Runcorn.

Increase in activity in the Warrington area required a new depot to be established at Haydock. The collapse of a Cheshire operator Lofty's of Mickle Trafford saw further growth in the mid Cheshire area and new Cheshire workings took vehicles as far south as Whitchurch.

In 1997, Arriva acquired the residue of South Lancs Transport following that operator's withdrawal from Chester, and the business was put under the supervision of North Western.

In 1998, some bus operations of Timeline in the North West were purchased along with some vehicles, though the majority went to First Group. Arriva North West manages the bus and coach facilities at the Trafford Centre on behalf of the owners of this striking shopping centre which is located four miles west of Manchester. Arriva branding initially used the identity 'Arriva serving the North West'.

In 1999, the Winsford-based Nova Scotia operation was acquired, its services being integrated into the fleet. In 2000, Arriva acquired MTL, and the bus operations were put under the control of Arriva North West, those operations being branded 'Arriva serving Merseyside' and early in 2002 the head office functions of Arriva Cymru were transferred to Aintree. Upon full integration in the later months, the company was re-titled Arriva North West and Wales.

In August 2005 the vehicle and services of Blue Bus of Bolton were acquired, taking Arriva into the northern part of Greater Manchester conurbation.

Yorkshire Bus Group to Arriva Yorkshire

The West Riding Automobile Company and Yorkshire Woollen District Transport were put under common management by NBC and, when privatisation happened in January 1987, the management team bought both companies. Selby and District was a trading title turned into a separate company by the new owners' Caldaire Holding company. While Caldaire became involved in the North East, the core business in West Yorkshire changed very little but there was steady investment in fleet replacement and upgrade.

There was involvement in the splitting up of National Travel East leaving a residue of operations on National Express contracts, and also competitive operations in Sheffield that led to corresponding competition in Wakefield.

The South Yorkshire Road Transport Company of Pontefract was purchased in July 1994, and maintained a separate trading identity for a time. In March 1995, the Caldaire Group was acquired by British Bus. Jaronda Travel of Selby was acquired in August 1999.

The Arriva identities used were 'Arriva serving Yorkshire' and 'Arriva serving Selby' seeing a merging together of the West Riding and Yorkshire identities for the first time. Arriva Yorkshire partnered with First Leeds in the extension to the East Leeds Guided Bus Corridor along the A64 York Road. This initiative saw both operators together contributing nearly half the scheme cost of around £9.9m with the other half coming from a partnership of Leeds City Council and West Yorkshire PTE.

United, Tees and District, and Teesside Motor Services Ltd become Arriva North East

United Automobile Services Ltd was another NBC subsidiary divided up in preparation for privatisation. In 1986, the northern part of the operating area was hived off into a new company called Northumbria. United continued to trade south of the Tyne, with its head office in Darlington. The operations in Scarborough and Pickering were transferred to a subsidiary of East Yorkshire Motor Services.

In December 1987, United was bought from NBC by Caldaire Holdings, the management buyout vehicle of the West Riding management team. In 1989, the National Express coaching activities of United were sold off to a joint venture company Durham Travel Services, set up by two former United managers with National Express Ltd.

In 1990, United was split into two parts, the Durham and North Yorkshire section continuing to trade as United, the section in Cleveland trading as Tees and District. At this time, the associated businesses of Trimdon Motor Services and Teeside Motor Services were acquired, with the Trimdon business being absorbed into United and the Teeside business continuing.

In the summer of 1992, there was a demerger of the Caldaire Group, with the North East operations passing to the Westcourt Group, and Caldaire North East becoming North East Bus.

In 1994, a new head office and engineering works in Morton Road, Darlington allowed the vacation of the Grange Road site for redevelopment. Also in 1994, the Westcourt Group sold to West Midlands Travel in the November, and North East Bus became part of the National Express Group following the merger with that group in 1995.

Eden Bus Services of Bishop Auckland was acquired in October 1995 and was absorbed into the main operation.

National Express Group sold North East Bus to the Cowie Group on the last day of July 1996 and, in October, the Ripon depot operations were sold to Harrogate and District Travel.

Northumbria Motor Services Ltd into Arriva Northumbria

In 1986, the operations of United Auto were split into two parts in preparation for privatisation. The dormant Southern National Omnibus Company Ltd was renamed Northumbria and took over operations in September 1986 with a new head office in Jesmond.

In October 1987, Northumbria was acquired from NBC by its management using Proudmutual as a holding company. Proudmutual also acquired Kentish Bus in March 1988. Other acquisitions included Moor-Dale Coaches and Hunters. In 1994 the Proudmutual group was acquired by British Bus while, at the same time, Moor-Dale Coaches was sold back to former directors.

In the Arriva era, two trading identities were used: 'Arriva serving Northumbria' and 'Arriva serving the North East'.

Crosville Cymru into Arriva Cymru

Crosville Wales Ltd was, until August 1986, the Welsh and Shropshire operations of Crosville Motor Services Ltd based in Chester. In 1986, it was resolved that the Crosville company was too large to be offered for privatisation as a whole, and the then dormant Devon General Omnibus and Touring Company Ltd was revived by NBC in order to take over the assets and business of Crosville in Wales, to be renamed Crosville Wales. The management team of Crosville Wales purchased the company from NBC in December 1987.

In January 1989, the company was bought by National Express Holdings Ltd. In July of that year, it purchased a subsidiary company called Amberline, based at Speke in Liverpool, and added a bus operation to the mainly National Express coach contracts operated.

In July 1991, the National Express group was purchased by a consortium of banks led by Drawlane, as explained earlier. Ultimately, this led to Crosville Wales becoming a full member of the Drawlane Group shortly before its transformation into British Bus plc. In January 1992, the Oswestry depot and its outstation at Abermule were sold to Midland Red North.

Crosville Wales took advantage of second hand vehicles from other group companies and other operators, building a fleet of Leyland Lynx and National 2s while concurrently buying further new Mercedes minibuses and Dennis Darts.

In 1995, some of the services, but no vehicles, of Alpine Travel were acquired, leading to an operation of certain services as Alpine Bus in a red and white livery. This was superseded by a Shoreline livery of blue, white and yellow, which has been phased out and replaced by route branding.

All operations were branded 'Arriva serving Wales/gwansanaethu Cymru', including those of the two acquisitions in 1998. The first was Devaway of Bretton, Chester. This brought a mixed fleet of VRTs, Nationals, and more Lynx and a depot from which to operate Chester area services. The second acquisition was Purple Motors of Bethesda. Further low floor buses arrived during 1999 to provide the Arriva share of a Quality Partnership Corridor on Deeside jointly provided with First Crosville. At the start of 2000 a large batch of low-floor Darts joined the fleet, and these displaced the last examples of the National in the fleet.

In February 2000, low-floor vehicles were introduced on low-volume rural services as north Wales authorities chose to use their share of the expanded Rural Bus Grant in improving quality rather than widening availability. Some vehicles are equipped with a bike racks.

Arriva Cymru is now managed under the Arriva North West and Wales umbrella.

Clydeside Buses Ltd into Arriva Scotland West Ltd

Clydeside Buses and its predecessors have been serving its core area of Renfrewshire and Inverclyde since 1928. Prior to 1985, the operation had formed the northern section of Western Scottish, part of the Scottish Bus Group (SBG). In preparation for the deregulation of local bus services, Clydeside Scottish assumed responsibility for the Glasgow, Renfrewshire and Inverclyde operations of Western Scottish in 1985. Over the next six years, there was a complex series of reorganisations between Clydeside and Western until, in 1991, Clydeside became the last SBG subsidiary to be privatised when it was purchased by its employees with assistance from Luton and District Transport Group, emerging as Clydeside 2000 plc.

After 1986, there were numerous competitors in the core area and trading proved extremely difficult. When the LDT group sold to British Bus, an offer put to the shareholders of Clydeside was accepted and Clydeside joined British Bus. There was immediate effort to update the fleet against a background of tightening up of enforcement generally in the area. Some of the competitive battles had led to the Traffic Commissioner taking steps to control the number of departures and waiting times in certain town centres.

The development of services has seen Flagship Routes introduced to raise quality levels. Additionally, opportunity was taken to acquire various smaller operators in the area such as Ashton Coaches of Greenock, and a significant share in Dart Buses of Paisley. Operations from the Greenock base were restyled as GMS-Greenock Motor Services with a separate livery. McGills Bus Service Ltd of Barrhead was acquired by the group in 1997 and for a time was kept as a separate entity from Clydeside Buses. Clydeside also acquired Bridge Coaches of Paisley which was fully absorbed into Clydeside.

During 2001, the shareholding in Dart Buses was sold to Stagecoach Western and the dormant McGills company used as a vehicle to sell off all remaining Inverclyde operations which ceased trading at the end of June. The redundant depot at Greenock and subsequently former McGill's site at Barrhead were demolished with all operations spread between remaining sites at Inchinnan and Johnstone. In a final move to consolidate the business the remote head office site located in Renfrew was vacated and all employees subsequently relocated within a refurbished facility at Inchinnan depot. The 'Arriva serving Scotland' branding covers all operations.

Expansion into Europe

September 1997	Unibus Holdings, Denmark
January 1998	Vancom Nederland
December 1998	Veonn & Hanze, Netherlands
March 1999	Bus Danmark
July 1999	Mercancias Ideal Gallego, Spain
September 1999	Transportes Finisterre, Spain
November 2000	Ami-Transportes, Portugal
December 2000	Abilio da Costa Moreira, Portugal
April 2001	Combus, Denmark
January 2002	Autocares Mallorca
June 2002	Transportes Sul ode Tejo, Portugal
July 2002	SAB Autoservizi, Italy
April 2004	Prignitzer Eisenbahn Gruppe, Germany
October 2004	Regentalbahn, Bavaria, Germany
February 2005	Sippel, Germany
July 2005	SAVDA Group, Italy

During 2003, Arriva completed its purchase of Transportes Sul do Tejo by acquiring the Barraqueiro Group's remaining 49%. It also began to operate its Danish rail franchises in Mid and North Jutland.

In 2004, the Group entered the German public transport market with the acquisition of Prignitzer Eisenbahn Gruppe and in October purchased a stake in Regentalbahn AG from the Bavarian Stae and now has a 90% shareholding. A further acquisiton in Germany was the bus businness of Sippel which operates throughout the Rhine-Main area.

Arriva also grew its position in the Italian public transport market with the acquisition of Società Autoservizi FVG SpA. In July 2005 it was announced that Arriva had also agreed to acquire

80 per cent of the operations of the SAVDA Group and it has an option to acquire the remaining 20 per cent in 2008.

These acquisitions continue the strategy of developing Arriva's mainland European transport business, which is now a major contributor to the Group's results. Arriva now has significant positions in the Netherlands, Denmark, Portugal and Italy, with smaller positions in Germany, Spain and Sweden.

Denmark

The first acquisition in mainland Europe was Unibus in Denmark, which was acquired in 1997. Unibus operated approximately 8% of the tendered market in Copenhagen and within that area is also the largest private sector provider of services for handicapped persons transport. Additionally, it had operations throughout Jutland and Zealand. Founded in 1985, Unibus grew by winning tendered bus operations for the Transport Authority for Copenhagen - HT. Unibus was the biggest coach operator in Copenhagen until in 1995, when the coaching business was sold to Lyngby Turistfart.

This involvement within the Danish bus market led to the acquisition of Bus Danmark (now Arriva Danmark) in 1999 and its wholly owned subsidiary Odakra Buss based in southern Sweden. In April 2000, Arriva Danmark acquired the former state owned Company, COMBUS. Part of the company was sold on to Connex but Arriva kept the majority of its regional and provincial bus operations throughout Denmark. Arriva Danmark operates a fleet of approximately 1150 buses, including demand responsive vehicles, and 43 train sets. During 2001 the first double-deck buses for the Danish fleet were delivered.

Arriva Danmark was also successful with its bid in respect of the first rail passenger franchises to be announced in Denmark. The package consists of two rail passenger franchises connecting Mid and North Jutland with Arhus. The franchises commenced operation in January 2003. Twenty-nine new Coradia Lint trains were delivered in 2004.

The Netherlands

Arriva entered the Dutch market through the acquisition of Vancom Nederland (now Arriva Nederland) in 1998, which operated the former municipal undertaking in the city of Groningen together with demand responsive services in the region and a joint venture in the Maastricht area of Zuid Limburg.

Arriva Nederland subsequently acquired the former VSN subsidiary companies of Veonn and Hanze covering the provinces of Friesland, Groningen and Drenthe. The companies operate an extensive network of urban and interurban bus services, and demand responsive transit.

In June 1999, Arriva made its first move into rail with NoordNed, a joint venture with Dutch Rail which represented the first rail privatisation in the Netherlands. This franchise operates bus and train services in Friesland and train services in the Province of Groningen. Arriva took full control of Noordned in 2003.

Arriva Nederland, now operates some 1200 vehicles, 51 train sets, has 2700 employees and is the geographic hub for the Group's potential interests in the Benelux countries.

Spain

Arriva's interest in the Spanish market commenced with the acquisition of IASA and Finisterre, both located in the Galicia region. Branded Arriva Noroeste, the company operates throughout Galicia with substantial facilities at La Coruña, Lugo and Santiago de Compostela providing regular, schools and discretional services. Arriva also operates buses in Mallorca. Its combined Spanish businesses have a fleet of over 300 vehicles and 500 employees.

Sweden

Arriva first entered the Swedish bus market when it acquired the Danish company Unibus Holdings in 1997. It operates 200 vehicles and employs around 500 people in the south of Sweden. Arriva Sverige (Odakra Buss) activities are focused in the Skane Lan region of southern Sweden operating 160 buses. In 2005 a new contract called for a large fleet of MAN buses to operate in the city of Helsingborg.

Portugal

Arriva's presence in Iberia was further strengthened through its entry into Portuguese public transport. This was achieved through the acquisition of Ami-Transportes SA, Joao Carlos Soares and Filhos SA, Viaco Costa Lino SA and Abilio da Costa Moreira SA. Collectively, these companies operate some 250 buses, with 340 employees on regional bus services in the northern half of Portugal.

In June 2002, Arriva acquired a 51% controlling interest in Transportes Sul ode Tejo (TST), Portugal, from the Barraqueiro Group, with an option to acquire the remaining 49% by 31 December 2003. TST is the leading operator of scheduled bus and coach services in the growing commuter region south of Lisbon. The company also operates schools and works contracts. The region has a large and growing population, and much of TST's operations involve the carriage of Lisbon commuters to ferry services on the River Tejo (Tagus) and the new cross-river railway. Arriva exercised its option to acquire the remaining 49% of TST in August 2003.

Arriva Portugal's combined business has a fleet of over 900 vehicles and 1,750 employees.

Italy

In July 2002, Arriva made its first acquisition in Italy with the purchase of SAB Autoservizi SrL, the largest private-sector bus operator in Italy, from parent company Italmobilare. The company operates mainly in the Lombardi (Lombardy) region of northern Italy, where it has a 13% share of the bus transport market. The majority of the region's other services are operated by municipal authorities. The passenger transport market in Italy is one of the largest in Europe with both bus and rail sectors moving rapidly to a competitive tendering environment.

Arriva made a further acquisition in April 2004 when it acquired Società Autoservizi F.V.G. S.p.A. in the Udine area of the Friuli Venezia Giulia region. Arriva's combined Italian businesses operate around 1,800 vehicles and employ around 2,600 staff.

The SAVDA Group bus businesses acquired in July 2005 operate in the Piemonte (Piedmont) and Valle d'Aosta regions of Northern Italy to the west of Arriva's current operations. Their main activity is the operation of public transport bus services as well as commercial, contract and private hire services. The operations include a 50 per cent holding in Autostradale, which operates scheduled bus services in Lombardy and Piemonte as well as operating airport shuttle services.

The Italian passenger market is the third largest in Europe and is evolving rapidly towards competitive tendering of all bus operations so the purchase offers significant opportunities for expansion.

Germany

Arriva entered the German public transport market - the largest in Europe - in April 2004, with the acquisition of rail company Prignitzer Eisenbahn Gruppe (PEG). PEG runs services in the federal states of North Rhine-Westphalia, Brandenburg and Mecklenburg-West Pomerania. With 21 train sets and 250 employees, Arriva now operates five franchises, two of which involve a joint venture. In February 2005 Arriva acquired German bus business Sippel which operates throughout the Rhine-Main area.

Arriva Trains

In 2000, Arriva acquired two British rail franchises as part of its purchase of MTL, the Liverpool-based transport company. The refranchising process has been protracted.

Arriva failed to make the shortlist of bidders for the Merseyrail franchise although it was rated the best mainland operator in terms of punctuality and reliability in the latest figures published by the SRA.

Arriva's UK Trains division operates two rail passenger operating Companies. Arriva Trains Wales/Trenau Arriva Cymru operates interurban, commuter and rural passenger services throughout Wales and the border counties. Arriva Trains Northern which operates extensively across the north of England.

Arriva Vehicle Rental

Arriva Vehicle Rental continues to perform strongly and is expected to grow over the next five years as Government's 'Best Value Initiative' encourages the public sector to outsource vehicle fleets. The current fleet is around 11,000 vehicles based at 42 locations. Vehicle Rental has been trading with six business brands, but each is now migrating to the Arriva brand.

Arriva operates several services in Denmark. Arriva was the top performing rail operator in Denmark with a total reliability of 98 per cent and won bonuses under its contract for each of the last three quarters of 2003. During 2004, Arriva introduced 29 new Alstom Coradia Lint trains fitted with a new generation of environmentally friendly EURO III engines. One of the new arrivals, AR26, is pictured at Viborg rail station where the single line has two passing loops. *Bill Potter*

ARRIVA SCOTLAND

Arriva Scotland West Ltd, Old Greenock Road, Inchinnan, PA4 9PG

2740	JO	N803BKN	Optare MetroRider MR15		Optare		B29F	1996	Arriva Southern Counties, 2004
2741	JO	N804BKN	Optare MetroRider MR15		Optare		B29F	1996	Arriva Southern Counties, 2004
195	JO	P895XCU	Optare MetroRider		Optare		B31F	1996	Arriva North East, 2000
196	JO	P896XCU	Optare MetroRider		Optare		B31F	1996	Arriva North East, 2000

201-208
Optare MetroRider MR17 — Optare — B29F — 1996

201	IN	N201NHS	203	IN	N203NHS	205	IN	N205NHS	207	IN	N207NHS
202	IN	N202NHS	204	IN	N204NHS	206	IN	N206NHS	208	IN	N208NHS

217-227
Optare MetroRider MR17 — Optare — B29F — 1996

217	IN	P217SGB	220	IN	P220SGB	224	IN	P224SGB	226	IN	P226SGB
218	IN	P218SGB	221	IN	P221SGB	225	IN	P225SGB	227	JO	P227SGB
219	IN	P219SGB	223	IN	P223SGB						

267	JO	N81PUS	Mercedes-Benz 811D	Marshall C16	B33F	1996	Ashton Group, Greenock, 1997
268	IN	N82PUS	Mercedes-Benz 811D	Marshall C16	B33F	1996	Ashton Group, Greenock, 1997
269	JO	N26KYS	Mercedes-Benz 811D	Plaxton Beaver	B33F	1995	Ashton Group, Greenock, 1997
270	JO	N27KYS	Mercedes-Benz 811D	Plaxton Beaver	B33F	1995	Ashton Group, Greenock, 1997
271	IN	P932YSB	Mercedes-Benz 811D	Mellor	B33F	1997	Ashton Group, Greenock, 1997
273	JO	P937YSB	Mercedes-Benz 811D	Mellor	B33F	1997	Ashton Group, Greenock, 1997
276	JO	P492TGA	Mercedes-Benz 711D	UVG CitiStar	B29F	1996	Ashton Group, Greenock, 1997
277	JO	P527UGA	Mercedes-Benz 711D	Marshall C19	B29F	1996	Ashton Group, Greenock, 1997
298	JO	P931YSB	Mercedes-Benz 709D	Plaxton Beaver	B29F	1997	Ashton Group, Greenock, 1997
299	JO	P529UGA	Mercedes-Benz 709D	Plaxton Beaver	B29F	1997	Ashton Group, Greenock, 1997
300	JO	P528UGA	Mercedes-Benz 709D	Plaxton Beaver	B29F	1997	Ashton Group, Greenock, 1997
303	IN	M878DDS	Mercedes-Benz 709D	WS Wessex II	B29F	1994	Ashton Group, Greenock, 1997
401	IN	M65FDS	Dennis Dart 9.8m	Plaxton Pointer	B41F	1995	
402	IN	M67FDS	Dennis Dart 9.8m	Plaxton Pointer	B41F	1995	
403	IN	K538ORH	Dennis Dart 9m	Plaxton Pointer	B34F	1992	Arriva London, 2002
404	IN	K539ORH	Dennis Dart 9m	Plaxton Pointer	B34F	1992	Arriva London, 2002
405	IN	K540ORH	Dennis Dart 9m	Plaxton Pointer	B34F	1992	Arriva London, 2002
406	IN	K541ORH	Dennis Dart 9m	Plaxton Pointer	B34F	1992	Arriva London, 2002
407	IN	N681GUM	Dennis Dart 9.8m	Plaxton Pointer	B40F	1995	Arriva London, 2002
408	IN	N684GUM	Dennis Dart 9.8m	Plaxton Pointer	B40F	1995	Arriva London, 2002
409	IN	P822RWU	Dennis Dart 9.8m	Plaxton Pointer	B40F	1996	Arriva London, 2002
410	IN	N710GUM	Dennis Dart 9m	Plaxton Pointer	B34F	1995	Arriva London, 2003
411	IN	N711GUM	Dennis Dart 9m	Plaxton Pointer	B34F	1995	Arriva London, 2003
412	IN	N712GUM	Dennis Dart 9m	Plaxton Pointer	B34F	1995	Arriva London, 2003
413	IN	P913PWW	Dennis Dart 9m	Plaxton Pointer	B34F	1996	Arriva London, 2003
414	IN	P914PWW	Dennis Dart 9m	Plaxton Pointer	B34F	1996	Arriva London, 2003
415	IN	P915PWW	Dennis Dart 9m	Plaxton Pointer	B34F	1996	Arriva London, 2003
416	JO	P962RUL	Dennis Dart SLF 10.2m	Alexander ALX200	N36F	1997	Arriva London, 2003
417	JO	P963RUL	Dennis Dart SLF 10.2m	Alexander ALX200	N36F	1997	Arriva London, 2003
418	IN	N708GUM	Dennis Dart 9.0m	Plaxton Pointer	B34F	1995	Arriva London, 2003
419	IN	N709GUM	Dennis Dart 9.0m	Plaxton Pointer	B34F	1995	Arriva London, 2003

420-424
Dennis Dart SLF 10.2m — Alexander ALX200 — N36F — 1997 — Arriva London, 2003

420	JO	P964RUL	422	JO	P966RUL	423	JO	P967RUL	424	JO	P968RUL
421	JO	P965RUL								

425-433
Dennis Dart 9.8m — Plaxton Pointer — B40F — 1995-96 — Arriva London, 2003

425	IN	N672GUM	428	IN	N683GUM	430	IN	N686GUM	432	IN	N688GUM
426	IN	N675GUM	429	IN	N685GUM	431	IN	N687GUM	433	IN	N691GUM
427	IN	N677GUM								

504	IN	M104RMS	Scania L113CRL	Alexander Strider	B51F	1995	
506	IN	M106RMS	Scania L113CRL	Alexander Strider	B51F	1995	
507	IN	M107RMS	Scania L113CRL	Alexander Strider	B51F	1995	

508-513
Scania N113CRL — East Lancs European — N45F* — 1995 — *509 is N51F

508	IN	M108RMS	510	IN	M110RMS	512	IN	M112RMS	513	IN	M113RMS
509	JO	M109RMS							

Arriva Scotland operates in an area to the south-west of the River Clyde, with Renfrew in the north and Johnstone further south. Many of the routes are operated by minibuses and Darts. In the centre of the operating area is Glasgow Airport, where MetroRider 201, N201NHS, was pictured in May 2005. *Mark Doggett*

514-521

			Scania L113CRL			East Lancs European		N51F	1995		
514	IN	M114RMS	516	IN	M116RMS	518	IN	M118RMS	520	IN	M120RMS
515	IN	M115RMS	517	IN	M117RMS	519	JO	M119RMS	521	JO	M121RMS

525	IN	L25LSX	Scania N113CRL			East Lancs European		N51F	1993	Scania demonstrator, 1995	

798	JO	WSU475	Dennis Dart SLF 10.7m			Plaxton Pointer 2		N43F	1999		
799	JO	WSU476	Dennis Dart SLF 10.7m			Plaxton Pointer 2		N43F	1999		
800	JO	GSU347	Dennis Dart SLF 10.7m			Plaxton Pointer 2		N43F	1999		

801-805

			Dennis Dart SLF			Plaxton Pointer		N35F	1996		
801	JO	P801RWU	803	JO	P803RWU	804	JO	P804RWU	805	JO	P805RWU
802	JO	P802RWU									

806-815

			Dennis Dart SLF			Alexander ALX200		N40F	1997		
806	JO	P806DBS	809	JO	P809DBS	812	JO	P812DBS	814	JO	P814DBS
807	JO	P807DBS	810	JO	P810DBS	813	JO	P813DBS	815	JO	P815DBS
808	JO	P808DBS	811	JO	P811DBS						

816-840

			Dennis Dart SLF			Plaxton Pointer		N40F	1997		
816	JO	P816GMS	823	JO	P823GMS	829	JO	P829KES	835	IN	P835KES
817	JO	P817GMS	824	JO	P824GMS	830	JO	P830KES	836	IN	P836KES
818	JO	P818GMS	825	JO	P825KES	831	JO	P831KES	837	IN	P837KES
819	JO	P819GMS	826	IN	P826KES	832	JO	P832KES	838	JO	P838KES
820	JO	P820GMS	827	IN	P827KES	833	JO	P833KES	839	JO	P839KES
821	IN	P821GMS	828	JO	P828KES	834	JO	P834KES	840	JO	P840KES
822	JO	P822GMS									

841	IN	N439GHG	Dennis Dart 9.8m	Northern Counties Paladin	B39F	1995	
842	IN	N440GHG	Dennis Dart 9.8m	Northern Counties Paladin	B39F	1995	
843	IN	N473MUS	Dennis Dart 9.8m	Northern Counties Paladin	B39F	1995	
844	IN	N474MUS	Dennis Dart 9.8m	Northern Counties Paladin	B39F	1995	
845	IN	K946SGG	Dennis Dart 9m	Plaxton Pointer	B35F	1993	
846	IN	K947SGG	Dennis Dart 9m	Plaxton Pointer	B35F	1993	

All seven of Arriva Scotland's double-deck buses are Volvo Citybus models transferred from the south. Pictured in Paisley, 882, H675GPF, illustrates the East Lancs bodywork. *Richard Godfrey*

847-851

						Dennis Dart SLF	Alexander ALX200	N40F	1998

847	JO	R381JYS	**849**	JO	R383JYS	**850**	JO	R384JYS	**851**	JO	R385JYS
848	JO	R382JYS									

852	IN	M248SPP	Dennis Dart 9.8m	Wright Handy-bus	B40F	1994	The Shires, 1998
853	IN	M250SPP	Dennis Dart 9.8m	Wright Handy-bus	B40F	1994	The Shires, 1998
854	JO	H242MUK	Dennis Dart 9.8m	Carlyle Dartline	B40F	1991	The Shires, 1998
855	IN	M251SPP	Dennis Dart 9.8m	Wright Handy-bus	B40F	1994	The Shires, 1998
856	IN	M249SPP	Dennis Dart 9.8m	Wright Handy-bus	B40F	1994	The Shires, 1998
857	JO	H244MUK	Dennis Dart 9.8m	Carlyle Dartline	B40F	1991	The Shires, 1998
858	IN	M247SPP	Dennis Dart 9.8m	Wright Handy-bus	B40F	1994	The Shires, 1998

860-869

						Dennis Dart SLF	Alexander ALX200	N40F	1998-99

860	JO	S860OGB	**863**	JO	S863OGB	**866**	JO	S866OGB	**868**	JO	S868OGB
861	JO	S861OGB	**864**	JO	S864OGB	**867**	JO	S867OGB	**869**	JO	HIL2148
862	JO	S862OGB	**865**	JO	S865OGB						

880-885

					Volvo Citybus B10M-50	East Lancs	B45/31F	1990-91	London South, 1998-99

880	JO	H668GPF	**882**	JO	H675GPF	**884**	IN	H677GPF	**885**	IN	H670GPF
881	JO	H681GPF	**883**	JO	H676GPF						

954	IN	G154TYT	Volvo Citybus B10M-55	Alexander RV	B46/33F	1990	Arriva London (NE), 1999
1001	JO	N750LUS	Mercedes-Benz OH1416	Wright Urbanranger	B47F	1995	
1918	JO	W78PRG	DAF SB120	Wright Cadet	N39F	2000	Arriva North East, 2005
1919	JO	W79PRG	DAF SB120	Wright Cadet	N39F	2000	Arriva North East, 2005
1951	IN	YJ54CKG	VDL Bus SB120	Wrightbus Cadet 2	N30F	2004	
1952	IN	YJ54CKK	VDL Bus SB120	Wrightbus Cadet 2	N30F	2004	

Ancillary vehicles:

701	JO	E26ECH	Scania K92CRB	Alexander PS	TV	1988	Arriva Midlands, 2003
9985	JO	H31PAJ	Leyland Lynx LX2R11C15Z4S	Leyland Lynx 2	TV	1991	Arriva North East, 2004
9989	JO	G511EAJ	Leyland Lynx LX2R11C15Z4S	Leyland Lynx	TV	1990	Arriva North East, 2003

Previous registrations:

GSU347	V313NGD	TUP572V	TUP572V, HIL2148
HIL2148	S869OGB	WSU475	V311NGD
LAZ5785	C203PCD	WSU476	V312NGD
N750LUS	N750LUS, WSU476		

Allocations:

Inchinnan (Greenock Road) - IN

MetroRider	201	202	203	204	205	206	207	208
	217	218	219	220	223	224	225	226
Mercedes-Benz	268	271	303					
Dart	401	402	403	404	405	406	407	408
	409	410	411	412	413	414	415	418
	419	425	426	427	428	429	430	431
	432	433	821	826	827	835	836	837
	841	842	843	844	845	846	852	853
	855	858						
SB120/Cadet	1951	1952						
Scania sd	504	506	507	508	510	512	513	514
	515	516	517	518	520	525		
Volvo Citybus	884	885	954					

Johnstone (Cochranemill Road) - JO

MetroRider	105	196	227					
Mercedes-Benz	267	269	270	273	276	277	298	299
	300							
Dart	401	416	417	420	421	422	423	424
	798	799	800	801	802	803	804	805
	806	807	808	809	810	811	812	813
	815	816	817	818	819	820	822	823
	824	825	828	829	830	831	832	833
	834	838	839	840	847	848	849	850
	851	854	857	860	861	862	863	864
	865	866	867	868	869			
SB120/Cadet	1918	1919						
MB Urbanranger	1001							
Scania SD	509	519	521					
Volvo Citybus	880	881	882	883				
Ancillary	701	9985	9989					

Scania buses were selected by British Bus in 1995 and these are the only full-length single-decks now operated. East Lancs European body styling is seen on 519, N119RMS, which operates alongside three with Alexander bodywork. *Mark Lyons*

ARRIVA NORTH EAST

Arriva North East Ltd, Arriva House, Admiral Way, Sunderland, SR3 3XP

142	NE	V142EJR	DAF SB3000	Van Hool T9 Alizée	C44FT	1999	
143	NE	X143WNL	DAF SB3000	Van Hool T9 Alizée	C49FT	2000	
144	NE	X144WNL	DAF SB3000	Van Hool T9 Alizée	C49FT	2000	
145	NE	NL52XZV	DAF SB4000XF	Van Hool T9 Alizée	C49FT	2002	
146	NE	NL52XZW	DAF SB4000XF	Van Hool T9 Alizée	C49FT	2002	
147	NE	NL52XZX	DAF SB4000XF	Van Hool T9 Alizée	C49FT	2002	
148	NE	NL52XZY	DAF SB4000XF	Van Hool T9 Alizée	C49FT	2002	
214	w	XSV691	Leyland Tiger TRCTL11/3ARZA	Plaxton Paramount 3200 III	C53F	1988	Maidstone & District, 1998
215	w	YSU870	Leyland Tiger TRCTL11/3ARZ	Plaxton Paramount 3500 III	C53F	1988	Maidstone & District, 1998
216	w	YSU871	Leyland Tiger TRCTL11/3ARZ	Plaxton Paramount 3500 III	C53F	1988	Maidstone & District, 1998
217	w	F188HKK	Leyland Tiger TRCL10/3ARZA	Duple 340	C53F	1989	Maidstone & District, 1998
247	w	B277KPF	Leyland Tiger TRCTL11/3RH	Plaxton Paramount 3200 IIE	C51F	1985	Kentish Bus, 1992

271-280
Scania L113CRL — East Lancs European — NC45F — 1996

271	NE	P271VRG	274	AS	P274VRG	277	BL	P277VRG	279	BL	P279VRG
272	NE	P272VRG	275	BL	P275VRG	278	BL	P278VRG	280	BL	P814VTY
273	AS	P273VRG	276	BL	P276VRG						

281-290
Scania L113CRL — East Lancs European — NC45F — 1995

281	AS	N281NCN	284	AS	N284NCN	287	BL	N287NCN	289	AS	N289NCN
282	AS	N282NCN	285	BL	N285NCN	288	BL	N288NCN	290	AS	N290NCN
283	AS	N283NCN									

601	w	BYX210V	MCW Metrobus DR101/12	MCW		B43/28F	1980	London North, 1998
604	DU	KYV646X	MCW Metrobus DR101/14	MCW		B43/28F	1982	London North, 1998
611	NE	GYE396W	MCW Metrobus DR101/12	MCW		B43/28F	1980	Arriva London, 2000
614	w	GYE515W	MCW Metrobus DR101/14	MCW		B43/28F	1981	Arriva London, 2000
615	w	KYV671X	MCW Metrobus DR101/14	MCW		B43/28F	1982	Arriva London, 2000
617	DU	OJD858Y	MCW Metrobus DR101/16	MCW		B43/28F	1983	Arriva London, 2000
620	w	WLT954	MCW Metrobus DR101/16	MCW		B43/28F	1984	Arriva London, 2000

621-631
MCW Metrobus DR101/17 — MCW — B43/28D* — 1984-85 — Arriva London, *621-5 B43/28F

621	w	A959SYF	624	NE	B116WUL	626	NE	B86WUL	630	NE	B90WUL
622	DU	A973SYF	625	HX	C354BUV	629	NE	B89WUL	631	NE	B91WUL
623	w	B112WUL									

Arriva North East's 2733, M447HPF, is seen on former Green Bus service 17a, the Newton Aycliffe circular.
Bob Downham

The Plaxton Prima Interurban is a development of the earlier Premiere Interurban model and continues to include many bus features in the coach shell to allow service operation. Arriva North East operates two batches, among which is 1207, V207DJR, carrying route lettering for the Middlesbrough to Scarborough service.

871-875
Optare MetroRider   Optare MR17   B31F   1995

871	BA	M871LBB	872	RD	M872LBB	873	RD	M873LBB	875	BL	M875LBB

877-894
Optare MetroRider   Optare MR17   B31F   1996

877	BL	N877RTN	882	BL	N882RTN	887	BL	N887RTN	891	AS	N891RTN
878	BL	N878RTN	883	BL	N883RTN	888	SN	N192RVK	892	AS	P892XCU
879	HX	N879RTN	884	BL	N884RTN	889	AS	N889RTN	893	SN	P893XCU
880	BL	N880RTN	885	DU	N885RTN	890	AK	N890RTN	894	PE	P894XCU
881	BL	N881RTN	886	AK	N886RTN						

897-901
Optare MetroRider   Optare MR17   B31F   1996   Arriva Scotland, 2002

897	SN	P56XTN	899	DU	P58XTN	900	NE	P59XTN	901	NE	P61XTN
898	BL	P57XTN									

902-923
Optare MetroRider MR15   Optare   B31F   1997-98

902	BL	P902DRG	908	AK	R908JNL	914	AS	R914JNL	919	AS	R919JNL
903	SN	P903DRG	909	AK	R909JNL	915	AS	R915JNL	920	BL	R920JNL
904	AS	P904DRG	910	AS	R910JNL	916	AS	R916JNL	921	NE	R921JNL
905	AS	P905JNL	911	AS	R251JNL	917	AS	R917JNL	922	HX	R922JNL
906	AS	P906JNL	912	AS	R912JNL	918	AS	R918JNL	923	HX	R923JNL
907	AS	R907JNL	913	AS	R913JNL						

937
937   AS   L700BUS   Optare MetroRider MR11   Optare   B32F   1996   Arriva The Shires, 2002

1201-1205
DAF SB3000   Plaxton Prima Interurban   BC51F   1997

1201	HX	R291KRG	1203	HX	R293KRG	1204	HX	R294KRG	1205	HX	R295KRG
1202	HX	R292KRG									

1206-1214
DAF SB3000   Plaxton Prima Interurban   BC51F   1999

1200	LS	V206DJR	1209	LS	V209DJR	1211	AK	V211DJR	1213	AK	V213DJR
1207	LS	V207DJR	1210	AK	V210DJR	1212	AK	V212DJR	1214	HX	V214DJR
1208	LS	V208DJR									

Vehicle rationalisation saw all the Optare Vecta buses move to the North East fleet, where the majority already operated. Illustrating the type is 1548, L548GHN, which is seen in Durham while operating route 5 from Shildon and Bishop Auckland. *Bob Downham*

| 1502 | u | J620UHN | MAN 11.190 | | | | Optare Vecta | | B42F | 1991 | |

1504-1517
			MAN 11.190				Optare Vecta		B42F	1993	*1509-13 are BC42F
1504	SN	K504BHN	1508	SN	K508BHN	1512	LS	K512BHN	1515	LS	K515BHN
1505	SN	K505BHN	1509	SN	K509BHN	1513	SN	K513BHN	1516	u	K516BHN
1506	SN	K506BHN	1510	RR	K510BHN	1514	SN	K514BHN	1517	BA	K517BHN
1507	SN	K507BHN	1511	u	K511BHN						

1519-1551
			MAN 11.190				Optare Vecta		B42F	1994	
1519	SN	L519FHN	1528	LS	L528FHN	1536	LS	L536FHN	1545	BA	L545GHN
1521	SN	L521FHN	1529	SN	L529FHN	1537	RR	L537FHN	1546	u	L546GHN
1522	u	L522FHN	1530	SN	L530FHN	1539	u	L539FHN	1547	BA	L547GHN
1523	u	L523FHN	1531	SN	L531FHN	1540	BA	L540FHN	1548	BA	L548GHN
1524	LS	L524FHN	1532	u	L532FHN	1541	BA	L541FHN	1549	BA	L549GHN
1525	SN	L525FHN	1533	SN	L533FHN	1542	SN	L542FHN	1550	BA	L550GHN
1526	SN	L526FHN	1534	LS	L534FHN	1543	RR	L543FHN	1551	RR	L551GHN
1527	RR	L527FHN	1535	BA	L535FHN	1544	SN	L544GHN			

1552	u	M501AJC	MAN 11.190	Optare Vecta	B42F	1995	Arriva Cymru, 1998
1553	RR	M502AJC	MAN 11.190	Optare Vecta	B42F	1995	Arriva Cymru, 1999
1554	u	M503AJC	MAN 11.190	Optare Vecta	B42F	1995	Arriva Cymru, 1999
1555	RR	M504AJC	MAN 11.190	Optare Vecta	B42F	1995	Arriva Cymru, 1999
1556	SN	UOI772	MAN 11.190	Optare Vecta	BC42F	1993	Arriva Midlands North, 1999
1557	u	L102MEH	MAN 11.190	Optare Vecta	B42F	1994	Arriva Midlands North, 1999
1558	SN	K140RYS	MAN 11.190	Optare Vecta	BC42F	1993	Arriva Midlands North, 1999

1636-1643
			Dennis Dart SLF 10.1m			Plaxton Pointer 2		N39F	1999	
1636	PE	S636KHN	1638	PE	S638KHN	1640	PE	S640KHN	1642	PE	S642KHN
1637	PE	S637KHN	1639	PE	S639KHN	1641	PE	S641KHN	1643	PE	S643KHN

1701	NE	T701RCN	Dennis Dart SLF 8.8m	Plaxton Pointer MPD	N29F	1999
1702	BL	T702RCN	Dennis Dart SLF 8.8m	Plaxton Pointer MPD	N29F	1999

A recently arrival to meet small vehicle needs is a batch of Alexander Dennis Mini Pointers. Illustrating the delivery is the first numerically, 1760, NK05GVX, seen on Hexham town service 802. *Bob Downham*

1703-1723

				Dennis Dart SLF 8.8m			Plaxton Pointer MPD		N29F	1999		
1703	DU	V703DNL	1709	DU	V709DNL	1714	BA	V714DNL	1719	SN	V719DNL
1704	DU	V612DNL	1710	DU	V710DNL	1715	BA	V715DNL	1720	SN	V720DNL
1705	DU	V705DNL	1711	BA	V711DNL	1716	PE	V716DNL	1721	SN	V721DNL
1706	DU	V706DNL	1712	BA	V712DNL	1717	RD	V717DNL	1722	SN	V722DNL
1707	DU	V707DNL	1713	BA	V713DNL	1718	RR	V718DNL	1723	SN	V723DNL
1708	PE	V708DNL									

1724-1742

				Dennis Dart SLF 8.8m			Plaxton Pointer MPD		N29F	1999		
1724	BL	V724DNL	1729	NE	V729DNL	1734	AS	V734DNL	1739	AS	V739DNL
1725	BL	V725DNL	1730	NE	V730DNL	1735	AS	V735DNL	1740	NE	V740DNL
1726	BL	V726DNL	1731	BL	V731DNL	1736	AS	V736DNL	1741	NE	V741DNL
1727	BL	V727DNL	1732	HX	V732DNL	1737	AS	V737DNL	1742	NE	V742DNL
1728	NE	V728DNL	1733	BL	V733DNL	1738	AS	V738DNL			

1743-1749

				Dennis Dart SLF 8.8m			Plaxton Pointer MPD		N29F	2000		
1743	SN	V743ECU	1745	DL	V745ECU	1747	SN	V747ECU	1749	HX	V749ECU
1744	SN	V744ECU	1746	DL	V746ECU	1748	SN	V748ECU			

1750-1757

				Dennis Dart SLF 8.8m			Plaxton Pointer MPD		N29F	2000		
1750	NE	W751SBR	1752	NE	W753SBR	1754	RR	W756SBR	1756	LS	W758SBR
1751	NE	W752SBR	1753	RR	W754SBR	1755	LS	W757SBR	1757	SN	W759SBR
1758	BL	NK53HJA	TransBus Dart SLF 8.8m		TransBus Mini Pointer			N29F	2003		
1759	SN	NK53VKA	TransBus Dart SLF 8.8m		TransBus Mini Pointer			N20F	2004		

1760-1775

				Alexander Dennis Dart 8.8m			Alexander Dennis Mini Pointer	NC29F	2005			
1760	HX	NK05GVX	1764	DU	NK05GWC	1768	DU	NK05GWG	1772	DU	NK05GWO
1761	DL	NK05GVY	1765	DU	NK05GWD	1769	DU	NK05GWJ	1773	DU	NK05GWU
1762	DL	NK05GVG	1766	DU	NK05GWE	1770	DU	NK05GWM	1774	u	NK05GWV
1763	DU	NK05GWA	1767	DU	NK05GWF	1771	DU	NK05GWN	1775	u	NK05GWW

1801	BL	NK53HHX	VDL Bus SB200	Wrightbus Commander	N44F	2003
1802	BL	NK53HHY	VDL Bus SB200	Wrightbus Commander	N44F	2003
1803	BL	NK53HHZ	VDL Bus SB200	Wrightbus Commander	N44F	2003

1901-1922

| | | | DAF SB120 | Wright Cadet | N39F | 2000 |

1901	SN	W301PPT	1906	SN	W308PPT	1911	SN	W314PPT	1916	RR	W72PRG
1902	SN	W302PPT	1907	SN	W309PPT	1912	SN	W315PPT	1917	SN	W76PRG
1903	SN	W303PPT	1908	SN	W311PPT	1913	SN	W317PPT	1920	RR	W81PRG
1904	SN	W304PPT	1909	SN	W312PPT	1914	SN	W319PPT	1921	RR	W82PRG
1905	SN	W307PPT	1910	SN	W313PPT	1915	RR	W69PRG	1922	RR	W83PRG

2606-2645

| | | | Optare MetroRider MR35 | Optare | | B25F | 1996-97 |

2606	SN	P606FHN	2616	DL	P616FHN	2627	PE	P627FHN	2637	LS	P637FHN
2607	SN	P607FHN	2617	PE	P617FHN	2628	PE	P628FHN	2638	LS	P638FHN
2608	SN	P608FHN	2618	LS	P618FHN	2629	u	P629FHN	2639	LS	P639FHN
2609	SN	P609FHN	2619	RD	P619FHN	2630	DL	P630FHN	2640	DL	P640FHN
2610	DL	P610FHN	2620	w	P620FHN	2631	DL	P631FHN	2641	RD	P641FHN
2611	BA	P611FHN	2621	RD	P621FHN	2632	RD	P632FHN	2642	DL	P642FHN
2612	DL	P612FHN	2622	u	P622FHN	2633	RD	P633FHN	2643	DL	P643FHN
2613	RD	P613FHN	2623	BA	P623FHN	2634	RD	P634FHN	2644	BA	P644FHN
2614	SN	P614FHN	2624	PE	P624FHN	2635	LS	P635FHN	2645	BA	P645FHN
2615	SN	P615FHN	2625	RD	P625FHN	2636	SN	P636FHN			

2646-2655

| | | | Mercedes-Benz Vario O814 | Alexander ALX100 | | B27F | 2001 |

2646	BL	X646WTN	2649	BL	X649WTN	2652	BL	X652WTN	2654	BL	X654WTN
2647	BL	X647WTN	2650	BL	X657WTN	2653	BL	X653WTN	2655	BL	X656WTN
2648	BL	X648WTN	2651	BL	X651WTN						

2656	u	R110GNW	Mercedes-Benz Vario O814	Plaxton Beaver 2	B27F	1998	Arriva North West, 2005
2657	u	R130GNW	Mercedes-Benz Vario O814	Alexander ALX100	B27F	1998	Arriva North West, 2005
2658	BL	S822MCC	Mercedes-Benz Vario O814	Plaxton Beaver 2	B27F	1998	Arriva North West, 2005
2659	LS	R113GNW	Mercedes-Benz Vario O814	Plaxton Beaver 2	B33F	1998	Arriva North West, 2005
2660	BL	R112GNW	Mercedes-Benz Vario O814	Plaxton Beaver 2	B33F	1998	Arriva North West, 2005
2661	u	R129GNW	Mercedes-Benz Vario O814	Alexander ALX100	B27F	1998	Arriva North West, 2005
2662	u	S350PGA	Mercedes-Benz Vario O814	Plaxton Beaver 2	B27F	1998	Arriva North West, 2005
2663	u	S353PGA	Mercedes-Benz Vario O814	Plaxton Beaver 2	B27F	1998	Arriva North West, 2005
2664	BL	R798DUB	Mercedes-Benz Vario O810	Plaxton Beaver 2	B31F	1997	Arriva North West, 2005
2665	LS	S354PGA	Mercedes-Benz Vario O814	Plaxton Beaver 2	B27F	1998	Arriva North West, 2005
2666	LS	S823MCC	Mercedes-Benz Vario O814	Plaxton Beaver 2	B27F	1998	Arriva North West, 2005
2667	u	S351PGA	Mercedes-Benz Vario O814	Plaxton Beaver 2	B27F	1998	Arriva North West, 2005
2668	BL	R792DUB	Mercedes-Benz Vario O810	Plaxton Beaver 2	B31F	1997	Arriva North West, 2005
2669	BL	S352PGA	Mercedes-Benz Vario O814	Plaxton Beaver 2	B27F	1998	Arriva North West, 2005
2670	u	R792DUB	Mercedes-Benz Vario O810	Plaxton Beaver 2	B31F	1997	Arriva North West, 2005
2671	u	R795DUB	Mercedes-Benz Vario O810	Plaxton Beaver 2	B31F	1997	Arriva North West, 2005
2672	u	R796DUB	Mercedes-Benz Vario O810	Plaxton Beaver 2	B31F	1997	Arriva North West, 2005
2673	u	R794DUB	Mercedes-Benz Vario O810	Plaxton Beaver 2	B31F	1997	Arriva North West, 2005

2701-2725

| | | | Optare MetroRider MR15 | Optare | | B31F | 1997-98 |

2701	DL	R701MHN	2708	RD	R708MHN	2714	AS	R714MHN	2720	DL	R720MHN
2702	DL	R702MHN	2709	PE	R709MHN	2715	DL	R715MHN	2721	DL	R721MHN
2703	DL	R703MHN	2710	PE	R710MHN	2716	PE	R716MHN	2722	DL	R722MHN
2704	DL	R704MHN	2711	AS	R711MHN	2717	DL	R717MHN	2723	DL	R723MHN
2705	DL	R705MHN	2712	DL	R712MHN	2718	AS	R718MHN	2724	DL	R724MHN
2706	DL	R706MHN	2713	AS	R713MHN	2719	AS	R719MHN	2725	PE	R725MHN
2707	RD	R707MHN									

2726-2737

| | | | Optare MetroRider MR17 | Optare | | B29F | 1994 | Arriva Southern Counties, 2004 |

2726	LS	M440HPF	2729	u	M443HPF	2732	w	M446HPF	2735	u	M449HPF
2727	BA	M441HPF	2730	SN	M444HPF	2733	DL	M447HPF	2736	DU	M452HPG
2728	LS	M442HPF	2731	u	M445HPF	2734	w	M448HPF	2737	u	M453HPG

2738	DL	N801BKN	Optare MetroRider MR15	Optare	B29F	1996	Arriva Southern Counties, 2004
2739	DL	N802BKN	Optare MetroRider MR15	Optare	B29F	1996	Arriva Southern Counties, 2004
2742	PE	P472APJ	Optare MetroRider MR17	Optare	B29F	1996	Arriva Southern Counties, 2004
2872	RR	H923XYT	Volvo Citybus B10M-55	East Lancashire EL2000	B41F	1990	Arriva Scotland, 2004
2873	LS	H925XYT	Volvo Citybus B10M-55	East Lancashire EL2000	B41F	1990	Arriva Scotland, 2004
2875	RR	H917XYT	Volvo Citybus B10M-55	East Lancashire EL2000	B41F	1990	Arriva Scotland, 2004

3001-3025			Mercedes-Benz O405			Optare Prisma			B49F			1995		
3001	RR	M301SAJ	3008	RR	N808XHN	3014	RR	N514XVN	3020	RR	N520XVN
3002	RR	M302SAJ	3009	RR	N809XHN	3015	RR	N515XVN	3021	RR	N521XVN
3003	RR	M303SAJ	3010	RR	N810XHN	3016	RR	N516XVN	3022	RR	N522XVN
3004	RR	M304SAJ	3011	RR	N511XVN	3017	RR	N517XVN	3023	RR	N523XVN
3005	RR	M305SAJ	3012	RR	N512XVN	3018	BA	N518XVN	3024	RR	N524XVN
3006	RR	N806XHN	3013	RR	N513XVN	3019	BA	N519XVN	3025	LS	N525XVN
3007	RR	N807XHN									

3026	RR	L100SBS	Mercedes-Benz O405		Wright Cityranger		B51F		1993		Arriva Midlands North, 1999
4002	DL	G210HCP	DAF SB200		Optare Delta		B51F		1990		
4005	PE	G214HCP	DAF SB200		Optare Delta		B51F		1990		
4006	PE	J866UPY	DAF SB200		Optare Delta		B49F		1992		

4008-4022			DAF SB220			Optare Delta			B49F			1993		
4008	PE	K408BHN	4012	DU	K412BHN	4016	RR	K416BHN	4020	DU	L420FHN
4009	PE	K409BHN	4013	PE	K413BHN	4017	RR	K417BHN	4021	DL	L421FHN
4010	PE	K410BHN	4014	RR	K414BHN	4018	RR	L418FHN	4022	RD	L422FHN
4011	PE	K411BHN	4015	RR	K415BHN	4019	DL	L419FHN			

4023-4058			DAF SB220			Plaxton Prestige			N45F			1998		
4023	LS	R423RPY	4032	SN	R432RPY	4041	DL	S341KHN	4050	DL	S350KHN
4024	DL	R424RPY	4033	SN	R433RPY	4042	SN	S342KHN	4051	LS	S351KHN
4025	LS	R425RPY	4034	SN	R434RPY	4043	SN	S343KHN	4052	DL	S352KHN
4026	LS	R426RPY	4035	DU	R435RPY	4044	SN	S344KHN	4053	LS	S353KHN
4027	LS	R427RPY	4036	DU	R436RPY	4045	SN	S345KHN	4054	LS	S354KHN
4028	BA	R428RPY	4037	SN	R437RPY	4046	SN	S346KHN	4055	DL	S355KHN
4029	BA	R429RPY	4038	SN	R438RPY	4047	BA	S347KHN	4056	RR	S356KHN
4030	SN	R430RPY	4039	SN	R439RPY	4048	SN	S348KHN	4057	RR	S357KHN
4031	SN	R431RPY	4040	SN	R440RPY	4049	SN	S349KHN	4058	RR	S358KHN

4059	DU	R701KCU	DAF SB220		Northern Counties Paladin		B41F		1997	

4060-4073			DAF SB220			Plaxton Prestige			N41F			1998		
4060	DU	S702KFT	4064	DU	S706KFT	4068	DU	S710KFT	4071	DU	S713KRG
4061	DU	S703KFT	4065	DU	S707KFT	4069	DU	S711KFT	4072	DU	S714KRG
4062	DU	S704KFT	4066	DU	S708KFT	4070	DU	S712KRG	4073	DU	S715KRG
4063	DU	S705KFT	4067	DU	S709KFT						

4074-4082			DAF SB220			Ikarus CitiBus			N43F*			1999		*4079-82 are N39F
4074	LS	T74AUA	4077	LS	T78AUA	4079	LS	T83AUA	4081	LS	T82AUA
4075	LS	T75AUA	4078	LS	T79AUA	4080	DL	T81AUA	4082	DL	V653LWT
4076	LS	T76AUA									

4083	AS	J926CYL	DAF SB220	Ikarus CitiBus	B48F	1992	Arriva London, 2000
4084	AK	J927CYL	DAF SB220	Ikarus CitiBus	B48F	1992	Arriva London, 2000
4085	RD	J931CYL	DAF SB220	Ikarus CitiBus	B48F	1992	Arriva London, 2000
4086	DL	J413NCP	DAF SB220	Ikarus CitiBus	B48F	1992	Arriva London, 2000
4087	RD	J414NCP	DAF SB220	Ikarus CitiBus	B48F	1992	Arriva London, 2000
4088	u	J929CYL	DAF SB220	Ikarus CitiBus	B48F	1992	Arriva London, 2000
4089	RD	J930CYL	DAF SB220	Ikarus CitiBus	B48F	1992	Arriva London, 2000

The first Plaxton, low-floor, full-length bus was the Prestige, seen here on the DAF SB220. Pictured in Durham is 4061, S703KFT.
Mat Southart

33

4090-4097 DAF SB220 Optare Delta BC48F 1989-90

4090	DL	G251SRG	**4093**	PE	G254SRG	**4095**	DL	G256UVK	**4097**	PE	G258UVK
4091	DU	G252SRG	**4094**	AK	G255UVK	**4096**	RD	G257UVK			

4098	PE	P130RWR	DAF SB220	Optare Delta	B44D	1997	Blue Bus, Bolton, 2004
4104	w	H266CFT	DAF SB220	Optare Delta	BC48F	1990	
4105	PE	H267CFT	DAF SB220	Optare Delta	BC48F	1990	
4106	DL	F701ECC	DAF SB220	Optare Delta	BC48F	1989	Crosville Cymru, 1997
4108	SN	L532EHD	DAF SB220	Ikarus CitiBus	B48F	1994	North Western, 1997
4109	SN	L533EHD	DAF SB220	Ikarus CitiBus	B48F	1994	North Western, 1997

4501-4515 Volvo B10BLE Wright Renown N44F 1999

4501	NE	V501DFT	**4505**	NE	V505DFT	**4509**	NE	V509DFT	**4513**	NE	V513DFT
4502	NE	V502DFT	**4506**	NE	V506DFT	**4510**	NE	V510DFT	**4514**	NE	V514DFT
4503	NE	V503DFT	**4507**	NE	V507DFT	**4511**	NE	V511DFT	**4515**	NE	V515DFT
4504	NE	V504DFT	**4508**	NE	V508DFT	**4512**	NE	V512DFT			

4516-4523 Volvo B10BLE Alexander ALX300 N44F 2000

4516	NE	W292PPT	**4518**	NE	W294PPT	**4520**	NE	W296PPT	**4522**	NE	W298PPT
4517	NE	W293PPT	**4519**	NE	W295PPT	**4521**	NE	W297PPT	**4523**	NE	W299PPT

4524-4530 Volvo B10BLE Wright Renown N44F 1999 Arriva Scotland, 2003

4524	HX	V530GDS	**4526**	HX	V532GDS	**4528**	HX	V534GDS	**4530**	HX	V536GDS
4525	HX	V531GDS	**4527**	HX	V533GDS	**4529**	HX	V535GDS			

4646-4659 Scania OmniCity CN94UB Scania N42F 2005

4646	DU	NK05GXW	**4650**	DU	NK05GXD	**4654**	DU	NK05GXH	**4657**	DU	NK05GXM
4647	DU	NK05GXA	**4651**	DU	NK05GXE	**4655**	DU	NK05GXJ	**4658**	DU	NK05GXN
4648	DU	NK05GXB	**4652**	DU	NK05GXF	**4656**	DU	NK05GXL	**4659**	DU	NK05GXO
4649	DU	NK05GXC	**4653**	DU	NK05GXG						

5009-5018 Leyland Lynx LX2R11C15Z4S Leyland Lynx 2 B49F 1991-92

5009	BA	H253PAJ	**5012**	BA	J652UHN	**5016**	BA	J656UHN	**5018**	BA	J658UHN
5011	BA	J651UHN	**5013**	BA	J653UHN	**5017**	BA	J657UHN			

5019	BA	H338TYG	Leyland Lynx LX2R11C15Z4S	Leyland Lynx 2	B49F	1990	Arriva Yorkshire, 2005
5020	BA	H338UWT	Leyland Lynx LX2R11C15Z4S	Leyland Lynx 2	B49F	1990	Arriva Yorkshire, 2005
5021	u	J371TWX	Leyland Lynx LX2R11C15Z4S	Leyland Lynx 2	B49F	1991	Arriva Yorkshire, 2005

7215-7222 Leyland Olympian ONLXB/1RH Eastern Coach Works B42/29F 1986-87 Arriva London, 2003

7215	NE	D155FYM	**7217**	NE	D165FYM	**7219**	PE	D216FYM	**7221**	BL	D157FYM
7216	PE	D160FYM	**7218**	BL	D189FYM	**7220**	AS	D178FYM	**7222**	AK	D174FYM

7242	u	A242GHN	Leyland Olympian ONLXB/1R	Eastern Coach Works	B45/32F	1985	KentishBus, 1998
7244	AS	A244GHN	Leyland Olympian ONLXB/1R	Eastern Coach Works	B45/32F	1985	KentishBus, 1998

7250-7258 Scania N113DRB Northern Counties Palatine B42/29F 1994-95 Arriva London, 2002

7250	BL	L159GYL	**7253**	AK	M178LYP	**7255**	AK	M180LYP	**7257**	AK	N182OYH
7251	AK	L160GYL	**7254**	AK	M179LYP	**7256**	BL	N181OYH	**7258**	AK	N183OYH
7252	AK	L161GYL									

7263	u	TPD116X	Leyland Olympian ONTL11/1R	Roe	B43/29F	1982	Arriva Scotland, 2005
7265	w	CWR519Y	Leyland Olympian ONLXB/1R	Eastern Coach Works	B45/32F	1982	Arriva Scotland, 2005
7266	DL	CWR518Y	Leyland Olympian ONLXB/1R	Eastern Coach Works	B45/32F	1983	Arriva Scotland, 2005
7267	w	A567NWX	Leyland Olympian ONLXB/1R	Eastern Coach Works	B45/32F	1984	Arriva Scotland, 2003
7268	DL	C268XEF	Leyland Olympian ONLXB/1R	Eastern Coach Works	B42/30F	1986	

7271-7275 Leyland Olympian ON2R50C13Z4 Alexander RH B45/29F 1993

7271	RD	L271FVN	**7273**	DU	L273FVN	**7274**	DU	L274FVN	**7275**	BA	L275FVN
7272	BA	L272FVN									

7276	u	G21HHG	Leyland Olympian ONCL10/1RZ	Leyland	B47/31F	1989	Atlas Bus, 1994

7279-7285 Leyland Olympian ONCL10/1R Northern Counties B43/32F 1989 Atlas Bus, 1994

7279	RR	G756UYT	**7283**	RR	G760UYT	**7284**	u	G761UYT	**7285**	BA	G762UYT
7280	RR	G757UYT									

7286	BL	UWW13X	Leyland Olympian ONLXB/1R	Roe	B47/29F	1982	Metrobus, Orpington, 1997
7292	BL	CUB66Y	Leyland Olympian ONLXB/1R	Roe	B47/29F	1983	Metrobus, Orpington, 1997
7293	NE	CUB68Y	Leyland Olympian ONLXB/1R	Roe	B47/29F	1983	Metrobus, Orpington, 1997
7302	w	C264XEF	Leyland Olympian ONLXB/1R	Eastern Coach Works	BC42/30F	1986	United, 1986

Seen arriving in Newcastle, Volvo B10BLE 4506, V506DFT, carries Wright Renown bodywork. The entire batch is based in the city. Expected shortly is a delivery of integral Scania OmniCity buses. *Richard Godfrey*

7370-7377
Volvo Olympian YN2RC18Z4   Northern Counties Palatine II   BC43/27F   1994

7370	AS	M370FTY	**7372**	AS	M372FTY	**7374**	AS	M374FTY	**7376**	AS	M376FTY
7371	AS	M371FTY	**7373**	AS	M373FTY	**7375**	AS	M375FTY	**7377**	AS	M377FTY

7381-7393
Scania N113DRB   East Lancs Cityzen   BC43/31F   1996

7381	BL	N381OTY	**7385**	BL	N385OTY	**7388**	BL	N388OTY	**7391**	BL	N391OTY
7382	BL	N382OTY	**7386**	BL	N386OTY	**7389**	BL	N389OTY	**7392**	BL	N392OTY
7383	BL	N383OTY	**7387**	BL	N387OTY	**7390**	BL	N390OTY	**7393**	BL	N393OTY
7384	BL	N384OTY								

7410-7420
Volvo Olympian   Northern Counties Palatine II   B43/29F   1997

7410	AS	P410CCU	**7413**	AS	P413CCU	**7416**	NE	P416CCU	**7419**	NE	P419CCU
7411	AS	P411CCU	**7414**	NE	P414CCU	**7417**	NE	P417CCU	**7420**	NE	P420CCU
7412	AS	P412CCU	**7415**	NE	P415CCU	**7418**	NE	P418CCU			

7421-7429
Volvo Olympian YN2RV16Z4   East Lancs   B44/30F   1994   Arriva Southern Counties, 1998

7421	AS	M685HPF	**7424**	NE	M688HPF	**7426**	DU	M690HPF	**7428**	DU	M692HPF
7422	NE	M686HPF	**7425**	DU	M689HPF	**7427**	DU	M691HPF	**7429**	DU	M693HPF
7423	AS	M687HPF								

7430-7435
Dennis Trident   Alexander ALX400   N51/31F   2000

7430	NE	W395RBB	**7432**	NE	W397RBB	**7434**	NE	W399RBB	**7435**	NE	W501RBB
7431	NE	W396RBB	**7433**	NE	W398RBB					

7436-7444
DAF DB250   East Lancs Lowlander   N44/29F   2001

7436	BL	Y686EBR	**7439**	BL	Y689FRR	**7441**	BL	Y691EBR	**7443**	DL	Y693EBR
7437	DL	Y687EBR	**7440**	BL	Y685EBR	**7442**	BL	Y692EBR	**7444**	DL	Y694EBR
7438	BL	Y688EBR								

7445	DL	NK05GWX	Volvo B7TL	Alexander Dennis ALX400	N	2005
7446	DL	NK05GWY	Volvo B7TL	Alexander Dennis ALX400	N	2005

The days of the Lynx are numbered as the type moves to driver training or disposal. However, still looking smart and operating in Darlington while on all-day service from Bishop Auckland, is 5020, H338UWT. This joined the fleet from Yorkshire. The type is to be found on routes 5 and 6 to Durham and 46 to Crook. Interestingly, only four pre-privatisation vehicles remain in the current fleet. *Bob Downham*

Ancillary vehicles:

9964	SN	N743AVM	Iveco TurboDaily 59.12	Marshall C31	Staff	1995	
9965	BL	L603FHN	Optare MetroRider MR33	Optare	Staff	1994	
9984	SN	M734AOO	Iveco TurboDaily 59.12	Marshall C31	Staff	1995	Arriva The Shires, 2002
9986	SN	G508EAJ	Leyland Lynx LX2R11C15Z4S	Leyland Lynx	TV	1990	
9987	SN	G509EAJ	Leyland Lynx LX2R11C15Z4S	Leyland Lynx	TV	1990	
9988	SN	G510EAJ	Leyland Lynx LX2R11C15Z4S	Leyland Lynx	TV	1990	
9990	SN	G512EAJ	Leyland Lynx LX2R11C15Z4S	Leyland Lynx	TV	1990	
9991	SN	H32PAJ	Leyland Lynx LX2R11C15Z4S	Leyland Lynx 2	TV	1991	
9992	AS	H339UWT	Leyland Lynx LX2R11C15Z4S	Leyland Lynx 2	TV	1990	
9993	SN	H755WWW	Leyland Lynx LX2R11C15Z4S	Leyland Lynx 2	TV	1990	

Previous registrations:

UOI772	K141RYS		YSU870	E186XKO
WLT954	A954SUL		YSU871	E187XKO
XSV691	E91OJT			

Allocations:-

Alnwick (Lisburn Street) - AK

MetroRider	886	890	908	909			
DAF SB3000	1210	1211	1212	1213			
DAF Delta	4084	4094					
Olympian	7222						
Scania dd	7251	7252	7253	7254	7255	7257	7258

Ashington (Lintonville Terrace) - AS

MetroRider	889	891	892	904	905	906	907	910
	911	912	913	914	915	916	917	918
	919	937	2711	2713	2714	2716	2718	2719
Scania sd	273	274	281	282	283	284	286	289
	290							
SB220	4083							
Olympian	7220	7370	7371	7372	7373	7374	7375	7376
	7377	7410	7411	7412	7413	7421	7423	

Ancillary	9988	9991	9992

Bishop Auckland (Morland Street) - BA

MetroRider	2611	2623	2644	2645	2727			
Dart	1711	1712	1713	1714	1715			
MAN Vecta	1517	1535	1540	1541	1545	1547	1548	1549
	1550							
Lynx	5009	5011	5012	5013	5016	5017	5018	5019
	5020							
Mercedes-Benz O405	3018	3019						
SB220 Prestige	4028	4029	4047					
Olympian	7272	7275	7285					

Blyth (Bridge Street) - BL

MetroRider	877	878	880	881	882	883	884	887
	898	902	920					
Mercedes-Benz	2646	2647	2648	2649	2650	2651	2652	2653
	2654	2655	2658	2660	2664	2668	2669	
Dart	1702	1724	1725	1726	1727	1731	1733	1758
Scania sd	275	276	277	278	279	280	285	287
	288							
VDL Bus Commander	1801	1802	1803					
Olympian	7218	7286	7292	7221				
Scania dd	7250	7256	7381	7382	7383	7384	7385	7386
	7387	7388	7389	7390	7391	7392	7393	
DAF DB250	7436	7437	7438	7439	7440	7441	7442	

Ancillary	9965

Darlington (Feethams) - DL - North East

Outstation: Barnard Castle

MetroRider	2610	2612	2616	2630	2631	2640	2642	2643
	2701	2702	2703	2704	2705	2706	2712	2715
	2717	2720	2721	2722	2723	2724	2733	2738
	2739							
Dart	1734	1735	1736	1737	1738	1739	1745	1746
	1761	1762						
SB220 Delta	4002	4019	4021	4090	4091	4095	4106	
SB220 Ikarus	4086							
SB220 Prestige	4024	4041	4050	4052	4055	4080	4082	
DB250 Lowlander	7443	7444						
Olympian	7266	7268						
Volvo B7TL	7445	7446						

Durham (Waddington Steet) - DU - North East

MetroRider	885	899						
Dart	1703	1704	1705	1706	1707	1709	1710	1763
	1764	1765	1766	1767	1768	1769	1770	1771
	1772	1773						
DAF Delta	4012	4020						
DAF Prestige	4035	4036	4059	4060	4061	4063	4064	4065
	4066	4067	4068	4069	4070	4071	4072	4073
Scania Omnicity	4646	4647	4648	4649	4650	4651	4652	4653
	4654	4655	4656	4657	4658	4659		
Metrobus	604	617	622					
Olympian	7425	7426	7427	7428	7429			

Hexham (Burn Lane) - HX

MetroRider	879	922	923				
Dart	1732	1749	1760				
DAF interurban	1201	1202	1203	1204	1205	1214	
Volvo B10BLE	4524	4525	4526	4527	4528	4529	4530
Metrobus	625						

Loftus (Whitby Road) - LS

Outstation: Whitby

MetroRider	2618	2635	2637	2638	2639	2726	2728
Mercedes-Benz	2659	2665	2666	2760	2673		
Dart	1755	1756					
MAN Vecta	1512	1515	1524	1528	1534	1536	
MB Prisma	3025						
Volvo B10M bus	2873						
DAF Prestige	4023	4025	4026	4027	4051	4053	4054
DAF Ikarus	4074	4075	4076	4077	4078	4079	4081
DAF Interurban	1206	1207	1208	1209			

Newcastle (Jesmond Road) - NE

MetroRider	900	901	921					
DAF coach	142	143	144	145	146	147	148	
Dart	1701	1728	1729	1730	1740	1741	1742	1750
	1751	1752						
Scania sd	271	272						
Volvo B10BLE	4501	4502	4503	4504	4505	4506	4507	4508
	4509	4510	4511	4512	4513	4514	4515	4516
	4517	4518	4519	4520	4521	4522	4523	
Metrobus	611	624	626	629	630	631		
Olympian	7215	7217	7293	7414	7415	7416	7417	7418
	7419	7420	7422	7435				
Trident	7430	7431	7432	7433	7434	7435		

Peterlee (Davey Drive) - PE

MetroRider	894	2617	2624	2627	2628	2709	2710	2725
	2742							
Dart	1636	1637	1638	1639	1640	1641	1642	1643
	1708	1716						
SB220 Delta	4005	4006	4008	4009	4010	4011	4013	4093
	4097	4098	4105					
Olympian	7216	7219	7273	7274				

Redcar (Ennis Road, Dormanstown) - RR

Dart	1601	1602	1718	1753	1754			
MAN Vecta	1510	1527	1537	1543	1551	1553	1555	1557
SB120 Cadet	1915	1916	1920	1921	1922			
SB220 Prestige	4056	4057	4058					
Volvo B10M bus	2872	2875						
Mercedes Prisma	3001	3002	3003	3004	3005	3006	3007	3008
	3009	3010	3011	3012	3013	3014	3015	3016
	3017	3020	3021	3022	3023	3024	3026	
Olympian	7279	7280	7283					

Richmond (Station Yard) - RD

MetroRider	872	873	2613	2619	2621	2625	2632	2633
	2634	2641	2707	2708				
Dart	1717							
SB220 Delta	4022	4096						
SB220 Ikarus	4085	4087	4089					
Olympian	7271							

Stockton (Boathouse Lane) - SN

MetroRider	875	888	893	897	903	2606	2607	2608
	2609	2614	2615	2636	2730			
Dart	1719	1720	1721	1722	1723	1743	1744	1747
	1748	1757	1759					
SB120 Cadet	1901	1902	1903	1904	1905	1906	1907	1908
	1909	1910	1911	1912	1913	1914	1917	
MAN Vecta	1504	1505	1506	1507	1508	1509	1513	1514
	1519	1521	1525	1526	1529	1530	1531	1533
	1542	1544	1556	1558				
SB220 Ikarus	4108	4109						
SB220 Prestige	4030	4031	4032	4033	4034	4037	4038	4039
	4040	4042	4043	4044	4045	4046	4048	4049
Ancillary	9964	9984	9986	9987	9989	9990	9991	9992
	9993							

Unallocated or stored - u/w

MetroRider	863	866	867	870	871	876	2604	2620
	2622	2629	2729	2731	2732	2734	2735	2736
	2737							
MAN Vecta	1502	1511	1516	1520	1522	1523	1532	1539
	1546	1552	1554					
Tiger	214	215	216	217	247	5021		
SB220	4001	4068	4104					
Metrobus	601	614	620	621	623			
Olympian	7242	7244	7263	7265	7276	7284	7302	7407
	7408	7409						

ARRIVA YORKSHIRE

Arriva Yorkshire Ltd; Arriva Yorkshire North Ltd,
24 Barnsley Road, Wakefield, West Yorkshire, WF1 5JX
Arriva Yorkshire West Ltd, Mill Street East, Dewsbury, West Yorkshire, WF12 9AG

11	DY	SB220AL	DAF SB220			Ikarus CitiBus	B49F	1997	K-Line Travel, 2000
12	DY	J802KHD	DAF SB220			Ikarus CitiBus	BC48F	1992	K-Line Travel, 2000
13	DY	R69GNW	DAF SB220			Ikarus CitiBus	B49F	1998	K-Line Travel, 2000
14	DY	PIL9735	DAF SB220			Ikarus CitiBus	B48F	1993	K-Line Travel, 2000
16	DY	PIL9730	DAF SB220			Ikarus CitiBus	B48F	1992	K-Line Travel, 2000
17	DY	PIL9732	DAF SB220			Ikarus CitiBus	B48F	1992	K-Line Travel, 2000
18	DY	PIL9733	DAF SB220			Ikarus CitiBus	B48F	1993	K-Line Travel, 2000
19	DY	PIL9734	DAF SB220			Ikarus CitiBus	B48F	1993	K-Line Travel, 2000
20	DY	PIL9731	DAF SB220			Ikarus CitiBus	B48F	1992	K-Line Travel, 2000

21-29
DAF SB220   Ikarus CitiBus   B49F   1994   K-Line Travel, 2000

21	DY	M811RCP	24	DY	M814RCP	26	DY	M816RCP	28	DY	M818RCP
22	DY	M812RCP	25	DY	M815RCP	27	DY	M817RCP	29	DY	M819RCP
23	DY	M813RCP									

51	DY	H512YCX	DAF SB220	Optare Delta	B48F	1991	K-Line Travel, 2000
52	DY	J23GCX	DAF SB220	Optare Delta	B49F	1991	K-Line Travel, 2000
53	DY	N51FWU	DAF SB220	Ikarus CitiBus	B49F	1995	Arriva Bus & Coach, 2004
54	DY	P202RUM	DAF SB220	Ikarus CitiBus	B49F	1996	Arriva Bus & Coach, 2004
55	DY	MOI2836	DAF SB220	Ikarus CitiBus	BC42F	1992	Arriva Bus & Coach, 2004
56	DY	N52FWU	DAF SB220	Ikarus CitiBus	B49F	1995	Arriva Bus & Coach, 2004
57	DY	YD02RJO	DAF SB220	Ikarus CitiBus	N44F	2002	Arriva Bus & Coach, 2004
58	DY	YD02RJJ	DAF SB220	Ikarus CitiBus	N44F	2002	Arriva Bus & Coach, 2004

102-109
Volvo B10BLE   Wright Renown   NC44F   2000

102	SB	W102EWU	104	SB	W104EWU	107	SB	W107EWU	109	SB	W109EWU
103	SB	W103EWU	106	SB	W106EWU	108	SB	W108EWU			

135-149
Dennis Dart 9m   Northern Counties Paladin   B35F   1994   Arriva Southern Counties, 2001

135	WF	L127YVK	139	CD	L129YVK	143	WF	L159BFT	147	WF	L157YVK
136	WF	L136YVK	140	WF	L140YVK	144	CD	L114YVK	148	WF	L131YVK
137	WF	L137YVK	141	CD	L141YVK	145	CD	L149YVK	149	WF	L130YVK
138	CD	L128YVK	142	CD	L152YVK	146	CD	L146YVK			

150	CD	K601HWR	Dennis Dart 9.8m	Plaxton Pointer	B43F	1992	K-Line Travel, 2000
152	SB	H878LOX	Dennis Dart 9m	Duple Dartline	B39F	1990	K-Line Travel, 2000
153	CD	J220HGY	Dennis Dart 9m	Plaxton Pointer	B35F	1992	Arriva Southern Counties, 2001
154	CD	J221HGY	Dennis Dart 9m	Plaxton Pointer	B35F	1992	Arriva Southern Counties, 2001
155	CD	J467OKP	Dennis Dart 9.8m	Plaxton Pointer	B40F	1992	Arriva Southern Counties, 2001
156	SB	K320CVX	Dennis Dart 9m	Plaxton Pointer	B35F	1992	Arriva Southern Counties, 2004
157	CD	J465MKL	Dennis Dart 9.8m	Plaxton Pointer	B40F	1991	Arriva Southern Counties, 2004
158	CD	J466OKP	Dennis Dart 9.8m	Plaxton Pointer	B40F	1992	Arriva Southern Counties, 2004
159	CD	J468OKP	Dennis Dart 9.8m	Plaxton Pointer	B40F	1992	Arriva Southern Counties, 2004
160	CD	K471SKO	Dennis Dart 9.8m	Plaxton Pointer	B40F	1992	Arriva Southern Counties, 2004
165	SB	W165HBT	Dennis Dart SLF	Alexander ALX200	N40F	2000	
166	SB	W166HBT	Dennis Dart SLF	Alexander ALX200	N40F	2000	
167	SB	TWY7	Dennis Dart SLF	Alexander ALX200	N40F	2000	

170-199
Dennis Dart SLF   Alexander ALX200   N40F   1997

170	DY	P170VUA	178	SB	P178VUA	186	DY	P186VUA	193	DY	P193VUA
171	DY	P171VUA	179	SB	P179VUA	187	DY	P187VUA	194	DY	P194VUA
172	DY	P172VUA	180	SB	P180VUA	188	HE	P188VUA	195	DY	P195VUA
173	DY	P173VUA	181	SB	P181VUA	189	DY	P189VUA	196	DY	P196VUA
174	DY	P174VUA	182	DY	P182VUA	190	DY	P190VUA	197	DY	P197VUA
175	DY	P175VUA	183	SB	P183VUA	191	DY	P191VUA	198	DY	P198VUA
176	DY	P176VUA	184	DY	P184VUA	192	DY	P192VUA	199	DY	P199VUA
177	SB	P177VUA	185	DY	P185VUA						

Pictured in Leeds, Yorkshire's 219, V219PCX, has recently been transferred to Selby and along with the others at that depot has been re-registered with one of the YBG marks owned. *Mark Lyons*

200	DY	R103GNW	Dennis Dart SLF			UVG Urbanstar		N40F	1998	Jaronda Travel, Cawood, 1999

201-229
Dennis Dart SLF — Plaxton Pointer MPD — N29F — 2000

201	WF	V201PCX	208	WF	V208PCX	215	WF	V215PCX	223	CD	V223PCX
202	SB	A1YBG	209	WF	V209PCX	216	CD	V216PCX	224	CD	V224PCX
203	SB	V203PCX	210	WF	V210PCX	217	CD	V217PCX	225	WF	V225PCX
204	SB	V204PCX	211	WF	V211PCX	218	CD	V218PCX	226	CD	V226PCX
205	WF	V205PCX	212	WF	V212PCX	219	SB	A4YBG	227	CD	V227PCX
206	WF	V206PCX	213	WF	V213PCX	220	CD	V220PCX	228	CD	V228PCX
207	WF	V207PCX	214	SB	A2YBG	221	CD	V221PCX	229	CD	V229XUB

344	CD	H344UWX	Leyland Lynx LX2R11C15Z4S	Leyland Lynx 2	B49F	1990-91

344-382
Leyland Lynx LX2R11C15Z4S — Leyland Lynx 2 — B49F — 1990-91

344	CD	H344UWX	363	CD	J363YWX	376	CD	J376AWT	381	CD	J381BWU
358	CD	H358WWY	365	CD	J365YWX	379	CD	J379BWU	382	CD	J382BWU
361	CD	H393WWY									

401-405
Volvo B10B-58 — Alexander Strider — B51F — 1993

401	CD	K401HWW	403	WF	K403HWW	404	WF	K404HWW	405	WF	K405HWX
402	WF	K402HWW									

406	WF	L406NUA	Volvo B10B-58	Wright Endeavour	BC49F	1993
407	WF	L407NUA	Volvo B10B-58	Wright Endeavour	BC49F	1993
408	WF	L408NUA	Volvo B10B-58	Wright Endeavour	BC49F	1993
409	WF	L409NUA	Volvo B10B-58	Wright Endeavour	BC49F	1993

410-433
Volvo B10B-58 — Alexander Strider — B51F — 1994

410	CD	M410UNW	416	CD	M416UNW	422	CD	M422UNW	428	CD	M428UNW
411	CD	M411UNW	417	WF	M417UNW	423	CD	M423UNW	429	CD	M429UNW
412	CD	M412UNW	418	CD	M418UNW	424	CD	M424UNW	430	CD	M430UNW
413	WF	M413UNW	419	CD	M419UNW	425	WF	M425UNW	431	CD	M431UNW
414	WF	M414UNW	420	CD	M420UNW	426	CD	M426UNW	432	CD	M432UNW
415	WF	M415UNW	421	CD	M421UNW	427	CD	M427UNW	433	CD	M433UNW

Arriva's bus dealership, Arriva Bus and Coach are the principal UK dealers for VDL Bus, the successor to DAF. Following orders for the original SB220, and its low floor successor, Arriva Yorkshire took a further five in 2004. These are designated the SB200, and feature an engine that meets the latest environmental standards and carry Wrightbus Commander bodywork. 496, YJ04HJD, is seen in Leeds having arrived from its base in Wakefield. *Mark Lyons*

435	WF	P10LPG	DAF SB220			Northern Counties Paladin		B42F	1997	Arriva Bus & Coach, 2004
436	WF	R989FNW	DAF SB220			Northern Counties Paladin		B42F	1997	Arriva Bus & Coach, 2004
437	WF	R985FNW	DAF SB220			Northern Counties Paladin		B42F	1997	Arriva Bus & Coach, 2004
438	WF	R28GNW	DAF SB220			Northern Counties Paladin		B41F	1998	Arriva Bus & Coach, 2004
439	WF	R29GNW	DAF SB220			Northern Counties Paladin		B41F	1998	Arriva Bus & Coach, 2005

440-471   DAF SB220   Alexander ALX300   N42F   1998

440	WF	R440GWY	449	WF	R449KWT	457	WF	R457KWT	465	WF	S465GUB
441	WF	R441KWT	450	DY	R450KWT	458	DY	R458KWT	466	DY	S466GUB
442	WF	R442KWT	451	WF	R451KWT	459	DY	R459KWT	467	WF	S467GUB
443	WF	R443KWT	452	DY	R452KWT	460	WF	R460KWT	468	WF	S468GUB
445	WF	R445KWT	453	DY	R453KWT	461	WF	R461KWT	469	WF	S469GUB
446	WF	R446KWT	454	WF	R454KWT	462	DY	S462GUB	470	WF	S470GUB
447	WF	R447KWT	455	WF	R455KWT	463	DY	S463GUB	471	WF	S471GUB
448	WF	R448KWT	456	DY	R456KWT	464	WF	S464GUB			

472-491   DAF SB220   Alexander ALX300   N42F   1998

472	WF	S472ANW	477	WF	S477ANW	482	WF	S482ANW	487	WF	S487ANW
473	WF	S473ANW	478	WF	S478ANW	483	WF	S483ANW	488	WF	S488ANW
474	WF	S474ANW	479	WF	S479ANW	484	WF	S484ANW	489	WF	S489ANW
475	WF	S475ANW	480	WF	S480ANW	485	WF	S485ANW	490	WF	S490ANW
476	WF	S476ANW	481	WF	S481ANW	486	WF	S486ANW	491	WF	S491ANW

495-499   VDL Bus SB200   Wrightbus Commander   N44F   2004

| 495 | WF | YJ04HJC | 497 | WF | YJ04HJE | 498 | WF | YJ04HJF | 499 | WF | YJ04HJG |
| 496 | WF | YJ04HJD | | | | | | | | | |

501-510   Dennis Arrow   East Lancs Pyoneer   B45/35F*   1996   Arriva Southern Counties, 1999
*509/10 are BC45/31F

501	HE	N801TPK	504	HE	N804TPK	507	HE	N807TPK	509	HE	N809TPK
502	HE	N802TPK	505	HE	N805TPK	508	HE	N808TPK	510	HE	N810TPK
503	HE	N803TPK	506	HE	N806TPK						

Rationalisation of models has seen the ten Dennis Arrow buses transferred to Heckmondwike. Pictured in Leeds on the Huddersfield service, 504, N804TPK, was new to London & Country at Crawley. *Mark Doggett*

511-521

Volvo Olympian YN2RV16Z4 — East Lancs — B44/30F — 1994 — Arriva London, 2004-05

511	HE	M694HPF	514	HE	M697HPF	517	HE	M700HPF	520	HE	M703HPF
512	HE	M702HPF	515	HE	M698HPF	518	HE	M701HPF	521	HE	M704HPF
513	HE	M696HPF	516	HE	M699HPF	519	HE	M695HPF			

541	HW	EWW541Y	Leyland Olympian ONLXB/1R	Eastern Coach Works	B45/33F	1982-83
542	WF	EWW542Y	Leyland Olympian ONLXB/1R	Eastern Coach Works	B45/33F	1982-83

565-612

Leyland Olympian ONLXB/1R — Eastern Coach Works — B45/32F* — 1983-85 — *seating varies

565	SB	A565NWX	580	WF	A580NWX	599	SB	B599SWX	607	WF	B607UUM
566	WF	A566NWX	581	WF	A581NWX	600	SB	B600UUM	609	WF	B609UUM
569	HE	A569NWX	584	WF	A584NWX	603	WF	B603UUM	610	WF	C610ANW
574	WF	A574NWX	586	HE	A586NWX	604	WF	B604UUM	611	WF	C611ANW
575	WF	A575NWX	590	SB	A590NWX	606	WF	B606UUM	612	WF	C612ANW
577	WF	A577NWX	591	SB	B591SWX						

615	WF	H106RWT	Leyland Olympian ON2R50C13Z4	Northern Counties	B43/28F	1990	South Yorkshire, Pontefract, 1995
616	WF	H108RWT	Leyland Olympian ON2R50C13Z4	Northern Counties	B43/28F	1990	South Yorkshire, Pontefract, 1995
621	SB	N621KUA	Volvo Olympian YN2RV18Z4	Northern Counties Palatine II	B43/30F	1996	
622	SB	N622KUA	Volvo Olympian YN2RV18Z4	Northern Counties Palatine II	B43/30F	1996	
623	SB	N623KUA	Volvo Olympian YN2RV18Z4	Northern Counties Palatine II	B43/30F	1996	

624-641

DAF DB250 — Optare Spectra — B48/29F — 1999

624	DY	T624EUB	629	DY	T629EUB	634	DY	T634EUB	638	DY	T638EUB
625	DY	T625EUB	630	DY	T630EUB	635	DY	T635EUB	639	WF	T639EUB
626	DY	T626EUB	631	DY	T631EUB	636	DY	T636EUB	640	WF	V640KVH
627	DY	T627EUB	632	DY	T632EUB	637	DY	T637EUB	641	WF	V641KVH
628	DY	T628EUB	633	WF	T633EUB						

651-674

Volvo B7L — Alexander ALX400 — N47/28F — 2000

651	CD	W651CWX	657	CD	W657CWX	663	CD	W663CWX	669	CD	W669CWX
652	CD	W652CWX	658	CD	W658CWX	664	CD	W664CWX	671	CD	W671CWX
653	CD	W653CWX	659	CD	W659CWX	665	CD	W665CWX	672	CD	W672CWX
654	CD	W654CWX	661	CD	W661CWX	667	CD	W667CWX	673	CD	W673CWX
656	CD	W656CWX	662	CD	W662CWX	668	CD	W668CWX	674	CD	W674CWX

675-696 — Volvo B7L — Plaxton President — N47/28F — 2001

675	SB	X675YUG	681	SB	X681YUG	686	SB	X686YUG	692	HE	X692YUG
676	SB	X676YUG	682	SB	X682YUG	687	HE	X687YUG	693	HE	X693YUG
677	SB	X677YUG	683	SB	X683YUG	688	HE	X688YUG	694	HE	X694YUG
678	SB	X678YUG	684	SB	X684YUG	689	HE	X689YUG	695	HE	X695YUG
679	SB	X679YUG	685	SB	X685YUG	691	HE	X691YUG	696	HE	X696YUG

700-723 — DAF DB250 — Optare Spectra — N47/27F — 2002

700	WF	YD02PXW	706	WF	YG52CFE	712	WF	YG52CFN	718	HE	YD02PYU
701	WF	YD02PXX	707	WF	YG52CFF	713	WF	YG52CFO	719	HE	YD02PYV
702	WF	YD02PXY	708	WF	YG52CFJ	714	WF	YG52CFP	720	HE	YD02PYW
703	WF	YD02PXZ	709	WF	YG52CFK	715	WF	YG52CFU	721	HE	YD02PYX
704	WF	YG52CFA	710	WF	YG52CFL	716	WF	YG52CFV	722	HE	YD02PYY
705	WF	YG52CFD	711	WF	YG52CFM	717	WF	YG52CFX	723	HE	YD02PYZ

746	DY	M746WWR	Optare MetroRider MR15	Optare	B31F	1995	
749	DY	M749WWR	Optare MetroRider MR15	Optare	B31F	1995	
755	WF	N755LWW	Optare MetroRider MR15	Optare	B31F	1996	
756	WF	N756LWW	Optare MetroRider MR15	Optare	B31F	1996	
757	DY	N757LWW	Optare MetroRider MR15	Optare	B31F	1996	
760	DY	N172WNF	Mercedes-Benz 709D	Alexander Sprint	B23F	1995	Arrive North West & Wales, 2004

761-765 — Volvo Citybus B10M-50 — East Lancs — B49/39F — 1989 — Arriva Southern Counties, 2004

761	HE	G612BPH	763	HE	G619BPH	764	HE	G620BPH	765	HE	G622BPH
762	HE	G618BPH							

766	HE	G637BPH	Volvo Citybus B10M-50	Northern Counties	B45/31F	1989	Arriva Southern Counties, 2004
768	HE	G639BPH	Volvo Citybus B10M-50	Northern Counties	B45/31F	1989	Arriva Southern Counties, 2004

801-830 — Dennis Lance 11m — Alexander Strider — B47F — 1993

801	HE	K801HWW	809	HE	L809NNW	817	HE	L817NWY	824	HE	L824NWY
802	HE	K802HWW	810	HE	L810NNW	818	HE	L818NWY	825	HE	L825NWY
803	HE	K803HWW	811	HE	L811NNW	819	HE	L819NWY	826	HE	L826NYG
804	HE	K804HWW	812	HE	L812NNW	820	HE	L820NWY	827	HE	L827NYG
805	HE	K805HWX	813	HE	L813NNW	821	HE	L821NWY	828	HE	L828NYG
806	HE	L806NNW	814	HE	L814NNW	822	HE	L822NWY	829	HE	L829NYG
807	HE	L807NNW	815	HE	L815NNW	823	HE	L823NWY	830	HE	L830NYG
808	HE	L808NNW	816	HE	L816NWY						

Ancillary vehicles

252	WF	C920FMP	Leyland Lynx LX1126LXCTFR1	Leyland Lynx	TV	1986	Leyland Bus, 1987
322	WF	G322NNW	Leyland Lynx LX2R11C15Z4S	Leyland Lynx	TV	1990	
329	WF	CWR519Y	Leyland Olympian ONLXB/1R	Eastern Coach Works	TV	1982	
330	WF	G330NUM	Leyland Lynx LX2R11C15Z4S	Leyland Lynx	TV	1990	
331	WF	G331NUM	Leyland Lynx LX2R11C15Z4S	Leyland Lynx	TV	1990	
332	WF	G332NUM	Leyland Lynx LX2R11C15Z4S	Leyland Lynx	TV	1990	

Previous registrations:

A1YBG	V202PCX	PIL9731	K123TCP
A2YBG	V214PCX	PIL9732	J54GCX
A4YBG	V219PCX	PIL9733	K506RJX
MOI2836	J804KHD	PIL9734	K507RJX
P10LPG	P10LPG, 99D73675	PIL9735	L512EHD
PIL9730	J412NCP	TWY7	W167HBT

Allocations:-

Castleford (Wheldon Road) - CD

Dart	138	139	141	142	144	145	146	150
	153	154	155	157	158	159	160	216
	217	218	220	221	223	224	226	227
	228							
Lynx	344	358	360	361	363	365	366	367
	368	369	370	371	372	373	374	376
	379	381	382					
Volvo B10B	401	402	403	404	410	411	412	416
	418	419	420	421	422	423	424	426
	427	428	429	430	431	432	433	
Volvo B7L	651	652	653	654	656	657	658	659
	661	662	663	664	665	667	668	669
	671	672	673	674				

Dewsbury (Mill Street East) - DY

MetroRider	746	749	757					
Mercedes-Benz	760							
Dart	135	170	171	172	173	174	175	176
	182	184	185	186	187	188	189	190
	191	192	193	194	195	196	197	198
	199	200						
SB220 Ikarus	11	12	13	14	16	17	18	19
	20	21	22	23	24	25	26	27
	28	29	53	54	55	56	57	58
SB220 Delta	51	52						
SB220 ALX300	450	452	453	456	458	459	462	463
	466							
DB250 Spectra	624	625	626	627	628	629	630	631
	632	634	635	636	637	638	639	

Heckmondwike (Beck Lane) - HE

Dart	188							
Lance	801	802	803	804	805	806	807	808
	809	810	811	812	813	814	815	816
	817	818	819	820	821	822	823	824
	825	826	827	828	829	830		
Arrow	501	502	503	504	505	506	507	508
	509	510						
Volvo Citybus	765	766	768					
Olympian	511	512	513	514	515	516	517	518
	519	520	521	569	586	601		
Volvo B7L	687	688	689	691	692	693	694	695
	696							
DAF Spectra	718	719	720	721	722	723		

Selby (Cowie Drive, Ousegate) - SB

Dart	152	156	165	166	167	177	178	179
	180	181	183	202	203	204	214	219
Volvo B10BLE	102	103	104	106	107	108	109	
Olympian	565	590	591	599	600	621	622	623
Volvo B7L	675	676	677	678	679	681	682	683
	684	685	686					

The Optare Spectra has been the staple double-deck bus built by Optare for several years. Based on the DAF DB250 chassis it developed from standard floor to low floor. From a 1999 delivery and based at Wakefield, 633, T633EUB, is seen heading out of Leeds on route 117. *Mark Lyons*

Wakefield (Belle Isle, Barnsley Road) - WF

MetroRider	755	756					
Dart	135	136	137	140	143	147	148	149
	201	205	206	207	208	209	210	211
	212	213	215	225				
Volvo B10B	405	406	407	408	409	413	414	415
	417	425						
SB220 ALX300	440	441	442	443	445	446	447	448
	449	451	454	455	457	460	461	464
	465	467	468	469	470	471	472	473
	474	475	476	477	478	479	480	481
	482	483	484	485	486	487	488	489
	490	491						
SB220 Paladin	435	436	437	438	439			
SB200 Commander	495	496	497	498	499			
Olympian	541	542	566	574	575	577	580	581
	584	603	604	606	607	609	610	611
	612	615	616	629				
DAF Spectra	633	640	641	700	701	702	703	704
	705	706	707	708	709	710	711	712
	713	714	715	716	717l			

Unallocated or stored - u/w

Lynx	377	378	
Volvo B10B	407		
Olympian	521	528	583

ARRIVA NORTH WEST & WALES

Arriva North West Ltd, Arriva Merseyside Ltd,
Arriva Cymru Ltd, Arriva Manchester Ltd, Arriva Liverpool Ltd,
73 Ormskirk Road, Aintree, Liverpool, L9 5AE

70	BN	N220BAL	Optare MetroRider MR15	Optare	B31F	1996	Blue Bus, Bolton, 2005
71	BN	N221BAL	Optare MetroRider MR15	Optare	B31F	1996	Blue Bus, Bolton, 2005
72	BN	N272BAL	Optare MetroRider MR15	Optare	B31F	1996	Blue Bus, Bolton, 2005
73	BN	M23UUA	Optare MetroRider MR15	Optare	B29F	1995	Blue Bus, Bolton, 2005
74	BN	N224BAL	Optare MetroRider MR15	Optare	B31F	1996	Blue Bus, Bolton, 2005
75	BN	P225FRB	Optare MetroRider MR15	Optare	B31F	1996	Blue Bus, Bolton, 2005
76	EC	R226SCH	Optare MetroRider MR15	Optare	B31F	1997	Blue Bus, Bolton, 2005
77	EC	R227SCH	Optare MetroRider MR15	Optare	B31F	1997	Blue Bus, Bolton, 2005
78	EC	R228SCH	Optare MetroRider MR15	Optare	B31F	1997	Blue Bus, Bolton, 2005
79	EC	R229SCH	Optare MetroRider MR15	Optare	B31F	1997	Blue Bus, Bolton, 2005
80	EC	L190DDW	Optare MetroRider MR15	Optare	B31F	1994	Blue Bus, Bolton, 2005
81	EC	M621PDP	Optare MetroRider MR17	Optare	B25F	1994	Blue Bus, Bolton, 2005
82	EC	M622PDP	Optare MetroRider MR17	Optare	B25F	1994	Blue Bus, Bolton, 2005
83	EC	M623PDP	Optare MetroRider MR17	Optare	B25F	1994	Blue Bus, Bolton, 2005
84	BN	M214STO	Optare MetroRider MR15	Optare	B30F	1994	Blue Bus, Bolton, 2005
85	BN	M215TNU	Optare MetroRider MR15	Optare	B30F	1995	Blue Bus, Bolton, 2005
86	BN	L686SUM	Optare MetroRider MR15	Optare	B28F	1994	Blue Bus, Bolton, 2005
87	BN	N217VVO	Optare MetroRider MR15	Optare	B30F	1995	Blue Bus, Bolton, 2005
88	BN	L208ONU	Optare MetroRider MR15	Optare	B30F	1994	Blue Bus, Bolton, 2005
89	BN	L209ONU	Optare MetroRider MR15	Optare	B30F	1994	Blue Bus, Bolton, 2005
95	BN	P310CXW	Optare MetroRider MR17	Optare	B30F	1996	Blue Bus, Bolton, 2005
147	CH	J3SLT	Mercedes-Benz 711D	Plaxton Beaver	B27F	1997	
148	WI	P658KEY	Mercedes-Benz 711D	Plaxton Beaver	B27F	1997	
149	CH	P473APJ	Mercedes-Benz 711D	Plaxton Beaver	B23F	1996	Arriva Southern Counties, 2001
151	WI	P688KCC	Mercedes-Benz 709D	Plaxton Beaver	B27F	1997	

158-163

			Mercedes-Benz 709D	Alexander Sprint	B23F	1996	Timeline, Leigh, 1998

158	CH	P178FNF	160	WX	P180FNF	162	WY	P182FNF	163	WY	P183FNF
159	WY	P179FNF	161	WY	P181FNF						

164	WI	P524UGA	Mercedes-Benz 709D	Plaxton Beaver	B27F	1996	Nova Scotia, Winsford, 2000
165	WI	P525UGA	Mercedes-Benz 709D	Plaxton Beaver	B27F	1996	Nova Scotia, Winsford, 2000

178-184

			Mercedes-Benz 811D	Plaxton Beaver	B31F	1996	

178	MF	N178DWM	180	WY	P180GND	182	WI	P182GND	184	MF	P184GND
179	MF	N179DWM	181	WY	P181GND	183	CH	P183GND			

191	CW	N781EUA	Mercedes-Benz 811D	Plaxton Beaver	B31F	1995	Arriva Yorkshire, 2000
192	CW	N782EUA	Mercedes-Benz 811D	Plaxton Beaver	B31F	1995	Arriva Yorkshire, 2000
193	CW	N783EUA	Mercedes-Benz 811D	Plaxton Beaver	B31F	1995	Arriva Yorkshire, 2000
198	WI	N718DJC	Mercedes-Benz 811D	Alexander Sprint	B31F	1995	
199	WI	N719DJC	Mercedes-Benz 811D	Alexander Sprint	B31F	1995	

301-321

			Mercedes-Benz Vario 0814	Plaxton Beaver 2	B27F	1998	320 Southern Counties, 2000

301	CW	R801YJC	307	WI	R807YJC	312	AB	R812YJC	317	LJ	R817YJC
302	CW	R802YJC	308	WI	R808YJC	313	AB	R813YJC	318	LJ	R818YJC
303	CW	R803YJC	309	LJ	R809YJC	314	RH	R814YJC	319	BG	R819YJC
304	CW	R804YJC	310	WI	R810YJC	315	RH	R815YJC	320	LJ	R114TKO
305	CW	R805YJC	311	WI	R811YJC	316	RH	R816YJC	321	LJ	R821YJC

329	AB	R799DUB	Mercedes-Benz Vario 0810	Plaxton Beaver 2	B31F	1997	Arriva Yorkshire, 2000

331-340

			Mercedes-Benz Vario 0810	Plaxton Beaver 2	B27F	1998	Arriva Southern Counties, 2000

331	LJ	R101TKO	334	WI	R104TKO	337	WX	R107TKO	339	LJ	R109TKO
332	LJ	R102TKO	335	AB	R105TKO	338	AB	R108TKO	340	RH	R110TKO
333	LJ	R103TKO									

Liveried for the Liverpool city circular, S2, Optare Solo 655, MK05MKM, is seen outside the City Hall. Like many other operators, Arriva operates buses on behalf of local authorities using their vehicles. Two further Solo buses are operated for Flintshire. *Mat Southart*

341	AB	R341KGG	Mercedes-Benz Vario O814	Alexander ALX100	B27F	1998	Arriva Scotland, 2001
342	AB	R112TKO	Mercedes-Benz Vario O810	Plaxton Beaver 2	B27F	1998	Arriva Southern Counties, 2000
343	RH	R113TKO	Mercedes-Benz Vario O810	Plaxton Beaver 2	B27F	1998	Arriva Southern Counties, 2000
344	AB	R344KGG	Mercedes-Benz Vario O814	Alexander ALX100	B27F	1998	Arriva Scotland, 2001
345	AB	R115TKO	Mercedes-Benz Vario O810	Plaxton Beaver 2	B27F	1998	Arriva Southern Counties, 2000
346	RH	R116TKO	Mercedes-Benz Vario O810	Plaxton Beaver 2	B27F	1998	Arriva Southern Counties, 2000
347	LJ	R117TKO	Mercedes-Benz Vario O810	Plaxton Beaver 2	B27F	1998	Arriva Southern Counties, 2000
353	RH	R123TKO	Mercedes-Benz Vario O810	Plaxton Beaver 2	B27F	1998	Arriva Southern Counties, 2001
354	LJ	R124TKO	Mercedes-Benz Vario O810	Plaxton Beaver 2	B27F	1998	Arriva Southern Counties, 2001
355	LJ	R962FYS	Mercedes-Benz Vario O810	Mellor	C33F	1998	D & G, Rachub, 2000
356	AB	R486UCC	Mercedes-Benz Vario O814	Plaxton Beaver 2	B27F	1997	
357	LJ	R487UCC	Mercedes-Benz Vario O814	Plaxton Beaver 2	B27F	1997	
365	WI	S355PGA	Mercedes-Benz Vario O814	Plaxton Beaver 2	B27F	1998	Arriva Scotland, 2001
374	u	S824MCC	Mercedes-Benz Vario O814	Plaxton Beaver 2	BC29F	1998	
375	u	S825MCC	Mercedes-Benz Vario O814	Plaxton Beaver 2	BC29F	1998	
391	WX	W191CDN	Mercedes-Benz Vario O814	Alexander ALX100	B27F	2000	Arriva Bus & Coach, 2000
392	WX	W192CDN	Mercedes-Benz Vario O814	Alexander ALX100	B27F	2000	Arriva Scotland, 2001
393	BG	W193CDN	Mercedes-Benz Vario O814	Alexander ALX100	B27F	2000	Arriva Scotland, 2001
394	BG	W194CDN	Mercedes-Benz Vario O814	Alexander ALX100	B27F	2000	Arriva Scotland, 2001
395	BN	V951KAG	Mercedes-Benz Vario O814	Plaxton Beaver 2	B27F	1999	Blue Bus, Bolton, 2005
396	BN	MV02XYJ	Mercedes-Benz Vario O814	Plaxton Beaver 2	B27F	2002	Blue Bus, Bolton, 2005
397	BN	MV02XYK	Mercedes-Benz Vario O814	Plaxton Beaver 2	B27F	2002	Blue Bus, Bolton, 2005
398	BN	MK52XNS	Mercedes-Benz Vario O814	Plaxton Beaver 2	B27F	2002	Blue Bus, Bolton, 2005
601	BO	M301YBG	Neoplan N4009	Neoplan	N23F	1995	
602	BO	M302YBG	Neoplan N4009	Neoplan	N23F	1995	
603	BO	M303YBG	Neoplan N4009	Neoplan	N23F	1995	
611	CH	YP52JWW	Optare Alero	Optare	N12F	2003	Operated for Flintshire CC
612	CH	YP52JWO	Optare Alero	Optare	N12F	2003	Operated for Flintshire CC
613	CH	YP52JWU	Optare Alero	Optare	N12F	2003	Operated for Flintshire CC
619	WX	YN04XZH	Optare Alero	Optare	N12F	2004	Operated for Flintshire CC
620	CH	YK05CAA	Optare Solo M880	Optare	N23F	2005	Operated for Flintshire CC
621	CH	YK05CAE	Optare Solo M880	Optare	N23F	2005	Operated for Flintshire CC

651-656 Optare Solo M850 Optare N28F 2005

651	BO	MK54YLR	653	BO	MK54YLU	655	BO	MK05MKM	656	BO	MK05MKN
652	BO	MK54YLT	654	BO	MK05MKL						

The competitor to the Optare Solo, with similar seating capacity and access, is the Mini Pointer Dart, or the Pointer MPD as it was sold for a while. Arriva North West and Wales operates a number of these, mainly in rural Cheshire and Wales. Seen near Penrhyncoch on Aberystwyth local service is 834, X274RFF. *A Moyes*

| 801 | WY | R546ABA | Dennis Dart SLF 8.8m | | Plaxton Pointer MPD | | N28F | 1997 | |

802-809
			Dennis Dart SLF 8.8m		Plaxton Pointer MPD		N25F	1998	
802	AB	S872SNB	804	LJ	S874SNB	806	HU	S876SNB	808	RU	S878SNB
803	WY	S873SNB	805	RU	S875SNB	807	MF	S877SNB	809	RU	S879SNB

810-813
			Dennis Dart SLF 8.8m		Plaxton Pointer MPD		N29F	1999	Nova Scotia, Winsford, 2000
810	WY	T62JBA	811	WY	T63JBA	812	WY	T64JBA	813	WY	T65JBA

814-820
			Dennis Dart SLF 8.8m		Plaxton Pointer MPD		N27F	1999	
814	LJ	T564JJC	816	BG	T566JJC	818	BG	T568JJC	820	AB	T570JJC
815	LJ	T565JJC	817	BG	T567JJC	819	BG	T569JJC			

821-852
			Dennis Dart SLF 8.8m		Plaxton Pointer MPD		N27F	2000-01	
821	BG	W269NFF	831	RH	X271RFF	841	AB	Y541UJC	847	RH	Y547UJC
822	BG	W394OJC	832	RH	X272RFF	842	AB	Y542UJC	848	WX	Y548UJC
823	AB	V553ECC	833	BG	X273RFF	843	RH	Y543UJC	849	WX	Y549UJC
824	AB	V554ECC	834	RH	X274RFF	844	RH	Y544UJC	851	WX	Y551UJC
826	AB	V556ECC	838	WX	Y538VFF	846	RH	Y546UJC	852	WX	Y552UJC
827	BG	V557ECC	839	WX	Y539VFF						

856-859
			Dennis Dart SLF 8.8m		Plaxton Pointer MPD		N29F	1999	Arriva Midlands North, 2003
856	MF	T526AOB	857	MF	T527AOB	858	MF	T528AOB	859	MF	T529AOB

860-886
			Dennis Dart SLF 8.8m		Plaxton Pointer MPD		N29F	2000-01	
860	WI	X209JOF	865	WI	X215JOF	869	WI	X32KON	878	CW	Y38TDA
861	WI	X211JOF	866	WI	X216JOF	872	CW	Y32TDA	879	CW	Y39TDA
862	WI	X212JOF	867	MF	X217JOF	876	CW	Y36TDA	882	CW	Y42TDA
863	WI	X213JOF	868	MF	X218JOF	877	CW	Y37TDA	886	CW	Y46TDA
804	WI	X214JOF									

887	WY	SN03DZY	TransBus Dart SLF 8.8m	TransBus Mini Pointer	N29F	2003	Operated for Cheshire CC
888	WY	SN03DZZ	TransBus Dart SLF 8.8m	TransBus Mini Pointer	N29F	2003	Operated for Cheshire CC
890	EC	T10BLU	Dennis Dart SLF	Plaxton Pointer MPD	N29F	2002	Blue Bus, Bolton, 2005
891	EC	T11BLU	Dennis Dart SLF	Plaxton Pointer MPD	N29F	2002	Blue Bus, Bolton, 2005
892	EC	W12LUE	Dennis Dart SLF	Plaxton Pointer MPD	N29F	2002	Blue Bus, Bolton, 2005
893	EC	X13LUE	Dennis Dart SLF	Plaxton Pointer MPD	N29F	2002	Blue Bus, Bolton, 2005
894	EC	X14LUE	Dennis Dart SLF	Plaxton Pointer MPD	N29F	2002	Blue Bus, Bolton, 2005

1035-1040

Scania L113CRL East Lancs Flyte B47F 1996

1035	JS	P135GND	1037	JS	P137GND	1039	JS	P139GND	1040	JS	P140GND
1036	JS	P136GND	1038	JS	P138GND						

1041-1061

Scania L113CRL Northern Counties Paladin B47F 1997

1041	RU	P41MVU	1047	RU	R47XVM	1052	JS	P52MVU	1057	JS	R57XVM
1042	RU	P42MVU	1048	RU	R48XVM	1053	JS	P53MVU	1058	JS	P58MVU
1043	RU	P43MVU	1049	RU	P49MVU	1054	JS	R54XVM	1059	JS	R59XVM
1044	RU	P244NBA	1050	RU	P250NBA	1055	JS	R255WRJ	1060	JS	P260NBA
1045	RU	P45MVU	1051	JS	R51XVM	1056	JS	P56MVU	1061	JS	P61MVU
1046	RU	P46MVU									

1062	JS	M102RMS	Scania L113CRL	Northern Counties Paladin	B51F	1995	Arriva Scotland West, 2002
1063	JS	M103RMS	Scania L113CRL	Northern Counties Paladin	B51F	1995	Arriva Scotland West, 2002
1065	JS	M105RMS	Scania L113CRL	Alexander Strider	B51F	1995	Arriva Scotland West, 2002
1068	JS	L588JSG	Scania L113CRL	Northern Counties Paladin	B51F	1994	Arriva Scotland West, 2002

1101-1110

Dennis Dart 9m Plaxton Pointer B31F 1993 Arriva London, 2001

1101	WX	L941GYL	1105	WX	L935GYL	1107	BG	L937GYL	1109	LJ	L939GYL
1104	WX	L934GYL	1106	WX	L936GYL	1108	BG	L938GYL	1110	CH	L940GYL

1111	SK	J311WHJ	Dennis Dart 9m	Plaxton Pointer	B35F	1991	Arriva London, 2000
1112	BG	J312WHJ	Dennis Dart 9m	Plaxton Pointer	B35F	1991	Arriva London, 2000
1113	WX	J313WHJ	Dennis Dart 9m	Plaxton Pointer	B35F	1991	Arriva London, 2000
1114	WX	J314XVX	Dennis Dart 9m	Wright Handybus	B35F	1992	East Herts & Essex, 1998
1115	WX	J315XVX	Dennis Dart 9m	Wright Handybus	B35F	1992	East Herts & Essex, 1998
1116	AB	L150WAG	Dennis Dart 9m	Plaxton Pointer	B34F	1993	Arriva London, 2001
1117	CH	L247WAG	Dennis Dart 9m	Plaxton Pointer	B34F	1993	Arriva London, 2001
1118	BG	L148WAG	Dennis Dart 9m	Plaxton Pointer	B34F	1993	Arriva London, 2001
1119	BG	L149WAG	Dennis Dart 9m	Plaxton Pointer	B34F	1993	Arriva London, 2001

1120-1125

Dennis Dart 9m Northern Counties Paladin B35F 1994 Arriva London, 2000

1120	RH	L120YVK	1122	MA	L126YVK	1124	JS	L123YVK	1125	JS	L121YVK
1121	MA	L125YVK	1123	MA	L151YVK						

1126	RH	N676GUM	Dennis Dart 9.8m	Plaxton Pointer	B40F	1995	Arriva London, 2001
1127	CH	N671GUM	Dennis Dart 9.8m	Plaxton Pointer	B40F	1995	Arriva London, 2001
1128	RH	N682GUM	Dennis Dart 9.8m	Plaxton Pointer	B40F	1995	Arriva London, 2001
1129	AB	N704GUM	Dennis Dart 9m	Plaxton Pointer	B34F	1995	Arriva London, 2001
1130	AB	N707GUM	Dennis Dart 9m	Plaxton Pointer	B34F	1995	Arriva London, 2001
1131	WI	H851NOC	Dennis Dart 9.8m	Carlyle Dartline	B43F	1991	Arriva Midlands North, 2003
1132	WI	G122RGT	Dennis Dart 9m	Carlyle Dartline	B33F	1990	Arriva Midlands North, 2003
1133	WI	G123RGT	Dennis Dart 9m	Carlyle Dartline	B36F	1990	Arriva Midlands North, 2003
1135	WI	G125RGT	Dennis Dart 9m	Carlyle Dartline	B36F	1990	Arriva Midlands North, 2003
1138	WI	J328VAW	Dennis Dart 9.8m	Carlyle Dartline	B40F	1991	Arriva Midlands North, 2003
1139	LJ	J556GTP	Dennis Dart 9m	Wadham Stringer Portsdown	B35F	1991	Arriva Midlands North, 2003
1140	WI	H192JNF	Dennis Dart 9m	Wadham Stringer Portsdown	B35F	1990	Arriva Midlands North, 2003
1141	MA	L115YVK	Dennis Dart 9m	Northern Counties Paladin	B35F	1994	Arriva Southern Counties, 2003
1142	MA	L116YVK	Dennis Dart 9m	Northern Counties Paladin	B35F	1994	Arriva Southern Counties, 2003
1143	MA	L117YVK	Dennis Dart 9m	Northern Counties Paladin	B35F	1994	Arriva Southern Counties, 2003
1146	RH	L122YVK	Dennis Dart 9m	Northern Counties Paladin	B35F	1994	Arriva Southern Counties, 2003
1148	CH	J701NHA	Dennis Dart 9.8m	East Lancs EL2000	B40F	1991	Arriva Midlands North, 2003
1149	WI	L618BNX	Dennis Dart 9m	East Lancs EL2000	B33F	1994	Arriva Midlands North, 2003
1150	BO	L150SBG	Dennis Dart 9m	East Lancs	B32F	1993	
1151	BO	L151SBG	Dennis Dart 9m	East Lancs	B32F	1993	
1152	BO	L152SBG	Dennis Dart 9m	East Lancs	B32F	1993	
1153	CH	L153UKB	Dennis Dart 9m	Plaxton Pointer	B34F	1994	
1154	BG	L154UKB	Dennis Dart 9m	Plaxton Pointer	B34F	1994	
1155	CH	L155UKB	Dennis Dart 9m	Plaxton Pointer	B34F	1994	
1156	WX	L156UKB	Dennis Dart 9m	Plaxton Pointer	B34F	1994	

1157-1170

Dennis Dart 9.8m East Lancs B40F 1994-95

1157	RU	M157WKA	1161	RU	M161WKA	1165	LJ	M165WKA	1168	RU	M168WKA
1158	RU	M158WKA	1162	RU	M162WKA	1166	RU	M166WKA	1169	RU	M169WKA
1159	RU	M159WKA	1163	RU	M163WKA	1167	RU	M167WKA	1170	RU	M170WKA
1160	RU	M160WKA	1164	SK	M164WKA						

1171-1187 — Dennis Dart 9.8m — Plaxton Pointer — B40F — 1995

1171	HU	M171YKA	1176	HU	M176YKA	1180	HU	M180YKA	1184	HU	M184YKA
1172	BD	M172YKA	1177	HU	M177YKA	1181	BD	M181YKA	1185	BD	M185YKA
1173	HU	M173YKA	1178	HU	M178YKA	1182	SO	M182YKA	1186	JS	M186YKA
1174	BD	M174YKA	1179	HU	M179YKA	1183	HU	M183YKA	1187	HU	M187YKA
1175	BD	M175YKA									

1188-1199 — Dennis Dart 9.8m — Plaxton Pointer — B40F — 1995

1188	WY	M188YKA	1191	HU	M191YKA	1194	HU	M194YKA	1197	BD	M197YKA
1189	SO	M189YKA	1192	HU	M192YKA	1195	HU	M195YKA	1198	BD	M198YKA
1190	SO	M190YKA	1193	BD	M193YKA	1196	HU	M196YKA	1199	WY	M199YKA

1211	BD	M211YKD	Dennis Dart 9.8m	Plaxton Pointer	B40F	1995
1212	BD	M212YKD	Dennis Dart 9.8m	Plaxton Pointer	B40F	1995
1213	BD	M213YKD	Dennis Dart 9.8m	Plaxton Pointer	B40F	1995
1214	BD	M214YKD	Dennis Dart 9.8m	Plaxton Pointer	B40F	1995
1215	BD	M215YKD	Dennis Dart 9.8m	Plaxton Pointer	B40F	1995
1216	BD	M216YKD	Dennis Dart 9.8m	Plaxton Pointer	B40F	1995

1217-1264 — Dennis Dart 9.8m — East Lancs — B40F — 1995

1217	WY	M217AKB	1229	SK	M229AKB	1241	BO	N241CKA	1253	SK	N253CKA
1218	WY	M218AKB	1230	BD	M230AKB	1242	BO	N242CKA	1254	MA	N254CKA
1219	SK	M219AKB	1231	WY	M231AKB	1243	BO	N243CKA	1255	WY	N255CKA
1220	RU	M220AKB	1232	WY	M232AKB	1244	BO	N244CKA	1256	WY	N256CKA
1221	RU	M221AKB	1233	LJ	N233CKA	1245	BO	N245CKA	1257	WY	N257CKA
1222	RU	M322AKB	1234	BO	N234CKA	1246	BO	N246CKA	1258	WY	N258CKA
1223	MA	M223AKB	1235	BO	N235CKA	1247	BO	N247CKA	1259	SK	N259CKA
1224	MA	M224AKB	1236	BO	N236CKA	1248	BO	N248CKA	1260	MA	N260CKA
1225	MA	M225AKB	1237	BO	N237CKA	1249	MA	N249CKA	1261	WY	N261CKA
1226	MA	M226AKB	1238	BO	N238CKA	1250	MA	N250CKA	1262	WY	N262CKA
1227	MA	M227AKB	1239	BO	N239CKA	1251	MA	N251CKA	1263	BD	N263CKA
1228	LJ	M228AKB	1240	BO	N240CKA	1252	SK	N252CKA	1264	MA	N264CKA

1265	WY	K877UDB	Dennis Dart 9.8m	Plaxton Pointer	B40F	1992	Star Line, 1995
1266	WY	M370KVR	Dennis Dart 9.8m	Northern Counties Paladin	B40F	1994	Star Line, 1995
1267	WY	M371KVR	Dennis Dart 9.8m	Northern Counties Paladin	B40F	1994	Star Line, 1995
1268	WY	M372KVR	Dennis Dart 9.8m	Northern Counties Paladin	B40F	1995	Star Line, 1995
1269	WY	M841RCP	Dennis Dart 9.8m	Northern Counties Paladin	B39F	1995	Wigan Bus Company, 1995
1270	WY	M842RCP	Dennis Dart 9.8m	Northern Counties Paladin	B39F	1995	Wigan Bus Company, 1995
1271	WY	M843RCP	Dennis Dart 9.8m	Northern Counties Paladin	B39F	1995	Wigan Bus Company, 1995
1272	BO	K911OEM	Dennis Dart 9.8m	Plaxton Pointer	B38F	1993	Blue Triangle, 1994
1273	SK	K73SRG	Dennis Dart 9.8m	Plaxton Pointer	B43F	1993	Northumbria (Hunters), 1997
1274	SK	K74SRG	Dennis Dart 9.8m	Plaxton Pointer	B43F	1993	Northumbria (Hunters), 1997
1275	SK	K75SRG	Dennis Dart 9.8m	Plaxton Pointer	B43F	1993	Northumbria (Hunters), 1997
1276	SK	J6SLT	Dennis Dart 9.8m	Plaxton Pointer	B40F	1996	South Lancashire, 1997
1277	SK	J7SLT	Dennis Dart 9.8m	Plaxton Pointer	B38F	1996	South Lancashire, 1997
1278	SK	J8SLT	Dennis Dart 9.8m	Plaxton Pointer	B38F	1992	South Lancashire, 1997
1279	SK	J9SLT	Dennis Dart 9.8m	Plaxton Pointer	B38F	1992	South Lancashire, 1997
1280	HU	L11SLT	Dennis Dart 9.8m	Plaxton Pointer	B38F	1993	South Lancashire, 1997
1281	RH	L1SLT	Dennis Dart 9m	Plaxton Pointer	B35F	1993	South Lancashire, 1997
1282	HU	L2SLT	Dennis Dart 9m	Plaxton Pointer	B35F	1993	South Lancashire, 1997
1283	SO	K817NKH	Dennis Dart 9m	Plaxton Pointer	B34F	1992	London Northern, 1994
1284	SK	K955PBG	Dennis Dart 9.8m	Plaxton Pointer	B36F	1993	Blue Triangle, 1994
1285	HU	M5SLT	Dennis Dart 9.8m	Plaxton Pointer	B40F	1994	South Lancashire, 1997
1286	HU	M950LYR	Dennis Dart 9.8m	Plaxton Pointer	B40F	1995	Arriva London, 2000
1287	WY	M20GGY	Dennis Dart 9.8m	Plaxton Pointer	B40F	1994	David Ogden, Haydock, 1995
1288	WY	M30GGY	Dennis Dart 9.8m	Plaxton Pointer	B40F	1994	David Ogden, Haydock, 1995
1289	SO	N678GUM	Dennis Dart 9.8m	Plaxton Pointer	B40F	1995	Arriva London, 2003
1300	SK	P3SLT	Dennis Dart 9.8m	Plaxton Pointer	B40F	1996	South Lancashire, 1997

1301-1310 — Dennis Dart 9.8m — East Lancs EL2000 — B34F* — 1995 — Arriva Southern Counties, 2001

1301	BG	M521MPF	1303	BG	M523MPF	1308	BG	N528SPA	1310	BG	N530SPA
1302	BG	M522MPF	1304	BG	M524MPF	1309	BG	N529SPA			

1311-1318 — Dennis Dart 9m — Plaxton Pointer — B34F — 1995-96 — Arriva London, 2005

1311	SK	N705GUM	1313	u	N703GUM	1316	HU	P916PWW	1318	HU	P918PWW
1312	SK	N706GUM	1314	u	N701GUM	1317	HU	P917PWW			

The vehicles and services of Blue Bus of Bolton were acquired in July 2005. Blue Bus had been established some 14 years earlier and operated to the north of Manchester, providing services in and around Bolton and to Manchester city centre. Pictured shortly after gaining Arriva names and dual fleet numbers is 1, K1BLU, also numbered 1344. Within a few days, the white Arriva names were replaced with black ones. *Bill Potter*

1323-1338

				Dennis Dart 9.8m			Plaxton Pointer		B40F	1996	Arriva London, 2001-03

1323	RH	P823RWU	1327	CH	P827RWU	1330	CH	P830RWU	1333	BG	P833RWU
1325	RH	P825RWU	1328	AB	P828RWU	1331	CH	P831RWU	1334	CH	P834RWU
1326	AB	P826RWU	1329	CH	P829RWU	1332	SO	P832RWU	1338	RH	P838RWU

1340	BG	M160SKR	Dennis Dart 9m	Plaxton Pointer	B35F	1995	Arriva Southern Counties, 1999
1341	RH	M161SKR	Dennis Dart 9m	Plaxton Pointer	B35F	1995	Arriva Southern Counties, 1999
1342	RH	M162SKR	Dennis Dart 9m	Plaxton Pointer	B35F	1995	Arriva Southern Counties, 1999
1343	RH	M163SKR	Dennis Dart 9m	Plaxton Pointer	B35F	1995	Arriva Southern Counties, 1999
1344	BN	K1BLU	Dennis Dart 9.8m	East Lancs EL2000	B40F	1993	Blue Bus, Bolton, 2005
1345	BN	M2BLU	Dennis Dart 9.8m	East Lancs EL2000	B40F	1994	Blue Bus, Bolton, 2005
1346	BN	N4BLU	Dennis Dart 9.8m	Alexander Dash	B40F	1995	Blue Bus, Bolton, 2005
1743	CW	G49CVC	Leyland Lynx LX112L10ZR1R	Leyland Lynx	B51F	1990	Arriva Midlands North, 2003
1747	CW	G327NUM	Leyland Lynx LX2R11C15Z4S	Leyland Lynx	B49F	1990	Arriva Midlands North, 2003
1750	BG	H130LPU	Leyland Lynx LX2R11C15Z4R	Leyland Lynx 2	B49F	1990	Colchester, 1994
1752	CW	H254PAJ	Leyland Lynx LX2R11C15Z4S	Leyland Lynx 2	B49F	1991	Arriva North East, 1999
1753	CW	H733HWK	Leyland Lynx LX2R11C15Z4R	Leyland Lynx 2	B51F	1990	Clydeside (McGills), 1997
1754	CW	J654UHN	Leyland Lynx LX2R11C15Z4S	Leyland Lynx 2	B49F	1991	Arriva North East, 1998
1755	BG	J655UHN	Leyland Lynx LX2R11C15Z4S	Leyland Lynx 2	B49F	1991	Arriva North East, 1999
1757	CH	K27EWC	Leyland Lynx LX2R11C15Z4R	Leyland Lynx 2	B49F	1992	Colchester, 1994
1772	AB	E52UNE	Leyland Tiger TRBTL11/3ARZA	Alexander N	B53F	1988	Arriva Midlands North, 2003
1773	BN	F902JBB	Leyland Tiger TRBTL11/2RP	Duple 300	B55F	1989	Blue Bus, Bolton, 2005
1774	BN	WJI9072	Leyland Tiger TRBTL11/2R	East Lancs EL2000	B55F	1982	Blue Bus, Bolton, 2005
1775	BN	WJI9074	Leyland Tiger TRBTL11/2R	East Lancs EL2000	B55F	1982	Blue Bus, Bolton, 2005
1776	AB	H278LEF	Leyland Tiger TRCL10/3ARZA	Alexander Q	B55F	1990	Arriva Midlands North, 2003
1777	AB	H279LEF	Leyland Tiger TRCL10/3ARZA	Alexander Q	B55F	1990	Arriva Midlands North, 2003

1778-1788

				Volvo B10M-50 Citybus			Alexander Q		B55F	1992	Timeline, Leigh, 1998

1778	AB	H78DVM	1785	AB	H85DVM	1787	AB	H87DVM	1788	AB	H588DVM
1779	AB	H79DVM	1786	AB	H86DVM						

Yellow school buses are spreading in Britain, although its unique benefit, America's school bus traffic legislation has not been applied. Pictured at Aberystwyth on its first outing on school contract is yellow-liveried **1788, H588DVM.** *Tony Moyes*

1790-1794

			DAF SB220			Ikarus CitiBus		B48F	1993	
1790	BD	K130TCP	**1792**	BD	K132TCP	**1793**	BD	K133TCP	**1794**	BD	K510RJX
1791	BD	K131TCP								

1795	AB	N25FWU	DAF SB220			Northern Counties Paladin	B49F	1995	West Coast Motors, 1996
1796	AB	N24FWU	DAF SB220			Northern Counties Paladin	B49F	1995	West Coast Motors, 1996
1797	AB	M847RCP	DAF SB220			Northern Counties Paladin	B49F	1995	Citybus, Southampton, 1996
1799	AB	M849RCP	DAF SB220			Northern Counties Paladin	B49F	1995	Citybus, Southampton, 1996

1900	BN	L205VAG	Dennis Lance 11m			Plaxton Verde	B46F	1994	Blue Bus, Bolton, 2005

1901-1910

			Dennis Lance 11m			Plaxton Verde		B49F	1995	
1901	BO	M201YKA	**1904**	BO	M204YKA	**1907**	BO	M207YKA	**1909**	BO	M209YKA
1902	BO	M202YKA	**1905**	BO	M205YKA	**1908**	BO	M208YKA	**1910**	BO	M210YKA
1903	BO	M203YKA	**1906**	BO	M206YKA					

1911-1920

			Dennis Lance 11m			Plaxton Verde		B49F	1994	
1911	BO	M931EYS	**1914**	BO	M934EYS	**1917**	BO	M927EYS	**1919**	BO	M929EYS
1912	BO	M932EYS	**1915**	BO	M935EYS	**1918**	BO	M928EYS	**1920**	BO	M930EYS
1913	BO	M933EYS	**1916**	BO	M936EYS					

1921-1935

			Dennis Lance 11m			Alexander PS		B47F	1992	Blue Bus, Bolton, 2005
1921	BN	J101WSC	**1925**	EC	J105WSC	**1929**	EC	J109WSC	**1933**	BN	J113WSC
1922	BN	J102WSC	**1926**	EC	J106WSC	**1930**	EC	J110WSC	**1934**	BN	J114WSC
1923	BN	J103WSC	**1927**	EC	J107WSC	**1931**	EC	J411WSC	**1935**	BN	J115WSC
1924	EC	J104WSC	**1928**	EC	J108WSC	**1932**	EC	J112WSC			

1940-1949

			Dennis Lance 11m			East Lancs		B49F	1996	Arriva London, 2001
1940	BO	N210TPK	**1943**	BO	N213TPK	**1946**	BO	N216TPK	**1948**	BO	N218TPK
1941	BO	N211TPK	**1944**	BO	N214TPK	**1947**	BO	N217TPK	**1949**	BO	N219TPK
1942	BO	N212TPK	**1945**	BO	N215TPK					

1950	BO	H163DJU	Dennis Javelin 11m			Duple 300	B55F	1991	Blue Bus, Bolton, 2005

In mid-July 2005 Arriva took over the operation of service 500 from Liverpool centre to the city's John Lennon Airport. Three Scania OmniCity integral buses have been acquired for the service and these carry a special livery as illustrated by 2063, CX05EDY, in this view taken when new. *Mat Southart*

2001-2005

Scania L113CRL — Wright Axcess-ultralow — N42F — 1996

2001	JS	N101YVU	2003	JS	N103YVU	2004	JS	N104YVU	2005	JS	N105YVU
2002	GL	M2SLT									

2006-2034

Scania L113CRL — Wright Axcess-ultralow — N43F — 1996

2006	GL	N106DWM	2014	JS	N114DWM	2021	JS	N121DWM	2028	GL	N128DWM
2007	JS	N107DWM	2015	JS	N115DWM	2022	JS	N122DWM	2029	JS	N129DWM
2008	GL	N108DWM	2016	JS	N116DWM	2023	JS	N123DWM	2030	GL	N130DWM
2009	GL	N109DWM	2017	JS	N117DWM	2024	GL	N124DWM	2031	GL	N131DWM
2010	GL	N110DWM	2018	JS	N118DWM	2025	GL	N125DWM	2032	JS	N132DWM
2011	GL	N211DWM	2019	JS	N119DWM	2026	GL	N126DWM	2033	GL	N133DWM
2013	JS	N113DWM	2020	JS	N120DWM	2027	JS	N127DWM	2034	GL	N134DWM

2041-2054

Scania N113CRL — Wright Pathfinder — B37D — 1994 — Arriva London, 1999

2041	JS	RDZ1701	2045	JS	RDZ1705	2049	RU	RDZ1709	2052	RU	RDZ1712
2042	JS	RDZ1702	2046	JS	RDZ1706	2050	RU	RDZ1710	2053	RU	RDZ1713
2043	JS	RDZ1703	2047	JS	RDZ1707	2051	RU	RDZ1711	2054	RU	RDZ1714
2044	JS	RDZ1704	2048	RU	RDZ1708						

2061	SP	CX05EOV	Scania OmniCity CN94UB	Scania	N44F	2005
2062	SP	CX05EOX	Scania OmniCity CN94UB	Scania	N44F	2005
2063	SP	CX05EOY	Scania OmniCity CN94UB	Scania	N44F	2005

2101-2109

Dennis Dart SLF 10.1m — Plaxton Pointer 2 — N39F — 1997 — Arriva North East, 2003

2101	WX	R601MHN	2104	WX	R604MHN	2106	WX	R606MHN	2108	WX	R608MHN
2102	WX	R602MHN	2105	WX	R685MHN	2107	WX	R607MHN	2109	WX	R609MHN
2103	WX	R603MHN									

2110-2135

Dennis Dart SLF 10.1m — Plaxton Pointer 2 — N39F — 1999 — being transferred from North East

2110	LJ	S610KHN	2117	u	S617KHN	2124	u	S624KHN	2130	u	S630KHN
2111	u	S611KHN	2118	u	S618KHN	2125	u	S625KHN	2131	u	S631KHN
2112	u	S612KHN	2119	u	S619KHN	2126	u	S626KHN	2132	u	S632KHN
2113	u	S613KHN	2120	u	S620KHN	2127	u	S627KHN	2133	u	S633KHN
2114	u	S614KHN	2121	u	S621KHN	2128	u	S628KHN	2134	u	S634KHN
2115	u	S615KHN	2122	u	S622KHN	2129	u	S629KHN	2135	u	S635KHN
2116	u	S616KHN	2123	u	S623KHN						

2201-2262 Dennis Dart SLF 10.1m Plaxton Pointer 2 N36F 2000-01

2201	HU	X201ANC	2217	BO	X217ANC	2234	BO	X234ANC	2248	MA	X248HJA
2202	HU	X202ANC	2218	BO	X218ANC	2235	BO	X235ANC	2249	MA	X249HJA
2203	HU	X203ANC	2219	BO	X219ANC	2236	BO	X236ANC	2251	MA	X251HJA
2204	HU	X204ANC	2221	BO	X221ANC	2237	BO	X237ANC	2252	MA	X252HJA
2207	HU	X207ANC	2223	BO	X223ANC	2238	MA	X238ANC	2253	MA	X253HJA
2208	HU	X208ANC	2224	BO	X224ANC	2239	MA	X239ANC	2254	MA	X254HJA
2209	HU	X209ANC	2226	BO	X226ANC	2241	MA	X241ANC	2256	MA	X256HJA
2211	HU	X211ANC	2227	BO	X227ANC	2242	MA	X242ANC	2257	CH	X257HJA
2212	HU	X212ANC	2228	BO	X228ANC	2243	MA	X243HJA	2258	CH	X258HJA
2213	HU	X213ANC	2229	BO	X229ANC	2244	MA	X244HJA	2259	BD	X259HJA
2214	HU	X214ANC	2231	BO	X231ANC	2246	MA	X246HJA	2261	BD	X261OBN
2215	BO	X215ANC	2232	BO	X232ANC	2247	MA	X247HJA	2262	BD	X262OBN
2216	BO	X216ANC	2233	BO	X233ANC						

2263-2272 Dennis Dart SLF 10.2m Alexander ALX200 N40F 2000-01

2263	BO	X263OBN	2266	BO	X266OBN	2268	BO	X268OBN	2271	BO	X271OBN
2264	BO	X264OBN	2267	BO	X267OBN	2269	BO	X269OBN	2272	BO	X272OBN
2265	BO	X265OBN									

2273	LJ	S558MCC	Dennis Dart SLF 10.2m	Alexander ALX200	N40F	1998
2274	LJ	S559MCC	Dennis Dart SLF 10.2m	Alexander ALX200	N40F	1998

2276-2279 Dennis Dart SLF 10.2m Alexander ALX200 N36F 1997 Arriva London, 2002-03

2276	LJ	P953RUL	2277	LJ	P959RUL	2278	LJ	P960RUL	2279	LJ	P961RUL

2280-2284 Dennis Dart SLF 10.1m Plaxton Pointer N40F 1996 Arriva Southern Counties, 2004

2280	GL	P180LKL	2282	GL	P182LKL	2283	GL	P183LKL	2284	GL	P214LKJ

2285-2288 Dennis Dart SLF 10.1m Plaxton Pointer N39F 1996 Arriva Southern Counties, 2004

2285	GL	P419HVX	2286	GL	P420HVX	2287	GL	P422HVX	2288	GL	P430HVX

2291-2294 Dennis Dart SLF 10.1m Plaxton Pointer N41F 1996 formerly CNG buses

2291	u	S248UVR	2292	u	S249UVR	2293	u	S250UVR	2294	u	S251UVR

2296-2300 Dennis Dart SLF 10.1m Plaxton Pointer N34F 1997 Arriva London, 2003

2296	RH	R416COO	2298	RH	R418COO	2299	RH	R419COO	2300	RH	R420COO
2297	RH	R417COO									

2301	WX	R301PCW	Dennis Dart SLF 10.1m	Plaxton Pointer 2	N39F	1998

2302-2313 Dennis Dart SLF 10.2m Alexander ALX200 N40F 1998

2302	WY	R302CVU	2305	WY	R305CVU	2309	WY	R309CVU	2312	WY	R312CVU
2303	WY	R303CVU	2306	WY	R606FBU	2310	WY	R310CVU	2313	WY	R313CVU
2304	WY	R304CVU	2308	WY	R308CVU	2311	WY	R311CVU			

2314-2324 Dennis Dart SLF 10.1m Plaxton Pointer 2 N36F 1999

2314	BO	T314PNB	2317	BO	T317PNB	2320	BO	T320PNB	2323	BO	T323PNB
2315	BO	T315PNB	2318	BO	T318PNB	2321	BO	T821PNB	2324	BO	T324PNB
2316	BO	T316PNB	2319	BO	T319PNB	2322	BO	T322PNB			

2325	BG	R521UCC	Dennis Dart SLF 10.1m	Plaxton Pointer	N39F	1997	
2326	BG	R522UCC	Dennis Dart SLF 10.1m	Plaxton Pointer	N39F	1997	
2328	CH	S848RJC	Dennis Dart SLF 10.1m	Plaxton Pointer 2	N39F	1998	Ieuan Williams, Deiniolen, 1999
2330	BG	T560JJC	Dennis Dart SLF 10.1m	Plaxton Pointer 2	N39F	1999	
2331	LJ	T561JJC	Dennis Dart SLF 10.1m	Plaxton Pointer 2	N39F	1999	
2332	AB	T562JJC	Dennis Dart SLF 10.1m	Plaxton Pointer 2	N39F	1999	
2333	AB	T563JJC	Dennis Dart SLF 10.1m	Plaxton Pointer 2	N39F	1999	

2341-2361 Dennis Dart SLF 10.1m Plaxton Pointer 2 N39F* 1999-2000 *2341/2 are N33F

2341	CH	V571DJC	2347	LJ	V577DJC	2352	RH	V582DJC	2357	CH	V587DJC
2342	CH	V572DJC	2348	LJ	V578DJC	2353	RH	V583DJC	2358	CH	V588DJC
2343	LJ	V573DJC	2349	RH	V670DJC	2354	RH	V584DJC	2359	CH	V580ECC
2344	LJ	V574DJC	2350	RH	V580DJC	2355	CH	V585DJC	2360	CH	V590DJC
2345	LJ	V575DJC	2351	RH	V581DJC	2356	CH	V586DJC	2361	CH	V591DJC
2346	LJ	V576DJC									

2391	BO	M517KPA	Dennis Lance SLF 11m	Wright Pathfinder	N40F	1995	Arriva Southern Counties, 2002
2392	BO	M518KPA	Dennis Lance SLF 11m	Wright Pathfinder	N40F	1995	Arriva Southern Counties, 2002
2393	BO	M519KPA	Dennis Lance SLF 11m	Wright Pathfinder	N40F	1995	Arriva Southern Counties, 2002
2394	BO	N527SPA	Dennis Lance SLF 11m	Wright Pathfinder	N39F	1995	Arriva Southern Counties, 2002

Three Plaxton Prestige-bodied DAF SB220s from Southern Counties were transferred north in 2004 and are now allocated to Aberystwyth. Pictured arriving from Lampeter, where the company has an outstation, they join an increasing number of DAF buses in the fleet from the Dutch manufacturer. *Tony Moyes*

2395	BO	M761JPA	Dennis Lance SLF 11m		Wright Pathfinder	N39F	1995	Arriva Southern Counties, 2004
2396	BO	M762JPA	Dennis Lance SLF 11m		Wright Pathfinder	N39F	1995	Arriva Southern Counties, 2004
2397	BO	M763JPA	Dennis Lance SLF 11m		Wright Pathfinder	N39F	1995	Arriva Southern Counties, 2004
2400	BN	R91GNW	DAF SB220		Plaxton Prestige	N40F	1998	Blue Bus, Bolton, 2005
2401	SP	R151GNW	DAF SB220		Plaxton Prestige	N38F	1998	Arriva London, 1999
2402	SP	R152GNW	DAF SB220		Plaxton Prestige	N38F	1998	Arriva London, 1999
2403	SP	R153GNW	DAF SB220		Plaxton Prestige	N38F	1998	Arriva London, 1999

2404-2415　DAF SB220　Alexander ALX300　N42F　2000

2404	BD	V404ENC	2407	HU	V407ENC	2410	SP	V410ENC	2413	SP	V413ENC
2405	BD	V405ENC	2408	BD	V408ENC	2411	BD	V411ENC	2414	BD	V414ENC
2406	BD	V406ENC	2409	BD	V409ENC	2412	BD	V412ENC	2415	SP	V415ENC

2416-2449　DAF SB120　Wright Cadet　N39F　2000-01

2416	SP	X416AJA	2426	SP	X426AJA	2434	SP	X434HJA	2442	BD	X442HJA
2417	SP	X417AJA	2427	SP	X427AJA	2435	BD	X435HJA	2443	BD	X443HJA
2418	SP	X418AJA	2428	BD	X428HJA	2436	BD	X436HJA	2445	BD	X445HJA
2419	SP	X419AJA	2429	SP	X429HJA	2437	BD	X437HJA	2446	BD	X446HJA
2421	SP	X421AJA	2431	SP	X431HJA	2438	BD	X438HJA	2447	BD	X447HJA
2422	SP	X422AJA	2432	SP	X432HJA	2439	BD	X439HJA	2448	BD	X448HJA
2423	SP	X423AJA	2433	SP	X433HJA	2441	BD	X441HJA	2449	BD	X449HJA
2424	SP	X424AJA									

2450	BN	V33BLU	DAF SB220		East Lancs Myllennium	N42F	1999	Blue Bus, Bolton, 2005

2451-2474　DAF SB220　East Lancs Myllennium　N44F　2001

2451	BD	Y451KBU	2457	BD	Y457KBU	2463	SP	Y463KNF	2469	SP	Y469KNF
2452	BD	Y452KBU	2458	BD	Y458KBU	2464	SP	Y464KNF	2470	SP	Y733KNF
2453	BD	Y453KBU	2459	BD	Y459KBU	2465	SP	Y465KNF	2471	SP	Y471KNF
2454	BD	Y454KBU	2460	BD	Y243KBU	2466	SP	Y466KNF	2472	SP	Y472KNF
2455	BD	Y241KBU	2461	BD	Y461KNF	2467	SP	Y467KNF	2473	SP	Y473KNF
2456	BD	Y242KBU	2462	SP	Y462KNF	2468	SP	Y468KNF	2474	SP	Y744KNF

2475	AB	T917KKM	DAF SB220		Plaxton Prestige	N39F	1999	Arriva Southern Counties, 2004
2476	AB	T920KKM	DAF SB220		Plaxton Prestige	N39F	1999	Arriva Southern Counties, 2004
2477	AB	T922KKM	DAF SB220		Plaxton Prestige	N39F	1999	Arriva Southern Counties, 2004
2479	SP	X782NWX	DAF SB120		Wrightbus Cadet	N39F	1999	Selwyns, Runcorn, 2005

The hourly X94 plies between Wrexham and Barmouth connecting many of the centres across north Wales. In 2005 the service received low-floor VDL Bus SB200s with high-back seating. These buses carry route branding as Illustrated by 2510, CX05AAF. *Mat Southart*

2480-2488   VDL Bus SB120   Wrightbus Cadet 2   N39F   2004

2480	BG	CX04AXW	2483	BG	CX04AYA	2485	BG	CX04AYC	2487	WX	CX04EHW
2481	BG	CX04AXY	2484	BG	CX04AYB	2486	WX	CX04EHV	2488	WX	CX04EHY
2482	BG	CX04AXZ									

2489-2503   VDL Bus SB120   Wrightbus Cadet 2   N39F   2004

2489	JS	CX54DKD	2493	JS	CX54DKK	2497	CW	CX54DKU	2501	CW	CX54DLF
2490	JS	CX54DKE	2494	JS	CX54DKL	2498	CW	CX54DKV	2502	CW	CX54DLJ
2491	JS	CX54DKF	2495	JS	CX54DKN	2499	CW	CX54DKY	2503	CW	CX54DLK
2492	JS	CX54DKJ	2496	JS	CX54DKO	2500	CW	CX54DLD			

2504-2513   VDL Bus SB200   Wrightbus Commander   NC43F   2005

2504	AB	CX54EPJ	2507	AB	CX54EPN	2510	AB	CX05AAF	2512	AB	CX05AAK
2505	BG	CX54EPK	2508	AB	CX54EPO	2511	AB	CX05AAJ	2513	WX	CX05AAN
2506	AB	CX54EPL	2509	AB	CX05AAE						

2514-2555   VDL Bus SB120   Wrightbus Cadet 2   N39F   On order

2514	-		2525	-		2536	-		2546	-
2515	-		2526	-		2537	-		2547	-
2516	-		2527	-		2538	-		2548	-
2517	-		2528	-		2539	-		2549	-
2518	-		2529	-		2540	-		2550	-
2519	-		2530	-		2541	-		2551	-
2520	-		2531	-		2542	-		2552	-
2521	-		2532	-		2543	-		2553	-
2522	-		2533	-		2544	-		2554	-
2523	-		2534	-		2545	-		2555	-
2524	-		2535	-						

2556	BN	Y20BLU	DAF SB120	Wrightbus Cadet	N36F	2001	Blue Bus, Bolton, 2005
2557	BN	Y21BLU	DAF SB120	Wrightbus Cadet	N36F	2001	Blue Bus, Bolton, 2005
2558	BN	MM02ZVH	DAF SB120	Wrightbus Cadet	N39F	2002	Blue Bus, Bolton, 2005
2559	BN	MM02ZVJ	DAF SB120	Wrightbus Cadet	N39F	2002	Blue Bus, Bolton, 2005
2560	BN	V34ENC	DAF SB220	Ikarus Citibus 481	N42F	1999	Blue Bus, Bolton, 2005

2561	BN	V35ENC	DAF SB220	Ikarus Citibus 481	N42F	1999	Blue Bus, Bolton, 2005
2562	BN	W174CDN	DAF SB220	Ikarus Citibus 481	N42F	2000	Blue Bus, Bolton, 2005
2563	EC	Y36KNB	DAF SB220	Ikarus Polaris	N42F	2001	Blue Bus, Bolton, 2005
2564	EC	Y37KNB	DAF SB220	Ikarus Polaris	N42F	2001	Blue Bus, Bolton, 2005
2565	EC	Y38KNB	DAF SB220	Ikarus Polaris	N42F	2001	Blue Bus, Bolton, 2005
2566	EC	MK52XNN	DAF SB220	Ikarus Polaris	N44F	2002	Blue Bus, Bolton, 2005
2567	EC	MK52XNO	DAF SB220	Ikarus Polaris	N44F	2002	Blue Bus, Bolton, 2005
2568	EC	MK52XNP	DAF SB220	Ikarus Polaris	N44F	2002	Blue Bus, Bolton, 2005
2569	EC	MK52XNR	DAF SB220	Ikarus Polaris	N44F	2002	Blue Bus, Bolton, 2005

2701-2730 Volvo B10BLE Wrightbus Renown N44F 2001

2701	JS	X701DBT	2709	JS	X709DBT	2717	SP	Y717KNF	2724	SO	Y724KNF
2702	JS	X702DBT	2710	JS	X956DBT	2718	SP	Y718KNF	2725	SO	Y475KNF
2703	JS	X703DBT	2711	JS	Y711KNF	2719	SP	Y719KNF	2726	SO	Y726KNF
2704	JS	X704DBT	2712	JS	Y712KNF	2720	SP	Y457KNF	2727	SO	Y727KNF
2705	JS	X705DBT	2713	JS	Y713KNF	2721	SP	Y721KNF	2728	SO	Y728KNF
2706	JS	X706DBT	2714	JS	Y714KNF	2722	SO	Y722KNF	2729	JS	Y729KNF
2707	JS	X707DBT	2715	SP	Y715KNF	2723	SP	Y723KNF	2730	JS	Y458KNF
2708	JS	X708DBT	2716	SP	Y716KNF						

2732	BN	V22BLU	Volvo B10BLE	Wright Renown	N42F	1999	Blue Bus, Bolton, 2005
2733	BN	X23BLU	Volvo B10BLE	Wright Renown	N42F	2000	Blue Bus, Bolton, 2005
2800	JS	Y22CJW	Volvo B7L	Wrightbus Eclipse	N41F	2001	

2801-2822 Volvo B6BLE Wright Crusader 2 N39F 2000

2801	SO	X801AJA	2806	JS	X806AJA	2812	JS	X812AJA	2817	SO	X817AJA
2802	SO	X802AJA	2807	JS	X807AJA	2813	SO	X813AJA	2818	SO	X818AJA
2803	SO	X803AJA	2808	JS	X808AJA	2814	SO	X814AJA	2819	SO	X819AJA
2804	SO	X804AJA	2809	JS	X809AJA	2815	SO	X815AJA	2821	SO	X821AJA
2805	JS	X805AJA	2811	JS	X811AJA	2816	SO	X816AJA	2822	SO	X822AJA

2825	BN	T222MTB	MAN 18.220	Alexander ALX300	N42F	1999	Blue Bus, Bolton, 2005
2826	BN	MF52LYY	MAN 14.220	East Lancs Myllennium	N39F	2002	Blue Bus, Bolton, 2005
2827	BN	MF52LYZ	MAN 14.220	East Lancs Myllennium	N39F	2002	Blue Bus, Bolton, 2005
2828	BN	MF52LZA	MAN 14.220	East Lancs Myllennium	N39F	2002	Blue Bus, Bolton, 2005
2829	BN	MF52LZB	MAN 14.220	East Lancs Myllennium	N39F	2002	Blue Bus, Bolton, 2005
3022	CW	A152UDM	Leyland Olympian ONLXB/1R	Eastern Coach Works	B45/32F	1984	Arriva Midlands North, 2003
3038	CW	B198DTU	Leyland Olympian ONLXB/1R	Eastern Coach Works	B45/32F	1985	Arriva Midlands North, 2003
3039	CW	A139MRN	Leyland Olympian ONLXB/1R	Eastern Coach Works	B45/32F	1984	Arriva Midlands North, 2003
3041	CW	A141MRN	Leyland Olympian ONLXB/1R	Eastern Coach Works	B45/32F	1984	Arriva Midlands North, 2003
3049	CH	B149TRN	Leyland Olympian ONLXB/1R	Eastern Coach Works	B45/32F	1985	Crosville, 1986
3064	CH	B964WRN	Leyland Olympian ONLXB/1R	Eastern Coach Works	B45/32F	1985	Arriva Midlands North, 2003
3071	BO	B251NVN	Leyland Olympian ONLXB/1R	Eastern Coach Works	B45/32F	1985	Arriva North East, 2000
3073	WI	B513LFP	Leyland Olympian ONLXB/1R	Eastern Coach Works	B45/32F	1984	Fox County, 1998

3101-3115 Leyland Olympian ON2R50C13Z4 Northern Counties B47/30F 1990 Arriva London, 2000

3101	MA	H101GEV	3105	BD	H105GEV	3109	MA	H109GEV	3113	BD	H113GEV
3102	MA	H102GEV	3106	MA	H106GEV	3110	MA	H110GEV	3114	BD	H114GEV
3103	MA	H103GEV	3107	MA	H107GEV	3112	BD	H112GEV	3115	BD	H115GEV
3104	MA	H104GEV	3108	MA	H108GEV						

3122	BO	C212GTU	Leyland Olympian ONLXB/1R	Eastern Coach Works	B42/27F	1985	Crosville, 1986
3146	WI	G916LHA	Leyland Olympian ON2R50G16ZA	East Lancs	B45/29F	1989	Arriva Midlands North, 2003
3147	WI	G917LHA	Leyland Olympian ON2R50G16ZA	East Lancs	B45/29F	1989	Arriva Midlands North, 2003
3148	WI	G918LHA	Leyland Olympian ON2R50G16ZA	East Lancs	B45/29F	1989	Arriva Midlands North, 2003
3149	WI	G919LHA	Leyland Olympian ON2R50G16ZA	East Lancs	B45/29F	1989	Arriva Midlands North, 2003

3206-3213 Leyland Olympian ONCL10/1RZ Northern Counties B47/30F 1989 Arriva Fox County, 1999

3206	SP	G506SFT	3209	SP	G509SFT	3212	BG	G512SFT	3213	SP	G513SFT
3208	BD	G508SFT									

3214	WI	G754UYT	Leyland Olympian ONCL10/1R	Northern Counties	B43/32F	1989	Arriva Midlands North, 2003
3215	WI	G755UYT	Leyland Olympian ONCL10/1R	Northern Counties	B43/32F	1989	Arriva Midlands North, 2003
3218	WI	G758UYT	Leyland Olympian ONCL10/1R	Northern Counties	B43/32F	1989	Arriva Midlands North, 2003
3219	JS	G759UYT	Leyland Olympian ONCL10/1R	Northern Counties	B43/32F	1989	Arriva Midlands North, 2003

3221-3225 Leyland Olympian ONLXB/1RZ Alexander RL B45/30F 1989 Arriva Fox County, 1999

3221	SP	G521WJF	3223	SP	G523WJF	3224	SP	G524WJF	3225	SP	G525WJF
3222	SP	G522WJF									

3226	WI	F96PRE	Leyland Olympian ONCL10/1RZ	Alexander RL	B47/32F	1988	Arriva Midlands North, 2003
3227	WI	F97PRE	Leyland Olympian ONCL10/1RZ	Alexander RL	B47/32F	1988	Arriva Midlands North, 2003

The two Alexander-bodied Olympians new to Stevensons have now moved to Winsford depot following a period during which they gradually migrated north from their original base. Seen leaving Crewe for Northwich, 3227, F97PRE, illustrates the model. *Mat Southart*

3251-3270   Leyland Olympian ONCL10/1RZ   Northern Counties   B45/30F   1989

3251	BD	F251YTJ	3256	SP	F256YTJ	3261	SP	F261YTJ	3266	BO	F266YTJ
3252	SP	F252YTJ	3257	SP	F257YTJ	3262	BD	F262YTJ	3268	BO	F268YTJ
3253	BD	F253YTJ	3258	SP	F258YTJ	3263	BD	F263YTJ	3269	BO	F269YTJ
3254	SP	F254YTJ	3259	SP	F259YTJ	3264	BD	F264YTJ	3270	BO	F270YTJ
3255	SP	F255YTJ	3260	SP	F260YTJ					

3271-3308   Volvo Olympian YN2RV18Z4   Northern Counties Palatine II B47/30F   1995-96

3271	BD	N271CKB	3281	BD	N281CKB	3290	BD	N290CKB	3299	BD	N299CKB
3272	BD	N272CKB	3282	BD	N282CKB	3291	BD	N291CKB	3301	BD	N301CKB
3273	BD	N273CKB	3283	BD	N283CKB	3292	BD	N292CKB	3302	BD	N302CKB
3274	BD	N274CKB	3284	BD	N284CKB	3293	BD	N293CKB	3303	BD	N303CLV
3275	BD	N275CKB	3285	BD	N285CKB	3294	BD	N294CKB	3304	BD	N304CLV
3276	BD	N276CKB	3286	BD	N286CKB	3295	BD	N295CKB	3305	BD	N305CLV
3277	BD	N277CKB	3287	BD	N287CKB	3296	BD	N296CKB	3306	BD	N306CLV
3278	BD	N278CKB	3288	BD	N288CKB	3297	BD	N297CKB	3307	BD	N307CLV
3279	BD	N279CKB	3289	BD	N289CKB	3298	BD	N298CKB	3308	BD	N308CLV

3309-3337   Volvo Olympian YN2RV18Z4   Northern Counties Palatine II   B47/30F   1998

3309	GL	R309WVR	3315	GL	R315WVR	3326	SP	R326WVR	3332	SP	R332WVR
3310	GL	R310WVR	3317	GL	R317WVR	3327	SP	R327WVR	3334	SP	R334WVR
3311	GL	R311WVR	3319	GL	R319WVR	3329	SP	R329WVR	3335	SP	R335WVR
3312	GL	R312WVR	3321	SP	R321WVR	3330	SP	R330WVR	3336	SP	R336WVR
3313	GL	R313WVR	3322	GL	R322WVR	3331	SP	R331WVR	3337	SP	R337WVR
3314	GL	R314WVR	3324	GL	R324WVR					

3338	SP	M218YKC	Volvo Olympian YN2RV18Z4	Northern Counties Palatine II	B47/29F	1995
3339	SP	M219YKC	Volvo Olympian YN2RV18Z4	Northern Counties Palatine II	B47/29F	1995
3340	HU	M921PKN	Volvo Olympian YN2R50C16Z4	Northern Counties Palatine	B47/30F	1994
3341	SP	L211SBG	Volvo Olympian YN2RV18Z4	Northern Counties Palatine II	B47/29F	1993

3343-3349   Volvo Olympian   Northern Counties Palatine I   B47/29F   1998

3343	AB	R233AEY	3345	AB	R235AEY	3347	SP	R237AEY	3349	SP	R239AEY
3344	HU	R234AEY	3346	SP	R236AEY	3348	SP	R238AEY			

The 1998 intake of Olympians carries Northern Counties Palatine II bodywork which are allocated between Green Lane and Speke depots. Tree guards have been fitted to the front dome as illustrated by 3315, R315WVR. This model was the final high-floor design from Northern Counties before the launch of the low-floor President. *Mat Southart*

3350-3354 — Volvo Olympian YN2RV18Z4 — Northern Counties Palatine — B47/30F — 1996 — Arriva Southern Counties, 2004

3350	HU	N705TPK	3352	HU	N707TPK	3353	HU	N708TPK	3354	HU	N709TPK
3351	HU	N706TPK								

3355-3360 — Volvo Olympian — Northern Counties Palatine — B45/30F — 1997 — Arriva Southern Counties, 2004

3355	BG	P938MKL	3357	BG	P940MKL	3359	BG	P942MKL	3360	BG	P943MKL
3356	BG	P939MKL	3358	BG	P941MKL					

3361	BN	V41DJA	Volvo Olympian	East Lancs Pyoneer	B47/30F	1999	Blue Bus, Bolton, 2005
3362	BN	T42PVM	Volvo Olympian	East Lancs Pyoneer	B47/30F	1999	Blue Bus, Bolton, 2005
3363	BN	S43BLU	Volvo Olympian	East Lancs Pyoneer	B47/30F	1998	Blue Bus, Bolton, 2005
3364	BN	R44BLU	Volvo Olympian	East Lancs Pyoneer	BC45/30F	1998	Blue Bus, Bolton, 2005
3365	BN	S45BLU	Volvo Olympian	East Lancs Pyoneer	B47/30F	1998	Blue Bus, Bolton, 2005

3601-3613 — DAF DB250 — Northern Counties Palatine II — B47/30F — 1995 — Arriva London, 2001

3601	SP	N601DWY	3605	SP	N605DWY	3608	SP	N608DWY	3611	SP	N611DWY
3602	SP	N602DWY	3606	SP	N606DWY	3609	SP	N609DWY	3612	SP	N612DWY
3603	SP	N603DWY	3607	SP	N607DWY	3610	SP	N610DWY	3613	SP	N613DWY
3604	SP	N604DWY								

3614-3618 — DAF DB250 — Northern Counties Palatine 2 — B43/28F — 1998 — Arriva London/SC, 2003/04

3614	SP	R213CKO	3616	SP	R201CKO	3617	SP	R202CKO	3618	SP	R203CKO
3615	SP	V715LWT								

3646	JS	G661DTJ	Volvo Citybus B10M-50	East Lancs	B49/39F	1990	Arriva Southern Counties, 1998
3647	JS	G647EKA	Volvo Citybus B10M-50	East Lancs	B49/39F	1990	Arriva Southern Counties, 1998
3650	JS	G650EKA	Volvo Citybus B10M-50	East Lancs	B49/39F	1990	
3651	JS	G651EKA	Volvo Citybus B10M-50	East Lancs	B49/39F	1990	
3652	JS	G652EKA	Volvo Citybus B10M-50	East Lancs	B49/39F	1990	
3653	JS	G653EKA	Volvo Citybus B10M-50	East Lancs	B49/39F	1990	
3671	BN	H113ABV	Volvo Citybus B10M-50	Alexander RH	B47/31F	1991	Blue Bus, Bolton, 2005
3672	BN	H115ABV	Volvo Citybus B10M-50	Alexander RH	BC47/31F	1991	Blue Bus, Bolton, 2005

3674-3682 — Volvo Citybus B10M-50 — Alexander RV — B47/32F — 1989 — Arriva London, 2000

3674	SO	F104TML	3677	SO	F107TML	3679	SO	F109TML	3682	SO	F112TML
3676	SO	F106TML	3678	SO	F108TML	3680	SO	F110TML			

Following an incident while at Fox County, Scania 3995, G35KHY was transferred for use on the North Wales coast. Since the arrival at Rhyl of Metrobuses from the London Sightseeing fleet, the Scania has now moved to Llandudno. *Mat Southart*

3690-3699

		Volvo Citybus B10M-50			East Lancs			B45/34F	1991	London South, 1998	

3690	BO	H660GPF	3692	BO	H662GPF	3697	BO	H667GPF	3699	BD	H679GPF
3691	BO	H661GPF	3695	BD	H665GPF						

3831-3836

		Dennis Dominator DDA1032*			East Lancs			B47/29F	1990	*3833-6 are DDA1031

3831	CH	G801THA	3833	CH	H803AHA	3835	CH	H805AHA	3836	CH	H806AHA
3832	CH	G802THA	3834	CH	H804AHA						

3837	CH	N716TPK	Dennis Dominator DDA2006	East Lancs	B45/31F	1996	
3975	RH	GYE365W	MCW Metrobus DR101/12	MCW	O43/28D	1980	Original Sightseeing Tour, 2004
3976	RH	GYE456W	MCW Metrobus DR101/12	MCW	O43/28D	1980	Original Sightseeing Tour, 2004
3977	RH	KYV663X	MCW Metrobus DR101/14	MCW	PO43/28D	1981	Original Sightseeing Tour, 2004
3978	RH	KYV689X	MCW Metrobus DR101/14	MCW	O43/28D	1981	Original Sightseeing Tour, 2004
3980	SO	GKA449L	Leyland Atlantean AN68/1R	Alexander AL	O43/32F	1973	
3981	SO	OLV551M	Leyland Atlantean AN68/1R	Alexander AL	O43/32F	1974	
3984	RH	E224WBG	Leyland Olympian ONCL10/1RZ	Alexander RL	O43/30F	1988	
3987	RH	E227WBG	Leyland Olympian ONCL10/1RZ	Alexander RL	O43/30F	1988	
3992	RH	YMB512W	Bristol VRT/SL3/6LXB	Eastern Coach Works	O43/31F	1981	Crosville, 1986
3995	LD	G35HKY	Scania N113DRB	Northern Counties	O47/33F	1990	Arriva Fox County, 2002
4000	BN	Y46ABA	Dennis Trident	Plaxton President	N47/28F	2001	Blue Bus, Bolton, 2005
4001	BN	Y47ABA	Dennis Trident	Plaxton President	N47/28F	2001	Blue Bus, Bolton, 2005
4002	BN	Y48ABA	Dennis Trident	Plaxton President	N47/28F	2001	Blue Bus, Bolton, 2005
5003	AB	M945LYR	DAF SB3000	Van Hool Alizée	C49FT	1995	London North East, 1998
5004	AB	NEY819	DAF SB3000	Van Hool Alizée	C49FT	1995	London North East, 1998

5301-5320

			Scania L113CRL			Wright Axcess-ultralow		N40F	1996	

5301	GL	P301HEM	5307	GL	P307HEM	5312	GL	P312HEM	5317	GL	P317HEM
5302	GL	P302HEM	5308	GL	P308HEM	5313	GL	P313HEM	5318	GL	P318HEM
5303	GL	P303HEM	5309	GL	P309HEM	5314	GL	P314HEM	5319	GL	P319HEM
5305	GL	P305HEM	5310	GL	P310HEM	5315	GL	P315HEM	5320	GL	P320HEM
5306	GL	P306HEM	5311	GL	P311HEM	5316	GL	P316HEM			

6301	SP	L301TEM	Volvo B10B	Alexander Strider	B49F	1994	
6302	SP	L302TEM	Volvo B10B	Alexander Strider	B49F	1994	
6303	SP	L303TEM	Volvo B10B	Alexander Strider	B49F	1994	

6402-6413   Neoplan N4016   Neoplan   N39F   1994

6402	GL	L402TKB	6405	GL	L405TKB	6408	GL	L408TKB	6411	GL	L411UFY
6403	GL	L403TKB	6406	GL	L406TKB	6409	GL	L409TKB	6412	GL	L412UFY
6404	GL	L404TKB	6407	GL	L407TKB	6410	GL	L410TKB	6413	GL	L413TKB

6501-6543   Volvo B10B   Wright Endurance   BC49F   1994

6501	JS	L501TKA	6512	JS	L512TKA	6523	BO	M523WHF	6533	JS	M533WHF
6502	JS	L502TKA	6513	JS	L513TKA	6524	SP	M524WHF	6534	SP	M534WHF
6503	JS	L503TKA	6514	SO	M514WHF	6525	BO	M525WHF	6535	SP	M535WHF
6504	JS	L504TKA	6515	SO	M515WHF	6526	BO	M526WHF	6536	SP	M536WHF
6505	JS	L505TKA	6516	SO	M516WHF	6527	SP	M527WHF	6537	SP	M537WHF
6506	JS	L506TKA	6517	BO	M517WHF	6528	SP	M528WHF	6538	SP	M538WHF
6507	SO	L507TKA	6518	BO	M518WHF	6529	BO	M529WHF	6540	GL	M540WHF
6508	JS	L508TKA	6519	GL	M519WHF	6530	JS	M530WHF	6541	SP	M541WHF
6509	JS	L509TKA	6520	BO	M520WHF	6531	BO	M531WHF	6542	SP	M542WHF
6510	JS	L510TKA	6521	BO	M521WHF	6532	JS	M532WHF	6543	SP	M543WHF
6511	JS	L511TKA	6522	BO	M522WHF						

6544-6623   Volvo B10B   Wright Endurance   BC49F   1994-96

6544	SO	M544WTJ	6565	BO	M565YEM	6584	GL	N584CKA	6605	JS	N605CKA
6545	SO	M545WTJ	6566	GL	M566YEM	6585	GL	N585CKA	6606	JS	N606CKA
6546	SO	M546WTJ	6567	GL	M567YEM	6586	SP	N586CKA	6607	JS	N607CKA
6547	SP	M547WTJ	6568	GL	M568YEM	6587	HU	N587CKA	6608	JS	N608CKA
6548	SO	M548WTJ	6569	GL	M569YEM	6588	SP	N588CKA	6609	JS	N609CKA
6549	SP	M549WTJ	6570	GL	M570YEM	6589	SP	N589CKA	6610	JS	N610CKA
6550	SP	M550WTJ	6571	GL	M571YEM	6590	SP	N590CKA	6611	JS	N611CKA
6551	SP	M551WTJ	6572	GL	M572YEM	6591	SP	N591CKA	6612	JS	N612CKA
6552	HU	M552WTJ	6573	GL	M573YEM	6592	SP	N592CKA	6613	SP	N613CKA
6553	JS	M553WTJ	6574	SP	M574YEM	6593	SP	N593CKA	6614	SP	N614CKA
6554	SO	M554WTJ	6575	GL	M575YEM	6594	SP	N594CKA	6615	SP	N615CKA
6556	HU	M556WTJ	6576	GL	N576CKA	6595	SP	N595CKA	6616	SP	N616CKA
6557	HU	M557WTJ	6577	GL	N577CKA	6596	SP	N596CKA	6617	SP	N617CKA
6558	SO	M558WTJ	6578	GL	N578CKA	6597	SP	N597CKA	6618	SP	N618CKA
6559	SO	M559WTJ	6579	GL	N579CKA	6598	SP	N598CKA	6619	SP	N619CKA
6561	BO	M561WTJ	6580	GL	N580CKA	6599	GL	N599CKA	6620	SP	N620CKA
6562	BO	M562WTJ	6581	GL	N581CKA	6601	GL	N601CKA	6621	SP	N621CKA
6563	GL	M563WTJ	6582	GL	N582CKA	6603	GL	N603CKA	6622	GL	N622CKA
6564	BO	M564YEM	6583	GL	N583CKA	6604	GL	N604CKA	6623	HU	N623CKA

6901-6913   Volvo B10B   Northern Counties Paladin   B51F   1993-95   Liverbus, 1995

6901	HU	K101OHF	6904	HU	K104OHF	6907	HU	K107OHF	6910	HU	M110XKC
6902	HU	K102OHF	6905	HU	K105OHF	6908	HU	K108OHF	6912	HU	M112XKC
6903	HU	K103OHF	6906	HU	K106OHF	6909	HU	M109XKC	6913	HU	M113XKC

7201-7244   Volvo B6 9.9M   Plaxton Pointer   B38F   1994

7201	JS	L201TKA	7213	JS	L213TKA	7224	JS	L224TKA	7235	SK	L235TKA
7202	JS	L202TKA	7214	JS	L214TKA	7225	JS	L225TKA	7236	JS	L236TKA
7203	JS	L203TKA	7215	RU	L215TKA	7226	JS	L226TKA	7237	JS	L237TKA
7204	SO	L204TKA	7216	JS	L216TKA	7227	JS	L227TKA	7238	SK	L238TKA
7205	RU	L205TKA	7217	SO	L217TKA	7228	JS	L228TKA	7239	JS	L239TKA
7206	JS	L206TKA	7218	JS	L218TKA	7229	JS	L229TKA	7240	SK	L240TKA
7208	SO	L208TKA	7219	RU	L219TKA	7230	JS	L230TKA	7241	SK	L241TKA
7209	JS	L209TKA	7220	RU	L220TKA	7231	JS	L231TKA	7242	SK	L242TKA
7210	JS	L210TKA	7221	JS	L221TKA	7232	RU	L232TKA	7243	SK	L243TKA
7211	JS	L211TKA	7222	JS	L222TKA	7233	JS	L233TKA	7244	SK	L244TKA
7212	JS	L212TKA	7223	JS	L223TKA	7234	JS	L234TKA			

7531-7545   Dennis Dart SLF 9.8m   Plaxton Pointer   N38F   1996-97

7531	RH	N531DWM	7535	RU	P535MBU	7539	RU	P539MBU	7543	RU	P543MBU
7532	RH	N532DWM	7536	HU	P536MBU	7540	GL	P540MBU	7544	RU	P544MBU
7533	RU	P533MBU	7537	HU	P537MBU	7541	RU	P541MBU	7545	RU	P545MBU
7534	RU	P534MBU	7538	HU	P538MBU	7542	RU	P542MBU			

Birkenhead is the base for 2456, Y242KBU, one of the 2001 intake of East Lancs Myllennium-bodied DAF SB220s. Launched two years earlier the model has been very successful for the bodybuilder, though none have yet been built on the later VDL low floor chassis. *Tony Cutler*

7547-7571 — Dennis Dart SLF 9.8m — Plaxton Pointer — N38F — 1998

7547	HU	R547ABA	7553	WX	R553ABA	7560	BG	R560ABA	7566	LJ	R566ABA
7548	HU	R548ABA	7554	BD	R554ABA	7561	HU	R561ABA	7567	HU	R567ABA
7549	HU	R549ABA	7556	BD	R556ABA	7562	LJ	R562ABA	7568	HU	R568ABA
7550	BD	R550ABA	7557	BD	R557ABA	7563	LJ	R563ABA	7569	HU	R569ABA
7551	BD	R551ABA	7558	BD	R558ABA	7564	LJ	R564ABA	7570	HU	R570ABA
7552	BD	R552ABA	7559	GL	R559ABA	7565	LJ	R565ABA	7571	HU	R571ABA

7612-7623 — Dennis Dart SLF 10.5m — Marshall Capital — N38F — 1999

7612	BO	T612PNC	7615	HY	T615PNC	7618	RU	T618PNC	7621	WY	T621PNC
7613	BO	T613PNC	7616	HY	T616PNC	7619	RU	T619PNC	7622	WY	T622PNC
7614	BO	T614PNC	7617	RU	T617PNC	7620	RU	T620PNC	7623	BO	T623PNC

7624-7676 — Dennis Dart SLF 10.5m — Marshall Capital — N38F — 1999-2000

7624	BO	V624DBN	7637	SK	V637DVU	7650	SK	V650DVU	7663	SK	V663DVU
7625	GL	V625DVU	7638	SK	V638DVU	7651	SO	V651DVU	7664	GL	V664DVU
7626	SO	V626DVU	7639	SK	V639DVU	7652	SO	V652DVU	7665	GL	V665DVU
7627	SO	V627DVU	7640	SK	V640DVU	7653	SO	V653DVU	7667	SK	V667DVU
7628	SO	V628DVU	7641	SK	V641DVU	7654	SO	V654DVU	7668	GL	V668DVU
7629	SO	V629DVU	7642	SK	V642DVU	7655	GL	V655DVU	7669	GL	V669DVU
7630	SO	V630DVU	7643	SK	V643DVU	7656	SO	V656DVU	7670	GL	V670DVU
7631	SO	V631DVU	7644	SK	V644DVU	7657	SO	V657DVU	7671	GL	V671DVU
7632	SO	V632DVU	7645	SK	V645DVU	7658	GL	V658DVU	7672	GL	V672DVU
7633	SK	V633DVU	7646	SK	V646DVU	7659	SK	V659DVU	7673	SK	V673DVU
7634	SK	V634DVU	7647	SK	V647DVU	7660	SK	V660DVU	7674	SK	V674DVU
7635	SK	V635DVU	7648	SK	V648DVU	7661	SK	V661DVU	7675	SK	V675DVU
7636	SK	V636DVU	7649	SK	V649DVU	7662	SK	V662DVU	7676	WY	V676DVU

Ancillary vehicles:-

1751	BG	H34PAJ	Leyland Lynx LX2R11C15Z4R	Leyland	TV	1989	Arriva North East, 2004
8165	WX	E49WEM	Leyland Lynx LX112L10ZR1R	Leyland Lynx	TV	1988	Travel West Midlands, 2005
8166	SP	DOC26V	Leyland National 2 NL116L11/1R		TV	1980	West Midlands Travel, 1996
8167	BO	DOC37V	Leyland National 2 NL116L11/1R		TV	1980	West Midlands Travel, 1996
8168	CW	124YTW	Volvo B58-61	Plaxton Supreme IV	TV	1980	G M Buses, 1986
8169	LJ	C324LDT	Volvo B9M	Plaxton Paramount 3200 II	TV	1986	D&G ,Rachub, 2000
8170	u	G137EOG	Leyland Lynx LX2R11C15Z4R	Leyland	TV	1989	Travel West Midlands, 2005
8171	BO	G175EOG	Leyland Lynx LX2R11C15Z4R	Leyland	TV	1989	Travel West Midlands, 2005
8172	RU	G129EOG	Leyland Lynx LX2R11C15Z4R	Leyland	TV	1989	Travel West Midlands, 2005
8173	RU	G282EOG	Leyland Lynx LX2R11C15Z4R	Leyland	TV	1989	Travel West Midlands, 2005
8177	u	G286EOG	Leyland Lynx LX2R11C15Z4R	Leyland	TV	1989	Travel West Midlands, 2005
8178	JS	G803EKA	Leyland Lynx LX2R11G15Z4R	Leyland Lynx	TV	1991	Colchester, 1994
8179	WY	H542FWM	Leyland Lynx LX2R11G15Z4R	Leyland Lynx	TV	1991	
8180	SP	H543FWM	Leyland Lynx LX2R11G15Z4R	Leyland Lynx	TV	1991	
8181	SP	J249KWM	Leyland Lynx LX2R11G15Z4R	Leyland Lynx	TV	1991	
8182	SP	J251KWM	Leyland Lynx LX2R11G15Z4R	Leyland Lynx	TV	1991	
8183	GL	F301AWW	Leyland Lynx LX112L10ZR1S	Leyland Lynx	TV	1989	
8184	BO	H28MJN	Leyland Lynx LX2R11G15Z4R	Leyland Lynx	TV	1991	Colchester, 1994
8185	BO	G149CHP	Leyland Lynx LX112L10ZR1S	Leyland Lynx	TV	1989	Arriva Midlands North, 2003
8186	HU	E642VFY	Leyland Lynx LX112L10ZR1R	Leyland Lynx	TV	1988	Devaway, Bretton, 1998
8187	JS	G324NWW	Leyland Lynx LX2R11C15Z4S	Leyland Lynx	TV	1990	Arriva Yorkshire, 1999
8188	-	G45VME	Leyland Lynx LX2R11C15Z4S	Leyland Lynx 2	TV	1989	Boro'line, Maidstone, 1992
8189	-	G329NUM	Leyland Lynx LX2R11C15Z4S	Leyland Lynx	TV	1990	Arriva Yorkshire, 2000
8190	SP	BCW824V	Leyland National 2 NL106L11/1R		TV	1980	Liverbus, 1999
8191	-	F61PRE	Leyland Lynx LX112L10ZR1R	Leyland Lynx	TV	1989	Arriva Midlands, 2004
8192	BG	E641VFY	Leyland Lynx LX112L10ZR1R	Leyland Lynx	TV	1988	Devaway, Bretton, 1998
8193	MA	D634BBV	Leyland Lynx LX112L10ZR1	Leyland Lynx	TV	1987	Nova Scotia, Winsford, 2000
8194	BG	D108NDW	Leyland Lynx LX112TL11ZR1R	Leyland Lynx	TV	1987	Arriva Southern Counties, 2000
8195	SK	D155HML	Leyland Lynx LX112TL11ZR1S	Leyland Lynx	TV	1987	Arriva Southern Counties, 2000
8196	GL	D157HML	Leyland Lynx LX112TL11ZR1S	Leyland Lynx	TV	1987	Arriva Southern Counties, 2000
8197	RU	PUK637R	Leyland National 11351A/1R	East Lancs Greenway (1994)	TV	1977	Arriva Midlands North, 2003
8272	-	PFY72J	Leyland Panther	Marshall	TV	1971	

Previous registrations:

124YTW	DEN247W	R91GNW	R91GNW, R33GNW
H192JNF	H1JYM	T10BLU	MF51TVV
J6SLT	N192BNB	T11BLU	MF51TVW
K250CBA	K133TCP	V580ECC	V589DJC
L411UFY	L175THF	W12LUE	MF51TVX
L412UFY	L176THF	WJI9072	MNS6Y
L588JJG	94D28205	WJI9073	EWR657Y
M2SLT	N102YVU	X13LUE	MF51TVY
M5SLT	M20CLA	X14LUE	MV02XYH
NEY819	M944LYR		

Allocations:-

Aberystwyth (Park Avenue) - AB

Outstations: Dolgellau, Lampeter, Machynlleth and New Quay

Mercedes-Benz	171	312	313	329	335	338	341	342
	344	345	356					
Dart	802	820	823	824	826	841	842	1116
	1129	1130	1326	1328	2332	2333		
SB120 Cadet	2504	2506	2507	2508	2509	2510	2511	2512
Tiger bus	1772	1776	1777					
Lynx	1739							
Volvo B10M bus	1778	1779	1785	1786	1787	1788		
SB220 Paladin	1795	1796	1797	1799				
SB220 Prestige	2475	2476	2477					
DAF coach	5003	5004						
Olympian	3345							

Bangor (Beach Road) - BG

Outstations: Amlwch; Caernarfon; Holyhead and Pwllheli

Mercedes-Benz	319	372	393	394				
Dart	816	817	818	819	821	822	827	833
	834	1107	1108	1112	1118	1119	1154	1164
	1301	1302	1303	1304	1308	1309	1310	1333
	1340	2325	2326	2330	7560			
SB120 Cadet	2480	2481	2482	2483	2484	2485	2505	
Lynx	1750	1755						
Olympian	3212							
Ancillary	1751	8173	8192	8195				

Birkenhead (Laird Street) - BD

Dart	1172	1174	1175	1181	1185	1193	1197	1198
	1211	1212	1213	1214	1215	1216	1230	1263
	1272	2259	2261	2262	7550	7551	7552	7554
	7556	7557	7558					
Volvo B10M bus	3695	3699						
DAF Cadet	2435	2436	2437	2438	2439	2441	2442	2443
	2445	2446	2447	2448	2449			
DAF Ikarus	1790	1791	1792	1793	1794			
DAF ALX300	2411	2412	2414					
DAF Myllennium	2451	2452	2453	2454	2455	2456	2457	2458
	2459	2460	2461					
Olympian	3105	3112	3113	3114	3115	3208	3251	3253
	3262	3263	3264	3271	3272	3273	3274	3275
	3276	3277	3278	3279	3281	3282	3283	3284
	3285	3286	3287	3288	3289	3290	3291	3292
	3293	3294	3295	3296	3297	3298	3299	3301
	3302	3303	3304	3305	3306	3307	3308	

Bolton (Folds Road) - BN

Outstation: Leyland

MetroRider	70	71	72	73	74	75	84	85
	86	87	88	89	95			
Mercedes-Benz	395	396	397	398				
Dart	1344	1345	1346					
SB120	2556	2557	2558	2559				
Tiger	1773	1774	1775					
Lance	1900	1921	1922	1923	1933	1934	1935	
Javelin	1950							
SB220	2400	2450	2560	2561	2562			
Volvo B10BLE	2732	2733						
MAN bus	2825	2826	2827	2828	2829			
Volvo Citybus	3671	3672						
Olympian	3361	3362	3363	3364	3365			
Trident	4000	4001	4002					

Bootle (Hawthorne Road) - BO

Neoplan N4009	601	602	603					
Solo	651	652	653	654	655	656		
Dart	1150	1151	1152	1233	1234	1235		
	1236	1237	1238	1239	1240	1241	1242	1243
	1244	1245	1246	1247	1248	2215	2216	2217
	2218	2219	2221	2223	2224	2226	2227	2228
	2229	2231	2232	2233	2234	2235	2236	2237
	2263	2264	2265	2266	2267	2268	2269	2271
	2272	2314	2315	2316	2317	2318	2319	2320
	2321	2322	2323	2324	7612	7613	7614	7623
	7624							
SB120 Cadet	2404	2405	2408	2409				
Lance	1901	1902	1903	1904	1905	1906	1907	1908
	1909	1910	1911	1912	1913	1914	1915	1916
	1917	1918	1919	1920	1940	1941	1942	1943
	1944	1945	1946	1947	1948	1949	2391	2392
	2393	2394	2395	2396	2397			
Volvo B10B	6517	6518	6520	6521	6522	6523	6525	
	6526	6529	6531	6561	6562	6564	6565	
Olympian	3071	3122	3266	3268	3269	3270		
Volvo Citybus	3690	3691	3692	3697				
Ancillary	3267	8164	8167	8170				

Chester (Manor Lane, Hawarden) - CH

Alero	611	612	613	620	621			
Mercedes-Benz	147	149	158	160	182	183	194	373
Dart	1110	1111	1117	1127	1148	1153	1155	1327
	1329	1330	1331	1334	2257	2258	2328	2341
	2342	2355	2356	2357	2358	2359	2360	2361
Dominator	3831	3832	3833	3834	3835	3836	3837	
Ancillary	8198							

Crewe (Delamere Street) - CW

Outstation: Macclesfield (MF)

Mercedes-Benz	178	179	184	191	192	301	302	303
	304	305						
Dart	807	856	857	858	859	867	868	872
	876	877	878	879	882	886		
SB120 Cadet	2497	2498	2499	2500	2501	2502	2503	
Lynx	1732	1743	1747	1752	1753	1754	1757	
Olympian	3022	3038	3039	3041	3049	3064		

Huyton (Wilson Road) - HU

Dart	806	1171	1173	1176	1177	1178	1179	1180
	1183	1184	1187	1191	1192	1194	1195	1196
	1280	1282	1285	1286	2201	2202	2203	2204
	2207	2208	2209	2211	2212	2213	2214	7536
	7537	7538	7561	7567	7568	7569	7570	7571
Volvo B6	7547	7548	7549					
SB120 Cadet	2406	2407						
Volvo B10B	6552	6556	6557	6587	6623	6901	6902	6903
	6904	6095	6906	6907	6908	6909	6910	6912
	6913							
Olympian	3340	3344	3350	3351	3352	3353	3354	
Ancillary	8186							

Liverpool (Green Lane) - GL

Dart	2280	2282	2283	2284	2285	2286	2287	2288
	7540	7559	7625	7655	7657	7658	7664	7665
	7668	7669	7670	7671	7672			
Neoplan	6402	6403	6404	6405	6406	6407	6408	6409
	6410	6411	6412	6413				
Volvo B10B	6519	6540	6563	6566	6567	6568	6569	6570
	6571	6572	6573	6575	6576	6577	6578	6579
	6580	6581	6582	6583	6584	6585	6599	6601
	6603	6604	6606	6622				
Scania sd	2002	2006	2008	2009	2010	2011	2024	2025
	2026	2028	2030	2031	2032	2033	2034	5301
	5302	5303	5305	5306	5307	5308	5309	5310
	5311	5312	5313	5314	5315	5316	5317	5318
	5319	5320						
Olympian	3309	3310	3311	3312	3313	3314	3315	3317
	3319	3322	3324					
Ancillary	8183	8196						

Liverpool (Shaw Road, Speke) - SP

SB120 Cadet	2416	2417	2418	2419	2421	2422	2423	2424
	2426	2427	2428	2429	2431	2432	2433	2434
Volvo B10BLE	2715	2716	2717	2718	2719	2720	2721	2723
	6301	6302	6303	6524	6527	6528	6534	6535
	6536	6537	6538	6541	6542	6543	6547	6549
	6550	6551	6574	6586	6588	6589	6590	6591
	6592	6593	6594	6595	6596	6597	6598	6613
	6614	6615	6616	6617	6618	6619	6620	6621
	6622							
SB220 Prestige	2401	2402	2403					
SB220 Paladin	3614	3615	3616	3617	3618			
SB220 ALX300	2404	2405	2406	2407	2408	2409	2410	2413
	2415							
DB250 Myllennium	2462	2463	2464	2465	2466	2467	2468	2469
	2470	2471	2472	2473	2474			
DB250 Palatine	3601	3602	3603	3604	3605	3606	3607	3608
	3609	3610	3611	3612	3613			
Olympian	3206	3209	3213	3221	3222	3223	3224	3225
	3252	3254	3255	3256	3257	3258	3259	3260
	3261	3321	3326	3327	3329	3330	3331	3332
	3334	3335	3336	3337	3338	3339	3341	3346
	3348	3349						

Llandudno Junction (Glan-y-mor Road) - LJ

Mercedes-Benz	309	317	318	320	321	322	323	324
	325	326	327	328	331	332	333	339
	347	354	355	356	357	364		
Dart	804	814	815	1109	1139	1165	1228	1233
	2110	2273	2274	2276	2277	2278	2279	2301
	2331	2343	2344	2345	2346	2347	2348	7562
	7563	7564	7565	7566				
Scania open-top	3905							

Manchester (St Andrew's Square, Piccadilly) - MA

MetroRider	76	77	78	79	80	81	82	83
Dart	112	890	891	892	893	894	1122	1123
	1141	1142	1143	1223	1224	1225	1226	1227
	1249	1250	1251	1254	1260	1264	2238	2239
	2241	2242	2243	2244	2246	2247	2248	2249
	2251	2252	2253	2254	2256			
Lance	1924	1925	1926	1927	1928	1929	1930	1931
	1932							
SB220 Ikarus	2563	2564	2565	2566	2567	2568	2569	
Olympian	3102	3103	3104	3106	3107	3108	3109	3110
Ancillary	8189	8193						

Rhyl (Ffynnongroew Road) - RH

Mercedes-Benz	314	315	316	340	343	346	353	
Dart	831	832	843	844	846	847	1120	1126
	1126	1128	1146	1281	1323	1325	1338	1341
	1342	1343	2296	2297	2298	2299	2300	2349
	2350	2351	2352	2353	2354	7531	7532	
Bristol VR open-top	3992							
Metrobus open-top	3975	3976	3977	3978				
Olympian open-top	3984	3987						

Runcorn (Beechwood) - RU

Dart	805	808	809	1157	1158	1159	1160	1161
	1162	1163	1166	1167	1168	1169	1170	1220
	1221	1222	7505	7515	7519	7520	7532	7533
	7534	7535	7539	7541	7542	7543	7544	7545
	7618	7619	7620					
Scania sd	1041	1042	1043	1044	1045	1046	1047	1048
	1049	1050	2048	2049	2050	2051	2052	2053
	2054							

St Helens (Jackson Street) - JS

Dart	1124	1125	1186	7539				
Volvo B6	2805	2806	2807	2808	2809	2811	2812	7201
	7202	7203	7206	7209	7210	7211	7212	7213
	7214	7216	7218	7221	7222	7223	7224	7225
	7226	7227	7228	7229	7230	7231	7233	7234
	7236	7237						
SB120 Cadet	2489	2490	2491	2492	2493	2494	2495	2496
Scania sd	1035	1036	1037	1038	1039	1040	1050	1051
	1052	1053	1054	1055	1056	1057	1058	1059
	1060	1061	1062	1063	1065	1068	2001	2003
	2004	2005	2007	2013	2014	2015	2016	2017
	2018	2019	2020	2021	2022	2023	2027	2029
	2041	2042	2043	2044	2045	2046	2047	
Volvo B10B	2701	2702	2703	2704	2705	2706	2707	2708
	2709	2710	2711	2712	2713	2714	2729	2730
	6501	6502	6503	6504	6505	6506	6508	6509
	6510	6511	6512	6513	6530	6532	6533	6553
	6605	6607	6608	6609	6610	6611	6612	
Volvo B7	2800							
Volvo Citybus	3219	3646	3647	3650	3651	3652	3653	
Ancillary	8178	8187	8191					

An extensive busway operation is undertaken at Runcorn for which new buses are expected later in 2005. One of the current fleet is Scania 1046, P46MVU, seen here shortly after repainting. Only three of the Northern Counties Paladin bodies were constructed on Scania chassis after this batch was complete, the Wigan assembly plant concentrating thereafter on double-decks. *Mat Southart*

Skelmersdale (Neverstitch Road) - SK

Dart								
	1164	1219	1229	1252	1253	1259	1273	1274
	1275	1276	1277	1278	1279	1284	1300	1311
	1312	1316	1317	1318	7535	7633	7634	7635
	7636	7637	7638	7639	7640	7641	7642	7643
	7644	7645	7646	7647	7648	7649	7650	7659
	7660	7661	7662	7663	7667	7673	7674	7675
Volvo B6	7238	7240	7241	7242	7243	7244		
Ancillary	1918	8195						

Southport (Canning Road) - SO

Dart								
	1182	1189	1190	1283	1289	1332	6248	6249
	6250	6251	7504	7508	7517	7624	7625	7626
	7627	7628	7629	7630	7631	7632	7651	7652
	7653	7654	7655	7656	7657	7658		
Volvo B6	2801	2802	2803	2804	2813	2814	2815	2816
	2817	2818	2819	2821	2822			
Volvo B10B	2722	2724	2725	2726	2727	2728	6507	6514
	6515	6516	6544	6545	6546	6548	6554	6558
	6559							
Volvo Citybus	3674	3676	3677	3678	3679	3680	3682	
Open-top	3980	3981						
Ancillary	8185							

Winsford (Winsford Industrial Estate) - WI

Mercedes-Benz	148	151	164	165	182	198	199	307
	308	310	311	334	358	359	365	
Dart	860	861	862	863	864	865	866	869
	1131	1132	1133	1135	1138	1140	1149	
Lynx	1724							
DAF SB220	1799							
Olympian	3073	3146	3147	3148	3149	3214	3215	3218
	3226	3227						

Wrexham (Berse Road, Caego) - WX

Alero	619							
Mercedes-Benz	160	327	350	351	352	360	361	362
	363	391	392					
Dart	838	839	848	849	851	852	1101	1104
	1105	1106	1113	1114	1115	1156	2301	2601
	2602	2603	2604	2605	2606	2607	2608	7553
VDL Bus Cadet	2486	2487	2513					
Olympian	3101	3343	3345					

Wythenshawe (Greeba Road) - WY

Mercedes-Benz	158	159	161	162	163	168	169	
Dart	801	803	810	811	812	813	1188	1199
	1217	1218	1231	1232	1255	1256	1257	1261
	1262	1263	1265	1266	1267	1268	1269	1270
	1271	1287	1288	2302	2303	2304	2305	2306
	2307	2308	2309	2310	2311	2312	2313	2601
	2602	2603	2604	2605	2606	2607	2608	7621
	7622	7676						

Unallocated or stored - u/w

Mercedes-Benz	374	375						
Dart	1156	1313	1314	2111	2112	2113	2114	2115
	2116	2117	2118	2119	2120	2121	2122	2123
	2124	2125	2126	2127	2128	2129	2130	2131
	2132	2133	2134	2135	2291	2292	2293	2294
	7540							

On order

SB120	2514	2515	2516	2517	2518	2519	2520	2521
	2522	2523	2524	2525	2526	2527	2528	2529
	2530	2531	2532	2533	2534	2535	2536	2537
	2538	2539	2540	2541	2542	2543	2544	2545
	2546	2547	2548	2549	2550	2551	2552	2553
	2554	2555						

ARRIVA MIDLANDS

Arriva Midlands North Ltd, Arriva Derby Ltd; Stevensons of Uttoxeter Ltd;
Arriva Fox County Ltd, PO Box 613, Melton Road, Thurmaston, Leicester, LE4 8ZN

127	SD	Y207RJU	Vauxhall Zafira	Vauxhall	M6	2001
129	SD	Y189RJU	Vauxhall Zafira	Vauxhall	M6	2001
1001	MH	BU53AWP	Mercedes-Benz Sprinter 412	Koch	N15	2003
1002	MH	BU53AWR	Mercedes-Benz Sprinter 412	Koch	N15	2003

1129-1146   Mercedes-Benz Vario O814   Plaxton Beaver 2   B27F   1997

1129	HY	R129LNR	1133	HY	R133LNR	1138	SD	R138LNR	1144	HY	R144LNR
1130	HY	R130LNR	1134	HY	R134LNR	1141	HY	R141LNR	1145	HY	R145LNR
1131	HY	R131LNR	1135	HY	R135LNR	1142	HY	R142LNR	1146	HY	R146LNR
1132	HY	R132LNR	1136	HY	R136LNR	1143	HY	R143LNR			

1147-1170   Mercedes-Benz Vario O814   Alexander ALX100   B27F   1998

1147	CK	R147UAL	1153	CV	R153UAL	1159	CK	R159UAL	1165	WG	R165UAL
1148	CK	R148UAL	1154	CV	R154UAL	1160	CK	R160UAL	1166	WG	R166UAL
1149	CK	R149UAL	1155	CV	R155UAL	1161	CV	R161UAL	1167	WG	R167UAL
1150	CK	R150UAL	1156	CV	R156UAL	1162	WG	R162UAL	1168	SS	R168UAL
1151	SD	R151UAL	1157	CV	R157UAL	1163	CK	R163UAL	1169	SD	R169UAL
1152	CV	R152UAL	1158	CK	R158UAL	1164	WG	R164UAL	1170	CK	R170UUT

1171-1180   Mercedes-Benz Vario O814   Plaxton Beaver 2   B27F   1997   Arriva Yorkshire, 1999

1171	CK	R765DUB	1175	WG	R785DUB	1177	CK	R788DUB	1179	MH	R790DUB
1172	WG	R768DUB	1176	WG	R787DUB	1178	WG	R789DUB	1180	CK	R791DUB
1174	WG	R770DUB									

1243-1252   Mercedes-Benz 811D   Alexander Sprint   B31F   1995

1243	SY	N463EHA	1247	SY	N467EHA	1250	BT	N470EHA	1252	BT	N472EHA
1246	SC	N466EHA	1249	ST	N469EHA	1251	BT	N471EHA			

Both Alexander and Plaxton bodywork are featured on the Vario minibuses operated by Arriva Midlands. Seen in Hinckley, 1134, R134LNR, illustrates the Plaxton Beaver product. During 2004 and the early part of 2005 more of the older minibuses have been replaced by Darts and Solos. *Mark Doggett*

New for use in London, Dart 2024, P824RWU, is now allocated to Leicester where it is seen at work on route 56.
Dave Heath

1260	TF	P438HKN	Mercedes-Benz 811D	Plaxton Beaver	B31F	1994	Arriva North West, 2000
1357	SY	N357OBC	Mercedes-Benz 709D	Alexander Sprint	B27F	1996	Arriva Fox County, 2002
1358	SY	N358OBC	Mercedes-Benz 709D	Alexander Sprint	B27F	1996	Arriva Fox County, 2002
1359	SY	P608JJU	Mercedes-Benz 709D	Reeve Burgess Beaver	B27F	1996	
1360	SY	P296OOA	Mercedes-Benz 709D	Alexander Sprint	B27F	1995	?, 2003
1372	CK	N472XRC	Mercedes-Benz 709D	Alexander Sprint	B27F	1996	

1373-1381

			Mercedes-Benz 709D	Alexander Sprint	B27F	1996		
1373	DE	N473XRC	**1376**	DE	N476XRC	**1378**	DE	N478XRC	**1380**	DE	N480XRC
1374	DE	N474XRC	**1377**	DE	N477XRC	**1379**	DE	N479XRC	**1381**	DE	N481XRC
1375	DE	N475XRC						

1382-1391

			Mercedes-Benz 709D	Plaxton Beaver	B27F	1996		
1382	CK	P482CAL	**1385**	TF	P485CAL	**1387**	DE	P487CAL	**1390**	TF	P490CAL
1383	DE	P483CAL	**1386**	SY	P486CAL	**1388**	DE	P488CAL	**1391**	DE	P491CAL
1384	DE	P484CAL						

1931	SC	J31SFA	Leyland Swift ST2R44C97A4	Wright Handybus	B39F	1992
1932	SC	J32SFA	Leyland Swift ST2R44C97A4	Wright Handybus	B39F	1992
1934	SC	J34SRF	Leyland Swift ST2R44C97A4	Wright Handybus	B39F	1992

2001	OS	H501GHA	Dennis Dart 8.5m	East Lancs EL2000	B35F	1991

2002-2023

			Dennis Dart 9m	East Lancs EL2000	B33F	1994		
2002	SC	L502BNX	**2008**	BT	L508BNX	**2013**	SY	L513BNX	**2019**	CK	L519BNX
2003	SC	L503BNX	**2009**	BT	L509BNX	**2014**	SY	L514BNX	**2020**	CK	L620BNX
2004	SC	L504BNX	**2010**	CK	L510BNX	**2015**	SY	L515BNX	**2021**	TF	L521BNX
2005	CK	L605BNX	**2011**	TF	L511BNX	**2016**	SY	L516BNX	**2022**	CK	L522BNX
2006	SC	L506BNX	**2012**	TF	L512BNX	**2017**	BT	L517BNX	**2023**	SC	L523BNX
2007	BT	L507BNX						

2024	LE	P824RWU	Dennis Dart 9.8m	Plaxton Pointer	B40F	1996	Arriva London, 2001
2025	SD	N680GUM	Dennis Dart 9.8m	Plaxton Pointer	B40F	1995	Arriva London, 2002
2026	SD	N673GUM	Dennis Dart 9.8m	Plaxton Pointer	B40F	1995	Arriva London, 2002
2027	SD	N674GUM	Dennis Dart 9.8m	Plaxton Pointer	B40F	1995	Arriva London, 2002
2028	TF	N679GUM	Dennis Dart 9.8m	Plaxton Pointer	B40F	1995	Arriva London, 2002
2029	BT	L300SBS	Dennis Dart 9.8m	Plaxton Pointer	B40F	1994	
2030	CK	J327VAW	Dennis Dart 9.8m	Carlyle Dartline	B40F	1991	Williamsons, Shrewsbury, 1998
2032	SD	M802MOJ	Dennis Dart 9.8m	Marshall C37	B40F	1994	
2033	SD	M803MOJ	Dennis Dart 9.8m	Marshall C37	B40F	1994	
2034	BT	M804MOJ	Dennis Dart 9.8m	Marshall (2001)	B35F	1994	
2035	CV	P835RWU	Dennis Dart 9.8m	Plaxton Pointer	B40F	1996	Arriva London, 2001
2036	CV	P836RWU	Dennis Dart 9.8m	Plaxton Pointer	B40F	1996	Arriva London, 2001
2037	LE	P837RWU	Dennis Dart 9.8m	Plaxton Pointer	B40F	1996	Arriva London, 2001
2038	OS	M30MPS	Dennis Dart 9.8m	Marshall C37	BC40F	1995	Arriva Southern Counties, 1999

2039-2055 — Dennis Dart 9.8m — Plaxton Pointer — B40F — 1996 — Arriva London, 2001-02

2039	LE	P839RWU	2044	MH	P844PWW	2048	SS	P848PWW	2052	LE	P852PWW
2040	CV	P840PWW	2045	MH	P845PWW	2049	SS	P849PWW	2053	LE	P853PWW
2041	LE	P841PWW	2046	LE	P846PWW	2050	SS	P850PWW	2054	LE	P854PWW
2042	CV	P842PWW	2047	SS	P847PWW	2051	LE	P851PWW	2055	LE	P855PWW
2043	SS	P843PWW									

2058	CK	G218LGK	Dennis Dart 9m	Duple Dartline	B36F	1990	Arriva Southern Counties, 1999
2060	BT	M20MPS	Dennis Dart 9.8m	Marshall C37	B40F	1994	Arriva Southern Counties, 1999
2061	CK	G141GOL	Dennis Dart 9m	Duple Dartline	B39F	1990	Arrowline, Knutsford, 1992

2062-2070 — Dennis Dart 9m — Plaxton Pointer — B34F — 1992 — Arriva London, 2002

2062	BT	K542ORH	2064	SY	K544ORH	2067	SY	K547ORH	2069	SY	K549ORH
2063	BT	K543ORH	2065	SY	K545ORH	2068	SY	K548ORH	2070	SY	K550ORH

2081	SY	K551ORH	Dennis Dart 9m	Plaxton Pointer	B34F	1992	Arriva London, 2001
2082	SY	K552ORH	Dennis Dart 9m	Plaxton Pointer	B34F	1992	Arriva London, 2001
2083	BT	L503CPB	Dennis Dart 9.8m	East Lancs EL2000	B40F	1994	Arriva Southern Counties, 2004
2084	BT	L504CPB	Dennis Dart 9.8m	East Lancs EL2000	B40F	1994	Arriva Southern Counties, 2004
2085	CK	L139YVK	Dennis Dart 9m	Northern Counties Paladin	B35F	1994	Arriva The Shires, 2002
2086	CK	L142YVK	Dennis Dart 9m	Northern Counties Paladin	B35F	1994	Arriva The Shires, 2002
2087	CK	L144YVK	Dennis Dart 9m	Northern Counties Paladin	B35F	1994	Arriva The Shires, 2002
2089	SS	N689GUM	Dennis Dart 9.8m	Plaxton Pointer	B40F	1995	Arriva London, 2002
2090	SS	N690GUM	Dennis Dart 9.8m	Plaxton Pointer	B40F	1995	Arriva London, 2002

2091-2095 — Dennis Dart 9.8m — Plaxton Pointer — B40F — 1994

2091	BT	L301NFA	2093	BT	L303NFA	2094	BT	L304NFA	2095	BT	L305NFA
2092	BT	L302NFA									

2096	OS	N806EHA	Dennis Dart 9.8m	East Lancs	B40F	1995	
2097	OS	N807EHA	Dennis Dart 9.8m	East Lancs	B40F	1995	
2098	BT	N808EHA	Dennis Dart 9.8m	East Lancs	B40F	1995	
2099	SD	M805MOJ	Dennis Dart 9.8m	Marshall C37	B40F	1994	
2100	BT	L766DPE	Dennis Dart 9.8m	Wadham Stringer Winchester	C39F	1993	Arriva Southern Counties, 1999

2194-2198 — Dennis Dart 9.8m — East Lancs EL2000 — B40F — 1994

2194	DE	L34PNN	2196	DE	L36PNN	2197	DE	L37PNN	2198	DE	L38PNN
2195	DE	L35PNN									

2201-2206 — Dennis Dart SLF — Plaxton Pointer — N39F — 1997

2201	LE	P201HRY	2203	SS	P203HRY	2205	CV	P205HRY	2206	CV	P206HRY
2202	LE	P202HRY	2204	LE	P204HRY						

2207	TH	S207DTO	Dennis Dart SLF	Plaxton Pointer 2	N39F	1998	
2208	LE	S208DTO	Dennis Dart SLF	Plaxton Pointer 2	N39F	1998	

2209-2212 — TransBus Dart SLF 8.8m — TransBus Mini Pointer — N29F — 2003

2209	SS	SN03LGC	2210	SS	SN03LGD	2211	SS	SN03LGE	2212	SS	SN03LGF

2214	HY	P954RUL	Dennis Dart SLF 10.2m	Alexander ALX200	N36F	1997	Arriva London, 2002
2215	DF	R45VJF	Dennis Dart SLF 10.2m	Alexander ALX200	N40F	1997	
2216	DE	R46VJF	Dennis Dart SLF 10.2m	Alexander ALX200	N40F	1997	

Though built in the former Alexander factory at Falkirk, Mini Pointer Dart 2272, SK52MLN, was one of the last constructed by TransBus with Plaxton names, before they were badged with their own name. Since the collapse of TransBus, a new company, Alexander Dennis has acquired the factory and the badge now carried by the product has again changed, this time to the full name Alexander Dennis. *Dave Heath*

2217-2224

Dennis Dart SLF 9.8m · Plaxton Pointer 2 · N33F · 1999

2217	DE	T47WUT	2219	TH	T49JJF	2222	DE	T52JJF	2224	DE	T54JJF
2218	DE	T48WUT	2221	DE	T51JJF	2223	DE	T53JJF			

2226-2238

Dennis Dart SLF 10.2m · Alexander ALX200 · N40F · 2000

2226	DE	W226SNR	2229	DE	W229SNR	2233	DE	W233SNR	2236	DE	W236SNR
2227	DE	W227SNR	2231	DE	W231SNR	2234	DE	W234SNR	2237	DE	W237SNR
2228	DE	W228SNR	2232	DE	W232SNR	2235	DE	W235SNR	2238	DE	W238SNR

2239-2251

Dennis Dart SLF 8.8m · Plaxton Pointer MPD · N29F · 2000

2239	HY	W239SNR	2243	LE	W243SNR	2247	LE	W247SNR	2249	HY	W249SNR
2241	LE	W241SNR	2244	LE	W244SNR	2248	LE	W248SNR	2251	CV	W251SNR
2242	HY	W242SNR	2246	LE	W246SNR						

2252	DE	X252HBC	Dennis Dart SLF 10.2m	Alexander ALX200	N40F	2000

2253-2267

Dennis Dart SLF 8.8m · Plaxton Pointer MPD · N29F · 2001

2253	LE	Y253YBC	2258	LE	Y258YBC	2262	LE	Y262YBC	2265	LE	Y265YBC
2254	LE	Y254YBC	2259	LE	Y259YBC	2263	LE	Y263YBC	2266	LE	Y266YBC
2256	LE	Y256YBC	2261	LE	Y261YBC	2264	LE	Y264YBC	2267	LE	Y267YBC
2257	LE	Y257YBC									

2268-2275

Dennis Dart SLF 8.8m · Plaxton Pointer MPD · N29F · 2002

2268	LE	SK52MLE	2270	LE	SK52MLJ	2272	LE	SK52MLN	2274	MH	FK52MML
2269	LE	SK52MLF	2271	LE	SK52MLL	2273	LE	SK52MLO	2275	MH	FL52MML

2276-2280

TransBus Dart SLF 8.8m · TransBus Mini Pointer · N29F · 2003

2276	DE	SN53ESG	2277	DE	SN53ESO	2279	TF	SN03LDV	2280	TF	SN03LDX

2281-2288

Dennis Dart SLF · Plaxton Pointer MPD · N29F · 1999

2281	SD	V201KDA	2283	SD	V203KDA	2285	SD	V205KDA	2287	CK	V207KDA
2282	SD	V202KDA	2284	SD	V204KDA	2286	CK	V206KDA	2288	CK	V208KDA

Five East Lancs-bodied Darts were supplied for service improvements in Stafford during 1996. These feature the attractive Spryte styling as illustrated by 2314, P314FEA, which carries lettering for route 8. *Mark Doggett*

2289-2297

Dennis Dart SLF 8.8m — Plaxton Pointer MPD — N29F — 2001-02

2289	CK	BU51KWJ	2292	CK	BU51KWL	2294	CK	Y184TUK	2296	OS	BF52NZO
2290	CK	BU51KWN	2293	CK	BU51KWK	2295	OS	BF52NZN	2297	OS	BF52NZP
2291	CK	BU51KWM								

2299	BT	T61JBA	Dennis Dart SLF 10.6m	Marshall Capital	N37F	1999	Arriva North West, 2000

2301-2305

Dennis Dart SLF 10.6m — Plaxton Pointer — N37F — 1996

2301	SY	N301ENX	2303	SY	N303ENX	2304	SY	N304ENX	2305	SY	N305ENX
2302	SY	N302ENX								

2306-2310

Dennis Dart SLF 10.6m — Plaxton Pointer — NC37F — 1996

2306	SY	P306FEA	2308	SY	P308FEA	2309	SY	P309FEA	2310	SY	P310FEA
2307	SY	P307FEA								

2311-2315

Dennis Dart SLF 10.6m — East Lancs Spryte — N41F — 1996

2311	SD	P311FEA	2313	SD	P313FEA	2314	SD	P314FEA	2315	SD	P315FEA
2312	SD	P312FEA								

2316-2327

Dennis Dart SLF 10.6m — Plaxton Pointer — NC39F — 1997

2316	BT	P316FEA	2319	BT	P319HOJ	2322	SC	P322HOJ	2325	CK	P325HOJ
2317	BT	P317FEA	2320	BT	P320HOJ	2323	CK	P323HOJ	2326	SC	P326HOJ
2318	CK	P318FEA	2321	SC	P321HOJ	2324	SC	P324HOJ	2327	SC	P327HOJ

2329-2344

Dennis Dart SLF 10.6m — Plaxton Pointer 2 — NC39F — 1997-98

2329	SD	R329TJW	2334	SD	R334TJW	2338	SD	R338TJW	2342	SY	R342TJW
2330	SD	R330TJW	2335	SD	R335TJW	2339	SY	R339TJW	2343	SY	R343TJW
2331	SD	R331TJW	2336	SD	R336TJW	2340	SY	R340TJW	2344	SY	R344TJW
2332	SD	R332TJW	2337	SD	R337TJW	2341	SY	R341TJW			

2345-2353

Dennis Dart SLF 10.6m — Plaxton Pointer 2 — NC44F — 1999

2345	SY	S345YOG	2348	OS	S348YOG	2350	OS	S350YOG	2352	OS	S352YOG
2346	SY	S346YOG	2349	OS	S349YOG	2351	OS	S351YOG	2353	OS	S353YOG
2347	OS	S347YOG								

2354-2358 — Dennis Dart SLF 10.2m — Alexander ALX200 — N36F — 1997 — Arriva London, 2002

2354	CK	P952RUL	2356	CK	P956RUL	2357	CK	P957RUL	2358	CK	P958RUL
2355	CK	P955RUL									

2359-2366 — Dennis Dart SLF 9.5m — East Lancs Spryte — N31F — 1996 — Arriva Southern Counties, 2002

2359	TF	N238VPH	2361	TF	N241VPH	2363	TF	N243VPH	2365	TF	N248VPH
2360	TF	N240VPH	2362	TF	N242VPH	2364	TF	N244VPH	2366	TF	N249VPH

2367-2379 — Alexander Dennis Dart 10.7m — Alexander Dennis Pointer — N41F* — 2004-05 — *2371-7 are NC41F

2367	OS	FJ54OTN	2371	SD	FJ55BWA	2374	SD	FJ55BWD	2377	SD	FJ55BWG
2368	OS	FJ54OTP	2372	SD	FJ55BWB	2375	SD	FJ55BWE	2378	OS	FJ55BVT
2369	OS	FJ54OTR	2373	SD	FJ55BWC	2376	SD	FJ55BWF	2379	OS	FJ55BVU
2370	OS	FJ54OTT									

2613-2642 — Volvo B6BLE — Wright Crusader 2 — N40F — 1999-2000

2613	TH	V213KDA	2621	TH	V221KDA	2629	TH	V229KDA	2636	TF	V236KDA
2614	TH	V214KDA	2622	TH	V212KDA	2630	TF	V230KDA	2637	TF	V237KDA
2615	TH	V215KDA	2623	TH	V223KDA	2631	TF	V231KDA	2638	TF	V238KDA
2616	TH	V216KDA	2624	TH	V224KDA	2632	TF	V232KDA	2639	TF	V239KDA
2617	TH	V217KDA	2625	TH	V225KDA	2633	TF	V233KDA	2640	TH	V210KDA
2618	TH	V218KDA	2626	TH	V226KDA	2634	TF	V234KDA	2641	TH	V211KDA
2619	TH	V219KDA	2627	TH	V227KDA	2635	TF	V235KDA	2642	TH	V209KDA
2620	TH	V220KDA	2628	TH	V228KDA						

2701	CK	YJ54CKE	DAF SB120 9.4m	Wrightbus Cadet	N30F	2004
2702	CK	YJ54CKF	DAF SB120 9.4m	Wrightbus Cadet	N30F	2004

2703-2707 — DAF SB120 10.8m — Wrightbus Cadet — N39F — 2002

2703	SY	BU02URX	2705	SY	BU02URZ	2706	SY	BU02USB	2707	SY	BU02USC
2704	SY	BU02URY									

2708-2727 — DAF SB120 10.8m — Wrightbus Cadet — N39F — 2001

2708	TF	Y348UON	2715	TF	Y365UON	2720	TF	Y347UON	2724	TF	Y364UON
2711	TF	Y351UON	2716	TF	Y356UON	2721	TF	Y361UON	2725	TF	Y346UON
2712	TF	Y352UON	2717	TF	Y357UON	2722	TF	Y362UON	2726	TF	Y366UON
2713	TF	Y353UON	2718	TF	Y358UON	2723	TF	Y363UON	2727	TF	Y367UON
2714	TF	Y354UON	2719	TF	Y349UON						

2728-2736 — DAF SB120 10.8m — Wrightbus Cadet — N39F — 2002-03

2728	TF	BF52OAG	2731	SD	BU03HRD	2733	SD	BU03HRF	2735	SD	BU03HRJ
2729	SY	BF52NZM	2732	SD	BU03HRE	2734	SD	BU03HRG	2736	SD	BU03HRK
2730	SD	BU03HRC									

2737	OS	CX04EHZ	DAF SB120 10.8m	Wrightbus Cadet	N39F	2004	Arriva North West & Wales, 2004
2738	u	X781NWX	DAF SB120 9.4m	Wrightbus Cadet	N30F	2001	Arriva North West & Wales, 2005
2739	u	X783NWX	DAF SB120 9.4m	Wrightbus Cadet	N30F	2001	Arriva North West & Wales, 2005
2998	SC	P315FAW	Optare Excel L1150	Optare	N40F	1997	Williamsons, Shrewsbury, 1998
2999	SC	P316FAW	Optare Excel L1150	Optare	N40F	1997	Williamsons, Shrewsbury, 1998
3039	TF	49XBF	Leyland Tiger TRBTL11/2RP	Plaxton Derwent 2	B54F	1988	Arriva North West, 2000
3053	SY	F33ENF	Leyland Tiger TRBL10/3ARZA	Alexander N	B53F	1989	Timeline, 1994

3071-3079 — Dennis Falcon HC SDA421 — East Lancs EL2000 — B48F — 1990 — London & Country, 1991

3071	BT	G301DPA	3074	TF	G304DPA	3076	u	G306DPA	3078	OS	G308DPA
3072	u	G302DPA	3075	TF	G305DPA	3077	TF	G307DPA	3079	BT	G309DPA
3073	TH	G303DPA									

3081-3088 — Dennis Falcon HC SDA423 — East Lancs EL2000 — B48F — 1992-93

3081	TF	K211UHA	3082	TF	K212UHA	3085	TF	K215UHA	3087	TF	K217UHA
3083	TF	K213UHA	3084	SC	K214UHA	3086	TF	K216UHA	3088	SY	K218UHA

3091-3098 — Dennis Falcon SDA421 — East Lancs EL2000 — B48F — 1990

3091	TF	G381EKA	3093	u	G383EKA	3095	OS	G385EKA	3097	TF	G387EKA
3092	TF	G382EKA	3094	TF	G384EKA	3096	u	G386EKA	3098	u	G388EKA

3101	CK	F258GWJ	Leyland Lynx LX112L10ZR1R	Leyland Lynx	B51F	1989	The Wright Company, 1993
3102	CK	E72KBF	Leyland Lynx LX112L10ZR1	Leyland Lynx	B51F	1988	
3103	CK	F284AWW	Leyland Lynx LX112L10ZR1S	Leyland Lynx	B49F	1989	Arriva Yorkshire (W), 1999
3104	TH	G110OUG	Leyland Lynx LX2R11C15Z4S	Leyland Lynx	B49F	1990	Arriva Yorkshire (W), 2000
3105	TH	G324NUM	Leyland Lynx LX2R11C15Z4S	Leyland Lynx	B51F	1990	Arriva Yorkshire (W), 2000
3106	CK	F281AWW	Leyland Lynx LX112L10ZR1S	Leyland Lynx	B49F	1989	Arriva Yorkshire (W), 2000
3107	CK	G108OUG	Leyland Lynx LX2R11C15Z4S	Leyland Lynx	B49F	1990	Arriva Yorkshire (W), 2000

Three further VDL Bus SB120s were delivered in 2004, two of which, including 2701, YJ54CKE, were allocated to Cannock where it is seen on the Brownhills service. *Mark Doggett*

3108	BT	G38YHJ	Leyland Lynx LX2R11C15Z4R	Leyland Lynx	B49F	1989	Arriva The Shires, 2002	
3109	BT	G40YHJ	Leyland Lynx LX2R11C15Z4R	Leyland Lynx	B49F	1989	Arriva The Shires, 2002	
3110	u	F48ENF	Leyland Lynx LX112L10ZR1R	Leyland Lynx	B49F	1988	Arriva Southern Counties, 2004	
3111	u	E966PME	Leyland Lynx LX112TL11ZR1R	Leyland Lynx	B49F	1988	Arriva Southern Counties, 2005	
3202	SS	YJ54CPE	VDL Bus SB4000	Van Hool T9 Alizée	C49FT	2004		
3203	SS	YJ53VFY	DAF SB4000	Van Hool T9 Alizée	C49FT	2003		
3204	SS	YJ03PFX	DAF SB4000	Van Hool T9 Alizée	C49FT	2003		
3205	SS	P205RWR	DAF SB3000	Van Hool Alizée	C51FT	1997	Arriva Yorkshire, 2000	
3206	SS	YJ04BKF	VDL Bus SB4000	Van Hool T9 Alizée	C49FT	2004		
3207	SS	YJ54CPF	VDL Bus SB4000	Van Hool T9 Alizée	C49FT	2004		
3208	SS	YJ05PVT	VDL Bus SB4000	Van Hool T9 Alizée	C49FT	2005		
3209	SS	T209XVO	DAF SB3000	Van Hool T9 Alizée	C51FT	1999		
3301	SD	H914XYT	Volvo Citybus B10M-55	East Lancs EL2000	B41F	1990	Arriva London (NE), 1999	
3302	SD	H918XYT	Volvo Citybus B10M-55	East Lancs EL2000	B41F	1990	Arriva London (NE), 1999	
3303	SD	H919XYT	Volvo Citybus B10M-55	East Lancs EL2000	B41F	1990	Arriva London (NE), 1999	

3304-3313 Volvo Citybus B10M-50   Alexander Q   B55F 1991 Timeline, Leigh, 1998

3304	SY	H73DVM	3307	SD	H76DVM	3310	SY	H81DVM	3312	SD	H83DVM
3305	SY	H74DVM	3308	SD	H577DVM	3311	SD	H82DVM	3313	SD	H84DVM
3306	SD	H575DVM	3309	SY	H580DVM						

3415-3429 Scania L113CRL   Plaxton Paladin   NC45F* 1998 *3415-19 are NC47F

3415	TH	R415TJW	3419	TH	R419TJW	3423	TH	R423TJW	3427	SY	R427TJW
3416	TH	R416TJW	3420	TH	R420TJW	3424	TH	R424TJW	3428	SY	R428TJW
3417	TH	R417TJW	3421	TH	R421TJW	3425	SY	R425TJW	3429	SY	R429TJW
3418	TH	R418TJW	3422	TH	R422TJW	3426	SY	R426TJW			

3466-3479 Scania L113CRL   East Lancs European   NC51F* 1996 *3476-9 are NC49F

3466	SS	N166PUT	3470	SS	N170PUT	3474	SS	N174PUT	3477	CV	N177PUT
3467	SS	N167PUT	3471	SS	N171PUT	3475	SS	N175PUT	3478	CV	N178PUT
3468	SS	N168PUT	3472	SS	N172PUT	3476	CV	N176PUT	3479	CV	N179PUT
3469	SS	N169PUT	3473	SS	N173PUT						

3489-3493 — Scania L113CRL — East Lancs European — N51F — 1996

3489	SS	N429XRC	3491	SS	N431XRC	3492	DE	N432XRC	3493	DE	N433XRC
3490	CV	N430XRC								

3501-3504 — Scania N113CRL — East Lancs European — B42F — 1995

3501	SY	M401EFD	3502	SY	M402EFD	3503	SY	M403EFD	3504	SY	M404EFD

3601-3612 — Volvo B10BLE — Alexander ALX300 — N44F — 2000

3601	HY	V601DBC	3604	DE	V604DBC	3607	SS	V607DBC	3610	CV	V610DBC
3602	HY	V602DBC	3605	DE	V605DBC	3608	SS	V608DBC	3611	CV	V611DBC
3603	HY	V603DBC	3606	DE	V606DBC	3609	CV	V609DBC	3612	CV	V612DBC

3701-3704 — DAF SB200 — Wrightbus Commander — N44F — 2003

3701	LE	FD52GGO	3702	LE	FD52GGP	3703	LE	FD52GGU	3704	LE	FD52GGV

3705-3718 — DAF SB200 — Wrightbus Commander — N44F — 2002

3705	TF	BF52NZR	3709	TF	BF52NZV	3713	TF	BF52NZZ	3716	TF	BF52OAC
3706	TF	BF52NZS	3710	TF	BF52NZW	3714	TF	BF52OAA	3717	TF	BF52OAD
3707	TF	BF52NZT	3711	TF	BF52NZX	3715	TF	BF52OAB	3718	TF	BF52OAE
3708	TF	BF52NZU	3712	TF	BF52NZY						

4001	MH	L94HRF	DAF DB250		Optare Spectra	B48/29F	1993	Midland (Stevensons), 1998
4002	MH	L95HRF	DAF DB250		Optare Spectra	B48/29F	1993	Midland (Stevensons), 1998

4134-4145 — Scania N113DRB — Northern Counties — B47/33F — 1990-91 — Arriva North West, 1999

4134	WG	G34HKY	4138	WG	G38HKY	4142	WG	G714LKW	4144	WG	H804RWJ
4136	WG	G36HKY	4141	WG	G711LKW	4143	WG	H803RWJ	4145	WG	H805RWJ
4137	WG	G37HKY									

4153-4158 — Scania N113DRB — Alexander RH — B47/33F — 1989 — BTS, Borehamwood, 1993

4153	WG	F153DET	4155	WG	F155DET	4157	WG	F157DET	4158	WG	F158DET
4154	WG	F154DET									

4159-4178 — Scania N113DRB — East Lancs — B47/33F — 1994-95

4159	WG	M159GRY	4165	WG	M165GRY	4171	SS	M171GRY	4175	SS	M175GRY
4160	WG	M160GRY	4166	WG	M166GRY	4172	SS	M172GRY	4176	SS	M176GRY
4161	WG	M161GRY	4168	WG	M168GRY	4173	SS	M173GRY	4177	SS	M177GRY
4162	MH	M162GRY	4169	SS	M169GRY	4174	SS	M174GRY	4178	SS	M178GRY
4163	WG	M163GRY	4170	SS	M170GRY						

4180-4184 — Scania N113DRB — East Lancs — B45/33F — 1995

4180	SS	N160VVO	4182	SS	N162VVO	4183	SS	N163VVO	4184	SS	N164VVO
4181	SS	N161VVO									

4191-4195 — Scania N113DRB — East Lancs — BC43/29F* — 1995 — 4194/5 are B45/33F

4191	TH	M831SDA	4193	TH	M833SDA	4194	TH	M834SDA	4195	TH	M835SDA
4192	TH	M832SDA									

4301	DE	GTO301V	Leyland Fleetline FE30AGR		Northern Counties	B43/30F	1980	

4320-4334 — Volvo Citybus B10M-50 — East Lancs — B45/33F — 1990-91 — London South, 1998

4320	DE	H650GPF	4324	DE	H655GPF	4328	DE	H669GPF	4332	DE	H680GPF
4321	DE	H652GPF	4325	DE	H659GPF	4329	DE	H671GPF	4333	DE	H682GPF
4322	DE	H653GPF	4326	DE	H663GPF	4330	DE	H672GPF	4334	DE	H684GPF
4323	DE	H654GPF	4327	DE	H664GPF	4331	DE	H674GPF			

4335-4343 — Volvo Citybus B10M-50 — Marshall — B45/33F — 1984

4335	DE	B135GAU	4339	DE	B139GAU	4341	DE	B141GAU	4342	DE	B142GAU
4336	DE	B136GAU	4337	DE	B137GAU	4338	DE	B138GAU	4343	DE	B143GAU

4344-4353 — Volvo Citybus B10M-50 — Northern Counties — B42/33F — 1986/88

4344	DE	C144NRR	4347	DE	C147NRR	4350	DE	E150BTO	4352	DE	E152BTO
4345	DE	C145NRR	4348	DE	C148NRR	4351	DE	E151BTO	4353	DE	E153BTO
4346	DE	C146NRR	4349	DE	E149BTO						

4354	DE	F114TML	Volvo Citybus B10M-50		Alexander RV	B47/31F	1989	Arriva London, 1999
4355	DE	F111TML	Volvo Citybus B10M-50		Alexander RV	B47/31F	1989	Arriva London, 1999

Around a third of the Arriva Midlands double-deck fleet are East Lancs-bodied DAF DB250s, with forty-five of the Lowlander model now in service. Illustrating the type is Wigston's 4708, FE51YWH, seen here heading out of Leicester. *Dave Heath*

4389-4393

			Volvo Citybus B10M-50	East Lancs		B45/34F	1990	London South, 1998
4389	DE	H649GPF	**4390**	CK	H651GPF	**4391**	DE	H656GPF	**4393**	DE	H658GPF

4389	DE	H649GPF	4390	CK	H651GPF	4391	DE	H656GPF	4393	DE	H658GPF

4396	CK	G646BPH	Volvo Citybus B10M-50	Northern Counties Palatine	B45/35F	1989	Bee Line Buzz, 1993
4397	CK	G647BPH	Volvo Citybus B10M-50	Northern Counties Palatine	B45/35F	1989	Bee Line Buzz, 1993
4501	CV	A501EJF	Leyland Olympian ONLXB/1R	Eastern Coach Works	B45/33F	1983	
4509	CK	A509EJF	Leyland Olympian ONLXB/1R	Eastern Coach Works	B45/33F	1983	
4514	WG	B514LFP	Leyland Olympian ONLXB/1R	Eastern Coach Works	O45/32F	1984	
4516	WG	A132SMA	Leyland Olympian ONLXB/1R	Eastern Coach Works	B45/32F	1983	
4518	WG	A134SMA	Leyland Olympian ONLXB/1R	Eastern Coach Works	O45/32F	1983	
4527	CV	B187BLG	Leyland Olympian ONLXB/1RZ	Eastern Coach Works	B45/32F	1984	Crosville Cymru, 1990
4528	LE	B190BLG	Leyland Olympian ONLXB/1RZ	Eastern Coach Works	B45/32F	1984	Crosville Cymru, 1990

4531-4534

			Leyland Olympian ONCL10/1RZ	Northern Counties Palatine	B47/30F	1989	Arriva Southern Counties, 2000
4531	SE	G501SFT	**4532**	SE	G502SFT	**4533**	BT	G503SFT	**4534**	BT	G504SFT

4535-4541

			Leyland Olympian ONCL10/1RZ	Northern Counties Palatine	B47/30F	1989	Bee Line Buzz, 1993
4535	BT	G505SFT	**4537**	BT	G507SFT	**4540**	BT	G510SFT	**4541**	BT	G511SFT

4545	SE	B274LPH	Leyland Olympian ONTL11/1R	Eastern Coach Works	B43/29F	1985	Arriva Southern Counties, 1998
4546	TF	B275LPH	Leyland Olympian ONTL11/1R	Eastern Coach Works	B43/29F	1985	Arriva Southern Counties, 1998

4558-4561

			Leyland Olympian ONLXB/1RH	Optare	B47/29F	1989	Arriva Southern Counties, 2001
4558	LE	E158OMD	**4559**	LE	E159OMD	**4560**	HY	E160OMD	**4561**	LE	E161OMD

4569	CK	D190FYM	Leyland Olympian ONLXB/1RH	Eastern Coach Works	B42/30F	1986	Arriva London, 2003
4570	BT	D170FYM	Leyland Olympian ONLXB/1RH	Eastern Coach Works	B42/30F	1986	Arriva London, 2003
4571	CK	D171FYM	Leyland Olympian ONLXB/1RH	Eastern Coach Works	B42/30F	1986	Arriva London, 2003

4601-4613

Volvo Olympian YN2RV18Z4   Northern Counties Palatine   B47/29F   1996

4601	LE	P601CAY	**4605**	LE	P605CAY	**4608**	LE	P608CAY	**4611**	WG	P611CAY
4602	LE	P602CAY	**4606**	WG	P606CAY	**4609**	WG	P609CAY	**4612**	WG	P612CAY
4603	LE	P603CAY	**4607**	WG	P607CAY	**4610**	WG	P610CAY	**4613**	SS	P613CAY
4604	LE	P604CAY									

4614-4643   Volvo Olympian   Northern Counties Palatine   B47/29F   1998

4614	CV	R614MNU	4621	CV	R621MNU	4629	DE	R629MNU	4637	LE	R637MNU
4615	CV	R615MNU	4622	CV	R622MNU	4630	DE	R630MNU	4638	LE	R638MNU
4616	LE	R616MNU	4623	CV	R623MNU	4631	DE	R631MNU	4639	DE	R639MNU
4617	LE	R617MNU	4624	LE	R624MNU	4632	LE	R632MNU	4640	DE	R640MNU
4618	LE	R618MNU	4625	DE	R625MNU	4633	LE	R633MNU	4641	DE	R641MNU
4619	LE	R619MNU	4626	DE	R626MNU	4634	LE	R634MNU	4642	DE	R642MNU
4620	CV	R620MNU	4627	DE	R627MNU	4636	LE	R636MNU	4643	DE	R643MNU

4644-4653   Volvo Olympian   Northern Counties Palatine   B47/29F   1998

4644	SS	S644KJU	4647	SS	S647KJU	4650	SS	S650KJU	4652	SS	S652KJU
4645	LE	S645KJU	4648	SS	S648KJU	4651	SS	S651KJU	4653	SS	S653KJU
4646	SS	S646KJU	4649	SS	S649KJU						

4665-4669   Volvo Olympian YN2RV18Z4   Northern Counties Palatine   B47/30F   1996

4665	DE	N165XVO	4667	DE	P167BTV	4668	LE	P168BTV	4669	LE	P169BTV
4666	DE	N166XVO									

4701-4716   DAF DB250   East Lancs Lowlander   N44/29F   2001

4701	WG	Y701XJF	4705	WG	Y705XJF	4709	WG	Y709XJF	4714	WG	FE51YWM
4702	WG	Y702XJF	4706	WG	Y706XJF	4711	WG	FE51YWJ	4715	WG	FE51WSU
4703	WG	Y703XJF	4707	WG	Y707XJF	4712	WG	FE51YWK	4716	WG	FE51WSV
4704	WG	Y704XJF	4708	WG	FE51YWH	4713	WG	FE51YWL			

4717-4733   DAF DB250   East Lancs Lowlander   N44/29F   2002

4717	WG	FD02UKB	4722	SS	FN52XBG	4726	SS	PN52XBF	4730	SS	FD02UKR
4718	WG	FD02UKC	4723	SS	FD02UKJ	4727	SS	FD02UKN	4731	SS	FD02UKS
4719	SS	FD02UKE	4724	SS	FD02UKK	4728	SS	FD02UKO	4732	SS	FD02UKT
4720	SS	PN52XBH	4725	SS	FD02UKL	4729	SS	FD02UKP	4733	SS	FD02UKU
4721	SS	FD02UKG									

4734-4745   DAF DB250   East Lancs Lowlander   N44/29F   2003

4734	DE	PN52XRJ	4737	DE	PN52XRM	4740	WG	PN52XRR	4743	DE	PN52XRU
4735	WG	PN52XRK	4738	WG	PN52XRO	4741	WG	PN52XRS	4744	DE	PN52XRV
4736	DE	PN52XRL	4739	DE	PN52XRP	4742	DE	PN52XRT	4745	DE	PN52XRW

6000-6006   Optare Solo M850   Optare   N24F   2003   Operated for Shropshire CC

6000	SY	BU03HRL	6002	SY	BU03HPX	6004	SY	BU03HPZ	6006	SY	FJ04PFX
6001	SY	BU03HPV	6003	SY	BU03HPY	6005	SY	BU03HRA			

6007	SH	FN04AFJ	Optare Solo M920	Optare	N33F	2004	Operated for Shropshire CC
6008	SY	FJ54OTV	Optare Solo M850	Optare	N29F	2004	Operated for Shropshire CC
6009	SY	FJ54OTW	Optare Solo M850	Optare	N29F	2004	Operated for Shropshire CC
6010	SH	FJ54OTX	Optare Solo M920	Optare	N30F	2004	Operated for Shropshire CC

Ancillary vehicles:

9501	TH	F51ENF	Leyland Lynx LX112L10ZR1R	Leyland Lynx	TV	1988	Shearings, 1991

9504-9509   Leyland Tiger TRBL10/3ARZA   Alexander N   B53F   1989   Timeline, 1994

9504	WG	F34ENF	9506	DE	F40ENF	9508	WG	F36ENF	9509	TH	F39ENF
9505	TF	F35ENF									

9510	WG	E25ECH	Scania K92CRB	Alexander PS	TV	1988	
9511	WG	F27JRC	Scania K93CRB	Alexander PS	TV	1989	
9512	DE	E23ECH	Scania K92CRB	Alexander PS	TV	1988	
9513	DE	F28JRC	Scania K93CRB	Alexander PS	TV	1989	
9514	SW	F406DUG	Volvo B10M-60	Plaxton Paramount 3500	TV	1989	Wallace Arnold, 1992

Previous registrations:

49XBF	F603CET, A19RBL, F603CET	M100PHA	M30MPS
D170FYM	D170FYM, 7CLT	P608JJU	P111MML
D190FYM	D190FYM, 319CLT		

Arriva Midlands operates Optare Solo buses on behalf of Shropshire Bus and which are liveried for the local authority. Pictured in North Shropshire is one of two longer M920 variants based at Telford's outstation at Shifnal. Illustrated here is 6007, FN04AFJ. *Tom Johnson*

Allocations

Burton-on-Trent (Wetmore Road) - BT

Mercedes-Benz	1249	1250	1251	1252				
Dart	2007	2008	2009	2017	2029	2034	2057	2060
	2062	2063	2083	2084	2091	2092	2093	2094
	2095	2098	2100	2299	2316	2317	2319	2320
Lynx	3108	3109						
Falcon	3071	3079						
Olympian	4533	4534	4535	4537	4540	4541	4570	

Cannock (Delta Way) - CK

Mercedes-Benz	1147	1148	1149	1150	1158	1159	1160	1163
	1170	1171	1177	1180	1372	1382		
Dart	2005	2010	2019	2020	2022	2058	2061	2073
	2074	2078	2085	2086	2087	2286	2287	2288
	2289	2290	2291	2292	2293	2294	2318	2323
	2325	2354	2355	2356	2357	2358		
SB120 Cadet	2701	2702						
Lynx	3101	3102	3103	3106				
Citybus	4390	4396	4397					
Olympian	4569	4571						

Coalville (Ashby Road) - CV

Mercedes-Benz	1152	1153	1154	1155	1156	1157	1161	
Dart	2035	2036	2040	2042	2205	2206	2251	
Volvo B10BLE	3609	3610	3611	3612				
Scania	3476	3477	3478	3479	3490			
Olympian	4501	4509	4527	4614	4615	4620	4621	4622
	4623							

Derby (London Road) - DE

Mercedes-Benz	1373	1374	1375	1376	1377	1378	1379	1380
	1381	1383	1384	1387	1391			
Dart	2194	2195	2196	2197	2198	2215	2216	2217
	2218	2221	2222	2223	2224	2226	2227	2228
	2229	2231	2232	2233	2234	2235	2236	2237
	2238	2252	2276	2277				
Scania sd	3492	3493						
Volvo B10BLE	3604	3605	3606					
Fleetline	4301							
Volvo Citybus	4320	4321	4322	4323	4324	4325	4326	4327
	4328	4329	4330	4331	4332	4333	4334	4335
	4336	4337	4338	4339	4341	4342	4343	4344
	4345	4346	4347	4348	4349	4350	4351	4352
	4353	4354	4355	4389	4391	4396		
Olympian	4625	4626	4627	4629	4630	4631	4639	4640
	4641	4642	4643	4665	4666	4667		
DAF Lowlander	4734	4736	4737	4739	4742	4743	4744	4745
Ancillary	9506	9512	9513					

Hinckley (Jacknell Road, Dodwells Bridge) - HY

Mercedes-Benz	1129	1130	1131	1132	1133	1134	1135	1136
	1141	1142	1143	1144	1145	1146		
Dart	2214	2239	2242	2249				
Volvo B10M coach	3213							
Volvo B10BLE	3601	3602	3603					
Olympian	4560							

Leicester (Melton Road, Thurmaston) - LE

Dart	2024	2037	2039	2041	2046	2047	2050	2051
	2052	2053	2054	2201	2202	2204	2207	2208
	2219	2241	2243	2244	2246	2247	2248	2253
	2254	2256	2257	2258	2259	2261	2262	2263
	2264	2265	2266	2267	2268	2269	2270	2271
	2272	2273						
SB200 Commander	3701	3702	3703	3704				
Volvo Citybus	4389	4391	4393					
Olympian	4528	4558	4559	4561	4601	4602	4603	4604
	4605	4608	4616	4617	4618	4619	4624	4632
	4633	4634	4636	4637	4638	4645	4668	4669

Leicester (Peacock Lane, Southgates) - SS

Mercedes-Benz	1168							
Dart	2048	2049	2089	2090	2203	2209	2210	2211
	2212							
DAF coach	3201	3202	3203	3204	3205	3206	3207	3208
	3209							
Scania SD	3466	3467	3468	3469	3470	3471	3472	3473
	3474	3475	3489	3491				
Volvo B10BLE	3607	3608						
Scania DD	4169	4170	4171	4172	4173	4174	4175	4176
	4177	4178	4180	4181	4182	4183	4184	
Olympian	4516	4613	4644	4646	4647	4648	4649	4650
	4651	4652	4653					
DAF Lowlander	4719	4720	4721	4722	4723	4724	4725	4726
	4727	4728	4729	4730	4731	4732	4733	

Market Harborough - MH

Mercedes-Benz	1001	1002	1179	
Dart	2044	2045	2274	2275
DAF Spectra	4001	4002		
Scania DD	4162			

Oswestry (Salop Road) - OS

Dart	2001	2096	2097	2295	2296	2297	2347	2348
	2349	2350	2351	2352	2353	2367	2368	2369
	2370	2378	2379					
Tiger	3038							
Falcon	3078	3095						

Shrewsbury (Spring Gardens) - SY

Mercedes-Benz	1243	1247	1357	1358	1359	1360	1386	1390
Solo	6000	6001	6002	6003	6004	6005	6006	6008
	6009							
Dart	2013	2014	2015	2016	2070	2064	2065	2067
	2068	2069	2081	2082	2301	2302	2303	2304
	2305	2306	2307	2308	2309	2310	2339	2340
	2341	2342	2343	2344	2345	2346		
SB120 Cadet	2703	2704	2705	2706	2707	2729		
Tiger	3053							
Volvo B10M bus	3215	3304	3305	3309	3310			
Scania sd	3425	3426	3427	3428	3429	3501	3502	3503
	3504							

Stafford (Dorrington Park Industrial Estate, Common Road) - SD

Zafira	127	129						
Mercedes-Benz	1138	1151	1169					
Dart	2025	2026	2027	2032	2033	2038	2099	2281
	2282	2283	2284	2285	2311	2312	2313	2314
	2315	2329	2330	2331	2332	2334	2335	2336
	2337	2338	2371	2372	2373	2374	2375	2376
	2377							
SB120 Cadet	2708	2730	2731	2732	2733	2734	2735	2736
Volvo B10M bus	3301	3302	3303	3306	3307	3308	3311	3312
	3313							

Swadlincote (Midland Road) - SC

Mercedes-Benz	1246							
Swift	1931	1932	1934					
Dart	2002	2003	2004	2006	2023	2030	2321	2322
	2324	2326	2327					
Optare Excel	2998	2999						
Falcon	3084							
Olympian	4531	4532	4545					
Ancillary	9514							

Tamworth (Aldergate) - TH

Dart	2060							
Volvo B6	2613	2614	2615	2616	2617	2618	2619	2620
	2621	2622	2623	2624	2625	2626	2627	2628
	2629	2640	2641	2642				
Falcon	3073							
Scania sd	3415	3416	3417	3418	3419	3420	3421	3422
	3423	3424	3425	3426				
Scania dd	4191	4192	4193	4194	4195			
Ancillary	9509							

Telford (Charlton Street, Wellington) - TF

Outstation: Shifnal

Solo	6007	6010						
Mercedes-Benz	1260	1385	1390					
Dart	2011	2012	2021	2028	2279	2280	2299	2359
	2360	2361	2362	2363	2364	2365	2366	
Volvo B6	2630	2631	2632	2633	2634	2635	2636	2637
	2638	2639						
SB120 Cadet	2708	2711	2712	2713	2714	2715	2716	2717
	2718	2719	2720	2721	2722	2723	2724	2725
	2726	2727	2728					
Falcon	3074	3075	3077	3081	3082	3083	3085	3086
	3087	3088	3091	3092	3094	3097		
SB200 Commander	3705	3706	3707	3708	3709	3710	3711	3712
	3713	3714	3715	3716	3717	3718		
Volvo Olympian	4546							
Ancillary	9505							

Wigston (Station Street, South Wigston) - WG

Mercedes Benz	1162	1164	1165	1166	1167	1172	1174	1175
	1176	1178						
Scania dd	4134	4136	4137	4138	4141	4142	4143	4144
	4145	4153	4154	4155	4157	4158	4159	4160
	4161	4163	4165	4166	4168			
Olympian open-top	4514	4518						
Olympian	4516	4606	4607	4609	4610	4611	4612	
DAF Lowlander	4701	4702	4703	4704	4705	4706	4707	4708
	4709	4711	4712	4713	4714	4715	4716	4717
	4718	4735	4738	4740	4741			
Ancillary	9504	9508	9510	9511				

Unallocated and withdrawn - u/w

SB120 Cadet	2738	2739			
Falcon	3072	3076	3093	3096	3098
Lynx	3107	3110	3111		

ARRIVA THE SHIRES & ESSEX

Arriva The Shires Ltd; Arriva East Herts & Essex Ltd
487 Dunstable Road, Luton, LU4 8DS

245-268			Mercedes-Benz 308D		Leicester Carriage		M7L	1992-9	Op'd for Hertfordshire CC
245	GR	M425BLU	258	GR	N108EVS	263	GR	P403MLD	266	GR	S356KJU
246	GR	M426BLU	259	GR	N109EVS	264	GR	P404MLD	267	GR	S537KJU
256	GR	N106EVS	262	GR	P402MLD	265	GR	P405MLD	268	GR	N248GBM
257	GR	N107EVS									

442	HW	Y42HBT	Optare Solo M850	Optare	N23F	2001	Op'd for Buckinghamshire CC
443	HA	YS02UBX	Optare Alero	Optare	N14F	2002	Operated for Essex CC
444	HA	YS02UBY	Optare Alero	Optare	N14F	2002	Operated for Essex CC
446	AY	Y46HBT	Optare Solo M850	Optare	N23F	2001	Op'd for Buckinghamshire CC
447	AY	Y47HBT	Optare Solo M850	Optare	N23F	2001	Op'd for Buckinghamshire CC
448	AY	Y48HBT	Optare Solo M850	Optare	N23F	2001	Op'd for Buckinghamshire CC
449	AY	Y49HBT	Optare Solo M850	Optare	N23F	2001	Op'd for Buckinghamshire CC
454	AY	YN04LXF	Optare Alero	Optare	N17F	2004	Op'd for Buckinghamshire CC
455	AY	YN04LXG	Optare Alero	Optare	N17F	2004	Op'd for Buckinghamshire CC
456	AY	YN04LXH	Optare Alero	Optare	N17F	2004	Op'd for Buckinghamshire CC
1258	HA	KS05JJE	Mercedes-Benz Vito 110CDi	Traveliner	M6	2005	
2105	u	M45WUR	Mercedes-Benz 709D	Plaxton Beaver	B27F	1995	
2106	u	M46WUR	Mercedes-Benz 709D	Plaxton Beaver	B27F	1995	
2107	HI	M47WUR	Mercedes-Benz 709D	Plaxton Beaver	B27F	1995	
2113	SV	M43WUR	Mercedes-Benz 709D	Plaxton Beaver	B27F	1995	
2114	u	N918ETM	Mercedes-Benz 709D	Plaxton Beaver	B27F	1995	

2116-2136			Mercedes-Benz 709D		Plaxton Beaver		B27F*	1995	*2116 is BC27F
2116	HA	N186EMJ	2121	HA	N191EMJ	2126	HA	N196EMJ	2131	LU	N911ETM
2118	HA	N188EMJ	2122	HA	N192EMJ	2127	AY	N907ETM	2132	LU	N912ETM
2119	HA	N189EMJ	2123	HA	N193EMJ	2128	LU	N908ETM	2133	LU	N913ETM
2120	HA	N190EMJ	2124	HA	N194EMJ	2129	LU	N909ETM	2136	LU	N916ETM

Arriva The Shires operates Optare Solo and Alero buses for the county councils while their own minibuses are all Mercedes-Benz. Shown en route for Buckingham is 2240, R760DUB, which was new to the Yorkshire operation.
Dave Heath

2138-2162 — Mercedes-Benz 709D — Plaxton Beaver — B27F — 1996

2138	u	N368JGS	2145	HA	N375JGS	2151	HA	N381JGS	2157	HI	N387JGS
2139	SV	N369JGS	2146	u	N376JGS	2152	u	N382JGS	2158	HA	N366JGS
2140	u	N370JGS	2147	u	N377JGS	2153	HI	N383JGS	2159	HA	N367JGS
2141	HI	N371JGS	2148	SV	N378JGS	2154	HI	N384JGS	2160	HI	P670PNM
2142	SV	N372JGS	2149	HA	N379JGS	2155	HI	N385JGS	2161	HI	P671PNM
2143	HA	N373JGS	2150	SV	N380JGS	2156	HI	N386JGS	2162	HI	P669PNM
2144	u	N374JGS									

2166	GR	J465UFS	Mercedes-Benz 609D	Crystals	BC24F	1992	Checker, Garston, 1997

2171-2195 — Mercedes-Benz Vario 0810 — Plaxton Beaver 2 — B27F — 1997-98

2171	HW	R171VBM	2177	HA	R177VBM	2182	HH	R182DNM	2189	HA	R189DNM
2172	HA	R172VBM	2178	HH	R178VBM	2183	HH	R183DNM	2190	HA	R190DNM
2173	AY	R173VBM	2179	HH	R179VBM	2184	HH	R184DNM	2194	HA	R194DNM
2175	HA	R175VBM	2180	HH	R180VBM	2185	HH	R185DNM	2195	HA	R195DNM
2176	AY	R176VBM	2181	HH	R181DNM						

2196	HW	R196DNM	Mercedes-Benz Vario 0814	Plaxton Beaver 2	B31F	1998	
2197	HW	R197DNM	Mercedes-Benz Vario 0814	Plaxton Beaver 2	B31F	1998	
2198	HW	R198DNM	Mercedes-Benz Vario 0814	Plaxton Beaver 2	B31F	1998	

2240-2249 — Mercedes-Benz Vario 0810 — Plaxton Beaver 2 — B27F — 1997 — Arriva Yorkshire, 1999-2003

2240	AY	R760DUB	2242	HH	R762DUB	2246	HH	R766DUB	2248	HA	R758DUB
2241	HH	R761DUB	2244	AY	R764DUB	2247	AY	R767DUB	2249	HH	R759DUB

2370-2377 — Mercedes-Benz Vario 0810 — Plaxton Beaver 2 — B25F* — 1998 — *2373 is BC25F

2370	HA	R940VPU	2373	WR	R943VPU	2375	WR	R945VPU	2377	WR	R947VPU
2371	HA	R941VPU	2374	WR	R944VPU	2376	WR	R946VPU			

2408	SV	M455UUR	Mercedes-Benz 811D	Plaxton Beaver	B31F	1995	Sovereign, Stevenage, 2005
2409	SV	M456UUR	Mercedes-Benz 811D	Plaxton Beaver	B31F	1995	Sovereign, Stevenage, 2005
2415	LU	N175DWM	Mercedes-Benz 811D	Plaxton Beaver	B31F	1996	Arriva North West, 2002
2416	AY	N176DWM	Mercedes-Benz 811D	Plaxton Beaver	B31F	1996	Arriva North West, 2002
2417	HA	N177DWM	Mercedes-Benz 811D	Plaxton Beaver	B31F	1996	Arriva North West, 2002
2457	HA	KE04PZF	Optare Solo M880	Optare	N29F	2004	
2458	HA	KE04PZG	Optare Solo M880	Optare	N29F	2004	
2459	HA	KE04OSU	Optare Solo M950	Optare	N33F	2004	
2460	HA	KE04OSV	Optare Solo M950	Optare	N33F	2004	
3079	GR	F151KGS	Volvo B10M-56	Plaxton Derwent II	B54F	1988	Buffalo, Flitwick, 1995
3080	HW	F152KGS	Volvo B10M-56	Plaxton Derwent II	B54F	1988	Buffalo, Flitwick, 1995
3081	GR	F153KGS	Volvo B10M-56	Plaxton Derwent II	B54F	1988	Buffalo, Flitwick, 1995
3085	SV	KE53KBO	TransBus Dart 8.8m	TransBus Mini Pointer	N29F	2003	Sovereign, Stevenage, 2005
3086	SV	KE53KBP	TransBus Dart 8.8m	TransBus Mini Pointer	N29F	2003	Sovereign, Stevenage, 2005
3089	GR	L133HVS	Volvo B10B-58	Alexander Strider	B51F	1993	Buffalo, Flitwick, 1995
3099	AY	K447XPA	Dennis Dart 9.8m	Plaxton Pointer	B40F	1992	Buffalo, Flitwick, 1995
3100	HA	K448XPA	Dennis Dart 9.8m	Plaxton Pointer	B40F	1992	Buffalo, Flitwick, 1995
3101	AY	L460NMJ	Dennis Dart 9.8m	Plaxton Pointer	B40F	1994	Lucky Bus, Watford, 1997
3102	GR	L200BUS	Dennis Dart 9.8m	Plaxton Pointer	B40F	1994	Lucky Bus, Watford, 1997
3103	u	L300BUS	Dennis Dart 9m	Marshall C36	B34F	1994	Lucky Bus, Watford, 1997
3104	AY	L400BUS	Dennis Dart 9m	Marshall C36	B34F	1994	Lucky Bus, Watford, 1997

3105-3136 — Volvo B6-9.9M — Northern Counties Paladin — N40F — 1994

3105	SV	L305HPP	3113	HI	L313HPP	3121	LU	M721OMJ	3129	SV	M729OMJ
3106	SV	L306HPP	3114	HI	L314HPP	3122	LU	M722OMJ	3130	LU	M730OMJ
3107	HW	L307HPP	3115	HW	L315HPP	3123	WR	M723OMJ	3131	LU	M711OMJ
3108	SV	L308HPP	3116	HW	L316HPP	3124	WR	M724OMJ	3132	LU	M712OMJ
3109	SV	L309HPP	3117	AY	M717OMJ	3125	u	M725OMJ	3133	LU	M713OMJ
3110	HW	L310HPP	3118	AY	M718OMJ	3126	HW	M726OMJ	3134	LU	M714OMJ
3111	HI	L311HPP	3119	AY	M719OMJ	3127	HW	M727OMJ	3135	LU	M715OMJ
3112	HI	L312HPP	3120	LU	M720OMJ	3128	SV	M728OMJ	3136	LU	M716OMJ

3137	AY	L43MEH	Volvo B6-9.9M	Plaxton Pointer	B40F	1994	Stevensons, 1994
3138	HW	L922LJO	Volvo B6-9.9M	Northern Counties Paladin	B40F	1994	Yellow Bus, Stoke Mandeville
3139	HW	L923LJO	Volvo B6-9.9M	Northern Counties Paladin	B40F	1994	Yellow Bus, Stoke Mandeville

Transferred with two other liquid petroleum gas (LPG) buses from Scotland to Luton, 3279, T495KGB, is seen on the airport service. The Plaxton Prestige body, here with high-back seating, was the first low-floor body from Plaxton, and was built on the later low-floor variant of the DAF SB220. *Dave Heath*

3143-3149

Scania L113CRL · East Lancs European · N51F · 1995

3143	LU	N693EUR	3145	HW	N695EUR	3147	LU	N697EUR	3149	LU	N699EUR
3144	HW	N694EUR	3146	HW	N696EUR	3148	LU	N698EUR			

3151-3166

Scania L113CRL · East Lancs European · NC47F · 1995

3151	HH	N701EUR	3155	HH	N705EUR	3159	HH	N709EUR	3163	HW	N713EUR
3152	HH	N702EUR	3156	HH	N706EUR	3160	HH	N710EUR	3164	AY	N714EUR
3153	HH	N703EUR	3157	HH	N707EUR	3161	HH	N711EUR	3165	AY	N715EUR
3154	HH	N704EUR	3158	HW	N708EUR	3162	HH	N712EUR	3166	AY	N716EUR

3167	LU	N28KGS	Scania L113CRL	East Lancs European	N51F	1996
3168	LU	N29KGS	Scania L113CRL	East Lancs European	N51F	1996
3169	HW	N31KGS	Scania L113CRL	East Lancs European	N51F	1996
3170	LU	N32KGS	Scania L113CRL	East Lancs European	N51F	1996
3171	HH	P671OPP	Dennis Dart SLF	East Lancs Flyte	N41F	1996
3172	AY	P672OPP	Dennis Dart SLF	East Lancs Flyte	N41F	1996
3173	HH	P673OPP	Dennis Dart SLF	East Lancs Flyte	N41F	1996
3174	SV	P674OPP	Dennis Dart SLF	East Lancs Flyte	N41F	1996

3175-3190

Dennis Dart SLF · Plaxton Pointer · N39F* · 1997 · *3175-8 are N41F

3175	HH	P175SRO	3179	GR	P179SRO	3183	GR	P183SRO	3187	GR	P187SRO
3176	HH	P176SRO	3180	GR	P180SRO	3184	GR	P184SRO	3188	GR	P188SRO
3177	HH	P177SRO	3181	HW	P181SRO	3185	GR	P185SRO	3189	GR	P189SRO
3178	AY	P178SRO	3182	GR	P182SRO	3186	GR	P186SRO	3190	GR	P190SRO

3191-3205

Scania L113CRL · Northern Counties Paladin · N51F* · 1997 · *3196-9,3201-5 are NC47F

3191	LU	R191RBM	3195	LU	R195RBM	3199	LU	R199RBM	3203	AY	R203RBM
3192	LU	R192RBM	3196	SV	R196RBM	3201	HI	R201RBM	3204	AY	R204RBM
3193	LU	R193RBM	3197	SV	R197RBM	3202	HI	R202RBM	3205	AY	R205RBM
3194	LU	R194RBM	3198	LU	R198RBM						

3206-3215 — Dennis Dart SLF — Plaxton Pointer — N31F — 1997-98

3206	GR	R206GMJ	3209	GR	R209GMJ	3212	GR	R212GMJ	3214	GR	R214GMJ
3207	GR	R207GMJ	3210	GR	R210GMJ	3213	GR	R213GMJ	3215	HH	R215GMJ
3208	GR	R208GMJ	3211	GR	R211GMJ						

3216-3229 — Dennis Dart SLF — Plaxton Pointer 2 — N39F* — 1998-98 — *seating varies

3216	HH	S216XPP	3219	SV	T219NMJ	3228	HH	T828NMJ	3229	HH	T829NMJ
3217	HH	S217XPP	3227	SV	T827NMJ						

3230-3239 — Dennis Dart SLF — Plaxton Pointer MPD — N29F — 1999-2000

3230	HA	V230HBH	3233	HH	V233HBH	3236	HH	V236HBH	3238	HH	V238HBH
3231	HA	V231HBH	3234	HH	V234HBH	3237	HH	V237HBH	3239	HH	V239HBH
3232	HH	V232HBH	3235	HH	V235HBH						

3240	SV	P601RGS	Volvo B6LE		Wright Crusader	NC38F	1997	Sovereign, Stevenage, 2005
3241	SV	R602WMJ	Volvo B6LE		Wright Crusader	NC38F	1998	Sovereign, Stevenage, 2005
3242	HW	M842DDS	Volvo B6-9.9		Alexander Dash	B45F	1993	Scotland West, 1998
3243	HW	M843DDS	Volvo B6-9.9		Alexander Dash	B45F	1993	Scotland West, 1998
3244	SV	M844DDS	Volvo B6-9.9		Alexander Dash	B45F	1993	Scotland West, 1998
3245	SV	R603WMJ	Volvo B6LE		Wright Crusader	NC38F	1998	Sovereign, Stevenage, 2005
3248	SV	R604WMJ	Volvo B6LE		Wright Crusader	NC38F	1998	Sovereign, Stevenage, 2005
3249	SV	R605WMJ	Volvo B6LE		Wright Crusader	NC38F	1998	Sovereign, Stevenage, 2005

3250-3260 — Volvo B6BLE — Wright Crusader 2 — N40F* — 1999 — *3258-60 are N33D

3250	HA	V250HBH	3253	HA	V253HBH	3256	HA	V256HBH	3259	GR	V259HBH
3251	HA	V251HBH	3254	HA	V254HBH	3257	HA	V257HBH	3260	GR	V260HBH
3252	HA	V252HBH	3255	HA	V255HBH	3258	GR	V258HBH			

3261-3268 — Volvo B10BLE — Wright Renown — N44F — 1999

3261	LU	V261HBH	3263	LU	V263HBH	3265	LU	V265HBH	3267	LU	V267HBH
3262	LU	V262HBH	3264	LU	V264HBH	3266	LU	V266HBH	3268	LU	V268HBH

3269	WR	T493KGB	DAF SB220 LPG		Plaxton Prestige	N42F	1999	Arriva Scotland West, 2000

3270-3276 — DAF SB220 LPG — Plaxton Prestige — N39F — 1999

3270	GR	V270HBH	3272	GR	V272HBH	3274	GR	V274HBH	3276	GR	V276HBH
3271	GR	V271HBH	3273	GR	V273HBH	3275	GR	V275HBH			

3277	GR	T491KGB	DAF SB220 LPG		Plaxton Prestige	N42F	1999	Arriva Scotland West, 2000
3278	GR	T492KGB	DAF SB220 LPG		Plaxton Prestige	N42F	1999	Arriva Scotland West, 2000
3279	GR	T495KGB	DAF SB220 LPG		Plaxton Prestige	N42F	1999	Arriva Scotland West, 2000

3280-3297 — Dennis Dart SLF — Plaxton Pointer MPD — N29F — 1999-2000

3280	LU	V280HBH	3285	LU	V285HBH	3290	LU	V290HBH	3294	HI	V294HBH
3281	LU	V281HBH	3286	LU	V286HBH	3291	LU	V291HBH	3295	HH	X295MBH
3282	LU	V282HBH	3287	LU	V287HBH	3292	LU	V292HBH	3296	u	X296MBH
3283	LU	V283HBH	3288	LU	V288HBH	3293	HI	V293HBH	3297	u	X297MBH
3284	LU	V284HBH	3289	LU	V289HBH						

3298	SV	R607WMJ	Volvo B6LE		Wright Crusader	NC38F	1998	Sovereign, Stevenage, 2005
3299	SV	R608WMJ	Volvo B6LE		Wright Crusader	NC38F	1998	Sovereign, Stevenage, 2005
3300	SV	R524TWR	Volvo B10BLE		Wright Renown	BC47F	1998	Sovereign, Stevenage, 2005

3301-3310 — Volvo B10BLE — Wright Renown — NC47F — 2000 — Sovereign, Stevenage, 2005

3301	SV	W128XRO	3304	SV	W132XRO	3307	SV	W136XRO	3309	SV	W138XRO
3302	SV	W129XRO	3305	SV	W133XRO	3308	SV	W137XRO	3310	SV	W139XRO
3303	SV	W131XRO	3306	SV	W134XRO						

3311-3314 — Volvo B10BLE — Wright Renown — NC47F — 2002 — Sovereign, Stevenage, 2005

3311	SV	PN02HVS	3312	SV	PN02HVL	3313	SV	PN02HVM	3314	SV	PN02HVO

3321	u	B861XYR	Volvo B10M-61		East Lancashire(1992)	B55F	1985	Grey Green, 1997
3322	SV	PN02HVR	Volvo B10BLE		Wright Renown	NC47F	2002	Sovereign, Stevenage, 2005
3323	SV	PN02HVP	Volvo B10BLE		Wright Renown	NC47F	2002	Sovereign, Stevenage, 2005
3324	u	E564BNK	Volvo B10M-56		Plaxton Derwent II	B54F	1988	Sampsons, Hoddesdon, 1989
3328	u	G621YMG	DAF SB220		Optare Delta	B47F	1992	West's, Woodford Green, 1997
3329	GR	K760JVX	DAF SB220		Optare Delta	B49F	1992	West's, Woodford Green, 1997
3330	SV	M234TBV	Volvo B10M-55		Alexander PS	BC48F	1995	Sovereign, Stevenage, 2005
3331	SV	M782PRS	Volvo B10M-55		Alexander PS	BC48F	1994	Sovereign, Stevenage, 2005
3332	SV	M783PRS	Volvo B10M-55		Alexander PS	BC48F	1994	Sovereign, Stevenage, 2005
3334	HI	L124YVK	Dennis Dart 9m		Northern Counties Paladin	B35F	1994	Arriva London, 2003
3352	HA	J402XVX	Dennis Dart 9.8m		Wright Handybus	B40F	1992	

Luton depot operates all eight of the 1999 Volvo B10BLEs that carry Wright Renown bodywork. Further examples have joined the fleet with the acquisition of Sovereign's routes and depot at Stevenage. Representing the type is 3267, V267HBH, as it heads for Dunstable. *Dave Heath*

3353	HA	J403XVX	Dennis Dart 9.8m			Wright Handybus		B40F	1992	
3354	AY	J404XVX	Dennis Dart 9.8m			Wright Handybus		B40F	1992	

3355-3364			Dennis Dart 9.8m			Plaxton Pointer		B40F	1993	
3355	AY	K405FHJ	**3358**	HA	K408FHJ	**3361**	GR	K411FHJ	**3363**	HA	K413FHJ
3356	HA	K406FHJ	**3359**	HA	K409FHJ	**3362**	HA	K412FHJ	**3364**	HA	K414FHJ
3357	HA	K407FHJ	**3360**	HA	K410FHJ					

3365	HW	L415NHJ	Dennis Dart 9.8m			Wright Handybus		B40F	1994	
3366	HA	J64BJN	Dennis Dart 9m			Wright Handybus		BC40F	1992	West's, Woodford Green, 1997
3367	HA	J65BJN	Dennis Dart 9m			Wright Handybus		B35F	1992	West's, Woodford Green, 1997

3368-3372			Dennis Dart 9m			Plaxton Pointer		B35F	1992	
3368	HA	K318CVX	**3369**	HA	K319CVX	**3371**	HA	K321CVX	**3372**	HA	K322CVX

3374	AY	K761JVX	Dennis Dart 9m	Wright Handybus	B40F	1992	West's, Woodford Green, 1997
3375	u	K762JVX	Dennis Dart 9m	Wright Handybus	B40F	1992	West's, Woodford Green, 1997
3376	u	M266VPU	Dennis Lance SLF	Wright Pathfinder	N40F	1994	
3377	AY	M267VPU	Dennis Lance SLF	Wright Pathfinder	N40F	1994	
3378	AY	M268VPU	Dennis Lance SLF	Wright Pathfinder	N40F	1994	
3385	GR	M951LYR	Dennis Dart 9.8m	Plaxton Pointer	B40F	1995	Grey Green, 1996
3386	HI	P256FPK	Dennis Dart SLF	Plaxton Pointer	N39F	1997	
3398	WR	L118YVK	Dennis Dart 9m	Northern Counties Paladin	B35F	1994	Arriva London, 2003
3399	WR	L119YVK	Dennis Dart 9m	Northern Counties Paladin	B35F	1994	Arriva London, 2003
3413	HA	P833HVX	Dennis Dart 9m	Plaxton Pointer	B34F	1996	
3414	HA	P334HVX	Dennis Dart 9m	Plaxton Pointer	B34F	1996	
3416	WR	R416HVX	Dennis Dart SLF	Wright Crusader	N41F	1998	
3417	WR	R417HVX	Dennis Dart SLF	Wright Crusader	N41F	1998	
3418	WR	R418HVX	Dennis Dart SLF	Wright Crusader	N41F	1998	
3435	WR	R165GNW	Dennis Dart SLF	Wright Crusader	N36F	1997	
3439	WR	R169GNW	Dennis Dart SLF	Wright Crusader	N36F	1997	
3440	WR	R170GNW	Dennis Dart SLF	Wright Crusader	N36F	1997	

Pictured in June 2005 while at Stevenage, 3453, W453XKX, of the Shires fleet is a Volvo B10BLE with Alexander ALX300 bodywork. This body features in the Arriva fleets on sixty-three DAF buses, one MAN and twenty-five other Volvo buses. *Dave Heath*

3441-3449

| | | | | | | | | | | DAF SB220 | | Plaxton Prestige | | NC37F | 1997 |

3441	WR	R201VPU	3444	WR	R204VPU	3446	HA	R206VPU	3448	HA	R208VPU
3442	WR	R202VPU	3445	HA	R205VPU	3447	HA	R207VPU	3449	HA	R209VPU
3443	WR	R203VPU									

3452-3459

Volvo B10BLE   Alexander ALX300   N44F   2000

| 3452 | SV | W452XKX | 3454 | SV | W454XKX | 3458 | SV | W458XKX | 3459 | SV | W459XKX |
| 3453 | SV | W453XKX | 3457 | SV | W457XKX | | | | | | |

3482-3498

Dennis Dart SLF   Plaxton Pointer MPD   N39F   2000

3482	HW	W482YGS	3486	AY	W486YGS	3491	HI	W491YGS	3495	HI	W495YGS
3483	WR	W483YGS	3487	AY	W487YGS	3492	AY	W492YGS	3496	HI	W496YGS
3484	AY	W484YGS	3488	LU	W488YGS	3493	HI	W493YGS	3497	AY	W497YGS
3485	AY	W485YGS	3489	LU	W489YGS	3494	HI	W494YGS	3498	HI	W498YGS

3500	GR	KE51PSZ	Dennis Dart SLF 8.8m	Alexander Pointer MPD	N28F	2001
3501	GR	KE51PTO	Dennis Dart SLF 8.8m	Alexander Pointer MPD	N28F	2001
3502	GR	KE51PTU	Dennis Dart SLF 8.8m	Alexander Pointer MPD	N28F	2001
3509	GR	KE51PTX	Dennis Dart SLF 8.8m	Alexander Pointer MPD	N28F	2001

3601-3619

Scania L94UB   Wrightbus Solar   N43F   2005

3601	-	K	3606	-	K	3611	-	K	3616	-	K
3602	-	K	3607	-	K	3612	-	K	3617	-	K
3603	-	K	3608	-	K	3613	-	K	3618	-	K
3604	-	K	3609	-	K	3614	-	K	3619	-	K
3605	-	K	3610	-	K	3615	-	K			

3701	HW	KE55CKU	VDL Bus SB120	Wrightbus Cadet	N35F	2005	
3702	HW	KE55CKO	VDL Bus SB120	Wrightbus Cadet	N35F	2005	
3703	HW	KE55CKP	VDL Bus SB120	Wrightbus Cadet	N35F	2005	
3806	SV	KC03PGE	TransBus Dart 10.1m	TransBus Pointer	N37F	2003	Sovereign, Stevenage, 2005
3807	SV	KC03PGF	TransBus Dart 10.1m	TransBus Pointer	N37F	2003	Sovereign, Stevenage, 2005
3808	SV	SN54GPK	Alexander Dennis Dart 10.1m	Alexander Dennis Pointer	N37F	2004	Sovereign, Stevenage, 2005
3809	SV	SN54GPO	Alexander Dennis Dart 10.1m	Alexander Dennis Pointer	N37F	2004	Sovereign, Stevenage, 2005
3810	SV	SN54GPU	Alexander Dennis Dart 10.1m	Alexander Dennis Pointer	N37F	2004	Sovereign, Stevenage, 2005

3811-3815	Dennis Dart 8.5m	Wright Handybus	B30F	1991	Wycombe Bus, 2000

3811	HW	G554SGT	**3812**	u	G552SGT	**3814**	u	G570SGT	**3815**	u	JDZ2353

3817-3820	Dennis Dart 8.5m	Wright Handybus	B29F	1991	Wycombe Bus, 2000

3817	u	H367XGC	**3818**	HA	H368XGC	**3819**	AY	H369XGC	**3820**	HW	H370XGC

3821-3827	Dennis Dart SLF	Plaxton Pointer 2	N36F	1996	Wycombe Bus, 2000

3821	HW	N521MJO	**3823**	AY	N523MJO	**3825**	HW	P525YJO	**3827**	HW	P527YJO
3822	HW	N522MJO	**3824**	HW	N524MJO	**3826**	HW	P526YJO			

3828	WR	KE03UKK	TransBus Dart 8.8m	TransBus Mini Pointer	N29F	2003	
3829	AY	KE53NFG	TransBus Dart 8.8m	TransBus Mini Pointer	N29F	2003	
3830	WR	KE04CZF	VDL Bus SB120	Wrightbus Cadet	N35F	2004	
3831	WR	KE04CZG	VDL Bus SB120	Wrightbus Cadet	N35F	2004	
3832	WR	KE04CZH	VDL Bus SB120	Wrightbus Cadet	N35F	2004	
3833	AY	M503VJO	Dennis Dart 9m	Marshall C37	B38F	1995	Wycombe Bus, 2000
3834	AY	M504VJO	Dennis Dart 9m	Marshall C37	B38F	1995	Wycombe Bus, 2000

3835-3839	TransBus Dart 8.8m	TransBus Mini Pointer	N29F	2003-04	

3835	HH	KE53NFD	**3837**	HW	KE53NEU	**3838**	HW	KE53NFA	**3839**	HW	KE53NFC
3836	HH	KE53NFF									

3840	SV	M101UKX	Volvo B10B	Wright Endurance	BC49F	1996	Sovereign, Stevenage, 2005

3841-3844	Volvo B10B	Plaxton Verde	B51F	1995-96	Wycombe Bus, 2000

3841	HW	N621FJO	**3842**	HW	N622FJO	**3843**	HW	N623FJO	**3844**	HW	N624FJO

3845-3848	Volvo B10B	Wright Endurance	BC49F	1995	Sovereign, Stevenage, 2005

3845	SV	M102UKX	**3846**	SV	M103UKX	**3847**	SV	M104UKX	**3848**	SV	M105UKX

3849-3852	Volvo B10B	Wright Endurance	BC49F	1997	Sovereign, Stevenage, 2005

3849	SV	R369TWR	**3850**	SV	R370TWR	**3851**	SV	R371TWR	**3852**	SV	R372TWR

3853-3855	Volvo B10B	Plaxton Verde	B51F	1995-96	Wycombe Bus, 2000

3853	HW	N415NRG	**3854**	HW	N414NRG	**3855**	HW	N415NRG

3856-3867	Volvo B7RLE	Wrightbus Eclipse Urban	N43F	2005	

3856	HA	KE54LNR	**3859**	HA	KE54LPJ	**3862**	HW	KE05FMV	**3865**	HW	KE05FMP
3857	HA	KE54LPC	**3860**	HA	KE54HHF	**3863**	HW	KE05GOH	**3866**	HW	KE05FMO
3858	HA	KE54LPF	**3861**	HW	KE05FMX	**3864**	HW	KE05FMU	**3867**	HW	KE05FMM

During 2005 Wrightbus bodies are being supplied on both Volvo and Scania chassis for Arriva The Shires. One of the first to arrive was Volvo 3863, KE05MFU, seen here on 'green' route 31. *Mark Lyons*

4001-4006 DAF SB4000 Van Hool T9 Alizée C53F 2005

4001	-	-	4003	-	-	4005	-	-	4006	-	-
4002	-	-	4004	-	-						

4012	SV	P316RGS	Volvo B10M-62	Plaxton Première 320	C53F	1996	Sovereign, Stevenage, 2005
4013	SV	P317RGS	Volvo B10M-62	Plaxton Première 320	C53F	1996	Sovereign, Stevenage, 2005
4014	LU	P318RGS	Volvo B10M-62	Plaxton Première 320	C53F	1996	Sovereign, Stevenage, 2005
4015	GR	HIL7595	Volvo B10M-61	Plaxton Paramount 3500 III	C53F	1988	Moor-Dale, 1994
4016	GR	SIB4846	Leyland Tiger TRCTL11/3ARZA	Plaxton Paramount 3200 III	C53F	1988	London Country NW, 1990
4020	u	SIB7480	Leyland Tiger TRCTL11/3ARZA	Plaxton Paramount 3200 III	C51F	1988	London Country NW, 1990
4023	GR	E323OMG	Leyland Tiger TRCTL11/3ARZA	Plaxton Paramount 3200 III	C53F	1988	London Country NW, 1990
4025	u	SIB8529	Leyland Tiger TRCTL11/3ARZA	Plaxton Paramount 3500 III	C51FT	1988	London Country NW, 1990
4026	GR	SIB7481	Leyland Tiger TRCTL11/3ARZA	Plaxton Paramount 3500 III	C51FT	1988	London Country NW, 1990
4028	GR	MIL2350	Dennis Javelin 12m	Duple 320	C57F	1990	Lucky Bus, Watford, 1997
4029	SV	M101CCD	Dennis Javelin 11m	Plaxton Première Interurban	BC49F	1994	Sovereign, Stevenage, 2005
4030	SV	L105SDY	Dennis Javelin 11m	Plaxton Première Interurban	BC47F	1994	Sovereign, Stevenage, 2005
4031	SV	L149BFV	Dennis Javelin 11m	Plaxton Première Interurban	BC49F	1993	Sovereign, Stevenage, 2005
4032	SV	L159CCW	Dennis Javelin 11m	Plaxton Première Interurban	BC47F	1993	Sovereign, Stevenage, 2005
4035	GR	H199AOD	Volvo B10M-60	Plaxton Expressliner	C46FT	1996	Trathens, Plymouth, 1996
4037	GR	P100LOW	Dennis Javelin 11m	UVG Unistar	C55FTL	1996	Lucky Bus, Watford, 1997
4040	u	YIB2396	Volvo B10M-61	Plaxton Paramount 3200 II	C53F	1986	Checker, Garston, 1997
4041	SV	KE51WUO	Volvo B10M-62	Plaxton Première 350	C53F	2001	Sovereign, Stevenage, 2005
4042	SV	KE51WUP	Volvo B10M-62	Plaxton Première 350	C53F	2001	Sovereign, Stevenage, 2005
4043	GR	YIB2397	Leyland Tiger TRCTL11/3RZ	Duple 320	C57F	1987	Checker, Garston, 1997

4047-4054 DAF SB3000 Plaxton Prima Interurban C53F 1997

4047	HH	R447SKX	4049	HH	R449SKX	4051	LU	R451SKX	4053	LU	R453SKX
4048	HH	R448SKX	4050	LU	R450SKX	4052	LU	R452SKX	4054	LU	R454SKX

4057-4063 DAF SB3000 Van Hool Alizée HE C53F* 1994-95 London North East, 1998
*4057/8 are C51F

4057	HH	M947LYR	4059	GR	M942LYR	4061	HH	M949LYR	4063	HH	M943LYR
4058	HH	M946LYR	4060	HH	M948LYR						

4064	LU	P201RWR	DAF DE33WSSB3000	Van Hool Alizée	C51FT	1997	First Edinburgh, 2001

4325-4333 Volvo B10M-60 Plaxton Paramount 3200 III C53F 1989-91 Express Travel, 1995

4325	u	F425UVW	4327	u	F467UVW	4332	u	H567MPD	4333	u	H845AHS

4352	GR	M52AWW	Scania K113CRB	Van Hool Alizée	C44FT	1995	Arriva Southern Counties, 2004
4353	GR	M53AWW	Scania K113CRB	Van Hool Alizée	C51F	1995	Arriva Southern Counties, 2004

4359-4369 DAF SB3000 Plaxton Prima Interurban C53F 2000

4359	LU	W359XKX	4363	LU	W363XKX	4366	LU	W366XKX	4368	LU	W368XKX
4361	LU	W361XKX	4364	LU	W364XKX	4367	LU	W367XKX	4369	LU	W369XKX
4362	LU	W362XKX	4365	LU	W365XKX						

4370	GR	D196WJC	Leyland Tiger TRCTL11/3RZ	Plaxton Paramount 3200 II	C49F	1987	Arriva North West & Wales, 2004
4371	GR	J26UNY	Leyland Tiger TRCL10/3ARZM	Plaxton 321	C53F	1992	Arriva Southern Counties, 2004
4400	GR	H616UWR	Volvo B10M-60	Plaxton Paramount 3500 III	C50F	1991	Arriva Southern Counties, 2002
4426	GR	S426MCC	DAF SB220	Plaxton Prestige	N42F	1999	Arriva North West, 2003
4427	GR	S427MCC	DAF SB220	Plaxton Prestige	N42F	1999	Arriva North West, 2003
4428	GR	S428MCC	DAF SB220	Plaxton Prestige	N42F	1999	Arriva Southern Counties, 2005
4429	GR	S429MCC	DAF SB220	Plaxton Prestige	N42F	1999	Arriva North West, 2003
4490	GR	T490KGB	DAF SB220	Plaxton Prestige	N42F	1999	Arriva Scotland, 2002
4491	GR	T494KGB	DAF SB220	Plaxton Prestige	N42F	1999	Arriva Scotland, 2002

4514-4518 DAF SB120 9.4m Wrightbus Cadet N35F 2002

4514	GR	KE51PVF	4516	SV	KE51PVK	4517	SV	KL52CWJ	4518	SV	KL52CWK
4515	GR	KE51PVZ									

4519-4525 VDL Bus SB120 9.4m Wrightbus Cadet N35F 2003

4519	HI	KE03OUN	4521	WR	KE03OUS	4523	HH	KE03OUK	4525	HI	KE03OUM
4520	HI	KE03OUP	4522	WR	KE03OUU	4524	HH	KE03OUL			

Buses allocated to the Shires route 280, which links Aylesbury with Oxford through Thame and Wheatley, carry a special livery comprising more than route branding. Dedicated buses are Olympians with Northern Counties Palatine II bodywork featuring high-back seating. Pictured here is 5158, S158KNK. *Dave Heath*

5000	LU	BKE847T	Bristol VRT/SL3/6LXB	Eastern Coach Works	B43/31F	1979	Maidstone & District, 1997
5033	LU	SNV933W	Bristol VRT/SL3/6LXB	Eastern Coach Works	B43/31F	1980	United Counties, 1986

5084-5094			Leyland Olympian ONCL10/1RZ	Alexander RL	B47/32F*	1988	*5091 is BC47/29F

5084	LU	F634LMJ	5089	LU	F639LMJ	5091	LU	F641LMJ	5093	LU	F643LMJ
5086	LU	F636LMJ	5090	LU	F640LMJ	5092	LU	F642LMJ	5094	LU	F644LMJ
5087	LU	F637LMJ									

5095-5107			Leyland Olympian ON2R50C13Z4	Alexander RL	B47/32F	1989-90	*5104 is BC47/29F 5099-5103 are B47/34F

5095	LU	G645UPP	5099	AY	G649UPP	5102	AY	G652UPP	5105	LU	G655UPP
5096	LU	G646UPP	5100	AY	G650UPP	5103	AY	G653UPP	5106	LU	G656UPP
5097	AY	G647UPP	5101	AY	G651UPP	5104	AY	G654UPP	5107	LU	G657UPP
5098	LU	G648UPP									

5108	HW	F506OYW	Leyland Olympian ONTL11/1RH	Northern Counties	B47/30F	1988	Yellow Bus, Stoke Mandeville
5109	HW	G129YEV	Leyland Olympian ONCL10/2RZ	Northern Counties	B49/33F	1989	London Country NW, 1990
5110	HW	G130YEV	Leyland Olympian ONCL10/2RZ	Northern Counties	B49/33F	1989	London Country NW, 1990

5113-5124			Leyland Olympian ONCL10/1RZ	Leyland	B47/31F	1989-90	London Country NW, 1990

5113	GR	G283UMJ	5118	GR	G288UMJ	5121	AY	G291UMJ	5123	GR	G293UMJ
5116	GR	G286UMJ	5120	HW	G290UMJ	5122	HW	G292UMJ	5124	AY	G294UMJ
5117	AY	G287UMJ									

5126	HH	H196GRO	Leyland Olympian ON2R50C13Z4	Leyland	B47/31F	1991	
5127	HH	H197GRO	Leyland Olympian ON2R50C13Z4	Leyland	B47/31F	1991	
5128	HH	H198GRO	Leyland Olympian ON2R50C13Z4	Leyland	B47/31F	1991	
5130	HW	F747XCS	Leyland Olympian ONCL10/1RZ	Alexander RL	B47/32F	1989	A1 Service (McMenemy), 1995
5132	HW	H202GRO	Leyland Olympian ON2R50C13Z4	Leyland	B47/31F	1991	
5133	HW	H203GRO	Leyland Olympian ON2R50C13Z4	Leyland	B47/31F	1991	
5134	HW	G131YWC	Leyland Olympian ONCL10/2RZ	Northern Counties	B49/33F	1989	Ensign, Purfleet, 1991
5135	HW	G132YWC	Leyland Olympian ONCL10/2RZ	Northern Counties	B49/33F	1989	London Country NW, 1990

5136-5145 — Volvo Olympian YN2RV18Z4 — Northern Counties Palatine — B47/30F — 1996

5136	LU	N36JPP	5139	LU	N39JPP	5142	LU	N42JPP	5144	HW	N35JPP
5137	LU	N37JPP	5140	LU	N46JPP	5143	LU	N43JPP	5145	HW	N45JPP
5138	LU	N38JPP	5141	LU	N41JPP						

5146-5161 — Volvo Olympian — Northern Counties Palatine II — BC39/29F — 1998

5146	GR	S146KNK	5150	GR	S150KNK	5154	GR	S154KNK	5159	AY	S159KNK
5147	HH	S147KNK	5151	GR	S151KNK	5156	AY	S156KNK	5160	AY	S160KNK
5148	HH	S148KNK	5152	HH	S152KNK	5157	AY	S157KNK	5161	AY	S161KNK
5149	GR	S149KNK	5153	GR	S153KNK	5158	AY	S158KNK			

5165	LU	EWW544Y	Leyland Olympian ONLXB/1R	Eastern Coach Works	B45/32F	1983	Arriva Yorkshire, 1998
5170	LU	B605UUM	Leyland Olympian ONLXB/1R	Eastern Coach Works	B45/32F	1983	Arriva Yorkshire, 1998
5171	LU	CWR524Y	Leyland Olympian ONLXB/1R	Eastern Coach Works	B45/32F	1983	Arriva Yorkshire, 2004
5381	LU	MUH281X	Leyland Olympian ONLXB/1R	Eastern Coach Works	B45/32F	1982	Rhondda, 1992

5421-5433 — Dennis Trident — Alexander ALX400 — N47/31F — 2000

5421	LU	W421XKX	5424	LU	W424XKX	5427	LU	W427XKX	5431	LU	W431XKX
5422	LU	W422XKX	5425	LU	W425XKX	5428	LU	W428XKX	5432	LU	W432XKX
5423	LU	W423XKX	5426	LU	W426XKX	5429	LU	W429XKX	5433	LU	W433XKX

5442-5451 — Dennis Trident — Alexander ALX400 — N47/31F — 2000 — Arriva Southern Counties, 2005

5442	WR	W442XKX	5445	WR	W445XKX	5447	WR	W447XKX	5451	WR	W451XKX
5443	WR	W443XKX	5446	WR	W446XKX						

5826	AY	E226CFC	Leyland Olympian ONLXB/1RH	Alexander RH	B47/26D	1988	Wycombe Bus, 2000

5830-5835 — Leyland Olympian ON2R50G16Z4 — Alexander RH — B47/29F — 1990 — Wycombe Bus, 2000

5830	AY	G230VWL	5832	AY	G232VWL	5834	AY	G234VWL	5835	LU	G235VWL
5831	LU	G231VWL									

5836-5856 — Leyland Olympian ONLXB/1RH — Eastern Coach Works — B42/26D — 1986-87 — Arriva London, 2003

5836	AY	WLT916	5841	WR	D203FYM	5846	WR	D240FYM	5853	HW	D166FYM
5837	WR	D187FYM	5842	WR	D146FYM	5847	WR	D224FYM	5854	u	D167FYM
5838	WR	C38CHM	5843	u	D242FYM	5849	HW	C31CHM	5855	u	D168FYM
5839	WR	D181FYM	5844	HW	D211FYM	5850	WR	C59CHM	5856	u	D169FYM
5840	WR	D215FYM	5845	WR	D231FYM	5851	WR	C36CHM			

5866	LU	FKM866V	Bristol VRT/SL3/6LXB	Eastern Coach Works	B43/31F	1979	Maidstone & District, 1997

Former London Buses Olympians with Eastern Coach Works bodies operate with several of the Arriva fleets. One recently photographed in High Wycombe, while heading for Maidenhead, was 5853, D166FYM.
Dave Heath

DAF DB250   Alexander ALX400   N45/20D   2002-03

6000	GR	KL52CWN	6007	GR	KL52CWW	6013	GR	KL52CXE	6019	GR	KL52CXM
6001	GR	KL52CWO	6008	GR	KL52CWZ	6014	GR	KL52CXF	6020	GR	KL52CXN
6002	GR	KL52CWP	6009	GR	KL52CXA	6015	GR	KL52CXG	6021	GR	KL52CXO
6003	GR	KL52CWR	6010	GR	KL52CXB	6016	GR	KL52CXH	6022	GR	KL52CXP
6004	GR	KL52CWT	6011	GR	KL52CXC	6017	GR	KL52CXJ	6023	GR	KL52CXR
6005	GR	KL52CWU	6012	GR	KL52CXD	6018	GR	KL52CXK	6024	GR	KL52CXS
6006	GR	KL52CWV								

6025	GR	YJ54CFG	DAF DB250	Alexander ALX400	N45/20D	2005

Special event vehicle:

5301	LU	JHK495N	Leyland Atlantean AN68/1R	Eastern Coach Works	O43/31F	1975

Ancillary vehicles:

1251	GR	P137MTU	LDV Convoy	LDV		Staff	1996
1252	GR	P697UFR	LDV Convoy	LDV		Staff	1996
2070	GR	J65UNA	Mercedes-Benz 709D	Reeve Burgess Beaver	TV	1992	South Lancashire, 1996
2108	AY	M38WUR	Mercedes-Benz 811D	Plaxton Beaver	BC31F	1995	
2235	GR	N935ETU	Iveco TurboDaily 59-12	Mellor	TV	1995	Cymru, 1998
2236	u	N936ETU	Iveco TurboDaily 59-12	Mellor	TV	1995	Cymru, 1998
2346	GR	M726UTW	Iveco TurboDaily 59.12	Marshall C31	TV	1994	
3067	u	H407ERO	Leyland Lynx LX2R11C15Z4S	Leyland Lynx	TV	1990	
3074	LU	F404PUR	Leyland Lynx LX112L10ZR1R	Leyland Lynx	TV	1989	
3087	GR	G97VMM	Leyland Swift LBM6T/2RS	Wadham Stringer Vanguard II	TV	1989	London Country NW, 199
3315	GR	A855UYM	Volvo B10M-61	East Lancs (1992)	TV	1984	Grey Green, 1997
3316	GR	A856UYM	Volvo B10M-61	East Lancs (1992)	TV	1984	Grey Green, 1997
3325	LU	E565BNK	Volvo B10M-56	Plaxton Derwent II	TV	1988	Sampsons, Hoddesdon, 1989
3344	GR	H254GEV	Leyland Lynx LX2R11C15Z4S	Leyland Lynx	B49F	1990	
4036	GR	L500BUS	Iveco 480-10-21	Wadham Stringer	TV	1995	Lucky Bus, Watford, 1997
4038	GR	ADZ4731	Volvo B10M-56	Plaxton Viewmaster IV Exp	TV	1982	
4039	GR	WIB1113	Volvo B10M-61	Plaxton Paramount 3200 II	TV	1985	Checker, Garston, 1997
5073	GR	A153FPG	Leyland Olympian ONTL11/1R	Roe	TV	1984	London Country NW, 1990
5380	GR	TPD110X	Leyland Olympian ONTL11/1R	Roe	TV	1982	
5889	GR	A889PKR	Leyland Olympian ONLXB/1R	Eastern Coach Works	TV	1984	

Previous registrations:

ADZ4731	KNP3X	J64BJN	J9BUS
815DYE	D900STU, NEY819, D196WJC	J65BJN	J6BUS
D215FYM	D215FYM, B15DYE	J65UNA	J59MHF, J6SLT
EWW544Y	EWW544Y, 544WRA	K760JVX	K5BUS
F425UVW	F449PSL, NXI9004	K761JUX	K2BUS
F467UVW	F450PSL, NXI9005	L500BUS	M289OUR
G552SGT	JDZ2346, WLT346	MIL2350	G171BLH
G554SGT	JDZ2345, 545CLT	SIB4846	E321OMG
G621YMG	G259EHO, A10BUS	SIB7481	E326OMG
H350PNO	H550AMT, A19BUS, H20BUS	WIB1113	B504CGP
H567MPD	H842AHS, NXI9001	WLT916	C816BYY
HIL7595	E663UNE	YIB2397	D296RKW

Allocations

Aylesbury (Smeaton Close, Brunel Park) - AY

Outstation - Leighton Buzzard

Alero	454	455	456				
Mercedes-Benz	2127	2173	2176	2240	2244	2247	2416
Optare Solo	446	447	448	449			
Dart	3099	3101	3104	3172	3178	3354	3374	3355
	3484	3485	3486	3487	3492	3497	3819	3823
	3829	3833	3834					
Volvo B6	3117	3118	3119	3137			
Lance	3377	3378					
Scania sd	3164	3165	3166	3203	3204	3205	
Olympian	5097	5099	5100	5101	5102	5103	5104	5117
	5121	5124	5156	5157	5158	5159	5160	5161
	5826	5830	5832	5834	5836			
Ancillary	2108						

The 2005-2006 Arriva Bus Handbook   **95**

Harlow (Fourth Avenue) - HA

Outstation - Langston Road, Debden

Mercedes-Benz Vito	1258						
Optare Alero	443	444					
Mercedes-Benz	2116	2118	2119	2120	2121	2122	2123	2124
	2126	2143	2145	2149	2151	2158	2159	2172
	2175	2177	2189	2190	2194	2195	2248	2370
	2371	2417						
Solo	2457	2458	2459	2460				
Dart	3100	3230	3231	3352	3353	3356	3357	
	3358	3359	3360	3362	3363	3364	3366	3367
	3368	3369	3371	3372	3413	3414		
	3818							
Volvo B6	3250	3251	3252	3253	3254	3255	3256	3257
Volvo B7RLE	3856	3857	3858	3859	3860			
DAF Prestige	3445	3446	3447	3448	3449			

Hemel Hempstead (Whiteleaf Road) - HH

Mercedes-Benz	2178	2179	2180	2181	2182	2183	2184	2185
	2241	2242	2246	2249				
Dart	3171	3173	3175	3176	3177	3215	3216	3217
	3228	3229	3232	3233	3234	3235	3236	3237
	3238	3239	3295	3835	3836			
DAF Cadet	4523	4524						
Scania sd	3151	3152	3153	3154	3155	3156	3157	3159
	3160	3161	3162					
DAF coach	4057	4058	4059	4060	4061	4063		
DAF Prima	4047	4048	4049					
Olympian	5126	5127	5128	5147	5148	5152		

Not all the buses on the Two-eighty are in route colours. Pictured in Oxford's St Clements, Alexander-bodied Olympian 5830, G230WVL which joined the fleet from Wycombe Bus, is seen heading for the city centre.
Mark Lyons

High Wycombe (Newlands bus station) - HW

Outstation: Old Amersham

Mercedes-Benz	2171	2196	2197	2198			
Solo	442						
Dart	3181	3365	3482	3811	3820	3821	3822	3824
	3825	3826	3827	3837	3838	3839		
Volvo B6	3107	3110	3115	3116	3126	3127	3138	3139
	3242							
SB120 Cadet	3701	3702	3703					
Volvo B10M bus	3080							
Volvo B10B	3841	3842	3843	3844	3853	3854	3855	
Scania sd	3144	3145	3146	3158	3163	3169		
Volvo B7RLE	3861	3862	3863	3864	3865	3866	3867	
Olympian	5108	5109	5110	5120	5122	5130	5132	5133
	5134	5135	5144	5145	5844	5849	5851	
	5853							

Hitchin (Fishponds Road) - HI

Outstation: Norton Green Road, Stevenage

Mercedes-Benz	2107	2113	2153	2154	2155	2156	2157	2160
	2161	2162						
Dart	3293	3294	3334	3386	3491	3493	3494	
Volvo B6	3111	3112	3113	3114				
DAF Cadet	4519	4520	4525					
Scania sd	3201	3202						

The long-established Green Line name associated with the longer commuting services of London Transport is now owned by Arriva, and continues to be used on a selection or services. Seen operating route 757 between Luton Airport and central London is 4054, R454SKX. This is one of the express service buses based on the Plaxton Prima body and marketed as Interurbans. *Mark Lyons*

Having entered The Shires fleet along with the Wycombe Bus operation, Dart 3819, H369XGC, is now one of a reducing number of older Wright-bodied Darts in the fleet. *Dave Heath*

Luton (Dunstable Road) - LU

Mercedes-Benz	2128	2129	2131	2132	2133	2136	2415	
Dart	3280	3281	3282	3283	3284	3285	3286	3287
	3288	3289	3290	3291	3292	3488	3489	
Volvo B6	3120	3121	3122	3130	3131	3132	3133	3134
	3135	3136						
DAF suburban	4050	4051	4052	4053	4054	4064	4359	4361
	4362	4363	4364	4365	4366	4367	4368	4369
Scania sd	3143	3147	3148	3149	3167	3168	3170	3191
	3192	3193	3194	3195	3198	3199		
Volvo B10M bus	4014							
Volvo B10BLE	3261	3262	3263	3264	3265	3266	3267	3268
Bristol VR	5000	5033	5866					
Olympian	5084	5086	5087	5091	5093	5094	5095	5096
	5098	5105	5106	5107	5136	5137	5138	5139
	5140	5141	5142	5143	5165	5170	5831	5381
	5835							
Trident	5421	5422	5423	5424	5425	5426	5427	5428
	5429	5431	5432	5433				
Ancillary	3074	3325						

Stevenage (Babbage Road) - SV

Mercedes-Benz	2113	2139	2142	2148	2150	2408	2409	
Dart	3085	3086	3174	3219	3227	3294	3495	3496
	3498	3806	3807	3808	3809	3810		
Volvo B6	3105	3106	3108	3109	3128	3129	3240	3241
	3244	3245	3248	3249	3298	3299		
SB120	4516	4517	4518					
Volvo B10M coach	4012	4013	4041	4042				
Javelin coach	4029	4030	4031	4032				
Volvo B10M bus	3330	3331	3332					
Scania L113	3196	3197						
Volvo B10B	3840	3845	3846	3847	3848	3849	3850	3851
	3852							
Volvo B10BLE	3300	3301	3302	3303	3304	3306	3307	3308
	3309	3310	3311	3312	3313	3314	3322	3323
	3330	3452	3453	3454	3458	3459		

Ware (Marsh Lane) - WR

Outstation - Pindar Road, Hoddesdon

Mercedes-Benz	2373	2374	2375	2376	2377			
Volvo B6	2123	3124						
Dart	3352	3398	3399	3416	3417	3418	3428	3435
	3439	3440	3483	3828				
SB120 Cadet	3830	3831	3832	4521	4522			
DAF SB220	3269	3441	3442	3443	3444			
Olympian	5837	5838	5839	5840	5842	5845	5846	5847
	5850							
Trident	5442	5443	5445	5446	5447	5451		

Watford (St Albans Road, Garston) - GR - includes private hire fleet and Dial a Ride

Mercedes-Benz	245	246	256	257	258	259	262	263
	264	265	266	267	268	2166		
Dart	3102	3179	3180	3182	3183	3184	3185	3186
	3187	3188	3189	3190	3206	3207	3208	3209
	3210	3211	3212	3213	3214	3361	3385	3500
	3501	3502	3509					
Volvo B6	3258	3259	3260					
DAF Cadet	4514							
Volvo B10M bus	3081	3089	3321	3324				
DAF SB220	3270	3271	3272	3273	3274	3275	3276	3277
	3278	3279	3328	3329	4426	4427	4428	4429
	4490	4491						
DAF coach	4059							
Volvo B10M coach	4015	4035	4400					
Tiger coach	4016	4020	4023	4026	4043	4370	4371	
Javelin coach	4028	4037						
Scania coach	4352	4353						
Olympian	5113	5116	5118	5123	5146	5149	5150	5151
	5153	5154						
DAF President	6000	6001	6002	6003	6004	6005	6006	6007
	6008	6009	6010	6011	6012	6013	6014	6015
	6016	6017	6018	6019	6020	6021	6022	6023
	6024	6025						
Ancillary	1251	1252	2346	3087	3315	3316	3344	4036
	4038	4039	5073	5380	5889			

Unallocated and stored

Remainder

ARRIVA LONDON

Arriva London North Ltd, 16 Watsons Road, Wood Green, London, N22 4TZ
Arriva London South Ltd, Croydon Bus Garage, Brighton Road, South Croydon, CR2 6EL

ADL1	DX	V701LWT			Dennis Dart SLF 10.2m			Alexander ALX200		N27D	1999	

ADL2-8

Dennis Dart SLF 10.2m — Alexander ALX200 — N30D — 2000

2	EC	W602VGJ	4	EC	W604VGJ	6	EC	W606VGJ	8	EC	W608VGJ
3	EC	W603VGJ	5	EC	W605VGJ	7	EC	W607VGJ			

ADL9-23

Dennis Dart SLF 10.8m — Alexander ALX200 — N33D — 1999

9	TC	V609LGC	13	TC	V613LGC	17	TC	V617LGC	21	TC	V621LGC
10	TC	V610LGC	14	TC	V614LGC	18	TC	V618LGC	22	TC	V622LGC
11	TC	V611LGC	15	TC	V615LGC	19	TC	V619LGC	23	TC	V623LGC
12	TC	V612LGC	16	TC	V616LGC	20	TC	V620LGC			

ADL61-81

Dennis Dart SLF 9.4m — Alexander ALX200 — N26D — 2000 — Arriva The Shires, 2005

61	EC	W461XKX	66	EC	W466XKX	72	EC	W472XKX	77	EC	W477XKX
62	EC	W462XKX	67	EC	W467XKX	73	EC	W473XKX	78	EC	W478XKX
63	EC	W463XKX	68	EC	W468XKX	74	EC	W474XKX	79	EC	W479XKX
64	EC	W464XKX	69	EC	W469XKX	75	EC	W475XKX	81	EC	W481XKX
65	EC	W465XKX	71	EC	W471XKX	76	EC	W476XKX			

ADL969-983

Dennis Dart SLF 10.2m — Alexander ALX200 — N27D — 1998

969	DX	S169JUA	973	DX	S173JUA	977	DX	S177JUA	981	DX	S181JUA
970	DX	S170JUA	974	DX	S174JUA	978	DX	S178JUA	982	DX	S182JUA
971	DX	S171JUA	975	DX	S175JUA	979	DX	S179JUA	983	DX	S183JUA
972	DX	S172JUA	976	DX	S176JUA	980	DX	S180JUA			

CW1	WN	W218CDN	DAF SB120 10.2m		Wright Cadet		N31D	2000			

The first Wright Cadet with Arriva London is dual-doored CW1, W218CDN, seen at Arnos Grove. After this the manufacturer was re-named Wrightbus and further Cadets arrived as DWL/DWS classes. *Colin Lloyd*

The ALD class comprises Alexander-bodied Darts that feature the ALX200 styling. Pictured in Croydon, ALD15, V615LGC, is one of the 10.8 metre examples from 1999. *Gerry Mead*

DDL1-18

DDL1-18			Dennis Dart SLF 10.1m			Plaxton Pointer 2		N26D	1998		
1	TH	S301JUA	6	TH	S306JUA	11	TH	S311JUA	15	EC	S315JUA
2	TH	S302JUA	7	TH	S307JUA	12	TH	S312JUA	16	DX	S316JUA
3	TH	S303JUA	8	TH	S308JUA	13	TH	S313JUA	17	DX	S317JUA
4	TH	S304JUA	9	TH	S309JUA	14	TH	S314JUA	18	DX	S318JUA
5	TH	S305JUA	10	TH	S310JUA						

DI4	EC	480CLT	DAF SB3000	Ikarus Blue Danube 396	C53F	1997	Arriva E Herts & Essex, 1998
DI7	EC	593CLT	DAF SB3000	Ikarus Blue Danube 396	C49FT	1999	Teamdeck, Honley, 2004

DLA1-64

DLA1-64			DAF DB250 10.6m			Alexander ALX400		N45/21D	1998-99		
1	WN	R101GNW	17	CT	S217JUA	33	WN	S233JUA	49	TH	S249JUA
2	TH	S202JUA	18	CT	S218JUA	34	WN	S234JUA	50	TH	S250JUA
3	TH	S203JUA	19	CT	S219JUA	35	WN	S235JUA	51	TH	S251JUA
4	TH	S204JUA	20	CT	S220JUA	36	WN	S236JUA	52	TH	S252JUA
5	TH	S205JUA	21	CT	S221JUA	37	WN	S237JUA	53	TH	S253JUA
6	TH	S206JUA	22	WN	S322JUA	38	TH	S238JUA	54	TH	S254JUA
7	TH	S207JUA	23	WN	S223JUA	39	TH	S239JUA	55	TH	S255JUA
8	TH	S208JUA	24	WN	S224JUA	40	TH	S240JUA	56	TH	S256JUA
9	TH	S209JUA	25	WN	S225JUA	41	TH	S241JUA	57	TH	S257JUA
10	TH	S210JUA	26	WN	S226JUA	42	TH	S242JUA	58	TH	S258JUA
11	CT	S211JUA	27	WN	S227JUA	43	TH	S243JUA	59	TH	S259JUA
12	CT	S212JUA	28	WN	S228JUA	44	TH	S244JUA	60	TH	S260JUA
13	CT	S213JUA	29	WN	S229JUA	45	WN	S245JUA	61	TH	S261JUA
14	CT	S214JUA	30	WN	S230JUA	46	WN	S246JUA	62	TH	S262JUA
15	CT	S215JUA	31	WN	S231JUA	47	WN	S247JUA	63	TH	S263JUA
16	CT	S216JUA	32	WN	S232JUA	48	TH	S248JUA	64	TH	S264JUA

DLA65-92

DLA65-92			DAF DB250 10.6m			Alexander ALX400		N45/10D	1999		
65	WN	S265JUA	72	WN	S272JUA	79	WN	S279JUA	86	WN	S286JUA
66	WN	S266JUA	73	WN	S273JUA	80	WN	S280JUA	87	WN	S287JUA
67	WN	S267JUA	74	WN	S274JUA	81	WN	S281JUA	88	WN	S288JUA
68	WN	S268JUA	75	WN	S275JUA	82	WN	S282JUA	89	WN	S289JUA
69	WN	S269JUA	76	WN	S276JUA	83	WN	S283JUA	90	WN	S290JUA
70	WN	S270JUA	77	WN	S277JUA	84	WN	S284JUA	91	WN	S291JUA
71	WN	S271JUA	78	WN	S278JUA	85	WN	S285JUA	92	WN	S292JUA

DLA93-125   DAF DB250 10.6m   Alexander ALX400   N45/19D*   1999   *DLA124/5 are N45/17D

93	WN	T293FGN	102	SF	T302FGN	110	SF	T310FGN	118	E	T318FGN
94	E	T294FGN	103	SF	T303FGN	111	SF	T311FGN	119	E	T319FGN
95	E	T295FGN	104	SF	T304FGN	112	SF	T312FGN	120	E	T320FGN
96	SF	T296FGN	105	SF	T305FGN	113	SF	T313FGN	121	E	T421GGO
97	SF	T297FGN	106	SF	T306FGN	114	SF	T314FGN	122	E	T322FGN
98	SF	T298FGN	107	SF	T307FGN	115	SF	T315FGN	123	E	T323FGN
99	SF	T299FGN	108	SF	T308FGN	116	E	T316FGN	124	WN	T324FGN
100	SF	T110GGO	109	SF	T309FGN	117	E	T317FGN	125	EC	T325FGN
101	SF	T301FGN									

DLA126-189   DAF DB250 10.2m   Alexander ALX400   N43/21D*   2000   *seating varies

126	TH	V326DGT	142	BN	V342DGT	159	BN	V359DGT	175	TC	W432WGJ
127	TH	V327DGT	143	BN	V343DGT	160	BN	V660LGC	176	TC	W376VGJ
128	TH	V628LGC	144	BN	V344DGT	161	BN	V361DGT	177	TC	W377VGJ
129	TH	V329DGT	145	BN	V345DGT	162	BN	V362DGT	178	TC	W378VGJ
130	TH	V330DGT	146	BN	V346DGT	163	BN	V363DGT	179	TC	W379VGJ
131	TH	V331DGT	147	BN	V347DGT	164	BN	V364DGT	180	TC	W433WGJ
132	TH	V332DGT	148	BN	V348DGT	165	BN	V365DGT	181	TC	W381VGJ
133	TC	V633LGC	149	BN	V349DGT	166	N	W366VGJ	182	TC	W382VGJ
134	TC	V334DGT	150	BN	V650LGC	167	N	W367VGJ	183	TC	W383VGJ
135	TC	V335DGT	151	BN	V351DGT	168	N	W368VGJ	184	TC	W384VGJ
136	TC	V336DGT	152	BN	V352DGT	169	N	W369VGJ	185	TC	W385VGJ
137	EC	V337DGT	153	BN	V353DGT	170	N	W431WGJ	186	TC	W386VGJ
138	EC	V338DGT	154	TC	V354DGT	171	TC	W371VGJ	187	TC	W387VGJ
139	EC	V339DGT	155	TC	V355DGT	172	TC	W372VGJ	188	TC	W388VGJ
140	N	V640LGC	156	TC	V356DGT	173	TC	W373VGJ	189	TC	W389VGJ
141	N	V341DGT	158	TC	V358DGT	174	TC	W374VGJ			

DLA190-223   DAF DB250 10.2m   Alexander ALX400   N43/21D   2000

190	E	W434WGJ	199	E	W399VGJ	208	N	W408VGJ	216	TC	X416FGP
191	E	W391VGJ	200	E	W435WGJ	209	N	W409VGJ	217	TC	X417FGP
192	E	W392VGJ	201	CT	W401VGJ	210	E	W438WGJ	218	TC	X418FGP
193	E	W393VGJ	202	CT	W402VGJ	211	E	W411VGJ	219	TC	X419FGP
194	E	W394VGJ	203	CT	W403VGJ	212	E	W412VGJ	220	TC	X501GGO
195	E	W395VGJ	204	N	W404VGJ	213	WN	W413VGJ	221	TC	X421FGP
196	E	W396VGJ	205	N	W436WGJ	214	WN	W414VGJ	222	TC	X422FGP
197	E	W397VGJ	206	N	W437WGJ	215	TC	X415FGP	223	TC	X423FGP
198	E	W398VGJ	207	N	W407VGJ						

DLA224-321   DAF DB250 10.2m   Alexander ALX400   N43/20D*   2000-01   *seating varies

224	TC	X424FGP	249	CT	X449FGP	274	AR	Y474UGC	298	CT	Y498UGC
225	E	X425FGP	250	TC	X506GGO	275	AR	Y475UGC	299	CT	Y499UGC
226	E	X426FGP	251	TC	X451FGP	276	E	Y476UGC	300	CT	Y524UGC
227	E	X427FGP	252	TC	X452FGP	277	AR	Y477UGC	301	CT	Y501UGC
228	WN	X428FGP	253	TC	X453FGP	278	AR	Y478UGC	302	CT	Y502UGC
229	WN	X429FGP	254	TC	X454FGP	279	AR	Y479UGC	303	CT	Y503UGC
230	AR	X502GGO	255	TC	X507GGO	280	AR	Y522UGC	304	CT	Y504UGC
231	AR	X431FGP	256	TC	X508GGO	281	AR	Y481UGC	305	CT	Y526UGC
232	AR	X432FGP	257	TC	X457FGP	282	AR	Y482UGC	306	CT	Y506UGC
233	E	X433FGP	258	TC	X458FGP	283	AR	Y483UGC	307	CT	Y507UGC
234	AR	X434FGP	259	TC	X459FGP	284	AR	Y484UGC	308	CT	Y508UGC
235	AR	X435FGP	260	TC	Y451UGC	285	AR	Y485UGC	309	CT	Y509UGC
236	N	X436FGP	261	TC	Y461UGC	286	AR	Y486UGC	310	CT	Y527UGC
237	E	X437FGP	262	TC	Y462UGC	287	AR	Y487UGC	311	N	Y511UGC
238	E	X438FGP	263	TC	Y463UGC	288	AR	Y488UGC	312	N	Y512UGC
239	AR	X439FGP	264	TC	Y464UGC	289	AR	Y489UGC	313	N	Y513UGC
240	AR	X503GGO	265	TC	Y465UGC	290	SF	Y523UGC	314	N	Y514UGC
241	AR	X441FGP	266	TC	Y466UGC	291	CT	Y491UGC	315	N	Y529UGC
242	AR	X442FGP	267	TC	Y467UGC	292	CT	Y492UGC	316	N	Y516UGC
243	AR	X443FGP	268	TC	Y468UGC	293	CT	Y493UGC	317	N	Y517UGC
244	AR	X504GGO	269	TC	Y469UGC	294	CT	Y494UGC	318	N	Y518UGC
245	AR	X445FGP	270	CT	Y452UGC	295	CT	Y495UGC	319	N	Y519UGC
246	AR	X446FGP	271	CT	Y471UGC	296	CT	Y496UGC	320	N	Y531UGC
247	AR	X447FGP	272	N	Y472UGC	297	CT	Y497UGC	321	N	Y521UGC
248	CT	X448FGP	273	AR	Y473UGC						

Displaying the oval TransBus badge, DLA381, LJ03MTZ, is seen in London's Bishopsgate while operating route 242. Almost four hundred of the DAF double-decks have the ALX400 body while a further hundred have the President style and sixty-seven Wrightbus. *Colin Lloyd*

DLA322-336

			DAF DB250 10.2m			TransBus ALX400				N45/20D	2003
322	TH	LG52DAO	326	TH	LG52DBV	330	TH	LG52DCF	334	TH	LG52DCX
323	TH	LG52DAU	327	TH	LG52DBY	331	TH	LG52DCO	335	TH	LG52DCY
324	TH	LG52DBO	328	TH	LG52DBZ	332	TH	LG52DCU	336	TH	LG52DCZ
325	TH	LG52DBU	329	TH	LG52DCE	333	TH	LG52DCV			

DLA337-389

			DAF DB250 10.2m			TransBus ALX400				N45/20D	2003
337	TH	LJ03MFX	351	EC	LJ03MKZ	364	EC	LJ03MKL	377	CT	LJ03MTK
338	TH	LJ03MFY	352	EC	LJ03MLE	365	EC	LJ03MWE	378	CT	LJ03MTU
339	TH	LJ03MFZ	353	EC	LJ03MLF	366	EC	LJ03MWF	379	CT	LJ03MTV
340	TH	LJ03MGE	354	EC	LJ03MLK	367	EC	LJ03MWG	380	CT	LJ03MTY
341	TH	LJ03MGU	355	EC	LJ03MJX	368	EC	LJ03MWK	381	CT	LJ03MTZ
342	TH	LJ03MGV	356	EC	LJ03MJY	369	EC	LJ03MWL	382	CT	LJ03MUA
343	TH	LJ03MDV	357	EC	LJ03MKA	370	CT	LJ03MUY	383	CT	LJ03MUB
344	TH	LJ03MDX	358	EC	LJ03MKC	371	CT	LJ03MVC	384	CT	LJ03MYU
345	TH	LJ03MDY	359	EC	LJ03MKD	372	CT	LJ03MVD	385	CT	LJ03MYV
346	CT	LJ03MDZ	360	EC	LJ03MKE	373	CT	LJ03MVE	386	CT	LJ03MYX
347	TH	LJ03MEU	361	EC	LJ03MKF	374	CT	LJ03MSY	387	CT	LJ03MYY
348	EC	LJ03MKU	362	EC	LJ03MKG	375	CT	LJ03MTE	388	CT	LJ03MYZ
349	EC	LJ03MKV	363	EC	LJ03MKK	376	CT	LJ03MTF	389	TH	LJ03MZD
350	EC	LJ03MKX									

DLP1-20

			DAF DB250 10.6m			Plaxton President				N45/19D	1999
1	E	V601LGC	6	E	T206XBV	11	E	T211XBV	16	F	T216XBV
2	E	T202XBV	7	E	T207XBV	12	E	T212XBV	17	E	T217XBV
3	C	T203XBV	8	E	T208XBV	13	E	T213XBV	18	E	T218XBV
4	E	T204XBV	9	E	T209XBV	14	E	T214XBV	19	E	T219XBV
5	E	T205XBV	10	E	T210XBV	15	E	T215XBV	20	E	T220XBV

DLP40-75 DAF DB250 10.6m Plaxton President N45/24D 2001

40	WN	Y532UGC	49	WN	Y549UGC	58	WN	LJ51DKF	67	WN	LJ51DLD
41	WN	Y541UGC	50	WN	LJ51DJU	59	WN	LJ51DKK	68	WN	LJ51DLF
42	WN	Y542UGC	51	WN	LJ51DJV	60	WN	LJ51DKL	69	WN	LJ51DLK
43	WN	Y543UGC	52	WN	LJ51DJX	61	WN	LJ51DKN	70	WN	LJ51DLN
44	WN	Y544UGC	53	WN	LJ51DJY	62	WN	LJ51DKO	71	WN	LJ51DLU
45	WN	Y533UGC	54	WN	LJ51DJZ	63	WN	LJ51DKU	72	WN	LJ51DLV
46	WN	Y546UGC	55	WN	LJ51DKA	64	WN	LJ51DKV	73	WN	LJ51DLX
47	WN	Y547UGC	56	WN	LJ51DKD	65	WN	LJ51DKX	74	WN	LJ51DLY
48	WN	Y548UGC	57	WN	LJ51DKE	66	WN	LJ51DKY	75	WN	LJ51DLZ

DLP76-90 DAF DB250 10.2m Plaxton President N43/20D 2002

76	E	LJ51OSX	80	E	LJ51ORC	84	E	LJ51ORK	88	E	LF02PKD
77	E	LJ51OSY	81	E	LJ51ORF	85	E	LJ51ORL	89	E	LF02PKE
78	E	LJ51OSZ	82	E	LJ51ORG	86	E	LF02PKA	90	E	LF02PKJ
79	E	LJ51ORA	83	E	LJ51ORH	87	E	LF02PKC			

DLP91-110 DAF DB250 10.6m Plaxton President N45/20D 2002

91	E	LF52URS	96	E	LF52URX	101	E	LF52URG	106	E	LF52URM
92	E	LF52URT	97	E	LF52URB	102	E	LF52URH	107	E	LF52UPP
93	E	LF52URU	98	E	LF52URC	103	E	LF52URJ	108	E	LF52UPR
94	E	LF52URV	99	E	LF52URD	104	E	LF52URK	109	E	LF52UPS
95	E	LF52URW	100	E	LF52URE	105	E	LF52URL	110	E	LF52UPT

DP1	EC	217CLT	DAF SB3000	Plaxton Première 350	C49FT	1996	Arriva East Herts & Essex, 1998
DP2	EC	398CLT	DAF SB3000	Plaxton Première 350	C53F	1996	Arriva East Herts & Essex, 1998
DP3	EC	319CLT	DAF SB3000	Plaxton Première 350	C53F	1997	Arriva East Herts & Essex, 1998
DP5	EC	519CLT	DAF SB3000	Plaxton Excalibur	C53F	1998	Westbus, Hounslow, 2002
DP6	EC	330CLT	DAF SB3000	Plaxton Première 350	C53F	1999	On Time, Wandsworth, 2002

DPP421-431 Dennis Dart SLF 10m Plaxton Pointer N34F 1997 Arriva East Herts & Essex, 1998

421	TC	R421COO	424	TC	R424COO	427	TC	R427COO	430	TC	R430COO
422	TC	R422COO	425	TC	R425COO	428	TC	R428COO	431	EC	R431COO
423	TC	R423COO	426	TC	R426COO	429	TC	R429COO			

DVH6	EC	VLT27	DAF MB230	Van Hool Alizée H	C53F	1990	Arriva East Herts & Essex, 1998
DVH8	EC	VLT47	DAF MB230	Van Hool Alizée H	C49FT	1990	Arriva East Herts & Essex, 1998

DW1-50 DAF DB250 10.3m Wrightbus Pulsar Gemini N43/22D 2003

1	TC	801DYE	14	TC	LJ03MWC	27	TC	LJ53BGK	39	CN	LJ53NHF
2	TC	LJ03MWN	15	TC	LJ03MWD	28	TC	LJ53BGO	40	CN	LJ53NHG
3	TC	LJ03MWP	16	TC	LJ03MVF	29	TC	LJ53BGU	41	CN	LJ53NHH
4	TC	LJ03MWU	17	TC	LJ03MVG	30	TC	LJ53NHV	42	CN	LJ53NHK
5	TC	LJ03MWV	18	TC	LJ53NHT	31	TC	LJ53NHX	43	CN	LJ53NHL
6	TC	LJ03MVT	19	TC	WLT719	32	TC	WLT531	44	CN	VLT244
7	TC	WLT807	20	TC	LJ53BFP	33	TC	LJ53NHZ	45	CN	LJ53NHN
8	TC	LJ03MVV	21	TC	LJ53BFU	34	TC	734DYE	46	CN	LJ53NHO
9	TC	LJ03MVW	22	TC	822DYE	35	CN	LJ53NJF	47	CN	LJ53NHP
10	TC	LJ03MVX	23	TC	LJ53BFX	36	TC	LJ53NJK	48	CN	WLT348
11	TC	LJ03MVY	24	TC	LJ53BFY	37	CN	LJ53NJN	49	CN	LJ53NGU
12	TC	LJ03MVZ	25	TC	725DYE	38	CN	LJ53NHE	50	CN	LJ53NGV
13	TC	LJ03MWA	26	TC	LJ53BGF						

DW51-93 VDL Bus DB250 10.3m Wrightbus Pulsar Gemini N43/22D 2004

51	CN	LJ04LDX	62	BN	LJ04LDC	73	BN	LJ04LGK	84	BN	LJ04LFX
52	CN	LJ04LDY	63	BN	LJ04LDD	74	BN	LJ04LGL	85	BN	LJ04LFY
53	BN	LJ04LDZ	64	BN	LJ04LDE	75	BN	LJ04LGN	86	BN	LJ04LFZ
54	BN	LJ04LEF	65	BN	LJ04LDF	76	BN	LJ04LGU	87	BN	LJ04LGA
55	BN	LJ04LEU	66	BN	LJ04LDK	77	BN	LJ04LGK	88	BN	LJ04LGC
56	BN	LJ04LFA	67	BN	LJ04LDL	78	BN	LJ04LGW	89	BN	LJ04LGD
57	BN	LJ04LFB	68	BN	LJ04LDN	79	BN	LJ04LGX	90	BN	LJ04LGE
58	BN	LJ04LFD	69	BN	LJ04LDU	80	BN	LJ04LGY	91	BN	LJ04LFG
59	BN	LJ04LFE	70	BN	LJ04LDV	81	BN	LJ04LFU	92	BN	LJ04LFH
60	BN	LJ04LFF	71	BN	LJ04LGF	82	BN	LJ04LFV	93	BN	LJ04LFK
61	BN	LJ04LDA	72	BN	LJ04LGG	83	BN	LJ04LFW			

Arriva joined the 'Back the Bid' campaign for the 2012 Olympics. One of several London Buses to receive overall adverts in support was Arriva's DW41, LJ53NHH, seen here in Croydon. *Mark Lyons*

DW94-102
VDL Bus DB250 10.3m   Wrightbus Pulsar Gemini   N43/22D   2004

94	CN	LJ54BFP	97	CN	LJ54BFX	99	CN	LJ54BFZ	101	CN	LJ54BGF
95	CN	LJ54BFU	98	CN	LJ54BFY	100	CN	LJ54BGE	102	CN	LJ54BGK
96	CN	LJ54BFV									

DW103-134
VDL Bus DB250 10.3m   Wrightbus Pulsar Gemini   N43/22D   2005

103	BA	LJ05BJV	111	BA	LJ05BHP	119	BA	LJ05BMY	127	BA	LJ05BNL
104	BA	LJ05BJX	112	BA	LJ05BHU	120	BA	LJ05BMZ	128	BA	LJ05GKX
105	BA	LJ05BJY	113	BA	LJ05BHV	121	BA	LJ05BNA	129	BA	LJ05GKY
106	BA	LJ05BJZ	114	BA	LJ05BHW	122	BA	LJ05BNB	130	BA	LJ05GKZ
107	BA	LJ05BKA	115	BA	LJ05BHX	123	BA	LJ05BND	131	BA	LJ05GLF
108	BA	LJ05BHL	116	BA	LJ05BHY	124	BA	LJ05BNE	132	BA	LJ05GLK
109	BA	LJ05BHN	117	BA	LJ05BHZ	125	BA	LJ05BNF	133	BA	LJ05GLV
110	BA	LJ05BHO	118	BA	LJ05BMV	126	BA	LJ05BNK	134	BA	LJ05GLY

DWL1-22
DAF SB120 10.2m   Wrightbus Cadet   N31D   2001

1	BS	Y801DGT	7	BS	LJ51DDK	13	BS	LJ51DDX	18	BS	LJ51DFC
2	BS	Y802DGT	8	BS	LJ51DDL	14	BS	LJ51DDY	19	BS	LJ51DFD
3	BS	Y803DGT	9	BS	LJ51DDN	15	BS	LJ51DDZ	20	BS	LJ51DFE
4	BS	Y804DGT	10	BS	LJ51DDO	16	BS	LJ51DEU	21	BS	LJ51DFF
5	BS	Y805DGT	11	BS	LJ51DDU	17	BS	LJ51DFA	22	BS	LJ51DFG
6	BS	Y806DGT	12	BS	LJ51DDV						

DWL23-29
DAF SB120 10.8m   Wrightbus Cadet   N34D   2002

| 23 | E | LF02PLU | 25 | E | LF02PLX | 27 | E | LF02PMO | 29 | E | LF02PMV |
| 24 | E | LF02PLV | 26 | E | LF02PLZ | | | | | | |

DWL30-55
DAF SB120 10.2m   Wrightbus Cadet   N30D   2002

30	WN	LF02PMX	37	WN	LF02PNU	44	WN	LF52UTB	50	WN	LF52UOB
31	WN	LF02PMY	38	WN	LF02PNU	45	WN	LF52UNW	51	WN	LF52UOC
32	WN	LF02PNE	39	WN	LF02PNV	46	WN	LF52UNX	52	WN	LF52UOD
33	WN	LF02PNJ	40	WN	LF02PNX	47	WN	LF52UNY	53	WN	LF52UOE
34	WN	LF02PNK	41	WN	LF02PNY	48	WN	LF52UNZ	54	WN	LF52USZ
35	WN	LF02PNL	42	WN	LF02POA	49	WN	LF52UOA	55	WN	LF52UTA
36	WN	LF02PNN	43	WN	LF02POH						

Following on from CW1, further Wrightbus Cadets have been numbered in the DWS and DWL classes. The Cadet, which is built on the VDL Bus SB120 chassis is available in three lengths, 9.4m, 10.2m and 10.8m. Pictured in Croydon is DWL61, LJ03MYG. *Mark Doggett*

DWL56-67

DAF SB120 10.2m · Wrightbus Cadet · N30D · 2003

56	E	LJ03MUW	59	CN	LJ03MZG	62	CN	LJ03MYH	65	CN	LJ03MYM
57	CN	LJ03MZE	60	CN	LJ03MZL	63	CN	LJ03MYK	66	CN	LJ53NGX
58	CN	LJ03MZF	61	CN	LJ03MYG	64	CN	LJ03MYL	67	CN	LJ53NGY

DWS1-18

VDL Bus SB120 9.4m · Wrightbus Cadet · N26D · 2003

1	CN	LJ53NGZ	6	CN	LJ53NFT	11	CN	LJ53NFZ	15	CN	LJ53NGN
2	CN	LJ53NHA	7	CN	LJ53NFU	12	CN	LJ53NGE	16	CN	LJ53NFE
3	CN	LJ53NHB	8	CN	LJ53NFV	13	CN	LJ53NGF	17	CN	LJ53NFF
4	CN	LJ53NHC	9	CN	LJ53NFX	14	CN	LJ53NGG	18	CN	LJ53NFG
5	CN	LJ53NHD	10	CN	LJ53NFY						

L24-230

Leyland Olympian ONLXB/1RH · Eastern Coach Works · B42/26D · 1986-87 · London Buses, 1994-95

24	w	C24CHM	162	N	D162FYM	198	N	D198FYM	223	N	D223FYM
25	N	C25CHM	180	N	D180FYM	201	N	D201FYM	230	w	D230FYM
37	N	C37CHM	191	w	D191FYM	214	N	D214FYM			

L315-354

Leyland Olympian ON2R50C13Z4 · Alexander RH · B43/25D · 1992 · London Buses, 1994

315	DX	J315BSH	331	DX	J331BSH	339	DX	J339BSH	352	EC	WLT372
319	DX	J319BSH	332	DX	J332BSH	346	DX	J346BSH	353	EC	VLT173
324	DX	J324BSH	334	DX	J334BSH	350	DX	J352BSH	354	EC	WLT554
328	EC	324CLT	337	DX	J337BSH	351	EC	WLT751			

L526-546

Leyland Olympian ON2R50C13Z4 · Northern Counties · B47/27D · 1990 · Kentish Bus, 1996

526	N	G526VBB	532	DX	G532VBB	534	DX	G534VBB	545	DX	G545VBB
530	DX	G530VBB	533	DX	G533VBB	535	DX	G535VBB	546	DX	G546VBB
531	DX	G531VBB									

M537	EC	GYE537W	MCW Metrobus DR101/14	MCW	B43/28D	1981	London Buses, 1994
M573	EC	GYE575W	MCW Metrobus DR101/14	MCW	B43/28D	1981	London Buses, 1994
M617	EC	KYC617X	MCW Metrobus DR101/14	MCW	B43/28D	1981	London Buses, 1994
M772	EC	KYV772X	MCW Metrobus DR101/14	MCW	B43/28D	1981	London Buses, 1994
M777	EC	KYV777X	MCW Metrobus DR101/14	MCW	B43/28D	1981	London Buses, 1994

Several of the Olympians have now been painted into dedicated training livery. Illustrating the scheme is former KentishBus example L553, G553VBB. Only fifty former London Buses vehicles remain in the operational fleet.
Colin Lloyd

M1075-1300   MCW Metrobus DR101/17   MCW   B43/28D   1984-85

1075	EC	B75WUL	1130	EC	B130WUL	1248	EC	B248WUL	1254	EC	B254WUL
1124	EC	B124WUL	1136	EC	B136WUL	1253	EC	B253WUL	1300	EC	B300WUL
1126	EC	B126WUL	1231	EC	B231WUL						

M1312-1405   MCW Metrobus DR101/17   MCW   B43/28D   1985

1312	EC	C312BUV	1320	EC	C320BUV	1327	EC	C327BUV	1379	EC	VLT88
1313	EC	C313BUV	1326	EC	C326BUV	1367	EC	C367BUV	1405	AR	C405BUV
1314	EC	C314BUV									

M1437   EC   VLT12   MCW Metrobus DR101/17   MCW   BC43/24F   1986   Arriva East Herts & Essex, 1998

MA1-76   Mercedes-Benz O530G 18m   Mercedes-Benz Citaro   AB49T   2004

1	LV	BX04MWW	20	LV	BX04MXU	39	LV	BX04NEJ	58	LV	BX04MZL
2	LV	BX04MWY	21	LV	BX04MXV	40	LV	BX04MYG	59	LV	BX04MZN
3	LV	BX04MWZ	22	LV	BX04MXW	41	LV	BX04MYH	60	LV	BX04NBK
4	LV	BX04MXA	23	LV	BX04MXY	42	LV	BX04MYJ	61	LV	BX04NBL
5	LV	BX04MXB	24	LV	BX04MXZ	43	LV	BX04MYK	62	LV	BX04NCF
6	LV	BX04MXC	25	LV	BX04MYA	44	LV	BX04MYL	63	LV	BX04NCJ
7	LV	BX04MXD	26	LV	BX04MYB	45	LV	BX04MYM	64	LV	BX04NCN
8	LV	BX04MXE	27	LV	BX04MYC	46	LV	BX04MYN	65	LV	BX04NCU
9	LV	BX04MXG	28	LV	BX04MYD	47	LV	BX04MYR	66	LV	BX04NCV
10	LV	BX04MXH	29	LV	BX04MYF	48	LV	BX04MYS	67	LV	BX04NCY
11	LV	BX04MXJ	30	LV	BX04MYY	49	LV	BX04MYT	68	IV	BX04NCZ
12	IV	BX04MXK	31	LV	BX04MYZ	50	LV	BX04MYU	69	LV	BX04NDC
13	LV	BX04MXL	32	LV	BX04NDD	51	LV	BX04MYV	70	LV	BX04NDE
14	LV	BX04MXM	33	LV	BX04NDG	52	LV	BX04MYW	71	LV	BX04NDF
15	LV	BX04MXN	34	LV	BX04NDU	53	LV	BX04MYZ	72	LV	BX04NDJ
16	LV	BX04MXP	35	LV	BX04NDV	54	LV	BX04MZD	73	LV	BX04NDK
17	LV	BX04MXR	36	LV	BX04NDY	55	LV	BX04MZE	74	LV	BX04NDL
18	LV	BX04MXS	37	LV	BX04NDZ	56	LV	BX04MZG	75	LV	BX04NDN
19	LV	BX04MXT	38	LV	BX04NEF	57	LV	BX04MZJ	76	LV	BX04NEN

Current deliveries of the articulated Citaro will take the type to over one hundred and fifty with Arriva. Pictured on route 73, MA69, BX04NDC, illustrates the model now becoming a feature of the London scene with the type in service with most major service providers. *Mark Lyons*

MA77-157 Mercedes-Benz O530G 18m   Mercedes-Benz Citaro   AB49T   2005

77	TM	BX05UWV	98	TM	BX55FUV	118	TM	BX55FVU	138	-
78	TM	BX05UWW	99	TM	BX55FUW	119	TM	BX55FVV	139	-
79	TM	BX05UWY	100	TM	BX55FUY	120	TM	BX55FVW	140	-
80	TM	BX05UWZ	101	TM	BX55FVA	121	TM	BX55FVY	141	-
81	TM	BU05VFE	102	TM	BX55FVB	122	TM	BX55FVZ	142	-
82	TM	BU05VFF	103	TM	BX55FVC	123	-		143	-
83	TM	BX05UXC	104	TM	BX55FVD	124	-		144	-
84	TM	BU05VFG	105	TM	BX55FVF	125	-		145	-
85	TM	BU05VFD	106	TM	BX55FVG	126	-		146	-
86	TM	BU05VFH	107	TM	BX55FVH	127	-		147	-
87	TM	BU05VFJ	108	TM	BX55FVJ	128	-		148	-
88	TM	BX05UXD	109	TM	BX55FVK	129	-		149	-
89	TM	BX55FWA	110	TM	BX55FVL	130	-		150	-
90	TM	BX55FWB	111	TM	BX55FVM	131	-		151	-
91	TM	BX55FUH	112	TM	BX55FVN	132	-		152	-
92	TM	BX55FUJ	113	TM	BX55FVQ	133	-		153	-
93	TM	BX55FUM	114	TM	BX55FVP	134	-		154	-
94	TM	BX55FUO	115	TM	BX55FVR	135	-		155	-
95	TM	BX55FUP	116	TM	BX55FVS	136	-		156	-
96	TM	BX55FUT	117	TM	BX55FVT	137	-		157	-
97	TM	BX55FUU								

The Mini Pointer Dart has proved to be a useful tool to Arriva, with the model operating in all the English fleets. Carrying Arriva's red scheme for TfL work, PDL72, LF52UOH, is seen on route 377. *Ian Jordan*

PDL1-18

Dennis Dart SLF 8.8m   Plaxton Pointer MPD   N29F*   2000   *16-18 are N21F

1	EC	V421DGT	6	EC	V426DGT	11	EC	V431DGT	15	EC	V435DGT
2	EC	V422DGT	7	EC	V427DGT	12	EC	V432DGT	16	CN	W136VGJ
3	EC	V423DGT	8	EC	V428DGT	13	EC	V433DGT	17	CN	W137VGJ
4	EC	V424DGT	9	EC	V429DGT	14	EC	V434DGT	18	CN	W138VGJ
5	EC	V425DGT	10	EC	V430DGT						

PDL19-38

Dennis Dart SLF 10.7m   Plaxton Pointer 2   N31D   2000

19	CN	X519GGO	24	CN	X524GGO	29	DX	X529GGO	34	DX	X534GGO
20	CN	X471GGO	25	CN	X475GGO	30	DX	X481GGO	35	DX	X485GGO
21	CN	X521GGO	26	CN	X526GGO	31	DX	X531GGO	36	DX	X536GGO
22	CN	X522GGO	27	CN	X527GGO	32	DX	X532GGO	37	DX	X537GGO
23	CN	X523GGO	28	CN	X478GGO	33	DX	X533GGO	38	DX	X538GGO

PDL39-49

Dennis Dart SLF 8.8m   Plaxton Pointer MPD   N29F   2001

39	AR	X239PGT	42	AR	X242PGT	45	AR	X546GGO	48	AR	X248PGT
40	AR	X541GGO	43	AR	X243PGT	46	AR	X246PGT	49	AR	X249PGT
41	AR	X241PGT	44	AR	X244PGT	47	AR	X247PGT			

PDL50-69

Dennis Dart SLF 8.8m   Plaxton Pointer MPD   N29F   2001-02

50	TH	LJ51DAA	55	TH	LJ51DBV	60	TH	LJ51DCF	65	E	LJ51DCY
51	TH	LJ51DAO	56	TH	LJ51DBX	61	TH	LJ51DCO	66	E	LJ51DCZ
52	TH	LJ51DAU	57	TH	LJ51DBY	62	CN	LJ51DCU	67	E	LJ51DDA
53	TH	LJ51DBO	58	TH	LJ51DBZ	63	CN	LJ51DCV	68	E	LJ51DDE
54	TH	LJ51DBU	59	TH	LJ51DCE	64	E	LJ51DCX	69	E	LJ51DDF

PDL70-94

TransBus Dart 8.8m   TransBus Mini Pointer   N29F   2002

70	EC	LF02PTZ	77	EC	LF52UON	83	E	LF52URZ	89	E	LF52USJ
71	TH	LF52UOG	78	EC	LF52UOO	84	E	LF52USB	90	u	LF52USL
72	EC	LF52UOH	79	EC	LF52UOP	85	E	LF52USC	91	E	LF52URN
73	EC	LF52UOJ	80	EC	LF52UOR	86	E	LF52USD	92	E	LF52URO
74	EC	LF52UOK	81	EC	LF52UNV	87	E	LF52USG	93	E	LF52URP
75	EC	LF52UOL	82	E	LF52URY	88	E	LF52USH	94	E	LF52URR
76	EC	LF52UOM									

PDL95-116 Alexander Dennis Dart 10.1m Alexander Dennis Pointer N27D 2004

95	EC	LJ54BCX	101	EC	LJ54BBF	107	EC	LJ54LHG	112	EC	LJ54LHN
96	EC	LJ54BAA	102	EC	LJ54BBK	108	EC	LJ54LHH	113	EC	LJ54LHO
97	EC	LJ54BAO	103	EC	LJ54BBN	109	EC	LJ54LHK	114	EC	LJ54LHP
98	EC	LJ54BAU	104	EC	LJ54BBO	110	EC	LJ54LHL	115	EC	LJ54LHR
99	EC	LJ54BAV	105	EC	LJ54BBU	111	EC	LJ54LHM	116	EC	LJ54LGV
100	EC	LJ54BBE	106	EC	LJ54LHF						

PDL117-123 Alexander Dennis Dart 10.1m Alexander Dennis Pointer N27D 2005

117	TC	LJ05GOP	119	TC	LJ05GOX	121	TC	LJ05GPK	123	TC	LJ05GPU
118	TC	LJ05GOU	120	TC	LJ05GPF	122	TC	LJ05GPO			

RM5-875 AEC Routemaster R2RH Park Royal B36/28R 1959-61

5	AR	VLT5	54	BN	LDS279A	652	CT	WLT652	848	CT	WLT848
6	N	VLT6	85	BN	VLT85	713	BN	TSK270	871	BN	WLT871
25	BN	855UXC	346	BN	SVS615	838	BN	XYJ440	875	BN	DVS940
29	BN	OYM453A	548	BN	SVS618						

RML884-901 AEC Routemaster R2RH/1 Park Royal B40/32R 1961

884	w	WLT884	892	BN	WLT892	897	CT	WLT897	901	CT	WLT901
888	CT	WLT888	895	BN	WLT895						

RM909 BN WLT909 AEC Routemaster R2RH Park Royal B36/28R 1961 preservation, 2002

RM1124-1312 AEC Routemaster R2RH Park Royal B36/28R 1961-65

1124	BN	VYJ806	1164	CT	NSG636A	1280	BN	280CLT	1312	CT	MFF509
1145	CT	LDS402A	1185	CT	XYJ427	1292	BN	NVS485			

RMC1453 EC 453CLT AEC Routemaster R2RH Park Royal B36/28R 1962 Arriva East Herts & Essex, 1998
RMC1464 EC 464CLT AEC Routemaster R2RH Park Royal O36/28R 1962 Arriva East Herts & Essex, 1998

RM1640-2217 AEC Routemaster R2RH Park Royal B36/28R 1961-65

1640	CT	640CLT	1968	CT	ALD968B	2050	CT	ALM50B	2122	CT	CUV122C
1776	CT	776DYE	1975	BN	ALD975B	2060	CT	ALM60B	2217	BN	CUV217C
1941	CT	ALD941B									

RML2264-2359 AEC Routemaster R2RH/1 Park Royal B40/32R 1965

2264	BN	CUV264C	2307	BN	CUV307C	2346	AR	CUV346C	2346	CT	CUV346C
2277	CT	CUV277C	2315	CT	CUV315C	2333	BN	CUV333C	2355	CT	CUV355C
2280	CT	CUV280C	2324	BN	CUV324C	2334	CT	CUV334C	2356	CT	CUV356C
2287	CT	CUV287C	2325	CT	CUV325C	2344	CT	CUV344C	2359	CT	CUV359C
2304	CT	CUV304C									

RML2366-2597 AEC Routemaster R2RH/1 Park Royal B40/32R 1966

2366	BN	JJD366D	2434	CT	JJD434D	2525	CT	JJD525D	2562	CT	JJD562D
2370	CT	JJD370D	2457	CT	JJD457D	2526	CT	JJD526D	2567	CT	JJD567D
2375	BN	JJD375D	2468	G	JJD468D	2528	CT	JJD528D	2571	CT	JJD571D
2386	CT	JJD386D	2483	CT	JJD483D	2533	BN	JJD533D	2572	BN	JJD572D
2387	BN	JJD387D	2491	BN	JJD491D	2534	CT	JJD534D	2573	BN	JJD573D
2401	CT	JJD401D	2492	CT	JJD492D	2544	CT	JJD544D	2577	BN	JJD577D
2406	CT	JJD406D	2494	CT	JJD494D	2545	BN	JJD545D	2586	BN	JJD586D
2408	CT	JJD408D	2503	CT	JJD503D	2546	CT	JJD546D	2591	w	JJD591D
2409	CT	JJD409D	2521	BN	JJD521D	2549	BN	JJD549D	2597	CT	JJD597D
2416	CT	JJD416D									

RML2619-2655 AEC Routemaster R2RH/1 Park Royal B40/32R 1967

2619	BN	NML619E	2636	BN	NML636E	2638	CT	NML638E	2655	CT	NML655E

RML2675-2759 AEC Routemaster R2RH/1 Park Royal B40/32R 1968

2675	CT	SMK675F	2715	w	SMK715F	2750	CT	SMK750F	2753	BN	SMK753F
2688	CT	SMK688F	2730	BN	SMK730F	2752	BN	SMK752F	2759	BN	SMK759F

TPL1	EC	124CLT	Leyland Tiger TRCTL11/3ARZM	Plaxton Paramount 3200 III	C53F	1989	Arriva East Herts & Essex, 1998
TPL2	EC	361CLT	Leyland Tiger TRCTL11/3ARZM	Plaxton Paramount 3200 III	C53F	1989	Arriva East Herts & Essex, 1998
TPL8	EC	70CLT	Leyland Tiger TRCT10/3ARZA	Plaxton Paramount 3200 III	C53F	1991	Arriva East Herts & Essex, 1998
TPL518	EC	530MUY	Leyland Tiger TRCTL11/3ARZ(Vo)	Plaxton Paramount 3500 III	C51FT	1988	Arriva East Herts & Essex, 1998

With the arrival of more Citaro buses, and further double-decks due, the days of the Routemaster in service are numbered. Pictured on route159, which will be converted to double-deck Volvo B7 operation by the end of 2005, RM1124, VYJ806, is one of those that have already had their original index mark transferred to another vehicle. In this case, 124CLT is now on coach TPL1. *Mark Lyons*

VLA1-55

Volvo B7TL 10.6m   TransBus ALX400 4.4m   N49/22D   2003

1	N	LJ03MYP	15	N	LJ03M**XH**	29	N	LJ53BDO	43	N	LJ53BCV
2	N	LJ03MYR	16	N	LJ03MXK	30	N	LJ53BDU	44	N	LJ53BCX
3	N	LJ03MYS	17	N	LJ03MXL	31	N	LJ53BDV	45	N	LJ53BCY
4	N	LJ03MYT	18	N	LJ03MXM	32	N	LJ53BDX	46	N	LJ53BAA
5	N	LJ03MXV	19	N	LJ03MXN	33	N	LJ53BDY	47	N	LJ53BAO
6	N	LJ03MXW	20	N	LJ03MXP	34	N	LJ53BDZ	48	N	LJ53BAU
7	N	LJ03MXX	21	N	LJ53BFK	35	N	LJ53BEO	49	N	LJ53BAV
8	N	LJ03MXY	22	N	LJ53BFL	36	N	LJ53BBV	50	N	LJ53BBE
9	N	LJ03MXZ	23	N	LJ53BFM	37	N	LJ53BBX	51	N	LJ53BBF
10	N	LJ03MYA	24	N	LJ53BFN	38	N	LJ53BBZ	52	N	LJ53BBK
11	N	LJ03MYB	25	N	LJ53B**FO**	39	N	LJ53BCF	53	N	LJ53BBN
12	N	LJ03MYC	26	N	LJ53BCZ	40	N	LJ53BCK	54	N	LJ53BBO
13	N	LJ03MYD	27	N	LJ53BDE	41	N	LJ53BCO	55	N	LJ53BBU
14	N	LJ03MYF	28	N	LJ53BDF	42	N	LJ53BCU			

VLA56-73

Volvo B7TL 10.6m   TransBus ALX400 4.4m   N49/22D   2004

56	WD	LJ04LFL	61	WD	LJ04LFS	66	WD	LJ04YWV	70	N	LJ04YWZ
57	WD	LJ04LFM	62	WD	LJ04LFT	67	WD	LJ04YWW	71	N	LJ04YXA
58	WD	LJ04LFN	63	WD	LJ04YWS	68	WD	LJ04YWX	72	N	LJ04YXB
59	WD	LJ04LFP	64	WD	LJ04YWT	69	WD	LJ04YWY	73	N	LJ04YWE
60	WD	LJ04LFR	65	WD	LJ04YWU						

VLA74-128

Volvo B7TL 10.1m   Alexander-Dennis ALX400   N49/22D   2004-05

74	AR	LJ54BGO	88	AR	LJ54BDF	102	AR	LJ54BCU	116	N	LJ54BKG
75	AR	LJ54BEO	89	AR	LJ54BDO	103	AR	LJ54BCV	117	N	LJ54BKK
76	AR	LJ54BEU	90	AR	LJ54BDU	104	N	LJ05BKY	118	N	LJ54BKL
77	AR	LJ54BFA	91	AR	LJ54BDV	105	N	LJ05BKZ	119	N	LJ54BKN
78	AR	LJ54BFE	92	AR	LJ54BDX	106	N	LJ05BLF	120	N	LJ54BKO
79	AR	LJ54BFF	93	AR	LJ54BDY	107	N	LJ05BLK	121	N	LJ54BKU
80	AR	LJ54BFK	94	AR	LJ54BDZ	108	N	LJ05BLN	122	N	LJ54BKV
81	AR	LJ54BFL	95	AR	LJ54BBV	109	N	LJ05BLV	123	N	LJ54BKX
82	AR	LJ54BFM	96	AR	LJ54BBX	110	N	LJ05BLX	124	N	LJ54BJE
83	AR	LJ54BFN	97	AR	LJ54BBZ	111	N	LJ05BLY	125	N	LJ54BJF
84	AR	LJ54BFO	98	AR	LJ54BCE	112	N	LJ05BMO	126	N	LJ54BJK
85	AR	LJ54BCY	99	AR	LJ54BCF	113	N	LJ05BMU	127	N	LJ54BJO
86	AR	LJ54BCZ	100	AR	LJ54BCK	114	N	LJ05BKD	128	N	LJ54BJU
87	AR	LJ54BDE	101	AR	LJ54BCO	115	N	LJ05BKF			

Arriva's choice of low-floor double-deck chassis has been between the DAF DB250 and the Volvo B7TL. Illustrating an Alexander-bodied Volvo is VLA57, LJ04LFM, seen in Putney while operating route 337. *Mark Lyons*

VLA129-143

Volvo B7TL 10.1m | Alexander-Dennis ALX400 | N41/22D | 2005

129	DX	LJ05GLZ	133	DX	LJ05GPY	137	DX	LJ05GRU	141	DX	LJ05GSU
130	DX	LJ05GME	134	DX	LJ05GPZ	138	DX	LJ05GRX	142	DX	LJ05GOH
131	DX	LJ05GMF	135	DX	LJ05GRF	139	DX	LJ05GRZ	143	DX	LJ05GOK
132	DX	LJ05GPX	136	DX	LJ05GRK	140	DX	LJ05GSO			

VLA144-179

Volvo B7TL 10.1m | Alexander-Dennis ALX400 | N41/22D | On order

144	BN	L	153	BN	L	162	BN	L	171	BN	L
145	BN	L	154	BN	L	163	BN	L	172	BN	L
146	BN	L	155	BN	L	164	BN	L	173	BN	L
147	BN	L	156	BN	L	165	BN	L	174	BN	L
148	BN	L	157	BN	L	166	BN	L	175	BN	L
149	BN	L	158	BN	L	167	BN	L	176	BN	L
150	BN	L	159	BN	L	168	BN	L	177	BN	L
151	BN	L	160	BN	L	169	BN	L	178	BN	L
152	BN	L	161	BN	L	170	BN	L	179	BN	L

VLW1-41

Volvo B7TL 10.1m | Wrightbus Eclipse Gemini | N41/22D | 2001-02

1	WN	Y581UGC	12	WN	LJ51DFV	22	WN	LJ51DGY	32	WN	LJ51DHN
2	WN	Y102TGH	13	WN	LJ51DFX	23	WN	LJ51DGZ	33	WN	LJ51DHO
3	WN	LJ51DJF	14	WN	LJ51DFY	24	WN	LJ51DHA	34	WN	LJ51DHP
4	WN	LJ51DJK	15	WN	LJ51DFZ	25	WN	LJ51DHC	35	WN	LJ51DHV
5	WN	LJ51DJO	16	WN	LJ51DGE	26	WN	LJ51DHD	36	WN	LJ51DHX
6	WN	LJ51DFK	17	WN	LJ51DGF	27	WN	LJ51DHE	37	WN	LJ51DHY
7	WN	LJ51DFL	18	WN	LJ51DGO	28	WN	LJ51DHF	38	WN	LJ51DHZ
8	WN	LJ51DFN	19	WN	LJ51DGU	29	WN	LJ51DHG	39	WN	LJ51DJD
9	WN	LJ51DFO	20	WN	LJ51DGV	30	WN	LJ51DHK	40	WN	LJ51DJE
10	WN	LJ51DFP	21	WN	LJ51DGX	31	WN	LJ51DHL	41	WN	LJ51OSK
11	WN	LJ51DFU									

VLW42-104 — Volvo B7TL 10.1m — Wrightbus Eclipse Gemini — N41/22D — 2002-03

42	WN	LF02PKO	58	WN	LF02PTU	74	WN	LF52UTM	90	DX	LF52URA
43	WN	LF02PKU	59	WN	LF02PTX	75	WN	LF52USM	91	DX	LF52UPD
44	WN	LF02PKV	60	WN	LF02PTY	76	WN	LF52USN	92	DX	LF52UPE
45	WN	LF02PKX	61	WN	LF02PVE	77	WN	LF52USO	93	DX	LF52UPG
46	WN	LF02PKY	62	WN	LF02PVJ	78	WN	LF52USS	94	DX	LF52UPH
47	WN	LF02PKZ	63	WN	LF02PVK	79	WN	LF52UST	95	DX	LF52UPJ
48	WN	LF02PLJ	64	WN	LF02PVL	80	WN	LF52USU	96	DX	LF52UPK
49	WN	LF02PLN	65	WN	LF02PVN	81	WN	LF52USV	97	AR	LF52UPL
50	WN	LF02PLO	66	WN	LF02PVO	82	WN	LF52USW	98	AR	LF52UPM
51	WN	LF02PRZ	67	WN	LF52UTC	83	WN	LF52USX	99	AR	LG52DDA
52	WN	LF02PSO	68	WN	LF52UTE	84	WN	LF52USY	100	AR	LG52DDE
53	WN	LF02PSU	69	EC	VLT25	85	DX	LF52UPV	101	AR	LG52DDF
54	WN	LF02PSX	70	WN	LF52UTG	86	DX	LF52UPW	102	AR	LG52DDJ
55	WN	LF02PSY	71	WN	LF52UTH	87	DX	LF52UPX	103	AR	LG52DDK
56	WN	LF02PSZ	72	WN	LF52UTJ	88	DX	LF52UPY	104	AR	LG52DDL
57	WN	LF02PTO	73	WN	LF52UTL	89	DX	LF52UPZ			

VLW105-179 — Volvo B7TL 10.1m — Wrightbus Eclipse Gemini — N41/22D — 2002-03

105	DX	LJ03MHU	124	AR	LF52UOX	143	SF	LG03MFA	162	SF	LG03MRX
106	DX	LJ03MHV	125	AR	LF52UOY	144	SF	LG03MFE	163	SF	LG03MRY
107	DX	LJ03MHX	126	AR	LF52UPA	145	SF	LG03MFF	164	SF	LG03MSU
108	DX	LJ03MHY	127	AR	LF52UPB	146	SF	LG03MFK	165	SF	LG03MSV
109	DX	LJ03MHZ	128	AR	LF52UPC	147	SF	LG03MBF	166	SF	LG03MSX
110	DX	LJ03MJE	129	AR	LG52DAA	148	SF	LG03MBU	167	SF	LG03MMU
111	DX	LJ03MJF	130	AR	LJ03MGZ	149	SF	LG03MBV	168	SF	LG03MMV
112	DX	LJ03MJK	131	AR	LJ03MHA	150	SF	LG03MBX	169	AR	LG03MMX
113	DX	LJ03MJU	132	AR	LJ03MHE	151	SF	LG03MBY	170	AR	LG03MOA
114	DX	LJ03MJV	133	AR	LJ03MHF	152	SF	LG03MDE	171	AR	LG03MOF
115	DX	LJ03MGX	134	AR	LJ03MHK	153	SF	LG03MDF	172	AR	LG03MOV
116	DX	LJ03MGY	135	AR	LJ03MHL	154	SF	LG03MDK	173	AR	LG03MPE
117	AR	LF52UPN	136	AR	LJ03MHM	155	SF	LG03MDN	174	AR	LG03MPF
118	AR	LF52UPO	137	AR	LJ03MHN	156	SF	LG03MDU	175	AR	LG03MPU
119	AR	LF52UOS	138	AR	LJ03MFN	157	SF	LG03MPX	176	AR	LG03MPV
120	AR	LF52UOT	139	AR	LJ03MFP	158	SF	LG03MPY	177	AR	LG03MLL
121	AR	LF52UOU	140	SF	LJ03MFU	159	SF	LG03MPZ	178	AR	LG03MLN
122	AR	LF52UOV	141	SF	LJ03MFV	160	SF	LG03MRU	179	AR	LG03MLV
123	AR	LF52UOW	142	SF	LG03MEV	161	SF	LG03MRV			

VLW180-199 — Volvo B7TL 10.8m — Wrightbus Eclipse Gemini — N45/24D — 2003

180	AR	LJ03MLX	185	AR	LJ03MMF	190	AR	LJ03MXR	195	AR	LJ53BEU
181	AR	LJ03MLY	186	AR	LJ03MMK	191	AR	LJ03MXS	196	AR	LJ53BEY
182	AR	LJ03MLZ	187	AR	LJ03MKM	192	AR	LJ03MXT	197	AR	LJ53BFA
183	AR	LJ03MMA	188	AR	LJ03MKN	193	AR	LJ03MXU	198	AR	LJ53BFE
184	AR	LJ03MME	189	AR	LJ03MYN	194	AR	LJ03MWX	199	AR	LJ53BFF

VPL3	EC	185CLT	Volvo B10M-61	Plaxton Paramount 3200 II	C53F	1986	Arriva East Herts & Essex, 1998
VPL4	EC	205CLT	Volvo B10M-61	Plaxton Paramount 3200 II	C53F	1986	Arriva East Herts & Essex, 1998
VPL503	EC	VLT32	Volvo B10M-60	Plaxton Paramount 3500 III	C49FT	1991	Arriva East Herts & Essex, 1998

Special event vehicle:

RV1	EC	GJG750D	AEC Regent V 2D3RA	Park Royal	B40/32F	1966	Arriva East Herts & Essex, 1998

Ancillary vehicles:

L515-556 — Leyland Olympian ON2R50C13Z4* Northern Counties — B47/27D — 1990 — *541/3/4/7/8/50-4 ONCL10/1RZA

515	TCt	G515VBB	525	SFt	G525VBB	541	SFt	G541VBB	550	TCt	G550VBB
516	TCt	G516VBB	526	Nt	G526VBB	542	SFt	G542VBB	551	TCt	G551VBB
517	TCt	G517VBB	536	SFt	G536VBB	543	SFt	G543VBB	552	SFt	G552VBB
518	TCt	G518VBB	537	TCt	G537VBB	544	BKt	G544VBB	553	TCt	G553VBB
519	TCt	G519VBB	538	TCt	G538VBB	547	TCt	G547VBB	554	TCt	G554VBB
520	TCt	G520VBB	539	SFt	G539VBB	548	SFt	G548VBB	555	TCt	G555VBB
521	TCt	G521VBB	540	TCt	G540VBB	549	SFt	C549VDD	556	TCt	G556VBB
523	u	G523VBB									

M537	GYE537W	MCW Metrobus DR101/14	MCW	TV	1981	London Buses, 1994
M752	KVY752X	MCW Metrobus DR101/14	MCW	TV	1981	London Buses, 1994
M770	KVY770X	MCW Metrobus DR101/14	MCW	TV	1981	London Buses, 1994
M773	KVY773X	MCW Metrobus DR101/14	MCW	TV	1981	London Buses, 1994

M903	A903SUL	MCW Metrobus DR101/16	MCW		TV	1983	London Buses, 1994
M984	A984SYF	MCW Metrobus DR101/17	MCW		TV	1983	London Buses, 1994
M1000	A700THV	MCW Metrobus DR101/17	MCW		TV	1984	London Buses, 1994

M1084-1105   MCW Metrobus DR134/1   MCW   TV   1984   London Buses, 1994

1084	B84WUL	**1095**	B95WUL	**1098**	B98WUL	**1103**	B103WUL
1092	B92WUL	**1096**	B96WUL	**1100**	B100WUL	**1104**	B104WUL
1094	B94WUL	**1097**	B97WUL	**1101**	B101WUL	**1105**	B105WUL

M1124-1399   MCW Metrobus DR101/17   MCW   TV   1984   London Buses, 1994

1124	B124WUL	**1170**	B170WUL	**1214**	B214WUL	**1399**	C399BVU
1140	B140WUL						

Previous registrations:

70CLT	H643GRO	OYM453A	VLT29
124CLT	G661WMD	SVS615	WLT346
185CLT	C874CYX	SVS618	WLT548
205CLT	C876CYX	TSK270	WLT713
217CLT	N551LUA	T324FGN	T324FGN, 99D53451
319CLT	P753RWU	T325FGN	T325FGN, 99D53440
324CLT	J328BSH	V423DGT	V435DGT
330CLT	T56AUA	V435DGT	V423DGT
361CLT	G662WMD	VLT12	C437BUV
398CLT	N552LUA	VLT25	LF52USE
480CLT	P754RWU	VLT27	G906TYR
519CLT	R162GNW	VLT32	H903AHS
530MUY	E118KFV	VLT47	G908TYR
593CLT	T110AUA	VLT88	C379BUV
725DYE	LJ53BGE	VLT173	J353BSH
734DYE	LJ53NJE	VLT244	LJ53NHM
801DYE	LJ03MWM	VYJ806	124CLT
822DYE	LJ53BFV	WLT348	LJ53NGO
852UXC	324CLT, VYJ807, 324CLT	WLT372	J352BSH
855UXC	VLT25	WLT531	LJ53NHX
D180FYM	D180FYM, 480CLT	WLT554	J354BSH, VLT32, J354BSH
LDS279A	VLT54	WLT719	LJ53NHU
LDS402A	145CLT	WLT751	J351BSH
LJ03MMX	LJ03MMX, VLT25	WLT807	LJ03MVU
MFF509	312CLT	WTS418A	WLT909
NSG636A	164CLT	XYJ427	185CLT
NVS485	292CLT	XYJ440	WLT838
OVS940	WLT875		

Allocations

Barking (Ripple Road) - DX

Dart	ADL1	DDL16	DDL17	DDL18	PDL29	PDL30	PDL31	PDL32
	PDL33	PDL34	PDL35	PDL36	PDL37	PDL38	ADL969	ADL970
	ADL971	ADL972	ADL973	ADL974	ADL975	ADL976	ADL977	ADL978
	ADL979	ADL980	ADL981	ADL982	ADL983			
Olympian	L315	L319	L324					
	L331	L332	L334	L337	L339	L346	L350	
	L530	L531						
	L532	L533	L534	L535	L545			
Volvo B7TL	VLA129	VLA130	VLA131	VLA132	VLA133	VLA134	VLA135	VLA136
	VLA137	VLA138	VLA139	VLA140	VLA141	VLA142	VLA143	VLW85
	VLW86	VLW87	VLW88	VLW89	VLW90	VLW91	VLW92	VLW93
	VLW94	VLW95	VLW96	VLW105	VLW106	VLW107	VLW108	VLW109
	VLW110	VLW111	VLW112	VLW113	VLW114	VLW115	VLW116	

Battersea (Hester Road) - BA

DB250	DW103	DW104	DW105	DW106	DW107	DW108	DW109	DW110
	DW111	DW112	DW113	DW114	DW115	DW116	DW117	DW118
	DW119	DW120	DW121	DW122	DW123	DW124	DW125	DW126
	DW127	DW128	DW129	DW130	DW131	DW132	DW133	DW134

Wrightbus introduced the Eclipse Gemini double-deck in the summer of 2001, and currently available on Volvo B7TL and VDL DB250. Arriva was an early customer. Here, VLW196, LJ53BEY, is seen outside St Paul's Cathedral while operating route 76. *Mark Lyons*

Brixton (Streatham Hill) - BN *Sub-depot: Old Tram Depot, Brixton Hill*

DAF Cadet	DWL1	DWL2	DWL3	DWL4	DWL5	DWL6	DWL7	DWL8
	DWL9	DWL10	DWL11	DWL12	DWL13	DWL14	DWL15	DWL16
	DWL17	DWL18	DWL19	DWL20	DWL21	DWL22		
Routemaster	RM25	RM29	RM54	RM85	RM346	RM548	RM713	RM838
	RM871	RM875	RML892	RML895	RM1124	RM1280	RM1292	RM1975
	RML2264	RML2307	RML2324	RML2333	RML2366	RML2375	RML2387	RLM2491
	RML2521	RML2533	RML2545	RML2549	RML2572	RML2573	RML2577	RML2586
	RML2619	RML2636	RML2730	RML2752	RML2753	RML2759		
DB250	DLA142	DLA143	DLA144	DLA145	DLA146	DLA147	DLA148	DLA149
	DLA150	DLA151	DLA152	DLA153	DLA159	DLA160	DLA161	DLA162
	DLA163	DLA164	DLA165	DW53	DW54	DW55	DW56	DW57
	DW58	DW59	DW60	DW61	DW62	DW63	DW64	DW65
	DW66	DW67	DW68	DW69	DW70	DW71	DW72	DW73
	DW74	DW75	DW76	DW77	DW78	DW79	DW80	DW81
	DW82	DW83	DW84	DW85	DW86	DW87	DW88	DW89
	DW90	DW91	DW92	DW93				

Clapton (Bohemia Place, Hackney) - CT

Dart	PDL16	PDL17	PDL18					
Routemaster	RM652	RM848	RML888	RML897	RML901	RM909	RM1145	RM1164
	RM1185	RM1312	RM1640	RM1776	RM1941	RM1968	RM2050	RM2060
	RM2122	RML2277	RML2280	RML2287	RML2304	RML2315	RML2325	RML2328
	RML2334	RML2344	RML2346	RML2355	RML2356	RML2359	RML2370	RML2386
	RML2401	RML2406	RML2408	RML2409	RML2416	RML2434	RML2457	RML2468
	RML2483	RML2492	RML2494	RML2503	RML2525	RML2526	RML2528	RML2534
	RML2544	RML2546	RML2562	RML2567	RML2571	RML2597	RML2638	RML2655
	RML2675	RML2688	RML2750					

DAF ALX400	DLA11	DLA12	DLA13	DLA14	DLA15	DLA16	DLA17	DLA18
	DLA19	DLA20	DLA21	DLA201	DLA202	DLA203	DLA248	DLA249
	DLA270	DLA271	DLA291	DLA292	DLA293	DLA294	DLA295	DLA296
	DLA297	DLA298	DLA299	DLA300	DLA301	DLA302	DLA303	DLA304
	DLA305	DLA306	DLA307	DLA308	DLA309	DLA310	DLA346	DLA370
	DLA371	DLA372	DLA373	DLA374	DLA375	DLA376	DLA377	DLA378
	DLA379	DLA380	DLA381	DLA382	DLA383	DLA384	DLA385	DLA386
	DLA387	DLA388						

Croydon (Beddington Farm Road) - CN

Dart	PDL19	PDL20	PDL21	PDL22	PDL23	PDL24	PDL25	PDL26
	PDL27	PDL28	PDL62	PDL63				
SB120	DWL57	DWL58	DWL59	DWL60	DWL61	DWL62	DWL63	DWL64
	DWL65	DWL66	DWL67	DWS1	DWS2	DWS3	DWS4	DWS5
	DWS6	DWS7	DWS8	DWS9	DWS10	DWS11	DWS12	DWS13
	DWS14	DWS15	DWS16	DWS17	DWS18			
DB250	DW35	DW37	DW38	DW39	DW40	DW41	DW42	DW43
	DW44	DW45	DW46	DW47	DW48	DW49	DW50	DW51
	DW52	DW94	DW95	DW96	DW97	DW98	DW99	DW100
	DW101	DW102						

Croydon (Brighton Road, South Croydon) - TC

Dart	ADL9	ADL10	ADL11	ADL12	ADL13	ADL14	ADL15	ADL16
	ADL17	ADL18	ADL19	ADL20	ADL21	ADL22	ADL23	DPP421
	DPP422	DPP423	DPP424	DPP425	DPP426	DPP427	DPP428	DPP429
	DPP430	PDL117	PDL118	PDL119	PDL120	PDL121	PDL122	PDL123
DB250	DLA133	DLA134	DLA135	DLA136	DLA154	DLA155	DLA156	DLA157
	DLA158	DLA171	DLA172	DLA173	DLA174	DLA175	DLA176	DLA177
	DLA178	DLA179	DLA180	DLA181	DLA182	DLA183	DLA184	DLA185
	DLA186	DLA187	DLA188	DLA189	DLA215	DLA216	DLA217	DLA218
	DLA219	DLA220	DLA221	DLA222	DLA223	DLA224	DLA250	DLA251
	DLA252	DLA253	DLA254	DLA255	DLA256	DLA257	DLA258	DLA259
	DLA260	DLA261	DLA262	DLA263	DLA264	DLA265	DLA266	DLA267
	DLA268	DLA269	DW1	DW2	DW3	DW4	DW5	DW6
	DW7	DW8	DW9	DW10	DW11	DW12	DW13	DW14
	DW15	DW16	DW17	DW18	DW19	DW20	DW21	DW22
	DW23	DW24	DW25	DW26	DW27	DW28	DW29	DW30
	DW31	DW32	DW33	DW34	DW36			

Edmonton (Towpath Road, Stonehill Business Park) - EC

Dart	ADL2	ADL3	ADL4	ADL5	ADL6	ADL7	ADL8	ADL61
	ADL62	ADL63	ADL64	ADL65	ADL66	ADL67	ADL68	ADL69
	ADL71	ADL72	ADL73	ADL74	ADL75	ADL76	ADL77	ADL78
	ADL79	ADL81	DDL15	DPP431	PDL1	PDL2	PDL3	PDL4
	PDL5	PDL6	PDL7	PDL8	PDL9	PDL10	PDL11	PDL12
	PDL13	PDL14	PDL15	PDL70	PDL72	PDL73	PDL74	PDL75
	PDL76	PDL77	PDL78	PDL79	PDL80	PDL81	PDL95	PDL96
	PDL97	PDL98	PDL99	PDL100	PDL101	PDL102	PDL103	PDL104
	PDL105	PDL106	PDL107	PDL108	PDL109	PDL110	PDL111	PDL112
	PDL113	PDL114	PDL115	PDL116				
Volvo B10M	VPL3	VPL4	VPL503					
Tiger coach	TPL1	TPL2	TPL8	TPL518				
DAF coach	DP1	DP2	DP3	DI4	DP5	DP6	DI7	DVH6
	DVH8							
AEC Regent V	RV1							
Routemaster	RMC1453	RMC1464						
Metrobus	M537	M573	M617	M772	M777	M1075	M1124	M1126
	M1130	M1136	M1231	M1248	M1253	M1254	M1300	M1312
	M1313	M1314	M1320	M1326	M1327	M1367	M1379	M1405
	M1437							

Olympian	L328	L351	L352	L353	L354			
Volvo B7TL	VLW69							
DAF/VDL DB250	DLA125	DLA136	DLA137	DLA138	DLA139	DLA348	DLA349	DLA350
	DLA351	DLA352	DLA353	DLA354	DLA355	DLA356	DLA357	DLA358
	DLA359	DLA360	DLA361	DLA362	DLA363	DLA364	DLA365	DLA366
	DLA367	DLA368	DLA369					

Enfield (Southbury Road, Ponders End) - E

Dart	PDL64	PDL65	PDL66	PDL67	PDL68	PDL69	PDL82	PDL83
	PDL84	PDL85	PDL86	PDL87	PDL88	PDL89	PDL90	PDL91
	PDL92	PDL93	PDL94					
Cadet	DWL23	DWL24	DWL25	DWL26	DWL27	DWL29	DWL56	
DAF/VDL DB250	DLA94	DLA95	DLA116	DLA117	DLA118	DLA119	DLA120	DLA121
	DLA122	DLA123	DLA190	DLA191	DLA192	DLA193	DLA194	DLA195
	DLA196	DLA197	DLA198	DLA199	DLA200	DLA210	DLA211	DLA212
	DLA225	DLA226	DLA227	DLA233	DLA237	DLA238	DLA276	DLP1
	DLP2	DLP3	DLP4	DLP5	DLP6	DLP7	DLP8	DLP9
	DLP10	DLP11	DLP12	DLP13	DLP14	DLP15	DLP16	DLP17
	DLP18	DLP19	DLP20	DLP76	DLP77	DLP78	DLP79	DLP80
	DLP81	DLP82	DLP83	DLP84	DLP85	DLP86	DLP87	DLP88
	DLP89	DLP90	DLP91	DLP92	DLP93	DLP94	DLP95	DLP96
	DLP97	DLP98	DLP99	DLP100	DLP101	DLP102	DLP103	DLP104
	DLP105	DLP106	DLP107	DLP108	DLP109	DLP110		

Lea Valley (Leeside Road, Edmonton) - LV

Citaro	MA1	MA2	MA3	MA4	MA5	MA6	MA7	MA8
	MA9	MA10	MA11	MA12	MA13	MA14	MA15	MA16
	MA17	MA18	MA19	MA20	MA21	MA22	MA23	MA24
	MA25	MA26	MA27	MA28	MA29	MA30	MA31	MA32
	MA33	MA34	MA35	MA36	MA37	MA38	MA39	MA40
	MA41	MA42	MA43	MA44	MA45	MA46	MA47	MA48
	MA49	MA50	MA51	MA52	MA53	MA54	MA55	MA56
	MA57	MA58	MA59	MA60	MA61	MA62	MA63	MA64
	MA65	MA66	MA67	MA68	MA69	MA70	MA71	MA72
	MA73	MA74	MA75	MA76	MA77	MA78	MA79	MA80
	MA81	MA82	MA83	MA84	MA85	MA86	MA87	MA88
	MA89	MA90	MA91	MA92	MA93	MA94	MA95	MA96
	MA97	MA98	MA99	MA100	MA101	MA102	MA103	MA104
	MA105	MA106	MA107	MA108	MA109	MA110	MA111	MA112
	MA113	MA114	MA115	MA116	MA117	MA118	MA119	MA120
	MA121	MA122						

Norwood (Knights Hill, West Norwood) - N

Routemaster	RM2	RML2217						
Olympian	L25	L37	L102	L162	L180	L198	L214	L223
DAF ALX400	DLA140	DLA141	DLA166	DLA167	DLA168	DLA169	DLA170	DLA236
	DLA272	DLA311	DLA312	DLA313	DLA314	DLA315	DLA316	
	DLA317	DLA318	DLA319	DLA320	DLA321			
Volvo B7TL ALX400	VLA1	VLA2	VLA3	VLA4	VLA5	VLA6	VLA7	VLA8
	VLA9	VLA10	VLA11	VLA12	VLA13	VLA14	VLA15	VLA16
	VLA17	VLA18	VLA19	VLA20	VLA21	VLA22	VLA23	VLA24
	VLA25	VLA26	VLA27	VLA28	VLA29	VLA30	VLA31	VLA32
	VLA33	VLA34	VLA35	VLA36	VLA37	VLA38	VLA39	VLA40
	VLA41	VLA42	VLA43	VLA44	VLA45	VLA46	VLA47	VLA48
	VLA49	VLA50	VLA51	VLA52	VLA53	VLA54	VLA55	VLA70
	VLA71	VLA72	VLA73	VLA104	VLA105	VLA106	VLA107	VLA108
	VLA109	VLA110	VLA111	VLA112	VLA113	VLA114	VLA115	VLA116
	VLA117	VLA118	VLA119	VLA120	VLA121	VLA122	VLA123	VLA124
	VLA125	VLA126	VLA127	VLA128				

Two orders for more Mercedes-Benz Citaro articulated buses will see the conversion of route 38 from Routemaster operation at Clapton and a further thirty-three are planned for the conversion of route 29 early in 2006. From the initial delivery, MA39, BX04NEJ, is seen in Lewisham. *Gerry Mead*

Stamford Hill (Rookwood Road) - SF

DAF ALX400	DLA38	DLA96	DLA97	DLA98	DLA99	DLA100	DLA101	DLA102
	DLA103	DLA104	DLA105	DLA106	DLA107	DLA108	DLA109	DLA110
	DLA111	DLA112	DLA113	DLA114	DLA115	DLA290		
Volvo B7 Gemini	VLW140	VLW141	VLW142	VLW143	VLW144	VLW145	VLW146	VLW147
	VLW148	VLW149	VLW150	VLW151	VLW152	VLW153	VLW154	VLW155
	VLW156	VLW157	VLW158	VLW159	VLW160	VLW161	VLW162	VLW163
	VLW164	VLW165	VLW166	VLW167	VLW168			

Thornton Heath (719 London Road) - TH

Dart	DDL1	DDL2	DDL3	DDL4	DDL5	DDL6	DDL7	DDL8
	DDL9	DDL10	DDL11	DDL12	DDL13	DDL14	PDL50	PDL51
	PDL52	PDL53	PDL54	PDL55	PDL56	PDL57	PDL58	PDL59
	PDL60	PDL61	PDL71					
DAF ALX400	DLA2	DLA3	DLA4	DLA5	DLA6	DLA7	DLA8	DLA9
	DLA10	DLA38	DLA39	DLA40	DLA41	DLA42	DLA43	DLA44
	DLA48	DLA49	DLA50	DLA51	DLA52	DLA53	DLA54	DLA55
	DLA56	DLA57	DLA58	DLA59	DLA60	DLA61	DLA62	DLA63
	DLA64	DLA126	DLA127	DLA128	DLA129	DLA130	DLA131	DLA132
	DLA322	DLA323	DLA324	DLA325	DLA326	DLA327	DLA328	DLA329
	DLA330	DLA331	DLA332	DLA333	DLA334	DLA335	DLA336	DLA337
	DLA338	DLA339	DLA340	DLA341	DLA342	DLA343	DLA344	DLA345
	DLA347	DLA389						

Tottenham (Philip Lane) - AR

Dart	PDL39	PDL40	PDL41	PDL42	PDL43	PDL44	PDL45	PDL46
	PDL47	PDL48	PDL49					
Routemaster	RM5							
DAF ALX400	DLA230	DLA231	DLA232	DLA234	DLA235	DLA239	DLA240	DLA241
	DLA242	DLA243	DLA244	DLA245	DLA246	DLA247	DLA273	DLA274
	DLA275	DLA277	DLA278	DLA279	DLA280	DLA281	DLA282	DLA283
	DLA284	DLA285	DLA286	DLA287	DLA288	DLA289		
Volvo B7 Gemini	VLA74	VLA75	VLA76	VLA77	VLA78	VLA79	VLA80	VLA81
	VLA82	VLA83	VLA84	VLA85	VLA86	VLA87	VLA88	VLA89
	VLA90	VLA91	VLA92	VLA93	VLA94	VLA95	VLA96	VLA97
	VLA98	VLA99	VLA100	VLA101	VLA102	VLA103	VLW85	VLW97
	VLW98	VLW99	VLW100	VLW101	VLW102	VLW103	VLW104	VLW117
	VLW118	VLW119	VLW120	VLW121	VLW122	VLW123	VLW124	VLW125
	VLW126	VLW127	VLW128	VLW129	VLW130	VLW131	VLW132	VLW133
	VLW134	VLW135	VLW136	VLW137	VLW138	VLW139	VLW169	VLW170
	VLW171	VLW172	VLW173	VLW174	VLW175	VLW176	VLW177	VLW178
	VLW179	VLW180	VLW181	VLW182	VLW183	VLW184	VLW185	VLW186
	VLW187	VLW188	VLW189	VLW190	VLW191	VLW192	VLW193	VLW194
	VLW195	VLW196	VLW197	VLW198	VLW199			

Wood Green (High Road) - WN (sub depot at Regent's Avenue, Palmers Green - AD)

SB120 Cadet	CW1	DWL30	DWL31	DWL32	DWL33	DWL34	DWL35	DWL36
	DWL37	DWL38	DWL39	DWL40	DWL41	DWL42	DWL43	DWL44
	DWL45	DWL46	DWL47	DWL48	DWL49	DWL50	DWL51	DWL52
	DWL53	DWL54	DWL55					
DAF/VDL DB250	DLA1	DLA22	DLA23	DLA24	DLA25	DAL26	DLA27	DLA28
	DLA29	DLA30	DLA31	DLA32	DLA33	DLA34	DLA35	DLA36
	DLA37	DLA45	DLA46	DLA47	DLA65	DLA66	DLA67	DLA68
	DLA69	DLA70	DLA71	DLA72	DLA73	DLA74	DLA75	DLA76
	DLA77	DLA78	DLA79	DLA80	DLA81	DLA82	DLA83	DLA84
	DLA85	DLA86	DLA87	DLA88	DLA89	DLA90	DLA91	DLA92
	DLA124	DLA125	DLA213	DLA214	DLA228	DLA229	DLP40	DLP41
	DLP42	DLP43	DLP44	DLP45	DLP46	DLP47	DLP48	DLP49
	DLP50	DLP51	DLP52	DLP53	DLP54	DLP55	DLP56	DLP57
	DLP58	DLP59	DLP60	DLP61	DLP62	DLP63	DLP64	DLP65
	DLP66	DLP67	DLP68	DLP69	DLP70	DLP71	DLP72	DLP73
	DLP74	DLP75						
Volvo B7TL	VLW1	VLW2	VLW3	VLW4	VLW5	VLW6	VLW7	VLW8
	VLW9	VLW10	VLW11	VLW12	VLW13	VLW14	VLW15	VLW16
	VLW17	VLW18	VLW19	VLW20	VLW21	VLW22	VLW23	VLW24
	VLW25	VLW26	VLW27	VLW28	VLW29	VLW30	VLW31	VLW32
	VLW33	VLW34	VLW35	VLW36	VLW37	VLW38	VLW39	VLW40
	VLW41	VLW42	VLW43	VLW44	VLW45	VLW46	VLW47	VLW48
	VLW49	VLW50	VLW51	VLW52	VLW53	VLW54	VLW55	VLW56
	VLW57	VLW58	VLW59	VLW60	VLW61	VLW62	VLW63	VLW64
	VLW65	VLW66	VLW67	VLW68	VLW70	VLW71	VLW72	VLW73
	VLW74	VLW75	VLW76	VLW77	VLW78	VLW79	VLW80	VLW81
	VLW82	VLW83	VLW84					

Unallocated

Routemaster	RML884	RML2350	RML2360	RML2403	RML2477	RML2588	RML2591	RML2602
	RML2684	RML2715	RML2742					
Olympian	L24	L159	L191	L230	L329	L546	L549	
Metrobus	M757	M1322						

ORIGINAL LONDON SIGHTSEEING TOUR

The Original London Sightseeing Tour Ltd, Jews Road, Wandsworth, SW18 1TB

DD202	VVN202Y	Dennis Dominator DDA149	Northern Counties	PO43/31D	1983	London Pride, 2001
EMB763	D553YNO	MCW Metrobus DR115/4	MCW	PO61/35D	1987	New World FirstBus, 2001
EMB764	E964JAR	MCW Metrobus DR115/4	MCW	PO61/35D	1987	New World FirstBus, 2001
EMB765	E965JAR	MCW Metrobus DR115/4	MCW	PO61/35D	1987	New World FirstBus, 2001
EMB767	E767JAR	MCW Metrobus DR115/4	MCW	PO61/35D	1987	New World FirstBus, 2001
EMB768	E768JAR	MCW Metrobus DR115/4	MCW	PO61/35D	1987	New World FirstBus, 2001
EMB769	E769JAR	MCW Metrobus DR115/4	MCW	PO61/35D	1987	New World FirstBus, 2001
EMB770	E770JAR	MCW Metrobus DR115/4	MCW	PO61/35D	1987	New World FirstBus, 2001
EMB771	E771JAR	MCW Metrobus DR115/4	MCW	PO61/35D	1987	New World FirstBus, 2001
EMB772	E772JAR	MCW Metrobus DR115/4	MCW	PO61/35D	1987	New World FirstBus, 2001
EMB773	E773JAR	MCW Metrobus DR115/4	MCW	PO61/35D	1987	New World FirstBus, 2001
EMB775	D675YNO	MCW Metrobus DR115/4	MCW	PO61/35D	1987	New World FirstBus, 2001
MB121	BYX121V	MCW Metrobus DR101/9	MCW	PO43/28D	1979	Cowie South London, 1996
MB296	BYX296V	MCW Metrobus DR101/12	MCW	PO43/28D	1980	London South, 1998
MB353	GYE353W	MCW Metrobus DR101/12	MCW	PO43/28D	1980	London General, 1997
MB495	GYE495W	MCW Metrobus DR101/14	MCW	PO43/28D	1980	Cowie South London, 1996
MB500	GYE500W	MCW Metrobus DR101/14	MCW	PO43/28D	1980	Arriva London, 1999
MB509	GYE509W	MCW Metrobus DR101/14	MCW	PO43/28D	1980	Arriva London, 1998
MB525	GYE525W	MCW Metrobus DR101/14	MCW	PO43/28D	1981	London South, 1998
MB533	GYE533W	MCW Metrobus DR101/14	MCW	PO43/28D	1981	London South, 1998
MB539	GYE539W	MCW Metrobus DR101/14	MCW	PO43/28D	1981	Cowie South London, 1996
MB553	GYE553W	MCW Metrobus DR101/14	MCW	PO43/28D	1981	Cowie South London, 1996
MB555	GYE555W	MCW Metrobus DR101/14	MCW	PO31/14F	1981	Arriva London, 2000
MB558	GYE558W	MCW Metrobus DR101/14	MCW	PO43/28D	1981	Cowie South London, 1996
MB603	GYE603W	MCW Metrobus DR101/14	MCW	PO43/28D	1981	Arriva London, 2000
MB663	KYV663X	MCW Metrobus DR101/14	MCW	PO43/28D	1981	London North, 1998
MB672	KYV672X	MCW Metrobus DR101/14	MCW	PO43/28D	1981	London North, 1998

Stars of the Original Sightseeing Tour are a batch of ten Ayats Bravo City open-top buses. The model is not new to Arriva, which uses two in its Italian operation, although these vehicles have closed tops with high back seating. Seen in London service is 602, LX02GDZ. *Mark Lyons*

As well as The Original Tour, Arriva now operate under the City Sightseeing brand. An integral tri-axle Metroliner, B825AAT, was initially new for National Express service, though since it has been converted for open-top tour duties. It is seen passing the Palace of Westminster. *David Longbottom*

MB707	KYV707X	MCW Metrobus DR101/14	MCW		PO43/28D	1981	London North, 1998
MB710	KYV710X	MCW Metrobus DR101/14	MCW		B43/28D	1981	Arriva London, 2000
MB724	KYV724X	MCW Metrobus DR101/14	MCW		B43/28D	1981	Arriva London, 2002
MB729	KYV729X	MCW Metrobus DR101/14	MCW		B43/28D	1981	Arriva London, 2000
MB748	KYV748X	MCW Metrobus DR101/14	MCW		PO43/28D	1982	London North, 1998
MB840	OJD840Y	MCW Metrobus DR101/16	MCW		PO43/28D	1983	Cowie South London, 1996
MB863	OJD863Y	MCW Metrobus DR101/16	MCW		B43/28D	1983	Arriva London, 2000
MB895	A895SUL	MCW Metrobus DR101/16	MCW		PO43/28D	1983	Arriva London, 2000
MB927	A927SUL	MCW Metrobus DR101/16	MCW		PO43/28D	1983	London South, 1998
MB1227	B227WUL	MCW Metrobus DR101/17	MCW		PO43/28D	1983	Arriva London, 1999
MB1239	B239WUL	MCW Metrobus DR101/17	MCW		B43/28D	1983	Arriva London, 2002
MB1265	B265WUL	MCW Metrobus DR101/17	MCW		B43/28D	1983	Arriva London, 2002
MB1310	C310BUV	MCW Metrobus DR101/17	MCW		B43/28D	1983	Arriva London, 2002
MB1401	C401BUV	MCW Metrobus DR101/17	MCW		B43/28D	1983	Arriva London, 2002
ML10	B240LRA	MCW Metroliner DR130/7	MCW		O63/23F	1986	Dunn Line, Nottingham, 1994
ML11	B241LRA	MCW Metroliner DR130/7	MCW		O63/23F	1986	Dunn Line, Nottingham, 1994
ML12	A112KFX	MCW Metroliner DR130/5	MCW		O67/22F	1984	London Pride, 2001
ML13	A113KFX	MCW Metroliner DR130/5	MCW		O67/20F	1984	London Pride, 2001
ML14	A114KFX	MCW Metroliner DR130/5	MCW		O67/20F	1984	London Pride, 2001
ML15	B115ORU	MCW Metroliner DR130/7	MCW		O63/20F	1984	London Pride, 2001
ML17	C907GUD	MCW Metroliner DR130/21	MCW		O63/17F	1985	London Pride, 2001
ML19	IIL7269	MCW Metroliner DR130/3	MCW		O63/20F	1984	London Pride, 2001
ML20	B224VHW	MCW Metroliner DR130/3	MCW		O63/20F	1984	London Pride, 2001
ML21	B121ORU	MCW Metroliner DR130/3	MCW		O63/20F	1984	London Pride, 2001
ML22	B222VHW	MCW Metroliner DR130/3	MCW		O63/16F	1984	London Pride, 2001
ML24	B224VHW	MCW Metroliner DR130/3	MCW		O63/18F	1984	London Pride, 2001
ML25	B225VHW	MCW Metroliner DR130/3	MCW		O63/18F	1984	London Pride, 2001
ML27	A667XDA	MCW Metroliner DR130/6	MCW		O63/23F	1984	London Pride, 2001
ML28	B824AAT	MCW Metroliner DR130/3	MCW		O63/16F	1984	London Pride, 2001
ML29	B825AAT	MCW Metroliner DR130/3	MCW		O63/16F	1984	London Pride, 2001
ML33	C133CFB	MCW Metroliner DR130/24	MCW		O63/18F	1986	London Pride, 2001

At one time Britain exported its older buses for use elsewhere in the world. Now we bring in some that are time-expired from Hong Kong! Pictured with its partial open-top form, tri-axle Metrobus EMB771, E771JAR, was new to China Motor Bus, based on Hong Kong island. It is seen at Hyde Park Corner. *Steve Rice*

OA320-349

			Leyland Olympian ON2R50C13Z4 Alexander RH			PO43/25D* 1992	Arriva London, 2003

*320 is PO42/25D, 321 is O42/25D.

320	J320BSH	327	J327BSH	338	J338BSH	344	J344BSH
321	J321BSH	330	J330BSH	340	J340BSH	345	J345BSH
322	J320BSH	333	J433BSH	341	J341BSH	347	J347BSH
323	J320BSH	335	J335BSH	342	J342BSH	348	J348BSH
325	J325BSH	336	J336BSH	343	J343BSH	349	J349BSH
326	J326BSHx						

VLY601-610

		Volvo B7L			Ayats Bravo City	O51/24F	2005

601	LX05GDV	604	LX05GEJ	607	LX05KNZ	609	EU05DVW
602	LX05GDY	605	LX05HRO	608	LX05KOA	610	EU05DVX
603	LX05GDZ	606	LX05HSC				

Ancillary vehicle:

MB1152	B152WUL	MCW Metrobus DR101/17	MCW	TV	1983	Arriva London, 1999

Previous registrations:

B240LRA	B901XJO, A5BOB	E771JAR	DT9187 (HK)
B241LRA	B904XJO, A4BOB	E772JAR	DV2896 (HK)
D553YNO	DV471 (HK)	E773JAR	DU3481 (HK)
E767JAR	DU3460 (HK)	E964JAR	DT4549 (HK)
E768JAR	DU8346 (HK)	E965JAR	DV4883 (HK)
E769JAR	DT7256 (HK)	E966JAR	DV3433 (HK)
E770JAR	DU8506 (HK)	IIL7269	B117ORU

Depot: Jews Road, Wandsworth

ARRIVA SOUTHERN COUNTIES

Arriva Southern Counties Ltd, Arriva West Sussex Ltd,
Arriva Kent Thameside Ltd; Arriva Kent & Sussex Ltd; New Enterprise Ltd
Arriva Medway Towns Ltd, Arriva Guildford & West Surrey Ltd;
Arriva Southend Ltd
Invicta House, Armstrong Road, Maidstone, Kent, ME15 6TX

1118-1143   Mercedes-Benz Vario O810   Plaxton Beaver 2   B27F   1998

1118	GI	R118TKO	1120	GI	R120TKO	1122	GI	R122TKO	1143	u	R763DUB
1119	GI	R119TKO	1121	GI	R121TKO						

1172-1183   Mercedes-Benz Vario O810   Plaxton Beaver 2   B25F   1998

1174	u	R174VBM	1179	GI	R949VPU	1180	GI	R950VPU	1183	SI	R953VPU
1178	GI	R948VPU									

1186	SI	R186DNM	Mercedes-Benz Vario O810	Plaxton Beaver 2	B27F	1997	
1187	SW	R187DNM	Mercedes-Benz Vario O810	Plaxton Beaver 2	B27F	1997	
1188	SE	R188DNM	Mercedes-Benz Vario O810	Plaxton Beaver 2	B27F	1997	
1189	SI	P478DPE	Mercedes-Benz 711D	Plaxton Beaver 2	B27F	1997	
1190	SI	P481DPE	Mercedes-Benz 711D	Plaxton Beaver 2	B27F	1997	
1191	w	R191DNM	Mercedes-Benz Vario O810	Plaxton Beaver 2	B27F	1998	
1192	w	R192DNM	Mercedes-Benz Vario O810	Plaxton Beaver 2	B27F	1998	
1193	w	R193DNM	Mercedes-Benz Vario O810	Plaxton Beaver 2	B27F	1998	
1450	TW	M450HPF	Optare MetroRider MR17	Optare	B29F	1994	Londonlinks, 1997
1451	TW	M451HPF	Optare MetroRider MR17	Optare	B29F	1994	Londonlinks, 1997
1455	TW	YN53ELU	Optare Solo M850	Optare	N25F	2003	Operated for Sussex CC
1475	TW	P475DPE	Mercedes-Benz 711D	Plaxton Beaver	B27F	1997	
1476	TW	P476DPE	Mercedes-Benz 711D	Plaxton Beaver	B27F	1997	
1477	TW	P477DPE	Mercedes-Benz 711D	Plaxton Beaver	B27F	1997	
1479	TW	P479DPE	Mercedes-Benz 711D	Plaxton Beaver	B27F	1997	

1601-1605   Dennis Dart SLF   Plaxton Pointer MPD   N29F   2000

1601	TW	W601YKN	1603	TW	W603YKN	1604	TW	W604YKN	1605	TW	W605YKN
1602	TW	W602YKN									

An interesting paint scheme was applied to Dennis Dart 3176, P176LKL. To celebrate a hundred years of public transport in Maidstone, it received a livery using the former corporation colours but in Arriva style. It is seen heading for Coxheath.
Mark Lyons

1606-1617   TransBus Dart 8.8m   TransBus Mini Pointer   N29F   2004

1606	GI	GN04UCW	1609	GI	GN04UCZ	1612	GI	GN04UDE	1615	GI	GN04UDJ
1607	GI	GN04UCX	1610	GI	GN04UDB	1613	GI	GN04UDG	1616	GI	GN04UDK
1608	GI	GN04UCY	1611	GI	GN04UDD	1614	GI	GN04UDH	1617	GI	GN04UDL

1618-1623   Alexander Dennis Dart 8.8m   Alexander Dennis Mini Pointer   N29F   2005

| 1618 | NF | GN05ANU | 1620 | NF | GN05ANX | 1622 | NF | GN05AOB | 1623 | NF | GN05AOC |
| 1619 | NF | GN05ANV | 1621 | NF | GN05AOA | | | | | | |

1751-1756   Mercedes-Benz Sprinter 411CDi   Mercedes-Benz   N15F   2002

| 1751 | SE | DE52OKV | 1753 | SE | DE52OKX | 1755 | SE | DE52OLM | 1756 | SE | DE52OLN |
| 1752 | SE | DE52OKW | 1754 | SE | DE52OKZ | | | | | | |

1805-1808   Optare MetroRider MR15   Optare   B29F   1996

| 1805 | u | N805BKN | 1806 | u | N806BKN | 1807 | NF | N807BKN | 1808 | u | N808BKN |

1809-1814   Optare MetroRider MR15   Optare   B29F   1998

| 1809 | NF | R809TKO | 1811 | NF | R811TKO | 1813 | NF | R813TKO | 1814 | NF | R814TKO |
| 1810 | NF | R810TKO | 1812 | NF | R812TKO | | | | | | |

1850	NF	L600BUS	Optare MetroRider MR11	Optare	B31F	1995	Arriva The Shires, 2001

2031	TO	UJI2338	Scania K113CRB	Plaxton Paramount 3500 III	C49FT	1990	Happy Days, Woodseaves, 1994
2051	TO	M51AWW	Scania K113CRB	Van Hool Alizée	C51F	1995	Arriva Yorkshire (W), 1999
2054	TO	M54AWW	Scania K113CRB	Van Hool Alizée	C49FT	1995	Arriva Yorkshire (W), 1999
2194	w	J25UNY	Leyland Tiger TRCL10/3ARZM	Plaxton 321	C53F	1992	Bebb, Llantwit Fardre, 1993
2830	TO	TIB5903	Volvo B10M-61	Van Hool Alizée H	C53F	1988	Jason, St Mary Cray, 1996
2831	TO	TIB5904	Volvo B10M-61	Van Hool Alizée H	C53F	1988	Jason, St Mary Cray, 1996
2835	TO	A11GTA	Volvo B10M-60	Plaxton Paramount 3500 III	C53F	1991	Kentish Bus, 1997
2846	ME	H846AHS	Volvo B10M-60	Plaxton Paramount 3500 III	C49FT	1991	Express Travel, Liverpool, 1995
2851	TO	G801BPG	Volvo B10M-60	Plaxton Paramount 3500 III	C37FT	1989	Speedlink, 1997
2894	TO	W183CDN	DAF SB3000	Van Hool T9 Alizée	C52F	2000	
2895	TO	SCZ9651	DAF SB3000	Van Hool T9 Alizée	C49F	1999	Eirebus, Dublin, 2003
2896	TO	SCZ9652	DAF SB3000	Van Hool T9 Alizée	C49F	1999	Eirebus, Dublin, 2003
2897	TO	R157GNW	DAF SB3000	Ikarus Blue Danube 396	C49F	1998	
2898	TO	W198CDN	DAF SB3000	Ikarus Blue Danube 396	C53F	2000	
2899	TO	F899GUM	DAF MB230	Plaxton Paramount 3500 III	C53F	1989	O'Sullivan, Killarney, 1997
2900	TO	F621HGO	DAF MB230	Van Hool Alizée H	C53FT	1989	London Coaches (Kent), 1997
2901	TO	F901GUM	DAF MB230	Plaxton Paramount 3500 III	C53F	1989	O'Sullivan, Killarney, 1996
2902	TO	J36GCX	DAF SB2305	Duple 320	C57F	1992	Eagle, Bristol, 1997

2903-2910   DAF SB3000   Plaxton Première 320   C53F   1998

| 2903 | ME | R903BKO | 2905 | ME | R905BKO | 2907 | ME | R907BKO | 2909 | ME | R909BKO |
| 2904 | ME | R904BKO | 2906 | ME | R906BKO | 2908 | ME | R908BKO | 2910 | ME | R910BKO |

2911	ME	R455SKX	DAF SB3000	Plaxton Prima	C53F	1997	Arriva The Shires, 2003
2912	ME	R456SKX	DAF SB3000	Plaxton Prima	C53F	1997	Arriva The Shires, 2003

3003	GU	R303CMV	Dennis Dart SLF	Plaxton Pointer 2	N39F	1997	

3004-3009   Dennis Dart 9.8m   East Lancs EL2000   B40F   1993

| 3004 | u | L504CPJ | 3006 | u | L506CPJ | 3008 | SE | L510CPJ | 3009 | SE | L511CPJ |
| 3005 | HK | L507CPJ | 3007 | SE | L509CPJ | | | | | | |

3014	ME	M525MPM	Dennis Dart 9.8m	East Lancs EL2000	B40F	1995	
3015	u	M526MPM	Dennis Dart 9.8m	East Lancs EL2000	B40F	1995	
3017	u	N540TPF	Dennis Dart 9.8m	East Lancs EL2000	B40F	1995	
3018	CR	M520KPA	Dennis Lance SLF	Wright Pathfinder	N40F	1995	
3019	WS	N539TPF	Dennis Dart 9.8m	East Lancs EL2000	B40F	1995	

3020-3024   Dennis Lance 11m   East Lancs   N49F   1996

| 3020 | TW | N220TPK | 3022 | TW | N322TPK | 3023 | GU | N223TPK | 3024 | GU | N224TPK |
| 3021 | GU | N221TPK | | | | | | | | | |

Not all low-floor Plaxton-bodied Dennis Darts carry Plaxton Pointer 2 bodywork, and here is an example. The early low-floor Dart SLFs continued with the styling of the original Pointer, as seen here on 3090, P290FPK. The Pointer 2 styling was introduced during the following year, 1998. *Dave Heath*

3025-3036

			Dennis Dart SLF			Plaxton Pointer 2		N35F	1996	North Western (Beeline), 1998
3025	CR	N225TPK	**3028**	CR	N228TPK	**3031**	CR	N231TPK	**3035**	CR	N235TPK
3026	CR	N226TPK	**3029**	GU	N229TPK	**3032**	HO	N232TPK	**3036**	CR	N236TPK
3027	GU	N227TPK	**3030**	CR	N230TPK	**3033**	CR	N233TPK			

3037	HO	N237VPH	Dennis Dart SLF			East Lancs Spryte	N31F	1996	
3038	SI	N245VPH	Dennis Dart SLF			East Lancs Spryte	N31F	1996	
3039	SI	N237VPH	Dennis Dart SLF			East Lancs Spryte	N31F	1996	
3045	TW	F45ENF	Leyland Lynx LX112L10ZR1R			Leyland Lynx	B49F	1988	Shearings, 1991
3046	NF	F46ENF	Leyland Lynx LX112L10ZR1R			Leyland Lynx	B49F	1988	Shearings, 1991
3047	GY	N247VPH	Dennis Dart SLF			East Lancs Spryte	N31F	1996	
3049	ME	H256YLG	Leyland Lynx LX2R11V18Z4R			Leyland Lynx 2	B49F	1990	Aintree Coachline, 1995
3050	GU	P250APM	Dennis Dart SLF			East Lancs Spryte	N31F	1996	
3051	NF	H814EKJ	Leyland Lynx LX2R11C15Z4S			Leyland Lynx 2	B49F	1991	Kentish Bus, 1997
3052	NF	H816EKJ	Leyland Lynx LX2R11C15Z4S			Leyland Lynx 2	B49F	1991	Kentish Bus, 1997
3053	GU	P253APM	Dennis Dart SLF			East Lancs Spryte	N31F	1997	
3054	u	H815EKJ	Leyland Lynx LX2R11C15Z4S			Leyland Lynx 2	B49F	1991	Boro'line, Maidstone, 1992
3055	SI	P255APM	Dennis Dart SLF			East Lancs Spryte	N31F	1997	
3065	HK	G45VME	Leyland Lynx LX2R11C15Z4S			Leyland Lynx 2	B49F	1989	Boro'line, Maidstone, 1992

3068-3096

			Dennis Dart SLF			Plaxton Pointer		N39F	1997	
3068	HO	P268FPK	**3075**	GI	P275FPK	**3084**	GU	P284FPK	**3091**	GU	P291FPK
3069	HO	P269FPK	**3076**	GI	P276FPK	**3085**	HO	P285FPK	**3092**	GU	P292FPK
3070	GI	P270FPK	**3077**	GI	P277FPK	**3086**	GU	P286FPK	**3093**	GU	P293FPK
3071	GI	P271FPK	**3080**	HO	P380FPK	**3087**	GU	P287FPK	**3094**	GU	P294FPK
3072	GI	P272FPK	**3081**	HO	P281FPK	**3088**	GU	P288FPK	**3095**	GU	P295FPK
3073	GI	P273FPK	**3082**	HO	P282FPK	**3089**	GU	P289FPK	**3096**	GU	P296FPK
3074	HO	P274FPK	**3083**	HO	P283FPK	**3090**	GU	P290FPK			

3097-3102

			Dennis Dart SLF			Plaxton Pointer 2		N39F	1997
3097	GU	R297CMV	**3099**	GU	R299CMV	**3101**	GU	R301CMV	**3102**	GU	R302CMV
3098	GU	R298CMV	**3100**	GU	R310CMV						

3103	HK	L500DKT	Dennis Dart 9m			WSC Portsdown	B43F	1994	Wealden Beeline, 1997
3104	HK	M501PKJ	Dennis Dart 9m			WSC Portsdown	B43F	1994	Wealden Beeline, 1997
3105	HK	M502RKO	Dennis Dart 9m			WSC Portsdown	B43F	1995	Wealden Beeline, 1997
3106	HK	L503HKM	Dennis Dart 9m			WSC Portsdown	B43F	1994	Wealden Beeline, 1997
3109	GU	T109LKK	Dennis Dart SLF 9m			Plaxton Pointer 2	N39F	1999	
3110	GU	T110LKK	Dennis Dart SLF 9m			Plaxton Pointer 2	N39F	1999	
3112	DA	L112YVK	Dennis Dart 9m			Northern Counties Paladin	B35F	1994	
3113	NF	L113YVK	Dennis Dart 9m			Northern Counties Paladin	B35F	1994	
3122	HO	N542TPK	Dennis Dart 9.8m			East Lancs EL2000	B40F	1996	
3124	SE	N544TPK	Dennis Dart 9.8m			East Lancs EL2000	B40F	1996	

3132-3145 — Dennis Dart 9m — Northern Counties Paladin — B35F — 1994

3132	NF	L132YVK	3134	NF	L134YVK	3138	SE	L138YVK	3145	SE	L145YVK
3133	NF	L133YVK	3135	NF	L135YVK	3143	NF	L143YVK			

3146	SI	N246VPH	Dennis Dart SLF 9m			East Lancs Spryte	N31F	1996	

3150-3158 — Dennis Dart 9m — Northern Counties Paladin — B35F — 1994

3150	SE	L150YVK	3154	SE	L154YVK	3156	NF	L156YVK	3158	NF	L158BFT
3153	SE	L153YVK	3155	NF	L155YVK						

3172	ME	N234TPK	Dennis Dart SLF 9m			Plaxton Pointer	N35F	1996	
3174	HK	M100CBB	Dennis Dart 9.8m			Plaxton Pointer	B40F	1995	Cardiff Bluebird, 1996
3175	SR	M200CBB	Dennis Dart 9.8m			Plaxton Pointer	B40F	1995	Cardiff Bluebird, 1996

3176-3191 — Dennis Dart SLF 10.1m — Plaxton Pointer — N40F — 1996

3176	ME	P176LKL	3181	ME	P181LKL	3186	NF	P186LKJ	3189	NF	P189LKJ
3177	ME	P177LKL	3184	TW	P184LKL	3187	NF	P187LKJ	3190	NF	P190LKJ
3178	GI	P178LKL	3185	TW	P185LKL	3188	NF	P188LKJ	3191	NF	P191LKJ
3179	DA	P179LKL									

3192-3247 — Dennis Dart SLF 10.1m — Plaxton Pointer — N40F — 1997

3192	ME	P192LKJ	3206	ME	P206LKJ	3221	GI	P221MKL	3235	GI	P235MKN
3193	ME	P193LKJ	3207	ME	P207LKJ	3223	GI	P223MKL	3236	GI	P236MKN
3194	ME	P194LKJ	3208	ME	P208LKJ	3224	GI	P224MKL	3237	GI	P237MKN
3195	ME	P195LKJ	3209	ME	P209LKJ	3225	GI	P225MKL	3238	GI	P238MKN
3196	ME	P196LKJ	3210	HK	P210LKJ	3226	GI	P226MKL	3239	GI	P239MKN
3197	DA	P197LKJ	3211	HK	P211LKJ	3227	GI	P227MKL	3240	GI	P240MKN
3198	NF	P198LKJ	3212	HK	P212LKJ	3228	GI	P228MKL	3241	GI	P241MKN
3199	SI	P199LKJ	3213	HK	P213LKJ	3229	GI	P229MKL	3242	GI	P242MKN
3201	SI	P201LKJ	3215	ME	P215LKJ	3230	GI	P230MKL	3243	GI	P243MKN
3202	ME	P202LKJ	3216	GI	P216LKJ	3231	GI	P231MKL	3244	GI	P244MKN
3203	ME	P203LKJ	3218	NF	P218MKL	3232	GI	P232MKL	3245	GI	P245MKN
3204	GY	P204LKJ	3219	GI	P219MKL	3233	GI	P233MKN	3246	GY	P246MKN
3205	ME	P205LKJ	3220	GI	P220MKL	3234	GI	P234MKN	3247	GY	P247MKN

3248	HO	P278FPK	Dennis Dart SLF 10.1m			Plaxton Pointer 2	N40F	1997	
3249	ME	P279FPK	Dennis Dart SLF 10.1m			Plaxton Pointer 2	N40F	1997	

3250-3259 — Scania L113CRL — Wright Axcess-ultralow — N43F — 1995

3250	NF	N250BKK	3253	NF	N253BKK	3256	NF	N256BKK	3258	NF	N258BKK
3251	NF	N251BKK	3254	NF	N254BKK	3257	NF	N257BKK	3259	NF	N259BKK
3252	NF	N252BKK	3255	NF	N255BKK						

3261-3272 — Dennis Dart SLF 10.1m — Plaxton Pointer 2 — N39F — 1998

3261	DA	R261EKO	3264	DA	R264EKO	3267	DA	R267EKO	3270	DA	R270EKO
3262	DA	R262EKO	3265	DA	R265EKO	3268	DA	R268EKO	3271	DA	R271EKO
3263	DA	R263EKO	3266	DA	R266EKO	3269	DA	R269EKO	3272	DA	R272EKO

3273-3289 — Dennis Dart SLF 10.1m — Plaxton Pointer 2 — N39F* — 1999 — *3276-81 are N37F

3273	NF	T273JKM	3278	DA	T278JKM	3282	DA	T282JKM	3286	DA	T286JKM
3274	NF	T274JKM	3279	DA	T279JKM	3283	DA	T283JKM	3287	DA	T287JKM
3275	NF	T275JKM	3280	DA	T280JKM	3284	DA	T284JKM	3288	DA	T288JKM
3276	DA	T276JKM	3281	DA	T281JKM	3285	DA	T285JKM	3289	NF	T289JKM
3277	DA	T277JKM									

Six 11.3 metre Super Pointer Darts were supplied to Arriva Southern Counties in 1998 for use at Maidstone. These are the only examples of this length within Arriva's British operation. Seen on route 82 that links Maidstone town centre with Park Wood, 3702, S702VKM, shows the length of the SPD. *Dave Heath*

3291-3303

			Dennis Dart SLF 10.1m		Plaxton Pointer 2		N34D		2001			
3291	DA	Y291TKJ	3294	DA	Y294TKJ	3297	DA	Y297TKJ	3301	DA	Y302TKJ
3292	DA	Y292TKJ	3295	DA	Y295TKJ	3298	DA	Y298TKJ	3302	DA	Y301TKJ
3293	DA	Y293TKJ	3296	DA	Y296TKJ	3299	DA	Y299TKJ	3303	DA	Y303TKJ

3304-3308

			Dennis Dart SLF 10.1m		Plaxton Pointer 2		N39F		1997			
3304	GU	R304CMV	3306	GU	R296CMV	3307	ME	R307CMV	3308	ME	R308CMV
3305	GU	R305CMV									

3318-3326

			Dennis Dart SLF		Plaxton Pointer 2		N33F*		1998		* E3224-6 are N39F	
3318	SE	T218NMJ	3321	SE	T821NMJ	3323	SE	T823NMJ	3325	SE	T825NMJ
3320	SE	T820NMJ	3322	SE	T822NMJ	3324	SE	T824NMJ	3326	SE	T826NMJ

3351	SI	P251APM	Dennis Dart SLF	East Lancs Spryte	N31F	1997		
3354	SI	P254APM	Dennis Dart SLF	East Lancs Spryte	N31F	1997		
3379	SE	M269VPU	Dennis Lance SLF 11m	Wright Pathfinder	N40F	1994		
3384	SE	M764JPA	Dennis Lance SLF 11m	Wright Pathfinder	N39F	1995		

3387-3397

			Dennis Dart SLF		Plaxton Pointer		N39F		1997			
3387	SE	P257FPK	3390	GY	P259FPK	3393	SE	P263FPK	3396	SE	P266FPK
3388	GY	P258FPK	3391	SE	P261FPK	3394	SE	P264FPK	3397	SE	P267FPK
3389	GY	P259FPK	3392	SE	P262FPK	3395	SE	P265FPK			

3400	GY	R310NGM	Dennis Dart SLF	Plaxton Pointer 2	N33F	1997	Town & Country, Corringham, '00
3401	GY	R311NGM	Dennis Dart SLF	Plaxton Pointer 2	N33F	1997	Town & Country, Corringham, '00
3402	GY	R312NGM	Dennis Dart SLF	Plaxton Pointer 2	N33F	1997	Town & Country, Corringham, '00
3403	GY	R313NGM	Dennis Dart SLF	Plaxton Pointer 2	N33F	1997	Town & Country, Corringham, '00

3404-3412

			Dennis Dart		Plaxton Pointer		B34F		1996			
3404	TW	P324HVX	3408	TW	P328HVX	3410	TW	P330HVX	3412	TW	P332HVX
3407	TW	P327HVX	3409	TW	P329HVX	3411	TW	P331HVX			

Arriva is the largest user of the Wrightbus Cadet, a body supplied on the former DAF and current VDL Bus SB120. As a replacement for the Volvo B6 series, Volvo is marketing the same product as a Merit. Route 21, on which VDL Bus 3932, GK51SZN, was operating when pictured, is one of three linking Guildford with Holmbury St Mary. *Dave Heath*

3421-3431

			Dennis Dart SLF			Plaxton Pointer			N39F	1996	
3421	GY	P421HVX	3425	GY	P425HVX	3427	GY	P427HVX	3429	GY	P429HVX
3423	GY	P423HVX	3426	GY	P426HVX	3428	GY	P428HVX	3431	GY	P431HVX
3424	GY	P424HVX									

3500-3510

			DAF SB120 10.2m			Wrightbus Cadet			N31D	2002	
3500	GY	KE51PTY	3503	GY	KE51PUF	3506	GY	KE51PUK	3509	GY	KE51PUV
3501	GY	KE51PTZ	3504	GY	KE51PUH	3507	GY	KE51PUO	3510	GY	KC51NFO
3502	GY	KE51PUA	3505	GY	KE51PUJ	3508	GY	KE51PUU			

3511	GY	KE51PUY	DAF SB120 9.4m	Wrightbus Cadet	N27F	2002	
3512	GY	KC51PUX	DAF SB120 9.4m	Wrightbus Cadet	N27F	2002	
3513	GY	KE51PVA	DAF SB120 9.4m	Wrightbus Cadet	N27F	2002	
3591	CR	T591CGT	Dennis Dart SLF 10.1m	Plaxton Pointer 2	N39F	1999	Operated for Surrey CC
3592	CR	T592CGT	Dennis Dart SLF 10.1m	Plaxton Pointer 2	N39F	1999	Operated for Surrey CC
3601	SE	L601EKM	Volvo B6-9.9M	Plaxton Pointer	B40F	1994	
3602	SE	L602EKM	Volvo B6-9.9M	Plaxton Pointer	B40F	1994	
3603	NF	L203YCU	Volvo B6-9.9M	Northern Counties Paladin	B39F	1994	Londonlinks, 1997
3604	NF	L204YCU	Volvo B6-9.9M	Northern Counties Paladin	B39F	1994	Londonlinks, 1997
3605	ME	L513CPJ	Volvo B6-9.9M	Plaxton Pointer	B41F	1994	

3606-3619

			Volvo B6-9.9M			Plaxton Pointer			B40F	1994-95	
3606	SR	L606EKM	3610	TW	L610EKM	3613	TW	M613PKP	3616	TW	M616PKP
3608	SE	L608EKM	3611	TW	M611PKP	3614	ME	M614PKP	3617	TW	M617PKP
3609	SI	L609EKM	3612	TW	M612PKP	3615	TO	M615PKP	3619	TO	M619PKP

3701-3706

			Dennis Dart SLF 11.3m			Plaxton Pointer SPD			N44F	1998	
3701	ME	S701VKM	3703	ME	S703VKM	3705	ME	S705VKM	3706	ME	S706VKM
3702	ME	S702VKM	3704	ME	S704VKM						

In 2004 more batches of Cadets and the longer Commanders were supplied to Southern Counties. Painted in Maidstone's Park & Ride livery is 3960, GN04UFX, which is seen passing through a festive town centre towards the Coombe Quarry car park. *Mark Lyons*

3730	GU	LF02PVA	Volvo B7L		Wrightbus Eclipse	N41F	2002	On loan from Arriva Bus & Coach

3731-3735

			Volvo B7RLE			Wrightbus Eclipse Urban	N44F	On order	
3731	GU	G-	3733	GU	G-	3734	GU	G-	3735	GU	G-
3732	GU	G-									

3911-3921

			DAF SB220			Plaxton Prestige	N39F	1999	
3911	NF	T911KKM	3914	NF	T914KKM	3916	NF	T916KKM	3919	TW	T919KKM
3912	NF	T912KKM	3915	NF	T915KKM	3918	TW	T918KKM	3921	NF	T921KKM
3913	NF	T913KKM									

3923-3932

			DAF SB120			Wrightbus Cadet	N39F	2002	
3923	CR	GK51SYY	3926	GU	GK51SZD	3929	GU	GK51SZG	3931	GU	GK51SZL
3924	CR	GK51SYZ	3927	GU	GK51SZE	3930	GU	GK51SZJ	3932	GU	GK51SZN
3925	GU	GK51SZC	3928	GU	GK51SZF						

3933-3944

			DAF SB120			Wrightbus Cadet	N39F	2002	
3933	GU	GK52YUW	3937	GU	GK52YVB	3940	GU	GK52YVF	3943	GU	GK52YVJ
3934	GU	GK52YUX	3938	GU	GK52YVC	3941	GU	GK52YVF	3944	GU	GK52YVL
3935	GU	GK52YUY	3939	GU	GK52YVD	3942	GU	GK52YVG			

3945-3960

			VDL Bus SB120			Wrightbus Cadet	N29F	2004	
3945	DA	GK53AOH	3949	DA	GK53AOO	3953	DA	GK53AOU	3957	DA	GK53AOY
3946	DA	GK53AOJ	3950	DA	GK53AOP	3954	DA	GK53AOV	3958	DA	GK53AOZ
3947	DA	GK53AOL	3951	DA	GK53AOR	3955	DA	GK53AOW	3959	ME	GN04UFW
3948	DA	GK53AON	3952	DA	GK53AOT	3956	DA	GK53AOX	3960	ME	GN04UFX

3961-3969

			VDL Bus SB200			Wrightbus Commander	N44F	2004	
3961	ME	GN04UFY	3964	ME	GN04UGB	3966	ME	GN04UGD	3968	ME	GN04UGF
3962	ME	GN04UFZ	3965	ME	GN04UGC	3967	ME	GN04UGE	3969	ME	GN04UGG
3963	ME	GN04UGA									

5089	SE	F639LMJ	Leyland Olympian ONCL10/1RZ	Alexander RL		B47/32F	1988	Arriva The Shires, 2005
5090	SE	F640LMJ	Leyland Olympian ONCL10/1RZ	Alexander RL		B47/32F	1988	Arriva The Shires, 2005
5092	SE	F642LMJ	Leyland Olympian ONCL10/1RZ	Alexander RL		B47/32F	1988	Arriva The Shires, 2005
5213	GU	N713TPK	Dennis Dominator DDA2006	East Lancs		B45/31F	1996	
5214	GU	N714TPK	Dennis Dominator DDA2006	East Lancs		B45/31F	1996	
5215	GU	N715TPK	Dennis Dominator DDA2006	East Lancs		B45/31F	1996	
5263	TO	B263WUL	MCW Metrobus DR101/17	MCW		B43/28D	1985	Arriva London, 1999
5275	TO	B275WUL	MCW Metrobus DR101/17	MCW		B43/28D	1985	Arriva London, 1999
5280	w	B280WUL	MCW Metrobus DR101/17	MCW		B43/28D	1985	Arriva London, 1999

5273-5278

Dennis Dominator DDA1031 — East Lancs — B43/25F — 1989-90 — Arriva Southern Counties, 1999

5273	SE	G663FKA	5276	SE	G626EKA	5277	SE	G665FKA	5278	SE	G628EKA
5274	SE	G664FKA						

5286	SE	K36XNE	Dennis Dominator DDA2005	East Lancs		B45/31F	1993	Arriva Southern Counties, 1999
5287	SE	K37XNE	Dennis Dominator DDA2005	East Lancs		B45/31F	1993	Arriva Southern Counties, 1999
5288	SE	K38YVM	Dennis Dominator DDA2005	East Lancs		B45/31F	1993	Arriva Southern Counties, 1999
5386	SE	C32CHM	Leyland Olympian ONLXB/1RH	Eastern Coach Works		B42/26D	1986	Arriva London, 2003
5387	SE	D172FYM	Leyland Olympian ONLXB/1RH	Eastern Coach Works		B42/26D	1986	Arriva London, 2003
5388	GY	D234FYM	Leyland Olympian ONLXB/1RH	Eastern Coach Works		B42/26D	1986	Arriva London, 2003

5392-5396

Leyland Olympian ONLXB/1RZ — Alexander RL — B47/32F — 1988 — London & Country (GWS), 1996

5392	SE	F572SMG	5394	SE	F574SMG	5395	SE	F575SMG	5396	SE	F576SMG
5393	SE	F573SMG						

5399	SE	F579SMG	Leyland Olympian ONLXB/1RZ	Alexander RL		B47/32F	1988	London & Country (GWS), 1996
5402	SE	H262GEV	Leyland Olympian ON2R50G13Z4	Leyland		B47/31F	1990	
5403	SE	H263GEV	Leyland Olympian ON2R50G13Z4	Leyland		B47/31F	1990	
5404	SE	H264GEV	Leyland Olympian ON2R50G13Z4	Leyland		BC43/29F	1990	
5405	SE	H265GEV	Leyland Olympian ON2R50G13Z4	Leyland		BC43/29F	1990	

5434-5441

Dennis Trident — Alexander ALX400 — N47/31F — 2000

5434	ME	W434XKX	5436	ME	W436XKX	5438	ME	W438XKX	5441	ME	W441XKX
5435	ME	W435XKX	5437	ME	W437XKX	5439	ME	W439XKX			

5557-5565

Volvo Olympian YN2RC16Z4* — Northern Counties Palatine II B47/30F — 1994 — *5565 is YN2RV18Z4

5557	NF	L557YCU	5559	NF	L559YCU	5562	SR	L562YCU	5564	ME	L564YCU
5558	NF	L558YCU	5561	ME	L561YCU	5563	ME	L563YCU	5565	SR	L565YCU

5765-5770

Leyland Olympian ON2R50C13Z4 — Northern Counties — B47/30F — 1991 — Boro'line, Maidstone, 1992

5765	GI	H765EKJ	5767	SR	H767EKJ	5769	SR	H769EKJ	5770	GI	H770EKJ
5766	SR	H766EKJ	5768	SR	H768EKJ						

5801	HO	F571SMG	Leyland Olympian ONLXB/1RZ	Alexander RL		B47/32F	1988	Alder Valley, 1990
5807	SE	F577SMG	Leyland Olympian ONLXB/1RZ	Alexander RL		B47/32F	1988	Alder Valley, 1990
5808	SE	F578SMG	Leyland Olympian ONLXB/1RZ	Alexander RL		B47/32F	1988	Alder Valley, 1990
5829	SD	E229CFC	Leyland Olympian ONLXB/1RH	Alexander RH		B47/26D	1988	Wycombe Bus, 2000
5881	SD	E225CFC	Leyland Olympian ONLXB/1RH	Alexander RH		B47/26D	1988	Wycombe Bus, 2000
5882	SD	E228CFC	Leyland Olympian ONLXB/1RH	Alexander RH		B47/26D	1988	Wycombe Bus, 2000

5891-5900

Leyland Olympian ONLXB/1RH — Northern Counties — B45/30F — 1988

5891	SE	E891AKN	5894	SE	F894BKK	5897	SE	F897DKK	5899	NE	F899DKK
5892	SE	F892BKK	5895	SE	F895BKK	5898	HK	F898DKK	5900	HK	F900DKK
5893	w	F893BKK	5896	HO	F896DKK						

5901-5905

Leyland Olympian ON2R50G13Z4 — Northern Counties Palatine — B45/30F — 1990

5901	HK	G901SKP	5903	HK	G903SKP	5904	TW	G904SKP	5905	TO	G905SKP
5902	HK	G902SKP									

5906-5910

Leyland Olympian ON2R50C13Z4 — Northern Counties Palatine — B45/30F — 1993

5906	TW	K906SKR	5908	TW	K908SKR	5909	HK	K909SKR	5910	HK	K910SKR
5907	TW	K907SKR									

5911-5925

Volvo Olympian YN2R50C16Z4 — Northern Counties Palatine — B47/30F — 1994-95 — 5913 rebodied 1995

5911	HK	M911MKM	5915	ME	M915MKM	5918	SR	M918MKM	5922	HK	M922PKN
5912	ME	M912MKM	5916	ME	M916MKM	5919	ME	M919MKM	5923	HK	M923PKN
5913	ME	M913MKM	5917	HK	M917MKM	5920	ME	M920MKM	5925	HK	M925PKN
5914	HK	M914MKM									

June 2004 saw the arrival of a large batch of Volvo B7TLs with TransBus ALX400 bodies. All forty-nine are allocated to Gillingham with many receiving route branding for specific key routes which also gained colour codes. The initial bus, 6401, GN04UDM, carries a promotion for the whole scheme and is seen here near Chatham bus station. The cover of this edition shows another from the delivery with route branding. *Mark Lyons*

5926-5937		Volvo Olympian			Northern Counties Palatine		B47/30F	1997		
5926	ME	P926MKL	**5929**	HK	P929MKL	**5932**	ME	P932MKL	**5935**	ME	P935MKL
5927	ME	P927MKL	**5930**	ME	P930MKL	**5933**	ME	P933MKL	**5936**	ME	P936MKL
5928	ME	P928MKL	**5931**	ME	P931MKL	**5934**	ME	P934MKL	**5937**	ME	P937MKL

6204-6212		DAF DB250			Northern Counties Palatine 2		B43/24D	1998		
6204	TW	R204CKO	**6207**	TW	R207CKO	**6209**	TW	R209CKO	**6211**	TW	R211CKO
6205	TW	R205CKO	**6208**	TW	R208CKO	**6210**	TW	R210CKO	**6212**	TW	R212CKO
6206	TW	R206CKO									

6213-6219		DAF DB250			Wrightbus Pulsar Gemini		N41/24D	2004		
6213	DA	GK53AOA	**6215**	DA	GK53AOC	**6217**	DA	GK53AOE	**6219**	DA	GK53AOG
6214	DA	GK53AOB	**6216**	DA	GK53AOD	**6218**	DA	GK53AOF			

6401-6449		Volvo B7TL			TransBus ALX400		N--/--F	2004		
6401	GI	GN04UDM	**6414**	GI	GN04UED	**6426**	GI	GN04UET	**6438**	GI	GN04UFG
6402	GI	GN04UDP	**6415**	GI	GN04UEE	**6427**	GI	GN04UEU	**6439**	GI	GN04UFH
6403	GI	GN04UDS	**6416**	GI	GN04UEF	**6428**	GI	GN04UEV	**6440**	GI	GN04UFJ
6404	GI	GN04UDT	**6417**	GI	GN04UEG	**6429**	GI	GN04UEW	**6441**	GI	GN04UFK
6405	GI	GN04UDU	**6418**	GI	GN04UEH	**6430**	GI	GN04UEX	**6442**	GI	GN04UFL
6406	GI	GN04UDV	**6419**	GI	GN04UEJ	**6431**	GI	GN04UEY	**6443**	GI	GN04UFM
6407	GI	GN04UDW	**6420**	GI	GN04UEK	**6432**	GI	GN04UEZ	**6444**	GI	GN04UFP
6408	GI	GN04UDX	**6421**	GI	GN04UEL	**6433**	GI	GN04UFA	**6445**	GI	GN04UFR
6409	GI	GN04UDY	**6422**	GI	GN04UEM	**6434**	CI	GN04UFB	**6446**	GI	GN04UFS
6410	GI	GN04UDZ	**6423**	GI	GN04UEP	**6435**	GI	GN04UFC	**6447**	GI	GN04UFT
6411	GI	GN04UEA	**6424**	GI	GN04UER	**6436**	GI	GN04UFD	**6448**	GI	GN04UFU
6412	GI	GN04UEB	**6425**	GI	GN04UES	**6437**	GI	GN04UFE	**6449**	GI	GN04UFV
6413	GI	GN04UEC									

7616	w	G616BPH	Volvo Citybus B10M-50		East Lancs		B49/39F	1989

Having originally operated in London Links livery, these Volvo Citybuses are now in Arriva's corporate scheme. The type is represented here by 7641, G641BPH. *Dave Heath*

7624-7643

Volvo Citybus B10M-50 Northern Counties B45/31F 1989 Londonlinks, 1997

7624	GI	G624BPH	7629	GI	G629BPH	7632	GI	G632BPH	7635	GI	G635BPH
7625	GI	G625BPH	7630	GI	G630BPH	7633	GI	G633BPH	7636	GI	G636BPH
7626	GI	G626BPH	7631	GI	G631BPH	7634	GI	G634BPH	7643	SR	G643BPH
7627	GI	G627BPH								

Ancillary vehicles:

T047	ME	F48ENF	Leyland Lynx LX112L10ZR1R	Leyland Lynx	TV	1988	Shearings, 1991
T148	NF	L148YVK	Dennis Dart 9m	Northern Counties Paladin	TV	1994	
T154	w	J154NKN	Mercedes-Benz 814D	Dormobile Routemaker	TV	1992	Crossways, Swanley, 1996
T162	-	J162REH	Leyland Swift ST2R44C97A4	Wadham Stringer Vanguard II	TV	1994	Arriva Midlands North, 2003
T169	-	J169REH	Leyland Swift ST2R44C97A4	Wadham Stringer Vanguard II	TV	1991	Arriva Midlands North, 2003

T205-212

Volvo B6-9.9M Northern Counties Paladin TV 1994 Londonlinks, 1997

205	GI	L205YCU	207	ME	L207YCU	209	ME	L209YCU	211	CH	L211YCU
206	GI	L206YCU	208	GI	L208YCU	210	GI	L210YCU	212	GI	L212YCU

T463	DA	J463MKL	Dennis Dart 9.8m	Plaxton Pointer	TV	1991	
T469	DA	J469SKO	Dennis Dart 9.8m	Plaxton Pointer	TV	1992	
T505	NF	L505CPJ	Dennis Dart 9.8m	East Lancs EL2000	TV	1993	
T512	ME	L512CPJ	Volvo B6-9.9M	Plaxton Pointer	TV	1994	
T514	ME	L514CPJ	Volvo B6-9.9M	Plaxton Pointer	TV	1994	
T515	ME	L515CPJ	Volvo B6-9.9M	Plaxton Pointer	TV	1994	
T603	ME	L603EKM	Volvo B6-9.9M	Plaxton Pointer	TV	1994	
T604	ME	L604EKM	Volvo B6-9.9M	Plaxton Pointer	TV	1994	
T605	ME	L605EKM	Volvo B6-9.9M	Plaxton Pointer	TV	1994	
T607	ME	L607EKM	Volvo B6-9.9M	Plaxton Pointer	TV	1994	
T833	ME	P833NAV	LDV Convoy	LDV	TV	?	
T888	w	E888KYW	Leyland Lynx LX1126LXCTZR1S	Leyland Lynx	TV	1987	Arriva The Shires, 2002

Previous registrations:

A11GTA	H832AHS	SCZ9652	99D81498, T179AUA
BAZ7384	C210PPE	SIB6709	LFR865X
L503HKM	L10FUG	SIB6711	HPF310N
PDZ6275	UFG54S	TIB5903	E316OPR
RDZ4279	KPA380P	TIB5904	E319OPR
SCZ9651	99D81499, T178AUA	UJI2338	G897DEH

Allocations

Cranleigh (Mansfield Park, Guildford Road) - CR

Dart	3025	3026	3028	3030	3031	3033	3035	3036
	3591	3592						
Lance	3018							
DAF Cadet	3923	3924						

Dartford (Central Road) - DA

MetroRider	1807	1850						
Dart	3112							
Dart SLF	3179	3197	3218	3261	3262	3263	3264	3265
	3266	3267	3268	3269	3270	3271	3272	3276
	3277	3278	3279	3280	3281	3282	3283	3284
	3285	3286	3287	3288	3291	3292	3293	3294
	3295	3296	3297	3298	3299	3301	3302	3303
SB120 Cadet	3945	3946	3947	3948	3949	3950	3951	3952
	3953	3954	3955	3956	3957	3958		
DAF Gemini	6213	6214	6215	6216	6217	6218	6219	

Gillingham (Nelson Road) - GI

Mercedes-Benz	1118	1119	1120	1121	1122			
Dart	1606	1607	1608	1609	1610	1611	1612	1613
	1614	1615	1616	1617	3070	3071	3072	3073
	3075	3076	3077	3178	3216	3219	3220	3221
	3223	3224	3225	3226	3227	3228	3229	3230
	3231	3232	3233	3234	3235	3236	3237	3238
	3239	3240	3241	3242	3243	3244	3245	
Olympian	5770							
Volvo Citybus	7624	7625	7626	7627	7629	7630	7631	7632
	7633	7634	7635	7636				
Volvo B7TL	6401	6402	6403	6404	6405	6406	6407	6408
	6409	6410	6411	6412	6413	6414	6415	6416
	6417	6418	6419	6420	6421	6422	6423	6424
	6425	6426	6427	6428	6429	6430	6431	6432
	6433	6434	6435	6436	6437	6438	6439	6440
	6441	6442	6443	6444	6445	6446	6447	6448
	6449							

Grays (Europa Park, London Road) - GY

Dart	3047	3204	3246	3247	3388	3389	3390	3400
	3401	3402	3403	3421	3423	3424	3425	3426
	3427	3428	3429	3431				
SB120 Cadet	3500	3501	3502	3503	3504	3505	3506	3507
	3508	3509	3510	3511	3512	3513		
Olympian	5388							

Guildford (Leas Road) - GU

Dart	3003	3027	3029	3050	3053	3084	3086	3087
	3088	3089	3090	3091	3092	3093	3094	3095
	3096	3097	3098	3099	3100	3101	3102	3109
	3110	3304	3305	3306				
DAF Cadet	3925	3926	3927	3928	3929	3930	3931	3932
	3933	3934	3935	3937	3938	3939	3940	3941
	3942	3943	3944					
Lance	3021	3023	3024					
Volvo B7L	3730							
Volvo B7RLE	3731	3731	3733	3734	3735			
Dominator	5213	5214	5215					

Hawkhurst (Rye Road) - HK

Outstation: Tenterden

Dart	3005	3103	3104	3105	3106	3174	3210	3211
	3212	3213						
Lynx	3065							
Olympian	5898	5900	5901	5902	5903	5909	5910	5911
	5914	5917	5920	5922	5923	5925	5929	

Horsham (Station Road, Warnham) - HO

Dart	3019	3032	3037	3068	3069	3080	3081	3082
	3083	3085	3122	3248				
Olympian	5801	5896						

Maidstone (Armstrong Road) - ME

Volvo B10M coach	2846							
DAF Première	2903	2904	2905	2906	2907	2908	2909	2910
	2911	2912						
Dart	3014	3172	3176	3177	3181	3192	3193	3194
	3195	3196	3202	3203	3205	3206	3207	3208
	3209	3215	3249	3307	3308	3701	3702	3703
	3704	3705	3706					
Volvo B6	3605	3614						
SB120 Cadet	3959	3960						
Lynx	3049							
SB220 Commander	3961	3962	3963	3964	3965	3966	3967	3968
	3969							
Olympian	5561	5563	5564	5912	5913	5915	5916	5919
	5926	5927	5928	5929	5930	5931	5932	5933
	5934	5935	5936	5937				
Trident	5434	5435	5436	5437	5438	5439	5441	

Northfleet (London Road) - NF

MetroRider	1809	1810	1811	1812	1813	1814		
Dart	1618	1619	1620	1621	1622	1623	3113	3132
	3133	3134	3135	3143	3155	3156	3158	3187
	3188	3189	3190	3191	3198	3273	3274	3275
	3289							
Volvo B6	3603	3604						
Lynx	3046	3051	3052					
Scania	3250	3251	3252	3253	3254	3255	3256	3257
	3258	3259						
SB220	3911	3912	3913	3914	3915	3916	3921	
Olympian	5557	5558	5907					

Route lettering for routes 700 and 701 is illustrated in this view of Volvo B7TL 6442, GK04UFL, seen heading for Wigmore. *Dave Heath*

Sheerness (Bridge Road) - SR

Dart	3175						
Volvo B6	3606						
Olympian	5562	5565	5765	5766	5767	5768	5769	5918
Volvo Citybus	7643						

Sittingbourne (Crown Quay Lane) - SI

Mercedes-Benz	1183	1186	1189	1190			
Dart	3038	3039	3055	3146	3199	3201	3351	3354
Volvo B6	3609						

Southend (Short Street) - SE

Mercedes-Benz	1188	1751	1752	1753	1754	1755	1756
Dart	3007	3008	3009	3124	3138	3145	3150	3153
	3154	3318	3320	3321	3322	3323	3324	3325
	3326	3398	3391	3392	3393	3394	3395	3396
	3397						
Volvo B6	3601	3602	3608				
Lance	3379	3384					
Dominator	5273	5274	5276	5277	5278	5286	5287	5288
Olympian	5089	5090	5092	5386	5387	5392	5393	5394
	5395	5396	5399	5402	5403	5404	5405	5807
	5808	5890	5829	5881	5882	5891	5892	5893
	5894	5895	5897				

Tonbridge (Cannon Lane) - NE - New Enterprise Coaches

Volvo B6	3615	3619						
Volvo B10M coach	2830	2831	2835	2851				
DAF coach	2894	2895	2896	2897	2898	2899	2900	2901
	2902							
Scania coach	2031	2051	2054					
MAN coach	2893							
Metrobus	5263	5275						
Volvo Citybus	5899							
Olympian	5905							

Tunbridge Wells (St John's Road) - TW

Mercedes-Benz	1178	1179	1187	1475	1476	1477	1479	
MetroRider	1450	1451						
Solo	1455							
Volvo B6	3610	3611	3612	3613	3616	3617		
Dart	1601	1602	1603	1604	1605	3184	3185	3404
	3407	3408	3409	3410	3411	3412		
Lance	3020	3022						
Lynx	3045							
SB220 Prestige	3918	3919						
Olympian	5559	5904	5906	5908				
DB250 Palatine	6204	6205	6206	6207	6208	6209	6210	6211
	6212							

Unallocated and stored - u/w

Mercedes-Benz	1180	T154	1172 on loan to Arriva Midlands		
MetroRider	1805	1806	1808	1851	
Swift	T162	T166	T169		
Tiger coach	2194				
Lynx	3041	3043	3044	3054	T888
Metrobus	5280				
Volvo Citybus	7616				

Vehicles on rental to Tellings-Golden Miller

Mercedes-Benz	1143	1174	1192	1192	1193		
Vovo B6	3141	3346	3607				
Dart	3004	3006	3015	3017	3121	3123	3406
Lynx	3341	3342	3343	3347	3348		
DAF SB220	3535	3539					
Olympian	5389	5397	5398	5407	5408	5409	
Citybus B10M	7613	7614	7615	7617			

ARRIVA DANMARK

Arriva Danmark A/S; Arriva Scandinavia A/S
Herstedvang 7C, DK-2650 Albertslund, Danmark

77	NJ89094		DAB GS200		DAB		AB60D	1993	
78	NU88541		Volvo B10M		Åbenrå		B	1994	
79	NU88542		Volvo B10M		Åbenrå		B	1994	

84-101   Volvo B10M   Åbenrå   B   1995-2001

84	NY92870	88	OS89960	92	NX90900	99	RS90131
85	NY92871	89	OS89961	93	RL92430	100	RS90289
86	NY92872	91	NX90899	94	RL92431	101	RT94703
87	NZ93570						

102-105   Volvo B10MA   Åbenrå   AB   2001

102	SB94592	103	SB94567	104	SB94594	105	SB94593

155	MY91485	DAB GS200 8.6m	DAB	N18D	1992	On loan from HT
156	MY91485	DAB GS200 8.6m	DAB	N18D	1992	On loan from HT
161	MY91439	DAB GS200 8.6m	DAB	N18D	1992	On loan from HT

400-404   Mercedes-Benz Sprinter 312   Mercedes-Benz   M8   1997   Handicap service

400	RN94522	402	OZ97632	403	OY95589	404	OX91313
401	OX90567						

407	OX91412	Mercedes-Benz Sprinter 310	Mercedes-Benz	M8	1992	Handicap service

408-411   Mercedes-Benz Sprinter 312   Mercedes-Benz   M8   1997   Handicap service

408	OX905607	409	OZ90635	410	OU96648	411	OU96505

414	SM90147	Mercedes-Benz Sprinter 312	Mercedes-Benz	M8	1998	Handicap service
416	SM90263	Mercedes-Benz Sprinter 312	Mercedes-Benz	M8	1998	Handicap service
417	SM90290	Mercedes-Benz Sprinter 312	Mercedes-Benz	M8	1998	Handicap service
418	NK91881	Mercedes-Benz 410	Mercedes-Benz	M8	1993	Handicap service
420	PE94546	Mercedes-Benz Sprinter 412	Mercedes-Benz	M8	1998	Handicap service
422	PE94547	Mercedes-Benz Sprinter 412	Mercedes-Benz	M8	1998	Handicap service
424	PE94548	Mercedes-Benz Sprinter 412	Mercedes-Benz	M8	1998	Handicap service
426	NR90952	Mercedes-Benz Sprinter 310	Mercedes-Benz	M8	1994	Handicap service
434	RH97631	Fiat Ducato 18.2.5	Fiat	M8	1996	Handicap service
435	OL96516	Fiat Ducato 18.2.5	Fiat	M8	1996	Handicap service
436	OU96508	Mercedes-Benz Sprinter 312	Mercedes-Benz	M8	1997	Handicap service
437	PE94549	Mercedes-Benz Sprinter 312	Mercedes-Benz	M8	1998	Handicap service
440	NU91449	Mercedes-Benz Sprinter 310	Mercedes-Benz	M8	1995	Handicap service
442	PE94550	Mercedes-Benz Sprinter 312	Mercedes-Benz	M8	1998	Handicap service
447	HD99516	Mercedes-Benz 609	Mercedes-Benz	M8	1987	Handicap service
448	DZ99640	Mercedes-Benz 609	Mercedes-Benz	M8	1987	Handicap service

451-466   Mercedes-Benz Sprinter 412   Mercedes-Benz   M-   1998-99   Handicap service

451	SB92849	455	PJ96270	459	TB94359	463	TC93363
452	SM90148	456	SM90201	460	TB94449	464	LS97271
453	SB92850	457	TB94338	461	TB94448	465	SV88830
454	SB92851	458	TB94358	462	TC93364	466	TC93409

467	TC93553	Mercedes-Benz Vario	Mercedes-Benz	M	1998	Handicap service
468	TC93647	Mercedes-Benz Vario	Mercedes-Benz	M	1998	Handicap service
469	TC93486	Mercedes-Benz Vario	Mercedes-Benz	M	1998	Handicap service

1001-1013   Volvo B10LE   Säffle   AN62D   1998

1001	PC90.745	1005	PC95.842	1008	PC95.862	1011	PC95.873
1002	PC95.805	1006	PC95.843	1009	PC95.872	1012	PC95.885
1003	PC95.830	1007	PC95.849	1010	PC95.863	1013	PC95.892
1004	PC95.836						

Arriva's Scandinavian buiness employs a fleet of over 1700 buses and coaches, with large operations on Jutland, Fyn and around Copenhagen in Denmark and Malmö, Helsingborg and Jönköping Vest in Sweden. Operating on Copenhagen service 184 from Kokkedal depot is 1007, PC95.849, a Volvo B10LE with Säffle bodywork. *Bill Potter*

1014-1027 Volvo B10BLE Åbenrå N43D 1998

1014	PJ88.334	1018	PJ88.338	1022	PJ88.342	1025	PJ88.345
1015	PJ88.335	1019	PJ88.339	1023	PJ88.343	1026	PJ88.346
1016	PJ88.336	1020	PJ88.340	1024	PJ88.344	1027	PJ88.347
1017	PJ88.337	1021	PJ88.341				

1028-1049 Volvo B10BLE Säffle N43D 1998

1028	PJ97.769	1034	PE94.601	1040	PE94.607	1045	PJ97.561
1029	PJ97.770	1035	PE94.591	1041	PE94.608	1046	PJ97.558
1030	PJ97.771	1036	PE94.592	1042	PE94.617	1047	PJ97.559
1031	PJ97.772	1037	PE94.602	1043	PE94.628	1048	PJ97.573
1032	PE94.590	1038	PE94.616	1044	PJ97.560	1049	PJ97.574
1033	PJ97.846	1039	PE94.603				

1084-1147 DAB Citibus S15 (lpg) DAB N43D 1998

1084	PE97.340	1096	PE97.352	1108	PJ96.904	1136	PM95.454
1085	PE97.341	1097	PE97.359	1109	PJ96.905	1137	PM95.455
1086	PE97.342	1098	PE97.424	1110	PJ96.906	1138	PM95.490
1087	PE97.343	1099	PE97.444	1127	PL96.059	1139	PM95.491
1088	PE97.344	1100	PE97.445	1128	PL96.060	1140	PM95.507
1089	PE97.345	1101	PE97.446	1129	PL96.061	1141	PM95.508
1090	PE97.346	1102	PJ96.813	1130	PM95.387	1142	PM95.509
1091	PE97.347	1103	PJ96.814	1131	PM95.388	1143	PP94.068
1092	PE97.348	1104	PJ96.815	1132	PM95.408	1144	PP94.069
1093	PE97.349	1105	PJ96.860	1133	PM95.409	1145	PP94.070
1094	PE97.350	1106	PJ96.861	1134	PM95.410	1146	PP94.071
1095	PE97.351	1107	PJ96.862	1135	PM95.453	1147	PP94.072

1148-1153 Volvo B10BLE Åbenrå AN43D 1994

1148	PP94.661	1149	PP94.663	1150	PP94.662	1153	PP94.659

1157-1171 Scania L113CLL Berkhof N43D 1998-99

1157	PP94.307	1161	PP94.355	1165	PR93.211	1169	PR93.373
1158	PP94.306	1162	PP94.356	1166	PR93.283	1170	PR93.374
1159	PP94.325	1163	PP94.280	1167	PR93.314	1171	PR93.328
1160	PP94.326	1164	PR93.210	1168	PR93.327		

Copenhagen services guaranteeing low-floor buses and high frequency have a red front nearside corner, while those on the 'S' express routes feature blue. Illustrating this feature is Volvo B10BLE 1402, RP88.738, which carries Åbenrå 13.7 metre bodywork. This example is operated from Bellerup. *Bill Potter*

1172-1181

		DAB Citibus S15 (lpg)		DAB		N43D	1999	
1172	PP94.305	1175	PZ89.716	1178	PZ89.855	1180	PZ89.893
1173	PZ90.195	1176	PZ89.723	1179	PZ89.856	1181	PZ89.894
1174	PZ90.196	1177	PZ89.838				

1182-1186

		Volvo B10BLE 12m		Åbenrå		NC39D	1999-2000	
1182	RE94.301	1184	RE94.302	1185	RE94.296	1186	RE94.303
1183	RE94.295						

1340-1384

		Volvo B10BLE 12m		Åbenrå		N36D	2000	
1340	RM90.995	1352	RM91.007	1363	RM91.018	1374	RM01.084
1341	RM90.996	1353	RM91.008	1364	RM91.019	1375	RN90.321
1342	RM90.997	1354	RM91.009	1365	RM91.020	1376	RN90.322
1343	RM90.998	1355	RM91.010	1366	RM91.021	1377	RN90.323
1344	RM90.999	1356	RM91.011	1367	RM91.022	1378	RN90.379
1345	RM91.000	1357	RM91.012	1368	RM91.023	1379	RN90.380
1346	RM91.001	1358	RM91.013	1369	RM91.024	1380	RN90.381
1347	RM91.002	1359	RM91.014	1370	RM91.025	1381	RN90.382
1348	RM91.003	1360	RM91.015	1371	RM91.026	1382	RN90.413
1349	RM91.004	1361	RM91.016	1372	RM91.082	1383	RN90.414
1350	RM91.005	1362	RM91.017	1373	RM91.083	1384	RP91.062
1351	RM91.006						

1385-1403

		Volvo B10BLE 13.7m		Åbenrå		NC41D	2000	
1385	SN89.817	1390	RN95.489	1395	RN95.514	1400	RP88.736
1386	RN90.444	1391	RN95.490	1396	RN95.515	1401	RP88.737
1387	RN95.486	1392	RN95.511	1397	RP88.732	1402	RP88.738
1388	RN95.487	1393	RN95.512	1398	RP88.733	1403	RP88.734
1389	RN95.488	1394	RN95.513	1399	RP88.735	

1404-1435

		Volvo B10BLE 13.7m		Åbenrå		NC41D	2001	
1404	RX93.855	1412	RX03.811	1420	RX93.891	1428	RX93.860
1405	RX93.854	1413	RX93.857	1421	RX93.892	1429	RV96.460
1406	RX93.856	1414	RV92.762	1422	RX93.893	1430	RV96.461
1407	RX93.853	1415	RX93.812	1423	RX93.894	1431	RV96.462
1408	RX93.882	1416	RX93.858	1424	RX93.895	1432	RX93.885
1409	RX93.883	1417	RX93.884	1425	RV92.764	1433	RV96.463
1410	RV92.761	1418	RX93.859	1426	RV92.765	1434	RV96.464
1411	RV92.729	1419	RV92.763	1427	RV96.459	1435	RX96.754

The only double-deck buses operated by Arriva in Denmark are fourteen East Lancs Nordic-bodied Volvo B7TLs. These currently operate route 15 with 1451, SB95.593 seen at Emdrup, while based at Ryvang depot. *Bill Potter*

1441-1454 — Volvo B7TL 12m — East Lancs Nordic — N(73)D — 2001

1441	RZ92.675	1445	RZ97.043	1449	RZ92.782	1452	SB95.711
1442	SB95.709	1446	RZ92.781	1450	RZ97.045	1453	SB95.712
1443	RZ92.799	1447	RZ97.044	1451	SB95.593	1454	SB95.594
1444	RZ92.676	1448	SB95.710				

1455-1473 — Volvo B10BLE 13.7m — Åbenrå — N41D — 2002

1455	SC90.610	1460	SC90.691	1465	SD88.214	1470	SD88.252
1456	SC90.611	1461	SD88.164	1466	SB93.616	1471	SD88.253
1457	SC90.651	1462	SD88.165	1467	SB93.617	1472	SD88.254
1458	SC90.652	1463	SD88.166	1468	SB93.618	1473	SD88.255
1459	SC90.677	1464	SD88.212	1469	SD88.251		

1700-1733 — Volvo B10BLE 12m — Åbenrå — AN38D — 1999

1700	PZ95.450	1709	PZ95.459	1718	PZ95.500	1726	PZ95.547
1701	PZ95.451	1710	PZ95.492	1719	PZ95.501	1727	PZ95.548
1702	PZ95.452	1711	PZ95.493	1720	PZ95.502	1728	PZ95.549
1703	PZ95.453	1712	PZ95.494	1721	PZ95.503	1729	PZ95.550
1704	PZ95.454	1713	PZ95.495	1722	PZ95.504	1730	PZ95.551
1705	PZ95.455	1714	PZ95.496	1723	PZ95.505	1731	PZ95.552
1706	PZ95.456	1715	PZ95.497	1724	PZ95.506	1732	PZ95.553
1707	PZ95.457	1716	PZ95.498	1725	PZ95.546	1733	PZ95.554
1708	PZ95.458	1717	PZ95.499				

1740	PZ95.592	Volvo B10BLE	Åbenrå	N68D	1999
1741	PZ95.593	Volvo B10BLE	Åbenrå	N68D	1999
1742	PZ95.594	Volvo B10BLE	Åbenrå	N68D	1999
1750	RU97.094	DAB	DAB	N14D	2001
1751	RU97.095	DAB	DAB	N14D	2002
1752	SR93.368	Volvo B10L	Åbenrå	N-	1996
1753	PP94.330	DAB	DAB	N14D	1998

1754-1760 — Optare Solo M920L · Optare · N23D · 2005

1754	TP97969	1756	TP97968	1758	TR88011	1760	TR88009
1755	TP97967	1757	TP97966	1759	TR88010		

1765	PC95.879	Volvo B10M	Åbenrå	B38D	1998
1766	PJ89239	Neoplan	Neoplan	N	1998
1767	PJ89235	Neoplan	Neoplan	N	1998
1768	PJ89236	Neoplan	Neoplan	N	1998
1770	OV91.913	Volvo B10BLE	Åbenrå	N32D	1997
1771	OV91.900	Volvo B10BLE	Åbenrå	N32D	1997
1772	PP89.362	Volvo B10BLE	Åbenrå	N32D	1997
1773	PP89.440	Volvo B10BLE	Åbenrå	N32D	1997
1777	PB91.328	DAB Citybus S15 III	DAB	N34D	1997
1778	PL97.752	Volvo B10BLE	Åbenrå	N32D	1998
1779	RC89.415	Volvo B10BLE	Åbenrå	N32D	1998
1780	RC89.416	Volvo B10BLE	Åbenrå	N32D	1998
1781	RC89.417	Volvo B10BLE	Åbenrå	N32D	1998
1782	RH97.569	Volvo B10BLE	Åbenrå	N32D	1998

1783-1794 — Scania OmniLink CL94UB 12m · Scania · N42D · 2003

1783	SU96.129	1786	SU96.126	1789	SU96.123	1792	SU96.135
1784	SU96.128	1787	SU96.125	1790	SU96.122	1793	SU96.148
1785	SU96.127	1788	SU96.124	1791	SU96.136	1794	SU96.147

1795-1813 — Scania OmniLink CL94UB 13.7m · Scania · N-D · 2003

1795	SV97.011	1800	SX90.752	1805	SY89.362	1810	SY89.417
1796	SV97.012	1801	SX90.819	1806	SY89.361	1811	SY89.416
1797	SV97.013	1802	SX90.854	1807	SY89.360	1812	SY89.479
1798	SV97.044	1803	SX90.839	1808	SY89.393	1813	SY89.496
1799	SX90.788	1804	SX90.875	1809	SY89.392		

1814-1818 — Volvo B10BLE 12m · Åbenrå · N32D · 1995-96

1814	NR88.857	1816	NY91.010	1817	NY91.011	1818	ST93942
1815	NY91.009						

1820	SR96.531	Volvo B10L	Åbenrå	N32D	1996
1821	SR96.545	Volvo B10L	Åbenrå	N32D	1996
1822	SR96.559	Volvo B10L	Åbenrå	N32D	1996
1823	ST94.135	MAN/DAB Citybus S15	DAB	N32D	1994
1824	ST94.140	MAN/DAB Citybus S15	DAB	N32D	1994
1825	ST93.232	Volvo B10L	Åbenrå	N32D	1996
1826	OM97.996	Volvo B10L	Åbenrå	N32D	1996

1827-1858 — Scania OmniLink CL94UB 13.7m · Scania · N-D · 2003-04

1827	SY93.825	1835	SY93.783	1843	TB88.449	1851	TB88.489
1828	SY93.784	1836	SZ91.745	1844	TB88.417	1852	TB88.477
1829	SY93.824	1837	SZ91.744	1845	TB88.418	1853	TB88.490
1830	SY93.774	1838	SZ91.749	1846	TB88.450	1854	TB88.491
1831	SY93.775	1839	SZ91.755	1847	TB88.444	1855	TB88.493
1832	SY93.776	1840	SZ91.756	1848	TB88.445	1856	TB88.492
1833	SY93.777	1841	SZ91.765	1849	TB88.483	1857	TB88.469
1834	SY93.778	1842	TB88.448	1850	TB88.484	1858	TB88.470

1859	OL88.346	Volvo B10BLE	Åbenrå	N32D	1996
1860	OV92.039	Volvo B10BLE	Åbenrå	N32D	1997
1861	RN88.117	Volvo B10BLE	Åbenrå	N32D	2000
1862	NV93.382	MAN/DAB Citybus S15	DAB	N32D	1994
1863	NV93.383	MAN/DAB Citybus S15	DAB	N32D	1994
1864	NY91.031	Volvo B10BLE	Åbenrå	N32D	1995
1865	NY91.032	Volvo B10BLE	Åbenrå	N32D	1995
1866	NY91.051	Volvo B10BLE	Åbenrå	N32D	1995

1912-1919 — DAB RS200L 12m · DAB · N26D · 1993

1912	SN94.318	1915	NJ97.882	1916	NJ97.883	1919	NK88.003
1914	NJ97.881						

1927-1934 — Volvo B10BLE 12m · Åbenrå · AN33D · 1994

1927	NU88.584	1929	NU88.590	1931	NU88.600	1933	NU88.603
1928	NU88.588	1930	NU88.591	1932	NU88.599	1934	NU88.631

An interesting additon to the Danish operation are seven Optare Solo buses used on rural links. Allocated to Roskilde 1757, TP97966, was about to start the day's duty when pictured outside the cathedral. These vehicle are dual doored and thus have a seating capacity of just twenty-three. *Bill Potter*

1946-1970

	DAB GS200		Silkeborg		NC34D	1995	
1946	OC93.611	**1953**	OC93.621	**1959**	OC93.650	**1965**	OD92.388
1947	OC93.618	**1954**	OC93.622	**1960**	OC93.651	**1966**	OD92.416
1948	OC93.592	**1955**	OC93.623	**1961**	OD92.384	**1967**	OD92.417
1949	OC93.612	**1956**	OC93.642	**1962**	OD92.385	**1968**	OD92.418
1950	OC93.613	**1957**	OC93.643	**1963**	OD92.386	**1969**	OD92.419
1951	OC93.619	**1958**	OC93.649	**1964**	OD92.387	**1970**	OD92.420
1952	OC93.620						

1971-1984

	Mercedes-Benz O405GN		Mercedes-Benz		AN54D	1995-96	
1971	OK94.243	**1975**	OK94.294	**1979**	OK94.484	**1982**	OM89.895
1972	OK94.242	**1976**	OK94.342	**1980**	OM89.830	**1983**	OM89.939
1973	OK94.241	**1977**	OK94.384	**1981**	OM89.857	**1984**	OM89.941
1974	OK94.240	**1978**	OK94.385				

1985	OK91.590	DAB GS200	Silkeborg	BC34D	1996	
1986	OK91.591	DAB GS200	Silkeborg	BC34D	1996	
1987	OK91.592	DAB GS200	Silkeborg	BC34D	1996	
1988	OP93.607	Mercedes-Benz O405N	Mercedes-Benz	N34D	1996	

1989-1998

	Volvo B10BLE		Åbenrå		N34D	1997	
1989	OV92.054	**1992**	OX94.338	**1995**	OX94.347	**1997**	OX94.366
1990	OX94.333	**1993**	OX94.339	**1996**	OX94.365	**1998**	OX94.372
1991	OX94.334	**1994**	OX94.346				

1999	PB91.329	DAB GS200	Silkeborg	BC37D	1997	
2007	LV91.554	Volvo B10M	Åbenrå	B39D	1989	
2012	NZ93.950	DAB	Silkeborg	B47F	1995	
2018	MB92.612	DAB	Silkeborg	B39D	1990	
2019	NX92.970	DAB	Silkeborg	B39D	1994	
2023	NX93.044	DAB	Silkeborg	B47F	1990	
2025	MV95.152	Setra	Setra	B44F	1992	
2039	NS91.543	Volvo B10	Åbenrå	B39F	1994	

2045-2057		Volvo B10B		Åbenrå		N29D	1997	

2045	OU92.250	**2049**	OU92.263	**2052**	OV91.884	**2055**	OV91.885
2046	OU92.249	**2050**	OU92.271	**2053**	OV91.887	**2056**	OV91.883
2047	OU92.248	**2051**	OU92.275	**2054**	OV91.886	**2057**	OV91.896
2048	OU92.255						

2059	PE91.021	Volvo B10BLE	Åbenrå	N44F	1998
2060	PP89.432	Volvo B10BLE	Åbenrå	N44F	?
2061	PP89.434	Volvo B10BLE	Åbenrå	N44F	1998
2062	RD91.902	Volvo B10BLE	Åbenrå	N44F	1999
2063	RD91.904	Volvo B10BLE	Åbenrå	N44F	1999
2064	RD91.919	Volvo B10BLE	Åbenrå	N44F	1999
2065	RN88.014	Volvo B10BLE	Åbenrå	N44F	?
2066	RV89.287	Mercedes-Benz Cito S	Mercedes-Benz	N29F	2002
2067	RV89.288	Mercedes-Benz Cito S	Mercedes-Benz	N29F	2002
2080	LH90.503	Volvo B10M	Åbenrå	B--D	1987
2084	TD95.436	Volvo B10M	Åbenrå	B--D	1987
2093	LC91641	Volvo B10M	Åbenrå	B--D	1987
2097	NM90252	DAB	Silkeborg	B39D	1993
2098	LD92341	Volvo B10M	Åbenrå	B--D	1987
2103	LD92390	Volvo B10M	Åbenrå	B--D	1987
2108	LD92538	Volvo B10M	Åbenrå	B--D	1987
2109	LD92539	Volvo B10M	Åbenrå	B--D	1987
2110	LD92540	Volvo B10M	Åbenrå	B--D	1987
2134	LP94.417	Volvo B10M	Åbenrå	B--D	1988
2136	LP94.443	Volvo B10M	Åbenrå	B--D	1988
2173	LX94.925	Volvo B10M	Åbenrå	B--D	1989
2193	LY93.236	Volvo B10BLE	Silkeborg	B--D	1989
2195	LY93.265	Volvo B10BLE	Silkeborg	B--D	1989
2212	MB92.838	Volvo B10BLE	Åbenrå	B--D	1990
2216	MC97.181	Volvo B10BLE	Åbenrå	B--D	1990

2230-2244		Volvo B10M		Silkeborg		B38D	1991

2230	MC92.667	**2242**	ME94.484	**2243**	ME94.488	**2244**	ME94.489
2241	ME94.483						

2249-2263		Volvo B10M		Åbenrå		B38D	1991

2249	MJ95.476	**2258**	MN92.151	**2261**	MN92.186	**2263**	MN92.282
2252	ML88.128	**2260**	MN92.185	**2262**	MN92.281		

2266	MR93.432	Volvo B10M	Silkeborg	B--D	1991
2268	MR93.469	Volvo B10M	Silkeborg	B--D	1991
2270	MR93.471	Volvo B10M	Silkeborg	B--D	1991
2285	MS91.111	Volvo B10M	Silkeborg	B--D	1991
2287	MS91.113	Volvo B10M	Silkeborg	B--D	1991
2291	MS97.752	Volvo B10M	Åbenrå	B--D	1991
2292	MS97.753	Volvo B10M	Åbenrå	B--D	1992

2303-2311		Volvo B10M		Åbenrå		B38D	1992

2303	NB97.060	**2304**	NB97.087	**2305**	NB97.088	**2311**	OE93.171

2312-2325		Volvo B10M		Silkeborg		B38D	1992

2312	NB89.308	**2315**	NB89.311	**2317**	NB89.355	**2325**	NB97.476
2314	NB89.310						

2327	MZ89.352	DAF/DAB Citybus	Silkeborg	B--D	1992
2328	NB97.583	DAF/DAB Citybus	Silkeborg	B--D	1992
2344	NB97.681	Volvo B10M	Silkeborg	B--D	1992
2345	NE89.728	Volvo B10M	Åbenrå	B--D	1993

2348-2354		Volvo B10M		Åbenrå		B38D	1993

2348	NJ93.668	**2350**	RS89.441	**2352**	NJ93.810	**2354**	NJ93.800
2349	NJ93.700	**2351**	NJ93.727	**2353**	NJ93.818		

2358	NK96.706	Volvo B10M	Åbenrå	BC35D	1993
2359	NK96.749	Volvo B10M	Åbenrå	BC35D	1993

2365-2379		Volvo B10M		Silkeborg		B38D	1993

2365	NN89.572	**2368**	NN89.574	**2370**	NN89.576	**2378**	NK96.626
2366	NN89.542	**2369**	NN89.575	**2377**	NN89.627	**2379**	NK96.625
2367	NN89.573						

The island of Fyn lies between Jylland (Jutland) and Sjælland (Zealand). From two depots in the island's capital Odense, Arriva provides the buses for the Fynbus operation in an all-over cream livery. Pictured in the bus station is one of the few Scania buses bodied by DAB/Silkeborg. Number 2683, RK95.314, was delivered in 2000.
Bill Potter

2390	NN91.909	Volvo B10BLE	Åbenrå	N44D	1994

2393-2425		Volvo B10M	Silkeborg	B38D	1994

2393	NN97.536	**2406**	NX93.002	**2417**	NX93.067	**2420**	NX93.070
2394	NN97.537	**2414**	NX93.041	**2418**	NX93.068	**2421**	NX93.071
2395	NN97.538	**2415**	NX93.042	**2419**	NX93.069	**2425**	NX90.912
2405	NX93.001	**2416**	NX93.066				

2427	NX90.942	Volvo B10M	Åbenrå	BC--D	1994
2442	NZ93.543	Volvo B10M	Åbenrå	BC--D	1995
2443	OB94.328	Volvo B10M	Åbenrå	B44D	1995
2456	OD92.566	Scania N113	Lahti	B39D	1995

2457-2463		Volvo B10M	Silkeborg	B38D	1995

2457	OD92.635	**2460**	OD92.657	**2462**	OD92.659	**2463**	OD92.660
2459	OD92.656	**2461**	OD92.658				

2473	OD97.349	Volvo B10M	Åbenrå	BC--D	1995
2474	OE94.307	Volvo B6LE	Vest	BC--D	1995
2475	OE94.308	Volvo B6LE	Vest	BC--D	1995

2481-2485		Volvo B10M	DAB/Silkeborg	B38D	1996

2481	OJ92.349	**2482**	OJ92.350	**2485**	OJ92.353

2486	OL97.128	Volvo B10LA	Saffle S	N--D	1996
2489	OL88.369	Volvo B10M	Åbenrå	B--D	1996
2490	OL96.926	Volvo B10M	Åbenrå	B--D	1996
2491	OL96.921	Volvo B10M	Åbenrå	B--D	1996
2506	OM97.903	Volvo B10M	Åbenrå	B--D	1996
2509	OM97.854	Volvo B10M	Åbenrå	B--D	1996
2510	OM97.918	Volvo B10M	Åbenrå	B--D	1996
2511	OM97.927	Volvo B10M	Åbenrå	B--D	1996
2512	OU94.973	Volvo B6LE	Vest	B--D	1997
2516	OV91.931	Volvo B9M	DAB/Silkeborg	B--D	1997

2521	OX91.625	Volvo B10M	DAB/Silkeborg	B--D	1997
2526	OX91.679	Volvo B10M	DAB/Silkeborg	B--D	1997
2527	OS89.334	DAF/DAB Citybus	DAB/Silkeborg	B--D	1997
2528	OS89.335	DAF/DAB Citybus	DAB/Silkeborg	B--D	1997
2531	OX94.453	Volvo B9M	DAB/Silkeborg	B--D	1997
2534	OX94.494	Volvo B10M	Åbenrå	B--D	1997
2535	OY97.183	Volvo B10M	Åbenrå	B--D	1997

2536-2543 — Scania N112CL — Scania — B--D — 1997

| 2536 | PB91.473 | 2538 | PB91.475 | 2541 | PB91.480 | 2543 | PB91.482 |
| 2537 | PB91.474 | 2539 | PB91.476 | 2542 | PB91.481 | | |

2544	PB89.173	Volvo B10M	Åbenrå	B--D	1997
2545	PB89.180	Volvo B10M	Åbenrå	B--D	1997
2546	PB91.477	Scania N112CL	Scania	B--D	1997
2547	PB91.478	Scania N112CL	Scania	B--D	1997
2548	PB89.069	Volvo B10M	Åbenrå	B--D	1997
2549	PB89.077	Volvo B10M	Åbenrå	B--D	1997

2550-2555 — Volvo B10M — Åbenrå — B--D — 1997

| 2550u | PB89.084 | 2552 | PB89.095 | 2554 | PB89.102 | 2555 | PB89.108 |
| 2551 | PB89.085 | 2553 | PB89.103 | | | | |

2556-2569 — Volvo B10M — Vest — B--D — 1997-98

2556	OZ94.278	2561	PC90.717	2564	PC95.835	2567	PC89.073
2559	OZ94.283	2562	PC90.719	2565	PC89.056	2568	PC89.080
2560	PC90.718	2563	PC90.720	2566	PC89.064	2569	PC89.105

2572	PC89.157	Volvo B10M	Åbenrå	B--D	1998
2574	PC97.949	Scania N112CL	Scania	B--D	1998
2575	PE92.039	Volvo B10M	Vest	B--D	1998
2576	PE92.042	Volvo B10M	Vest	B--D	1998
2578	PP89.431	Volvo B10M	Åbenrå	B--D	1998

2581-2589 — Volvo B10M — Vest — B--D — 1998

| 2581 | PE92.002 | 2585 | PP93.852 | 2587 | PP93.854 | 2589 | PR94.089 |
| 2582 | PE92.001 | 2586 | PP93.855 | 2588 | PP93.852 | | |

2590-2634 — Volvo B10M — Åbenrå — B--D — 1998-99

| 2590 | PE94.629 | 2596 | PP89.417 | 2633 | PT95.382 | 2634 | PT95.381 |
| 2595 | PP89.414 | 2619 | PT95.340 | | | | |

2647	PX96.158	Volvo B10M	Åbenrå	B--D	1999
2648	PX96.158	Volvo B10M	Åbenrå	B--D	1999
2649	PX96.158	Volvo B10M	Åbenrå	B--D	1999

2652-2656 — Volvo B10M — Vest — B--D — 1999

| 2652 | RC91.287 | 2654 | RC91.289 | 2655 | RC91.290 | 2656 | RC91.291 |
| 2653 | RC91.288 | | | | | | |

2658-2663 — Volvo B10M — Åbenrå — B--D — 1999

| 2658 | PX96.253 | 2660 | PX96.265 | 2662 | RC89.372 | 2663 | RC89.383 |
| 2659 | PX96.266 | 2661 | PX96.271 | | | | |

2664	RD94.746	DAF/DAB Citybus	DAB	B--D	1999
2665	RD94.747	DAF/DAB Citybus	DAB	B--D	1999
2666	RD90.971	Volvo B10M	Vest	B--D	1999
2667	RC89.395	Volvo B10M	Åbenrå	B--D	1999
2668	RC89.396	Volvo B10M	Åbenrå	B--D	1999
2669	RC89.397	Volvo B10M	Åbenrå	B--D	1999
2671	RD91.987	Volvo B10LA	Saffle S	N--D	1999

2672-2676 — Volvo B10M — Åbenrå — B--D — 1999

| 2672 | RD91.994 | 2674 | PX96.241 | 2675 | RE94.201 | 2676 | RD91.993 |
| 2673 | RD91.999 | | | | | | |

2682	RH97.538	Volvo B10M	Åbenrå	B--D	2000
2683	RK95.314	Scania	DAB/Silkeborg	N--D	2000
2701	RL92.435	Volvo B10LA	Saffle S	N--D	2000

Recent arrivals for the additional contracts gained on Jutland are six Scania OmniLine integral buses used on the X-series limited stop services. These are the only ones currently with corporate colours and 2848, SL95855, is seen pulling away from the bus station in Aarhus. *Bill Potter*

2707-2718

		Scania L113CLL		DAB/Silkeborg		N--D	2000	
2707	RM96.994	**2712**	RN96.024	**2715**	RN96.188	**2717**	RN95.954
2710	RM96.996	**2713**	RN96.048	**2716**	RN96.189	**2718**	RN95.953

2720	RN88.013	Volvo B10BLE	Åbenrå	N38D	2000
2723	RP91.142	Volvo B10BLE	Åbenrå	N38D	2000
2745	RN96.076	Scania	DAB/Silkeborg	N--D	2000
2746	RN96.123	Scania	DAB/Silkeborg	N--D	2000
2747	RN96.124	Scania	DAB/Silkeborg	N--D	2000
2749	RP91.084	Volvo B10M	Åbenrå	B--D	2000
2751	RT95.351	MAN NL223 9m	MAN	N--F	2001
2752	RT95.350	MAN NL223 9m	MAN	N--F	2001

2753-2769

		Volvo B10BLE		Åbenrå		N38D	2001	
2753	RT95.277	**2758**	RT95.268	**2762**	RT95.272	**2766**	RT95.276
2754	RT95.261	**2759**	RT95.269	**2763**	RT95.273	**2767**	RT95.267
2755	RT95.262	**2760**	RT95.270	**2764**	RT95.274	**2768**	RT95.266
2756	RT95.263	**2761**	RT95.271	**2765**	RT95.275	**2769**	RT95.265
2757	RT95.264						

2770-2819

		Scania OmniLine CL94UB 12m		Scania		N--D	2001	*2774 is an OmniLink
2770	RT96.882	**2787**	RV95.338	**2798**	RV95.384	**2809**	RV95.394
2774	RV95.418	**2788**	RV95.339	**2799**	RV95.347	**2810**	RV95.395
2777	RV95.328	**2789**	RV95.340	**2800**	RV95.385	**2811**	RV95.396
2778	RV95.329	**2790**	RV95.341	**2801**	RV95.386	**2812**	RV95.397
2779	RV95.330	**2791**	RV95.342	**2802**	RV95.387	**2813**	RV95.398
2780	RV95.331	**2792**	RV95.343	**2803**	RV95.388	**2814**	RV95.399
2781	RV95.332	**2793**	RV95.344	**2804**	RV95.389	**2815**	RV95.400
2782	RV95.333	**2794**	RV95.345	**2805**	RV95.390	**2816**	RV95.401
2783	RV95.334	**2795**	RV95.382	**2806**	RV95.391	**2817**	RV95.402
2784	RV95.335	**2796**	RV95.383	**2807**	RV95.392	**2818**	RV95.403
2785	RV95.336	**2797**	RV95.346	**2808**	RV95.393	**2819**	RV95.404
2786	RV95.337						

2820-2825

		Scania 13.6m		Lahti		N--D	2001-02	
2820	RV95.405	**2822**	RV95.407	**2824**	SJ94.192	**2825**	RX97.975
2821	RV95.406	**2823**	RV95.408				

2826	RX96.850	Volvo B10M 13.7m	Åbenrå	NC44D	2002
2827	SM97.944	Scania 13.6m	Lahti	N--D	2002
2830	RZ88.061	Scania OmniLine L94UB	DAB	N--D	2002
2831	RY88.058	Scania 13.6m	Lahti	N--D	2002
2837	RX96.843	Volvo B10M 13.7m	Åbenrå	NC44D	2002

2840-2844

		Scania OmniLine CL94UB 12m	Scania	N--D	2002	*2843 is an OmniLink
2840	RZ97.927	**2842**	SD91.475	**2843**	SJ93.967	**2844**	SH93.791
2841	RZ97.946						

| 2845 | SM95.889 | Volvo B12M | Vest | NC44D | 2002 |

2846-2851

		Scania OmniLine CL94UB 12m	Scania	N--D	2002
2846	SL96.650	**2848**	SL95.855	**2850**	SL95.857	**2851**	SL95.953
2847	SL95.830	**2849**	SL95.856				

2852-2865

		Scania OmniLink CL94UB 12m	Scania	N--D	2003
2852	SM97.681	**2856**	SX97.339	**2860**	SX97.367	**2863**	SX97.369
2853	SX97.361	**2857**	SX97.364	**2861**	SX97.340	**2864**	SX97.303
2854	SX97.362	**2858**	SX97.365	**2862**	SX97.368	**2865**	SX97.338
2855	SX97.363	**2859**	SX97.366				

2866-2871

		MAN 13.310	Jonckheere Modulo	C--D	2004
2866	SY89.049	**2868**	SY89.051	**2870**	SY89.081	**2871**	SY89.082
2867	SY89.050	**2869**	SY89.052				

2872-2882

		Scania OmniLink CL94UB 12m	Scania	N--D	2004
2872	TJ88585	**2875**	TJ88588	**2878**	TJ88591	**2881**	TJ88593
2873	TJ88586	**2876**	TJ88589	**2879**	TJ88555	**2882**	TJ88594
2874	TJ88587	**2877**	TJ88590	**2880**	TJ88592		

2883-2886

		Scania L94UB 13.6m	Lahti	N--D	2004
2883	TK94765	**2884**	TK94766	**2885**	TK94767	**2886**	TM88197

2887	TJ97221	Volvo B12BLE	Åbenrå	N--D	2004
2888	TM88244	Scania OmniLine CL94UB 12m	Scania	NC--D	2004
2890	TT88270	Scania OmniLink CL94UB 12m	Scania	N--D	2004
2891	TT88410	Scania OmniLink CL94UB 12m	Scania	N--D	2004

2892-2899

		Volvo B12M	Carrus	N--	2005
2892	TT90158	**2894**	TT90160	**2896**	I I90162	**2898**	TT90164
2893	TT90159	**2895**	TT90161	**2897**	TT90163	**2899**	TT90165

3000-3015

		Volvo B10BLE	Åbenrå	N30D	1997	Arriva Sweden, 2004-05
3000	TD89898	**3004**	TD89753	**3008**	TD89748	**3012**	TD89752
3001	TD89899	**3005**	TD89751	**3009**	TD89749	**3013**	TJ92701
3002	TD89710	**3006**	TD89711	**3010**	TD89707	**3014**	TJ92702
3003	TJ92700	**3007**	TD89750	**3011**	TD89706	**3015**	TJ92703

| 3025 | NV89.197 | Volvo B10BLE | Säffle | B36D | 1994 |
| 3026 | NV89.198 | Volvo B10BLE | Säffle | B36D | 1994 |

3050-3071

		Volvo B12BLE	Åbenrå	N36D	2004
3050	TJ91367	**3056**	TJ97103	**3062**	TJ97844	**3067**	TJ97896
3051	TJ91368	**3057**	TJ97105	**3063**	TJ97843	**3068**	TL89534
3052	TJ91375	**3058**	TJ97811	**3064**	TJ97870	**3069**	TL89537
3053	TJ97101	**3059**	TJ97812	**3065**	TJ97869	**3070**	TL89536
3054	TJ97102	**3060**	TJ97813	**3066**	TJ97889	**3071**	TL89535
3055	TJ97104	**3061**	TJ97842				

3100	JJ92242	Leyland/DAB	DAB	B--D	1983
3101	JS95579	Leyland/DAD	DAB	B--D	1985
3102	LY88528	Volvo B10M	Åbenrå	B--D	1985
3103	NB89216	Leyland/DAB	DAB	B--D	1986
3104	KR95939	Leyland/DAB	DAB	B--D	1986
3105	PL95856	Volvo B10M	Åbenrå	B--D	1986
3106	KV94917	Leyland/DAB	DAB	B--D	1986
3107	SJ92565	Leyland/DAB	DAB	B--D	1986
3108	KV94649	Volvo B10M	Åbenrå	B--D	1987
3109	LD92510	Leyland/DAB	DAB	B--D	1987
3110	LS89326	DAB	DAB	B--D	1988
3111	LP96030	Volvo B10M	Åbenrå	B--D	1988

3112	NK94883	Volvo B10M	Åbenrå	B--D	1988
3113	MR93264	Leyland/DAB	DAB	B--D	1989
3114	NV89288	Volvo B10M	Åbenrå	B--D	1989
3115	LV92590	DAB	DAB	B--D	1989
3116	NS88229	DAF/DAB	DAB	B--D	1989
3117	LV91530	Volvo B10M	Åbenrå	B--D	1989
3118	LT91490	Volvo B10M	Åbenrå	B--D	1989
3119	LX91252	Leyland/DAB	DAB	B--D	1989
3121	RU96982	Leyland/DAB	DAB	B--D	1989
3122	LY93298	DAF/DAB	DAB	B--D	1989
3123	LY93382	DAF/DAB	DAB	B--D	1989
3124	LZ92953	DAF/DAB	DAB	B--D	1989
3125	NX88081	Leyland/DAB	DAB	B--D	1989
3126	LZ92949	DAF/DAB	DAB	B--D	1989
3127	LZ93121	DAF/DAB	DAB	B--D	1990
3128	RZ93500	DAF/DAB	DAB	B--D	1990
3129	MB92831	Volvo B10M	Åbenrå	B--D	1990
3130	MB92879	Volvo B10M	Åbenrå	B--D	1990
3131	MC92668	Volvo B10M	Åbenrå	B--D	1990
3132	PJ95895	DAF/DAB	DAB	B--D	1990
3133	MD91762	DAF/DAB	DAB	B--D	1990
3134	NB89190	DAF/DAB	DAB	B--D	1990
3135	ME94496	Volvo B10M	Åbenrå	B--D	1990
3136	MJ92959	DAF/DAB	DAB	B--D	1990
3137	RS89264	Volvo B10M	Åbenrå	B--D	1991
3138	RS89265	Volvo B10M	Åbenrå	B--D	1991
3139	ML88076	Volvo B10M	Åbenrå	B--D	1991
3140	RP89285	DAF/DAB	DAB	B--D	1991
3141	MS0998	Volvo B10M	Åbenrå	B--D	1991
3142	MS91016	Volvo B10M	Åbenrå	B--D	1991
3143	RU94658	Scania/DAB	DAB	B--D	1991
3144	RK92117	DAF/DAB	DAB	B--D	1991
3145	ML93910	DAF/DAB	DAB	B--D	1991
3146	ML88147	Volvo B10M	Åbenrå	B--D	1991
3147	MN92231	Volvo B10M	Åbenrå	B--D	1991
3148	MR93298	DAF/DAB	DAB	B--D	1991
3149	MS91014	Volvo B10M	Åbenrå	B--D	1991
3150	ME94496	Volvo B10M	Åbenrå	B--D	1991
3151	OZ91963	DAF/DAB	DAB	B--D	1992
3152	MY91487	DAF/DAB	DAB	B--D	1992
3153	OJ94187	DAF/DAB	DAB	B--D	1992
3154	MZ89389	DAF/DAB	DAB	B--D	1992
3155	MZ93819	Volvo B10M	Åbenrå	B--D	1992
3156	NB89328	DAF/DAB	DAB	B--D	1992
3158	MY97786	Volvo B10M	Åbenrå	B--D	1993
3159	NC92046	Volvo B10M	Åbenrå	B--D	1993
3160	NJ89097	DAF/DAB	DAB	B--D	1993
3161	NC97647	MAN/DAB	DAB Citybus S15 Mk2	B--D	1993
3162	NJ89096	DAF/DAB	DAB	B--D	1993
3163	NJ89125	MAN/DAB	DAB Citybus S15 Mk2	B--D	1993
3164	NC92204	Volvo B10M	Åbenrå	B--D	1993
3165	TD89591	DAF/DAB	DAB	B--D	1993
3166	NV91273	Volvo B10M	Åbenrå	B--D	1993
3167	OS94520	DAF/DAB	DAB	B--D	1993
3168	SJ92752	DAF/DAB	DAB Citybus S15 Mk1	B--D	1993
3169	NU93403	DAF/DAB	DAB	B--D	1994
3170	NR96191	Volvo B10M	Åbenrå	B--D	1994
3171	NY91070	Volvo B10M	Åbenrå	B--D	1995
3172	NZ93969	DAF/DAB	DAB	B--D	1995
3173	NZ93981	DAF/DAB	DAB	B--D	1995
3174	MB92888	Volvo B10M	Åbenrå	B--D	1995
3175	OB93468	MAN/DAB	DAB Citybus S15 Mk2	B--D	1995
3176	OB93469	MAN/DAB	DAB Citybus S15 Mk2	B--D	1995
3177	OB93603	DAF/DAB	DAB	B--D	1995
3178	OB94382	Volvo B10M	Åbenrå	B--D	1995
3179	OB93603	DAF/DAB	DAB	B--D	1995
3180	OB93516	MAN/DAB	DAB Citybus S15 Mk2	B--D	1995
3181	OB94432	Volvo B10M	Åbenrå	B--D	1995
3182	OB94438	Volvo B10M	Åbenrå	B--D	1995
3183	OD97599	Volvo B10M	Åbenrå	B--D	1996
3184	NJ89095	DAF/DAB	DAB	B--D	1996
3185	RL91182	Volvo B10M	Åbenrå	B--D	1997
3186	OX89205	Volvo B10M	Åbenrå	B--D	1997

3187	PE94555	Volvo B10M	Åbenrå	B--D	1998
3188	OZ92476	Volvo B10M	Vest	B--D	1998
3189	PL97691	Volvo B10M	Åbenrå	B--D	1998
3190	PE94573	Volvo B10M	Åbenrå	B--D	1998
3191	PE94583	Volvo B10M	Åbenrå	B--D	1998
3192	PE94587	Volvo B10M	Åbenrå	B--D	1998
3193	OZ92475	Volvo B10M	Vest	B--D	1998
3194	OZ92511	Volvo B10M	Vest	B--D	1998
3195	OZ92510	Volvo B10M	Vest	B--D	1998
3196	PL97595	Volvo B10BLE	Åbenrå	B--D	1998
3197	PL97652	Volvo B10M	Vest	B--D	1998
3198	PP89464	Volvo B10M	Vest	B--D	1998
3199	PX96127	Volvo B10BLE	Åbenrå	B--D	1999
3200	PX96128	Volvo B10BLE	Åbenrå	N39D	1999
3201	PZ89728	Scania/DAB	DAB	B--D	1999
3202	PZ89729	Scania/DAB	DAB	B--D	1999
3203	PZ89726	Scania/DAB	DAB	B--D	1999
3204	PZ89727	Scania/DAB	DAB	B--D	1999
3205	RC89419	Volvo B10M	Vest	B--D	1999
3206	RC89418	Volvo B10M	Vest	B--D	1999
3207	RX96461	Scania/DAB	DAB	B--D	1999
3208	RD94888	Scania/DAB	DAB	B--D	1999
3209	RD94889	Scania/DAB	DAB	B--D	1999
3210	RP89275	DAF/DAB	DAB	B--D	1999

3211-3218   Volvo B10M   Åbenrå   B36D   2000

3211	RE92067	3213	RK97522	3215	RL91165	3217	RL91164
3212	RE92095	3214	RK97521	3216	RL91181	3218	RL91162

3219-3225   Volvo B10M   Åbenrå   B36D   2000

3219	RL91231	3221	RL91230	3223	RL91240	3225	RL91242
3220	RL91232	3222	RL91197	3224	RL91244		

3226	RL97017	Scania/DAB	DAB	B--D	2000
3227	RL97018	Scania/DAB	DAB	B--D	2000

3228-3232   Volvo B10M   Åbenrå   B36D   2000

3228	RL91163	3230	RL91229	3231	RL91241	3232	RL91161
3229	RL91245						

3233	RM91512	Volvo B10MA	Åbenrå	B	2000
3234	RM91513	Volvo B10MA	Åbenrå	B	2000

3235-3264   Scania OmniCity CL94UB   Scania   N32D   2000-01

3235	RP97560	3243	RS97157	3251	RT96583	3258	RP96894
3236	RP97561	3244	RS97158	3252	RT96584	3259	RP96891
3237	RP97562	3245	RS97266	3253	RT96585	3260	RP96895
3238	RP97563	3246	RS97267	3254	RT96586	3261	RP96896
3239	RP97564	3247	RS97268	3255	RT96587	3262	RP96897
3240	RS97154	3248	RS97269	3256	RT96892	3263	RP96898
3241	RS97155	3249	RS97270	3257	RT96893	3264	RP96899
3242	RS97156	3250	RT96582				

3265-3284   Volvo B12BLE   Åbenrå   N39D   2002

3265	SJ89558	3270	SJ89639	3275	SJ89651	3280	SJ89664
3266	SJ89569	3271	SJ89640	3276	SJ89650	3281	SJ89675
3267	SJ89581	3272	SJ89643	3277	SJ89649	3282	SJ89676
3268	SJ89633	3273	SJ89644	3278	SJ89663	3283	SJ89661
3269	SJ89634	3274	SJ89645	3279	SJ89662	3284	SJ89668

3285	SH90380	Volvo B12M	Åbenrå	NC39D	2002
3286	SH90382	Volvo B12M	Åbenrå	NC39D	2002
3287	SH90381	Volvo B12M	Åbenrå	NC39D	2002

3288-3307   Volvo B12BLE   Åbenrå   N39D   2002

3288	SJ89718	3293	SL91813	3298	SL91788	3303	SL91807
3289	SJ89724	3294	SL91821	3299	SL91791	3304	SL91811
3290	SJ89725	3295	SL91780	3300	SL91794	3305	SL91881
3291	SJ89732	3296	SL91786	3301	SL91798	3306	SL91883
3292	SJ89734	3297	SL91787	3302	SL91804	3307	SL91993

Arriva operates several of the town services in Aalborg and vehicles allocated there use two liveries, one yellow and one red. Illustrating the red version is Scania OmniCity 4427, TB90.831, seen here outside the rail station and carrying national flags commemorating the birthday of the Prince Regent. *Bill Potter*

3308-3311	MAN		MAN		N	2002	
3308	SM90243	**3309**	SM90244	**3310**	SM90244	**3311**	SM90245

3312-3316	Volvo B12M		Åbenrå		NC39D	2002-04	
3312	SM95991	**3314**	SM96002	**3315**	SM96003	**3316**	SX93476
3313	SM95992						

3317	TM88210	Scania OmniLine CL94UB 12m	Scania	N42D	2004
3318	TM88211	Scania OmniLine CL94UB 12m	Scania	N42D	2004
3319	TM88212	Scania OmniLine CL94UB 12m	Scania	N42D	2004
3320	OE93129	Scania OmniLine CL94UB 12m	Scania	N42D	1996
3321	PX91001	Setra S315	Setra	C--D	1998
3322	SD92675	Volvo B12M	Åbenrå	NC39D	2002
3323	SU94086	Scania OmniLine CL94UB 12m	Scania	N42D	2003
3324	RD94352	Volvo B10BLE	Åbenrå	N39D	1983
3325	NC97648	DAF/DAB	DAB	B--D	1990

3900	NX91857	Setra S215HD	Setra	C--F	1984
3901	NK88067	Leyland/DAB VIP bus	DAB	C--F	1987
3902	RV90715	Setra S215HD	Setra	C--F	1990
3904	OL89981	Setra S211	Setra	C--F	1992
3905	OB93545	Scania K113CLB	Lahti	C--F	1995
3906	NZ89326	Setra S328	Setra	C--/--F	1995
3907	OB96021	Volvo B10B	Carrus	C--F	1995
3909	OB89308	Scania K113CLB	Irizar Century	C--F	1997
3910	OP93816	Setra S328	Setra	C--/--F	1997
3911	OS94453	Setra	Setra (hotel bus)	C--F	1997
3912	OZ91566	Setra S315GT	Setra	C--F	1997
3913	PC90372	Scania K113CLB 13.7m	Irizar Century	C--F	1998
3914	PZ91224	Bova FHD	Bova Futura	C--F	1999
3915	PZ94396	MAN 13.7m	MAN	C--F	1999
3916	RH95630	Volvo B12M	Carrus	C--F	2000
3917	RK96669	Bova FHD	Bova Futura	C--F	2000
3919	RX88217	Bova FHD	Bova Futura	C--F	2001

3920	RZ93076	Mercedes-Benz	Mercedes-Benz	C--F	2001
3921	SP93749	Setra S431	Setra	C--F	2003
3922	SZ92739	MAN Lion Coach R08	MAN	C--F	2004
3923	SZ93981	MAN Lion Coach R08	MAN	C--F	2004
4001	OV92.022	Volvo B10L	Carrus	N40D	1997
4006	OP90.477	MAN/DAB	Silkeborg	N35D	1996
4007	OP90.478	MAN/DAB	Silkeborg	N35D	1996
4008	OY91.823	DAF/DAB	Silkeborg	N--D	1997

4021-4030 Volvo B10BLE Vest N36D 2002

4021	SN90.043	4024	SN90.046	4027	SM97.699	4029	SM97.737
4022	SN90.044	4025	SN90.047	4028	SM97.714	4030	SM97.752
4023	SN90.045	4026	SM97.688				

4050	SP88751	Scania OmniLink CL94UB 12m	Scania	N42D	2003

4307-4319 MAN/DAB Silkeborg N35D 1995

4307	OE92.914	4311	OE92.917	4319	OE92.963

4331	RP89.787	Volvo B10L	Carrus	N40D	1996
4355	OS89.286	DAF/DAB	Silkeborg	N--D	1996
4356	OS89.287	MAN/DAB	Silkeborg	N35D	1996

4361-4367 Volvo B10L Carrus N40D 1997

4361	PB89.204	4363	PB89.218	4365	PB89.226	4367	PB89.507
4362	PB89.215	4364	PB89.223	4366	PB89.488		

4368	PP94.329	DAB	Silkeborg	N35D	1998
4370	PP94.331	DAB	Silkeborg	N35D	1998
4371	PP94.332	DAB	Silkeborg	N35D	1998
4372	PX96.281	Volvo B7L	Åbenrå	N39D	1999

4375-4388 Volvo B10BLE Åbenrå N--D 2000

4375	RE94.369	4377	RE94.371	4386	RN88.149	4388	RN88.151
4376	RE94.370	4378	RE94.372	4387	RN88.150		

4389-4393 Scania OmniLink 13.7m N--D 2002

4389	RU97.030	4391	RU97.078	4392	RU97.079	4393	RU97.080
4390	RU97.031						

4394	SJ89.557	Volvo B10BLE 13.7m	Åbenrå	NC--D	2002

4395-4409 Volvo B10BLE Vest N--D 2002

4395	SJ88.780	4399	SJ88.784	4403	SJ88.788	4407	SJ88.792
4396	SJ88.781	4400	SJ88.785	4404	SJ88.789	4408	SJ88.793
4397	SJ88.782	4401	SJ88.786	4405	SJ88.790	4409	SJ88.794
4398	SJ88.783	4402	SJ88.787	4406	SJ88.791		

4410-4419 Mercedes-Benz Cito Mercedes-Benz N17F 2002

4410	SD96.842	4413	SD96.845	4416	SD96.848	4418	SD96.850
4411	SD96.843	4414	SD96.846	4417	SD96.849	4419	SD96.851
4412	SD96.844	4415	SD96.847				

4420-4430 Scania OmniLink CL94UB 12m Scania N42D 2004

4420	TB90824	4423	TB90827	4426	TB90830	4429	TB90833
4421	TB90825	4424	TB90828	4427	TB90831	4430	TB90834
4422	TB90826	4425	TB90829	4428	TB90832		

5047	KV94783	Volvo B10M	Åbenrå	B34D	1986
5063	KV94780	Volvo B10M	Åbenrå	B34D	1986
5097	RX94425	Volvo B10M	Åbenrå	B34D	1987

Vehicles 0xxx operate in Sweden

6101	HSO203	Scania L113CLB	Scania	B55D	1995
6102	HSL103	Scania L113CLB	Scania	B55D	1995
6103	PFT339	Scania L113CLB	Carrus	B52D	1994
6112	HLR063	Scania L113CLB	DAB	B55D	1995
6113	HTS063	Scania L113CLB	DAB	B55D	1995
6114	TFY796	Volvo B10B	Carrus Delta Star	B42D	1993
6117	GNX410	Scania CN113ALB	Scania	AB70D	1996
6118	GOE130	Scania CN113ALB	Scania	AB70D	1996
6119	GPR410	Scania CN113ALB	Scania	AB70D	1996

During the morning rush hour several of the Mercedes-Benz Cito buses at Aalborg perform extra (Ekstra) duties on University routes 2 and 12. Illustrating the model is yellow-liveried 4415, SD96847 which joined the fleet in 2002. *Bill Potter*

6125-6132
Scania L113TLL — Carrus — AB56D — 1996

6125	AER681	6127	AER941	6129	AES661	6131	ASX692
6126	AEO541	6128	AEO661	6130	AES611	6132	ASX602

6136-6142
Scania L94UB — Vest — N--D — 2001

6136	SCH145	6138	SCH094	6140	SCH106	6142	SKL304
6137	SCH103	6139	SCH175	6141	SKL439		

6143	DLE670	Volvo B10M-70	Vest	AB55D	1997
6144	DLE630	Volvo B10M-70	Vest	AB55D	1997

6146-6159
Scania L94UB 14.8m — Lahti — N38D — 2003

6146	STU583	6150	TPM226	6154	TPL931	6157	TPL703
6147	TPM241	6151	TPM082	6155	TPL922	6158	TPL691
6148	TPM238	6152	TPM079	6156	TPL916	6159	TPL673
6149	TPM232	6153	TPM073				

6160-6166
Scania L94UB 13.5m — Vest — N34D — 2003

6160	TPL913	6162	TPL955	6164	TPL712	6166	TPM811
6161	TPL940	6163	TPL685	6165	TPM802		

6167-6171
Scania L94UB 13.5m — Vest — N34D — 2003

6167	TSX610	6169	TSX601	6170	TSX559	6171	TSX583
6168	TSX562						

6172-6176
Scania L94UB 14.8m — Vest — N38D — 2003

6172	TSX574	6174	TSX532	6175	TSX538	6176	TSX547
6173	TSX580						

6198	RGP523	Scania L94UB	Vest	N34D	2000
6199	RGP529	Scania L94UB	Vest	N34D	2000
6388	TUS376	Volvo B10L	Åbenrå	N32D	1997
6389	TYJ706	Volvo B10L	Åbenrå	N32D	1997
6390	UAF976	Volvo B10L	Åbenrå	N32D	1997

6391-6398 Scania OmniLink CL94UB Scania N32D 2001

6391	SFW553	6393	SHA709	6395	SHB571	6397	SOB811
6392	SFW559	6394	SHA715	6396	SOB844	6398	SOB832

6399	TUS256	DAB GS200 8.6m	DAB		N18D	1996
6400	TWG436	DAB GS200 8.6m	DAB		N18D	1996

6403-6426 Volvo B10BLE Carrus City L N36D 1997

6403	DYE741	6421	DHD620	6423	DHE580	6425	DHE680
6411	DGZ660	6422	DHD690	6424	DHE670	6426	DHE960
6420	DHD590						

6451-6458 Scania OmniCity CN94UB (cng) Scania N32D 1998-99

6451	JKF208	6453	JJZ208	6455	JKA158	6457	DSO512
6452	JKA408	6454	JKC218	6456	JJZ138	6458	DSO632

6459	DKO530	Scania CN113CLL	Scania Maxi		N35D	1997
6460	JTM555	Scania CN113CLL	Scania Maxi		N35D	1997

6461-6480 Scania OmniCity CL94UB Scania N32D 2001

6461	SEA778	6466	SFA697	6471	SFA682	6476	SFW565
6462	SEA769	6467	SFC013	6472	SFA679	6477	SFW595
6463	SEA841	6468	SFA691	6473	SFW571	6478	SFW538
6464	SEA847	6469	SFA796	6474	SFW580	6479	SHA700
6465	SFA700	6470	SFA685	6475	SFX187	6480	SHA736

6481	DFS589	Scania OmniCity CN94UB	Scania		N32D	1997

6482-6487 DAB Citybus S11 DAB B36D 1994

6482	SHU676	6484	SGX301	6486	SJK781	6487	SGX289
6483	SJJ676	6485	SGW388				

6488-6495 DAB Citybus S11 DAB B36D 2000

6488	RGP517	6490	RGP574	6492	RGP568	6494	RGP535
6489	RGP442	6491	RGP577	6493	RGP610	6495	RGP587

6501-6515 Volvo B10L (cng) Carrus City L N36D 1997

6501	DSD690	6505	DSE550	6509	DSF570	6513	DSG850
6502	DSD780	6506	DSE590	6510	DSF590	6514	DSG940
6503	DSD870	6507	DSE650	6511	DSG560	6515	DSH520
6504	DSD890	6508	DSE580	6512	DSG590		

6516-6538 Volvo B10BLE (cng) Åbenrå N30D 2001

6516	SHC256	6522	SHC274	6528	SHC727	6534	SHB772
6517	SHC259	6523	SHC277	6529	SHC736	6535	SHB781
6518	SHC252	6524	SHC280	6530	SHC739	6536	SHD922
6519	SHC265	6525	SHC283	6531	SHC748	6537	SHD925
6520	SHC288	6526	SHC708	6532	SHB760	6538	SHD931
6521	SHC271	6527	SHC718	6533	SHB763		

6539-6544 Volvo B10LA (cng) Saffle AN48D 2001

6539	SHH016	6541	SHH025	6543	SHH031	6544	SHH034
6540	SHH019	6542	SHH028				

6545-6550 MAN NL313 (cng) MAN N30D 2005

6545	XBD788	6547	XBC066	6549	XBC047	6550	XBC057
6546	XBC056	6548	XBC202				

6551-6574 Volvo B10L (cng) Carrus N32D 1999

6551	DCH730	6557	DBT690	6563	DBX640	6569	DCC780
6552	DBU790	6558	DCA750	6564	DCD500	6570	OOP953
6553	DBS990	6559	DCA850	6565	DBU650	6571	EZZ628
6554	DCA880	6560	DBU720	6566	DBU610	6572	HKK690
6555	DCN930	6561	DBS960	6567	DCH510	6573	ELP614
6556	DBW580	6562	DBZ910	6568	DCE600	6574	LDP685

6575	CDR237	Volvo B10L (cng)	Säffle 3000		N32D	1998

Pictured in Copenhagen, 7116, NS96052, is one of the DAB Citybuses with Silkeborg bodywork. Many of the type carry liquid petroleum gas tanks on the roof. However, this batch is powered by the standard diesel engine.
Bill Potter

6576-6626

MAN NL313 (cng)   MAN   N30D   2005

6576	XBC076	6589	XBC107	6602	XBC211	6615	XBC241
6577	XBC091	6590	XBC152	6603	XBC212	6616	XBC261
6578	XBC071	6591	XBC171	6604	XBC176	6617	XBC257
6579	XBC077	6592	XBC067	6605	XBC206	6618	XBC231
6580	XBC092	6593	XBC157	6606	XBC217	6619	XBC247
6581	XBC117	6594	XBC177	6607	XBC221	6620	XBC256
6582	XBC136	6595	XBC192	6608	XBC232	6621	XBC291
6583	XBC132	6596	XBC141	6609	XBC216	6622	XBC262
6584	XBC082	6597	XBC187	6610	XBC227	6623	XBC236
6585	XBC131	6598	XBC196	6611	XBC242	6624	XBC252
6586	XBC142	6599	XBC222	6612	XBC237	6625	XBC266
6587	XBC156	6600	XBC207	6613	XBC197	6626	XBC267
6588	XBC166	6601	XBC201	6614	XBC246		

6701-6729

Scania Omnicity CN94UA 18m   Scania   AN44D   2001

6701	SCH208	6709	SDD967	6716	SDM457	6723	SFA859
6702	SCH223	6710	SDD955	6717	SEA832	6724	SFA721
6703	SCH199	6711	SDD952	6718	SEA820	6725	SFA706
6704	SCH181	6712	SDE007	6719	SEA817	6726	SFW556
6705	SCH184	6713	SDD958	6720	SEA784	6727	SFW568
6706	SCH226	6714	SDD949	6721	SEA775	6728	SFW547
6707	SCH220	6715	SDM460	6722	SEA766	6729	SFZ649
6708	SDD964						

6991	TXT772	Solaris	Solaris	N--D	2003
6992	TXT754	Solaris	Solaris	N--D	2003
6993	TXT763	Solaris	Solaris	N--D	2003

7077-7082

MAN 13.310   Jonckheere Modulo   C--D   2004

7077	SX88.391	7079	SX88.393	7081	SX88.395	7082	SX88.396
7078	SX88.392	7080	SX88.394				

7088-7122 — DAB Citybus S15 — Silkeborg — B26D — 1994

7088	NR96.589	7096	NR96.619	7107	NS95.974	7114	NS96.034
7089	NR96.590	7099	NR96.621	7108	NS95.987	7115	NS96.035
7091	NR96.592	7101	NS95.940	7109	NS95.988	7116	NS96.052
7092	NR96.593	7102	NS95.941	7110	NS95.989	7117	NS96.053
7093	NR96.594	7103	NS95.942	7111	NS95.990	7119	NS96.074
7094	NR96.595	7105	NS95.944	7113	NS96.013	7122	NV93.256
7095	NR96.618	7106	NS95.973				

7143-7159 — Volvo B10L — Åbenrå — B29D — 1996

7143	OL88.190	7148	OL88.238	7152	OL88.242	7156	OL88.261
7144	OL88.191	7149	OL88.239	7153	OL88.242	7157	OL88.262
7145	OL88.192	7150	OL88.240	7154	OL88.250	7158	OL88.279
7146	PC95.824	7151	OL88.241	7155	OL88.260	7159	OL88.280
7147	OL88.194						

7208	NR96.200	Volvo B10	Åbenrå	B39D	1994
7209	NN91.908	Volvo B10	Åbenrå	B39D	1994
7210	NX90.841	Volvo B10	Åbenrå	B39D	1994
7211	OB94.391	Volvo B10	Åbenrå	B39D	1995
7229	PX96.500	MAN NL233	MAN	N26F	1999
7230	PX96.499	MAN NL233	MAN	N26F	1999
8050	NX93.077	DAF SB220 12m	?	B47D	1994
8076	MR93.187	DAF/DAB Citybus	Silkeborg	B47D	1991
8094	ME91.072	Volvo B10M	Åbenrå	B36D	1990

8098-8281 — DAF/DAB Citybus — Silkeborg — B47D — 1991-95

8098	NM90.134	8120	ME94.417	8270	SB92.891	8281	NB97.670
8099	NM90.133						

8134	OD92514	Scania/DAB	Silkeborg	B47D	1995
8288	NU93379	MAN/DAB Citybus Mk2	Silkeborg	B35D	1994
8302	TU97352	Volvo B10M	Åbenrå	B39D	1997
8303	OV89881	DAF/DAB Citybus S12	Silkeborg	B47D	1997
8304	OV89882	DAF/DAB Citybus S12	Silkeborg	B47D	1997
8305	OV89883	DAF/DAB Citybus S12	Silkeborg	B47D	1997
8308	OZ91788	Scania/DAB	Silkeborg	N38D	1997
8323	NY91.120	Volvo B10M	Åbenrå	B39D	1995
8332	OD90.885	Scania N113CLB	Lahti	N--D	1995
8353	NY91.118	Volvo B10M	Åbenrå	B39D	1995
8354	NY91.119	Volvo B10M	Åbenrå	B39D	1995
8380	OY91.949	Scania OmniCity N94UB	DAB Silkeborg	N--D	1997

A recent additon to the fleet at Fyn is Volvo B10M 8345, NY91.119. It is seen at Odense interchange. The building in the background houses a museum for preserved railway engines and other items for railway enthusiasts.
Bill Potter

Recent arrivals for Roskilde are a batch of Volvo B12BLEs with Volvo-owned Åbenrå bodywork. Pictured leaving the bus station is 3050, TD91367, duly adorned with national flags. *Bill Potter*

8381-8390

						B--D	1994-95
		MAN/DAB 12m		Lavgulv			
8381	OS89.278	**8384**	NY93.044	**8387**	NX92.950	**8389**	NX92.952
8382	NZ93.971	**8385**	NY93.045	**8388**	NX92.951	**8390**	NS96.012
8383	NZ93.973	**8386**	NX92.949				

8392	OP90.576	DAF/DAB Citybus Mk III	Silkeborg	N--D	1996
8393	OP90.577	DAF/DAB Citybus Mk III	Silkeborg	N--D	1996
8398	ML93.951	DAF/DAB Citybus	Silkeborg	B38D	1991
8399	ML93.952	DAF/DAB Citybus	Silkeborg	B38D	1991
8417	MS97.695	Volvo B10M	Åbenrå	B39D	1992
8418	OD97.597	Volvo B10M	Vest	B--D	1996
8419	RH95.798	Volvo B10M	Vest	B--D	2000
8421	PX90675	Volvo B10M	Vest	B--D	1999
8422	PX90674	Volvo B10M	Vest	B--D	1999
8423	PX90671	Volvo B10M	Vest	B--D	1999
8424	PX90718	Volvo B10M	Vest	B--D	1999
8425	PZ96612	Volvo B10M	Vest	B--D	1999
8426	RK95274	Scania L94	DAB	B--D	2000
8427	RX97899	Scania OmniLink CL94UB 12m	Scania	N42D	2001
8428	SN97877	Volvo B12M	Åbenrå	B--D	2003
8429	OX91585	DAB Citybus Mk III	Silkeborg	B--D	1997
8430	TN94780	Volvo B10M	Vest	B--D	2000
8431	TN94781	Volvo B10M	Vest	B--D	2000
8432	TN94757	Volvo B10M	Vest	B--D	2000
8433	SL91898	Volvo B10M	Vest	B--D	2002
8434	TU9183	Scania OmniLink CL94UB 12m	Scania	N--D	1998
8435	RN88130	Volvo B10M	Åbenrå	B--D	2000
9060	KV94.741	Volvo B10M	DAB Silkeborg	B39D	1986
9061	KV94.742	Volvo B10M	DAB Silkeborg	B39D	1986
9978	OX93.195	Volvo B10M	Åbenrå	B39D	1984
9982	JR89.438	Volvo B10M	Åbenrå	B39D	1984
9985	JR89.456	Volvo B10M	Åbenrå	B39D	1984

ARRIVA NEDERLAND

Arriva Nederlands BV, Trambaan 3, postbus 626, 8440 AP Heerenveen

14	LS	BB-TD-03	Iveco 380.12.35HD	Berkhof E3000HD	C50F	19
15	WT	BB-GF-85	Bova FHD 12.340	Bova Futura	C50F	19
58	GR	BB-GF-85	Mercedes-Benz 0404	Mercedes-Benz	C	19
62	AS	VT-86-VP	DAF SB3000	Berkhof Axial	C	19
63	DR	VT-82-VP	DAF SB3000	Berkhof Axial	C	19
64	LS	BB-LV-58	Iveco 380.12.35HD	Berkhof E3000HD	C50F	19
65	GR	BD-BZ-68	DAF SB3000	Berkhof Axial	C	19
66	GR	BD-FV-42	Iveco 380.12.35HD	Berkhof E3000HD	C50F	19
67	GR	BF-DH-41	Iveco 380.12.35HD	Berkhof E3000HD	C50F	19

133-138

Mercedes-Benz 0405G — Mercedes-Benz — AB49D — 1990

133	GR	VJ-58-LT	135	GR	VJ-71-ZV	137	GR	VN-59-GX	138	GR	VN-19-HG
134	GR	VJ-77-TK	136	ML	VJ-75-TK						

139	SG	VN-72-JX	Mercedes-Benz 0405	Mercedes-Benz	C38F	1991

142-157

Mercedes-Benz 0405G — Mercedes-Benz — AB49D — 1992-93

142	GR	VR-27-LR	146	ZW	VR-85-JS	150	GR	VR-39-DF	154	GR	VV-72-XH
143	GR	VR-12-JT	147	GR	VR-98-JS	151	GR	VR-58-FJ	155	ML	VV-64-XH
144	GR	VR-09-XS	148	LS	VR-06-XS	152	ML	VR-10-LR	156	GR	VV-99-XB
145	GR	VR-13-XS	149	GR	VR-09-LR	153	AM	VV-69-XH	157	GR	VV-65-XH

158-165

Mercedes-Benz 0530G — Mercedes-Benz Citaro — AB50F — 1999-2002 Seating varies

158	GR	BH-VJ-15	160	GR	BH-XX-29	162	GR	BN-HN-57	164	GR	BN-HN-60
159	GR	BH-XX-31	161	GR	BH-XX-30	163	GR	BN-HN-59	165	GR	BN-HN-61

185	GR	VR-17-LK	Bova FHD 12.290	Bova Futura	C50F	1992
186	WT	VV-85-KK	DAF SB3000	Smit Orion Grandluxe	C50F	1993

189-199

Mercedes-Benz 0350 — Mercedes-Benz Tourismo — C51F — 1995-2002

189	GR	BB-ZP-54	192	GR	BG-NP-90	195	HV	BL-VH-80	198	SN	BJ-BG-36
190	GR	BD-RX-88	193	GR	BL-VH-95	196	WT	BH-FH-71	199	GR	BL-BG-74
191	GR	BF-LH-16	194	GR	BL-VH-96	197	WT	BH-HG-65			

Recent arrivals for the town services in Groningen are fourteen Mercedes-Benz Citaro articulated buses that have seen earlier models dispersed to other depots. Pictured in the town is the first to arrive, 221, BP-NH-41.
Harry Laming

Pictured at Groningen depot shortly after receiving Arriva corporate colours, 205, BD-FZ-08 is one of the LPG-powered DAB SB220 buses with Berkhof bodywork. Route 19, shown on the destination display, provides a link between the town and the depot. *Harry Laming*

201-206

			DAF SB220			Berkhof 2000NL		N36D	1995	LPG bus	
201	GR	BD-FZ-03	**203**	GR	BD-FZ-01	**205**	GR	BD-FZ-08	**206**	GR	BD-FZ-09
202	GR	BD-FZ-10	**204**	GR	BD-FZ-05						

221-234

			Mercedes-Benz Citaro O530 G			Mercedes-Benz		N--D	2004-05		
221	GR	BP-NH-41	**225**	GR	BP-NH-53	**229**	GR	BP-NH-59	**232**	GR	BP-NL-71
222	GR	BP-NH-50	**226**	GR	BP-NH-52	**230**	GR	BP-NH-39	**233**	GR	BP-NL-74
223	GR	BP-NH-51	**227**	GR	BP-NH-56	**231**	GR	BP-NL-69	**234**	GR	BP-NL-75
224	GR	BP-NH-54	**228**	GR	BP-NH-57						

451	GR	VV-78-GZ	Bova FHD 12.290	Bova Futura	C47F	1993	
452	GR	VV-89-GZ	Bova FHD 12.290	Bova Futura	C47F	1993	
453	LS	BB-LT-71	Iveco 380.12.35HD	Berkhof E3000HD	C50F	1994	
454	LS	BB-LT-69	Iveco 380.12.35HD	Berkhof E3000HD	C50F	1994	
456	DM	BD-BZ-70	Iveco 380.12.35HD	Berkhof E3000HD	C50F	1995	
457	GR	BP-LG-16	Setra S317 HDH	Setra	C	2005	
458	GR	BP-LH-10	Setra S317 HDH	Setra	C	2005	
459	HV	BP-LT-05	Setra S317 HDH	Setra	C	2005	
460	HV	BP-LV-72	Setra S317 HDH	Setra	C	2005	
501	WT	BJ-BB-12	DAF SB2305	Berkhof Esprit	C	19	
502	SN	BJ-JD-18	Mercedes-Benz O405	Mercedes-Benz	C38F	1991	

521-540

			Mercedes-Benz Citaro O530			Mercedes-Benz		N35D	2002-03		
521	GR	BN-JD-07	**526**	GR	BN-JD-02	**531**	GR	BN-JB-96	**536**	GR	BN-TS-65
522	GR	BN-JD-06	**527**	GR	BN-JD-01	**532**	GR	BN-JB-95	**537**	GR	BN-TS-66
523	GR	BN-JD-05	**528**	GR	BN-JB-99	**533**	GR	BN-JB-93	**538**	GR	BN-TS-67
524	GR	BN-JD-04	**529**	GR	BN-JB-98	**534**	GR	BN-TS-61	**539**	GR	BN-TS-62
525	GR	BN-JD-03	**530**	GR	BN-JB-97	**535**	GR	BN-TS-64	**540**	GR	BN-TS-68

551-557 — Mercedes-Benz Citaro O530 — Mercedes-Benz — N35D — 2005

551	GR	BP-NH-40	553	GR	BP-NH-44	555	GR	BP-NH-47	557	GR	BP-NH-49
552	GR	BP-NH-43	554	GR	BP-NH-46	556	GR	BP-NH-48			

551 GR BP-NH-40 553 GR BP-NH-44 555 GR BP-NH-47 557 GR BP-NH-49
552 GR BP-NH-43 554 GR BP-NH-46 556 GR BP-NH-48

1080-1086 — Volvo B10M-55 — Berkhof 2000NL — B45D — 1995

1080 DM BD-BG-94 1082 DM BD-BG-92 1084 DR BD-BG-29 1086 LS BD-BG-96
1081 DM BD-BG-33 1083 LS BD-BG-26 1085 LS BD-BG-98

1087-1096 — Iveco EuroRider 391.12.29A — Berkhof 2000NL — B44D — 1996

1087 SN BD-NN-44 1090 SN BD-NN-46 1092 SN BD-NN-48 1095 SN BD-NN-52
1088 SN BD-NN-21 1091 SN BD-NN-47 1094 SN BD-NN-50 1096 SN BD-NN-42
1089 SN BD-NN-51

1117-1126 — Mercedes-Benz O408 — Mercedes-Benz — B49D — 1995

1117 LK BD-FS-86 1120 SK BD-FX-84 1123 AS BD-FT-09 1125 UZ BD-FT-05
1118 LK BD-FS-87 1121 SK BD-FV-88 1124 AS BD-FT-06 1126 UZ BD-FT-03
1119 LK BD-FS-88 1122 UZ BD-TV-38

1138-1147 — Iveco EuroRider B89 — Den Oudsten — N45D — 1995

1138 DM BD-JB-29 1141 DM BD-HV-14 1144 LS BD-JP-95 1146 LS BD-JP-94
1139 DM BD-HV-12 1142 DM BD-JB-28 1145 LS BD-JP-96 1147 MG BD-HV-26
1140 DM BD-HV-13 1143 DM BD-HV-24

1152-1162 — Den Oudsten B91 — Den Oudsten Alliance — BC47D — 1996

1152 AP BD-BS-19 1155 GR BD-BS-18 1158 DR BD-BS-12 1161 LK BD-BS-09
1153 LK BD-BS-16 1156 UZ BD-BS-11 1159 LK BD-BS-21 1162 SV BD-RX-80
1154 GR BD-BS-15 1157 TG BD-BS-13 1160 LK BD-BS-20

1254-1257 — Den Oudsten B96 — Den Oudsten Alliance — N31D — 1996

1254 AS BD-ZJ-61 1255 TG BD-ZJ-52 1256 SG BD-ZJ-51 1257 AS BD-ZJ-66

1258-1267 — Mercedes-Benz O408 — Mercedes-Benz — B49D — 1996

1258 VD BD-ZB-16 1261 DM BD-ZF-13 1264 SK BD-ZF-10 1266 DM BD-ZF-16
1259 VD BD-ZF-18 1262 DM BD-ZF-05 1265 VD BD-ZF-14 1267 DM BD-ZF-15
1260 AS BD-ZF-03 1263 UZ BD-ZF-08

1268-1276 — Den Oudsten B95 — Den Oudsten Alliance — N45D — 1997

1268 UZ BD-TS-78 1271 LK BD-TS-66 1273 LK BD-TS-70 1275 SN BD-TS-72
1269 AP BD-TS-63 1272 AM BD-TS-69 1274 UZ BD-TS-71 1276 SN BD-TS-67
1270 AP BD-TS-64

1279-1288 — Iveco EuroRider — Berkhof 2000NL — N44D — 1997

1279 MG BF-GJ-28 1282 DM BF-GJ-34 1285 SN BF-GJ-29 1287 SN BF-GJ-86
1280 MG BF-GJ-38 1283 SN BF-GJ-31 1286 SN BF-GJ-26 1288 SN BF-GJ-13
1281 SN BF-GJ-36 1284 DM BF-GJ-30

2194-2203 — Den Oudsten B95 — Den Oudsten Alliance — B45D — 1997

2194 SN BF-LG-44 2197 LS BF-LG-87 2199 SN BF-LJ-29 2202 SN BF-LG-42
2195 ZW BF-LG-43 2198 SN BF-LG-83 2200 SN BF-LG-40 2203 SN BF-LH-20
2196 SN BF-LG-89

2217-2221 — Den Oudsten B95 — Den Oudsten Alliance — B45D — 1997

2217 ML BF-XV-78 2219 EM BF-XV-23 2220 EM BF-XV-22 2221 HV BF-XV-21
2218 ML BF-XV-24

4014-4076 — DAF MB230 — Den Oudsten B88 — B45D — 1988

4014 GR BZ-71-SV 4018 GR BZ-46-SP 4041 DV BZ-05-ZV 4045 GR VB-71-BN
4015 FM BZ-74-SV 4023 HV BZ-50-SP 4043 GR BZ-07-ZV 4076 WT VB-64-KJ
4016 VD BZ-73-SV 4024 GR BZ-44-SP 4044 GR BZ-98-7T

4116-4155 — DAF MB230 — Den Oudsten B88 — B45D — 1989

4118 GR VF-06-HY 4127 GR VF-79-GN 4146 GR VF-99-GG 4151 LS VF-27-GK
4119 GR VF-71-HX 4130 GR VF-25-HG 4148 GR VF-92-GG 4153 GR VF-87-GG
4122 GR VF-20-HY 4142 ZW VF-16-GH 4149 HV VF-86-GG 4154 DV VF-32-PP
4123 GR VF-18-HY 4144 GR VF-12-GH 4150 DR VF-02-GH 4155 GR VF-91-NP

During 2004 many of the Den Oudsten Alliance B95 intercity buses received corporate colours. Based on the DAF SB3000 chassis, 5574, BB-HJ-82, is seen at Dedemsvaart. This model features high-back seating for use on longer rural journeys. *Harry Laming*

4233	ML	VH-91-JX	DAF MB230			Den Oudsten B88		B45D	1990
4234	DV	VH-01-JY	DAF MB230			Den Oudsten B88		B45D	1990

4239-4267   DAF MB230   Den Oudsten B88   B45D   1990

4239	GR	VH-69-HF	**4245**	GR	VH-88-HF	**4259**	GR	VH-43-KD	**4264**	GR	VH-37-KD
4240	LS	VH-72-HF	**4252**	GR	VH-66-KD	**4261**	GR	VH-91-KB	**4265**	VD	VH-44-NR
4241	GR	VH-31-HG	**4255**	SK	VH-14-KP	**4262**	GR	VH-26-KD	**4267**	GR	VH-42-NR
4243	DV	VH-42-HG	**4257**	GR	VH-95-KB	**4263**	GR	VH-34-KD			

4299	LS	VS-31-RB	Mercedes-Benz O408			Mercedes-Benz/Zabo		BC49D	1992

4300-4328   DAF MB230   Den Oudsten B88   B45D   1990

4300	GR	VH-29-NK	**4304**	GR	VH-35-NX	**4309**	GR	VH-23-SV	**4327**	DV	VH-93-VX
4302	GR	VH-33-NK	**4306**	GR	VH-27-TF	**4310**	GR	VH-35-SV	**4328**	ED	VH-82-XG
4303	GR	VH-04-NX	**4307**	GR	VH-26-SV						

4458-4475   Mercedes-Benz O408   Mercedes-Benz/Zabo   BC49D   1991

4458	ND	VN-09-DF	**4459**	ND	VN-77-DL	**4466**	LS	VL-03-SZ	**4475**	SN	VL-14-SB

4577-4602   DAF MB230   Den Oudsten B88   B45D   1990-91

4577	ZW	VL-49-SY	**4585**	GR	VL-07-PB	**4595**	ZW	VL-92-PB	**4599**	DV	VL-98-RZ
4578	ZW	VL-52-SY	**4586**	GR	VL-93-PK	**4596**	DV	VL-05-SB	**4600**	GR	VL-96-RZ
4579	DV	VL-47-SY	**4590**	GR	VH-98-PK	**4597**	ML	VL-04-SB	**4601**	GR	VL-38-TL
4581	GR	VL-62-PG	**4591**	GR	VL-90-PB	**4598**	DV	VL-01-SB	**4602**	GR	VL-20-SB

4603-4632   DAF MB230   Den Oudsten Alliance B89   BC45D   1992

4603	HO	VR-03-GJ	**4611**	ZW	VR-22-GN	**4618**	GR	VP-72-XJ	**4625**	GR	VP-78-XX
4604	HO	VR-58-HH	**4612**	ZW	VR-27-GN	**4619**	ED	VP-48-XJ	**4626**	GR	VP-60-XJ
4605	ML	VR-11-GJ	**4613**	DV	VR-30-GN	**4620**	HV	VP-53-XJ	**4628**	GR	VP-41-XJ
4606	PP	VR-09-GJ	**4614**	DV	VR-28-GN	**4621**	GR	VP-12-XN	**4629**	GR	VP-14-YP
4607	EM	VR-06-GJ	**4615**	w	VP-80-XJ	**4622**	GR	VP-56-XJ	**4630**	VD	VP-05-YP
4608	EM	VR-18-GN	**4616**	w	VP-44-XJ	**4623**	GR	VP-59-XK	**4631**	GR	VP-78-YN
4609	ZW	VR-24-GN	**4617**	w	VP-77-XJ	**4624**	GR	VP-43-XK	**4632**	ED	VP-61-YN
4610	ZW	VR-21-GN									

4677-4684

			Mercedes-Benz 0408		Mercedes-Benz/Zabo		B49D	1992

4677	ML	VR-60-VG	4679	ML	VS-01-DB	4681	ML	VS-94-BZ	4683	ML	VS-87-BZ
4678	ML	VR-61-VG	4680	ML	VS-96-BZ	4682	ML	VS-90-BZ	4684	ML	VS-85-BZ

4700	DR	VR-23-GJ	DAF MB230		Den Oudsten Alliance B89		B45D	1992
4735	DM	VS-75-LN	Mercedes-Benz 0408		Mercedes-Benz/Zabo		B49D	1992
4736	LS	VS-84-LN	Mercedes-Benz 0408		Mercedes-Benz/Zabo		B49D	1992

4738-4652

			Volvo B10M-61		Berkhof 2000NL		B45D	1993

4738	HO	VV-14-XD	4742	HO	VV-23-XD	4747	MG	VV-29-XD	4750	MG	VX-09-DL
4739	HO	VV-17-XD	4743	HO	VV-24-XD	4748	MG	VX-66-DY	4751	LS	VX-18-DL
4740	HO	VV-20-XD	4744	LS	VV-25-XD	4749	MG	VX-36-DL	4752	LS	VX-58-DK
4741	HO	VV-22-XD	4746	ZW	VV-27-XD						

4753-4757

			Mercedes-Benz 0408		Mercedes-Benz/Zabo		B49D	1993

4753	AM	VX-27-GJ	4755	SN	VX-17-GJ	4756	SN	VX-15-GJ	4757	SN	VX-23-GJ
4754	ML	VX-35-GJ									

4771-4777

			Mercedes-Benz 0408		Mercedes-Benz		B49D	1993

4771	ZK	BB-DL-39	4773	LS	BB-DL-76	4775	VD	BB-DL-35	4777	VD	BB-DL-37
4772	UZ	BB-DL-31	4774	DM	BB-DL-33	4776	SK	BB-DL-86			

4833-4848

			DAF SB220		Den Oudsten B89 Alliance		BC47D	1992

4833	HO	BB-LB-10	4838	ZW	BB-JV-77	4842	LS	BB-JV-80	4846	DV	VX-07-LK
4835	ML	BB-JX-59	4839	ED	BB-NL-24	4843	LS	BB-JV-89	4847	WT	BB-LB-14
4836	ED	BB-JZ-94	4840	ZW	BB-NL-23	4845	HV	BB-LB-13	4848	HO	BB-LB-61
4837	DV	BB-LB-60	4841	WT	BB-JZ-95						

5531-5576

			DAF SB3000		Den Oudsten B95 Intercity		BC45D	1993-94

5531	EM	VV-23-JP	5536	EM	VV-25-JP	5569	DV	BB-HJ-76	5573	DV	BB-HJ-87
5532	ZW	VV-14-JP	5537	ML	VV-19-JP	5570	GR	BB-HJ-73	5574	DV	BB-HJ-82
5533	AP	VV-16-JP	5538	AS	VV-11-JP	5571	EM	BB-HJ-90	5575	EM	BB-HJ-80
5534	ED	VV-07-JV	5567	ED	BB-HJ-86	5572	AP	BB-HJ-88	5576	AP	BB-HJ-69
5535	ZW	VV-35-JV	5568	EM	BB-HJ-78						

5577-5586

			Den Oudsten B91 DM580		Den Oudsten Alliance		B47D	1993

5577	SK	BB-GS-55	5580	DR	BB-GS-03	5583	AS	BB-GR-98	5585	AS	BB-GT-03
5578	ZK	BB-GS-54	5581	AP	BB-GS-01	5584	AS	BB-GR-97	5586	AP	BB-GS-23
5579	ZK	BB-GS-02	5582	AP	BB-BR-99						

5700-5704

			DAF SBR3015 15m		Berkhof Excellence 500NL		BC45D	1994-95

5700	GR	BB-PP-08	5702	GR	BB-PD-64	5703	EM	BB-PD-63	5704	GR	BB-PD-62
5701	GR	BB-PP-11									

5742-5746

			DAF SBR3015 15m		Berkhof Excellence 500NL		BC44D	1995

5742	SN	BD-HG-61	5744	DR	BD-HG-64	5745	GR	BD-HG-69	5746	ED	BD-HH-22
5743	HV	BD-HG-59									

5747	GR	BB-HH-19	DAF SBR3015		Den Oudsten Interliner 500NL	BC44D	1995
5748	HV	BB-HG-38	DAF SBR3015		Den Oudsten Interliner 500NL	BC44D	1995
5783	GR	BF-XR-66	DAF SBR3015		Berkhof Radial	BC58D	1997
5784	HV	BF-XR-65	DAF SBR3015		Berkhof Radial	BC58D	1997
5785	EM	BF-XR-63	DAF SBR3015		Berkhof Radial	BC58D	1997
5800	AS	46-DL-RX	Mercedes-Benz Vito 208D		Mercedes-Benz	M8	1999
5802	HO	03-DN-BL	Mercedes-Benz Vito 208D		Mercedes-Benz	M8	1999
5803	DV	42-DL-XT	Mercedes-Benz Vito 208D		Mercedes-Benz	M8	1999

5810-5821

			Mercedes-Benz 0550ÜL		Mercedes-Benz Integro L		NC50D	2000

5810	EM	BH-TD-29	5813	LK	BH-TN-93	5816	GR	BH-TN-90	5819	GR	BH-TR-99
5811	GH	BH-TN-95	5014	DR	BH-TN-92	5817	GR	BH-TR-97	5820	LK	BH-TS-01
5812	GR	BH-TN-94	5815	LK	BH-TN-91	5818	GR	BH-TR-98	5821	LK	BH-TS-02

5822-5834

			DAF SB220		Berkhof Excellence 2000		N36D	2000

5822	SG	BJ-DF-10	5826	TG	BJ-DF-16	5829	TG	BJ-DF-21	5832	SG	BJ-DF-25
5823	AM	BJ-DF-12	5827	TG	BJ-DF-18	5830	LS	BJ-DF-23	5833	DR	BJ-DF-27
5824	DR	BJ-DF-14	5828	TG	BJ-DF-19	5831	SG	BJ-DF-24	5834	EM	BJ-DR-02
5825	AM	BJ-DF-15									

Inital deliveries of new buses for the Dutch operation were fifty Dennis Darts with Alexander ALX200 bodies. As the allocations show, these are now widely spread across the system, with 5853, BJ-XN-81, seen here in the city of **Emmen.** *Harry Laming*

5835-5845   DAF SB220   Berkhof Excellence 2000   N42D   2000

5835	EM	BJ-DP-99	5838	DV	BJ-DP-93	5841	ZW	BJ-DP-90	5844	ZW	BJ-DP-86
5836	HV	BJ-DP-96	5839	DV	BJ-DP-92	5842	ZW	BJ-DP-89	5845	ED	BJ-DP-83
5837	ML	BJ-DP-95	5840	DV	BJ-DP-91	5843	ZW	BJ-DP-88			

5846	DR	96-JS-XX	Mercedes-Benz Vito 208D	Mercedes-Benz	M8	2002
5847	DR	97-JS-XX	Mercedes-Benz Vito 208D	Mercedes-Benz	M8	2002
5848	OO	98-JS-XX	Mercedes-Benz Vito 208D	Mercedes-Benz	M8	2002
5849	HE	99-JS-XX	Mercedes-Benz Vito 208D	Mercedes-Benz	M8	2002

5850-5899   Dennis Dart SLF   Alexander ALX200   N39D   2000-01

5850	AS	BL-JD-45	5863	AS	BJ-ZF-51	5875	DR	BJ-ZT-87	5887	OO	BL-BJ-82
5851	WT	BJ-VB-33	5864	AP	BJ-ZF-50	5876	DR	BJ-ZT-90	5888	OO	BL-BJ-83
5852	DR	BJ-XN-84	5865	AS	BJ-ZF-46	5877	DR	BJ-ZT-89	5889	DR	BL-BJ-78
5853	EM	BJ-XN-81	5866	VD	BJ-ZT-77	5878	LS	BJ-ZT-91	5890	HV	BL-BJ-79
5854	WT	BJ-XN-82	5867	VD	BJ-ZJ-38	5879	LS	BJ-ZT-86	5891	HV	BL-BS-19
5855	EM	BJ-XN-78	5868	GR	BJ-ZJ-39	5880	DR	BJ-ZT-94	5892	DR	BL-BS-20
5856	EM	BJ-XN-80	5869	LS	BJ-ZJ-40	5881	DR	BJ-ZT-93	5893	LS	BL-BS-21
5857	WT	BJ-XN-77	5870	DM	BJ-ZJ-41	5882	DR	BJ-ZT-92	5894	HV	BL-BS-22
5858	EM	BJ-XN-83	5871	DM	BJ-ZJ-42	5883	DR	BL-DX-66	5895	HV	BL-BV-38
5859	SK	BL-BS-18	5872	LS	BJ-ZJ-43	5884	DR	BL-BJ-77	5896	HV	BL-BV-37
5860	SK	BJ-ZF-49	5873	DR	BJ-ZJ-44	5885	OO	BJ-ZT-76	5898	DR	BL-GN-77
5861	AP	BJ-ZF-48	5874	DR	BJ-ZJ-45	5886	OO	BL-BJ-80	5899	SK	BJ-TB-91
5862	AP	BJ-ZF-47									

5900-5919   Volvo B10BLE   Carrus   N40D   1997   Arriva Sverige, 2002

5900	GR	BL-SH-07	5906	ZK	BN-BS-01	5911	GR	BN-FN-94	5916	GR	BN-HT-39
5902	ZK	BL-VJ-93	5907	GR	BN-FJ-84	5912	GR	BL-TX-80	5917	GR	BN-FR-71
5903	ZK	BN-FH-34	5908	GR	BN-PJ-70	5913	GR	BL-ZP-63	5918	GR	BN-HV-20
5904	ZK	BL-VZ-99	5909	GR	BN-DG-29	5914	GR	BL-TN-74	5919	ZK	BL-SH-08
5905	ZK	BL-XR-75	5910	GR	BL-SP-71	5915	GR	BL-VF-77			

Arriva has been instrumental in exchanging buses between its operations is various countries. Now in Holland, 5908, BN-PJ-70, was included under Sweden in the 2004 edition of this publication. It is now in corporate colours and is seen in Groningen. *Harry Laming*

5920-5927

			DAF SB120			Wright Cadet		N24D	2002		
5920	LS	DL-TG 43	5922	LS	BL-TG-49	5924	LS	BL-TG-47	5926	LS	BL-TG-48
5921	LS	BL-TG-50	5923	LS	BL-TG-46	5925	LS	BL-TG-45	5927	LS	BL-TG 44

5928-5939

			DAF SB200			Wrightbus Commander		N37D	2002		
5928	LS	BL-XH-68	5931	LS	BL-XH-67	5934	LS	BL-XH-70	5937	LS	BL-XH-80
5929	LS	BL-XH-73	5932	LS	BL-XH-71	5935	LS	BL-XH-77	5938	LS	BL-XH-76
5930	LS	BL-XH-66	5933	LS	BL-XH-74	5936	LS	BL-XH-78	5939	LS	BL-XH-79

5940	SK	TD-GD-80	Fiat Ducato			Fiat		M8	1998		

5941-5999

			DAF SB200			Wrightbus Commander		N42D	2002	Seating varies	
5941	OO	BL-BP-84	5956	OO	BL-DS-81	5971	DR	BN-HD-75	5986	ED	BN-HS-82
5942	OO	BL-BP-85	5957	OO	BL-DS-82	5972	DR	BN-HD-76	5987	WT	BN-HS-66
5943	HV	BL-BP-86	5958	HV	BN-DS-83	5973	DR	BN-HD-78	5988	AP	BN-HS-67
5944	HV	BL-BP-87	5959	DR	BN-DS-84	5974	DR	BN-HD-79	5989	TI	BN-HS-68
5945	DR	BL-BP-89	5960	DR	BN-DS-85	5975	DR	BN-HD-81	5990	TI	BN-HS-69
5946	WT	BL-BP-90	5961	DR	BN-DS-86	5976	OO	BN-HD-87	5991	TI	BN-HS-83
5947	WT	BL-BP-91	5962	DR	BN-DS-87	5977	OO	BN-HD-73	5992	TI	BN-HS-76
5948	WT	BL-BP-92	5963	ZW	BN-DS-88	5978	OO	BN-HD-77	5993	TI	BN-HS-77
5949	WT	BL-BP-94	5964	ML	BN-DS-89	5979	OO	BN-HD-88	5994	TI	BN-HS-78
5950	WT	BL-BP-96	5965	ZW	BN-DS-90	5980	HV	BN-HD-89	5995	TI	BN-HS-80
5951	AP	DL BP 07	5966	ZW	BN-DS-91	5981	HV	BN-HD-90	5996	TI	BN-HS-81
5952	AP	BL-BP-82	5967	ZW	BN-DS-93	5982	DV	BN-HS-70	5997	TI	DN HS 73
5953	HV	BL-DS-78	5968	ZW	BN-DS-95	5983	DV	BN-HS-71	5998	TI	BN-HS-74
5954	OO	BL-DS-79	5969	ZW	BN-DS-96	5984	DV	BN-HS-72	5999	TI	BN-HS-75
5955	OO	BL-DS-80	5970	ZW	BN-DS-97	5985	ED	BN-HS-79			

6021	GR	BP-PN-13	Volkswagen City Bus			Volkswagen		M8	2004		
6022	GR	BP-PN-08	Volkswagen City Bus			Volkswagen		M8	2004		

Recent arrivals have seen further Mercedes-Benz Integro O550ÜLs placed in service for the *Qliner* routes, an inter-city express network which compares with Britain's National Express network. *Harry Laming*

6100-6109

			DAF SB200			Berkhof Ambassador		N43D	2002		
6100	SN	BN-HX-03	**6103**	SN	BN-JB-07	**6106**	SN	BN-HH-82	**6108**	SN	BN-JT-79
6101	SN	BN-HX-04	**6104**	SN	BN-JB-08	**6107**	SN	BN-HH-85	**6109**	SN	BN-JT-80
6102	SN	BN-HX-06	**6105**	SN	BN-JB-09						

6110	AS	BN-HP-85	Mercedes-Benz Sprinter 411 CDi	Mercedes-Benz	M8	2002				

6111-6122

			Mercedes-Benz Vito 208			Mercedes-Benz		M8	2003		
6111	SN	35-LD-NK	**6114**	TI	08-LF-XH	**6117**	TI	07-LF-XH	**6120**	PP	27-LK-BF
6112	SN	36-LD-NK	**6115**	TI	05-LF-XH	**6118**	PP	09-LF-XH	**6121**	PP	28-LK-BF
6113	DM	34-LD-NK	**6116**	TI	06-LF-XH	**6119**	PP	26-LK-BF	**6122**	PP	29-LK-BF

6131-6158

			Mercedes-Benz O550			Mercedes-Benz Integro		NC43D	2003		
6131	HE	BN-NF-13	**6138**	LS	BN-NF-24	**6145**	PP	BN-NG-16	**6152**	MK	BN-NF-98
6132	DR	BN-NF-15	**6139**	LS	BN-NF-25	**6146**	MK	BN-NG-13	**6153**	PP	BN-NG-40
6133	DR	BN-NF-17	**6140**	SN	BN-NF-06	**6147**	HV	BN-NG-08	**6154**	PP	BN-NX-74
6134	DR	BN-NF-20	**6141**	PP	BN-NG-39	**6148**	HV	BN-NG-04	**6155**	GR	BN-NX-78
6135	DR	BN-NF-21	**6142**	PP	BN-NG-38	**6149**	PP	BN-NG-02	**6156**	GR	BN-NX-76
6136	DR	BN-NF-22	**6143**	PP	BN-NG-34	**6150**	PP	BN-NG-01	**6157**	SN	BN-NX-77
6137	DR	BN-NF-23	**6144**	GR	BN-NG-19	**6151**	MK	BN-NF-99	**6158**	LS	BN-NX-73

6171-6189

			DAF SB200			Berkhof Ambassador		NC43D	2003		
6171	DM	BN-VX-54	**6176**	DM	BN-VX-59	**6181**	LS	BN-VX-64	**6186**	LS	BN-VX-69
6172	DM	BN-VX-55	**6177**	DM	BN-VX-60	**6182**	LS	BN-VX-65	**6187**	MG	BN-VX-70
6173	DM	BN-VX-56	**6178**	DM	BN-VX-61	**6183**	LS	BN-VX-66	**6188**	MG	BN-VX-71
6174	DM	BN-VX-57	**6179**	DM	BN-VX-62	**6184**	LS	BN-VX-67	**6189**	MG	BN-VX-72
6175	DM	BN-VX-58	**6180**	LS	BN-VX-63	**6185**	LS	BN-VX-68			

DAF SB200 Wrightbus Commander N42D 2003

6200	TI	BN-PN-23	6226	PP	BN-RP-10	6252	MK	BN-SG-15	6277	PP	BN-TB-25
6201	MK	BN-PN-27	6227	PP	BN-RP-11	6253	MK	BN-SG-17	6278	PP	BN-TB-26
6202	MK	BN-PN-30	6228	PP	BN-RP-12	6254	MK	BN-TB-43	6279	PP	BN-TB-27
6203	MK	BN-PN-32	6229	PP	BN-RP-13	6255	PP	BN-TB-45	6280	MK	BN-TB-28
6204	MK	BN-PN-33	6230	PP	BN-RP-15	6256	PP	BN-TB-47	6281	PP	BN-TB-29
6205	GR	BN-PN-38	6231	MK	BN-RP-17	6257	PP	BN-TB-49	6282	PP	BN-TB-30
6206	GR	BN-PN-39	6232	MK	BN-RP-18	6258	PP	BN-TB-51	6283	PP	BN-TB-31
6207	GR	BN-PN-35	6233	MK	BN-RP-20	6259	PP	BN-TB-53	6284	PP	BN-TB-32
6208	GR	BN-PN-41	6234	MK	BN-RP-21	6260	PP	BN-TR-56	6285	PP	BN-TB-33
6209	GR	BN-PN-42	6235	MK	BN-RP-23	6261	ML	BN-TR-58	6286	PP	BN-TB-35
6210	GR	BN-RD-38	6236	GR	BN-RP-26	6262	PP	BN-TR-59	6287	PP	BN-TB-37
6211	PP	BN-RD-39	6237	PP	BN-RP-28	6263	PP	BN-TR-61	6288	PP	BN-TB-38
6212	PP	BN-RD-40	6238	GR	BN-RP-30	6264	PP	BN-TR-62	6289	PP	BN-TB-41
6213	PP	BN-RD-41	6239	GR	BN-RP-32	6265	PP	BN-TR-63	6290	WT	BN-TR-69
6214	PP	BN-RD-47	6240	PP	BN-SF-92	6266	PP	BN-TR-64	6291	WT	BN-TR-70
6215	PP	BN-RD-48	6241	PP	BN-SF-94	6267	PP	BN-TR-66	6292	WT	BN-TR-71
6216	PP	BN-RD-49	6242	PP	BN-SF-96	6268	PP	BN-TR-67	6293	VD	BN-TR-76
6217	PP	BN-RD-50	6243	PP	BN-SF-98	6269	WT	BN-TR-68	6294	VD	BN-TR-77
6218	PP	BN-RD-51	6244	PP	BN-SF-99	6270	PP	BN-SG-19	6295	VD	BN-TR-78
6219	PP	BN-RD-52	6245	PP	BN-SG-01	6271	PP	BN-SG-24	6296	VD	BN-TR-79
6220	PP	BN-RN-83	6246	PP	BN-SG-03	6272	PP	BN-SG-25	6297	SK	BN-TR-81
6221	PP	BN-RN-87	6247	MK	BN-SG-04	6273	PP	BN-SG-26	6298	AS	BN-TR-83
6222	PP	BN-RN-84	6248	MK	BN-SG-06	6274	PP	BN-SG-27	6299	AS	BN-TR-84
6223	PP	BN-RN-85	6249	DR	BN-SG-08	6275	PP	BN-SG-28	6300	AS	BN-TR-85
6224	PP	BN-RN-86	6250	MK	BN-SG-11	6276	MK	BN-TB-24	6301	AS	BN-TR-86
6225	PP	BN-RP-08	6251	MK	BN-SG-13						

6381	SN	BD-VV-35	Iveco Daily 45.10	Iveco	M17	1996
6387	GR	BF-XL-12	MAN 11.220	Berkhof 2000NLE	B25D	1997
6388	GR	BF-XL-09	MAN 11.220	Berkhof 2000NLE	B25D	1997
6721	FA	BT-92-NP	DAF MB 230 10m	Den Oudsten Alliance	B26F	1987
7119	DV	VT-55-FG	DAF SBG220	Den Oudsten Alliance	AB61D	1992
7120	DV	VT-54-LD	DAF SBG220	Den Oudsten Alliance	AB61D	1992

7151-7174 Mercedes-Benz O550ÜL Mercedes-Benz Integro L NC50D 2004-05

7151	LK	BP-NN-71	7157	EM	BP-NN-86	7163	AS	BP-NT-61	7169	VD	BP-NT-55
7152	DR	BP-NN-73	7158	EM	BP-NN-76	7164	AS	BP-NT-63	7170	SK	BP-NT-54
7153	DR	BP-NN-74	7159	GR	BP-NN-78	7165	VD	BP-NT-59	7171	SK	BP-NT-53
7154	SK	BP-NN-77	7160	GR	BP-NN-79	7166	VD	BP-NT-58	7172	VD	BP-NT-51
7155	SK	BP-NN-80	7161	GR	BP-NN-81	7167	VD	RP-NT-56	7173	HV	BP-NT-47
7156	EM	BP-NN-84	7162	GR	BP-NT-60	7168	SK	BP-NT-57	7174	HV	BP-NT-46

7284	DM	RG-XN-42	Iveco 35.10	Iveco	M8	1997
7285	TI	RG-XN-44	Iveco 35.10	Iveco	M8	1997
7287	ML	RG-FG-89	Mercedes-Benz Sprinter 208D	Mercedes-Benz	M8	1996
7288	AS	RG-FG-86	Mercedes-Benz Sprinter 208D	Mercedes-Benz	M8	1996
7291	AP	RZ-XG-70	Mercedes-Benz Sprinter 208D	Mercedes-Benz	M8	1997
7301	AP	SN-FZ-80	Mercedes-Benz Sprinter 208D	Mercedes-Benz	M8	1997
7302	AS	SX-GZ-04	Mercedes-Benz Sprinter 208D	Mercedes-Benz	M8	1997
7303	ML	SX-PG-91	Mercedes-Benz Sprinter 208D	Mercedes-Benz	M8	1997
7304	DV	SX-GZ-02	Mercedes-Benz Sprinter 208D	Mercedes-Benz	M8	1997
7305	DR	SP-NG-36	Iveco 35.10	Iveco	M8	1997
7306	EM	SP-NG-38	Iveco 35.10	Iveco	M8	1997
7316	AS	TS-VV-22	Mercedes-Benz Sprinter 208D	Mercedes-Benz	M8	1998

7752-7759 Volvo B10MG-55 III Berkhof AB65D 1991

7752	ZW	VL-88-PB	7754	DV	VL-33-SB	7756	ZW	VL-48-TH	7758	ZW	VL-31-LN
7753	ZW	VL-21-SB	7755	DV	VL-97-SY	7757	LS	VL-98-SY	7759	ED	VL-17-LN

7801-7823 Mercedes-Benz Citaro O530G Mercedes-Benz AN--D 2004-05

7801	ZK	BP-NZ-00	7807	AP	BP-NZ-75	7813	EM	BP-NZ-85	7819	AS	BP-NZ-91
7802	ZK	BP-NZ-68	7808	GR	BP-NZ-76	7814	GR	BP-NZ-86	7820	AS	BP-NZ-92
7803	ZK	BP-NZ-69	7809	GR	BP-NZ-77	7815	GR	BP-NZ-87	7821	AS	BP-NZ-93
7804	ZK	BP-NZ-71	7810	SK	BP-NZ-81	7816	GR	BP-NZ-88	7822	AS	BP-NZ-94
7805	AP	BP-NZ-73	7811	LK	BP-NZ-83	7817	AS	BP-NZ-89	7823	AS	BP-NZ-95
7806	AP	BP-NZ-74	7812	VD	BP-NZ-84	7818	AS	BP-NZ-90			

7830	DR	BP-SG-53	Scania OmniCity CN94UA	Scania	AN48D	2004
7831	DR	BP-SG-52	Scania OmniCity CN94UA	Scania	AN48D	2004

Recent arrivals for the Arriva Nederlands are seventy VDL Bus SB200s with VDL Berkhof Ambassador bodies. These citybuses are allocated to many of the depots and have displaced Den Oudsten Alliance vehicles from the late 1980s. Illustrating the type is 8028, BP-LT-67. *Harry Laming*

8001-8070   VDL Bus SB200   VDL Berkhof Ambassador   N--D   2005

8001	VD	BP-LT-50	8019	AS	BP-LT-58	8037	AP	BP-LT-77	8054	SV	BP-NS-96
8002	VD	BP-LD-76	8020	AS	BP-LT-59	8038	AP	BP-LT-78	8055	SV	BP-NS-97
8003	SK	BP-LD-75	8021	EM	BP-LT-60	8039	AP	BP-LT-79	8056	SN	BP-LT-98
8004	SK	BP-LD-74	8022	EM	BP-LT-61	8040	SK	BP-LT-80	8057	HV	BP-NS-22
8005	ZK	BP-LT-51	8023	GR	BP-LT-62	8041	SK	BP-LT-81	8058	OO	BP-NS-23
8006	SK	BP-LD-72	8024	GR	BP-LT-63	8042	SK	BP-LT-82	8059	DR	BP-NS-26
8007	SK	BP-LD-71	8025	GR	BP-LT-64	8043	SK	BP-LT-84	8060	DR	BP-NS-27
8008	SK	BP-LD-71	8026	GR	BP-LT-65	8044	SK	BP-LT-85	8061	DR	BP-NS-28
8009	WT	BP-LT-52	8027	GR	BP-LT-66	8045	SK	BP-LT-87	8062	DR	BP-NS-29
8010	WT	BP-LD-70	8028	AP	BP-LT-67	8046	AP	BP-LT-88	8063	DR	BP-NS-30
8011	WT	RP-LD-68	8029	AP	BP-LT-68	8047	AP	BP-LT-89	8064	SN	BP-NS-14
8012	WT	BP-LD-67	8030	AP	BP-LT-69	8048	SN	BP-LT-90	8065	SN	BP-NS-16
8013	WT	BP-LD-66	8031	EM	BP-LT-70	8049	SN	BP-LT-91	8066	LS	BP-NS-18
8014	ZK	BP-LT-53	8032	EM	BP-LT-71	8050	SV	BP-LT-92	8067	LS	BP-NS-19
8015	ZK	BP-LT-54	8033	EM	BP-LT-73	8051	SV	BP-LT-93	8068	DM	BP-NS-20
8016	AP	BP-LT-55	8034	EM	BP-LT-74	8052	SV	BP-LT-94	8069	DM	BP-NS-21
8017	AP	BP-LT-56	8035	EM	BP-LT-75	8053	SN	BP-LT-95	8070	-	
8018	AP	BP-LT-57	8036	AP	BP-LT-76						

Depots and Codes:

AM	Ameland	GR	Groningen	SG	Schiermonnikoog
AP	Appingedam	HV	Heerenveen	SK	Stadskanaal
AS	Assen	LK	Groningen Srreek/Leek	SN	Sneek
DG	Dieverbrug	LS	Leeuwarden Stad	SV	Surhuisterveen
DM	Dokkum	MG	Minnertsga	TG	Terschelling
		MK	?	TL	Tiel
DR	Drachten	ML	Meppel	UZ	Uithuizen
DV	Dedernsvaart	ND	N Drenthe	VD	Veendam
ED	Emmeloord	OO	Oosterworlde	WT	Winschoten
EN	Emmen	PP	Papendrecht	ZW	Zwartsluis

SIPPEL

Autobus Sippel GmbH, Hessenstraße 16, 65719 Hofheim, Germany

1	WI-RS501	Mercedes-Benz Vario 0815	-	C	2003
3	WI-RS483	Mercedes-Benz 0307	Mercedes-Benz	B	1979
4	WI-RS214	Mercedes-Benz 0405	Mercedes-Benz	B	1986
6	WI-JP74	Mercedes-Benz 0405	Mercedes-Benz	B	1990
7	WI-RS507	Mercedes-Benz 0405	Mercedes-Benz	B	1991
9	WI-RS699	Mercedes-Benz 0405	Mercedes-Benz	B	1986
11	WI-RS512	Mercedes-Benz 0307	Mercedes-Benz	B55D	1983
13	WI-RS913	Mercedes-Benz Citaro 0530	Mercedes-Benz	B	2001
14	WI-RS514	Mercedes-Benz 614D	-	M	1992
15	WI-RS515	Mercedes-Benz 0405G	Mercedes-Benz	AB	1987
16	F-ST4169	Mercedes-Benz 0350 RHD	Mercedes-Benz	C	1999
17	WI-RS617	Mercedes-Benz Cito 0520	Mercedes-Benz	B	1999
18	WI-RS618	Mercedes-Benz 0815	Mercedes-Benz	C	2001
19	WI-RS	Mercedes-Benz Citaro 0530L	Mercedes-Benz	N49D	2003
20	WI-RS728	Mercedes-Benz 0405	Mercedes-Benz	B	1988
22	WI-RS722	Mercedes-Benz 0405G	Mercedes-Benz	AB	1986
23	WI-RS923	Mercedes-Benz Citaro 0530G	Mercedes-Benz	AN	2003
24	WI-RS724	Mercedes-Benz 0305G	Mercedes-Benz	B	1984
25	WI-RS625	Mercedes-Benz 0405N	Mercedes-Benz	N	1995
26	WI-RS726	Mercedes-Benz 0405N	Mercedes-Benz	N	1996
27	GG-PL427	Mercedes-Benz Citaro 0530	Mercedes-Benz	N	2002
29	WI-RS429	Mercedes-Benz Unimog 425	Mercedes-Benz		1976
30	WI-RS930	Mercedes-Benz 0405ST	Mercedes-Benz	B	1992
31	WI-RS931	Mercedes-Benz 0405GN	Mercedes-Benz	AB	1998
32	WI-RS632	Mercedes-Benz 0405N	Mercedes-Benz	B	1990
36	WI-RS736	Mercedes-Benz 0405GN	Mercedes-Benz	AB	1998
38	WI-RS538	Mercedes-Benz Citaro 0530G	Mercedes-Benz	AB	2000
40	WI-S4140	Mercedes-Benz 0405ST	Mercedes-Benz	B	1992
42	WI-RS942	Mercedes-Benz Citaro 0530N3	Mercedes-Benz	N	1998
43	WI-RS743	Mercedes-Benz 0405ST	Mercedes-Benz	N	1992
44	WI-RS244	Mercedes-Benz Citaro 0530N	Mercedes-Benz	N	1994
45	WI-RS245	Mercedes-Benz 0405N	Mercedes-Benz	B	1994
46	WI-XE846	Mercedes-Benz 0405ST	Mercedes-Benz	B	1985
47	WI-XE853	Mercedes-Benz 0407	Mercedes-Benz	B	1989
48	WI-RS448	Mercedes-Benz 0405ST	Mercedes-Benz	B	1992
49	WI-RS649	Mercedes-Benz 0405G	Mercedes-Benz	AB	1996
50	GG-PL450	Mercedes-Benz Citaro 0530	Mercedes-Benz	B	2002
53	WI-RS553	Setra S215 HR	Setra	C	1989
54	WI-RS754	Mercedes-Benz 0405ST	Mercedes-Benz	B	1986
55	WI-XR988	Mercedes-Benz 0405ST	Mercedes-Benz	B	1985
56	GG-PL456	Mercedes-Benz Citaro 0530	Mercedes-Benz	N	2002
57	GG-PL457	Mercedes-Benz Citaro 0530	Mercedes-Benz	N	2002
58	WI-RS758	Mercedes-Benz 0405N	Mercedes-Benz	B	1996
60	WI-RS836	Mercedes-Benz 0405ST	Mercedes-Benz	B	1991
62	WI-RS762	Mercedes-Benz Citaro 0530	Mercedes-Benz	N	2003
63	WI-RS563	Mercedes-Benz 0305	Mercedes-Benz	B	1985
64	WI-RS764	Mercedes-Benz 0305	Mercedes-Benz	B	1992
65	WI-RS465	Mercedes-Benz 0405ST	Mercedes-Benz	B	1985
67	WI-RS767	Mercedes-Benz Citaro 0530	Mercedes-Benz	N	2001
69	WI-RS269	Mercedes-Benz Citaro 0530N3	Mercedes-Benz	N	1998
70	WI-RS870	Mercedes-Benz 0305	Mercedes-Benz	B	1980
73	WI-RS173	Setra S213RL	Setra	BC	1986
74	Wi-RS774	Mercedes-Benz 0405N	Mercedes-Benz	B	1995
75	WI-RS775	Mercedes-Benz 0405N	Mercedes-Benz	B	1995
76	F-3T1270	Mercedes-Benz 0350 RHD	Mercedes-Benz	C	2000
77	WI-RS587	Mercedes-Benz Citaro 0530	Mercedes-benz	N	2000
78	WI-RS878	Mercedes-Benz 0350 RHD	Mercedes-Benz	C	2005
79	WI-RS879	Mercedes-Benz 0405G	Mercedes-Benz	AB	1987
80	WI-RS780	Mercedes-Benz 0405ST	Mercedes-Benz	B	1992
81	WI-RS781	Mercedes-Benz 0405GN	Mercedes-Benz	AB	1995
82	GG-PL982	Mercedes-Benz Citaro 0530N3	Mercedes-Benz	N	2001
83	GG-PL183	Mercedes-Benz 0405N	Mercedes-Benz	N	2000
84	WI-RS284	Mercedes-Benz 0405ST	Mercedes-Benz	B	1992
85	GG-PL185	Mercedes-Benz Citaro 0530	Mercedes-Benz	N	2002
86	WI-AS586	Mercedes-Benz 0405ST	Mercedes-Benz	B	1990

87	WI-AS687	Mercedes-Benz O405ST	Mercedes-Benz	B	1990
88	WI-RS688	Mercedes-Benz O405ST	Mercedes-Benz	B	1990
89	WI-RS489	Mercedes-Benz O405ST	Mercedes-Benz	B	1990
90	WI-S1090	Mercedes-Benz O405ST	Mercedes-Benz	B	1991
91	WI-RS191	Mercedes-Benz O303 10R	Mercedes-Benz	C	1984
93	WI-RS993	Mercedes-Benz O404 15RH	Mercedes-Benz	C	1993
94	WI-RS894	Mercedes-Benz O405ST	Mercedes-Benz	B	1993
95	WI-RS595	Mercedes-Benz O405ST	Mercedes-Benz	B	1993
96	WI-RS596	Mercedes-Benz O405ST	Mercedes-Benz	B	1993
97	WI-RS597	Mercedes-Benz O405ST	Mercedes-Benz	B	1993
98	WI-RS798	Mercedes-Benz O405ST	Mercedes-Benz	B	1993
99	WI-RS799	Mercedes-Benz O405G	Mercedes-Benz	AB	1990
100	WI-SG4444	Mercedes-Benz O404 15R	Mercedes-Benz	C	1994
101	WI-S1101	Mercedes-Benz Cito O520	Mercedes-Benz	N	2001
102	WI-S1102	Mercedes-Benz Cito O520	Mercedes-Benz	N	2001
103	GG-PL103	Mercedes-Benz Citaro O530G	Mercedes-Benz	N	2002
104	WI-RS704	Mercedes-Benz Citaro O530	Mercedes-Benz	N	2001
105	WI-RS105	Mercedes-Benz Citaro O530	Mercedes-Benz	N	2001
107	WI-RS907	Mercedes-Benz Citaro O530	Mercedes-Benz	N	2002
108	WI-RS908	Mercedes-Benz Citaro O530	Mercedes-Benz	N	2001
109	WI-S1313	Mercedes-Benz Citaro O530N3	Mercedes-Benz	N	2001
110	WI-S1323	Mercedes-Benz Citaro O530N3	Mercedes-Benz	N	2001
111	WI-S1324	Mercedes-Benz Citaro O530N3	Mercedes-Benz	N	2001
112	WI-RS712	Mercedes-Benz Citaro O815	-	B	2001
113	WI-RS613	Mercedes-Benz Citaro O815	-	B	2001
114	WI-RS914	Mercedes-Benz Citaro O530G	Mercedes-Benz	AN	2001
115	WI-S2305	Mercedes-Benz Citaro O530G	Mercedes-Benz	AN	2001
116	F-D1356	Mercedes-Benz Citaro Vario O814		C	1993
117	WI-RS317	Mercedes-Benz O405	Mercedes-Benz	B	1988
118	WI-RS318	Mercedes-Benz O405	Mercedes-Benz	B	1988
120	WI-RS137	Mercedes-Benz Citaro O530N3	Mercedes-Benz	N	1998
121	WI-RS731	Mercedes-Benz Citaro O530	Mercedes-Benz	N	2001
122	F-ST2122	Mercedes-Benz Citaro O350	Mercedes-Benz	C	2002
123	WI-RS163	Mercedes-Benz O405GN	Mercedes-Benz	AB	1992
124	WI-GS224	Mercedes-Benz O405GN	Mercedes-Benz	AB	1996
125	WI-GS225	Mercedes-Benz O405N	Mercedes-Benz	B	1996
126	WI-RS926	Mercedes-Benz Citaro O530N3	Mercedes-Benz	N	2002
131	WI-RS831	Mercedes-Benz O405GN	Mercedes-Benz	AB	1996
132	WI-RS832	Mercedes-Benz O405N	Mercedes-Benz	B	1996
134	WI-RS134	Mercedes-Benz Citaro O530	Mercedes-Benz	N	2002
136	WI-RS936	Mercedes-Benz Citaro O530	Mercedes-Benz	N	2001
138	WI-RS638	Setra S215 HR	Setra	C	1989
139	WI-RS339	Mercedes-Benz O405N	Mercedes-Benz	B	1997
140	WI-XW510	Mercedes-Benz O405ST	Mercedes-Benz	B	1986
141	WI-ZX281	Mercedes-Benz O405G	Mercedes-Benz	AB	1988
142	WI-ZX280	Mercedes-Benz O405G	Mercedes-Benz	AB	1988
143	WI-ZX279	Mercedes-Benz O405G	Mercedes-Benz	AR	1988
144	WI-XW509	Mercedes-Benz O405ST	Mercedes-Benz	B	1986
145	WI-XW515	Mercedes-Benz O405ST	Mercedes-Benz	B	1986
146	WI-XW506	Mercedes-Benz O405ST	Mercedes-Benz	B	1986
147	WI-RS147	Mercedes-Benz O350	Mercedes-Benz	C	2004
148	WI-RS748	Mercedes-Benz O405GN	Mercedes-Benz	AN	1997
149	WI-RS749	Mercedes-Benz Citaro O530	Mercedes-Benz	N	2003
150	WI-RS157	Mercedes-Benz O405N	Mercedes-Benz	B	1997
151	WI-RS851	Mercedes-Benz Citaro O530G	Mercedes-Benz	AN	2001
152	WI-XW513	Mercedes-Benz O405ST	Mercedes-Benz	B	1986
153	WI-XW504	Mercedes-Benz O405ST	Mercedes-Benz	B	1986
154	WI-RS854	Mercedes-Benz O405	Mercedes-Benz	B	1988
155	WI-RS955	Mercedes-Benz O404 RH	Mercedes-Benz	C49FT	2001
156	WI-RS956	Mercedes-Benz O550	Mercedes-Benz	C	1997
157	WI-RS247	Mercedes-Benz O405GN	Mercedes-Benz	AB	1997
158	WI-RS258	Mercedes-Benz O405N	Mercedes-Benz	B	1997
159	WI-RS759	Mercedes-Benz Citaro O530	Mercedes-Benz	N	2000
164	WI-RS464	Mercedes-Benz Citaro O530	Mercedes-Benz	N	2001
165	GG-PL965	Mercedes-Benz Citaro O530N3	Mercedes-Benz	N	2001
169	WI-RS569	Mercedes-Benz Citaro O530N3	Mercedes-Benz	N	1998
170	WI-S1170	Mercedes-Benz Citaro O530	Mercedes-Benz	N	2001
171	F-ST4171	Mercedes-Benz O350 RHD	Mercedes-Benz	C	1999
172	F-ST4172	Mercedes-Benz O350 RHD	Mercedes-Benz	C	1999
174	WI-RS674	Mercedes-Benz Citaro O530GN	Mercedes-Benz	AN	1999
175	WI-RS275	Mercedes-Benz Citaro O530GN	Mercedes-Benz	AN	1999
176	WI-RS976	Mercedes-Benz Citaro O530GN	Mercedes-Benz	AN	1999
177	WI-RS977	Mercedes-Benz Citaro O530GN	Mercedes-Benz	AN	1999

178	WI-RS378	Mercedes-Benz Citaro O530GN	Mercedes-Benz		AN	1999			
181	WI-RS981	Mercedes-Benz Citaro O405N	Mercedes-Benz		B	1999			
182	WI-RS982	Mercedes-Benz Citaro O405N	Mercedes-Benz		B	1999			
183	WI-RS983	Mercedes-Benz Citaro O530N	Mercedes-Benz		N	1999			
184	WI-RS684	Mercedes-Benz Citaro O530GN	Mercedes-Benz		AN	1999			
185	WI-RS675	Mercedes-Benz Citaro O530GN	Mercedes-Benz		AN	1999			
186	WI-RS886	Mercedes-Benz Citaro O530N	Mercedes-Benz		N	1999			
187	F-ST4174	Mercedes-Benz Citaro O580	Mercedes-Benz		C	1999			
188	WI-TK438	Mercedes-Benz O405ST	Mercedes-Benz		B	1986			
189	WI-RS389	Mercedes-Benz O303 15R	Mercedes-Benz		C	1978			
190	F-ST1190	Mercedes-Benz O350 RHD	Mercedes-Benz		C	2000			
191	WI-RS791	Mercedes-Benz O405N	Mercedes-Benz		B	2000			
192	WI-RS592	Mercedes-Benz Cito O520	Mercedes-Benz		N	1999			
193	WI-RS193	Mercedes-Benz Citaro O530N	Mercedes-Benz		N	1998			
194	WI-RS794	Mercedes-Benz Citaro O530G	Mercedes-Benz		AB	2000			
195	GG-PL195	Mercedes-Benz Citaro O530G	Mercedes-Benz		AB	2002			
196	WI-RS856	Mercedes-Benz Citaro O530G	Mercedes-Benz		AB	2001			
197	F-ST2197	Mercedes-Benz Citaro O530	Mercedes-Benz		C	2002			
198	WI-RS698	Mercedes-Benz Citaro O530N	Mercedes-Benz		N	2001			
199	F-ST2199	Mercedes-Benz Citaro O530	Mercedes-Benz		C	2002			
200	F-EF1000	Mercedes-Benz Travego O580	Mercedes-Benz		C	2000			

202-220

Mercedes-Benz Cito O520 Mercedes-Benz N 2000

202	F-V2082		207	F-V2087		212	F-V2092		217	F-V2097
203	F-V2083		208	F-V2088		213	F-V2093		218	F-V2098
204	F-V2084		209	F-V2089		214	F-V2094		219	F-V2099
205	F-V2085		210	F-V2090		215	F-V2095		220	F-AJ520
206	F-V2086		211	F-V2091		216	F-V2096			

224	F-V2104	Volkswagen	Volkswagen	M	1995	
301	WI-AP401	Mercedes-Benz Citaro O530	Mercedes-Benz	N	1999	
302	WI-TK447	Mercedes-Benz O405ST	Mercedes-Benz	B	1993	
303	WI-TK433	Mercedes-Benz O405ST	Mercedes-Benz	B	1991	
304	WI-TK434	Mercedes-Benz O405ST	Mercedes-Benz	B	1992	
306	WI-TK436	Mercedes-Benz O405ST	Mercedes-Benz	B	1989	
307	WI-TK437	Mercedes-Benz O405	Mercedes-Benz	B	1996	
308	WI-JP108	Mercedes-Benz Citaro O530	Mercedes-Benz	N	1998	
309	WI-JP109	Mercedes-Benz Citaro O530	Mercedes-Benz	N	1998	
310	WI-TK440	Mercedes-Benz O405ST	Mercedes-Benz	B	1986	
311	WI-TK441	Mercedes-Benz O405G	Mercedes-Benz	AB	1993	
312	WI-TK439	Mercedes-Benz O405N	Mercedes-Benz	B	1996	
314	WI-JP114	Mercedes-Benz Citaro O530	Mercedes-Benz	N	1998	
315	WI-JP115	Mercedes-Benz Citaro O530	Mercedes-Benz	N	1998	
316	WI-XW527	Mercedes-Benz O405ST	Mercedes-Benz	B	1986	
317	WI-TK417	Mercedes-Benz O405ST	Mercedes-Benz	B	1992	
318	WI-TK448	Mercedes-Benz O405ST	Mercedes-Benz	B	1995	
319	WI-XW519	Mercedes-Benz O405ST	Mercedes-Benz	B	1986	
321	WI-TK626	Opel	Opel	Taxi	1998	
322	WI-TK626	Opel	Opel	Taxi	1998	
325	WI-S1325	Mercedes-Benz Citaro O530	Mercedes-Benz	N	2001	
326	WI-S1326	Mercedes-Benz Citaro O530	Mercedes-Benz	N	2003	
327	WI-S1327	Mercedes-Benz Citaro O530	Mercedes-Benz	N	2003	
400	GI-YC400	Setra S315 UL	Setra	NC	2000	
401	GI-YC401	Setra S315 UL	Setra	NC	2000	
402	GI-YI402	Mercedes-Benz O550	Mercedes-Benz	C	2001	
403	GI-YI403	Mercedes-Benz O550	Mercedes-Benz	C	2001	
404	GI-ED404	Mercedes-Benz O408	Mercedes-Benz	N	1992	
405	GI-ED405	Mercedes-Benz O408	Mercedes-Benz	N	1991	
406	GI-ED292	MAN NL	MAN	N	1992	
407	GI-AD407	Mercedes-Benz Vario O815	-	C	1995	
416	HG-DC360	Setra S215 HR	Setra	C	1988	
417	HG-DC150	Mercedes-Benz O405	Mercedes-Benz	B	1997	
418	HG-DC250	Mercedes-Benz O405	Mercedes-Benz	B	1986	
419	HG-DC767	Mercedes-Benz O405	Mercedes-Benz	B	1992	
450	GI-AD420	Mercedes-Benz O350	Mercedes-Benz	C	2001	
462	GI-US768	Volkswagen	Volkswagen	M	1995	

ARRIVA PORTUGAL

Arriva Portugal, Edificio Guimarães, Rua Eduardo de Almeida, No 162, 2°Sala-C,
4810-440 Guimarães, Portugal

20	RT-83-65	Volvo B58-55	Irmãos Mota (1991)	BC53D	1971	Hotelcar, Lisboa, 1990
23	TM-67-93	AEC Reliance 10U3ZL	UTIC (Porto)	BC55D	1980	
48	OS-22-02	AEC Reliance 6U3ZL	UTIC (Porto)	B32D	1972	
52	MS-65-03	AEC Reliance 6U3ZL	UTIC (Porto)	BC59D	1972	
54	NN-94-78	AEC Reliance 6U3ZL	UTIC (Porto)	B34D	1975	
55	ON-25-62	AEC Reliance 6U3ZL	UTIC (Porto)	BC73D	1973	
62	NP-74-16	AEC Reliance 10U2L	UTIC (Lisboa)	C53D	1979	
64	NP-74-18	AEC Reliance 10U2L	UTIC (Lisboa)	C51D	1979	
65	EU-58-65	UTIC-AEC U2077	UTIC (Lisboa)	C51D	1980	
68	GR-84-44	UTIC-AEC U2077	UTIC (Lisboa)	C55D	1980	
69	IV-72-34	Scania BR116S	Irmãos Mota	BC47D	1981	
70	BZ-09-52	Scania BR116S	Irmãos Mota	C47D	1981	
71	BZ-09-50	Scania BR116S	Irmãos Mota	C49D	1981	
72	DO-02-26	Scania BR116S	Irmãos Mota	C55D	1982	
73	EB-09-81	Scania BR116S	Irmãos Mota	C55D	1982	
74	ND-16-05	Scania BR116S	Irmãos Mota	C49D	1983	Barraqueiro, Malaveira, 1999
75	CJ-48-40	Scania K112S	Alfredo Caetano	C51D	1984	Belos Transportes, Setúbal, 1999
78	NT-91-12	UTIC Leyland MTL11R	UTIC (Porto)	C54D	1983	
79	OT-51-12	Volvo B10M-60	Irmãos Mota	C49D	1983	
80	OT-51-13	Volvo B10M-60	Irmãos Mota	C49D	1983	
81	TN-95-90	Scania K112S	Irmãos Mota	C49D	1984	
82	TN-95-91	Scania K112S	Irmãos Mota	C49D	1984	
84	JS-97-52	Scania K112S	Irmãos Mota	C49D	1986	
85	JS-97-53	Scania K112S	Irmãos Mota	C49D	1986	
86	FQ-88-17	Scania K112S	Irmãos Mota	C49D	1987	
87	FQ-88-18	Scania K112S	Irmãos Mota	C49D	1987	
92	NR-36-07	AEC Reliance 6U3ZL	UTIC (Porto)	BC59D	1972	
94	DU-95-69	Scania BR116S	Irmãos Mota	C55D	1981	
95	DU-99-92	Scania BR86S	Irmãos Mota	BC51D	1981	
96	IM-02-26	Scania BR116S	Irmãos Mota	C55D	1981	
98	ND-16-04	Scania BR116S	Irmãos Mota	C49D	1983	
100	PA-65-24	Scania K112-60	Irmãos Mota	C53D	1989	
101	RF-74-82	Scania K113CLB	Irmãos Mota	C49D	1989	
102	RF-74-81	Scania K113CLB	Irmãos Mota	C49D	1989	

116-122
MAN SL200 — MAN — B39D — 1977 — Hamburg, 1992

116	56-18-AU	118	56-20-AU	121	56-16-AU	122	56-17-AU
117	56-19-AU	119	56-14-AU				

123-129
Mercedes-Benz O305 — Mercedes-Benz — B44D — 1981 — Germany 1993-94

123	23-36-CL	125	23-38-CL	127	23-40-CL	129	52-91-EC
124	23-37-CL	126	23-39-CL	128	52-90-EC		

130	99-70-EH	Mercedes-Benz O303	Mercedes-Benz	BC55D	1986	Germany, 1994

131-143
Mercedes-Benz O305 — Mercedes-Benz — B44D* — 1979-84 — Germany 1994-95
*131 is BC44D; 137-40 are B37D; 141/2 are B41D

131	99-74-EI	134	39-63-EJ	140	61-64-FU	142	98-37-FV
132	99-75-EI	137	79-05-FT	141	98-36-FV	143	21-02-FX
133	99-76-EI	139	12-22-FU				

145	GP-80-07	UTIC-AEC U2075	UTIC (Lisboa)	B40D	1977	VIMECA, Queiuz de Baixo, 1996
147	16-81-HT	Mercedes-Benz O303	Mercedes-Benz	C51D	1984	Germany, 1997
148	13-06-HJ	Mercedes-Benz O303	Mercedes-Benz	C51D	1988	Germany, 1996
150	08-86-DC	MAN SL200	MAN	B41D	1981	VIMECA, Queiuz de Baixo, 1997
152	63-36-CC	MAN SL200	MAN	B44D	1981	VIMECA, Queiuz de Baixo, 1997
154	55-39-KF	Mercedes-Benz O305	Mercedes-Benz	B44D	1983	Germany, 1997
155	64-00-JL	Mercedes-Benz O305	Mercedes-Benz	B44D	1982	Germany, 1998
156	56-56-JO	Mercedes-Benz O305	Mercedes-Benz	B37D	1983	Germany, 1998
157	95-75-MJ	Mercedes-Benz O303	Mercedes-Benz	B44D	1986	Germany, 1998
158	95-76-MJ	Mercedes-Benz O305	Mercedes-Benz	B44D	1986	Germany, 1998
159	46-36-ML	Mercedes-Benz O405	Mercedes-Benz	B44D	1986	Germany, 1998
160	46-37-ML	Mercedes-Benz O303	Mercedes-Benz	BC53D	1991	Germany, 1998

One of the benefits of the Arriva Group is its ability to transfer vehicles between operations. Now with Arriva Portugal, 388, 81-17-TH, is one of the former Copenhagen 'S service' buses based on a Volvo B10M chassis complete with DAB bodywork and high-back seating. *Harry Laming*

161	79-18-ML	Mercedes-Benz O305	Mercedes-Benz	B37D	1986	Germany, 1998
162	79-19-ML	Mercedes-Benz O305	Mercedes-Benz	B38D	1986	Germany, 1998

163-179		Mercedes-Benz O405	Mercedes-Benz	B44D	1987-91	Germany, 2003

163	98-34-VU	**168**	25-06-VU	**172**	45-10-VX	**176**	98-35-VU
164	25-10-VU	**169**	45-08-VX	**173**	98-36-VU	**177**	98-37-VU
165	25-08-VU	**170**	25-11-VU	**174**	45-09-VX	**178**	98-33-VU
166	25-09-VU	**171**	98-32-VU	**175**	25-12-VU	**179**	25-13-VU
167	25-07-VU						

196	OO-21-50	AEC Reliance U2076 (Volvo)	UTIC (Porto) (1988)	BC43D	1978	A V Minho, 1992
197	TM-30-63	AEC Reliance U2076 (Volvo)	UTIC (Porto)	B35D	1979	
206	IG-86-75	UTIC-AEC U2001	J D Martins (1985)	C47D	1963	
207	II-27-28	UTIC-AEC U2001	UTIC (Porto) (1981)	C47D	1964	
209	NN-56-30	UTIC-AEC U2047	UTIC (Lisboa)	BC73D	1974	
212	GI-41-27	UTIC-AEC U2001	J D Martins (1985)	C47D	1966	
218	ST-91-65	Volvo B58-60R	Irmãos Mota (1989)	BC53D	1976	
222	OR-84-90	Volvo B58-60R	J D Martins	BC73D	1977	
223	NN-99-29	Volvo B58-60R	Irmãos Mota (1988)	BC55D	1975	SOTUBE, 1982
240	RT-72-92	AEC Reliance U2021	J D Martins	C51D	1971	
243	RT-81-80	Volvo B58-55	Irmãos Mota	BC49D	1971	Machado Fernandes, 1983
246	OS-23-59	UTIC-AEC U2047	UTIC (Lisboa)	BC59D	1972	
248	NR-39-48	UTIC-AEC U2047	UTIC (Lisboa)	BC59D	1972	
251	AO-12-13	UTIC-AEC U2055	UTIC (Lisboa)	B39D	1973	RBI, Castelo Branco, 1996
252	OS-60-31	UTIC-AEC U2047	UTIC (Lisboa)	BC59D	1972	
253	NR-76-54	UTIC-AEC U2055	UTIC (Lisboa)	BC73D	1973	
254	NR-76-55	UTIC-AEC U2055	UTIC (Lisboa)	BC73D	1973	
255	AO-12-20	UTIC-AEC U2047	UTIC (Lisboa)	BC73D	1973	Covas & Filhos, 2001
259	PM-47-25	UTIC-AEC U2055	UTIC (Lisboa)	BC59D	1974	
261	72-54-HT	Mercedes-Benz O303/15R	Mercedes-Benz	C49D	1987	
263	PO-47-04	Magirus Deutz 260B120A	Salvador Caetano	C49D	1977	
264	PO-70-16	Volvo B58-60R	J D Martins	BC73D	1977	
265	SR-56-38	Volvo B58-60R	J D Martins	BC73D	1977	
267	PS-35-43	Volvo B58-60R	Irmãos Mota	BC53D	1977	

269	76-65-NM	Mercedes-Benz O303/15R		Mercedes-Benz		C49D	1987	
270	76-66-NM	Mercedes-Benz O303/15R		Mercedes-Benz		C49DT	1984	
271	SR-74-98	Volvo B58-60P		Irmãos Mota (1998)		C53D	1978	
273	PO-96-69	Magirus Deutz 260C120E		Salvador Caetano		C53D	1977	
275	OM-98-37	Volvo B10M-60		Alfredo Caetano		C49D	1982	Ag Viagens Sta Filomena, 1996
278	OO-39-95	Volvo B58-60R		J D Martins		BC59D	1979	
279	OO-39-88	Volvo B58-60P		Irmãos Mota (1993)		BC53D	1979	
284	HS-58-14	UTIC-AEC U2077		UTIC (Lisboa)		C49D	1979	
286	TS-22-34	UTIC-AEC U2077		UTIC (Lisboa)		C49D	1980	
291	RS-17-88	Volvo B10M-60		Ramp		C49D	1983	Ag Viagens Sta Filomena, 1996
292	OR-78-64	Volvo B58-60R		Salvador Caetano		C53F	1976	Ag Viagens Sta Filomena, 1996
293	TM-75-73	AEC Reliance 10U3ZL		UTIC (Lisboa)		BC53D	1980	
294	TM-75-74	AEC Reliance 10U3ZL		UTIC (Lisboa)		C55D	1980	
295	OO-99-57	Volvo B58-60P		J D Martins		B36D	1979	
296	TS-24-63	Volvo B58-60P		Irmãos Mota		C49D	1980	
298	SP-51-23	Volvo B10M-60		Irmãos Mota		C49D	1981	Ag Viagens Sta Filomena, 1996
299	RS-59-61	Pegaso 5036		Salvador Caetano		C47D	1983	
300	RS-59-62	Pegaso 5036		Salvador Caetano		C47D	1983	

301-308

		Volvo B10M-55G		CAMO		AB49D	1987	Acquired, 2002
301	QN-06-15	**303**	RP-69-35	**305**	QN-54-94	**307**	QT-33-69
302	QN-06-19	**304**	RP-95-43	**306**	QN-83-83	**308**	QQ-79-80

350	QS-93-85	Volvo B10R		Irmãos Mota		B36D	1990	TUG, Guimaraes, 2003
351	RQ-11-70	Volvo B10R		CAMO		B36D	1991	TUG, Guimaraes, 2003
352	SQ-29-93	Volvo B10R		Irmãos Mota		B36D	1992	TUG, Guimaraes, 2003
376	70-16-TI	Volvo B10M-60		DAB		BC51D	1988	Arriva Danmark, 2002
377	85-57-TL	Volvo B10M-60		Åbenrå		BC51D	1989	Arriva Danmark, 2002

378-390

		Volvo B10M-60		DAB		BC51D	1989-90	Arriva Danmark, 2001-03
378	81-15-TH	**381**	89-21-SR	**386**	97-07-TD	**389**	85-58-TL
379	70-18-TI	**383**	97-09-TD	**387**	81-16-TH	**390**	35-65-UP
380	70-17-TI	**384**	97-08-TD	**388**	81-17-TH		

391	89-73-UP	Volvo B10R		Åbenrå		BC49D	1987	Arriva Danmark, 2003

Arriva Portugal 123, 23-37-CL, is a Mercedes-Benz O305 imported from Germany. It is seen in Famalicão bus station. *Harry Laming*

392-400 Volvo B10M-60 Åbenrå BC51D* 1987-91 Arriva Denmark, 2003
*seating varies

392	59-25-UP	395	35-61-UP	397	35-59-UP	399	89-62-UP
393	35-64-UP	396	35-63-UP	398	35-62-UP	400	97-43-UZ
394	35-60-UP						

401-420 Mercedes-Benz OH1634L Irmãos Mota C51D 1994

401	23-30-EH	406	90-45-EI	411	79-16-EJ	416	42-79-EL
402	49-07-EH	407	90-46-EI	412	79-37-EJ	417	42-80-EL
403	49-08-EH	408	90-47-EI	413	79-38-EJ	418	42-81-EL
404	49-09-EH	409	90-48-EI	414	79-39-EJ	419	42-82-EL
405	90-35-EI	410	79-15-EJ	415	42-78-EL	420	42-88-EL

421	VI-16-66	Mercedes-Benz O303	Irmãos Mota	C51D	1990
501	75-37-DJ	Scania K113CLB	Irmãos Mota	C51D	1994
502	66-89-FI	Scania K113CLB	Irmãos Mota	C51D	1995
503	61-34-ND	Scania K124IB4	Irmãos Mota	C51D	1999
504	70-12-NT	Scania K124IB4	Irmãos Mota	C55D	1999

521-527 Scania K114IB4 Caetano Bus C59D 2002

521	10-70-TT	523	10-68-TT	525	10-66-TT	527	10-64-TT
522	10-69-TT	524	10-67-TT	526	10-65-TT		

581	JJ-81-37	Scania K112S	UTIC (Lisboa) (1990)	C49D	1984	EVA Transportes, Faro, 2002
582	JA-86-73	Scania K112S	UTIC (Lisboa) (1990)	C49D	1985	EVA Transportes, Faro, 2002
589	RD-57-84	Scania K113CLB	UTIC (Lisboa)	C49D	1988	
590	RG-68-73	Scania K113CLB	UTIC (Lisboa)	C51D	1989	
591	UA-48-65	Scania K113CLB	UTIC (Lisboa)	C49D	1989	Cruz e Neves, Ilhavo, 2002
592	UA-48-68	Scania K113CLB	UTIC (Lisboa)	C49D	1989	Cruz e Neves, Ilhavo, 2002
593	VC-38-22	Scania K113CLB	UTIC (Lisboa)	C49D	1990	EVA Transportes, Faro, 2002
594	VC-38-25	Scania K113CLB	UTIC (Lisboa)	C49D	1990	EVA Transportes, Faro, 2002
601	68-35-SD	Scania L94IB4	CAMO	B47D	2001	
602	68-34-SD	Scania L94IB4	CAMO	B47D	2001	
603	62-12-SG	Scania L94IB4	CAMO	B47D	2001	
604	62-06-SG	Scania L94IB4	CAMO	B47D	2001	
651	32-05-GU	Scania K113CLL	Irmãos Mota	B47D	1996	
652	32-06-GU	Scania K113CLL	Irmãos Mota	B47D	1996	
701	QX-01-42	Scania K113CLB	Irmãos Mota	C(63)DT	1991	
702	QX-01-43	Scania K113CLB	Irmãos Mota	C(63)DT	1991	
703	29-69-FB	Scania K113CLB	Irmãos Mota	C(61)DT	1995	
704	29-70-FB	Scania K113CLB	Irmãos Mota	C(61)DT	1995	
705	06-01-IG	Scania K113CLB	Irmãos Mota	C(59)DT	1997	
706	42-09-NH	Scania K124IB4	Irmãos Mota	C(59)DT	1999	

Scania chassis have been supplied to Arriva fleets with four delivered to the Portuguese fleet in 2001. Number 604, 62-06-SG illustrates the type.
Marco Antonio Lindo

ARRIVA NOROESTE

Arriva (Iasa-Finisterre), Poligono de Sabon, Parcela 31-32, 15142 Arteixo, La Coruña, España

0177	C-2375-Z	Setra S215HU	Setra	BC55D	1984
0178	C-5716-AC	Pegaso 5031-L4	Unicar	C55D	1986
0179	C-5717-AC	Pegaso 5031-L4	Unicar	C55D	1986
0180	C-8337-AC	Pegaso 5031-L4	Unicar	C55D	1986
0204	C-1248-AF	Volvo B10M-60	Irizar	C55D	1986
0205	C-1249-AF	Volvo B10M-60	Irizar	C55D	1986
0206	C-1813-AF	Mercedes-Benz O303	Irizar	C55D	1986
0207	C-1814-AF	Mercedes-Benz O303	Irizar	C55D	1986
0208	C-1918-AF	Pegaso 5036-S1	Castrosua	C55D	1986
0209	C-1919-AF	Pegaso 5036-S1	Castrosua	C55D	1986
0212	C-7688-AF	Pegaso 5036-S1	Castrosua	C55D	1987
0213	C-7689-AF	Pegaso 5036-S1	Castrosua	C55D	1987
0214	C-2324-A	Setra S215HU	Setra	BC55D	1989
0215	C-2325-A	Setra S215HU	Setra	BC55D	1989
0216	C-2326-A	Setra S215HU	Setra	BC55D	1989
0217	C-2327-A	Setra S215HU	Setra	BC55D	1989
0218	C-2328-A	Setra S215HU	Setra	BC55D	1989
0219	C-2329-A	Setra S215HU	Setra	BC55D	1989
0221	C-8224-AT	Setra S215HD	Setra	C55D	1990
0222	C-8225-AT	Setra S215HU	Setra	C55D	1990
0223	C-8226-AT	Setra S215HU	Setra	BC55D	1990
0224	C-8227-AT	Setra S215HD	Setra	C55D	1990
0225	C-8228-AT	Setra S215HU	Setra	BC55D	1990
0226	C-8229-AT	Setra S215HD	Setra	C55D	1990
0227	LU-9759-I	Mercedes-Benz O303	Hispano Carrocera	C55D	1987
0229	LU-5545-J	Mercedes-Benz O303/15	Irizar	C56F	1988
0231	C-6734-A	Setra S215HU	Setra	BC55D	1991
0232	C-6735-A	Setra S215HU	Setra	BC55D	1991
0233	C-6736-A	Setra S215HU	Setra	BC55D	1991
0234	C-6737-A	Setra S215HU	Setra	BC55D	1991
0235	LU-5547-J	Mercedes-Benz O303/15	Castrosua	C55D	1988
0236	LU-5546-J	Mercedes-Benz O303/15	Castrosua	C55D	1988
0243	C-1910-AY	DAF SB3000	Castrosua	C55D	1991
0245	C-1912-AY	DAF SB3000	Castrosua	C55D	1991
0246	C-1913-AY	DAF SB3000	Castrosua	C55D	1991
0248	C-0746-AZ	Mercedes-Benz O303/15	Irizar	C55D	1992
0249	C-0747-AZ	Mercedes-Benz O303/15	Irizar	C55D	1992
0250	C-2011-BB	Mercedes-Benz O303/15	Irizar	C55D	1992
0251	C-2012-BB	Mercedes-Benz O303/15	Irizar	C55D	1992
0254	LU-9758-I	Mercedes-Benz O303/15	Hispano Carrocera	C55D	1987
0255	C-7264-BB	Pegaso 5226	Castrosua	C55D	1992
0256	C-7265-BB	Pegaso 5226	Castrosua	C55D	1992
0257	C-7266-BB	Pegaso 5226	Castrosua	C55D	1992
0258	C-7267-BB	Pegaso 5226	Castrosua	C55D	1992
0264	C-9126-BD	Pegaso 5226	Castrosua	C55D	1993
0265	C-9127-BD	Pegaso 5226	Castrosua	C55D	1993
0266	C-9128-BD	Pegaso 5226	Castrosua	C55D	1993
0267	C-9129-BD	Pegaso 5226	Castrosua	C55D	1993
0268	LU-5964-O	Setra S215HD	Setra	C55D	1993
0269	LU-5965-O	Setra S215HD	Setra	C55D	1993
0270	C-9130-BD	Volvo B12	Irizar	C55D	1993
0271	C-9131-BD	Volvo B12	Irizar	C55D	1993
0279	M-4106-GK	Mercedes-Benz O303	Obradors	C54D	1985
0280	M-4916-GK	Mercedes-Benz O303	Obradors	C54D	1985
0281	M-4917-GK	Mercedes-Benz O303	Obradors	C54D	1985
0282	M-3844-GL	Mercedes-Benz O303	Obradors	C54D	1985
0283	M-3845-GL	Mercedes-Benz O303	Obradors	C54D	1985
0284	M-8982-JK	Mercedes-Benz	Ayats	C50D	1989
0285	O-8206-AH	Scania K113TLA	Irizar Dragon	C(75)D	1986
0286	C-1998-BH	Scania K113TLA	Irizar Dragon	C(81)D	1994
0291	C-2166-AB	Setra S215HU	Setra	C55D	1985
0292	C-8424-AC	Setra S215HU	Setra	C55D	1986
0293	C-8425-AC	Setra S215HU	Setra	C55D	1986
0294	C-0245-AH	Setra S215HU	Setra	C55D	1987
0295	C-5051-AK	Setra S215HU	Setra	C55D	1988

0296	C-7818-AM	Setra S215HU	Setra	C55D	1989
0297	C-7289-AW	Setra S215HU	Setra	C55D	1991
0298	C-9928-AX	Setra S215HD	Setra	C55D	1991
0299	C-0041-BD	Setra S215HD	Setra	C55D	1993
0300	C-4724-BJ	Mercedes-Benz O404 RH	Irizar	C55D	1994
0301	C-4725-BJ	Mercedes-Benz O404 RH	Irizar	C55D	1994
0302	S-7337-P	Scania K112TL	Ayats	BC75D	1988
0303	LU-4913-O	Pegaso 5226	Castrosua	C56D	1993
0304	C-2809-BK	Pegaso 5226	Hispano Carrocera	C55D	1994
0305	C-2808-BK	Pegaso 5226	Hispano Carrocera	C55D	1994
0306	C-9809-BK	Pegaso CC95.9.E18	Unvi	C36D	1995
0307	C-9810-BK	Pegaso CC95.9.E18	Unvi	C36D	1995
0308	C-3741-BL	Mercedes-Benz O1117	Ferqui	C36C	1995
0309	C-3742-BL	Mercedes-Benz O1117	Ferqui	C36C	1995
0310	S-7109-V	Scania K113	Ayats	BC75D	1990
0314	C-6100-BN	Mercedes-Benz O1117	Ferqui	C36C	1996
0315	C-6101-BN	Mercedes-Benz O1117	Ferqui	C36C	1996
0316	C-6424-BN	Mercedes-Benz O1117	Ferqui	C36C	1996
0317	C-6425-BN	Mercedes-Benz O1117	Ferqui	C36C	1996
0320	C-2523-BT	Mercedes-Benz O1829	Irizar	C55D	1997
0321	C-2524-BT	Mercedes-Benz O1829	Irizar	C55D	1997
0322	C-5538-BT	Setra Seida 412MH	Setra	C55D	1997
0323	C-5539-BT	Setra Seida 412MH	Setra	C55D	1997
0324	C-5748-BT	Setra Seida 412MH	Setra	C55D	1997
0325	C-5749-BT	Setra Seida 412MH	Setra	C55D	1997
0326	C-0297-BU	MAN 10.220	Ferqui	C38C	1997
0327	C-0358-BV	MAN 10.220	Ferqui	C38C	1997
0328	C-0359-BV	MAN 10.220	Ferqui	C38C	1997
0329	C-0360-BV	MAN 10.220	Ferqui	C38C	1997
0330	C-3683-BX	MAN 13.220	Ugarte	C43D	1998
0331	C-3684-BX	MAN 13.220	Ugarte	C43D	1998
0332	C-3685-BX	MAN 13.220	Ugarte	C43D	1998
0333	C-3686-BX	MAN 13.220	Ugarte	C43D	1998
0334	C-7698-BY	MAN 13.220	Ugarte	C43D	1998
0335	C-7699-BY	MAN 13.220	Ugarte	C43D	1998
0336	C-7700-BY	MAN 13.220	Ugarte	C43D	1998
0337	C-7701-BY	MAN 13.220	Ugarte	C43D	1998
0338	C-0336-CB	Scania K94IB	OVI	C47D	1999
0339	C-0337-CB	Scania K94IB	OVI	C47D	1999
0340	C-0338-CB	Scania K94IB	OVI	C47D	1999
0341	C-0339-CB	Scania K94IB	OVI	C47D	1999
0400	C-8493-BZ	Iveco Mago 59.12	Indcar	C27D	1999
0401	C-8494-BZ	Iveco Mago 59.12	Indcar	C27D	1999
0402	C-8495-BZ	Iveco Mago 59.12	Indcar	C27D	1999
0403	C-8496-BZ	Iveco Mago 59.12	Indcar	C27D	1999
0424	C-1285-AB	Setra S215HD	Setra	C55D	1985
0425	C-6884-AC	Setra S215HD	Setra	C56D	1986
0426	C-6885-AC	Setra S215HD	Setra	C56D	1986
0428	C-2204-AD	Pegaso 5031-S1	Unicar	C56D	1986
0429	C-2205-AD	Pegaso 5031-S1	Unicar	C56D	1986
0430	C-7120-AF	Setra S215HU	Setra	BC56D	1987
0431	C-7121-AF	Setra S215HU	Setra	BC56D	1987
0432	C-7122-AF	Setra S215HU	Setra	BC56D	1987
0433	C-0878-AH	Pegaso 5036-S1	Unicar	C56D	1987
0434	C-0228-A	Volvo B10M	Irizar	C56D	1987
0435	C-0229-A	Volvo B10M	Irizar	C56D	1987
0436	C-1675-AJ	DAF SB3000	Obradors	C54D	1988
0437	BI-1336-AU	MAN-Caetano	Caetano	C56D	1988
0439	C-5189-AJ	MAN-Caetano	Caetano	C56D	1988
0440	C-5190-AJ	MAN-Caetano	Caetano	C56D	1988
0441	C-5385-AJ	MAN-Caetano	Caetano	C56D	1988
0442	C-6357-AJ	MAN-Caetano	Caetano	C56D	1988
0443	C-6474-AJ	MAN-Caetano	Caetano	C56D	1988
0444	C-4538-BX	MAN-Caetano	Caetano	C56D	1988
0445	M-9035-IZ	Mercedes-Benz O303/15	Irizar	C56D	1988
0446	M-9036-IZ	Mercedes-Benz O303/15	Irizar	C54D	1988
0447	C-8875-BU	Setra S215HU	Setra	C56D	1988
0448	C-8743-BU	MAN 10.180	Hispano Carrocera	C37D	1989
0449	C-1365-BZ	DAF SB3000	Castrosua	C56D	1989
0450	O-1919-AU	MAN 16.360	Obradors	C55D	1989
0451	C-8874-BU	Setra S215HU	Setra	C56D	1989
0452	C-8352-AP	Setra S215HU	Setra	C56D	1989
0453	C-8986-AP	Setra S215HU	Setra	C56D	1989

Operating with Autocares Mallorca, 48, IB-790-CW is an Iveco EuroRider 391 with Unvi Cidade II bodywork. It is seen in Alcudia. *Colin Martin*

0454	C-9637-AP	Volvo B10M-60	Hispano Carrocera	C56D	1989
0455	C-9638-AP	Volvo B10M-60	Hispano Carrocera	C56D	1989
0456	C-6114-AS	Volvo B10M-60	Hispano Carrocera	C56D	1990
0457	C-4673-AU	DAF SB3000	Sunsundegui	C56D	1990
0458	C-5106-AU	DAF SB3000	Castrosua	C56D	1990
0459	C-5107-AU	DAF SB3000	Castrosua	C56D	1990
0460	C-5108-AU	DAF SB3000	Castrosua	C56D	1990
0462	C-5110-AU	DAF SB3000	Castrosua	C56D	1990
0463	C-9926-CB	DAF FA1000	Noge	C25D	1991
0464	C-9239-BX	MAN 16.360	Irizar	C64D	1991
0465	C-9360-BU	MAN 16.360	Irizar	C56D	1991
0466	C-2037-AX	Pegaso 5226	Beulas	C56D	1991
0467	C-5546-AX	DAF SB3000	Sunsundegui	C56D	1991
0468	C-0913-BC	DAF SB3000	Castrosua	C56D	1992
0469	C-0914-BC	DAF SB3000	Castrosua	C56D	1992
0470	C-0915-BC	DAF SB3000	Castrosua	C56D	1992
0471	C-0916-BC	DAF SB3000	Castrosua	C56D	1992
0472	C-1524-BC	Pegaso 5226	Castrosua	C56D	1992
0473	C-9452-BF	Pegaso 5226	Castrosua	C56D	1993
0474	C-9544-BF	Pegaso 5226	Castrosua	C56D	1993
0475	C-0017-BG	DAF SB3000	Castrosua	C56D	1993
0476	C-3745-BX	Pegaso CC95.9.E18	Indcar	C35D	1994
0477	C-7700-BJ	Mercedes-Benz OH 1627L	Castrosua	C56D	1994
0478	C-1177-BM	MAN 18.310	Irizar	C56D	1995
0479	C-4402-BM	MAN 18.310	Castrosua	C56D	1995
0480	C-3568-BP	MAN 18.310	Irizar	C57D	1996
0481	C-9560-BP	MAN 18.310	Castrosua	C56D	1996
0482	C-9561-BP	MAN 18.310	Castrosua	C56D	1996
0483	C-9562-BP	MAN 18.310	Castrosua	C56D	1996
0484	C-2371-BV	MAN 18.350	Irizar	C56D	1997
0486	C-5304-BX	MAN 18.350	Irizar	C57D	1999
0487	C-5305-BX	MAN 18.350	Irizar	C57D	1999
0488	C-1013-CD	MAN 18.310	Irizar	C56D	1999
0489	C-1014-CD	MAN 18.310	Irizar	C56D	1999
0490	C-1015-CD	MAN 18.310	Irizar	C56D	1999
0491	C-5395-CF	Volvo B12	Irizar Century	C50D	1999
0492	C-5396-CF	Volvo B12	Irizar Century	C50D	1999
0493	C-5397-CF	Volvo B12	Irizar Century	C50D	1999
0494	C-5398-CF	Volvo B12	Irizar Century	C50D	1999
0495	C-5399-CF	Volvo B12	Irizar Century	C50D	1999
0496	C-5400-CF	Volvo B12	Irizar Century	C50D	1999

Since the arrival of new Setra S317 coaches in Holland, this manufacturer is now represented in all Arriva's continental fleets. Seen in Inca bus station is Autocares Mallorca 32, PM-4524-AH, a Setra S215HD. *Colin Martin*

0497	C-5401-CF	Volvo B12	Irizar Century	C50D	1999
0498	C-5402-CF	Volvo B12	Irizar Century	C50D	1999
0499	C-8930-CF	Volvo B12	Irizar Century	C50D	1999
0500	C-8928-CF	Volvo B12	Irizar Century	C50D	1999
0501	C-8929-CF	Volvo B12	Irizar Century	C50D	1999
0502	C-9814-CF	Volvo B12	Irizar Century	C50D	1999
0503	C-9815-CF	Volvo B12	Irizar Century	C50F	1999
0504	C-9816-CF	Volvo B12	Irizar Century	C50F	1999
0505	C-9817-CF	Volvo B12	Irizar Century	C50F	1999
0506	C-0637-CG	Volvo B10M	Irizar InterCentury	C54F	1999
0507	C-0638-CG	Volvo B12	Irizar Century	C50F	1999
0508	C-0639-CG	Volvo B10M	Irizar InterCentury	C54F	1999
0509	C-0640-CG	Volvo B10M	Irizar InterCentury	C54F	1999
0510	C-0641-CG	Volvo B10M	Irizar InterCentury	C54F	1999
0511	C-0642-CG	Volvo B10M	Irizar InterCentury	C54F	1999
0512	C-0643-CG	Volvo B10M	Irizar InterCentury	C54F	1999
0513	C-0644-CG	Volvo B10M	Irizar InterCentury	C54F	1999
0514	C-0645-CG	Volvo B10M	Irizar InterCentury	C54F	1999
0515	C-0646-CG	Volvo B10M	Irizar InterCentury	C54F	1999
0516	C-0647-CG	Volvo B10M	Irizar InterCentury	C54F	1999
0517	C-0648-CG	Volvo B12	Irizar Century	C50F	1999
0518	C-0649-CG	Volvo B12	Irizar Century	C50F	1999
0519	C-0650-CG	Volvo B10M	Irizar InterCentury	C54F	1999
0520	C-0651-CG	Volvo B10M	Irizar InterCentury	C54F	1999
0521	C-0025-CG	Volvo B10M	Irizar InterCentury	C54F	1999
0522	C-0653-CG	Volvo B10M	Irizar InterCentury	C54F	1999
0523	C-0654-CG	Volvo B10M	Irizar InterCentury	C54F	1999
0524	C-0655-CG	Volvo B12	Irizar Century	C50F	1999
0525	C-0656-CG	Volvo B10M	Irizar InterCentury	C54F	1999
0526	C-0657-CG	Volvo B10M	Irizar InterCentury	C54F	1999
0527	C-0658-CG	Volvo B10M	Irizar InterCentury	C54F	1999
0528	C-0659-CG	Volvo B10M	Irizar InterCentury	C54F	1999
0529	C-0660-CG	Volvo B10M	Irizar InterCentury	C54F	1999
0530	C-0661-CG	Volvo B10M	Irizar InterCentury	C54F	1999

0531	4277-BSW	Volvo B12	Irizar Century	C55F	1995
0532	4278-BSW	Volvo B12	Irizar Century	C55F	1996
0533	4276-BSW	Volvo B12	Sunsundegui	C56F	1996
0534	3838-BWJ	Volvo B12	Irizar Century	C55F	1995
0535	3839-BWJ	Volvo B12	Irizar Century	C55F	1996
0536	4016-BWJ	Volvo B12	Irizar Century	C55F	1997
0537	0471-BZN	Scania 420	Irizar Century	C71F	2002
0538	0547-BZN	Scania 420	Irizar Century	C71F	2002
0539	0343-BZN	Scania K114	Irizar Century	C59F	2002
0540	0517-BZN	Scania K114	Irizar Century	C59F	2002
0541	7452-BZN	Scania K114	Irizar Century	C59F	2002
0542	0324-BZN	Scania K114	Irizar Century	C59F	2002
0543	9571-BZN	Scania K114	Irizar Century	C59F	2002
0544	0359-BZN	Scania K114	Irizar Century	C59F	2002
0545	0402-BZN	Scania K114	Irizar Century	C59F	2002

Autocares Mallorca

Camino Vell Mal Pas, Alcudia

Autocares Pujol

1	PM-1070-AB	Pegaso 5036	Beulas Super	C59D	1984
2	PM-0345-AN	Mercedes-Benz OH1628	Obradors Sagaro 3.50	C55D	1987
3	PM-0743-BN	MAN 11.190	Beulas Midi Star	C35D	1992
5	PM-2126-AV	Pegaso 5231	Beulas Stergo	C55D	1988

Palma de Mallorca

19	PM-2033-W	Setra S215H	Setra	C59D	1982
20	PM-1337-AB	Pegaso 5036	Camelsa Yhetero	C59D	1984
23	PM-2261-AF	Pegaso 6100S	Camelsa Yhetero	C55D	1984
25	PM-0091-AJ	Mercedes-Benz 180	Mercedes	M10	1986
32	PM-4524-AH	Setra S215HD	Setra	C55D	1986
33	PM-6726-BD	Pegaso 5231	Hispano Phoenix	C55D	1990
34	PM-9943-BD	Pegaso 5231	Hispano Phoenix	C55D	1990
35	PM-4846-BZ	Iveco 391E	Castrosua	B39D	1995
36	PM-4851-BZ	Iveco 391E	Castrosua	B39D	1995
37	PM-0457-CB	Iveco 391E	Ugarte CX-Elite	C55D	1995
38	PM-1248-CB	Iveco 391E	Ugarte CX-Elite	C55D	1995
39	PM-0304-CH	Iveco 391E	Castrosua	B39D	1996
40	PM-0305-CH	Iveco 391E	Castrosua	B39D	1995

Pictured in Puerto Pollensa, the colours of TIB are shown on Arriva's 73, 2671CHR. This bus is a Iveco EuroRider 397E Unvi Cidade II dating from 2003.
Colin Martin

41	PM-4402-CG	Ford Transit	Ford	C14D	1996
42	PM-1249-CM	Iveco 80E18	Indcar Mago	C30F	1997
43	PM-9734-CM	Iveco 391E	Irizar Century	BC55D	1997
44	PM-9735-CM	Iveco 391E	Irizar Century	BC55D	1997
45	PM-3530-CN	Iveco 391E	Castrosua	B39D	1997
46	PM-3531-CN	Iveco 391E	Castrosua	B39D	1997
47	IB-8194-CV	Iveco 391E	Irizar Century	C55D	1998
48	IB-7901-CW	Iveco 391E	Unvi Cidade II	B26D	1998
51	IB-2184-CZ	Mercedes-Benz O405	Mercedes-Benz	B55D	1998
53	IB-3540-DG	Iveco 391E	Ayats Atlas	C55D	1999
54	IB-0143-BM	Ford Transit	Ford	C14D	1992
55	IB-5156-DG	Iveco Daily 35-10	Iveco	C13D	1999
56	IB-5157-DG	Iveco Daily 35-10	Iveco	C13D	1999
57	IB-5158-DG	Iveco Daily 35-10	Iveco	C13D	1999
58	IB-3046-DN	Iveco 391E	Noge Touring	C27D	2000
60	IB-9413-DN	Iveco 391E	Unvi Cidade II	B44D	2000
61	IB-9414-DN	Iveco 391E	Unvi Cidade II	B44D	2000
62	IB-4796-DP	Iveco 391E	Ugarte Nobus	C36D	2000
63	IB-4737-CY	MAN 1190	Arabus	C35D	1988
64	IB-5685-CY	Iveco 391E	Irizar InterCentury	BC53D	1998
65	IB-5686-CY	Iveco 391E	Irizar InterCentury	BC53D	1998

66-70		Iveco EuroRider 397E.12.35	Irizar InterCentury	BC55D	2002-03
66	8867BWL	**68**	8784BWL	**69**	7280CHJ	**70**	7321CHJ
67	8678BWL						

71-76		Iveco EuroRider 397E	Unvi Cidade II	B44D	2003
71	2543CHR	**73**	2671CHR	**75**	6244CJD	**76**	6293CJD
72	2630CHR	**74**	2717CHR				

Bus Nort Balear, Palma

19 Gremi Fusters, Poligono Son Castello, Palma

44	IB-4854-AT	Scania K112	Irizar 360	C55D	1984
45	IB-8182-AT	Scania K112	Irizar 360	C55D	1984
46	IB-0596-BC	Ford Transit	Ford	M14	1989
49	IB-6800-CG	MAN 8150	Alvilla	C26D	1996
53	IB-2534-AU	MAN 16.290	Unicar 3000 GLS	C55D	1988
54	IB-2535-AS	Setra S215H	Setra	C55D	1988
57	IB-2038-AT	MAN 16.290	Caetano Algarve	C55D	1988
58	IB-2655-AY	MAN 22.360	Camelsa Yumbo	C(79)D	1989
59	IB-2124-DB	MAN 24.420	Obradors ST400	C(75)D	1995
60	IB-8635-BJ	Pegaso 5226	Beulas Stergo	C55D	1991
61	IB-1675-BM	Pegaso 5226	Camelsa	C55D	1991
62	IB-0120-DF	Iveco EuroRider 391E.12.29	OVI Radial	B44D	1999
63	IB-4614-BC	MAN 22.330	Camelsa Yumbo	BC(80)D	1990
65	M-1994-KT	Scania K93CLB	Burillo	B52D	1990
66	IB-2138-DT	MAN 22.360	Camelsa Yumbo	B80D	1989
71	IB-0365-BM	Pegaso 5226	Noge Xaloc II	C55D	1992
72	SE-8048-AY	MAN 16.290	Andecar Sahara	C55D	1989
73	M-3689-OC	Pegaso 5226	Ugarte 3000N	C55D	1993
74	IB-6814-AV	Scania K112	Castrosua Master 35	C55D	1988
75	IB-7717-CL	Ford Transit	Ford	M14	1997
76	IB-9451-DD	MAN 18.310	Sunsundegui Stylo	B55D	1999
78	IB-7573-CN	Iveco EuroRider 391E	Ugarte CX-Elite	C55D	1997
81	9830BWT	Iveco EuroRider 391E.12.35	Irizar InterCentury	C55D	2002
82	LU-1200-H	Mercedes-Benz	Irizar 360	C52D	1984
83	LU-1212-H	Mercedes-Benz	Irizar 360	C52D	1984
84	C-7724-AM	Mercedes-Benz O303	Castrosua Master 35	C54D	1990
85	C-7726-AM	Mercedes-Benz O303	Castrosua Master 35	C54D	1990
86	3283CHJ	Iveco EuroRider 397E.12.35	Irizar InterCentury	C55D	1996
87	3129CHG	Iveco EuroRider 397E.12.35	Irizar InterCentury	C55D	1996
88	3061CHG	Iveco EuroRider 397E.12.35	Irizar InterCentury	C55D	1996
89	3290CHG	Iveco EuroRider 397E.12.35	Irizar InterCentury	C55D	1996

ARRIVA ITALY

SAB Autoservizi srl, Piazza Marconi 4, 24122 Bergamo

6	BGA55461	Iveco Daily F35.12			Iveco		Regional bus	1991

26-38		Iveco 370.97.24			Portesi		Regional bus	1985-89
26	BG744315	30	BG776473	33	BG872091	36	BG922940	
27	BG758737	31	BG776492	34	BG876301	37	BG930888	
28	BG758736	32	BG819302	35	BG922939	38	BG940393	
29	BG776402							

39	BGA52588	Iveco 370.97.S24	Portesi	Regional bus	1991
40	BGA50162	Iveco 370.97.S24	Portesi	Regional bus	1991
41	BG794807	Iveco 315.8.17	Orlandi	Regional bus	1986
42	BGA50161	Iveco 370.97.S24	Portesi	Regional bus	1991
43	BGA48631	Iveco 370.97.S24	Portesi	Regional bus	1991
44	BGA50160	Iveco 370.97.S24	Portesi	Regional bus	1991
45	BGA34200	Iveco 370.97.S24	Portesi	Regional bus	1990
49	BG740961	Iveco 315.8.17	Garbarini	Regional bus	1984
50	BG777875	Iveco 315.8.17	Orlandi	Regional bus	1985

51-75		Mercedes-Benz 0303/10R			Bianchi		Regional bus	1981-87
51	BG626692	61	BGA17224	68	BG710038	72	BG825373	
52	BG626694	62	BGA17234	69	BG711242	73	BG825372	
55	BG627151	63	BGA17226	70	BG711243	74	BG828183	
59	BGA17233	64	BGA17232	71	BGD17574	75	BA759JL	
60	BGA17227	65	BGA17230					

76	AW749PY	Mercedes-Benz 0303/9R	Mercedes	Regional bus	1990
77	BA635JC	Mercedes-Benz 0303/9R	Mercedes	Coach	1991
79	AW288TM	Mercedes-Benz 0303/10R	Mercedes	Coach	1987
80	BGD12750	Mercedes-Benz 0303/10R	Mercedes	Coach	1994

81-84		Mercedes-Benz 0303/10R			Bianchi		Regional bus	1987-90
81	BG918869	82	AW092TN	83	BG918870	84	BGA40904	

85	AH913KM	Iveco 380.10.29 EuroClass	Orlandi	Regional bus	1996
86	AH911KM	Iveco 380.10.29 EuroClass	Orlandi	Regional bus	1996
87	AH915KM	Iveco 380.10.29 EuroClass	Orlandi	Regional bus	1996
88	AH128JK	Iveco 370.97.24	Portesi	Regional bus	1987

89-93		Iveco 370.10.24			Iveco		Regional bus	1986
89	BG787336	91	BG787337	92	BGB64702	93	BGB59004	
90	BG787335							

95	BG762751	Iveco 370.10.24	Portesi	Regional bus	1985
96	BG762752	Iveco 370.10.24	Portesi	Regional bus	1985
97	BG771140	Iveco 370.10.24	Portesi	Regional bus	1985
98	BG766040	Iveco 370.10.24	Iveco	Regional bus	1985
99	BG773987	Iveco 370.10.24	Bianchi	Regional bus	1985
100	BG865704	Iveco 370.10S.24	Portesi	Regional bus	1987
101	BG878119	Iveco 370.10S.24	Bianchi	Regional bus	1987
102	BG888744	Iveco 370.10S.24	Bianchi	Regional bus	1988
103	BG890276	Iveco 370.10S.24	Bianchi	Regional bus	1988

104-107		Iveco 370.10S.24			Iveco		Regional bus	1987-89
104	BG875640	105	BG877365	106	BG893072	107	BG952197	

108-113		Iveco 370.10S.24			Portesi		Regional bus	1989
108	BG952200	110	BG952198	112	BG960676	113	BG960675	
109	BG952199	111	BG953420					

114	AD666TP	Iveco 370.10S.24	Desimon	Regional bus	1990

Since the last edition of the book, further operators in Italy have been acquired by Arriva, all in the north-east of the country, principally in Lombardy. Now some 1700 buses are deployed in the area. While the buses conform to the national colours (orange for city buses and blue for urban buses) the coaches carry private colours. Here we see 80, BGD12750, a Mercedes-Benz O303 coach based in Bergamo. *Bill Potter*

115-120

		Iveco 380.10.29 EuroClass		Orlandi		Regional bus		1995
115	AH401KF	117	AH876KF	119	AH877KF	120	AH875KF
116	AH878KF	118	AH402KF				

121-135

		MAN SG 280		Portesi		City bus		1985-88
121	BG884606	123	BG744316	125	BGB34394	135	BG923925
122	BG814714	124	BGB34395				

138	BGA65439	Setra SG221 UL	Kassbohrer	Regional bus	1991
139	BGA74947	Setra SG221 UL	Kassbohrer	Regional bus	1991
140	BGB18812	Setra SG221 UL	Kassbohrer	Regional bus	1992

142-145

		Setra S 215 UL		Kassbohrer		Regional bus		1991-92
142	BGB51904	143	BGB51903	144	BGB01838	145	BGB01837

155	BG860952	Mercedes-Benz O303/10R	Bianchi	Regional bus	1987
156	BG861737	Mercedes-Benz O303/10R	Bianchi	Regional bus	1987
157	BG861736	Mercedes-Benz O303/10R	Bianchi	Regional bus	1987
159	BS458WY	Cacciamali TCI 970 Sigma 2	Cacciamali	Regional bus	2001
160	BS460WY	Cacciamali TCI 970 Sigma 2	Cacciamali	Regional bus	2001
161	BG886418	Iveco 315.8.17	Iveco	Regional bus	1988
162	BG886413	Iveco 315.8.17	Iveco	Regional bus	1988
163	AH669KM	Iveco 315.8.17	Iveco	Regional bus	1985
164	AN015PP	Iveco 315.8.18	Orlandi	Regional bus	1996
165	AN014PP	Iveco 315.8.18	Orlandi	Regional bus	1996
166	AN013PP	Iveco 315.8.18	Orlandi	Regional bus	1996
167	AW525RA	Iveco 315.8.17	Iveco	Regional bus	1986

168-186

		Cacciamali TCI 970 Sigma 2		Cacciamali		Regional bus		2001-03
168	BS456WY	172	BS790WZ	176	BS777WT	181	BV382VR
169	BS459WY	173	BS791WZ	177	BV355VS	185	BX177BE
170	BS457WY	174	BS895WZ	178	BV356VS	186	CE896TB
171	BS560WT	175	BS896WZ	179	BV357VS		

187	CW712PC	Irisbus EuroRider 397.10.31	10.8m	2004

222-227   Mercedes-Benz O303/15R   Bianchi   Regional bus   1983-85

222	BG942534	224	BG707215	226	BG754859	227	BG754860
223	BG707214	225	BG754858				

228-232   Mercedes-Benz O303/15R   Bianchi   Regional-Coach   1985

228	BG746477	230	BG752672	231	BG775999	232	BG757432
229	BG752671						

258	BG728280	Mercedes-Benz O303/15R	Bianchi	Regional bus	1984
259	BG741064	Mercedes-Benz O303/15R	Bianchi	Regional bus	1984

261-264   Iveco 370.12.S30   Bianchi   Regional bus   1991

261	BGA48629	262	BGA52589	263	BGA48630	264	BGA52590

304-309   Mercedes-Benz O303/15R   Bianchi   Regional bus   1985-91

304	BG781439	306	BG921921	308	BGA55605	309	BGA55606
305	BG781440	307	BGA52587				

310	BGB54150	Setra S215 HRI	Kassbohrer	Regional bus	1992
311	BGB54151	Setra S215 HRI	Kassbohrer	Regional bus	1992

321-329   Iveco 380.12.35 EuroClass   Orlandi   Regional bus   1995-96

321	AH880KF	324	AH882KF	326	AH912KM	328	AH914KM
322	AH403KF	325	AH400KF	327	AH910KM	329	AH909KM
323	AH881KF						

332-346   Iveco 393.12.35 My Way   Irisbus-Orlandi   Regional bus   2000

332	BG305PC	336	BG301PC	340	BG297PC	344	BG293PC
333	BG304PC	337	BG300PC	341	BG296PC	345	BG292PC
334	BG303PC	338	BG299PC	342	BG295PC	346	BG291PC
335	BG302PC	339	BG298PC	343	BG294PC		

347	CP755CX	Mercedes-Benz O405 NU	Mercedes	Regional bus	1992
348	AW278TP	Mercedes-Benz O404	Mercedes	Regional bus	1998
349	AW279TP	Mercedes-Benz O404	Mercedes	Regional bus	1998

350-364   Mercedes-Benz O408   Mercedes   Regional bus   1997

350	AT083SN	353	AT084SN	356	AT080SN	358	AT088SN
351	AT086SN	354	AT087SN	357	AT079SN	364	AT085SN
352	AT081SN	355	AT082SN				

365-387   Mercedes-Benz O405 NU   Mercedes   Regional bus   1998

365	AW205TM	371	AW386TM	377	AW383TM	383	AW396TM
366	AW220TM	372	AW387TM	378	AW395TM	384	AW392TM
367	AW203TM	373	AW388TM	379	AW384TM	385	AW394TM
368	AW206TM	374	AW382TM	380	AW391TM	386	BE193NY
369	AW204TM	375	AW389TM	381	AW393TM	387	BE194NY
370	AW219TM	376	AW390TM	382	AW397TM		

388-398   Mercedes-Benz Citaro O530 NU   Evobus   Regional bus   2001

388	BN683RW	391	BN689RW	394	BN681RW	397	BN690RW
389	BN688RW	392	BP287ZA	395	BN687RW	398	BP288ZA
390	BN677RW	393	BN693RW	396	BN694RW		

400-403   Setra S300 NC   Kassbohrer   City bus   1991-92

400	AT158SM	401	AT159SM	402	AT889SM	403	AT989SM

404	AN974PP	Menarini M 221.1	Menarini	City bus	14/01/1997

405-418   Mercedes-Benz Citaro O530 NU   Evobus   Regional bus   2000-01

405	BN678RW	412	BN691RW	415	BN679RW	417	BM871EW
406	BP289ZA	413	BP292ZA	416	BN686RW	418	BN680RW
407	BN684RW	414	BN682RW				

419-422   Mercedes-Benz O407   Mercedes   Regional bus   1992

419	BZ825WZ	420	BZ826WZ	421	BZ827WZ	422	BZ828WZ

423-429   Mercedes-Benz O407   Mercedes   Regional bus   1992

423	CP756CZ	425	CP757CZ	427	CP754CZ	429	CP496CZ
424	CP752DA	426	CP495CZ	428	CP753CZ		

430-447 — Iveco 393.12.35 My Way — Iveco — Regional bus — 2000

430	BM961EV	435	BM262EW	440	BM259EW	444	BM874EW
431	BM962EV	436	BM263EW	441	BM257EW	445	BM875EW
432	BM963EV	437	BM260EW	442	BM872EW	446	BM876EW
433	BM964EV	438	BM264EW	443	BM873EW	447	BM877EW
434	BM261EW	439	BM258EW					

448-452 — Iveco 393.12.35 My Way — Irisbus-Orlandi — Regional bus — 2000-03

448	BM569EY	450	BM570EY	451	BM568EY	452	CE897TB
449	BM571EY						

453	CH278PD	Setra S300 NC	Kassbohrer	City bus	1992
454	CH633NZ	Setra S300 NC	Kassbohrer	City bus	1992
455	CR546AH	Irisbus Domino 2001 HD	Irisbus Orlandi	Regional bus	2004
456	CR545AH	Irisbus Domino 2001 HD	Irisbus Orlandi	Regional bus	2004
457	CT986EC	Mercedes-Benz Citaro O530 NU	Mercedes-Benz	Regional bus	2005
458	CT987EC	Mercedes-Benz Citaro O530 NU	Mercedes-Benz	Regional bus	2005
459	CT988EC	Mercedes-Benz Integro O550 UL	Mercedes-Benz	Regional bus	2005

462-478 — Mercedes-Benz O303/15R — Bianchi — Coach — 1985-86

462	BG770681	465	BG776713	470	BG782510	474	BG806386
463	BG769199	466	BG777451	472	BG796681	475	BG807955
464	BG776712	467	AH342KN	473	BA800JC	478	BG818432

481-487 — Mercedes-Benz O303/15R — Bianchi — Regional-Coach — 1986-88

481	AH406KF	484	BG498PC	486	BG499PC	487	BG497PC
482	AH405KF						

488	BG907343	Mercedes-Benz O303/15R	Bianchi	Coach	1988
489	BG912768	Mercedes-Benz O303/15R	Bianchi	Coach	1988
490	BGA06869	Iveco 370.12.S30	Bianchi	Coach	1990
491	BGA09074	Iveco 370.12.S30	Bianchi	Coach	1990
492	BGA65274	Iveco 370.12.S30	Bianchi	Coach	1991
493	CB768MJ	Iveco 370.12.S30	Orlandi	Regional bus	1992
494	BGB29553	Iveco 370.12.S30	Orlandi	Coach	1992
495	BGB29554	Iveco 370.12.S30	Orlandi	Coach	1992
496	BGB31233	Iveco 370.12.S30	Orlandi	Coach	1992
497	AH404KF	Mercedes-Benz O303/15RHD	Mercedes	Coach	1992
498	AT356TE	Mercedes-Benz O350 Tourismo	Mercedes	Coach	1997
499	AT537TE	Mercedes-Benz O350 Tourismo	Mercedes	Coach	1997

501-511 — Mercedes-Benz O404 — Mercedes — Coach — 1992-93

501	AW352RV	505	AW145PZ	508	AW488RA	510	BE213NY
503	AW144PZ	506	AW146PZ	509	BE246NZ	511	BF264NR
504	AW786PZ	507	AW888PZ					

512	CD086FF	Mercedes-Benz O350 Tourismo	Mercedes	Coach	2002
513	CD743FE	Mercedes-Benz O350 Tourismo	Mercedes	Coach	2002

514-517 — Irisbus Domino 2001 HD — Irisbus Orlandi — Regional bus — 2004

514	CR045AH	515	CR046AH	516	CR991AH	517	CR992AH

550-555 — Mercedes-Benz O407 — Mercedes — Regional bus — 1994-95 Arriva Danmark, 2005

550	-	552	-	554	-	555	-
551	-	553	-					

556	CT698ZF	Mercedes-Benz Integro O550 UL	Mercedes-Benz	Regional bus	2001

600-603 — Mercedes-Benz Citaro O530NU — Mercedes-Benz — Regional bus — 2001

600	CT412ZF	601	BP695ZY	602	BP541ZY	603	CT104ZF

604-610 — Irisbus Turbocity U491.10.24 — De Simon — Regional bus — On order

604	-	606	-	608	-	610	-
605	-	607	-	609	-			

631-642 — Irisbus Ares N 10.6m — Irisbus — Regional bus — On order

631	-	634	-	637	-	640	-
632	-	635	-	638	-	641	-
633	-	636	-	639	-	642	-

978	BX755BF	Iveco Daily F45.12	Iveco	Regional bus	2001
979	BS105XA	Iveco EuroPolis 9.15	Iveco	City bus	2001

The older articulated buses are expected to be displaced shortly by Mercedes-Benz transferred from the Denmark operation. Pictured at the depot in Bergamo is Citybus 122, BG814714, an MAN SG280 with Portesi bodywork. *Bill Potter*

980	BS224XA	Iveco EuroPolis 9.15	Iveco	City bus	2001
981	AW170TP	Mercedes-Benz Vario O814	Beluga	Coach	1987 ex Zambetti
984	CE543TA	Fiat Ducato L2.8JTD	Fiat	Coach	2003
985	BX274BG	Iveco 65.C15 THESI	Cacciamali	Regional bus	2001
986	BY309EF	Iveco 65.C15 THESI	Cacciamali	Regional bus	2002
987	BX275BG	Iveco 65.C15 THESI	Cacciamali	Regional bus	2001
988	BY308EF	Iveco 65.C15 THESI	Cacciamali	Regional bus	2002
989	AW386TL	Mercedes-Benz O402	Mercedes	City bus	1987
990	AT431TG	Mercedes-Benz O402	Mercedes	City bus	1986
991	AT949TT	Iveco Daily F45.12	Iveco	Regional bus	1997
992	AT948TT	Iveco Daily F45.12	Iveco	Regional bus	1997
993	AT947TT	Iveco Daily F45.12	Iveco	Regional bus	1997
994	AT950TT	Iveco Daily F45.12	Iveco	Regional bus	1997
995	BE248NZ	Iveco Daily F45.12	Iveco	Regional bus	1999
996	BE249NZ	Iveco Daily F45.12	Iveco	Regional bus	1999
997	BY722EG	Fiat Ducato	Fiat	Regional bus	2002
998	AD923TB	Fiat Ducato	Fiat	Regional bus	1995
999	AW385TM	Fiat Ducato	Fiat	Regional bus	1996
1000	AF054JX	Fiat Ducato	Fiat	Regional bus	1996
1001	BG853433	Iveco 370.97.24	Portesi	Regional bus	1987
1004	BG963500	Iveco 370.97.S24	Portesi	Regional bus	1989
1011	BGB28561	Iveco 370.12.S30	Orlandi	Regional bus	1992
1013	BGB28562	Iveco 370.12.S30	Orlandi	Regional bus	1992
1026	BG834773	Mercedes-Benz O303/15R	Menarini	Regional bus	1987
1027	BG834774	Mercedes-Benz O303/15R	Menarini	Regional bus	1987
1041	BG756834	Menarini 110 M	Menarini	Regional bus	1985
1042	BG756835	Menarini 110 M	Menarini	Regional bus	1985
1043	BG774002	Mercedes-Benz O303/10R	Menarini	Regional bus	1985
1045	BG774004	Mercedes-Benz O303/10R	Menarini	Regional bus	1985
1046	BG803871	Menarini 110 M	Menarini	Regional bus	1986
1047	BG803869	Menarini 110 M	Menarini	Regional bus	1986
1049	AH745KN	Menarini 110 M	Menarini	Regional bus	1985
1051	BG883403	Iveco 370.97.S24	Portesi	Regional bus	1988
1053	BG874860	Iveco 370.12.L25	Portesi	Regional bus	1987
1054	BG853434	Iveco 370.12.L25	Portesi	Regional bus	1987
1055	BG874861	Iveco 370.12.L25	Portesi	Regional bus	1987

The SAB operation is based in Bergamo, the centre of Arriva's Italian operation. In the early 1990s several Setra S300NC buses were placed in service, and these can now be found at several of the operations. At Bergamo the depot and bus station are adjacent, and 401, AT159SM, is seen arriving at its terminus. *Bill Potter*

1056	BG874862	Iveco 370.12.L25	Portesi	Regional bus	1987
1057	BG853435	Iveco 370.12.L25	Portesi	Regional bus	1987
1058	BG963501	Iveco 370.97.S24	Portesi	Regional bus	1989
1059	BG860165	Iveco 370.97.24	Portesi	Regional bus	1987
1060	BG853436	Iveco 370.12.L25	Portesi	Regional bus	1907
1061	AI219SM	Iveco 370.12.L25	Portesi	Regional bus	1989
1062	BG969683	Iveco 370.12.L25	Portesi	Regional bus	1989
1063	BG970248	Iveco 370.12.L25	Portesi	Regional bus	1989
1064	BG970249	Iveco 370.12.L25	Portesi	Regional bus	1989
1067	BGA57919	Iveco 370.10S.24	Iveco	Regional bus	1991
1069	BGB11432	Setra SG 221 UL	Kassbohrer	Regional bus	1992

1081-1086		Mercedes-Benz O530GNU	Mercedes-Benz Citaro	Regional bus	2001

1081	BS585XB	**1083**	BS844XB	**1085**	BS988WY	**1086**	BS101WY
1082	BS455WY	**1084**	BS578WY				

1087	BB553TB	BredaMenarini M 321	BredaMenarini	City bus	1999
1106	BG692729	Mercedes-Benz O303/15R	Menarini	Regional bus	1983
1110	BG871072	Iveco 370.12.L25	Iveco	Regional bus	1987
1111	BG922858	Mercedes-Benz O303/10R	Bianchi	Regional bus	1988
1112	BG940225	Mercedes-Benz O303/10R	Menarini	Regional bus	1989
1113	BGA68889	Volvo B10M	Portesi	Regional bus	1991
1114	BGA68890	Volvo B10M	Portesi	Regional bus	1991

1201-1210		Volvo B7LA	Snodato	City/Regional bus	2000-01

1201	CH280PD	**1204**	CH483PD	**1207**	CH096NZ	**1209**	CH636NZ
1202	CH28IPD	**1205**	CH563PD	**1208**	CH140NZ	**1210**	CH636NZ
1203	CH484PD	**1206**	CH139NZ				

1211-1214		Mercedes-Benz O405GN	Mercedes-Benz	AN57D	1994	Arriva Denmark, 2005

1211	-	**1212**	-	**1213**	-	**1214**	-

4005	BE570BF	Iveco 370.10.25	Iveco	Regional bus	1982

SAL

SAL srl, Via della Pergola 2, 23900 Lecco

3002	AN848EV	MAN 11.190	MACCHI	City bus	1996
3005	AN942EW	MAN 11.190	MACCHI	City bus	1997
3013	COD59447	MAN 11.190	MACCHI	City bus	1994
3015	AN438EW	Setra S 300 NC	Setra	City bus	1992
3016	AN439EW	Setra S 300 NC	Setra	City bus	1997
3017	AN440EW	Setra S 300 NC	Setra	City bus	1993
3018	AN441EW	Setra S 300 NC	Setra	City bus	1993
3019	C0838445	Menarini M 201/2 LS	Menarini	City bus	1985
3020	CO838444	Menarini M 201/2 LS	Menarini	City bus	1985
3025	CO833367	Menarini M 201/2 LS	Menarini	City bus	1985
3026	AG533TR	BredaMenarini M 3001.12L	Bredamenarinbus	City bus	1996
3027	AG534TR	BredaMenarini M 3001.12L	Bredamenarinbus	City bus	1996
3029	AN731EW	BredaMenarini M 221	Bredamenarinbus	City bus	1997
3031	AN442EW	Setra S 300 NC	Setra	City bus	1992
3032	C0B03782	Setra S 210 H	Setra	City bus	1990
3033	COD39220	Iveco 370.97.24	Portesi	Regional bus	1985
3034	AN988EW	Setra S 300 NC	Setra	Regional bus	1991
3035	COB83012	BredaMenarini M120/1	Bredamenarinbus	City bus	1992
3036	COA95307	Iveco 370.97.24	Portesi	Regional bus	1990
3040	BB257KC	Inbus I 240	Desimon	Regional bus	1984
3043	COA01929	Iveco 370.97.24	Portesi	Regional bus	1989
3044	CO846144	Iveco 370.97.24	Portesi	Regional bus	1986
3048	COA95306	Mercedes-Benz O303/15R	Bianchi	Regional bus	1990
3052	CO825029	Mercedes-Benz O303/15R	Bianchi	Regional bus	1985
3053	CO846143	Mercedes-Benz O303/15R	Padane	Regional bus	1986
3054	CO951309	Mercedes-Benz O303/15R	Bianchi	Regional bus	1988
3055	CO956066	Mercedes-Benz O303/15R	Bianchi	Regional bus	1988
3056	COA05267	Mercedes-Benz O303/15R	Bianchi	Regional bus	1989
3057	COD59602	Setra S 212 H	Setra	Regional bus	1994
3058	COD61582	Iveco 370.12.L25	Iveco	Regional bus	1990
3059	COD61581	Iveco 370.12.L25	Iveco	Regional bus	1990
3060	BGB60678	Iveco 370.10.24	Desimon	Regional bus	1990
3062	AE270JA	Iveco 370.12.35	Iveco	Regional bus	1989
3063	AN080EZ	Mercedes-Benz O303/15R	Bianchi	Regional bus	1987
3064	AP574VZ	Mercedes-Benz O303/15R	Bianchi	Regional bus	1986
3065	AN939EY	Mercedes-Benz O303/15R	Bianchi	Coach	1986
3072	MI46254Z	Mercedes-Benz O303/15R	Bianchi	Coach	1986
3073	MI46255Z	Mercedes-Benz O303/15R	Bianchi	Regional bus	1986
3074	MI7G7326	Mercedes-Benz O303/15R	Bianchi	Regional bus	1988
3075	MI1N3923	Mercedes-Benz O303/15R	Padane	Regional bus	1989
3077	MI0U7810	Iveco 580.12.24	Iveco	Regional bus	1991
3096	AN570EV	MAN SR 280 F	Bianchi	Regional bus	1986
3098	AN943EW	Mercedes-Benz O303/10R	Menarini	City bus	1987
3105	BB764KB	Mercedes-Benz O303/9R	Mercedes	Regional bus	1986
3106	BB199KC	Mercedes-Benz O303/14R	Mercedes	Regional bus	1999
3109	BE328MY	Iveco Daily F45.12	Iveco	City bus	1999
3114	BF634TD	Mercedes-Benz O408	Mercedes	Regional bus	1997
3115	BF635TD	Mercedes-Benz O408	Mercedes	Regional bus	1997
3116	BF636TD	Mercedes-Benz O408	Mercedes	Regional bus	1997
3117	BF637TD	Mercedes-Benz O408	Mercedes	Regional bus	1997
3118	BF638TD	Mercedes-Benz O408	Mercedes	Regional bus	1997
3119	BF830TD	Iveco Daily F45.12	Iveco	Regional bus	1998
3120	BF829TD	Iveco Daily F45.12	Iveco	Regional bus	2000
3121	BF828TD	Iveco Daily F45.12	Iveco	School bus	2000
3122	BY901MN	Iveco 393.12.35 My Way	Iveco	School bus	2000
3123	BK965MA	Mercedes-Benz O404	Mercedes	School bus	1993
3124	BJ017NR	Iveco 393.12.35 My Way	Iveco	Regional bus	2000
3125	BJ015NR	Iveco 393.12.35 My Way	Iveco	Coach	2000
3126	BJ018NR	Iveco 393.12.35 My Way	Iveco	Regional bus	2000
3127	BJ016NR	Iveco 393.12.35 My Way	Iveco	Regional bus	2000
3128	BJ014NR	Iveco 393.12.35 My Way	Iveco	Regional bus	2000
3129	BJ012NR	Iveco 393.12.35 My Way	Iveco	Regional bus	2000
3130	BJ013NR	Iveco 393.12.35 My Way	Iveco	Regional bus	2000
3131	BP600PP	DeSimon Starline 55.12	Desimon	Regional bus	2001
3132	BP722PP	DeSimon Starline 55.12	Desimon	Regional bus	2001

The SAL operation is based at Lecco, on the southern shore of Lake Como from where the central depot supports many outstations. Illustrating the fleet is regional bus 3096, AN570EV, MAN SR280 with Bianchi bodywork. In the fleet list we show the group fleet number, although in practice the displayed number is 3000 less. *Bill Potter*

3133	BP262PR	Iveco EuroPolis 9.15	Iveco	City bus	2001
3134	BP261PR	Iveco EuroPolis 9.15	Iveco	Regional bus	2001
3135	BP260PR	Iveco EuroPolis 9.15	Iveco	City bus	2001
3136	BP259PR	Iveco EuroPolis 9.15	Iveco	City bus	2001
3137	BP694ZY	Iveco EuroPolis 10.50	Iveco	City bus	2001
3138	BP539ZY	Iveco EuroPolis 10.50	Iveco	Regional bus	2001
3143	BP538ZY	Mercedes-Benz Citaro O530 NU	Mercedes	City bus	2001
3144	BV031SY	Inbus 181	De Simon	City bus	1992
3145	BV004 SZ	Inbus 181	De Simon	Regional bus	1987
3146	BV937SX	Iveco Dayli F45.12	Iveco	City bus	2001
3147	BZ 262 SZ	Mercedes-Benz O350 TURISMO	Mercedes	Coach	2002
3148	CD147SA	DeSimon Starline 55.12	Desimon	School bus	2002
3149	BZ646TB	Cacciamali TCI 970 Sigma 2	Cacciamali	Coach	2002
3150	CL586JJ	Mercedes-Benz O340	Mercedes	Regional bus	2001
3151	CL587JJ	Mercedes-Benz O340	Mercedes	Regional bus	2001
3152	CL478JL	MAN 272 UL 12m	MAN	Regional bus	1993
3153	CL479JL	MAN 272 UL 12m	MAN	Regional bus	1993
3154	CL501JL	MAN 272 UL 12m	MAN	Regional bus	1993
3155	CL502JL	MAN 272 UL 12m	MAN	Regional bus	1995
3156	CL477JL	MAN 313 UL 12m	MAN	Regional bus	1997
3157	CL503JL	MAN 313 UL 10.4m	MAN	Regional bus	1997
3158	CR428PP	Mercedes-Benz O404	Noleggio	Coach	1992
3159	CR005PR	MAN 313 UL 10.4m	MAN	Regional bus	1999
3160	CR670PR	MAN 272 UL 12m	MAN	Regional bus	1994
3161	CR669PR	MAN 272 UL 12m	MAN	Regional bus	1994
3162	CR668PR	MAN 292 UL 12m	MAN	Regional bus	1993
3163	DN085RW	Mercedes-Benz Citaro O530	Mercedes	Regional bus	2001
3164	CR189PA	Mercedes-Benz Citaro O530	Mercedes	Regional bus	2001
3165	CR190PA	Mercedes-Benz Citaro O530	Mercedes	City bus	2001
3166	CR191PA	Mercedes-Benz Citaro O530	Mercedes	City bus	2001
3195	CM982NV	Mercedes-Benz Citaro O530	Mercedes	Regional bus	2001

SIA

Società Italiana Autoservizi Spa, Via Cassala 3/a, 25126 Brescia

16	BS985450	Iveco 370.12.35		Orlandi		Coach		1987
18	AZ 513NG	Iveco 370.12.35		Orlandi		Coach		1987
19	BSA23490	Iveco 370.12.35		Orlandi		Coach		1987

20-25 Iveco 370.12.30 — Dallavia — Coach — 1987-88

20	BSA21499	**22**	BSA41550	**24**	BSA83566	**25**	BSA83567
21	BSA41552	**23**	BSA41551				

26	BSB64403	BredaMenarini 5001.12SL	Bredabus	Regional bus	1990
28	BSD42532	Iveco 370.12.S30	Dallavia	Coach	1991
29	BSB69700	Iveco 370.12.30	Bianchi	Regional bus	1990
32	BSE05236	Iveco 370.12.S30	Orlandi	Coach	1992
33	BSE05235	Iveco 370.12.S30	Orlandi	Coach	1992
34	BSE72407	Iveco 315.8.18	Orlandi	Coach	1993
35	BSF08559	Iveco 370.12.S30	Dallavia	Coach	1994
36	AF 080XT	Iveco 370.12.SE35	Dallavia	Coach	1996
37	AF 330XW	Iveco 370.12.SE35	Dallavia	Coach	1996
38	AZ 085MC	Iveco 380.12.38 EuroClass HD	Orlandi	Coach	1998
39	AZ 423MC	Mercedes-Benz O404/15R HD	Mercedes-Benz	Coach	1998
40	AZ 431MC	Mercedes-Benz O404/15R HD	Mercedes-Benz	Coach	1998
41	BE 792ZJ	Iveco 380.12.38 EuroClass HD	Orlandi	Coach	1999
42	BT062GC	Iveco 391.12.35 EuroRider	Orlandi	Coach	2001
43	BSB41099	Mercedes-Benz O303/15R	Bianchi	Regional bus	1989
44	BSB73813	Mercedes-Benz O303/15R	Bianchi	Regional bus	1990
45	CD209BW	Mercedes-Benz O350	Mercedes-Benz Tourismo	Coach	2002
46	CD124BW	Mercedes-Benz O350	Mercedes-Benz Tourismo	Coach	2002
47	CD125BW	Mercedes-Benz O350	Mercedes-Benz Tourismo	Coach	2002
50	BS873474	Inbus I 330	Inbus	Regional bus	1984
55	BS937361	Inbus I 330	Inbus	Regional bus	1986
56	BS937360	Inbus I 330	Inbus	Regional bus	1986

63-66 Iveco 370.12.S30 — Iveco — Regional bus — 1987-89

63	BSA28909	**64**	BSA70782	**65**	BSA70783	**66**	BSB29140

74-79 BredaMenarini M 5001.12SL — Bredabus — Regional bus — 1990-95

74	BSD15607	**76**	BSD24107	**78**	BSD24110	**79**	AF 386XJ
75	BSD24109	**77**	BSD24108				

84-87 Iveco 370.12.SE35 12m — Orlandi — Regional bus — 1998

84	AZ 264MD	**85**	AZ 888MC	**86**	AZ 783MD	**87**	AZ 784MD

91-94 BredaMenarini M 3001.12L — Bredabus — City bus — 1989

91	BSB55791	**92**	BSB55781	**93**	BSB55771	**94**	BSB55779

95	BSB90063	BredaMenarini M 2001.10L	Bredabus	City bus	18/05/1990

102-115 Inbus AID 280 FT 17.5m — Inbus — Regional bus — 1985

102	BS897393	**105**	BS897395	**111**	BS899160	**114**	BS899157
103	BS897394	**106**	BS897396	**112**	BS899159	**115**	BS899156
104	BS899162	**110**	BS899161	**113**	BS899158		

116	BSE19611	Inbus AID 280 FT	Inbus	Regional bus	1992
117	BSE62370	MAN SG 292	Inbus	Regional bus	1993
118	AF 079XT	Inbus AID 280 FT	Inbus	Regional bus	1985
119	AF 078XT	Inbus AID 280 FT	Inbus	Regional bus	1985
121	AP 164NW	Inbus AID 280 FT	Inbus	Regional bus	1991

122-126 Mercedes-Benz O530 GNU 18m — Mercedes-Benz Citaro — Regional bus — 2001

122	BV 951 DY	**124**	BV 579 DW	**125**	BV 580 DW	**126**	BV 585 DW
123	BV 581 DW						

127	CP730TT	Mercedes-Benz O530 GNU 18m	Mercedes-Benz Citaro	Regional bus	1998
128	CN584HF	Mercedes-Benz O530 GNU 18m	Mercedes-Benz Citaro	Regional bus	1998
129	CN334HF	Mercedes-Benz O530 GNU 18m	Mercedes-Benz Citaro	Regional bus	1998

149-162
Iveco 315.8.17 7.5m | Iveco | Regional bus | 1983-87

149	AZ 177NG	153	BS917310	157	BS951858	160	BSA32181
150	BS814619	154	BS925626	158	BSA28908	161	BSB29110
151	BS814618	155	BS925628	159	BSA28907	162	BSB29130
152	BS912625	156	BS944758				

163-167
Iveco 315.8.18 7.6m | Orlandi | Regional bus | 1993

163	BSE62369	165	BSE62367	166	BSE62366	167	BSE62365
164	BSE62368						

168-172
Iveco 315.8.S18 7.6m | Orlandi | Regional bus | 1996-98

168	AF870XR	170	AF869XR	171	AZ350NF	172	AZ351NF
169	AF868XR						

250-290
Mercedes-Benz O408 | Mercedes-Benz | Regional bus | 1996-97

250	AF436XX	261	AF440XX	272	AP634NW	282	AP636NW
251	AF701XX	262	AF441XX	273	AP481NW	283	AP632NW
252	AF437XX	263	AF787XX	274	AP490NW	284	AP635NW
253	AF710XX	265	AF705XX	275	AP683NW	285	AP489NW
254	AF708XX	266	AF709XX	276	AP491NW	286	AP488NW
256	AF707XX	267	AP487NW	277	AP492NW	287	AP486NW
257	AF702XX	268	AP482NW	278	AP493NW	288	AP631NW
258	AF703XX	269	AP495NW	279	AP494NW	289	AP633NW
259	AF704XX	270	AP485NW	280	AP483NW	290	AP682NW
260	AF439XX	271	AP496NW	281	AP484NW		

291-295
Mercedes-Benz O405 NU | Mercedes-Benz | Regional bus | 1998

291	BH071WK	293	BH073WK	294	BH074WK	295	BH075WK
292	BH072WK						

296-322
Mercedes-Benz O530 NU | Mercedes-Benz Citaro | Regional bus | 2001

296	BT242GD	303	BT108GD	310	BT 763 GD	317	BV 403 DV
297	BT100GD	304	BT109GD	311	BT 107 GD	318	BV 582 DW
298	BT101GD	305	BT110GD	312	BT 244 GD	319	BV 402 DV
299	BT102GD	306	BT112GD	313	BT 764 GD	320	BV 583 DW
300	BT103GD	307	BT111GD	314	BT 761 GD	321	BV 401 DV
301	BT104GD	308	BT106GD	315	BT 243 GD	322	BV 584 DW
302	BT105GD	309	BV 404 DV	316	BT 762 GD		

350-362
Mercedes-Benz O345 | Mercedes-Benz Conecto | Regional bus | 2003-04

350	CL043AY	354	CL982AY	357	CL190AY	360	CL979AY
351	CL042AY	355	CL983AY	358	CL191AY	361	CL985AY
352	CL980AY	356	CL981AY	359	CL984AY	362	CL099AY
353	CL189AY						

405-414
Iveco 370.10.25 | Iveco | Regional bus | 1984-85

405	BS854525	408	BS854524	411	BS917311	413	BS917313
406	BS854522	409	BS878689	412	BS917312	414	BS925627
407	BS854520	410	BS912624				

Both SIA and SAIA operations are located in the Lombardy city of Brescia, each with its own services. Pictured outside one of the large garages on the Cassaia site Is 306, **BT112GD**, a Mercedes-Benz Citaro O530NU Regional bus.
Bill Potter

189

415	BS912626	Iveco 370.10.24	Dallavia	Regional bus	1985
416	BS912627	Iveco 370.10.24	Dallavia	Regional bus	1985
417	BS937362	Iveco 370.10.24	Dallavia	Regional bus	1986
418	BS981593	Iveco 370.97.24	Portesi	Regional bus	1987
419	BSA18358	Iveco 370.97.24	Portesi	Regional bus	1987
420	BSA32610	Iveco 370.97.S24	Portesi	Regional bus	1987

421-426 Iveco 370.10.S24 Iveco Regional bus 1989

421	BSA32612	**423**	BSA64151	**425**	BSB29120	**426**	BSB29080
422	BSA32611	**424**	BSA65280				

427-431 Iveco 370.97.S24 Portesi Regional bus 1990-91

427	BSD12666	**429**	BSD33608	**430**	BSD33604	**431**	BSD24106
428	BSD33607						

432	BSD39302	Iveco 370.10.S24	Iveco	Regional bus	1991
433	BSE53607	Iveco 370.97.24	Portesi	Regional bus	1987
434	BSE53610	Iveco 370.97.24	Portesi	Regional bus	1987
435	BSE53609	Iveco 370.97.24	Portesi	Regional bus	1987
436	BSE53606	Iveco 370.10.24	Iveco	Regional bus	1986
437	BSE53605	Iveco 370.10.24	Iveco	Regional bus	1986
438	AD 459WC	Iveco 370.97.S24	Portesi	Regional bus	1995
439	AD 458WC	Iveco 370.97.S24	Portesi	Regional bus	1995
501	BS925664	Iveco 370.12.L25	Portesi	Regional bus	1985
502	BSB36607	Mercedes-Benz O303/15R	Padane	Regional bus	1989
503	MI4S3982	Volvo B10M	Portesi	Regional bus	1995
504	BSE88082	Iveco 370.12.L25	Portesi	Regional bus	1993
505	BSE97138	Iveco 370.12.L25	Portesi	Regional bus	1993
506	AF649XH	Iveco 370.12.SE35	Orlandi	Regional bus	1994
507	AD126VP	Iveco 370.12.SE35	Orlandi	Regional bus	1995
508	AF784XJ	Iveco 370.12.SE35	Orlandi	Regional bus	1995
509	AP382NT	Mercedes-Benz O408	Mercedes-Benz	Regional bus	1997
510	AZ605ND	Mercedes-Benz O408	Mercedes-Benz	Regional bus	1998
511	AZ736NF	Mercedes-Benz O405 N2	Mercedes-Benz	City bus	1998
512	BE684ZJ	Iveco EuroRider 391.12.29	Orlandi	Regional bus	1999
513	BR642FF	Iveco EuroRider 391.12.29	Orlandi	Regional bus	2000
514	BR112FG	Iveco EuroRider 391.12.29	Orlandi	Regional bus	2000
642	BSD39306	Iveco 370.12.L25	Iveco	Regional bus	1991
643	BSD39402	Iveco 370.12.L25	Iveco	Regional bus	1991
644	BSD39303	Iveco 370.12.L25	Iveco	Regional bus	1991
645	BSD39308	Iveco 370.12.L25	Iveco	Regional bus	1991

646-658 Iveco 370.12.SE35 Iveco Regional bus 1995

646	AF 402XJ	**650**	AF 405XJ	**653**	AF 395XJ	**656**	AF 392XJ
647	AF 404XJ	**651**	AF 396XJ	**654**	AF 393XJ	**657**	AF 401XJ
648	AF 417XL	**652**	AF 406XJ	**655**	AF 403XJ	**658**	AF 391XJ
649	AF 394XJ						

659-690 Iveco 393.12.35 Iveco My Way Regional bus 2000

659	BM 314 FV	**676**	BM 417 FV	**681**	BM 689 FV	**686**	BM 692 FV
666	BM 685 FV	**677**	BM 418 FV	**682**	BM 690 FV	**687**	BM 555 FF
667	BM 321 FV	**678**	BM 687 FV	**683**	BM 420 FV	**688**	BM 554 FF
668	BM 686 FV	**679**	BM 419 FV	**684**	BM 691 FV	**689**	BM 553 FF
674	BM 416 FV	**680**	BM 688 FV	**685**	BM 326 FV	**690**	BM 552 FF
675	BM 325 FV						

802-810 Setra S300 NC Setra City bus 1992-94

802	AP 002NZ	**805**	AP 005NZ	**807**	AP 007NZ	**809**	AP 009NZ
803	AP 003NZ	**806**	AP 006NZ	**808**	AP 008NZ	**810**	AP 010NZ
804	AP 004NZ						

811-831 Mercedes-Benz O405N Mercedes-Benz City bus 1998-99

811	AZ 933NE	**817**	AZ 112NF	**822**	AZ 935NE	**827**	AZ 119NF
812	AZ 932NE	**818**	AZ 114NF	**823**	AZ 934NE	**828**	AZ 937NE
813	AZ 108NF	**819**	AZ 115NF	**824**	AZ 938NE	**829**	AZ 107NF
814	AZ 110NF	**820**	AZ 936NE	**825**	AZ 117NF	**830**	BE 794ZJ
815	AZ 109NF	**821**	AZ 116NF	**826**	AZ 118NF	**831**	BE 793ZJ
816	AZ 113NF						

832	CN335HF	Mercedes-Benz O530 NU 12m	Mercedes-Benz Citaro	Regional bus	1997

SAIA

SAIA Trasporti, Via Foro Boario 4/b, 25124 Brescia.

Additonal depots are located at Palazzolo sull'Oglio, Orzinuovi, Fiesse, Pralboino and Desenzano del Garda.

1	BSB72612	Menarini M101/1 12m	Menarini	Coach	1990
3	BS E64899	Iveco 370S 12.30	Domino	Coach	1996
9	AZ 528 NF	Renault FRI GTX	Renault	Coach	1993
11	AF 737 XL	Scania	Ikarus	Coach	1996
12	BS 792546	Iveco 370.12.25	Iveco	Regional bus	1982
13	AF 946 XR	Iveco 370E.12.35	DallaVia Palladio	Coach	1996
14	BS 793292	Iveco 370.12.25	Iveco	Regional bus	1982
15	AP 032 NY	Iveco 370E.12.35	Iveco	Coach	1997
17	AN 528 JX	Iveco 380.12.38.	Irisbus-Orlandi	Coach	1997
19	AP 139 NW	Renault Iliade GTX	Renault	Coach	1997
21	AP 209 NZ	Renault Iliade GTX	Renault	Coach	1998
23	AP 289 NZ	Iveco 380.12.38	Irisbus-Orlandi	Coach	1998
25	BR 459 ZT	Renault Iliade GTX	Renault	Coach	2001
26	BS 794053	Iveco 370.12.25	Iveco	Regional bus	1982
27	BS A42593	Iveco 49	Cacciamali	Coach	1988
28	BS 794048	Iveco 370.12.25	Iveco	Regional bus	1982
29	BS D23781	Iveco 70	Cacciamali	Coach	1990
30	BS B97299	Iveco 370.12.25	Iveco	Regional bus	1982
31	BS B97340	Irisbus 389E.12.43	Iveco	Coach	2003
32	BS B97296	Iveco.370.12.25	Iveco	Regional bus	1982
34	AZ 845 MC	Iveco.370.12.25	Inbus	Regional bus	1982
40	BS 902692	Iveco 370.12.30	Iveco	Regional bus	1984
42	BS 873470	Iveco 370.12.35	Iveco	Regional bus	1984
44	VR 674897	Iveco 370.12.25	Portesi	Regional bus	1984
46	BS 914719	Iveco 370.12.30	Padane	Regional bus	1985
48	AF 429 XP	Iveco.370.12.L.25	Iveco	Regional bus	1985
50	BS 920315	Iveco.370.12.L.25	Iveco	Regional bus	1985
52	BS 920316	Iveco.370.12.L.25	Iveco	Regional bus	1985
54	BS 897398	Inbus AID 280.FT	Inbus	Regional bus	1985
56	BS 897392	Inbus AID 280.FT	Inbus	Regional bus	1985
58	BS 887824	Iveco 370.12.35	Iveco	Regional bus	1983
60	BS 897397	Inbus AID 280.FT	Inbus	Regional bus	1985
62	BS 897399	Inbus AID 280.FT	Inbus	Regional bus	1985
64	BS 943084	Iveco 370.12.30	Iveco	Regional bus	1986
66	AZ 733 ND	Mercedes-Benz O402	Mercedes-Benz	Regional bus	1986
68	AZ 734 ND	Mercedes-Benz O402	Mercedes-Benz	Regional bus	1986
70	BS 932802	Iveco 370.12.25L	Portesi	Regional bus	1986
72	BS 974553	Iveco 370.12.L.25	Iveco	Regional bus	1986
74	AF 872 XN	Iveco 370.12.L.25	Iveco	Regional bus	1986
76	VR 732641	Iveco 370.12.L25	Iveco	Regional bus	1986
78	BV 263 DZ	Menarini 370.12.30	Breda Menarini	Regional bus	1987
80	BS A31136	Menarini 370.12.30	Breda Menarini	Regional bus	1987
82	BS A20189	Iveco 370.12.30	Portesi	Regional bus	1987
84	BG 301 NT	Inbus I.210	Inbus	Regional bus	1987
86	BS A11037	Iveco 370.12.L.25	Iveco	Regional bus	1987
88	BS A18977	Iveco 671.12.24	Iveco	Regional bus	1987
90	BS A18978	Iveco 671.12.24	Iveco	Regional bus	1987
92	BS A28911	Imbus I.330.30	Inbus	Regional bus	1987
96	VR 798892	Iveco 370.12.30S	Iveco	Regional bus	1987
98	BS A28910	Inbus I.330.30	Inbus	Regional bus	1987
100	BS A77137	Renault FRI R50	Renault	Regional bus	1988
102	BS A80969	Setra 215 UL	Setra	Regional bus	1988
104	AN 220 JY	Iveco 370.12.35	Orlandi	Regional bus	1988
106	BS A88951	Iveco 370.12.L25	Iveco	Regional bus	1988
108	BS A88952	Iveco 370.12.L25	Iveco	Regional bus	1988
110	BS B31560	Iveco 315.8.17	Iveco	Regional bus	1989
112	BS B46884	Mercedes-Benz O303	Padane	Regional bus	1989
114	BS B03701	Mercedes-Benz O303	Bianchi	Regional bus	1989
116	BS B40368	Inbus I.330.30	Inbus	Regional bus	1989
118	BS B94283	Bredabus 5001.12sl	Breda Menarini	Regional bus	1990
120	BS B40369	Inbus I.330.30	Inbus	Regional bus	1989
122	VR 864004	Iveco 370.12.30S	Iveco	Regional bus	1989

Mercedes-Benz Conecto O345 292, CL560AY, was heading for Roccafranca when is pictured leaving Brescia bus station. Brescia lies some 70km to the east of Milan with Roccafranca midway between. *Bill Potter*

124	BS D23647	Inbus AID 280 FT	Inbus	Regional bus	1990
126	BS D05104	Iveco 370.12.L.25	Iveco	Regional bus	1990
128	AP 354 NZ	Mercedes-Benz O405N	Mercedes-Benz	Regional bus	1991
130	MI 7T2510	Mercedes-Benz O303	Bianchi	Regional bus	1991
132	AF 503 XX	Iveco 370.12.30.	Orlandi	Regional bus	1991
134	BS D65556	Iveco 370.12.L.25	Iveco	Regional bus	1991
136	VR 955482	Inbus I 330	Inbus	Regional bus	1991
138	AP 163 NW	Inbus AID. 280.FT	Inbus	Regional bus	1991
140	BS D98773	Setra 215 UL	Setra	Regional bus	1992
142	BS D99326	Volvo B10M-60	Barbi	Regional bus	1992
144	BS D99327	Volvo B10M-60	Barbi	Regional bus	1992
146	BH 433WC	Iveco GTS	Irisbus-Orlandi Domino	Regional bus	1992
148	AP 001NZ	Setra S330 NC	Setra	Regional bus	1992
150	AP 425NW	MAN NG272	MAN	Regional bus	1993
152	BC 217VM	Iveco GTS	Irisbus-Orlandi Domino	Regional bus	1993
154	BF 021VJ	MAN NG272	MAN	Regional bus	1993
156	AF 284XK	Volvo B10B	Barbi	Regional bus	1995

158-178		Mercedes-Benz 0408	Mercedes-Benz	Regional bus	1996-97
158	AF 957XX	**164**	AF 706XX	**170**	AP 033NX	**176**	AP 036NX
160	AF 958XX	**166**	AF 438XX	**172**	AP 034NX	**178**	AP 037NX
162	AF 959XX	**168**	AP 032NX	**174**	AP 035NX

180	AZ 944NF	Mercedes-Benz O405 NU	Mercedes-Benz	Regional bus	1998
182	AZ 710NF	Mercedes-Benz O405 NU	Mercedes-Benz	Regional bus	1998
184	AZ 927NF	Mercedes-Benz O405 NU	Mercedes-Benz	Regional bus	1998
186	BS B93695	Iveco 370.12.25	Iveco	Regional bus	1982
188	BS B93698	Iveco 370.12.25	Iveco	Regional bus	1982
190	AY 420CV	De Simon UL Scania	Desimon	Regional bus	1998
192	BA 087SM	Iveco 391E.12.35/M	Padane	Regional bus	1999
194	BE 218DN	Mauri 18EP30-1	Mauri	Regional bus	1999
196	BN 300SX	Mercedes-Benz Integro O550	Mercedes-Benz	Regional bus	2000
198	BN 518SX	Mercedes-Benz Integro O550	Mercedes-Benz	Regional bus	2000
200	BN 695SX	Mercedes-Benz Integro O550	Mercedes-Benz	Regional bus	2000

202	BN 694SX		Ayats Bravo I	Ayats	Regional bus	2000
204	BR 094FE		Ayats Bravo I	Ayats	Regional bus	2000
206	BR 096FE		Mercedes-Benz Integro O550	Mercedes-Benz	Regional bus	2000
208	BR 095FE		Mercedes-Benz Integro O550	Mercedes-Benz	Regional bus	2000

210-236   Irisbus 393.12.35 My Way   Irisbus-Orlandi   Regional bus   2000

210	BR 928FE	**218**	BM 324FV	**226**	BM 320FV	**232**	BM 315FV
212	BR 964FE	**220**	BM 316FV	**228**	BM 323FV	**234**	BM 415FV
214	BR 772FE	**222**	BM 317FV	**230**	BM 313FV	**236**	BM 318FV
216	BM 322FV	**224**	BM 319FV				

238	BP 180BG	MAN NL263 F	Autodromo	Regional bus	2000
240	BP 177BG	MAN NL263 F	Autodromo	Regional bus	2000

242-254   Mercedes-Benz Citaro O530 NU   Mercedes-Benz   Regional bus   2001

242	BT 351GC	**246**	BT 348GC	**250**	BT 537GC	**254**	BT 204GD
244	BT 350GC	**248**	BT 349GC	**252**	BT 538GC		

256	BT203GD	Ayats Bravo I	Ayats	Regional bus	2000
258	BT941GD	Mercedes-Benz Citaro O530 NU	Mercedes-Benz	Regional bus	2001
260	BT940GD	Mercedes-Benz Citaro O530 NU	Mercedes-Benz	Regional bus	2001
262	BV410DV	Mercedes-Benz Citaro O530 NU	Mercedes-Benz	Regional bus	2001
264	AF359XE	Volvo B10M-60	Barbi	Regional bus	1985
266	BV873DZ	Irisbus Agora Moovy	Irisbus	Regional bus	2001
268	BV874DZ	Irisbus Agora Moovy	Irisbus	Regional bus	2001
270	BZ174XN	Setra S215 UL	Setra	Regional bus	1991
272	BZ169XN	MAN SU 313	MAN	Regional bus	2002
274	BZ170XN	MAN SU 313	MAN	Regional bus	2002
276	CF122JN	Irisbus 399E My Way	Irisbus Orlandi	Regional bus	2003
278	CJ391BX	Iveco 380.12.35	Orlandi	Regional bus	1995
280	CJ309BY	MAN SG292 18m	MAN	Regional bus	1993

282-300   Mercedes-Benz Conecto O345   Mercedes-Benz   Regional bus   2001

282	CL542AX	**288**	CL544AX	**294**	CL052AY	**298**	CM023EW
284	CL543AX	**290**	CL220AX	**296**	CL5624Y	**300**	CL561AY
286	CL541AX	**292**	CL560AY				

SAF

Società Autoservizi FVG SpA, Via Baldasseria Bassa 75, 33100 Udine, Italy

43	UD495990	Fiat 370.12.30 12m	Fiat	Regional	B55D	1985
44	UD496000	Fiat 370.12.30 12m	Fiat	Regional	B55D	1985
46	UD510965	Fiat 370.12.30 12m	Fiat	Regional	BC51D	1985
47	UD517390	Iveco 370.12.30 12m	Iveco	Regional	B55D	1986
52	UD662611	Iveco 370.12.25 12m	Iveco	Regional	B55D	1991
53	UD684276	Iveco 370.12.25 12m	Iveco	Regional	B55D	1991
54	UD684277	Iveco 370.12.25 12m	Iveco	Regional	B55D	1991
55	UD684278	Iveco 370.12.25 12m	Iveco	Regional	B55D	1991
56	UD744862	Iveco 370.12.30 12m	Iveco	Regional	B55D	1993
68	AG170CR	Iveco 380.12.35 12m	Iveco	Regional	B55D	1996
100	UD546469	Iveco 370.12.25 12m	Iveco	Regional	B55D	1987
101	AM920SR	Scania L94IB	Irizar InterCentury 12m	Regional	B55D	1997
104	BD181LG	Scania L94IB	Irizar InterCentury 12m	Regional	B55D	1999
106	GO178180	Mercedes-Benz O303 15R	Mercedes-Benz	Regional	B53D	1988
109	BD439LG	Scania L94IB	Irizar InterCentury 12m	Regional	B55D	1999
110	BV193MF	Mercedes-Benz O350 12m	Mercedes-Benz	Coach	C51F	2001
112	BV651MF	Mercedes-Benz O350 12m	Mercedes-Benz	Coach	C51F	2001
113	GO188450	Iveco 370.12.30 12m		Regional	B55D	1989
118	BV238MF	Mercedes-Benz O350 12m	Mercedes-Benz	Coach	C51F	2001
119	BV194MF	Mercedes-Benz O580 12m	Mercedes-Benz	Coach	C51F	2001
120	BV195MF	Mercedes-Benz O580 12m	Mercedes-Benz	Coach	C51F	2001
122	GO178310	Mercedes-Benz O303 12m	Mercedes-Benz	Regional	BC53D	1988
123	BV196MF	Mercedes-Benz O580 12m	Mercedes-Benz	Coach	B51D	2001
125	CD750SA	Fiat 343	11m	Schoolbus	B55F	1974
129	BW000WE	Neoplan N4426/3	Piani 12m	Regional	B86D	2001
134	AM880SS	De Simon IL3 260 Scania	12m	Regional	53+28+1	1997

135	AM870SS	De Simon IL3 260 Scania	12m		Regional	B53D	1997
136	AM879SS	De Simon IL3 260 Scania	12m		Regional	B53D	1997
137	BV289MG	Neoplan N4426/3	Piani 12m		Regional	B86D	2001
138	GO177720	Mercedes-Benz O303 15R 12m	Mercedes-Benz		Regional	B53D	1988
139	BV423MG	Neoplan N4426/3	Piani 12m		Regional	B86D	2001
140	GO164820	Mercedes-Benz O303 15R 12m	Mercedes-Benz		Regional	B55D	1986
141	GO171600	Mercedes-Benz O303 15R 12m	Mercedes-Benz		Regional	C55D	1987
142	GO171610	Mercedes-Benz O303 15R 12m	Mercedes-Benz		Regional	C55D	1987
143	GO164810	Mercedes-Benz O303 15R 12m	Mercedes-Benz		Regional	B55D	1986
144	BV497MG	Neoplan N4426/3	Piani 12m		Regional	B86D	2001
145	BV740MG	Neoplan N4426/3	Piani 12m		Regional	B86D	2001
146	GO232620	Volvo B10B	12m		Regional	B55D	1994
148	BJ715RC	Fiat 315.8.17	7.48m		Regional	BC30	1987
152	AG170CY	Iveco 370E.12.35 H	12m		Coach	BC55D	1996
163	PN219006	INBUS I.330.35	12m		Regional	B55D	1985
164	PN219007	INBUS I.330.35	12m		Regional	B55D	1985
165	PN219008	INBUS I.330.35	12m		Regional	B55D	1985
166	PN257385	Fiat 315.8.17T	7.56m		Regional	BC28D	1988

167-170

		Starbus LL30 12m		Regional bus		Regional	B55D	1988
167	PN257386	**169**	PN257728	**170**	PN257729	**171**	PN290200
168	PN257387						

174	AG150CR	Iveco 380.12.35	Iveco		Regional	B55D	1996
175	AG160CR	Iveco 380.12.35	Iveco		Regional	B55D	1996
176	AG180CR	Iveco 380.12.35	Iveco		Regional	B55D	1996
177	AG510CS	Iveco 370E.12.35	Iveco		Regional	B55D	1996
178	AG520CS	Iveco 370E.12.35	Iveco		Regional	B55D	1996
182	UD584970	Fiat 370.12.25	Fiat		Regional	B55D	1988
186	UD625580	Fiat 370.12.25	Fiat		Regional	B55D	1989
189	UD663432	Iveco 370.12.30	Iveco		Regional	B55D	1991
194	UD684510	Fiat 315.8.17	Fiat		Regional	BC28F	1991
198	UD739074	Iveco 680.18.29 Automat	17.81m		Regional	B73D	1993
213	UD675340	Mercedes-Benz O303/15R	12m		Coach	BC51F	1986
214	UD729328	Mercedes-Benz O303/9R	8.69		Regional	BC37F	1987
215	UD567020	Mercedes-Benz O303/15R	12m		Regional	B53D	1988
216	UD567030	Mercedes-Benz O303/15R	12m		Regional	B53D	1988
217	UD567040	Mercedes-Benz O303/15R	12m		Regional	B53D	1988
218	UD574070	Mercedes-Benz O303/15R	12m		Regional	B53D	1988
219	UD574060	Mercedes-Benz O303/15R	12m		Regional	B53D	1988
220	UD574050	Mercedes-Benz O303/15R	12m		Regional	B53D	1988
221	UD590656	Mercedes-Benz O303/15R	12m		Regional	B53D	1988
222	UD590653	Mercedes-Benz O303/15R	12m		Regional	B53D	198
224	UD586090	Mercedes-Benz O303/13R	10.55m		Regional	B47D	1988

225-255

		Mercedes-Benz O303/15R	12m		Regional	B53D	1988-90
225	UD590654	**234**	UD618930	**243**	UD607005	**250**	UD656413
226	UD590655	**235**	UD620370	**244**	UD607004	**251**	UD641020
227	UD565741	**236**	UD616563	**245**	UD655850	**252**	UD641030
228	UD565742	**237**	UD616564	**246**	UD639700	**253**	UD641740
229	UD572803	**240**	UD607006	**247**	UD639734	**254**	UD641040
230	UD620350	**241**	UD607007	**248**	UD640292	**255**	UD642450
233	UD618920	**242**	UD607008	**249**	UD644180		

256	UD675385	Mercedes-Benz O303/15R	12m		Coach	B51F	1991
257	UD682828	Mercedes-Benz O303/10R	9.28m		Regional	B39D	1991
258	UD682829	Mercedes-Benz O303/10R	9.23m		Regional	B39D	1991
259	UD683358	Mercedes-Benz O303/13R	10.55m		Regional	B47D	1991
260	UD702725	Mercedes-Benz O303/15R	12m		Coach	C36F	1992
261	UD703710	Mercedes-Benz O303/15R	12m		Coach	C57F	1992
262	UD709540	Mercedes-Benz O303/15R	12m		Regional	B55D	1992
263	UD711714	Mercedes-Benz O408	12m		Regional	B53D	1992
264	AG420CN	Mercedes-Benz O404	12m		Coach	C55F	1993
265	UD732805	Mercedes-Benz O408	12m		Regional	B53	1993
266	AA318WH	Mercedes-Benz O340	12m		Coach	C55F	1994
267	AA307WH	Mercedes-Benz O340	12m		Regional	C53D	1994
268	AA308WH	Mercedes-Benz O340	12m		Coach	B48D	1994
269	AA309WH	Mercedes-Benz O340	12m		Coach	B48D	1994
270	CR121TD	Mercedes-Benz O340	12m		Schoolbus	C55F	1994
271	AG170BX	Mercedes-Benz O340	12m		Coach	C55F	1994
272	AG130BZ	Mercedes-Benz O340	12m		Coach	C55F	1994
273	TS408719	Mercedes-Benz O340	12m		Coach	C55F	1994

274	AG199CJ	Mercedes-Benz O404	12m		Coach	C55F	1994
275	AE458RW	Mercedes-Benz O408	12m		Regional	B53D	1994
276	AE459RW	Mercedes-Benz O408	12m		Regional	B53D	1994

277-287   Mercedes-Benz O350   12m   Coach   C53F   1995-96

277	AG037BT	280	AG040BT	283	AG353CC	286	AK847RC
278	AG038BT	281	AG351CC	284	AG354CC	287	AG240CM
279	AG039BT	282	CR122TD	285	AG551CC		

288	AT460HV	Mercedes-Benz DF 412	6.94m		Coach	B16F	1997
290	CF317HL	Mercedes-Benz O350 RHD	12m		Coach	B51D	2003

291-305   Mercedes-Benz O408   12m   Regional   B53D   1996

291	AG347CC	295	AG355CC	299	AG359CC	303	AG363CC
292	AG348CC	296	AG356CC	300	AG360CC	304	AG364CC
293	AG349CC	297	AG357CC	301	AG361CC	305	AG365CC
294	AG350CC	298	AG358CC	302	AG362CC		

306	BB861RY	Mercedes-Benz DF 412 40	6.94m		Regional	B18F	1999
307	BB953RY	Mercedes-Benz DF 412 40	6.94m		Regional	B18F	1999
308	BV362MF	Mercedes-Benz DF 416 40	7.m		Regional	B18F	2001
309	BE837FE	Mercedes-Benz DF 412 40	6.94m		Regional	B18F	1999
310	BE838FE	Mercedes-Benz DF 412 40	6.94m		Regional	B18F	1999
311	BF907DX	Mercedes-Benz DF 412 40	6.94m		Regional	B18F	1999
312	AG190CY	Iveco 380.12.35	12m		Regional	B55D	1996
313	AG910CZ	Iveco 370E.12.35	12m		Regional	B55D	1996
314	AG900CZ	Iveco 370E.12.35	12m		Regional	B55D	1996
316	AT960HF	Iveco Daily	6.86m		Regional	B19F	1997
319	AZ300WB	Neoplan N 4026/3	12m		Regional	C88F	1998
320	AZ488VF	Iveco 315.8.18	7.58m		Regional	B30F	1998
321	AZ489VF	Iveco 391E.12.29	12m		Regional	B53D	1998
322	AZ490VF	Iveco 391E.12.29	12m		Regional	B53D	1998
324	AZ088WB	Iveco 391E.12.29	12m		Regional	B53D	1998
325	AZ089WB	Iveco 391E.12.29	12m		Regional	B53D	1998
326	AZ099WB	Iveco 391E.12.29	12m		Regional	B53D	1998
327	AZ100WB	Iveco 380.12.35	12m		Regional	B55D	1998
328	BD310FZ	Iveco 380.12.35	12m		Regional	B55D	1999
329	BF242DX	Neoplan N 4026/3	12m		Regional	C88F	1999
330	BH578XR	Neoplan N 4026/3	12m		Regional	C88F	2000

331-342   Volvo B10B 12m   -   Regional   B53D   2000

331	BH855XR	334	BH114XS	337	BH117XS	340	BH120XS
332	BV048MG	335	BH115XS	338	BH118XS	341	BH121XS
333	BH857XR	336	BH116XS	339	BH119XS	342	BH122XS

343	CH225AJ	Fiat 670.12.20	12m		Schoolbus	B69D	1982
344	CH542AJ	Fiat 670.12.20	12m		Schoolbus	B69D	1982
345	CH226AJ	Fiat 370.12.26	12m		Schoolbus	B68D	1977
347	CH819AH	Fiat 343 R	11.m		Schoolbus	B50D	1973
348	UD514645	MAN 16 280	12m		Regional	B55D	1986
353	UD535001	Setra S215 12m	Setra		Regional	B53D	1986
354	UD546572	Setra S215 12m	Setra		Regional	B53D	1987
355	UD623854	Setra S215 12m	Setra		Regional	B53D	1989
356	UD623864	Setra S215 12m	Setra		Regional	B53D	1989
357	AG560BV	Setra S228 DT 12m	Setra		Coach	C79F	1984
358	AG700CJ	Neoplan N122/3	12m		Coach	C79F	1996
359	AG490CL	Neoplan N4026/3	12m		Regional	C88F	1996
360	AG500CL	Neoplan N4026/3	12m		Regional	C88F	1996

361-368   Neoplan N316 SHD   12m   Coach   C53F   1998

361	AT191JA	363	BE331FE	365	AT590JA	368	AZ778VF
362	AT192JA	364	AT390JA	367	AZ760VF		

369-373   Neoplan N4026/3   12m   Regional   C88F   1998

369	AZ389VF	371	AZ840VF	372	AZ047VG	373	AZ411VG
370	AZ046VG						

374	AZ899VF	Neoplan N122/3	12m		Coach	C75F	1998
375	BH568XR	Neoplan N4026/3	12m		Regional	C88F	2000
376	BH569XR	Neoplan N4026/3	12m		Regional	C88F	2000
377	BH674XT	Volvo B10B 10.8m			Regional	B45D	2000
378	BH673XT	Volvo B10B 10.8m			Regional	B45D	2000

Arriva added to its Italian portfolio when in April 2004 it acquired Società Autoservizi FVG SpA in the Udine area of the Friuli-Venezia Giulia region. Arriva's combined Italian businesses operate around 1,800 vehicles and employ around 2,600 staff. Arriva made its first acquisition in Italy with the purchase of SAB Autoservizi SrL, and is now the largest private-sector bus operator in Italy. *Bill Potter*

379-368

Volvo B10B 12m   Regional   B53D   2000

379	BH229XV	385	BH235XV	391	BJ051RB	396	BJ056RB
380	BH230XV	386	BH236XV	392	BJ052RB	397	BJ057RB
381	BH231XV	387	BH237XV	393	BJ053RB	398	BJ058RB
382	BH232XV	388	BH238XV	394	BJ054RB	399	BJ059RB
383	BH233XV	389	BJ049RB	395	BJ055RB	400	BJ060RB
384	BH234XV	390	BJ050RB				

446-449

De Simon Intercity IL3   12m   Regional   B53D   2001

446	BS311RN	447	BS312RN	448	BS318RN	449	BS319RN

450	CF318HL	Mercedes-Benz O350	12m	Coach	B51D	2003
451	UD565507	De Simon Starbus LL24	12m	Regional	B55D	1988
452	UD565508	De Simon Starbus LL24	12m	Regional	B55D	1988
453	UD565509	De Simon Starbus LL24	12m	Regional	B55D	1988
454	UD565510	De Simon Starbus LL24	12m	Regional	B55D	1988
455	UD565511	De Simon Starbus LL24	12m	Regional	B55D	1988
456	UD579049	De Simon Starbus LN24	10.7m	Regional	B47D	1988
457	UD579051	De Simon Starbus LN24	10.7m	Regional	B47D	1988
458	UD579053	De Simon Starbus LN24	10.7m	Regional	B47D	1988
459	UD579052	De Simon Starbus LN24	10.7m	Regional	B47D	1988
460	UD579054	De Simon Starbus LN24	10.7m	Regional	B47D	1988
461	AZ090WB	Irizar Century 12.37A	12m	Coach	B38D	1998

462-476

De Simon Intercity IL3   12m   Regional   B53D   1999

462	AZ807WB	465	AZ810WB	470	AZ812WB	474	AZ816WB
466	AZ046WC	467	AZ047WC	471	AZ813WB	475	AZ858WB
463	AZ808WB	468	AZ048WC	472	AZ814WB	476	AZ859WB
464	AZ809WB	469	AZ811WB	473	AZ815WB		

477	BJ031RB	MAN 11.22 8.82m	De Simon	Regional	B34F	2000
478	BJ028RB	Iveco A45E12	6.86m	Regional	B19F	2000
479	BJ029RB	Iveco A45E12	6.86m	Regional	B19F	2000
480	BJ030RB	Iveco A45E12	6.86m	Regional	B19F	2000
481	BJ677RB	Volvo B10B	12m	Regional	B53F	2000

482-486 — Volvo B10B 10.8m — Regional — B45D — 2000

482	BJ493RB	484	BJ674RB	485	BJ675RB	486	BJ676RB
483	BJ673RB						

488-493 — Neoplan Euroliner N316 SHD — Neoplan — Coach — C51F — 2000

488	BJ450RC	490	BH780XY	492	BH782XY	493	BH783XY
489	BJ369RC	491	BH781XY				

494	BJ244RC	Iveco A45E12	6.86m	Regional	C19F	2000
495	BJ889RC	Mercedes-Benz 416 CDI T46	6.89m	Coach	B18D	2000
496	BV716ZB	Beulas Ministar N MAN	8.67m	Coach	B35D	2000
497	BJ473RD	De Simon Intercity IN3	10.67m	Regional	B47D	2000
498	BJ474RD	De Simon Intercity IN3	10.67m	Regional	B47D	2000
499	BS884RN	Beulas Ministar N MAN	8.67m	Coach	C35F	2001
500	BS441RN	Volvo B12B	12m	Coach	C46F	2001
503	UD677410	Volvo B10MA	18.m	Regional	B69D	1991
505	BE330FE	Volvo B12B	12m	Coach	C51F	1999
506	BM877SA	Iveco EuroRider 391E.12.35	12m	Coach	C48F	2001
507	BM837SA	Iveco EuroRider 391E.12.35	12m	Coach	C48F	2001
508	CN237SF	Iveco EuroRider 391E.12.35	12m	Coach	C48F	2001
509	BM809SA	Iveco EuroRider 391E.12.35	12m	Coach	C48F	2001
510	BM810SA	Iveco EuroRider 391E.12.35	12m	Regional	B53D	2001
511	BM832SA	Iveco EuroRider 391E.12.35	12m	Regional	B53D	2001
512	BM831SA	Iveco EuroRider 391E.12.35	12m	Regional	B53D	2001
513	BS487RN	Iveco EuroRider 391E.12.35	12m	Regional	B53D	2001
514	BM972SA	Iveco EuroRider 391E.12.35	12m	Regional	B53D	2001
515	BW410WE	Iveco EuroRider 391.10.35	10.8m	Regional	B45D	2002
516	BZ715EZ	Mercedes-Benz O350	12m	Coach	BC46F	1997
517	BW854WF	Mercedes-Benz O350	12m	Coach	BC46F	1997
518	CN236SF	Mercedes-Benz O350	12m	Coach	BC46F	1997
519	BZ548EZ	Mercedes-Benz O350	12m	Coach	BC46F	1997
520	CB526YE	Mercedes-Benz O350 RHD	12m	Coach	C53F	2003
523	BZ046FA	Iveco 370E.12.35	12m	Coach	C50F	2002
524	BZ047FA	Iveco 370E.12.35	12m	Coach	C50F	2002
525	BZ048FA	Iveco 370E.12.35	12m	Coach	C50F	2002
526	CF530HL	Neoplan N4426/3	12m	Regional	B86D	2003
527	CF531HL	Neoplan N4426/3	12m	Regional	B86D	2003
528	CF532HL	Neoplan N4426/3	12m	Regional	B86D	2003
529	CF533HL	Neoplan N4426/3	12m	Regional	B86D	2003
530	CF569HL	Mercedes-Benz O350 RHD	12m	Coach	C51F	2003
540	CF986HL	Mercedes-Benz O350 SHD	12m	Coach	C46F	2003
557	CR405TD	Scania L124UB6 13.7m	Beulas Aura	Coach	C43F	2005
558	CR406TD	Scania L124UB6 13.7m	Beulas Aura	Coach	C43F	2005
561	UD594539	Fiat 315.8.17	7.56m	Regional	C18F	1988
563	UD620380	Fiat 315.8.17	7.56m	Regional	C18F	1989
567	UD708010	Iveco 315.8.18	7.58m	Coach	C18F	1992

568-573 — Iveco 391E.12.29 — 12m — Regional — B53D — 2001

568	BM937SA	570	BM939SA	572	BM878SA	573	BM879SA
569	BM938SA	571	BS486RN				

574-600 — De Simon Intercity IL3. — 12m — Regional — B53D — 2001

574	BS017RN	581	BS098RN	588	BS062RN	595	BS291RN
575	BS003RN	582	BS001RN	589	BS061RN	596	BS290RN
576	BS018RN	583	BS126RN	590	BS139RN	597	BS176RN
577	BS019RN	584	BS138RN	591	BS161RN	598	BS288RN
578	BS063RN	585	BS002RN	592	BS162RN	599	BS310RN
579	BS099RN	586	BS137RN	593	BS163RN	600	BS265RN
580	BS097RN	587	BS125RN	594	BS175RN		

602-608 — De Simon Intercity IL3. — 12m — Regional — B53D — 2001

602	BV841MF	605	BV042MF	607	BV871MF	608	BW007WE

614	CR404TD	Beulas Ministar N MAN	9.8m	Coach	C39F	2005
615	ZA885BV	Fiat 470 12.20	12m	Schoolbus	B62D	1980
620	CR407TD	Beulas Ministar N MAN	13.7m	Coach	C63F	2005

622-642 — Mercedes-Benz Integro O550 U — Mercedes-Benz — Regional — B53D — 2003

622	CD882SA	628	CD888SA	633	CD893SA	638	CJ747PJ
623	CH505AJ	629	CD889SA	634	CD894SA	639	CJ748PJ
624	CD884SA	630	CD890SA	635	CD895SA	640	CN331SF
625	CD885SA	631	CD891SA	636	CD896SA	641	CN332SF
626	CD886SA	632	CD892SA	637	CD897SA	642	CN333SF
627	CD887SA						

643	CJ495PJ	De Simon Intercity IN3.	10.67m	Regional	B47D	2004
644	CJ496PJ	De Simon Intercity IN3.	10.67m	Regional	B47D	2004
689	CD751SA	Fiat 343	11.00m	Schoolbus	B50D	1976

711-718 — MAN 11.22 8.82m — De Simon — Regional — B34D — 1998

711	AT195HT	713	AT243JA	715	AT245JA	717	AT247JA
712	AT196HT	714	AT244JA	716	AT246JA	718	AT248JA

719-726 — Mercedes-Benz O404 10RH — Tiziano 9.22m — Regional — B39D — 2001-02

719	BS354RP	721	BS632RP	723	BS634RP	725	BZ915FA
720	BS631RP	722	BS633RP	724	BS635RP	726	BZ916FA

727-730 — De Simon Intercity IN3. — 10.67m — Regional — B47D — 2003

727	CD795SA	728	CD796SA	729	CD797SA	730	CD798SA

767	BF288DX	Volvo B10B	12m	Regional	B53D	1999
785	CN334SF	Bredamenarin M240 LU3	12m	City Bus	B22D	2004
786	CN335SF	Bredamenarin M240 LU3	12m	City Bus	B22D	2004
787	CN336SF	Bredamenarin M240 LU3	12m	City Bus	B22D	2004

727-730 — Bredamenarin M240 LU3 — 11.96m — City Bus — B22D — 2003

788	CF107HM	791	CF110HM	794	CH062AH	797	CH250AH
789	CF108HM	792	CH060AH	795	CH063AH	798	CH251AH
790	CF109HM	793	CH061AH	796	CH064AH	799	CH252AH

800	CD435SA	De Simon 15 MT	14.80m	Regional	B65D	2002
819	UD665332	Fiat 480.12.21 P	12m	City Bus	B20D	1991
822	BH018XV	Irisbus 491E.12.22 (cng)	12m	City Bus	B28D	2000
823	UD590602	Inbus U210 Mentano	12m	City Bus	B20D	1988
824	UD621733	Inbus U240	12m	City Bus	B20D	1989
825	AT029HT	MAN Bassotto Metano	12m	City Bus	B25D	1997
833	BH019XV	Irisbus 491E.12.22 (cng)	12m	City Bus	B28D	2000
835	AT718HV	MAN Bassotto Metano	12m	City Bus	B25D	1997
836	UD590603	Inbus U210 Dual Fuel	12m	City Bus	B20D	1988
838	AT031HT	MAN Bassotto Metano	12m	City Bus	B25D	1997
839	AT719HV	MAN Bassotto Metano	12m	City Bus	B25D	1997
840	BH020XV	Irisbus 491E.12.22 (cng)	12m	City Bus	B28D	2000
845	UD600103	Inbus U210	12m	City Bus	B20D	1989
846	UD621732	Inbus U240	12m	City Bus	B20D	1989
848	UD665335	Fiat 480.12.21 P	12m	City Bus	B20D	1991
849	UD665336	Fiat 480.12.21 P	12m	City Bus	B20D	1991
850	BV903MF	Irisbus 491E.12.22 (cng)	12m	City Bus	B28D	2000
851	AT720HV	MAN Bassotto Metano	12m	City Bus	B25D	1997
852	UD672465	Fiat 480.12.21 P	12m	City Bus	B20D	1991
853	UD672464	Fiat 480.12.21 P	12m	City Bus	B20D	1991
854	BH022XV	Irisbus 491E.12.22 (cng)	12m	City Bus	B28D	2000
855	BH023XV	Irisbus 491E.12.22 CNG	12m	City Bus	B28D	2000
856	BH024XV	Irisbus 491E.12.22 CNG	12m	City Bus	B28D	2000
857	AT721HV	MAN Bassotto Metano	12m	City Bus	B25D	1997
858	BH025XV	Irisbus 491E.12.22 CNG	12m	City Bus	B28D	2000
859	BH026XV	Irisbus 491E.12.22 CNG	12m	City Bus	B28D	2000
860	BH027XV	Irisbus 491E.12.22 CNG	12m	City Bus	B28D	2000
861	BH028XV	Irisbus 491E.12.22 CNG	12m	City Bus	B28D	2000
862	BH029XV	Irisbus 491E.12.22 CNG	12m	City Bus	B28D	2000
863	BH030XV	Irisbus 491E.12.22 CNG	12m	City Bus	B28D	2000
864	BH031XV	Irisbus 491E.12.22 CNG	12m	City Bus	B28D	2000
870	UD585917	Inbus U210 FTN	10.74m	City Bus	B18D	1988
872	UD600104	Inbus U210 DUAL FUEL	12m	City Bus	B20D	1989
873	UD621731	Inbus U240	12m	City Bus	B20D	1989
874	AT030HT	MAN Bassotto Metano	12m	City Bus	B25D	1997
875	AT032HT	MAN Bassotto Metano	12m	City Bus	B25D	1997
876	AT033HT	MAN Bassotto Metano	12m	City Bus	B25D	1997
877	AT034HT	MAN Bassotto Metano	12m	City Bus	B25D	1997
878	BM940SA	Iveco 491E.12.22 (methanol)	12m	City Bus	B28D	2001

879	BM941SA	Iveco 491E.12.22 METANO	12m	City Bus	B28D	2001
880	BM847SA	Iveco 491E.12.22 METANO	12m	City Bus	B28D	2001
881	BM848SA	Iveco 491E.12.22 METANO	12m	City Bus	B28D	2001
882	BM849SA	Iveco 491E.12.22 METANO	12m	City Bus	B28D	2001
883	BM880SA	Iveco 491E.12.22 METANO	12m	City Bus	B28D	2001
884	CD013SA	Mercedes-Benz Cito O520	9.59m	City Bus	B17D	2002
885	CD014SA	Mercedes-Benz Cito O520	9.59m	City Bus	B17D	2002
886	CD015SA	Mercedes-Benz Cito O520	9.59m	City Bus	B17D	2002
887	BZ627FA	Mercedes-Benz Cito O520	8.09m	City Bus	B11D	2002
888	BZ628FA	Mercedes-Benz Cito O520	8.09m	City Bus	B11D	2002
889	CD799SA	BMB M240GNC NU EXOBUS	10.79m	City Bus	B18D	2003
890	CD800SA	BMB M240GNC NU EXOBUS	10.79m	City Bus	B18D	2003
891	CD801SA	BMB M240GNC NU EXOBUS	10.79m	City Bus	B18D	2003
892	CD802SA	BMB M240GNC NU EXOBUS	10.79m	City Bus	B18D	2003
893	CD803SA	BMB M240GNC NU EXOBUS	10.79m	City Bus	B18D	2003
894	CH253AH	BMB M240GNC NU EXOBUS	10.79m	City Bus	B18D	2003
895	CH254AH	BMB M240GNC NU EXOBUS	10.79m	City Bus	B18D	2003
896	CH255AH	BMB M240GNC NU EXOBUS	10.79m	City Bus	B18D	2003
897	CH256AH	BMB M240GNC NU EXOBUS	10.79m	City Bus	B18D	2003
899	UD697536	Iveco 49.10.1/N-3,6 POLL	6.32m	City Bus	B9D	1992
900	CF714HL	Iveco 49.10.1/N-3,6 POLL	6.32m	City Bus	B9D	1992

KM

KM spa, Via Postumia 102, 26100 Cremona

3	CR389359	Iveco 280 RA7	Cacciamali	School bus	1988
4	BG451PH	Iveco 45.10	Iveco	School bus	1995
5	BH060WY	Iveco CC80E18M/86	Cacciamali	School bus	2000
6	BV937GP	Iveco Scuolabus Turbo Daily	Cacciamali	School bus	1989
58	CR384191	Inbus U210/FT	Breda	City bus	1987
59	CR384192	Inbus U210/FT	Breda	City bus	1987
61	CR384194	Inbus U210/FT	Breda	City bus	1987
62	CR384195	Inbus U210/FT	Breda	City bus	1987
63	CR389020	Menarini 201/2 LU	Menarini	City bus	1987
64	CR390912	Menarini M 201/2NU	Menarini	City bus	1988
66	CR410068	Inbus U210/FTN	Breda	City bus	1989
67	CR410069	Inbus U210/FTN	Breda	City bus	1989
68	CR410070	Inbus U210/FTN	Breda	City bus	1989
70	CR413848	Menarini M 201/2NU	Menarini	City bus	1989
71	CR413849	Menarini M 201/2NU	Menarini	City bus	1989
72	CR454939	Menarini M 220/NU	Menarini	City bus	1991
73	CR454940	Menarini M 220/NU	Menarini	City bus	1991
74	AL597GD	CAM Bussotto NL202 FU	Carrozzeria Autiromo	City bus	1996
75	AP257XK	Breda Menarini M 230/1E2	Bredamenarinbus	City bus	1998
76	AP258XK	Breda Menarini M 230/1E2	Bredamenarinbus	City bus	1998

78-82		Kronos 10KV23-U	Mauri	City bus	2001
78	BV620GK	**80**	BV621GK	**81** BV826GK	**82** BV827GK
79	BV680GK				

83-86		Mercedes-Benz Cito O520	Mercedes-Benz	City bus	2002
83	BV916GS	**84** BV014GT	**85** BV917GS	**86** BV936GP	

87	-	Iveco 491.12.27 - Cityclass	Iveco	City bus	On order
100	BS 814084	Iveco 370.12.25	Iveco	Regional bus	1983
101	BS 814083	Iveco 370.12.25	Iveco	Regional bus	1983
103	BS D05103	Iveco 370.12.25L	Iveco	Regional bus	1990
104	BS918590	Iveco 370.12.25L	Iveco	Regional bus	1985
105	AF778 XJ	Cam Busotto 2LS-SR	Carrozzeria Autiromo	City bus	1995
106	BS870148	Iveco 370.12.25	Portesi	Regional bus	1984
107	CR463164	Inbus S 210	Breada	City bus	1987
108	AW765 EJ	Breda Menarini M 230/01 MS	Bredamenarinbus	City bus	1998
109	BE301DN	Mercedes-Benz O405NU	Mercedes-Benz	Regional bus	1999

One of the Arriva's early requirements at Cremona was to replace the ageing trolleybus system - and thus for a few weeks Arriva did in fact operated the network. Now operating on the town services are four Mercedes-Benz Cito O520s, a type found in many of Arriva's continental operations. This model has been deleted from the Mercedes product list. Showing KM livery is 86, BV936GP. *Bill Potter*

110	AZ465 NF	Mercedes-Benz O405NU	Mercedes-Benz	Regional bus	1998
111	BM984FW	Mercedes-Benz O405NU	Mercedes-Benz	Regional bus	2000
112	BS918588	Iveco 370.12.25L	Iveco	Regional bus	1985
113	AF164 XD	Iveco 370.12.35	Dalla Via	Regional bus	1995
114	AZ469 NF	Mercedes-Benz O405NU	Mercedes-Benz	Regional bus	1998
115	AN900 JY	Iveco 370.12.25L	Dalla Via	Regional bus	1986
116	BS834021	Iveco 370.12.25	Portesi	Regional bus	1983
117	BS918589	Iveco 370.12.25L	Portesi	Regional bus	1985
118	BSA11038	Iveco 370.12.25L	Iveco	Regional bus	1987
119	BS902579	Iveco 370.12.25L	Iveco	Regional bus	1985
120	BS840857	Inbus I/330	Iveco	Regional bus	1994
121	BSA73986	Iveco 370.12.25L	Portesi	Regional bus	1988
122	BS920314	Iveco 370.12.25L	Iveco	Regional bus	1985
123	BSA11035	Iveco 370.12.25L	Portesi	Regional bus	1987
124	BS920313	Iveco 370.12.25L	Iveco	Regional bus	1985
125	BSA84583	Iveco 370.12.25L	Portesi	Regional bus	1988
126	BSA84584	Iveco 370.12.25L	Portesi	Regional bus	1988
127	BS967705	Iveco 370.12.25L	Portesi	Regional bus	1986
128	BSB69662	Iveco 370.12.25L	Iveco	Regional bus	1990
129	BSD05102	Iveco 370.12.25L	Iveco	Regional bus	1990
130	BH343WC	Iveco EuroRider 391E.12.29	Iveco	Regional bus	1998
131	BH342WC	Iveco EuroRider 391E.12.29	Iveco	Regional bus	1998
132	AZ 468NF	Mercedes-Benz O405 NU	Iveco	Regional bus	1998
133	BS 799902	Inbus S/210	Iveco	City bus	1983
134	BS 902580	Iveco 370.12.25	Iveco	Regional bus	1985
135	BS A11034	Iveco 370.12.25L	Portesi	Regional bus	1987
136	BS A84582	Iveco 370.12.25L	Portesi	Regional bus	1988

137-142

		Ayats 2 Piani		Ayats			Regional bus	2001

137	BM 281DX		139	BM 283DX		141	BR 776FE		142	BR 905FE
138	BM 282DX		140	BR 775FE						

143	AF 163 XD	Iveco 370.12.35	Dalla Via	Regional bus	1995
144	BM 280DX	Iveco 393E.12.35 My Way	Iveco	Regional bus	2001
145	BM 285DX	Iveco 393E.12.35 My Way	Iveco	Regional bus	2001
146	BM 290DX	Iveco 393E.12.35 My Way	Iveco	Regional bus	2001
147	AF 747 XF	Iveco 370.12.35	Dalla Via	Regional bus	1995

148-155			Iveco 393E.12.35 My Way	Iveco	Regional bus	2001
148	BM 291DX	150	BM 284DX	152	BM 288DX	154	BM 292DX
149	BM 286DX	151	BM 287DX	153	BM 289DX	155	CD523YR

157	AZ 470 NF	Mercedes-Benz O405NU	Mercedes-Benz	Regional bus	1998
159	AZ 467 NF	Mercedes-Benz O405NU	Mercedes-Benz	Regional bus	1998
160	BS 693LE	Iveco 491.12.27 - Cityclass	Iveco	City bus	2001
161	BS 694LE	Iveco 491.12.27 - Cityclass	Iveco	City bus	2001
162	BS 695LE	Iveco 491.12.27 - Cityclass	Iveco	City bus	2001
189	BS D09800	Iveco 370.12.30S	Portesi	Regional bus	1990
195	AZ 466 NF	Mercedes-Benz O405NU	Mercedes-Benz	Regional bus	1998
401	CR 508523	Iveco 370E.12.35 - Palladio	Dalla Via	Coach	1994
402	AL 285 GG	Iveco 370E.12.35 - Palladio	Dalla Via	Coach	1996
403	AW 021 EM	Iveco 370E.12.35 - Dornino	Iveco-Orlandi	Coach	1997
404	AW 491 EL	Iveco 370E.12.35 - Palladio	Dalla Via	Coach	1997
405	AP 785 XF	Iveco 370E.12.35 - Domino	Iveco-Orlandi	Coach	1998
406	AP 596 XG	Iveco 370E.12.35 - Palladio	Dalla Via	Coach	1998
407	BG 322PH	Mercedes-Benz 0404 V8	Dalla Via	Coach	2000
408	BG 323PH	Mercedes-Benz 0404 V8	Dalla Via	Coach	2000
409	BV103GM	Iveco GT 65C15	Cacciamali	Coach	2002

Trieste Trasporti

Trieste Trasporti Spa, Stazione Centrale di Plazza Della Liberta 8, Trieste

511-514		Europolis TCC760	Cacciamali	City bus	1999-2000
511	BG 401 BS	512	BG 402 BS	513	BH 096 XY	514	BH 095 XY

521-528		Breda Menarini 231 MU/3P	Bredamenarinbus	City bus	1999-2000
521	BG 845 BS	523	BH 624 XX	525	BH 623 XX	527	BM 161 RA
522	BG 846 BS	524	BH 622 XX	526	BM 139 RA	528	BM 160 RA

531	AN 099 ER	Europolis TCC 635 L	Cacciamali	City bus	1997
541	AN 159 EP	Breda Menarini M230/1E	Bredamenarinbus	City bus	1997
542	AN 120 ES	Breda Menarini M230/1E	Bredamenarinbus	City bus	1997
543	AT 320 FD	Breda Menarini M230/1E	Bredamenarinbus	City bus	1998
544	AX 127 ZT	Breda Menarini M230/1E	Bredamenarinbus	City bus	1998

551-562		Breda Menarini 240 NU	Bredamenarinbus	City bus	1999
551	BD 691 AF	554	BD 694 AF	557	BD 829 AF	560	BD 828 AF
552	BD 692 AF	555	BD 695 AF	558	BD 826 AF	561	BD 893 AF
553	BD 693 AF	556	BD 696 AF	559	BD 827 AF	562	BD 894 AF

571-587		Europolis TCN105	Cacciamali	City bus	1999
571	BF 203 AR	576	BF 207 AR	580	BF 208 AR	584	BF 267 AR
572	BF 204 AR	577	BF 362 AR	581	BF 265 AR	585	BF 210 AR
573	BF 205 AR	578	BF 363 AR	582	BF 209 AR	586	BF 268 AR
574	BF 424 AR	579	BF 364 AR	583	BF 266 AR	587	BF 211 AR
575	BF 206 AR						

591	CB 258 YE	Europolis 024	Cacciamali	City bus	2002
592	CB 350 YE	Europolis 924	Cacciamali	City bus	2002
593	CB 351 YE	Europolis 924	Cacciamali	City bus	2002
601	BM 667 RA	Setra S315 HD	Setra	Coach	1999
603	BM 762 RA	Mercedes-Benz 0404	Mercedes-Benz	Coach	1999
604	BM 761 RA	Iveco 370E.12.35H Palladio	Iveco	Coach	2000
605	BV 038 ZB	Neoplan N516SHD Starliner	Neoplan	Coach	2000
606	BV 678 ZC	Domino 2001 HDH	Orlandi	Coach	2002

611	AK 653 RA	Breda Menarini M220 LU 4P	Bredamenarinbus	City bus	1996
612	AN 263 EN	Breda Menarini M220 LU 4P	Bredamenarinbus	City bus	1996
615	BM 666 RA	Iveco 380.12.38 HD-T	Iveco	Coach	1996
616	BM 668 RA	Iveco 380.12.38 HD-T	Iveco	Coach	1998
641	BM 868 RA	Iveco CC80.E.18M	Cacciamali	School bus	1999
642	BV 039 ZB	Iveco CC80.E.18M	Cacciamali	School bus	1999
643	BV 074 ZB	Iveco CC80.E.18M	Cacciamali	School bus	1999
644	BV 088 ZB	Iveco 100.E.18E2	Cacciamali	School bus	1999
645	BV 073 ZB	Iveco 100.E.18E2	Cacciamali	School bus	1999
646	BV 072 ZB	Iveco CC80.E.18M	Cacciamali	School bus	2000
647	BM 605 RA	Iveco 100.E.18E2	Cacciamali	School bus	2000
648	CB 051 YE	Iveco 100.E.21N	Cacciamali	School bus	2002

712-767 — Iveco Turbocity-U — Desimon UN 70.02 — City bus — 1990-92

712	TS 349482	726	TS 350863	740	TS 352777	754	TS 361087
713	TS 349483	727	TS 350864	741	TS 353124	755	TS 377316
714	TS 349484	728	TS 350865	742	TS 353475	756	BD 503 AF
715	AN 522 ER	729	TS 350866	743	TS 353476	757	TS 377318
716	TS 350480	730	TS 350867	744	TS 353477	758	TS 377319
717	TS 349866	731	TS 350868	745	TS 353478	759	TS 377320
718	TS 349867	732	TS 350869	746	TS 353479	760	TS 377321
719	TS 349868	733	TS 350870	747	TS 353480	761	TS 377322
720	TS 349869	734	TS 351355	748	TS 353481	762	TS 377323
721	TS 349870	735	TS 351713	749	TS 353482	763	TS 377324
722	TS 350476	736	TS 351712	750	TS 353483	764	TS 377325
723	TS 350479	737	AK 663 RA	751	TS 361084	765	TS 377769
724	TS 350477	738	TS 352386	752	TS 361085	766	TS 377771
725	TS 350478	739	TS 352387	753	TS 361086	767	TS 377770

771-775 — Van Hool AG300RA01 — Desimon — City bus — 1999

| 771 | BD 795 AF | 773 | BF 005 AR | 774 | BF 007 AR | 775 | BF 006 AR |
| 772 | BF 008 AR | | | | | | |

781-790 — Breda Menarini M321/1 — Bredamenarinbus — City bus — 1999

781	BD 895 AF	784	BD 898 AF	787	BD 900 AF	789	BD 902 AF
782	BD 896 AF	785	BD 796 AF	788	BD 901 AF	790	BD 903 AF
783	BD 897 AF	786	BD 899 AF				

801-833 — Irisbus 491.12.29 CityClass — Irisbus — City bus — 2001

801	BM 827 RA	810	BM 595 RA	818	BM 681 RA	826	BM 599 RA
802	BM 399 RA	811	BM 518 RA	819	BM 597 RA	827	BM 601 RA
803	BM 398 RA	812	BM 455 RA	820	BM 519 RA	828	BM 520 RA
804	BM 397 RA	813	BM 596 RA	821	BM 453 RA	829	BM 678 RA
805	BM 396 RA	814	BM 454 RA	822	BM 456 RA	830	BM 602 RA
806	BM 521 RA	815	BM 395 RA	823	BM 517 RA	831	BM 603 RA
807	BM 680 RA	816	BM 452 RA	824	BM 677 RA	832	BM 604 RA
808	BM 457 RA	817	BM 522 RA	825	BM 598 RA	833	BM 679 RA
809	BM 594 RA						

861-892 — Iveco 490.E10.22 — Iveco — City bus — 1996-97

861	AK 005 RD	869	AN 418 EN	876	AN 425 EN	886	AN 335 ES
862	AN 016 EN	870	AN 419 EN	877	AN 869 EN	887	AN 336 ES
863	AK 006 RD	871	AN 420 EN	881	AN 330 ES	888	AN 337 ES
864	AN 773 EN	872	AN 421 EN	882	BV 602 ZC	889	AN 338 ES
865	AN 020 EN	873	AN 422 EN	883	AN 332 ES	890	AN 339 ES
866	AN 018 EN	874	AN 423 EN	884	AN 333 ES	891	AN 340 ES
867	AN 021 EN	875	AN 424 EN	885	AN 334 ES	892	AN 341 ES
868	AN 019 EN						

1001-1005 — ALE 7,7/3P E3 — Autiromo — City bus — 2001-03

| 1001 | BV 785 ZB | 1003 | BV 787 ZB | 1004 | BV 786 ZB | 1005 | CB 450 YE |
| 1002 | BV 788 ZB | | | | | | |

1011-1020 — Breda Menarini M231/E3 — Bredamenarinbus — City bus — 2001

1011	BV 501 ZB	1014	BV 562 ZB	1017	BV 561 ZB	1019	BV 656 ZB
1012	BV 502 ZB	1015	BV 503 ZB	1018	BV 637 ZB	1020	BV 655 ZB
1013	BV 635 ZB	1016	BV 636 ZB				

1031-1049	Breda Menarini M240/E3 NU	Bredamenarinbus	City bus	2001

1031	BV 504 ZB	1036	BV 507 ZB	1041	BV 567 ZB	1046	BV 559 ZB
1032	BV 505 ZB	1037	BV 508 ZB	1042	BV 512 ZB	1047	BV 560 ZB
1033	BV 506 ZB	1038	BV 509 ZB	1043	BV 513 ZB	1048	BV 570 ZB
1034	BV 565 ZB	1039	BV 510 ZB	1044	BV 568 ZB	1049	BV 571 ZB
1035	BV 566 ZB	1040	BV 511 ZB	1045	BV 569 ZB		

1050-1080	Breda Menarini M240/E3 NU	Bredamenarinbus	City bus	2002-03

1050	CB 352 YE	1058	CB 410 YE	1066	CB 413 YE	1074	CB 127 YE
1051	CB 180 YE	1059	CB 411 YE	1067	CB 414 YE	1075	CB 152 YE
1052	CB 181 YE	1060	CB 259 YE	1068	CB 415 YE	1076	CB 128 YE
1053	CB 409 YE	1061	CB 260 YE	1069	CB 416 YE	1077	CB 129 YE
1054	CB 182 YE	1062	CB 261 YE	1070	CB 417 YE	1078	CB 151 YE
1055	CB 183 YE	1063	CB 262 YE	1071	CB 418 YE	1079	CB 150 YE
1056	CB 195 YE	1064	CB 263 YE	1072	CB 125 YE	1080	CB 149 YE
1057	CB 196 YE	1065	CB 412 YE	1073	CB 126 YE		

1101-1110	Breda Menarini M240/E3 LU 3P	Bredamenarinbus	City bus	2002

1101	CB 264 YE	1104	CB 238 YE	1107	CB 240 YE	1109	CB 241 YE
1102	CB 197 YE	1105	CB 239 YE	1108	CB 198 YE	1110	CB 266 YE
1103	CB 237 YE	1106	CB 265 YE				

1151-1170	Breda Menarini M240/E3 LU 18m	Bredamenarinbus	City bus	2002-03

1151	CB 419 YE	1156	CB 355 YE	1161	CB 358 YE	1166	CB 425 YE
1152	CB 420 YE	1157	CB 430 YE	1162	CB 422 YE	1167	CB 426 YE
1153	CB 267 YE	1158	CB 421 YE	1163	CB 423 YE	1168	CB 427 YE
1154	CB 353 YE	1159	CB 356 YE	1164	CB 424 YE	1169	CB 359 YE
1155	CB 354 YE	1160	CB 357 YE	1165	CB 429 YE	1170	CB 428 YE

1201	CB 835 YE	Scania OmniCity CN94UB	Scania	City bus	2003

RT

RT buses are based in Imperia, in the region of Liguria.

RT3202	IM158620	Iveco A55 F 10	Iveco	Regional bus	1979
RT3211	BK398WN	Iveco A45 F 12	Iveco	Regional bus	2002
RT4150	IM155885	Iveco 315.8.13	Iveco	Regional bus	1979
RT4151	IM156272	Iveco 315.8.13	Iveco	Regional bus	1979
RT4153	IM158617	Iveco 315.8.13	Iveco	Regional bus	1979
RT4154	IM158618	Iveco 315.8.13	Iveco	Regional bus	1979
RT4156	IM168348	Iveco 315.8.13	Iveco	Regional bus	1980
RT4157	IM178086	Iveco 315.8.13	Iveco	Regional bus	1981
RT4159	IM178087	Iveco 315.8.13	Iveco	Regional bus	1981
RT4164	BG308BX	Iveco 315.8.18	Iveco	Regional bus	1999
RT4168	BH026VV	Iveco 315.8.18	Iveco	Regional bus	1999
RT4300	IM217583	Iveco 316.8.13	Viberti	Regional bus	1991
RT4305	IM274912	Iveco 316.8.13	Viberti	Regional bus	1991
RT4306	IM274942	Iveco 316.8.13	Viberti	Regional bus	1991
RT4308	IM2768001	Iveco 316.8.13	Viberti	Regional bus	1991
RT4309	IM276802	Iveco 316.8.13	Viberti	Regional bus	1991
RT5074	AG103DY	MAN 11.220	DeSimon	Regional bus	1996
RT5077	AG237DY	MAN 11.220	DeSimon	Regional bus	1996
RT5079	AG238DY	MAN 11.220	DeSimon	Regional bus	1996
RT5081	AG834DY	MAN 11.220	DeSimon	Regional bus	1996
RT5082	AG835DY	MAN 11.220	DeSimon	Regional bus	1996
RT5083	AG833DY	MAN 11.220	DeSimon	Regional bus	1996
RT5085	BD041RN	MAN 11.220	DeSimon	Regional bus	1999
RT5087	BK830WM	MAN 11.220	DeSimon	Regional bus	2000
RT5350	IM201418	Inbus S150	Sicca	Regional bus	1986
RTL001	BZ417CB	Iveco A50 C 15	Iveco	Regional bus	2002
RTL002	BZ980CB	Mercedes-Benz O303/10R	Bianchi	Regional bus	1981

Index to UK vehicles

Reg	Region	Reg	Region	Reg	Region	Reg	Region	Reg	Region
49XBF	Midlands	B91WUL	North East	BF52NZN	Midlands	BX04MYB	London
70CLT	London	B92WUL	London	BF52NZO	Midlands	BX04MYC	London
124CLT	London	B94WUL	London	BF52NZP	Midlands	BX04MYD	London
124YTW	North West & W	B95WUL	London	BF52NZR	Midlands	BX04MYF	London
217CLT	London	B96WUL	London	BF52NZS	Midlands	BX04MYG	London
280CLT	London	B97WUL	London	BF52NZT	Midlands	BX04MYH	London
319CLT	London	B98WUL	London	BF52NZU	Midlands	BX04MYJ	London
324CLT	London	B100WUL	London	BF52NZV	Midlands	BX04MYK	London
330CLT	London	B101WUL	London	BF52NZW	Midlands	BX04MYL	London
361CLT	London	B103WUL	London	BF52NZX	Midlands	BX04MYM	London
398CLT	London	B104WUL	London	BF52NZY	Midlands	BX04MYN	London
453CLT	London	B105WUL	London	BF52NZZ	Midlands	BX04MYR	London
464CLT	London	B112WUL	North East	BF52OAA	Midlands	BX04MYS	London
480CLT	London	B115ORU	Original SST	BF52OAB	Midlands	BX04MYT	London
519CLT	London	B116WUL	North East	BF52OAC	Midlands	BX04MYU	London
530MUY	London	B121ORU	Original SST	BF52OAD	Midlands	BX04MYV	London
593CLT	London	B124WUL	London	BF52OAE	Midlands	BX04MYW	London
640CLT	London	B124WUL	London	BF52OAG	Midlands	BX04MYY	London
700THV	London	B126WUL	London	BKEB47T	The Shires	BX04MYZ	London
725DYE	London	B130WUL	London	BU02URX	Midlands	BX04MYZ	London
734DYE	London	B135GAU	Midlands	BU02URY	Midlands	BX04MZD	London
776DYE	London	B136GAU	Midlands	BU02URZ	Midlands	BX04MZE	London
801DYE	London	B136WUL	London	BU02USB	Midlands	BX04MZG	London
822DYE	London	B137GAU	Midlands	BU02USC	Midlands	BX04MZJ	London
855UXC	London	B138GAU	Midlands	BU03HPV	Midlands	BX04MZL	London
903SUL	London	B139GAU	Midlands	BU03HPX	Midlands	BX04MZN	London
984SYF	London	B140WUL	London	BU03HPY	Midlands	BX04NBK	London
A1YBG	Yorkshire	B141GAU	Midlands	BU03HPZ	Midlands	BX04NBL	London
A2YBG	Yorkshire	B142GAU	Midlands	BU03HRA	Midlands	BX04NCF	London
A4YBG	Yorkshire	B143GAU	Midlands	BU03HRC	Midlands	BX04NCJ	London
A11GTA	Southern	B149TRN	North West & W	BU03HRD	Midlands	BX04NCN	London
A112KFX	Original SST	B152WUL	Original SST	BU03HRE	Midlands	BX04NCU	London
A113KFX	Original SST	B170WUL	London	BU03HRF	Midlands	BX04NCV	London
A114KFX	Original SST	B187BLG	Midlands	BU03HRG	Midlands	BX04NCY	London
A132SMA	Midlands	B190BLG	Midlands	BU03HRJ	Midlands	BX04NCZ	London
A134SMA	Midlands	B198DTU	North West & W	BU03HRK	Midlands	BX04NDC	London
A139MRN	North West & W	B214WUL	London	BU03HRL	Midlands	BX04NDD	London
A141MRN	North West & W	B222VHW	Original SST	BU05VFD	London	BX04NDE	London
A152UDM	North West & W	B224VHW	Original SST	BU05VFE	London	BX04NDF	London
A153FPG	The Shires	B224VHW	Original SST	BU05VFF	London	BX04NDG	London
A242GHN	North East	B225VHW	Original SST	BU05VFG	London	BX04NDJ	London
A244GHN	North East	B227WUL	Original SST	BU05VFH	London	BX04NDK	London
A501EJF	Midlands	B231WUL	London	BU05VFJ	London	BX04NDL	London
A509EJF	Midlands	B239WUL	Original SST	BU51KWJ	Midlands	BX04NDN	London
A565NWX	Yorkshire	B240LRA	Original SST	BU51KWK	Midlands	BX04NDU	London
A566NWX	Yorkshire	B241LRA	Original SST	BU51KWL	Midlands	BX04NDV	London
A567NWX	North East	B248WUL	London	BU51KWM	Midlands	BX04NDY	London
A569NWX	Yorkshire	B251NVN	North West & W	BU51KWN	Midlands	BX04NDZ	London
A574NWX	Yorkshire	B253WUL	London	BU53AWP	Midlands	BX04NEF	London
A575NWX	Yorkshire	B254WUL	London	BU53AWR	Midlands	BX04NEJ	London
A577NWX	Yorkshire	B263WUL	Southern	BX04MWW	London	BX04NEN	London
A580NWX	Yorkshire	B265WUL	Original SST	BX04MWY	London	BX05UWV	London
A581NWX	Yorkshire	B274LPH	Midlands	BX04MWZ	London	BX05UWW	London
A584NWX	Yorkshire	B275LPH	Midlands	BX04MXA	London	BX05UWY	London
A586NWX	Yorkshire	B275WUL	Southern	BX04MXB	London	BX05UWZ	London
A590NWX	Yorkshire	B277KPF	North East	BX04MXC	London	BX05UXC	London
A667XDA	Original SST	B280WUL	Southern	BX04MXD	London	BX05UXD	London
A855UYM	The Shires	B300WUL	London	BX04MXE	London	BX55FUH	London
A856UYM	The Shires	B513LFP	North West & W	BX04MXG	London	BX55FUJ	London
A889PKR	The Shires	B514LFP	Midlands	BX04MXH	London	BX55FUM	London
A895SUL	Original SST	B591SWX	Yorkshire	BX04MXJ	London	BX55FUO	London
A927SUL	Original SST	B599SWX	Yorkshire	BX04MXK	London	BX55FUP	London
A959SYF	North East	B600UUM	Yorkshire	BX04MXL	London	BX55FUT	London
A973SYF	North East	B603UUM	Yorkshire	BX04MXM	London	BX55FUU	London
ADZ4731	The Shires	B604UUM	Yorkshire	BX04MXN	London	BX55FUW	London
ALD941B	London	B605UUM	The Shires	BX04MXP	London	BX55FUY	London
ALD968B	London	B606UUM	Yorkshire	BX04MXR	London	BX55FVA	London
ALD975B	London	B607UUM	Yorkshire	BX04MXS	London	BX55FVB	London
ALM50B	London	B609UUM	Yorkshire	BX04MXT	London	BX55FVC	London
ALM60B	London	B824AAT	Original SST	BX04MXU	London	BX55FVD	London
B75WUL	London	B825AAT	Original SST	BX04MXV	London	BX55FVF	London
B84WUL	London	B861XYR	The Shires	BX04MXW	London	BX55FVF	London
B86WUL	North East	B964WRN	North West & W	BX04MXY	London	BX55FVG	London
B89WUL	North East	BCWB24V	North West & W	BX04MXZ	London	BX55FVH	London
B90WUL	North East	BF52NZM	Midlands	BX04MYA	London	BX55FVJ	London

Reg	Region	Reg	Region	Reg	Region	Reg	Region
BX55FVK	London	CWR519Y	North East	D242FYM	The Shires	F114TML	Midlands
BX55FVL	London	CWR519Y	Yorkshire	D553YNO	Original SST	F151KGS	The Shires
BX55FVM	London	CWR524Y	The Shires	D634BBV	North West & W	F152KGS	The Shires
BX55FVN	London	CX04AXW	North West & W	D675YNO	Original SST	F153DET	Midlands
BX55FVP	London	CX04AXY	North West & W	DE52OKV	Southern	F153KGS	The Shires
BX55FVQ	London	CX04AXZ	North West & W	DE52OKW	Southern	F154DET	Midlands
BX55FVR	London	CX04AYA	North West & W	DE52OKX	Southern	F155DET	Midlands
BX55FVS	London	CX04AYB	North West & W	DE52OKZ	Southern	F157DET	Midlands
BX55FVT	London	CX04AYC	North West & W	DE52OLM	Southern	F158DET	Midlands
BX55FVU	London	CX04EHV	North West & W	DE52OLN	Southern	F188HKK	North East
BX55FVV	London	CX04EHW	North West & W	DOC26V	North West & W	F251YTJ	North West & W
BX55FVW	London	CX04EHY	North West & W	DOC37V	North West & W	F252YTJ	North West & W
BX55FVY	London	CX04EHZ	Midlands	DVS940	London	F253YTJ	North West & W
BX55FVZ	London	CX05AAE	North West & W	E23ECH	Midlands	F254YTJ	North West & W
BX55FWA	London	CX05AAF	North West & W	E25ECH	Midlands	F255YTJ	North West & W
BX55FWB	London	CX05AAJ	North West & W	E26ECH	Scotland	F256YTJ	North West & W
BYX121V	Original SST	CX05AAK	North West & W	E52UNE	North West & W	F257YTJ	North West & W
BYX210V	North East	CX05AAN	North West & W	E72KBF	Midlands	F258GWJ	Midlands
BYX296V	Original SST	CX05EOV	North West & W	E149BTO	Midlands	F258YTJ	North West & W
C24CHM	London	CX05EOX	North West & W	E150BTO	Midlands	F259YTJ	North West & W
C25CHM	London	CX05EOY	North West & W	E151BTO	Midlands	F260YTJ	North West & W
C31CHM	The Shires	CX54DKD	North West & W	E152BTO	Midlands	F261YTJ	North West & W
C32CHM	Southern	CX54DKE	North West & W	E153BTO	Midlands	F262YTJ	North West & W
C36CHM	The Shires	CX54DKF	North West & W	E158OMD	Midlands	F263YTJ	North West & W
C37CHM	London	CX54DKJ	North West & W	E159OMD	Midlands	F264YTJ	North West & W
C38CHM	The Shires	CX54DKK	North West & W	E160OMD	Midlands	F266YTJ	North West & W
C59CHM	The Shires	CX54DKL	North West & W	E161OMD	Midlands	F268YTJ	North West & W
C133CFB	Original SST	CX54DKN	North West & W	E224WBG	North West & W	F269YTJ	North West & W
C144NRR	Midlands	CX54DKO	North West & W	E225CFC	Southern	F270YTJ	North West & W
C145NRR	Midlands	CX54DKU	North West & W	E227WBG	North West & W	F281AWW	Midlands
C146NRR	Midlands	CX54DKV	North West & W	E228CFC	Southern	F284AWW	Midlands
C147NRR	Midlands	CX54DKY	North West & W	E229CFC	Southern	F301AWW	North West & W
C148NRR	Midlands	CX54DLD	North West & W	E323OMG	The Shires	F404PUR	The Shires
C212GTU	North West & W	CX54DLF	North West & W	E49WEM	North West & W	F406DUG	Midlands
C260UAJ	North East	CX54DLJ	North West & W	E564BNK	The Shires	F425UVW	The Shires
C261UAJ	North East	CX54DLK	North West & W	E565BNK	The Shires	F467UVW	The Shires
C262UAJ	North East	CX54EPJ	North West & W	E641VFY	North West & W	F506OYW	The Shires
C264XEF	North East	CX54EPK	North West & W	E642VFY	North West & W	F571SMG	Southern
C268XEF	North East	CX54EPL	North West & W	E767JAR	Original SST	F572SMG	Southern
C310BUV	Original SST	CX54EPN	North West & W	E768JAR	Original SST	F573SMG	Southern
C312BUV	London	CX54EPO	North West & W	E769JAR	Original SST	F574SMG	Southern
C313BUV	London	D108NDW	North West & W	E770JAR	Original SST	F575SMG	Southern
C314BUV	London	D146FYM	The Shires	E771JAR	Original SST	F576SMG	Southern
C320BUV	London	D155FYM	North East	E772JAR	Original SST	F577SMG	Southern
C324LDT	North West & W	D155HML	North East	E773JAR	Original SST	F578SMG	Southern
C326BUV	London	D157FYM	North East	E888KYW	Southern	F579SMG	Southern
C327BUV	London	D157HML	North West & W	E891AKN	Southern	F621HGO	Southern
C354BUV	North East	D160FYM	North East	E964JAR	Original SST	F634LMJ	The Shires
C367BUV	London	D162FYM	London	E965JAR	Original SST	F636LMJ	The Shires
C399BVU	London	D165FYM	North East	E966PME	Midlands	F637LMJ	The Shires
C401BUV	Original SST	D166FYM	The Shires	EU05DVW	Original SST	F639LMJ	Southern
C405BUV	London	D167FYM	The Shires	EU05DVX	Original SST	F639LMJ	The Shires
C610ANW	Yorkshire	D168FYM	The Shires	EWW541Y	Yorkshire	F640LMJ	Southern
C611ANW	Yorkshire	D169FYM	The Shires	EWW542Y	Yorkshire	F640LMJ	The Shires
C612ANW	Yorkshire	D170FYM	Midlands	EWW544Y	The Shires	F641LMJ	The Shires
C907GUD	Original SST	D171FYM	Midlands	F27JRC	Midlands	F642LMJ	Southern
C920FMP	Yorkshire	D172FYM	Southern	F28JRC	Midlands	F642LMJ	The Shires
CUB66Y	North East	D174FYM	North East	F33ENF	Midlands	F643LMJ	The Shires
CUB68Y	North East	D178FYM	North East	F34ENF	Midlands	F644LMJ	The Shires
CUV122C	London	D180FYM	London	F35ENF	Midlands	F701ECC	North East
CUV217C	London	D181FYM	The Shires	F36ENF	Midlands	F747XCS	The Shires
CUV264C	London	D187FYM	The Shires	F39ENF	Midlands	F892BKK	Southern
CUV277C	London	D189FYM	North East	F40ENF	Midlands	F893BKK	Southern
CUV280C	London	D190FYM	Midlands	F45ENF	Southern	F894BKK	Southern
CUV287C	London	D191FYM	London	F46ENF	Southern	F895BKK	Southern
CUV304C	London	D196WJC	The Shires	F48ENF	Midlands	F896DKK	Southern
CUV307C	London	D198FYM	London	F48ENF	Southern	F897DKK	Southern
CUV315C	London	D201FYM	London	F51ENF	Midlands	F898DKK	Southern
CUV324C	London	D203FYM	The Shires	F61PRE	North West & W	F899DKK	Southern
CUV325C	London	D211FYM	The Shires	F96PRE	North West & W	F899GUM	Southern
CUV333C	London	D214FYM	London	F97PRE	North West & W	F900DKK	Southern
CUV334C	London	D215FYM	The Shires	F104TML	North West & W	F901GUM	Southern
CUV344C	London	D216FYM	North East	F106TML	North West & W	F902JBB	North West & W
CUV346C	London	D223FYM	London	F107TML	North West & W	FD02UKB	Midlands
CUV346C	London	D224FYM	The Shires	F108TML	North West & W	FD02UKC	Midlands
CUV355C	London	D230FYM	London	F109TML	North West & W	FD02UKE	Midlands
CUV356C	London	D231FYM	The Shires	F110TML	North West & W	FD02UKG	Midlands
CUV359C	London	D234FYM	Southern	F111TML	Midlands	FD02UKJ	Midlands
CWR518Y	North East	D240FYM	The Shires	F112TML	North West & W	FD02UKK	Midlands

Reg	Region	Reg	Region	Reg	Region	Reg	Region
FD02UKL	Midlands	G255UVK	North East	G535VBB	London	G758UYT	North West & W
FD02UKN	Midlands	G256UVK	North East	G536VBB	London	G759UYT	North West & W
FD02UKO	Midlands	G257UVK	North East	G537VBB	London	G760UYT	North East
FD02UKP	Midlands	G258UVK	North East	G538VBB	London	G761UYT	North East
FD02UKR	Midlands	G282EOG	North West & W	G539VBB	London	G762UYT	North East
FD02UKS	Midlands	G283UMJ	The Shires	G540VBB	London	G801BPG	Southern
FD02UKT	Midlands	G286EOG	North West & W	G541VBB	London	G801THA	North West & W
FD02UKU	Midlands	G286UMJ	The Shires	G542VBB	London	G802THA	North West & W
FD52GGO	Midlands	G287UMJ	The Shires	G543VBB	London	G803EKA	North West & W
FD52GGP	Midlands	G288UMJ	The Shires	G544VBB	London	G901SKP	Southern
FD52GGU	Midlands	G290UMJ	The Shires	G545VBB	London	G902SKP	Southern
FD52GGV	Midlands	G291UMJ	The Shires	G546VBB	London	G903SKP	Southern
FE51WSU	Midlands	G292UMJ	The Shires	G547VBB	London	G904SKP	Southern
FE51WSV	Midlands	G293UMJ	The Shires	G548VBB	London	G905SKP	Southern
FE51YWH	Midlands	G294UMJ	The Shires	G549VBB	London	G916LHA	North West & W
FE51YWJ	Midlands	G301DPA	Midlands	G550VBB	London	G917LHA	North West & W
FE51YWK	Midlands	G302DPA	Midlands	G551VBB	London	G918LHA	North West & W
FE51YWL	Midlands	G303DPA	Midlands	G552SGT	The Shires	G919LHA	North West & W
FE51YWM	Midlands	G304DPA	Midlands	G552VBB	London	GK51SYY	Southern
FJ04PFX	Midlands	G305DPA	Midlands	G553VBB	London	GK51SYZ	Southern
FJ54OTN	Midlands	G306DPA	Midlands	G554SGT	The Shires	GK51SZC	Southern
FJ54OTP	Midlands	G307DPA	Midlands	G554VBB	London	GK51SZD	Southern
FJ54OTR	Midlands	G308DPA	Midlands	G555VBB	London	GK51SZE	Southern
FJ54OTT	Midlands	G309DPA	Midlands	G556VBB	London	GK51SZF	Southern
FJ54OTV	Midlands	G322NNW	Yorkshire	G570SGT	The Shires	GK51SZG	Southern
FJ54OTW	Midlands	G324NUM	Midlands	G612BPH	Yorkshire	GK51SZJ	Southern
FJ54OTX	Midlands	G324NWW	North West & W	G616BPH	Southern	GK51SZL	Southern
FJ55BVT	Midlands	G327NUM	North West & W	G618BPH	Yorkshire	GK51SZN	Southern
FJ55BVU	Midlands	G329NUM	North West & W	G619BPH	Yorkshire	GK52YUW	Southern
FJ55BWA	Midlands	G330NUM	Yorkshire	G620BPH	Yorkshire	GK52YUX	Southern
FJ55BWB	Midlands	G331NUM	Yorkshire	G621YMG	The Shires	GK52YUY	Southern
FJ55BWC	Midlands	G332NUM	Yorkshire	G622BPH	Yorkshire	GK52YVB	Southern
FJ55BWD	Midlands	G381EKA	Midlands	G624BPH	Southern	GK52YVC	Southern
FJ55BWE	Midlands	G382EKA	Midlands	G625BPH	Southern	GK52YVD	Southern
FJ55BWF	Midlands	G383EKA	Midlands	G626BPH	Southern	GK52YVE	Southern
FJ55BWG	Midlands	G384EKA	Midlands	G626EKA	Southern	GK52YVF	Southern
FK52MML	Midlands	G385EKA	Midlands	G627BPH	Southern	GK52YVG	Southern
FKM866V	The Shires	G386EKA	Midlands	G628EKA	Southern	GK52YVJ	Southern
FL52MML	Midlands	G387EKA	Midlands	G629BPH	Southern	GK52YVL	Southern
FN04AFJ	Midlands	G388EKA	Midlands	G630BPH	Southern	GK53AOA	Southern
FN52XBG	Midlands	G501SFT	Midlands	G631BPH	Southern	GK53AOB	Southern
G21HHG	North East	G502SFT	Midlands	G632BPH	Southern	GK53AOC	Southern
G34HKY	Midlands	G503SFT	Midlands	G633BPH	Southern	GK53AOD	Southern
G35HKY	North West & W	G504SFT	Midlands	G634BPH	Southern	GK53AOE	Southern
G36HKY	Midlands	G505SFT	Midlands	G635BPH	Southern	GK53AOF	Southern
G37HKY	Midlands	G506SFT	North West & W	G636BPH	Southern	GK53AOG	Southern
G38HKY	Midlands	G507SFT	Midlands	G637BPH	Yorkshire	GK53AOH	Southern
G38YHJ	Midlands	G508EAJ	North East	G639BPH	Yorkshire	GK53AOJ	Southern
G40YHJ	Midlands	G508SFT	North West & W	G643BPH	Southern	GK53AOL	Southern
G45VME	North West & W	G509EAJ	North East	G645UPP	The Shires	GK53AON	Southern
G45VME	Southern	G509SFT	North West & W	G646BPH	Midlands	GK53AOO	Southern
G49CVC	North West & W	G510EAJ	North East	G646UPP	The Shires	GK53AOP	Southern
G97VMM	The Shires	G510SFT	Midlands	G647BPH	Midlands	GK53AOR	Southern
G108OUG	Midlands	G511EAJ	Scotland	G647EKA	North West & W	GK53AOT	Southern
G110OUG	Midlands	G511SFT	Midlands	G647UPP	The Shires	GK53AOU	Southern
G122RGT	North West & W	G512EAJ	North East	G648UPP	The Shires	GK53AOV	Southern
G123RGT	North West & W	G512SFT	North West & W	G649UPP	The Shires	GK53AOW	Southern
G125RGT	North West & W	G513SFT	North West & W	G650EKA	North West & W	GK53AOX	Southern
G129EOG	North West & W	G515VBB	London	G650UPP	The Shires	GK53AOY	Southern
G129YEV	The Shires	G516VBB	London	G651EKA	North West & W	GK53AOZ	Southern
G130YEV	The Shires	G517VBB	London	G651UPP	The Shires	GKA449L	North West & W
G131YWC	The Shires	G518VBB	London	G652EKA	North West & W	GN04UCW	Southern
G132YWC	The Shires	G519VBB	London	G652UPP	The Shires	GN04UCX	Southern
G137EOG	North West & W	G520VBB	London	G653EKA	North West & W	GN04UCY	Southern
G141GOL	Midlands	G521VBB	London	G653UPP	The Shires	GN04UCZ	Southern
G149CHP	North West & W	G521WJF	North West & W	G654UPP	The Shires	GN04UDB	Southern
G154TYT	Scotland	G522WJF	North West & W	G655UPP	The Shires	GN04UDD	Southern
G175EOG	North West & W	G523VBB	London	G656UPP	The Shires	GN04UDE	Southern
G210HCP	North East	G523WJF	North West & W	G657UPP	The Shires	GN04UDG	Southern
G214HCP	North East	G524WJF	North West & W	G661DTJ	North West & W	GN04UDH	Southern
G218LGK	Midlands	G525VBB	London	G663FKA	Southern	GN04UDJ	Southern
G230VWL	The Shires	G525WJF	North West & W	G664FKA	Southern	GN04UDK	Southern
G231VWL	The Shires	G526VBB	London	G665FKA	Southern	GN04UDL	Southern
G232VWL	The Shires	G526VBB	London	G711LKW	Midlands	GN04UDM	Southern
G234VWL	The Shires	G530VBB	London	G714LKW	Midlands	GN04UDP	Southern
G235VWL	The Shires	G531VBB	London	G754UYT	North West & W	GN04UDS	Southern
G251SRG	North East	G532VBB	London	G755UYT	North West & W	GN04UDT	Southern
G252SRG	North East	G533VBB	London	G756UYT	North East	GN04UDU	Southern
G254SRG	North East	G534VBB	London	G757UYT	North East	GN04UDV	Southern

Reg	Region	Reg	Region	Reg	Region	Reg	Region
GN04UDW	Southern	GYE603W	Original SST	H616UWR	The Shires	J102WSC	North West & W
GN04UDX	Southern	H31PAJ	Scotland	H649GPF	Midlands	J103WSC	North West & W
GN04UDY	Southern	H32PAJ	North East	H650GPF	Midlands	J104WSC	North West & W
GN04UDZ	Southern	H34PAJ	North West & W	H651GPF	Midlands	J105WSC	North West & W
GN04UEA	Southern	H73DVM	Midlands	H652GPF	Midlands	J106WSC	North West & W
GN04UEB	Southern	H74DVM	Midlands	H653GPF	Midlands	J107WSC	North West & W
GN04UEC	Southern	H78DVM	North West & W	H654GPF	Midlands	J108WSC	North West & W
GN04UED	Southern	H79DVM	North West & W	H655GPF	Midlands	J109WSC	North West & W
GN04UEE	Southern	H81DVM	Midlands	H656GPF	Midlands	J110WSC	North West & W
GN04UEF	Southern	H82DVM	Midlands	H658GPF	Midlands	J112WSC	North West & W
GN04UEG	Southern	H83DVM	Midlands	H659GPF	Midlands	J113WSC	North West & W
GN04UEH	Southern	H84DVM	Midlands	H660GPF	North West & W	J114WSC	North West & W
GN04UEJ	Southern	H85DVM	North West & W	H661GPF	North West & W	J115WSC	North West & W
GN04UEK	Southern	H86DVM	North West & W	H662GPF	North West & W	J154NKN	Southern
GN04UEL	Southern	H87DVM	North West & W	H663GPF	Midlands	J162REH	Southern
GN04UEM	Southern	H101GEV	North West & W	H664GPF	Midlands	J169REH	Southern
GN04UEP	Southern	H102GEV	North West & W	H665GPF	North West & W	J220HGY	Yorkshire
GN04UER	Southern	H103GEV	North West & W	H667GPF	North West & W	J221HGY	Yorkshire
GN04UES	Southern	H104GEV	North West & W	H668GPF	Scotland	J249KWM	North West & W
GN04UET	Southern	H105GEV	North West & W	H669GPF	Midlands	J251KWM	North West & W
GN04UEU	Southern	H106GEV	North West & W	H670GPF	Scotland	J311WHJ	North West & W
GN04UEV	Southern	H106RWT	Yorkshire	H671GPF	Midlands	J312WHJ	North West & W
GN04UEW	Southern	H107GEV	North West & W	H672GPF	Midlands	J313WHJ	North West & W
GN04UEX	Southern	H108GEV	North West & W	H674GPF	Midlands	J314XVX	North West & W
GN04UEY	Southern	H108RWT	Yorkshire	H675GPF	Scotland	J315BSH	London
GN04UEZ	Southern	H109GEV	North West & W	H676GPF	Scotland	J315XVX	North West & W
GN04UFA	Southern	H110GEV	North West & W	H677GPF	Scotland	J319BSH	London
GN04UFB	Southern	H112GEV	North West & W	H679GPF	North West & W	J320BSH	Original SST
GN04UFC	Southern	H113ABV	North West & W	H680GPF	Midlands	J320BSH	Original SST
GN04UFD	Southern	H113GEV	North West & W	H681GPF	Scotland	J320BSH	Original SST
GN04UFE	Southern	H114GEV	North West & W	H682GPF	Midlands	J321BSH	Original SST
GN04UFG	Southern	H115ABV	North West & W	H684GPF	Midlands	J324BSH	London
GN04UFH	Southern	H115GEV	North West & W	H733HWK	North West & W	J325BSH	Original SST
GN04UFJ	Southern	H130LPU	North West & W	H755WWW	North East	J326BSH	Original SST
GN04UFK	Southern	H163DJU	North West & W	H765EKJ	Southern	J327BSH	Original SST
GN04UFL	Southern	H192JNF	North West & W	H766EKJ	Southern	J327VAW	Midlands
GN04UFM	Southern	H196GRO	The Shires	H767EKJ	Southern	J328VAW	North West & W
GN04UFP	Southern	H197GRO	The Shires	H768EKJ	Southern	J330BSH	Original SST
GN04UFR	Southern	H198GRO	The Shires	H769EKJ	Southern	J331BSH	London
GN04UFS	Southern	H199AOD	The Shires	H76DVM	Midlands	J332BSH	London
GN04UFT	Southern	H202GRO	The Shires	H770EKJ	Southern	J334BSH	London
GN04UFU	Southern	H203GRO	The Shires	H803AHA	North West & W	J335BSH	Original SST
GN04UFV	Southern	H242MUK	Scotland	H803RWJ	Midlands	J336BSH	Original SST
GN04UFW	Southern	H243MUK	The Shires	H804AHA	North West & W	J337BSH	London
GN04UFX	Southern	H244MUK	Scotland	H804RWJ	Midlands	J338BSH	Original SST
GN04UFY	Southern	H253PAJ	North East	H805AHA	North West & W	J339BSH	London
GN04UFZ	Southern	H254GEV	The Shires	H805RWJ	Midlands	J340BSH	Original SST
GN04UGA	Southern	H254PAJ	North West & W	H806AHA	North West & W	J341BSH	Original SST
GN04UGB	Southern	H256YLG	Southern	H814EKJ	Southern	J342BSH	Original SST
GN04UGC	Southern	H262GEV	Southern	H815EKJ	Southern	J343BSH	Original SST
GN04UGD	Southern	H263GEV	Southern	H816EKJ	Southern	J344BSH	Original SST
GN04UGE	Southern	H264GEV	Southern	H845AHS	The Shires	J345BSH	Original SST
GN04UGF	Southern	H265GEV	Southern	H846AHS	Southern	J346BSH	London
GN04UGG	Southern	H266CFT	North East	H851NOC	North West & W	J347BSH	Original SST
GN05ANU	Southern	H267CFT	North East	H878LOX	Yorkshire	J348BSH	Original SST
GN05ANV	Southern	H278LEF	North West & W	H914XYT	Midlands	J349BSH	Original SST
GN05ANX	Southern	H279LEF	North West & W	H917XYT	North East	J352BSH	London
GN05AOA	Southern	H28MJN	North West & W	H918XYT	Midlands	J363YWX	Yorkshire
GN05AOB	Southern	H338TYG	North East	H919XYT	Midlands	J365YWX	Yorkshire
GN05AOC	Southern	H338UWT	North East	H922LOX	The Shires	J371TWX	North East
GSU347	Scotland	H339UWT	North East	H923XYT	North East	J376AWT	Yorkshire
GTO301V	Midlands	H344UWX	Yorkshire	H926LOX	The Shires	J379BWU	Yorkshire
GYE353W	Original SST	H344UWX	Yorkshire	HIL2148	Scotland	J381BWU	Yorkshire
GYE365W	North West & W	H358WWY	Yorkshire	HIL7595	The Shires	J382BWU	Yorkshire
GYE396W	North East	H367XGC	The Shires	IIL7269	Original SST	J402XVX	The Shires
GYE456W	North West & W	H368XGC	The Shires	J3SLT	North West & W	J403XVX	The Shires
GYE495W	Original SST	H369XGC	The Shires	J6SLT	North West & W	J404XVX	The Shires
GYE500W	Original SST	H370XGC	The Shires	J7SLT	North West & W	J411WSC	North West & W
GYE509W	Original SST	H393WWY	Yorkshire	J8SLT	North West & W	J413NCP	North East
GYE615W	North East	H407FRO	The Shires	J9SLT	North West & W	J414NCP	North East
GYE525W	Original SST	H501GHA	Midlands	J23GCX	Yorkshire	J433BSH	Original SST
GYE533W	Original SST	H512YCX	Yorkshire	J25UNY	Southern	J463MKL	Southern
GYE537W	London	H542FWM	North West & W	J26UNY	The Shires	J465MKL	Yorkshire
GYE537W	London	H543FWM	North West & W	J31SFA	Midlands	J465UFS	The Shires
GYE539W	Original SST	H567MPD	The Shires	J32SFA	Midlands	J466OKP	Yorkshire
GYE553W	Original SST	H575DVM	Midlands	J34SRF	Midlands	J467OKP	Yorkshire
GYE555W	Original SST	H577DVM	Midlands	J36GCX	Southern	J468OKP	Yorkshire
GYE558W	Original SST	H580DVM	Midlands	J64BJN	The Shires	J469SKO	Southern
GYE575W	London	H588DVM	North West & W	J101WSC	North West & W	J556GTP	North West & W

J620UHN	North East	K211UHA	Midlands	K817NKH	North West & W	KL52CWR	The Shires
J651UHN	North East	K212UHA	Midlands	K877UDB	North West & W	KL52CWT	The Shires
J652UHN	North East	K213UHA	Midlands	K906SKR	Southern	KL52CWU	The Shires
J653UHN	North East	K214UHA	Midlands	K907SKR	Southern	KL52CWV	The Shires
J654UHN	North West & W	K215UHA	Midlands	K908SKR	Southern	KL52CWW	The Shires
J655UHN	North West & W	K216UHA	Midlands	K909SKR	Southern	KL52CWZ	The Shires
J656UHN	North East	K217UHA	Midlands	K910SKR	Southern	KL52CXA	The Shires
J657UHN	North East	K218UHA	Midlands	K911OEM	North West & W	KL52CXB	The Shires
J658UHN	North East	K318CVX	The Shires	K946SGG	Scotland	KL52CXC	The Shires
J65BJN	The Shires	K319CVX	The Shires	K947SGG	Scotland	KL52CXD	The Shires
J65UNA	The Shires	K320CVX	Yorkshire	K955PBG	North West & W	KL52CXE	The Shires
J701NHA	North West & W	K321CVX	The Shires	KC03PGE	The Shires	KL52CXF	The Shires
J802KHD	Yorkshire	K322CVX	The Shires	KC03PGF	The Shires	KL52CXG	The Shires
J866UPY	North East	K401HWW	Yorkshire	KC51NFO	Southern	KL52CXH	The Shires
J926CYL	North East	K402HWW	Yorkshire	KC51PUX	Southern	KL52CXJ	The Shires
J927CYL	North East	K403HWW	Yorkshire	KE03OUK	The Shires	KL52CXK	The Shires
J929CYL	North East	K404HWW	Yorkshire	KE03OUL	The Shires	KL52CXM	The Shires
J930CYL	North East	K405FHJ	The Shires	KE03OUM	The Shires	KL52CXN	The Shires
J931CYL	North East	K405HWX	Yorkshire	KE03OUN	The Shires	KL52CXO	The Shires
JDZ2353	The Shires	K406FHJ	The Shires	KE03OUP	The Shires	KL52CXP	The Shires
JHK495N	The Shires	K407FHJ	The Shires	KE03OUS	The Shires	KL52CXR	The Shires
JJD366D	London	K408BHN	North East	KE03OUU	The Shires	KL52CXS	The Shires
JJD370D	London	K408FHJ	The Shires	KE03UKK	The Shires	KVY752X	London
JJD375D	London	K409BHN	North East	KE04CZF	The Shires	KVY770X	London
JJD386D	London	K409FHJ	The Shires	KE04CZG	The Shires	KVY773X	London
JJD387D	London	K410BHN	North East	KE04CZH	The Shires	KYC617X	London
JJD401D	London	K410FHJ	The Shires	KE04OSU	The Shires	KYV646X	North East
JJD406D	London	K411BHN	North East	KE04OSV	The Shires	KYV663X	North West & W
JJD408D	London	K411FHJ	The Shires	KE04PZF	The Shires	KYV663X	Original SST
JJD409D	London	K412BHN	North East	KE04PZG	The Shires	KYV671X	North East
JJD416D	London	K412FHJ	The Shires	KE05FMM	The Shires	KYV672X	Original SST
JJD434D	London	K413BHN	North East	KE05FMO	The Shires	KYV689X	North West & W
JJD457D	London	K413FHJ	The Shires	KE05FMP	The Shires	KYV707X	Original SST
JJD468D	London	K414BHN	North East	KE05FMU	The Shires	KYV710X	Original SST
JJD483D	London	K414FHJ	The Shires	KE05FMV	The Shires	KYV724X	Original SST
JJD491D	London	K415BHN	North East	KE05FMX	The Shires	KYV729X	Original SST
JJD492D	London	K416BHN	North East	KE05GOH	The Shires	KYV748X	Original SST
JJD494D	London	K417BHN	North East	KE51PSZ	The Shires	KYV772X	London
JJD503D	London	K447XPA	The Shires	KE51PTO	The Shires	KYV777X	London
JJD521D	London	K448XPA	The Shires	KE51PTU	The Shires	L1SLT	North West & W
JJD525D	London	K471SKO	Yorkshire	KE51PTX	The Shires	L2SLT	North West & W
JJD526D	London	K504BHN	North East	KE51PTY	Southern	L11SLT	North West & W
JJD528D	London	K505BHN	North East	KE51PTZ	Southern	L25LSX	Scotland
JJD533D	London	K506BHN	North East	KE51PUA	Southern	L34PNN	Midlands
JJD534D	London	K507BHN	North East	KE51PUF	Southern	L35PNN	Midlands
JJD544D	London	K508BHN	North East	KE51PUH	Southern	L36PNN	Midlands
JJD545D	London	K509BHN	North East	KE51PUJ	Southern	L37PNN	Midlands
JJD546D	London	K510BHN	North East	KE51PUK	Southern	L38PNN	Midlands
JJD549D	London	K510RJX	North West & W	KE51PUO	Southern	L43MEH	The Shires
JJD562D	London	K511BHN	North East	KE51PUU	Southern	L94HRF	Midlands
JJD567D	London	K512BHN	North East	KE51PUV	Southern	L95HRF	Midlands
JJD571D	London	K513BHN	North East	KE51PUY	Southern	L100SBS	North East
JJD572D	London	K514BHN	North East	KE51PVA	Southern	L102MEH	North East
JJD573D	London	K515BHN	North East	KE51PVF	The Shires	L105SDY	The Shires
JJD577D	London	K516BHN	North East	KE51PVK	The Shires	L112YVK	Southern
JJD586D	London	K517BHN	North East	KE51PVZ	The Shires	L113YVK	Southern
JJD591D	London	K538ORH	Scotland	KE51WUO	The Shires	L114YVK	Yorkshire
JJD597D	London	K539ORH	Scotland	KE51WUP	The Shires	L115YVK	North West & W
K1BLU	North West & W	K540ORH	Scotland	KE53KBO	The Shires	L116YVK	North West & W
K27EWC	North West & W	K541ORH	Scotland	KE53KBP	The Shires	L117YVK	North West & W
K36XNE	Southern	K542ORH	Midlands	KE53NEU	The Shires	L118YVK	The Shires
K37XNE	Southern	K543ORH	Midlands	KE53NFA	The Shires	L119YVK	The Shires
K38YVM	Southern	K544ORH	Midlands	KE53NFC	The Shires	L120YVK	North West & W
K73SRG	North West & W	K545ORH	Midlands	KE53NFD	The Shires	L121YVK	North West & W
K74SRG	North West & W	K547ORH	Midlands	KE53NFF	The Shires	L122YVK	North West & W
K75SRG	North West & W	K548ORH	Midlands	KE53NFG	The Shires	L123YVK	North West & W
K101OHF	North West & W	K549ORH	Midlands	KE54HHF	The Shires	L124YVK	The Shires
K102OHF	North West & W	K550ORH	Midlands	KE54LNR	The Shires	L125YVK	North West & W
K103OHF	North West & W	K551ORH	Midlands	KE54LPC	The Shires	L126YVK	North West & W
K104OHF	North West & W	K552ORH	Midlands	KE54LPF	The Shires	L127YVK	Yorkshire
K105OHF	North West & W	K601HWR	Yorkshire	KE54LPJ	The Shires	L128YVK	Yorkshire
K106OHF	North West & W	K760JVX	The Shires	KE55CKO	The Shires	L129YVK	Yorkshire
K107OHF	North West & W	K761JVX	The Shires	KE55CKP	The Shires	L130YVK	Yorkshire
K108OHF	North West & W	K762JVX	The Shires	KE55CKU	The Shires	L131YVK	Yorkshire
K130TCP	North West & W	K801HWW	Yorkshire	KL52CWJ	The Shires	L132YVK	Southern
K131TCP	North West & W	K802HWW	Yorkshire	KL52CWK	The Shires	L133HVS	The Shires
K132TCP	North West & W	K803HWW	Yorkshire	KL52CWN	The Shires	L133YVK	Southern
K133TCP	North West & W	K804HWW	Yorkshire	KL52CWO	The Shires	L134YVK	Southern
K140RYS	North East	K805HWX	Yorkshire	KL52CWP	The Shires	L135YVK	Southern

Reg	Area	Reg	Area	Reg	Area	Reg	Area
L136YVK	Yorkshire	L228TKA	North West & W	L504CPB	Midlands	L588JSG	North West & W
L137YVK	Yorkshire	L229TKA	North West & W	L504CPJ	Southern	L601EKM	Southern
L138YVK	Southern	L230TKA	North West & W	L504TKA	North West & W	L602EKM	Southern
L139YVK	Midlands	L231TKA	North West & W	L505CPJ	Southern	L603EKM	Southern
L140YVK	Yorkshire	L232TKA	North West & W	L505TKA	North West & W	L603FHN	North East
L141YVK	Yorkshire	L233TKA	North West & W	L506BNX	Midlands	L604EKM	Southern
L142YVK	Midlands	L234TKA	North West & W	L506CPJ	Southern	L605BNX	Midlands
L143YVK	Southern	L235TKA	North West & W	L506TKA	North West & W	L605EKM	Southern
L144YVK	Midlands	L236TKA	North West & W	L507BNX	Midlands	L606EKM	Southern
L145YVK	Southern	L237TKA	North West & W	L507CPJ	Southern	L607EKM	Southern
L146YVK	Yorkshire	L238TKA	North West & W	L507TKA	North West & W	L608EKM	Southern
L148WAG	North West & W	L239TKA	North West & W	L508BNX	Midlands	L609EKM	Southern
L148YVK	Southern	L240TKA	North West & W	L508TKA	North West & W	L610EKM	Southern
L149BFV	The Shires	L241TKA	North West & W	L509BNX	Midlands	L618BNX	North West & W
L149WAG	North West & W	L242TKA	North West & W	L509CPJ	Southern	L620BNX	Midlands
L149YVK	Yorkshire	L243TKA	North West & W	L509TKA	North West & W	L686SUM	North West & W
L150SBG	North West & W	L244TKA	North West & W	L510BNX	Midlands	L700BUS	North East
L150WAG	North West & W	L247WAG	North West & W	L510CPJ	Southern	L766DPE	Midlands
L150YVK	Southern	L271FVN	North East	L510TKA	North West & W	L806NNW	Yorkshire
L151SBG	North West & W	L272FVN	North East	L511BNX	Midlands	L807NNW	Yorkshire
L151YVK	North West & W	L273FVN	North East	L511CPJ	Southern	L808NNW	Yorkshire
L152SBG	North West & W	L274FVN	North East	L511TKA	North West & W	L809NNW	Yorkshire
L152YVK	Yorkshire	L275FVN	North East	L512BNX	Midlands	L810NNW	Yorkshire
L153UKB	North West & W	L300BUS	The Shires	L512CPJ	Southern	L811NNW	Yorkshire
L153YVK	Southern	L300SBS	Midlands	L512TKA	North West & W	L812NNW	Yorkshire
L154UKB	North West & W	L301NFA	Midlands	L513BNX	Midlands	L813NNW	Yorkshire
L154YVK	Southern	L301TEM	North West & W	L513CPJ	Southern	L814NNW	Yorkshire
L155UKB	North West & W	L302NFA	Midlands	L513TKA	North West & W	L815NNW	Yorkshire
L155YVK	Southern	L302TEM	North West & W	L514BNX	Midlands	L816NWY	Yorkshire
L156UKB	North West & W	L303NFA	Midlands	L514CPJ	Southern	L817NWY	Yorkshire
L156YVK	Southern	L303TEM	North West & W	L515BNX	Midlands	L818NWY	Yorkshire
L157YVK	Yorkshire	L304NFA	Midlands	L515CPJ	Southern	L819NWY	Yorkshire
L158BFT	Southern	L305HPP	The Shires	L516BNX	Midlands	L820NWY	Yorkshire
L158BFT	Yorkshire	L305NFA	Midlands	L517BNX	Midlands	L821NWY	Yorkshire
L159CCW	The Shires	L306HPP	The Shires	L519BNX	Midlands	L822NWY	Yorkshire
L159GYL	North East	L307HPP	The Shires	L519FHN	North East	L823NWY	Yorkshire
L160GYL	North East	L308HPP	The Shires	L521BNX	Midlands	L824NWY	Yorkshire
L161GYL	North East	L309HPP	The Shires	L521FHN	North East	L825NWY	Yorkshire
L190DDW	North West & W	L310HPP	The Shires	L522BNX	Midlands	L826NYG	Yorkshire
L200BUS	The Shires	L311HPP	The Shires	L522FHN	North East	L827NYG	Yorkshire
L201TKA	North West & W	L312HPP	The Shires	L523BNX	Midlands	L828NYG	Yorkshire
L202TKA	North West & W	L313HPP	The Shires	L523FHN	North East	L829NYG	Yorkshire
L203TKA	North West & W	L314HPP	The Shires	L524FHN	North East	L830NYG	Yorkshire
L203YCU	Southern	L315HPP	The Shires	L525FHN	North East	L922LJO	The Shires
L204TKA	North West & W	L316HPP	The Shires	L526FHN	North East	L923LJO	The Shires
L204YCU	Southern	L400BUS	The Shires	L527FHN	North East	L934GYL	North West & W
L205TKA	North West & W	L402TKB	North West & W	L528FHN	North East	L935GYL	North West & W
L205VAG	North West & W	L403TKB	North West & W	L529FHN	North East	L936GYL	North West & W
L205YCU	Southern	L404TKB	North West & W	L530FHN	North East	L937GYL	North West & W
L206TKA	North West & W	L405TKB	North West & W	L531FHN	North East	L938GYL	North West & W
L206YCU	Southern	L406NUA	Yorkshire	L532EHD	North East	L939GYL	North West & W
L207YCU	Southern	L406TKB	North West & W	L532FHN	North East	L940GYL	North West & W
L208ONU	North West & W	L407NUA	Yorkshire	L533EHD	North East	L941GYL	North West & W
L208TKA	North West & W	L407TKB	North West & W	L533FHN	North East	LDS279A	London
L208YCU	Southern	L408NUA	Yorkshire	L534FHN	North East	LDS402A	London
L209ONU	North West & W	L408TKB	North West & W	L535FHN	North East	LF02PKA	London
L209TKA	North West & W	L409NUA	Yorkshire	L536FHN	North East	LF02PKC	London
L209YCU	Southern	L409TKB	North West & W	L537FHN	North East	LF02PKD	London
L210TKA	North West & W	L410TKB	North West & W	L539FHN	North East	LF02PKE	London
L210YCU	Southern	L411UFY	North West & W	L540FHN	North East	LF02PKJ	London
L211SBG	North West & W	L412UFY	North West & W	L541FHN	North East	LF02PKO	London
L211TKA	North West & W	L413TKB	North West & W	L542FHN	North East	LF02PKU	London
L211YCU	Southern	L415NHJ	The Shires	L543FHN	North East	LF02PKV	London
L212TKA	North West & W	L418FHN	North East	L544GHN	North East	LF02PKX	London
L213TKA	North West & W	L419FHN	North East	L545GHN	North East	LF02PKY	London
L214TKA	North West & W	L420FHN	North East	L546GHN	North East	LF02PKZ	London
L215TKA	North West & W	L421FHN	North East	L547GHN	North East	LF02PLJ	London
L216TKA	North West & W	L422FHN	North East	L548GHN	North East	LF02PLN	London
L217TKA	North West & W	L460NMJ	The Shires	L549GHN	North East	LF02PLO	London
L218TKA	North West & W	L500BUS	The Shires	L550GHN	North East	LF02PLU	London
L219TKA	North West & W	L500UKI	Southern	L551GHN	North East	LF02PLV	London
L220TKA	North West & W	L501TKA	North West & W	L557YCU	Southern	LF02PLX	London
L221TKA	North West & W	L502BNX	Midlands	L558YCU	Southern	LF02PLZ	London
L222TKA	North West & W	L502TKA	North West & W	L559YCU	Southern	LF02PMO	London
L223TKA	North West & W	L503BNX	Midlands	L561YCU	Southern	LF02PMV	London
L224TKA	North West & W	L503CPB	Midlands	L562YCU	Southern	LF02PMX	London
L225TKA	North West & W	L503HKM	Southern	L563YCU	Southern	LF02PMY	London
L226TKA	North West & W	L503TKA	North West & W	L564YCU	Southern	LF02PNE	London
L227TKA	North West & W	L504BNX	Midlands	L565YCU	Southern	LF02PNJ	London

LF02PNK	London	LF52URC	London	LG03MRU	London	LJ03MKZ	London
LF02PNL	London	LF52URD	London	LG03MRV	London	LJ03MLE	London
LF02PNN	London	LF52URE	London	LG03MRX	London	LJ03MLF	London
LF02PNO	London	LF52URG	London	LG03MRY	London	LJ03MLK	London
LF02PNU	London	LF52URH	London	LG03MSU	London	LJ03MLX	London
LF02PNV	London	LF52URJ	London	LG03MSV	London	LJ03MLY	London
LF02PNX	London	LF52URK	London	LG03MSX	London	LJ03MLZ	London
LF02PNY	London	LF52URL	London	LG52DAA	London	LJ03MMA	London
LF02POA	London	LF52URM	London	LG52DAO	London	LJ03MME	London
LF02POH	London	LF52URN	London	LG52DAU	London	LJ03MMF	London
LF02PRZ	London	LF52URO	London	LG52DBO	London	LJ03MMK	London
LF02PSO	London	LF52URP	London	LG52DBU	London	LJ03MSY	London
LF02PSU	London	LF52URR	London	LG52DBV	London	LJ03MTE	London
LF02PSX	London	LF52URS	London	LG52DBY	London	LJ03MTF	London
LF02PSY	London	LF52URT	London	LG52DBZ	London	LJ03MTK	London
LF02PSZ	London	LF52URU	London	LG52DCE	London	LJ03MTU	London
LF02PTO	London	LF52URV	London	LG52DCF	London	LJ03MTV	London
LF02PTU	London	LF52URW	London	LG52DCO	London	LJ03MTY	London
LF02PTX	London	LF52URX	London	LG52DCU	London	LJ03MTZ	London
LF02PTY	London	LF52URY	London	LG52DCV	London	LJ03MUA	London
LF02PTZ	London	LF52URZ	London	LG52DCX	London	LJ03MUB	London
LF02PVA	Southern	LF52USB	London	LG52DCY	London	LJ03MUW	London
LF02PVE	London	LF52USC	London	LG52DCZ	London	LJ03MUY	London
LF02PVJ	London	LF52USD	London	LG52DDA	London	LJ03MVC	London
LF02PVK	London	LF52USG	London	LG52DDE	London	LJ03MVD	London
LF02PVL	London	LF52USH	London	LG52DDF	London	LJ03MVE	London
LF02PVN	London	LF52USJ	London	LG52DDJ	London	LJ03MVF	London
LF02PVO	London	LF52USL	London	LG52DDK	London	LJ03MVG	London
LF52UNV	London	LF52USM	London	LG52DDL	London	LJ03MVT	London
LF52UNW	London	LF52USN	London	LJ03MDV	London	LJ03MVV	London
LF52UNX	London	LF52USO	London	LJ03MDX	London	LJ03MVW	London
LF52UNY	London	LF52USS	London	LJ03MDY	London	LJ03MVX	London
LF52UNZ	London	LF52UST	London	LJ03MDZ	London	LJ03MVY	London
LF52UOA	London	LF52USU	London	LJ03MEU	London	LJ03MVZ	London
LF52UOB	London	LF52USV	London	LJ03MFN	London	LJ03MWA	London
LF52UOC	London	LF52USW	London	LJ03MFP	London	LJ03MWC	London
LF52UOD	London	LF52USX	London	LJ03MFU	London	LJ03MWD	London
LF52UOE	London	LF52USY	London	LJ03MFV	London	LJ03MWE	London
LF52UOG	London	LF52USZ	London	LJ03MFX	London	LJ03MWF	London
LF52UOH	London	LF52UTA	London	LJ03MFY	London	LJ03MWG	London
LF52UOJ	London	LF52UTB	London	LJ03MFZ	London	LJ03MWK	London
LF52UOK	London	LF52UTC	London	LJ03MGE	London	LJ03MWL	London
LF52UOL	London	LF52UTE	London	LJ03MGU	London	LJ03MWN	London
LF52UOM	London	LF52UTG	London	LJ03MGV	London	LJ03MWP	London
LF52UON	London	LF52UTH	London	LJ03MGX	London	LJ03MWU	London
LF52UOO	London	LF52UTJ	London	LJ03MGY	London	LJ03MWV	London
LF52UOP	London	LF52UTL	London	LJ03MGZ	London	LJ03MWX	London
LF52UOR	London	LF52UTM	London	LJ03MHA	London	LJ03MXH	London
LF52UOS	London	LG03MBF	London	LJ03MHE	London	LJ03MXK	London
LF52UOT	London	LG03MBU	London	LJ03MHF	London	LJ03MXL	London
LF52UOU	London	LG03MBV	London	LJ03MHK	London	LJ03MXM	London
LF52UOV	London	LG03MBX	London	LJ03MHL	London	LJ03MXN	London
LF52UOW	London	LG03MBY	London	LJ03MHM	London	LJ03MXP	London
LF52UOX	London	LG03MDE	London	LJ03MHN	London	LJ03MXR	London
LF52UOY	London	LG03MDF	London	LJ03MHU	London	LJ03MXS	London
LF52UPA	London	LG03MDK	London	LJ03MHV	London	LJ03MXT	London
LF52UPB	London	LG03MDN	London	LJ03MHX	London	LJ03MXU	London
LF52UPC	London	LG03MDU	London	LJ03MHY	London	LJ03MXV	London
LF52UPD	London	LG03MEV	London	LJ03MHZ	London	LJ03MXW	London
LF52UPE	London	LG03MFA	London	LJ03MJE	London	LJ03MXX	London
LF52UPG	London	LG03MFE	London	LJ03MJF	London	LJ03MXY	London
LF52UPH	London	LG03MFF	London	LJ03MJK	London	LJ03MXZ	London
LF52UPJ	London	LG03MFK	London	LJ03MJU	London	LJ03MYA	London
LF52UPK	London	LG03MLL	London	LJ03MJV	London	LJ03MYB	London
LF52UPL	London	LG03MLN	London	LJ03MJX	London	LJ03MYC	London
LF52UPM	London	LG03MLV	London	LJ03MJY	London	LJ03MYD	London
LF52UPN	London	LG03MMU	London	LJ03MKA	London	LJ03MYF	London
LF52UPO	London	LG03MMV	London	LJ03MKC	London	LJ03MYG	London
LF52UPP	London	LG03MMX	London	LJ03MKD	London	LJ03MYH	London
LF52UPR	London	LG03MOA	London	LJ03MKE	London	LJ03MYK	London
LF52UPS	London	LG03MOF	London	LJ03MKF	London	LJ03MYL	London
LF52UPT	London	LG03MOV	London	LJ03MKG	London	LJ03MYM	London
LF52UPV	London	LG03MPE	London	LJ03MKK	London	LJ03MYN	London
LF52UPW	London	LG03MPF	London	LJ03MKL	London	LJ03MYP	London
LF52UPX	London	LG03MPU	London	LJ03MKM	London	LJ03MYR	London
LF52UPY	London	LG03MPV	London	LJ03MKN	London	LJ03MYS	London
LF52UPZ	London	LG03MPX	London	LJ03MKU	London	LJ03MYT	London
LF52URA	London	LG03MPY	London	LJ03MKV	London	LJ03MYU	London
LF52URB	London	LG03MPZ	London	LJ03MKX	London	LJ03MYV	London

J03MYX	London	LJ05BJV	London	LJ51DDO	London	LJ51ORF	London
J03MYY	London	LJ05BJX	London	LJ51DDU	London	LJ51ORG	London
J03MYZ	London	LJ05BJY	London	LJ51DDV	London	LJ51ORH	London
J03MZD	London	LJ05BJZ	London	LJ51DDX	London	LJ51ORK	London
J03MZE	London	LJ05BKA	London	LJ51DDY	London	LJ51ORL	London
J03MZF	London	LJ05BKD	London	LJ51DDZ	London	LJ51OSK	London
J03MZG	London	LJ05BKF	London	LJ51DEU	London	LJ51OSX	London
J03MZL	London	LJ05BKY	London	LJ51DFA	London	LJ51OSY	London
J04LDA	London	LJ05BKZ	London	LJ51DFC	London	LJ51OSZ	London
J04LDC	London	LJ05BLF	London	LJ51DFD	London	LJ53BAA	London
J04LDD	London	LJ05BLK	London	LJ51DFE	London	LJ53BAO	London
J04LDE	London	LJ05BLN	London	LJ51DFF	London	LJ53BAU	London
J04LDF	London	LJ05BLV	London	LJ51DFG	London	LJ53BAV	London
J04LDK	London	LJ05BLX	London	LJ51DFK	London	LJ53BBE	London
J04LDL	London	LJ05BLY	London	LJ51DFL	London	LJ53BBF	London
J04LDN	London	LJ05BMO	London	LJ51DFN	London	LJ53BBK	London
J04LDU	London	LJ05BMU	London	LJ51DFO	London	LJ53BBN	London
J04LDV	London	LJ05BMV	London	LJ51DFP	London	LJ53BBO	London
J04LDX	London	LJ05BMY	London	LJ51DFU	London	LJ53BBU	London
J04LDY	London	LJ05BMZ	London	LJ51DFV	London	LJ53BBV	London
J04LDZ	London	LJ05BNA	London	LJ51DFX	London	LJ53BBX	London
J04LEF	London	LJ05BNB	London	LJ51DFY	London	LJ53BBZ	London
J04LEU	London	LJ05BND	London	LJ51DFZ	London	LJ53BCF	London
J04LFA	London	LJ05BNE	London	LJ51DGE	London	LJ53BCK	London
J04LFB	London	LJ05BNF	London	LJ51DGF	London	LJ53BCO	London
J04LFD	London	LJ05BNK	London	LJ51DGO	London	LJ53BCU	London
J04LFE	London	LJ05BNL	London	LJ51DGU	London	LJ53BCV	London
J04LFF	London	LJ05GKX	London	LJ51DGV	London	LJ53BCX	London
J04LFG	London	LJ05GKY	London	LJ51DGX	London	LJ53BCY	London
J04LFH	London	LJ05GKZ	London	LJ51DGY	London	LJ53BCZ	London
J04LFK	London	LJ05GLF	London	LJ51DGZ	London	LJ53BDE	London
J04LFL	London	LJ05GLK	London	LJ51DHA	London	LJ53BDF	London
J04LFM	London	LJ05GLV	London	LJ51DHC	London	LJ53BDO	London
J04LFN	London	LJ05GLY	London	LJ51DHD	London	LJ53BDU	London
J04LFP	London	LJ05GLZ	London	LJ51DHE	London	LJ53BDV	London
J04LFR	London	LJ05GME	London	LJ51DHF	London	LJ53BDX	London
J04LFS	London	LJ05GMF	London	LJ51DHG	London	LJ53BDY	London
J04LFT	London	LJ05GOH	London	LJ51DHK	London	LJ53BDZ	London
J04LFU	London	LJ05GOK	London	LJ51DHL	London	LJ53BEO	London
J04LFV	London	LJ05GOP	London	LJ51DHN	London	LJ53BEU	London
J04LFW	London	LJ05GOU	London	LJ51DHO	London	LJ53BEY	London
J04LFX	London	LJ05GOX	London	LJ51DHP	London	LJ53BFA	London
J04LFY	London	LJ05GPF	London	LJ51DHV	London	LJ53BFE	London
J04LFZ	London	LJ05GPK	London	LJ51DHX	London	LJ53BFF	London
J04LGA	London	LJ05GPO	London	LJ51DHY	London	LJ53BFK	London
J04LGC	London	LJ05GPU	London	LJ51DHZ	London	LJ53BFL	London
J04LGD	London	LJ05GPX	London	LJ51DJD	London	LJ53BFM	London
J04LGE	London	LJ05GPY	London	LJ51DJE	London	LJ53BFN	London
J04LGF	London	LJ05GPZ	London	LJ51DJF	London	LJ53BFO	London
J04LGG	London	LJ05GRF	London	LJ51DJK	London	LJ53BFP	London
J04LGK	London	LJ05GRK	London	LJ51DJO	London	LJ53BFU	London
J04LGL	London	LJ05GRU	London	LJ51DJU	London	LJ53BFX	London
J04LGN	London	LJ05GRX	London	LJ51DJV	London	LJ53BFY	London
J04LGU	London	LJ05GRZ	London	LJ51DJX	London	LJ53BGF	London
J04LGV	London	LJ05GSO	London	LJ51DJY	London	LJ53BGK	London
J04LGW	London	LJ05GSU	London	LJ51DJZ	London	LJ53BGO	London
J04LGX	London	LJ51DAA	London	LJ51DKA	London	LJ53BGU	London
J04LGY	London	LJ51DAO	London	LJ51DKD	London	LJ53NFE	London
J04YWE	London	LJ51DAU	London	LJ51DKE	London	LJ53NFF	London
J04YWS	London	LJ51DBO	London	LJ51DKF	London	LJ53NFG	London
J04YWT	London	LJ51DBU	London	LJ51DKK	London	LJ53NFT	London
J04YWU	London	LJ51DBV	London	LJ51DKL	London	LJ53NFU	London
J04YWV	London	LJ51DBX	London	LJ51DKN	London	LJ53NFV	London
J04YWW	London	LJ51DBY	London	LJ51DKO	London	LJ53NFX	London
J04YWX	London	LJ51DBZ	London	LJ51DKU	London	LJ53NFY	London
J04YWY	London	LJ51DCE	London	LJ51DKV	London	LJ53NFZ	London
J04YWZ	London	LJ51DCF	London	LJ51DKX	London	LJ53NGE	London
J04YXA	London	LJ51DCO	London	LJ51DKY	London	LJ53NGF	London
J04YXB	London	LJ51DCU	London	LJ51DLD	London	LJ53NGG	London
J05RHI	London	LJ51DCV	London	LJ51DLF	London	LJ53NGN	London
J05BHN	London	LJ51DCX	London	LJ51DLK	London	LJ53NGU	London
J05BHO	London	LJ51DCY	London	LJ51DLN	London	LJ53NGV	London
J05BHP	London	LJ51DCZ	London	LJ51DLU	London	LJ53NGX	London
J05BHU	London	LJ51DDE	London	LJ51DLV	London	LJ53NGY	London
J05BHV	London	LJ51DDF	London	LJ51DLX	London	LJ53NGZ	London
J05BHW	London	LJ51DDK	London	LJ51DLY	London	LJ53NHA	London
J05BHX	London	LJ51DDL	London	LJ51DLZ	London	LJ53NHB	London
J05BHY	London	LJ51DDL	London	LJ51ORA	London	LJ53NHC	London
J05BHZ	London	LJ51DDN	London	LJ51ORC	London	LJ53NHD	London

Reg	Region	Reg	Region	Reg	Region	Reg	Region
LJ53NHE	London	LJ54LGV	London	M162WKA	North West & W	M219AKB	North West & W
LJ53NHF	London	LJ54LHF	London	M163GRY	Midlands	M219YKC	North West & W
LJ53NHG	London	LJ54LHG	London	M163SKR	North West & W	M220AKB	North West & W
LJ53NHH	London	LJ54LHH	London	M163WKA	North West & W	M221AKB	North West & W
LJ53NHK	London	LJ54LHK	London	M164WKA	North West & W	M223AKB	North West & W
LJ53NHL	London	LJ54LHL	London	M165GRY	Midlands	M224AKB	North West & W
LJ53NHN	London	LJ54LHM	London	M165WKA	North West & W	M225AKB	North West & W
LJ53NHO	London	LJ54LHN	London	M166GRY	Midlands	M226AKB	North West & W
LJ53NHP	London	LJ54LHO	London	M166WKA	North West & W	M227AKB	North West & W
LJ53NHT	London	LJ54LHP	London	M167WKA	North West & W	M228AKB	North West & W
LJ53NHV	London	LJ54LHR	London	M168GRY	Midlands	M229AKB	North West & W
LJ53NHX	London	LX05GDV	Original SST	M168WKA	North West & W	M230AKB	North West & W
LJ53NHZ	London	LX05GDY	Original SST	M169GRY	Midlands	M231AKB	North West & W
LJ53NJF	London	LX05GDZ	Original SST	M169WKA	North West & W	M232AKB	North West & W
LJ53NJK	London	LX05GEJ	Original SST	M170GRY	Midlands	M234TBV	The Shires
LJ53NJN	London	LX05HRO	Original SST	M170WKA	North West & W	M247SPP	Scotland
LJ54BAA	London	LX05HSC	Original SST	M171GRY	Midlands	M248SPP	Scotland
LJ54BAO	London	LX05KNZ	Original SST	M171YKA	North West & W	M249SPP	Scotland
LJ54BAU	London	LX05KOA	Original SST	M172GRY	Midlands	M250SPP	Scotland
LJ54BAV	London	M2BLU	North West & W	M172YKA	North West & W	M251SPP	Scotland
LJ54BBE	London	M2SLT	North West & W	M173GRY	Midlands	M266VPU	The Shires
LJ54BBF	London	M5SLT	North West & W	M173YKA	North West & W	M267VPU	The Shires
LJ54BBK	London	M20MPS	Midlands	M174GRY	Midlands	M268VPU	The Shires
LJ54BBN	London	M23UUA	North West & W	M174YKA	North West & W	M269VPU	Southern
LJ54BBO	London	M30GGY	North West & W	M175GRY	Midlands	M301SAJ	North East
LJ54BBU	London	M30MPS	Midlands	M175YKA	North West & W	M301YBG	North West & W
LJ54BBV	London	M38WUR	The Shires	M176GRY	Midlands	M302SAJ	North East
LJ54BBX	London	M43WUR	The Shires	M176YKA	North West & W	M302YBG	North West & W
LJ54BBZ	London	M45WUR	The Shires	M177GRY	Midlands	M303SAJ	North East
LJ54BCE	London	M46WUR	The Shires	M177YKA	North West & W	M303YBG	North West & W
LJ54BCF	London	M47WUR	The Shires	M178GRY	Midlands	M304SAJ	North East
LJ54BCK	London	M51AWW	Southern	M178LYP	North East	M305SAJ	North East
LJ54BCO	London	M52AWW	The Shires	M178YKA	North West & W	M322AKB	North West & W
LJ54BCU	London	M53AWW	The Shires	M179LYP	North East	M370FTY	North East
LJ54BCV	London	M54AWW	Southern	M179YKA	North West & W	M370KVR	North West & W
LJ54BCX	London	M65FDS	Scotland	M180LYP	North East	M371FTY	North East
LJ54BCY	London	M67FDS	Scotland	M180YKA	North West & W	M371KVR	North West & W
LJ54BCZ	London	M100CBB	Southern	M181YKA	North West & W	M372FTY	North East
LJ54BDE	London	M101CCD	The Shires	M182YKA	North West & W	M372KVR	North West & W
LJ54BDF	London	M101UKX	The Shires	M183YKA	North West & W	M373FTY	North East
LJ54BDO	London	M102RMS	North West & W	M184YKA	North West & W	M374FTY	North East
LJ54BDU	London	M102UKX	The Shires	M185YKA	North West & W	M375FTY	North East
LJ54BDV	London	M103RMS	North West & W	M186YKA	North West & W	M376FTY	North East
LJ54BDX	London	M103UKX	The Shires	M187YKA	North West & W	M377FTY	North East
LJ54BDY	London	M104RMS	Scotland	M188YKA	North West & W	M401EFD	Midlands
LJ54BDZ	London	M104UKX	The Shires	M189YKA	North West & W	M402EFD	Midlands
LJ54BEO	London	M105RMS	North West & W	M190YKA	North West & W	M403EFD	Midlands
LJ54BEU	London	M105UKX	The Shires	M191YKA	North West & W	M404EFD	Midlands
LJ54BFA	London	M106RMS	Scotland	M192YKA	North West & W	M410UNW	Yorkshire
LJ54BFE	London	M107RMS	Scotland	M193YKA	North West & W	M411UNW	Yorkshire
LJ54BFF	London	M108RMS	Scotland	M194YKA	North West & W	M412UNW	Yorkshire
LJ54BFK	London	M109RMS	Scotland	M195YKA	North West & W	M413UNW	Yorkshire
LJ54BFL	London	M109XKC	North West & W	M196YKA	North West & W	M414UNW	Yorkshire
LJ54BFM	London	M110RMS	Scotland	M197YKA	North West & W	M415UNW	Yorkshire
LJ54BFN	London	M110XKC	North West & W	M198YKA	North West & W	M416UNW	Yorkshire
LJ54BFO	London	M112RMS	Scotland	M199YKA	North West & W	M417UNW	Yorkshire
LJ54BFP	London	M112XKC	North West & W	M200CBB	Southern	M418UNW	Yorkshire
LJ54BFU	London	M113RMS	Scotland	M201YKA	North West & W	M419UNW	Yorkshire
LJ54BFV	London	M113XKC	North West & W	M202YKA	North West & W	M420UNW	Yorkshire
LJ54BFX	London	M114RMS	Scotland	M203YKA	North West & W	M421UNW	Yorkshire
LJ54BFY	London	M115RMS	Scotland	M204YKA	North West & W	M422UNW	Yorkshire
LJ54BFZ	London	M116RMS	Scotland	M205YKA	North West & W	M423UNW	Yorkshire
LJ54BGE	London	M117RMS	Scotland	M206YKA	North West & W	M424UNW	Yorkshire
LJ54BGF	London	M118RMS	Scotland	M207YKA	North West & W	M425BLU	The Shires
LJ54BGK	London	M119RMS	Scotland	M208YKA	North West & W	M425UNW	Yorkshire
LJ54BGO	London	M120RMS	Scotland	M209YKA	North West & W	M426BLU	The Shires
LJ54BJE	London	M121RMS	Scotland	M20GGY	North West & W	M426UNW	Yorkshire
LJ54BJF	London	M157WKA	North West & W	M210YKA	North West & W	M427UNW	Yorkshire
LJ54BJK	London	M158WKA	North West & W	M211YKD	North West & W	M428UNW	Yorkshire
LJ54BJO	London	M159GRY	Midlands	M212YKD	North West & W	M429UNW	Yorkshire
LJ54BJU	London	M159WKA	North West & W	M213YKD	North West & W	M430UNW	Yorkshire
LJ54BKG	London	M160GRY	Midlands	M214STO	North West & W	M431UNW	Yorkshire
LJ54BKK	London	M160SKR	North West & W	M214YKD	North West & W	M432UNW	Yorkshire
LJ54BKL	London	M160WKA	North West & W	M215TNU	North West & W	M433UNW	Yorkshire
LJ54BKN	London	M161GRY	Midlands	M215YKD	North West & W	M440HPF	North East
LJ54BKO	London	M161SKR	North West & W	M216YKD	North West & W	M441HPF	North East
LJ54BKU	London	M161WKA	North West & W	M217AKB	North West & W	M442HPF	North East
LJ54BKV	London	M162GRY	Midlands	M218AKB	North West & W	M443HPF	North East
LJ54BKX	London	M162SKR	North West & W	M218YKC	North West & W	M444HPF	North East

Reg	Location	Reg	Location	Reg	Location	Reg	Location
1445HPF	North East	M567YEM	North West & W	M816RCP	Yorkshire	MOI2836	Yorkshire
1446HPF	North East	M568YEM	North West & W	M817RCP	Yorkshire	MUH281X	The Shires
1447HPF	North East	M569YEM	North West & W	M818RCP	Yorkshire	MV02XYJ	North West & W
1448HPF	North East	M570YEM	North West & W	M819RCP	Yorkshire	MV02XYK	North West & W
1449HPF	North East	M571YEM	North West & W	M831SDA	Midlands	N4BLU	North West & W
1450HPF	Southern	M572YEM	North West & W	M832SDA	Midlands	N25FWU	North West & W
1451HPF	Southern	M573YEM	North West & W	M833SDA	Midlands	N26KYS	Scotland
1452HPG	North East	M574YEM	North West & W	M834SDA	Midlands	N27KYS	Scotland
1453HPG	North East	M575YEM	North West & W	M835SDA	Midlands	N28KGS	The Shires
1455UUR	The Shires	M611PKP	Southern	M841RCP	North West & W	N29KGS	The Shires
1456UUR	The Shires	M612PKP	Southern	M842DDS	The Shires	N31KGS	The Shires
1501AJC	North East	M613PKP	Southern	M842RCP	North West & W	N32KGS	The Shires
1501PKJ	Southern	M614PKP	Southern	M843DDS	The Shires	N35JPP	The Shires
1502AJC	North East	M615PKP	Southern	M843RCP	North West & W	N36JPP	The Shires
1502RKO	Southern	M616PKP	Southern	M844DDS	The Shires	N37JPP	The Shires
1503AJC	North East	M617PKP	Southern	M847RCP	North West & W	N38JPP	The Shires
1503VJO	The Shires	M619PKP	Southern	M849RCP	North West & W	N39JPP	The Shires
1504AJC	North East	M621PDP	North West & W	M863KCU	North East	N42JPP	The Shires
1504VJO	The Shires	M622PDP	North West & W	M866KCU	North East	N43JPP	The Shires
1514WHF	North West & W	M623PDP	North West & W	M867KCU	North East	N45JPP	The Shires
1515WHF	North West & W	M685HPF	North East	M869KCU	North East	N46JPP	The Shires
1516WHF	North West & W	M686HPF	North East	M870KCU	North East	N51FWU	Yorkshire
1517KPA	North West & W	M687HPF	North East	M871LBB	North East	N52FWU	Yorkshire
1517WHF	North West & W	M688HPF	North East	M872LBB	North East	N81PUS	Scotland
1518KPA	North West & W	M689HPF	North East	M873LBB	North East	N82PUS	Scotland
1518WHF	North West & W	M690HPF	North East	M875LBB	North East	N101YVU	North West & W
1519KPA	North West & W	M691HPF	North East	M878DDS	Scotland	N103YVU	North West & W
1519WHF	North West & W	M692HPF	North East	M911MKM	Southern	N104YVU	North West & W
1520KPA	Southern	M693HPF	North East	M912MKM	Southern	N105YVU	North West & W
1520WHF	North West & W	M694HPF	Yorkshire	M913MKM	Southern	N106DWM	North West & W
1521MPF	North West & W	M695HPF	Yorkshire	M914MKM	Southern	N106EVS	The Shires
1521WHF	North West & W	M696HPF	Yorkshire	M915MKM	Southern	N107DWM	North West & W
1522MPF	North West & W	M697HPF	Yorkshire	M916MKM	Southern	N107EVS	The Shires
1522WHF	North West & W	M698HPF	Yorkshire	M917MKM	Southern	N108DWM	North West & W
1523MPF	North West & W	M699HPF	Yorkshire	M918MKM	Southern	N108EVS	The Shires
1523WHF	North West & W	M700HPF	Yorkshire	M919MKM	Southern	N109DWM	North West & W
1524MPF	North West & W	M701HPF	Yorkshire	M920MKM	Southern	N109EVS	The Shires
1524WHF	North West & W	M702HPF	Yorkshire	M921PKN	North West & W	N110DWM	North West & W
1525MPM	Southern	M703HPF	Yorkshire	M922PKN	Southern	N113DWM	North West & W
1525WHF	North West & W	M704HPF	Yorkshire	M923PKN	Southern	N114DWM	North West & W
1526MPM	Southern	M7110MJ	The Shires	M025PKN	Southern	N115DWM	North West & W
1526WHF	North West & W	M7120MJ	The Shires	M927EYS	North West & W	N116DWM	North West & W
1527WHF	North West & W	M7130MJ	The Shires	M928EYS	North West & W	N117DWM	North West & W
1528WHF	North West & W	M7140MJ	The Shires	M929EYS	North West & W	N118DWM	North West & W
1529WHF	North West & W	M7150MJ	The Shires	M930EYS	North West & W	N119DWM	North West & W
1530WHF	North West & W	M7160MJ	The Shires	M931EYS	North West & W	N120DWM	North West & W
1531WHF	North West & W	M7170MJ	The Shires	M932EYS	North West & W	N121DWM	North West & W
1532WHF	North West & W	M7180MJ	The Shires	M933EYS	North West & W	N122DWM	North West & W
1533WHF	North West & W	M7190MJ	The Shires	M934EYS	North West & W	N123DWM	North West & W
1534WHF	North West & W	M7200MJ	The Shires	M935EYS	North West & W	N124DWM	North West & W
1535WHF	North West & W	M7210MJ	The Shires	M936EYS	North West & W	N125DWM	North West & W
1536WHF	North West & W	M7220MJ	The Shires	M942LYR	The Shires	N126DWM	North West & W
1537WHF	North West & W	M7230MJ	The Shires	M943LYR	The Shires	N127DWM	North West & W
1538WHF	North West & W	M7240MJ	The Shires	M945LYR	North West & W	N128DWM	North West & W
1540WHF	North West & W	M7250MJ	The Shires	M946LYR	The Shires	N129DWM	North West & W
1541WHF	North West & W	M7260MJ	The Shires	M947LYR	The Shires	N130DWM	North West & W
1542WHF	North West & W	M726UTW	The Shires	M948LYR	The Shires	N131DWM	North West & W
1543WHF	North West & W	M7270MJ	The Shires	M949LYR	The Shires	N132DWM	North West & W
1544WTJ	North West & W	M7280MJ	The Shires	M950LYR	North West & W	N133DWM	North West & W
1545WTJ	North West & W	M7290MJ	The Shires	M951LYR	The Shires	N134DWM	North West & W
1546WTJ	North West & W	M7300MJ	The Shires	MF52LYY	North West & W	N160VVO	Midlands
1547WTJ	North West & W	M734A00	North East	MF52LYZ	North West & W	N161VVO	Midlands
1548WTJ	North West & W	M746WWR	Yorkshire	MF52LZA	North West & W	N162VVO	Midlands
1549WTJ	North West & W	M749WWR	Yorkshire	MF52LZB	North West & W	N163VVO	Midlands
1550WTJ	North West & W	M761JPA	North West & W	MFF509	London	N164VVO	Midlands
1551WTJ	North West & W	M762JPA	North West & W	MIL2350	The Shires	N165XVO	Midlands
1552WTJ	North West & W	M763JPA	North West & W	MK05MKL	North West & W	N166PUT	Midlands
1553WTJ	North West & W	M764JPA	Southern	MK05MKM	North West & W	N166XVO	Midlands
1554WTJ	North West & W	M782PRS	The Shires	MK05MKN	North West & W	N167PUT	Midlands
1556WTJ	North West & W	M783PRS	The Shires	MK52XNN	North West & W	N168PUT	Midlands
1557WTJ	North West & W	M802MOJ	Midlands	MK52XNO	North West & W	N169PUT	Midlands
1558WTJ	North West & W	M803MOJ	Midlands	MK52XNP	North West & W	N170PUT	Midlands
1559WTJ	North West & W	M804MOJ	Midlands	MK52XNR	North West & W	N171PUT	Midlands
1561WTJ	North West & W	M805MOJ	Midlands	MK52XNS	North West & W	N172PUT	Midlands
1562WTJ	North West & W	M811RCP	Yorkshire	MK54YLR	North West & W	N172WNF	Yorkshire
1563WTJ	North West & W	M812RCP	Yorkshire	MK54YLT	North West & W	N173PUT	Midlands
1564YEM	North West & W	M813RCP	Yorkshire	MK54YLU	North West & W	N174PUT	Midlands
1565YEM	North West & W	M814RCP	Yorkshire	MM02ZVH	North West & W	N175DWM	The Shires
1566YEM	North West & W	M815RCP	Yorkshire	MM02ZVJ	North West & W	N175PUT	Midlands

Reg	Region	Reg	Region	Reg	Region	Reg	Region
N176DWM	The Shires	N244VPH	Midlands	N302ENX	Midlands	N512XVN	North East
N176PUT	Midlands	N245CKA	North West & W	N303CLV	North West & W	N513XVN	North East
N177DWM	The Shires	N245VPH	Southern	N303ENX	Midlands	N514XVN	North East
N177PUT	North West & W	N246CKA	North West & W	N304CLV	North West & W	N515XVN	North East
N178DWM	North West & W	N246VPH	Southern	N304ENX	Midlands	N516XVN	North East
N178PUT	Midlands	N247CKA	North West & W	N305CLV	North West & W	N517XVN	North East
N179DWM	North West & W	N247VPH	Southern	N305ENX	Midlands	N518XVN	North East
N179PUT	Midlands	N248CKA	North West & W	N306CLV	North West & W	N519XVN	North East
N181OYH	North East	N248GBM	The Shires	N307CLV	North West & W	N520XVN	North East
N182OYH	North East	N248VPH	Midlands	N308CLV	North West & W	N521MJO	The Shires
N183OYH	North East	N249CKA	North West & W	N322TPK	Southern	N521XVN	North East
N186EMJ	The Shires	N249VPH	Midlands	N3570BC	Midlands	N522MJO	The Shires
N188EMJ	The Shires	N24FWU	North West & W	N3580BC	Midlands	N522XVN	North East
N189EMJ	The Shires	N250BKK	Southern	N366JGS	The Shires	N523MJO	The Shires
N190EMJ	The Shires	N250CKA	North West & W	N367JGS	The Shires	N523XVN	North East
N191EMJ	The Shires	N251BKK	Southern	N368JGS	The Shires	N524MJO	The Shires
N192EMJ	The Shires	N251CKA	North West & W	N369JGS	The Shires	N524XVN	North East
N192RVK	North East	N252BKK	Southern	N370JGS	The Shires	N525XVN	North East
N193EMJ	The Shires	N252CKA	North West & W	N371JGS	The Shires	N527SPA	North West & W
N194EMJ	The Shires	N253BKK	Southern	N372JGS	The Shires	N528SPA	North West & W
N196EMJ	The Shires	N253CKA	North West & W	N373JGS	The Shires	N529SPA	North West & W
N201NHS	Scotland	N254BKK	Southern	N374JGS	The Shires	N530SPA	North West & W
N202NHS	Scotland	N254CKA	North West & W	N375JGS	The Shires	N531DWM	North West & W
N203NHS	Scotland	N255BKK	Southern	N376JGS	The Shires	N532DWM	North West & W
N204NHS	Scotland	N255CKA	North West & W	N377JGS	The Shires	N539TPF	Southern
N205NHS	Scotland	N256BKK	Southern	N378JGS	The Shires	N540TPF	Southern
N206NHS	Scotland	N256CKA	North West & W	N379JGS	The Shires	N542TPK	Southern
N207NHS	Scotland	N257BKK	Southern	N380JGS	The Shires	N544TPK	Southern
N208NHS	Scotland	N257CKA	North West & W	N381JGS	The Shires	N576CKA	North West & W
N210TPK	North West & W	N258BKK	Southern	N381OTY	North East	N577CKA	North West & W
N211DWM	North West & W	N258CKA	North West & W	N382JGS	The Shires	N578CKA	North West & W
N211TPK	North West & W	N259BKK	Southern	N382OTY	North East	N579CKA	North West & W
N212TPK	North West & W	N259CKA	North West & W	N383JGS	The Shires	N580CKA	North West & W
N213TPK	North West & W	N260CKA	North West & W	N383OTY	North East	N581CKA	North West & W
N214TPK	North West & W	N261CKA	North West & W	N384JGS	The Shires	N582CKA	North West & W
N215TPK	North West & W	N262CKA	North West & W	N384OTY	North East	N583CKA	North West & W
N216TPK	North West & W	N263CKA	North West & W	N385JGS	The Shires	N584CKA	North West & W
N217TPK	North West & W	N264CKA	North West & W	N385OTY	North East	N585CKA	North West & W
N217VVO	North West & W	N271CKB	North West & W	N386JGS	The Shires	N586CKA	North West & W
N218TPK	North West & W	N272BAL	North West & W	N386OTY	North East	N587CKA	North West & W
N219TPK	North West & W	N272CKB	North West & W	N387JGS	The Shires	N588CKA	North West & W
N220BAL	North West & W	N273CKB	North West & W	N387OTY	North East	N589CKA	North West & W
N220TPK	Southern	N274CKB	North West & W	N388OTY	North East	N590CKA	North West & W
N221BAL	North West & W	N275CKB	North West & W	N389OTY	North East	N591CKA	North West & W
N221TPK	Southern	N276CKB	North West & W	N390OTY	North East	N592CKA	North West & W
N223TPK	Southern	N277CKB	North West & W	N391OTY	North East	N593CKA	North West & W
N224BAL	North West & W	N278CKB	North West & W	N392OTY	North East	N594CKA	North West & W
N224TPK	Southern	N279CKB	North West & W	N393OTY	North East	N595CKA	North West & W
N225TPK	Southern	N281CKB	North West & W	N41JPP	The Shires	N596CKA	North West & W
N226TPK	Southern	N281NCN	North East	N414NRG	The Shires	N597CKA	North West & W
N227TPK	Southern	N282CKB	North West & W	N415NRG	The Shires	N598CKA	North West & W
N228TPK	Southern	N282NCN	North East	N415NRG	The Shires	N599CKA	North West & W
N229TPK	Southern	N283CKB	North West & W	N429XRC	Midlands	N601CKA	North West & W
N230TPK	Southern	N283NCN	North East	N430XRC	Midlands	N601DWY	North West & W
N231TPK	Southern	N284CKB	North West & W	N431XRC	Midlands	N602DWY	North West & W
N232TPK	Southern	N284NCN	North East	N432XRC	Midlands	N603CKA	North West & W
N233CKA	North West & W	N285CKB	North West & W	N433XRC	Midlands	N603DWY	North West & W
N233TPK	Southern	N285NCN	North East	N439GHG	Scotland	N604CKA	North West & W
N234CKA	North West & W	N286CKB	North West & W	N440GHG	Scotland	N604DWY	North West & W
N234TPK	Southern	N287CKB	North West & W	N463EHA	Midlands	N605CKA	North West & W
N235CKA	North West & W	N287NCN	North East	N466EHA	Midlands	N605DWY	North West & W
N235TPK	Southern	N288CKB	North West & W	N467EHA	Midlands	N606CKA	North West & W
N236CKA	North West & W	N288NCN	North East	N469EHA	Midlands	N606DWY	North West & W
N236TPK	Southern	N289CKB	North West & W	N470EHA	Midlands	N607CKA	North West & W
N237CKA	North West & W	N289NCN	North East	N471EHA	Midlands	N607DWY	North West & W
N237VPH	Southern	N290CKB	North West & W	N472EHA	Midlands	N608CKA	North West & W
N237VPH	Southern	N290NCN	North East	N472XRC	Midlands	N608DWY	North West & W
N238CKA	North West & W	N291CKB	North West & W	N473MUS	Scotland	N609CKA	North West & W
N238VPH	Midlands	N292CKB	North West & W	N473XRC	Midlands	N609DWY	North West & W
N239CKA	North West & W	N293CKB	North West & W	N474MUS	Scotland	N610CKA	North West & W
N240CKA	North West & W	N294CKB	North West & W	N474XRC	Midlands	N610DWY	North West & W
N240VPH	Midlands	N295CKB	North West & W	N475XRC	Midlands	N611CKA	North West & W
N241CKA	North West & W	N296CKB	North West & W	N476XRC	Midlands	N611DWY	North West & W
N241VPH	Midlands	N297CKB	North West & W	N477XRC	Midlands	N612CKA	North West & W
N242CKA	North West & W	N298CKB	North West & W	N478XRC	Midlands	N612DWY	North West & W
N242VPH	Midlands	N299CKB	North West & W	N479XRC	Midlands	N613CKA	North West & W
N243CKA	North West & W	N301CKB	North West & W	N480XRC	Midlands	N613DWY	North West & W
N243VPH	Midlands	N301ENX	Midlands	N481XRC	Midlands	N614CKA	North West & W
N244CKA	North West & W	N302CKB	North West & W	N511XVN	North East	N615CKA	North West & W

Reg	Area	Reg	Area	Reg	Area	Reg	Area
N616CKA	North West & W	N718DJC	North West & W	NK05GXB	North East	P178VUA	Yorkshire
N617CKA	North West & W	N719DJC	North West & W	NK05GXC	North East	P179FNF	North West & W
N618CKA	North West & W	N743AVM	North East	NK05GXD	North East	P179LKL	Southern
N619CKA	North West & W	N750LUS	Scotland	NK05GXE	North East	P179SRO	The Shires
N620CKA	North West & W	N755LWW	Yorkshire	NK05GXF	North East	P179VUA	Yorkshire
N621CKA	North West & W	N756LWW	Yorkshire	NK05GXG	North East	P180FNF	North West & W
N621FJO	The Shires	N757LWW	Yorkshire	NK05GXH	North East	P180GND	North West & W
N621KUA	Yorkshire	N781EUA	North West & W	NK05GXJ	North East	P180LKL	North West & W
N622CKA	North West & W	N782EUA	North West & W	NK05GXL	North East	P180SRO	The Shires
N622FJO	The Shires	N783EUA	North West & W	NK05GXM	North East	P180VUA	Yorkshire
N622KUA	Yorkshire	N801BKN	North East	NK05GXN	North East	P181FNF	North West & W
N623CKA	North West & W	N801TPK	Yorkshire	NK05GXO	North East	P181GND	North West & W
N623FJO	The Shires	N802BKN	North East	NK05GXW	North East	P181LKL	Southern
N623KUA	Yorkshire	N802TPK	Yorkshire	NK53HHX	North East	P181SRO	The Shires
N624FJO	The Shires	N803BKN	Scotland	NK53HHY	North East	P181VUA	Yorkshire
N671GUM	North West & W	N803TPK	Yorkshire	NK53HHZ	North East	P182FNF	North West & W
N672GUM	Scotland	N804BKN	Scotland	NK53HJA	North East	P182GND	North West & W
N673GUM	Midlands	N804TPK	Yorkshire	NK53VKA	North East	P182LKL	North West & W
N674GUM	Midlands	N805TPK	Yorkshire	NL52XZV	North East	P182SRO	The Shires
N675GUM	Scotland	N806BKN	Southern	NL52XZW	North East	P182VUA	Yorkshire
N676GUM	North West & W	N806EHA	Midlands	NL52XZX	North East	P183FNF	North West & W
N677GUM	Scotland	N806TPK	Yorkshire	NL52XZY	North East	P183GND	North West & W
N678GUM	North West & W	N806XHN	North East	NML619E	London	P183LKL	North West & W
N679GUM	Midlands	N807BKN	Southern	NML636E	London	P183SRO	The Shires
N680GUM	Midlands	N807EHA	Midlands	NML638E	London	P183VUA	Yorkshire
N681GUM	Scotland	N807TPK	Yorkshire	NML655E	London	P184GND	North West & W
N682GUM	North West & W	N807XHN	North East	NSG636A	London	P184LKL	Southern
N683GUM	Scotland	N808BKN	Southern	NVS485	London	P184SRO	The Shires
N684GUM	Scotland	N808EHA	Midlands	OJD840Y	Original SST	P184VUA	Yorkshire
N685GUM	Scotland	N808TPK	Yorkshire	OJD858Y	North East	P185LKL	Southern
N686GUM	Scotland	N808XHN	North East	OJD863Y	Original SST	P185SRO	The Shires
N687GUM	Scotland	N809TPK	Yorkshire	OLV551M	North West & W	P185VUA	Yorkshire
N688GUM	Scotland	N809XHN	North East	OYM453A	London	P186LKJ	Southern
N689GUM	Midlands	N810TPK	Yorkshire	P3SLT	North West & W	P186SRO	The Shires
N690GUM	Midlands	N810XHN	North East	P10LPG	Yorkshire	P186VUA	Yorkshire
N691GUM	Scotland	N877RTN	North East	P41MVU	North West & W	P187LKJ	Southern
N693EUR	The Shires	N878RTN	North East	P42MVU	North West & W	P187SRO	The Shires
N694EUR	The Shires	N879RTN	North East	P43MVU	North West & W	P187VUA	Yorkshire
N695EUR	The Shires	N880RTN	North East	P45MVU	North West & W	P188LKJ	Southern
N696EUR	The Shires	N881RTN	North East	P46MVU	North West & W	P188SRO	The Shires
N697EUR	The Shires	N882RTN	North East	P49MVU	North West & W	P188VUA	Yorkshire
N698EUR	The Shires	N883RTN	North East	P52MVU	North West & W	P189LKJ	Southern
N699EUR	The Shires	N884RTN	North East	P53MVU	North West & W	P189SRO	The Shires
N701EUR	The Shires	N885RTN	North East	P56MVU	North West & W	P189VUA	Yorkshire
N701GUM	North West & W	N886RTN	North East	P56XTN	North East	P190LKJ	Southern
N702EUR	The Shires	N887RTN	North East	P57XTN	North East	P190SRO	The Shires
N703EUR	The Shires	N889RTN	North East	P58MVU	North West & W	P190VUA	Yorkshire
N703GUM	North West & W	N090RTN	North East	P58XTN	North East	P191LKJ	Southern
N704EUR	The Shires	N891RTN	North East	P59XTN	North East	P191VUA	Yorkshire
N704GUM	North West & W	N907ETM	The Shires	P61MVU	North West & W	P192LKJ	Southern
N705EUR	The Shires	N908ETM	The Shires	P61XTN	North East	P192VUA	Yorkshire
N705GUM	North West & W	N909ETM	The Shires	P100LOW	The Shires	P193LKJ	Southern
N705TPK	North West & W	N911ETM	The Shires	P130RWR	North East	P193VUA	Yorkshire
N706EUR	The Shires	N912ETM	The Shires	P135GND	North West & W	P194LKJ	Southern
N706GUM	North West & W	N913ETM	The Shires	P136GND	North West & W	P194VUA	Yorkshire
N706TPK	North West & W	N916ETM	The Shires	P137GND	North West & W	P195LKJ	Southern
N707EUR	The Shires	N918ETM	The Shires	P137MTU	The Shires	P195VUA	Yorkshire
N707GUM	North West & W	N935ETU	The Shires	P138GND	North West & W	P196LKJ	Southern
N707TPK	North West & W	N936ETU	The Shires	P139GND	North West & W	P196VUA	Yorkshire
N708EUR	The Shires	NEY819	North West & W	P140GND	North West & W	P197LKJ	Southern
N708GUM	Scotland	NK05GVG	North East	P167BTV	Midlands	P197VUA	Yorkshire
N708TPK	North West & W	NK05GVX	North East	P168BTV	Midlands	P198LKJ	Southern
N709EUR	The Shires	NK05GVY	North East	P169BTV	Midlands	P198VUA	Yorkshire
N709GUM	Scotland	NK05GWA	North East	P170VUA	Yorkshire	P199LKJ	Southern
N709TPK	North West & W	NK05GWC	North East	P171VUA	Yorkshire	P199VUA	Yorkshire
N710EUR	The Shires	NK05GWD	North East	P172VUA	Yorkshire	P201HRY	Midlands
N710GUM	Scotland	NK05GWE	North East	P173VUA	Yorkshire	P201LKJ	Southern
N711EUR	The Shires	NK05GWF	North East	P174VUA	Yorkshire	P202HRY	Midlands
N711GUM	Scotland	NK05GWG	North East	P175SRO	The Shires	P202LKJ	Southern
N712EUR	The Shires	NK05GWJ	North East	P175VUA	Yorkshire	P202RUM	Yorkshire
N712GUM	Scotland	NK05GWM	North East	P176I KI	Southern	P203HRY	Midlands
N713EUR	The Shires	NK05GWN	North East	P176SRO	The Shires	P203LKJ	Southern
N713TPK	Southern	NK05GWO	North East	P176VUA	Yorkshire	P204HRY	Midlands
N714EUR	The Shires	NK05GWU	North East	P177LKL	Southern	P204LKJ	Southern
N714TPK	Southern	NK05GWV	North East	P177SRO	The Shires	P205HRY	Midlands
N715EUR	The Shires	NK05GWW	North East	P177VUA	Yorkshire	P205LKJ	Southern
N715TPK	Southern	NK05GWX	North East	P178FNF	North West & W	P205RWR	Midlands
N716EUR	The Shires	NK05GWY	North East	P178LKL	Southern	P206HRY	Midlands
N716TPK	North West & W	NK05GXA	North East	P178SRO	The Shires	P206LKJ	Southern

Reg	Region	Reg	Region	Reg	Region	Reg	Region
P207LKJ	Southern	P274FPK	Southern	P329HVX	Southern	P605CAY	Midlands
P208LKJ	Southern	P274VRG	North East	P330HVX	Southern	P606CAY	Midlands
P209LKJ	Southern	P275FPK	Southern	P331HVX	Southern	P606FHN	North East
P210LKJ	Southern	P275VRG	North East	P332HVX	Southern	P607CAY	Midlands
P211LKJ	Southern	P276FPK	Southern	P334HVX	The Shires	P607FHN	North East
P212LKJ	Southern	P276VRG	North East	P380FPK	Southern	P608CAY	Midlands
P213LKJ	Southern	P277FPK	Southern	P402MLD	The Shires	P608FHN	North East
P214LKJ	North West & W	P277VRG	North East	P403MLD	The Shires	P608JJU	Midlands
P215LKJ	Southern	P278FPK	Southern	P404MLD	The Shires	P609CAY	Midlands
P216LKJ	Southern	P278VRG	North East	P405MLD	The Shires	P609FHN	North East
P217SGB	Scotland	P279FPK	Southern	P410CCU	North East	P610CAY	Midlands
P218MKL	Southern	P279VRG	North East	P411CCU	North East	P610FHN	North East
P218SGB	Scotland	P281FPK	Southern	P412CCU	North East	P611CAY	Midlands
P219MKL	Southern	P282FPK	Southern	P413CCU	North East	P611FHN	North East
P219SGB	Scotland	P283FPK	Southern	P414CCU	North East	P612CAY	Midlands
P220MKL	Southern	P284FPK	Southern	P415CCU	North East	P612FHN	North East
P220SGB	Scotland	P285FPK	Southern	P416CCU	North East	P613CAY	Midlands
P221MKL	Southern	P286FPK	Southern	P417CCU	North East	P613FHN	North East
P221SGB	Scotland	P287FPK	Southern	P418CCU	North East	P614FHN	North East
P223MKL	Southern	P288FPK	Southern	P419CCU	North East	P615FHN	North East
P223SGB	Scotland	P289FPK	Southern	P419HVX	North West & W	P616FHN	North East
P224MKL	Southern	P290FPK	Southern	P420CCU	North East	P617FHN	North East
P224SGB	Scotland	P291FPK	Southern	P420HVX	North West & W	P618FHN	North East
P225FRB	North West & W	P292FPK	Southern	P421HVX	Southern	P619FHN	North East
P225MKL	Southern	P293FPK	Southern	P422HVX	North West & W	P620FHN	North East
P225SGB	Scotland	P294FPK	Southern	P423HVX	Southern	P621FHN	North East
P226MKL	Southern	P295FPK	Southern	P424HVX	Southern	P622FHN	North East
P226SGB	Scotland	P296FPK	Southern	P425HVX	Southern	P623FHN	North East
P227MKL	Southern	P296OOA	Midlands	P426HVX	Southern	P624FHN	North East
P227SGB	Scotland	P301HEM	North West & W	P427HVX	Southern	P625FHN	North East
P228MKL	Southern	P302HEM	North West & W	P428HVX	Southern	P627FHN	North East
P229MKL	Southern	P303HEM	North West & W	P429HVX	Southern	P628FHN	North East
P230MKL	Southern	P305HEM	North West & W	P430HVX	North West & W	P629FHN	North East
P231MKL	Southern	P306FEA	Midlands	P431HVX	Southern	P630FHN	North East
P232MKL	Southern	P306HEM	North West & W	P438HKN	Midlands	P631FHN	North East
P233MKN	Southern	P307FEA	Midlands	P472APJ	North East	P632FHN	North East
P234MKN	Southern	P307HEM	North West & W	P473APJ	North West & W	P633FHN	North East
P235MKN	Southern	P308FEA	Midlands	P475DPE	Southern	P634FHN	North East
P236MKN	Southern	P308HEM	North West & W	P476DPE	Southern	P635FHN	North East
P237MKN	Southern	P309FEA	Midlands	P477DPE	Southern	P636FHN	North East
P238MKN	Southern	P309HEM	North West & W	P478DPE	Southern	P637FHN	North East
P239MKN	Southern	P310CXW	North West & W	P479DPE	Southern	P638FHN	North East
P240MKN	Southern	P310FEA	Midlands	P481DPE	Southern	P639FHN	North East
P241MKN	Southern	P310HEM	North West & W	P482CAL	Midlands	P640FHN	North East
P242MKN	Southern	P311FEA	Midlands	P483CAL	Midlands	P641FHN	North East
P243MKN	Southern	P311HEM	North West & W	P484CAL	Midlands	P642FHN	North East
P244MKN	Southern	P312FEA	Midlands	P485CAL	Midlands	P643FHN	North East
P244NBA	North West & W	P312HEM	North West & W	P486CAL	Midlands	P644FHN	North East
P245MKN	Southern	P313FEA	Midlands	P487CAL	Midlands	P645FHN	North East
P246MKN	Southern	P313HEM	North West & W	P488CAL	Midlands	P658KEY	North West & W
P247MKN	Southern	P314FEA	Midlands	P490CAL	Midlands	P669PNM	The Shires
P250APM	Southern	P314HEM	North West & W	P491CAL	Midlands	P670PNM	The Shires
P250NBA	North West & W	P315FAW	Midlands	P492TGA	Scotland	P671PNM	The Shires
P251APM	Southern	P315FEA	Midlands	P524UGA	North West & W	P672OPP	The Shires
P253APM	Southern	P315HEM	North West & W	P525UGA	North West & W	P673OPP	The Shires
P254APM	Southern	P316FAW	Midlands	P525YJO	The Shires	P674OPP	The Shires
P255APM	Southern	P316FEA	Midlands	P526YJO	The Shires	P688KCC	North West & W
P256FPK	The Shires	P316HEM	North West & W	P527UGA	Scotland	P697UFR	The Shires
P257FPK	Southern	P316RGS	The Shires	P527YJO	The Shires	P801RWU	Scotland
P258FPK	Southern	P317FEA	Midlands	P528UGA	Scotland	P802RWU	Scotland
P259FPK	Southern	P317HEM	North West & W	P529UGA	Scotland	P803RWU	Scotland
P259FPK	Southern	P317RGS	The Shires	P533MBU	North West & W	P804RWU	Scotland
P260NBA	North West & W	P318FEA	Midlands	P534MBU	North West & W	P805RWU	Scotland
P261FPK	Southern	P318HEM	North West & W	P535MBU	North West & W	P806DBS	Scotland
P262FPK	Southern	P318RGS	The Shires	P536MBU	North West & W	P807DBS	Scotland
P263FPK	Southern	P319HEM	North West & W	P537MBU	North West & W	P808DBS	Scotland
P264FPK	Southern	P319HOJ	Midlands	P538MBU	North West & W	P809DBS	Scotland
P265FPK	Southern	P320HEM	North West & W	P539MBU	North West & W	P810DBS	Scotland
P266FPK	Southern	P320HOJ	Midlands	P540MBU	North West & W	P811DBS	Scotland
P267FPK	Southern	P321HOJ	Midlands	P541MBU	North West & W	P812DBS	Scotland
P268FPK	Southern	P322HOJ	Midlands	P542MBU	North West & W	P813DBS	Scotland
P269FPK	Southern	P323HOJ	Midlands	P543MBU	North West & W	P814DBS	Scotland
P270FPK	Southern	P324HOJ	Midlands	P544MBU	North West & W	P814VTY	North East
P271FPK	Southern	P324HVX	Southern	P545MBU	North West & W	P815DBS	Scotland
P271VRG	North East	P325HOJ	Midlands	P601CAY	Midlands	P816GMS	Scotland
P272FPK	Southern	P326HOJ	Midlands	P601RGS	The Shires	P817GMS	Scotland
P272VRG	North East	P327HOJ	Midlands	P602CAY	Midlands	P818GMS	Scotland
P273FPK	Southern	P327HVX	Southern	P603CAY	Midlands	P819GMS	Scotland
P273VRG	North East	P328HVX	Southern	P604CAY	Midlands		

216

Registration	Fleet
820GMS	Scotland
821GMS	Scotland
822GMS	Scotland
822RWU	Scotland
823GMS	Scotland
823RWU	North West & W
824GMS	Scotland
824RWU	Midlands
825KES	Scotland
825RWU	North West & W
826KES	Scotland
826RWU	North West & W
827KES	Scotland
827RWU	North West & W
828KES	Scotland
828RWU	North West & W
829KES	Scotland
829RWU	North West & W
830KES	Scotland
830RWU	North West & W
831KES	Scotland
831RWU	North West & W
832KES	Scotland
832RWU	North West & W
833HVX	The Shires
833KES	Scotland
833NAV	Southern
833RWU	North West & W
834KES	Scotland
834RWU	North West & W
835KES	Scotland
835RWU	Midlands
836KES	Scotland
836RWU	Midlands
837KES	Scotland
837RWU	Midlands
838KES	Scotland
838RWU	North West & W
839KES	Scotland
839RWU	Midlands
840KES	Scotland
840PWW	Midlands
841PWW	Midlands
842PWW	Midlands
843PWW	Midlands
844PWW	Midlands
845PWW	Midlands
846PWW	Midlands
847PWW	Midlands
848PWW	Midlands
849PWW	Midlands
850PWW	Midlands
851PWW	Midlands
852PWW	Midlands
853PWW	Midlands
854PWW	Midlands
855PWW	Midlands
892XCU	North East
893XCU	North East
894XCU	North East
895XCU	Scotland
896XCU	Scotland
902DRG	North East
903DRG	North East
904DRG	North East
905JNL	North East
906JNL	North East
913PWW	Scotland
914PWW	Scotland
915PWW	Scotland
916PWW	North West & W
917PWW	North West & W
918PWW	North West & W
926MKL	Southern
927MKL	Southern
928MKL	Southern
929MKL	Southern
930MKL	Southern
931MKL	Southern
931YSB	Scotland
932MKL	Southern
932YSB	Scotland
933MKL	Southern
934MKL	Southern
935MKL	Southern
936MKL	Southern
937MKL	Southern
937YSB	Scotland
938MKL	North West & W
939MKL	North West & W
940MKL	North West & W
941MKL	North West & W
942MKL	North West & W
943MKL	North West & W
952RUL	Midlands
953RUL	North West & W
954RUL	Midlands
955RUL	Midlands
956RUL	Midlands
957RUL	Midlands
958RUL	Midlands
959RUL	North West & W
960RUL	North West & W
961RUL	North West & W
962RUL	Scotland
963RUL	Scotland
964RUL	Scotland
965RUL	Scotland
966RUL	Scotland
967RUL	Scotland
968RUL	Scotland
PFY72J	North West & W
PIL9730	Yorkshire
PIL9731	Yorkshire
PIL9732	Yorkshire
PIL9733	Yorkshire
PIL9734	Yorkshire
PIL9735	Yorkshire
PN02HVL	The Shires
PN02HVM	The Shires
PN02HVO	The Shires
PN02HVP	The Shires
PN02HVR	The Shires
PN02HVS	The Shires
PN52XBF	Midlands
PN52XBH	Midlands
PN52XRJ	Midlands
PN52XRK	Midlands
PN52XRL	Midlands
PN52XRM	Midlands
PN52XRO	Midlands
PN52XRP	Midlands
PN52XRR	Midlands
PN52XRS	Midlands
PN52XRT	Midlands
PN52XRU	Midlands
PN52XRV	Midlands
PN52XRW	Midlands
PUK637R	North West & W
R45VJF	Midlands
R46VJF	Midlands
R47XVM	North West & W
R48XVM	North West & W
R51XVM	North West & W
R54XVM	North West & W
R57XVM	North West & W
R59XVM	North West & W
R69GNW	Yorkshire
R101GNW	London
R101TKO	North West & W
R102TKO	North West & W
R103GNW	Yorkshire
R103TKO	North West & W
R104TKO	North West & W
R105TKO	North West & W
R107TKO	North West & W
R108TKO	North West & W
R109TKO	North West & W
R110GNW	North East
R110TKO	North West & W
R112GNW	North East
R112TKO	North West & W
R113GNW	North East
R113TKO	North West & W
R114TKO	North West & W
R115TKO	North West & W
R116TKO	North West & W
R117TKO	North West & W
R118TKO	Southern
R119TKO	Southern
R120TKO	Southern
R121TKO	Southern
R122TKO	Southern
R123TKO	North West & W
R124TKO	North West & W
R129GNW	North East
R129LNR	Midlands
R130GNW	North East
R130LNR	Midlands
R131LNR	Midlands
R132LNR	Midlands
R133LNR	Midlands
R134LNR	Midlands
R135LNR	Midlands
R136LNR	Midlands
R138LNR	Midlands
R141LNR	Midlands
R142LNR	Midlands
R143LNR	Midlands
R144LNR	Midlands
R145LNR	Midlands
R146LNR	Midlands
R147UAL	Midlands
R148UAL	Midlands
R149UAL	Midlands
R150UAL	Midlands
R151GNW	North West & W
R151UAL	Midlands
R152GNW	North West & W
R152UAL	Midlands
R153GNW	North West & W
R153UAL	Midlands
R154UAL	Midlands
R155UAL	Midlands
R156UAL	Midlands
R157GNW	Southern
R157UAL	Midlands
R158UAL	Midlands
R159UAL	Midlands
R160UAL	Midlands
R161UAL	Midlands
R162UAL	Midlands
R163UAL	Midlands
R164UAL	Midlands
R165GNW	The Shires
R165UAL	Midlands
R166UAL	Midlands
R167UAL	Midlands
R168UAL	Midlands
R169GNW	The Shires
R169UAL	Midlands
R170GNW	The Shires
R170UUT	Midlands
R171VBM	The Shires
R172VBM	The Shires
R173VBM	The Shires
R174VBM	Southern
R175VBM	The Shires
R176VBM	The Shires
R177VBM	The Shires
R178VBM	The Shires
R179VBM	The Shires
R180VBM	The Shires
R181DNM	The Shires
R182DNM	The Shires
R183DNM	The Shires
R184DNM	The Shires
R185DNM	The Shires
R186DNM	Southern
R187DNM	Southern
R188DNM	Southern
R189DNM	The Shires
R190DNM	The Shires
R191DNM	Southern
R191RBM	The Shires
R192DNM	Southern
R192RBM	The Shires
R193DNM	Southern
R193RBM	The Shires
R194DNM	The Shires
R194RBM	The Shires
R195DNM	The Shires
R195RBM	The Shires
R196DNM	The Shires
R196RBM	The Shires
R197DNM	The Shires
R197RBM	The Shires
R198DNM	The Shires
R198RBM	The Shires
R199RBM	The Shires
R201CKO	North West & W
R201RBM	The Shires
R201VPU	The Shires
R202CKO	North West & W
R202RBM	The Shires
R202VPU	The Shires
R203CKO	North West & W
R203RBM	The Shires
R203VPU	The Shires
R204CKO	Southern
R204RBM	The Shires
R204VPU	The Shires
R205CKO	Southern
R205RBM	The Shires
R205VPU	The Shires
R206CKO	Southern
R206GMJ	The Shires
R206VPU	The Shires
R207CKO	Southern
R207GMJ	The Shires
R207VPU	The Shires
R208CKO	Southern
R208GMJ	The Shires
R208VPU	The Shires
R209CKO	Southern
R209GMJ	The Shires
R209VPU	The Shires
R210CKO	Southern
R210GMJ	The Shires
R211CKO	Southern
R211GMJ	The Shires
R212CKO	Southern
R212GMJ	The Shires
R213CKO	North West & W
R213GMJ	The Shires
R214GMJ	The Shires
R215GMJ	The Shires
R226SCH	North West & W
R227SCH	North West & W
R228SCH	North West & W
R229SCH	North West & W
R233AEY	North West & W
R234AEY	North West & W
R235AEY	North West & W
R236AEY	North West & W
R237AEY	North West & W
R238AEY	North West & W
R239AEY	North West & W
R251JNL	North East
R255WRJ	North West & W
R261EKO	Southern
R262EKO	Southern
R263EKO	Southern
R264EKO	Southern
R265EKO	Southern
R266EKO	Southern

Reg	Region	Reg	Region	Reg	Region	Reg	Region
R267EKO	Southern	R371TWR	The Shires	R453SKX	The Shires	R638MNU	Midlands
R268EKO	Southern	R372TWR	The Shires	R454KWT	Yorkshire	R639MNU	Midlands
R269EKO	Southern	R381JYS	Scotland	R454SKX	The Shires	R640MNU	Midlands
R270EKO	Southern	R382JYS	Scotland	R455KWT	Yorkshire	R641MNU	Midlands
R271EKO	Southern	R383JYS	Scotland	R455SKX	Southern	R642MNU	Midlands
R272EKO	Southern	R384JYS	Scotland	R456KWT	Yorkshire	R643MNU	Midlands
R28GNW	Yorkshire	R385JYS	Scotland	R456SKX	Southern	R685MHN	North West & W
R291KRG	North East	R415TJW	Midlands	R457KWT	Yorkshire	R701KCU	North East
R292KRG	North East	R416COO	North West & W	R458KWT	Yorkshire	R701MHN	North East
R293KRG	North East	R416HVX	The Shires	R459KWT	Yorkshire	R702MHN	North East
R294KRG	North East	R416TJW	Midlands	R460KWT	Yorkshire	R703MHN	North East
R295KRG	North East	R417COO	North West & W	R461KWT	Yorkshire	R704MHN	North East
R296CMV	Southern	R417HVX	The Shires	R486UCC	North West & W	R705MHN	North East
R297CMV	Southern	R417TJW	Midlands	R487UCC	North West & W	R706MHN	North East
R298CMV	Southern	R418COO	North West & W	R521UCC	North West & W	R707MHN	North East
R299CMV	Southern	R418HVX	The Shires	R522UCC	North West & W	R708MHN	North East
R29GNW	Yorkshire	R418TJW	Midlands	R524TWR	The Shires	R709MHN	North East
R301PCW	North West & W	R419COO	North West & W	R546ABA	North West & W	R710MHN	North East
R302CVU	North West & W	R419TJW	Midlands	R547ABA	North West & W	R711MHN	North East
R303CMV	Southern	R420COO	North West & W	R548ABA	North West & W	R712MHN	North East
R303CVU	North West & W	R420TJW	Midlands	R549ABA	North West & W	R713MHN	North East
R304CMV	Southern	R421COO	London	R550ABA	North West & W	R714MHN	North East
R304CVU	North West & W	R421TJW	Midlands	R551ABA	North West & W	R715MHN	North East
R305CMV	Southern	R422COO	London	R552ABA	North West & W	R716MHN	North East
R305CVU	North West & W	R422TJW	Midlands	R553ABA	North West & W	R717MHN	North East
R307CMV	Southern	R423COO	London	R554ABA	North West & W	R718MHN	North East
R308CMV	Southern	R423RPY	North East	R556ABA	North West & W	R719MHN	North East
R308CVU	North West & W	R423TJW	Midlands	R557ABA	North West & W	R720MHN	North East
R309CVU	North West & W	R424COO	London	R558ABA	North West & W	R721MHN	North East
R309WVR	North West & W	R424RPY	North East	R559ABA	North West & W	R722MHN	North East
R310CMV	Southern	R424TJW	Midlands	R560ABA	North West & W	R723MHN	North East
R310CVU	North West & W	R425COO	London	R561ABA	North West & W	R724MHN	North East
R310NGM	Southern	R425RPY	North East	R562ABA	North West & W	R725MHN	North East
R310WVR	North West & W	R425TJW	Midlands	R563ABA	North West & W	R758DUB	The Shires
R311CVU	North West & W	R426COO	London	R564ABA	North West & W	R759DUB	The Shires
R311NGM	Southern	R426RPY	North East	R565ABA	North West & W	R760DUB	The Shires
R311WVR	North West & W	R426TJW	Midlands	R566ABA	North West & W	R761DUB	The Shires
R312CVU	North West & W	R427COO	London	R567ABA	North West & W	R762DUB	The Shires
R312NGM	Southern	R427RPY	North East	R568ABA	North West & W	R763DUB	Southern
R312WVR	North West & W	R427TJW	Midlands	R569ABA	North West & W	R764DUB	The Shires
R313CVU	North West & W	R428COO	London	R570ABA	North West & W	R765DUB	Midlands
R313NGM	Southern	R428RPY	North East	R571ABA	North West & W	R766DUB	The Shires
R313WVR	North West & W	R428TJW	Midlands	R601MHN	North West & W	R767DUB	The Shires
R314WVR	North West & W	R429COO	London	R602MHN	North West & W	R768DUB	Midlands
R315WVR	North West & W	R429RPY	North East	R602WMJ	The Shires	R770DUB	Midlands
R317WVR	North West & W	R429TJW	Midlands	R603MHN	North West & W	R785DUB	Midlands
R319WVR	North West & W	R430COO	London	R603WMJ	The Shires	R787DUB	Midlands
R321WVR	North West & W	R430RPY	North East	R604MHN	North West & W	R788DUB	Midlands
R322WVR	North West & W	R431COO	London	R604WMJ	The Shires	R789DUB	Midlands
R324WVR	North West & W	R431RPY	North East	R605WMJ	The Shires	R790DUB	Midlands
R326WVR	North West & W	R432RPY	North East	R606FBU	North West & W	R791DUB	Midlands
R327WVR	North West & W	R433RPY	North East	R606MHN	North West & W	R792DUB	North East
R329TJW	Midlands	R434RPY	North East	R607MHN	North West & W	R792DUB	North East
R329WVR	North West & W	R435RPY	North East	R607WMJ	The Shires	R794DUB	North East
R330TJW	Midlands	R436RPY	North East	R608MHN	North West & W	R795DUB	North East
R330WVR	North West & W	R437RPY	North East	R608WMJ	The Shires	R796DUB	North East
R331TJW	Midlands	R438RPY	North East	R609MHN	North West & W	R798DUB	North East
R331WVR	North West & W	R439RPY	North East	R614MNU	Midlands	R799DUB	North West & W
R332TJW	Midlands	R440GWY	Yorkshire	R615MNU	Midlands	R801YJC	North West & W
R332WVR	North West & W	R440RPY	North East	R616MNU	Midlands	R802YJC	North West & W
R334TJW	Midlands	R441KWT	Yorkshire	R617MNU	Midlands	R803YJC	North West & W
R334WVR	North West & W	R442KWT	Yorkshire	R618MNU	Midlands	R804YJC	North West & W
R335TJW	Midlands	R443KWT	Yorkshire	R619MNU	Midlands	R805YJC	North West & W
R335WVR	North West & W	R445KWT	Yorkshire	R620MNU	Midlands	R807YJC	North West & W
R336TJW	Midlands	R446KWT	Yorkshire	R621MNU	Midlands	R808YJC	North West & W
R336WVR	North West & W	R447KWT	Yorkshire	R622MNU	Midlands	R809YJC	North West & W
R337TJW	Midlands	R447SKX	The Shires	R623MNU	Midlands	R810YJC	North West & W
R337WVR	North West & W	R448KWT	Yorkshire	R624MNU	Midlands	R811TKO	Southern
R338TJW	Midlands	R448SKX	The Shires	R625MNU	Midlands	R811YJC	North West & W
R339TJW	Midlands	R449KWT	Yorkshire	R626MNU	Midlands	R812TKO	Southern
R340TJW	Midlands	R449SKX	The Shires	R627MNU	Midlands	R812YJC	North West & W
R341KGG	North West & W	R44BLU	North West & W	R629MNU	Midlands	R813TKO	Southern
R341TJW	Midlands	R450KWT	Yorkshire	R630MNU	Midlands	R813YJC	North West & W
R342TJW	Midlands	R450SKX	The Shires	R631MNU	Midlands	R814TKO	Southern
R343TJW	Midlands	R451KWT	Yorkshire	R632MNU	Midlands	R814YJC	North West & W
R344KGG	North West & W	R451SKX	The Shires	R633MNU	Midlands	R815YJC	North West & W
R344TJW	Midlands	R452KWT	Yorkshire	R634MNU	Midlands	R816YJC	North West & W
R369TWR	The Shires	R452SKX	The Shires	R636MNU	Midlands	R817YJC	North West & W
R370TWR	The Shires	R453KWT	Yorkshire	R637MNU	Midlands	R818YJC	North West & W

Reg	Location	Reg	Location	Reg	Location	Reg	Location
R819YJC	North West & W	S176JUA	London	S266JUA	London	S358KHN	North East
R821YJC	North West & W	S177JUA	London	S267JUA	London	S426MCC	The Shires
R903BKO	Southern	S178JUA	London	S268JUA	London	S427MCC	The Shires
R904BKO	Southern	S179JUA	London	S269JUA	London	S428MCC	The Shires
R905BKO	Southern	S180JUA	London	S270JUA	London	S429MCC	The Shires
R906BKO	Southern	S181JUA	London	S271JUA	London	S462GUB	Yorkshire
R907BKO	Southern	S182JUA	London	S272JUA	London	S463GUB	Yorkshire
R907JNL	North East	S183JUA	London	S273JUA	London	S464GUB	Yorkshire
R908BKO	Southern	S202JUA	London	S274JUA	London	S465GUB	Yorkshire
R908JNL	North East	S203JUA	London	S275JUA	London	S466GUB	Yorkshire
R909BKO	Southern	S204JUA	London	S276JUA	London	S467GUB	Yorkshire
R909JNL	North East	S205JUA	London	S277JUA	London	S468GUB	Yorkshire
R910BKO	Southern	S206JUA	London	S278JUA	London	S469GUB	Yorkshire
R910JNL	North East	S207DTO	Midlands	S279JUA	London	S470GUB	Yorkshire
R912JNL	North East	S207JUA	London	S280JUA	London	S471GUB	Yorkshire
R913JNL	North East	S208DTO	Midlands	S281JUA	London	S472ANW	Yorkshire
R914JNL	North East	S208JUA	London	S282JUA	London	S473ANW	Yorkshire
R915JNL	North East	S209JUA	London	S283JUA	London	S474ANW	Yorkshire
R916JNL	North East	S210JUA	London	S284JUA	London	S475ANW	Yorkshire
R917JNL	North East	S211JUA	London	S285JUA	London	S476ANW	Yorkshire
R918JNL	North East	S212JUA	London	S286JUA	London	S477ANW	Yorkshire
R919JNL	North East	S213JUA	London	S287JUA	London	S478ANW	Yorkshire
R91GNW	North West & W	S214JUA	London	S288JUA	London	S479ANW	Yorkshire
R920JNL	North East	S215JUA	London	S289JUA	London	S480ANW	Yorkshire
R921JNL	North East	S216JUA	London	S290JUA	London	S481ANW	Yorkshire
R922JNL	North East	S216XPP	The Shires	S291JUA	London	S482ANW	Yorkshire
R923JNL	North East	S217JUA	London	S292JUA	London	S483ANW	Yorkshire
R940VPU	The Shires	S217XPP	The Shires	S301JUA	London	S484ANW	Yorkshire
R941VPU	The Shires	S218JUA	London	S302JUA	London	S485ANW	Yorkshire
R943VPU	The Shires	S219JUA	London	S303JUA	London	S486ANW	Yorkshire
R944VPU	The Shires	S220JUA	London	S304JUA	London	S487ANW	Yorkshire
R945VPU	The Shires	S221JUA	London	S305JUA	London	S488ANW	Yorkshire
R946VPU	The Shires	S223JUA	London	S306JUA	London	S489ANW	Yorkshire
R947VPU	The Shires	S224JUA	London	S307JUA	London	S490ANW	Yorkshire
R948VPU	Southern	S225JUA	London	S308JUA	London	S491ANW	Yorkshire
R949VPU	Southern	S226JUA	London	S309JUA	London	S537KJU	The Shires
R950VPU	Southern	S227JUA	London	S310JUA	London	S558MCC	North West & W
R953VPU	Southern	S228JUA	London	S311JUA	London	S559MCC	North West & W
R962FYS	North West & W	S229JUA	London	S312JUA	London	S610KHN	North West & W
R985FNW	Yorkshire	S230JUA	London	S313JUA	London	S611KHN	North West & W
R989FNW	Yorkshire	S231JUA	London	S314JUA	London	S612KHN	North West & W
RDZ1701	North West & W	S232JUA	London	S315JUA	London	S613KHN	North West & W
RDZ1702	North West & W	S233JUA	London	S316JUA	London	S614KHN	North West & W
RDZ1703	North West & W	S234JUA	London	S317JUA	London	S615KHN	North West & W
RDZ1704	North West & W	S235JUA	London	S318JUA	London	S616KHN	North West & W
RDZ1705	North West & W	S236JUA	London	S322JUA	London	S617KHN	North West & W
RDZ1706	North West & W	S237JUA	London	S341KHN	North East	S618KHN	North West & W
RDZ1707	North West & W	S238JUA	London	S342KHN	North East	S619KHN	North West & W
RDZ1708	North West & W	S239JUA	London	S343KHN	North East	S620KHN	North West & W
RDZ1709	North West & W	S240JUA	London	S344KHN	North East	S621KHN	North West & W
RDZ1710	North West & W	S241JUA	London	S345KHN	North East	S622KHN	North West & W
RDZ1711	North West & W	S242JUA	London	S345YOG	Midlands	S623KHN	North West & W
RDZ1712	North West & W	S243JUA	London	S346KHN	North East	S624KHN	North West & W
RDZ1713	North West & W	S244JUA	London	S346YOG	Midlands	S625KHN	North West & W
RDZ1714	North West & W	S245JUA	London	S347KHN	North East	S626KHN	North West & W
S43BLU	North West & W	S246JUA	London	S347YOG	Midlands	S627KHN	North West & W
S45BLU	North West & W	S247JUA	London	S348KHN	North East	S628KHN	North West & W
S146KNK	The Shires	S248JUA	London	S348YOG	Midlands	S629KHN	North West & W
S147KNK	The Shires	S248UVR	North West & W	S349KHN	North East	S630KHN	North West & W
S148KNK	The Shires	S249JUA	London	S349YOG	Midlands	S631KHN	North West & W
S149KNK	The Shires	S249UVR	North West & W	S350KHN	North East	S632KHN	North West & W
S150KNK	The Shires	S250JUA	London	S350PGA	North East	S633KHN	North West & W
S151KNK	The Shires	S250UVR	North West & W	S350YOG	Midlands	S634KHN	North West & W
S152KNK	The Shires	S251JUA	London	S351KHN	North East	S635KHN	North West & W
S153KNK	The Shires	S251UVR	North West & W	S351PGA	North East	S636KHN	North East
S154KNK	The Shires	S252JUA	London	S351YOG	Midlands	S637KHN	North East
S156KNK	The Shires	S253JUA	London	S352KHN	North East	S644KJU	Midlands
S157KNK	The Shires	S254JUA	London	S352PGA	North East	S645KJU	Midlands
S158KNK	The Shires	S255JUA	London	S352YOG	Midlands	S646KJU	Midlands
S159KNK	The Shires	S256JUA	London	S353KHN	North East	S647KJU	Midlands
S160KNK	The Shires	S257JUA	London	S353PGA	North East	S648KJU	Midlands
S161KNK	The Shires	S258JUA	London	S353YOG	Midlands	S649KJU	Midlands
S169JUA	London	S259JUA	London	S354KHN	North East	S650KJU	Midlands
S170JUA	London	S260JUA	London	S354PGA	North East	S651KJU	Midlands
S171JUA	London	S261JUA	London	S355KHN	North East	S652KJU	Midlands
S172JUA	London	S262JUA	London	S355PGA	North West & W	S653KJU	Midlands
S173JUA	London	S263JUA	London	S356KHN	North East	S701VKM	Southern
S174JUA	London	S264JUA	London	S356KJU	The Shires	S702KFT	North East
S175JUA	London	S265JUA	London	S357KHN	North East	S702VKM	Southern

S703KFT	North East	T47WUT	Midlands	T310FGN	London	T702RCN	North East
S703VKM	Southern	T48WUT	Midlands	T311FGN	London	T820NMJ	Southern
S704KFT	North East	T49JJF	Midlands	T312FGN	London	T821NMJ	Southern
S704VKM	Southern	T51JJF	Midlands	T313FGN	London	T821PNB	North West & W
S705KFT	North East	T52JJF	Midlands	T314FGN	London	T822NMJ	Southern
S705VKM	Southern	T53JJF	Midlands	T314PNB	North West & W	T823NMJ	Southern
S706KFT	North East	T54JJF	Midlands	T315FGN	London	T824NMJ	Southern
S706VKM	Southern	T61JBA	Midlands	T315PNB	North West & W	T825NMJ	Southern
S707KFT	North East	T62JBA	North West & W	T316FGN	London	T826NMJ	Southern
S708KFT	North East	T63JBA	North West & W	T316PNB	North West & W	T827NMJ	The Shires
S709KFT	North East	T64JBA	North West & W	T317FGN	London	T828NMJ	The Shires
S710KFT	North East	T65JBA	North West & W	T317PNB	North West & W	T829NMJ	The Shires
S711KFT	North East	T74AUA	North East	T318FGN	London	T911KKM	Southern
S712KRG	North East	T75AUA	North East	T318PNB	North West & W	T912KKM	Southern
S713KRG	North East	T76AUA	North East	T319FGN	London	T913KKM	Southern
S714KRG	North East	T78AUA	North East	T319PNB	North West & W	T914KKM	Southern
S715KRG	North East	T79AUA	North East	T320FGN	London	T915KKM	Southern
S822MCC	North East	T81AUA	North East	T320PNB	North West & W	T916KKM	Southern
S823MCC	North East	T82AUA	North East	T322FGN	London	T917KKM	North West & W
S824MCC	North West & W	T83AUA	North East	T322PNB	North West & W	T918KKM	Southern
S825MCC	North West & W	T109LKK	Southern	T323FGN	London	T919KKM	Southern
S848RJC	North West & W	T110GGO	London	T323PNB	North West & W	T920KKM	North West & W
S8600GB	Scotland	T110LKK	Southern	T324FGN	London	T921KKM	Southern
S8610GB	Scotland	T202XBV	London	T324PNB	North West & W	T922KKM	North West & W
S8620GB	Scotland	T203XBV	London	T325FGN	London	TIB5903	Southern
S8630GB	Scotland	T204XBV	London	T421GGO	London	TIB5904	Southern
S8640GB	Scotland	T205XBV	London	T490KGB	The Shires	TPD110X	The Shires
S8650GB	Scotland	T206XBV	London	T491KGB	The Shires	TPD116X	North East
S8660GB	Scotland	T207XBV	London	T492KGB	The Shires	TSK270	London
S8670GB	Scotland	T208XBV	London	T493KGB	The Shires	TWY7	Yorkshire
S8680GB	Scotland	T209XBV	London	T494KGB	The Shires	UJI2338	Southern
S872SNB	North West & W	T209XVO	Midlands	T495KGB	The Shires	UOI772	North East
S873SNB	North West & W	T210XBV	London	T526AOB	North West & W	UWW13X	North East
S874SNB	North West & W	T211XBV	London	T527AOB	North West & W	V22BLU	North West & W
S875SNB	North West & W	T212XBV	London	T528AOB	North West & W	V33BLU	North West & W
S876SNB	North West & W	T213XBV	London	T529AOB	North West & W	V34ENC	North West & W
S877SNB	North West & W	T214XBV	London	T557UOX	The Shires	V35ENC	North West & W
S878SNB	North West & W	T215XBV	London	T560JJC	North West & W	V41DJA	North West & W
S879SNB	North West & W	T216XBV	London	T561JJC	North West & W	V142EJR	North East
SB220AL	Yorkshire	T217XBV	London	T562JJC	North West & W	V201KDA	Midlands
SCZ9651	Southern	T218NMJ	Southern	T563JJC	North West & W	V201PCX	Yorkshire
SCZ9652	Southern	T218XBV	London	T564JJC	North West & W	V202KDA	Midlands
SIB4846	The Shires	T219NMJ	The Shires	T565JJC	North West & W	V203KDA	Midlands
SIB7480	The Shires	T219XBV	London	T566JJC	North West & W	V203PCX	Yorkshire
SIB7481	The Shires	T220XBV	London	T567JJC	North West & W	V204KDA	Midlands
SIB8529	The Shires	T222MTB	North West & W	T568JJC	North West & W	V204PCX	Yorkshire
SK52MLE	Midlands	T273JKM	Southern	T569JJC	North West & W	V205KDA	Midlands
SK52MLF	Midlands	T274JKM	Southern	T570JJC	North West & W	V205PCX	Yorkshire
SK52MLJ	Midlands	T275JKM	Southern	T591CGT	Southern	V206DJR	North East
SK52MLL	Midlands	T276JKM	Southern	T592CGT	Southern	V206KDA	Midlands
SK52MLN	Midlands	T277JKM	Southern	T612PNC	North West & W	V206PCX	Yorkshire
SK52MLO	Midlands	T278JKM	Southern	T613PNC	North West & W	V207DJR	North East
SMK675F	London	T279JKM	Southern	T614PNC	North West & W	V207KDA	Midlands
SMK688F	London	T280JKM	Southern	T615PNC	North West & W	V207PCX	Yorkshire
SMK715F	London	T281JKM	Southern	T616PNC	North West & W	V208DJR	North East
SMK730F	London	T282JKM	Southern	T617PNC	North West & W	V208KDA	Midlands
SMK750F	London	T283JKM	Southern	T618PNC	North West & W	V208PCX	Yorkshire
SMK752F	London	T284JKM	Southern	T619PNC	North West & W	V209DJR	North East
SMK753F	London	T285JKM	Southern	T620PNC	North West & W	V209KDA	Midlands
SMK759F	London	T286JKM	Southern	T621PNC	North West & W	V209PCX	Yorkshire
SN03DZY	North West & W	T287JKM	Southern	T622PNC	North West & W	V210DJR	North East
SN03DZZ	North West & W	T288JKM	Southern	T623PNC	North West & W	V210KDA	Midlands
SN03LDV	Midlands	T289JKM	Southern	T624EUB	Yorkshire	V210PCX	Yorkshire
SN03LDX	Midlands	T293FGN	London	T625EUB	Yorkshire	V211DJR	North East
SN03LGC	Midlands	T294FGN	London	T626EUB	Yorkshire	V211KDA	Midlands
SN03LGD	Midlands	T295FGN	London	T627EUB	Yorkshire	V211PCX	Yorkshire
SN03LGE	Midlands	T296FGN	London	T628EUB	Yorkshire	V212DJR	North East
SN03LGF	Midlands	T297FGN	London	T629EUB	Yorkshire	V212KDA	Midlands
SN53ESG	Midlands	T298FGN	London	T630EUB	Yorkshire	V212PCX	Yorkshire
SN53ESO	Midlands	T299FGN	London	T631EUB	Yorkshire	V213DJR	North East
SN54GPK	The Shires	T301FGN	London	T632EUB	Yorkshire	V213KDA	Midlands
SN54GPO	The Shires	T302FGN	London	T633EUB	Yorkshire	V213PCX	Yorkshire
SN54GPU	The Shires	T303FGN	London	T634EUB	Yorkshire	V214DJR	North East
SNV933W	The Shires	T304FGN	London	T635EUB	Yorkshire	V214KDA	Midlands
SVS615	London	T305FGN	London	T636EUB	Yorkshire	V215KDA	Midlands
SVS618	London	T306FGN	London	T637EUB	Yorkshire	V215PCX	Yorkshire
T10BLU	North West & W	T307FGN	London	T638EUB	Yorkshire	V216KDA	Midlands
T11BLU	North West & W	T308FGN	London	T639EUB	Yorkshire	V216PCX	Yorkshire
T42PVM	North West & W	T309FGN	London	T701RCN	North East	V217KDA	Midlands

Reg	Region	Reg	Region	Reg	Region	Reg	Region
V217PCX	Yorkshire	V291HBH	The Shires	V515DFT	North East	V639DVU	North West & W
V218KDA	Midlands	V292HBH	The Shires	V530GDS	North East	V640DVU	North West & W
V218PCX	Yorkshire	V293HBH	The Shires	V531GDS	North East	V640KVH	Yorkshire
V219KDA	Midlands	V294HBH	The Shires	V532GDS	North East	V640LGC	London
V220KDA	Midlands	V326DGT	London	V533GDS	North East	V641DVU	North West & W
V220PCX	Yorkshire	V327DGT	London	V534GDS	North East	V641KVH	Yorkshire
V221KDA	Midlands	V329DGT	London	V535GDS	North East	V642DVU	North West & W
V221PCX	Yorkshire	V330DGT	London	V536GDS	North East	V643DVU	North West & W
V223KDA	Midlands	V331DGT	London	V553ECC	North West & W	V644DVU	North West & W
V223PCX	Yorkshire	V332DGT	London	V554ECC	North West & W	V645DVU	North West & W
V224KDA	Midlands	V334DGT	London	V556ECC	North West & W	V646DVU	North West & W
V224PCX	Yorkshire	V335DGT	London	V557ECC	North West & W	V647DVU	North West & W
V225KDA	Midlands	V336DGT	London	V571DJC	North West & W	V648DVU	North West & W
V225PCX	Yorkshire	V337DGT	London	V572DJC	North West & W	V649DVU	North West & W
V226KDA	Midlands	V338DGT	London	V573DJC	North West & W	V650DVU	North West & W
V226PCX	Yorkshire	V339DGT	London	V574DJC	North West & W	V650LGC	London
V227KDA	Midlands	V341DGT	London	V575DJC	North West & W	V651DVU	North West & W
V227PCX	Yorkshire	V342DGT	London	V576DJC	North West & W	V652DVU	North West & W
V228KDA	Midlands	V343DGT	London	V577DJC	North West & W	V653DVU	North West & W
V228PCX	Yorkshire	V344DGT	London	V578DJC	North West & W	V653LWT	North East
V229KDA	Midlands	V345DGT	London	V579DJC	North West & W	V654DVU	North West & W
V229XUB	Yorkshire	V346DGT	London	V580DJC	North West & W	V655DVU	North West & W
V230HBH	The Shires	V347DGT	London	V580ECC	North West & W	V656DVU	North West & W
V230KDA	Midlands	V348DGT	London	V581DJC	North West & W	V657DVU	North West & W
V231HBH	The Shires	V349DGT	London	V582DJC	North West & W	V658DVU	North West & W
V231KDA	Midlands	V351DGT	London	V583DJC	North West & W	V659DVU	North West & W
V232HBH	The Shires	V352DGT	London	V584DJC	North West & W	V660DVU	North West & W
V232KDA	Midlands	V353DGT	London	V585DJC	North West & W	V660LGC	London
V233HBH	The Shires	V354DGT	London	V586DJC	North West & W	V661DVU	North West & W
V233KDA	Midlands	V355DGT	London	V587DJC	North West & W	V662DVU	North West & W
V234HBH	The Shires	V356DGT	London	V588DJC	North West & W	V663DVU	North West & W
V234KDA	Midlands	V358DGT	London	V590DJC	North West & W	V664DVU	North West & W
V235HBH	The Shires	V359DGT	London	V591DJC	North West & W	V665DVU	North West & W
V235KDA	Midlands	V361DGT	London	V601DBC	Midlands	V667DVU	North West & W
V236HBH	The Shires	V362DGT	London	V601LGC	London	V668DVU	North West & W
V236KDA	Midlands	V363DGT	London	V602DBC	Midlands	V669DVU	North West & W
V237HBH	The Shires	V364DGT	London	V603DBC	Midlands	V670DVU	North West & W
V237KDA	Midlands	V365DGT	London	V604DBC	Midlands	V671DVU	North West & W
V238HBH	The Shires	V404ENC	North West & W	V605DBC	Midlands	V672DVU	North West & W
V238KDA	Midlands	V405ENC	North West & W	V606DBC	Midlands	V673DVU	North West & W
V239HBH	The Shires	V406ENC	North West & W	V607DBC	Midlands	V674DVU	North West & W
V230KDA	Midlands	V407ENC	North West & w	V608DBC	Midlands	V675DVU	North West & W
V250HBH	The Shires	V408ENC	North West & W	V609DBC	Midlands	V676DVU	North West & W
V251HBH	The Shires	V409ENC	North West & W	V609LGC	London	V701LWT	London
V252HBH	The Shires	V410ENC	North West & W	V610DBC	Midlands	V703DNL	North East
V253HBH	The Shires	V411ENC	North West & W	V610LGC	London	V705DNL	North East
V254HBH	The Shires	V412ENC	North West & W	V611DBC	Midlands	V706DNL	North East
V255HBH	The Shires	V413ENC	North West & W	V611LGC	London	V707DNL	North East
V256HBH	The Shires	V414ENC	North West & W	V612DBC	Midlands	V708DNL	North East
V257HBH	The Shires	V415ENC	North West & W	V612DNL	North East	V709DNL	North East
V258HBH	The Shires	V421DGT	London	V612LGC	London	V710DNL	North East
V259HBH	The Shires	V422DGT	London	V613LGC	London	V711DNL	North East
V260HBH	The Shires	V423DGT	London	V614LGC	London	V712DNL	North East
V261HBH	The Shires	V424DGT	London	V615LGC	London	V713DNL	North East
V262HBH	The Shires	V425DGT	London	V616LGC	London	V714DNL	North East
V263HBH	The Shires	V426DGT	London	V617LGC	London	V715DNL	North East
V264HBH	The Shires	V427DGT	London	V618LGC	London	V715LWT	North West & W
V265HBH	The Shires	V428DGT	London	V619LGC	London	V716DNL	North East
V266HBH	The Shires	V429DGT	London	V620LGC	London	V717DNL	North East
V267HBH	The Shires	V430DGT	London	V621LGC	London	V718DNL	North East
V268HBH	The Shires	V431DGT	London	V622LGC	London	V719DNL	North East
V270HBH	The Shires	V432DGT	London	V623LGC	London	V720DNL	North East
V271HBH	The Shires	V433DGT	London	V624DBN	North West & W	V721DNL	North East
V272HBH	The Shires	V434DGT	London	V625DVU	North West & W	V722DNL	North East
V273HBH	The Shires	V435DGT	London	V626DVU	North West & W	V723DNL	North East
V274HBH	The Shires	V501DFT	North East	V627DVU	North West & W	V724DNL	North East
V275HBH	The Shires	V502DFT	North East	V628DVU	North West & W	V725DNL	North East
V276HBH	The Shires	V503DFT	North East	V628LGC	London	V726DNL	North East
V280HBH	The Shires	V504DFT	North East	V629DVU	North West & W	V727DNL	North East
V281HBH	The Shires	V505DFT	North East	V630DVU	North West & W	V728DNL	North East
V282HBH	The Shires	V506DFT	North East	V631DVU	North West & W	V729DNL	North East
V283HBH	The Shires	V507DFT	North East	V632DVU	North West & W	V730DNL	North East
V284HBH	The Shires	V508DFT	North East	V633DVU	North West & W	V731DNL	North East
V285HBH	The Shires	V509DFT	North East	V633LGC	London	V732DNL	North East
V286HBH	The Shires	V510DFT	North East	V634DVU	North West & W	V733DNL	North East
V287HBH	The Shires	V511DFT	North East	V635DVU	North West & W	V734DNL	North East
V288HBH	The Shires	V512DFT	North East	V636DVU	North West & W	V735DNL	North East
V289HBH	The Shires	V513DFT	North East	V637DVU	North West & W	V736DNL	North East
V290HBH	The Shires	V514DFT	North East	V638DVU	North West & W	V737DNL	North East

V738DNL	North East	W243SNR	Midlands	W404VGJ	London	W496YGS	The Shires
V739DNL	North East	W244SNR	Midlands	W407VGJ	London	W497YGS	The Shires
V740DNL	North East	W246SNR	Midlands	W408VGJ	London	W498YGS	The Shires
V741DNL	North East	W247SNR	Midlands	W409VGJ	London	W501RBB	North East
V742DNL	North East	W248SNR	Midlands	W411VGJ	London	W601YKN	Southern
V743ECU	North East	W249SNR	Midlands	W412VGJ	London	W602VGJ	London
V744ECU	North East	W251SNR	Midlands	W413VGJ	London	W602YKN	Southern
V745ECU	North East	W269NFF	North West & W	W414VGJ	London	W603VGJ	London
V746ECU	North East	W292PPT	North East	W421XKX	The Shires	W603YKN	Southern
V747ECU	North East	W293PPT	North East	W422XKX	The Shires	W604VGJ	London
V748ECU	North East	W294PPT	North East	W423XKX	The Shires	W604YKN	Southern
V749ECU	North East	W295PPT	North East	W424XKX	The Shires	W605VGJ	London
V951KAG	North West & W	W296PPT	North East	W425XKX	The Shires	W605YKN	Southern
VLT5	London	W297PPT	North East	W426XKX	The Shires	W606VGJ	London
VLT6	London	W298PPT	North East	W427XKX	The Shires	W607VGJ	London
VLT12	London	W299PPT	North East	W428XKX	The Shires	W608VGJ	London
VLT25	London	W301PPT	North East	W429XKX	The Shires	W651CWX	Yorkshire
VLT27	London	W302PPT	North East	W431WGJ	London	W652CWX	Yorkshire
VLT47	London	W303PPT	North East	W431XKX	The Shires	W653CWX	Yorkshire
VLT85	London	W304PPT	North East	W432WGJ	London	W654CWX	Yorkshire
VLT88	London	W307PPT	North East	W432XKX	The Shires	W656CWX	Yorkshire
VLT173	London	W308PPT	North East	W433WGJ	London	W657CWX	Yorkshire
VLT244	London	W309PPT	North East	W433XKX	The Shires	W658CWX	Yorkshire
VVN202Y	Original SST	W311PPT	North East	W434WGJ	London	W659CWX	Yorkshire
VYJ806	London	W312PPT	North East	W434XKX	Southern	W661CWX	Yorkshire
W12LUE	North West & W	W313PPT	North East	W435WGJ	London	W662CWX	Yorkshire
W69PRG	North East	W314PPT	North East	W435XKX	Southern	W663CWX	Yorkshire
W72PRG	North East	W315PPT	North East	W436WGJ	London	W664CWX	Yorkshire
W76PRG	North East	W317PPT	North East	W436XKX	Southern	W665CWX	Yorkshire
W78PRG	Scotland	W319PPT	North East	W437WGJ	London	W667CWX	Yorkshire
W79PRG	Scotland	W359XKK	The Shires	W437XKX	Southern	W668CWX	Yorkshire
W81PRG	North East	W361XKK	The Shires	W438WGJ	London	W669CWX	Yorkshire
W82PRG	North East	W362XKK	The Shires	W438XKX	Southern	W671CWX	Yorkshire
W83PRG	North East	W363XKK	The Shires	W439XKX	Southern	W672CWX	Yorkshire
W102EWU	Yorkshire	W364XKK	The Shires	W441XKX	Southern	W673CWX	Yorkshire
W103EWU	Yorkshire	W365XKK	The Shires	W442XKX	The Shires	W674CWX	Yorkshire
W104EWU	Yorkshire	W366VGJ	London	W443XKX	The Shires	W751SBR	North East
W106EWU	Yorkshire	W366XKK	The Shires	W445XKX	The Shires	W752SBR	North East
W107EWU	Yorkshire	W367VGJ	London	W446XKX	The Shires	W753SBR	North East
W108EWU	Yorkshire	W367XKK	The Shires	W447XKX	The Shires	W754SBR	North East
W109EWU	Yorkshire	W368VGJ	London	W451XKX	The Shires	W756SBR	North East
W128XRO	The Shires	W368XKK	The Shires	W452XKX	The Shires	W757SBR	North East
W129XRO	The Shires	W369VGJ	London	W453XKX	The Shires	W758SBR	North East
W131XRO	The Shires	W369XKK	The Shires	W454XKX	The Shires	W759SBR	North East
W132XRO	The Shires	W371VGJ	London	W457XKX	The Shires	WIB1113	The Shires
W133XRO	The Shires	W372VGJ	London	W458XKX	The Shires	WJI9072	North West & W
W134XRO	The Shires	W373VGJ	London	W459XKX	The Shires	WJI9074	North West & W
W136VGJ	London	W374VGJ	London	W461XKX	London	WLT348	London
W136XRO	The Shires	W376VGJ	London	W462XKX	London	WLT372	London
W137VGJ	London	W377VGJ	London	W463XKX	London	WLT531	London
W137XRO	The Shires	W378VGJ	London	W464XKX	London	WLT554	London
W138VGJ	London	W379VGJ	London	W465XKX	London	WLT652	London
W138XRO	The Shires	W381VGJ	London	W466XKX	London	WLT719	London
W139XRO	The Shires	W382VGJ	London	W467XKX	London	WLT751	London
W165HBT	Yorkshire	W383VGJ	London	W468XKX	London	WLT808	London
W166HBT	Yorkshire	W384VGJ	London	W469XKX	London	WLT848	London
W174CDN	North West & W	W385VGJ	London	W471XKX	London	WLT871	London
W183CDN	Southern	W386VGJ	London	W472XKX	London	WLT884	London
W191CDN	North West & W	W387VGJ	London	W473XKX	London	WLT888	London
W192CDN	North West & W	W388VGJ	London	W474XKX	London	WLT892	London
W193CDN	North West & W	W389VGJ	London	W475XKX	London	WLT895	London
W194CDN	North West & W	W391VGJ	London	W476XKX	London	WLT897	London
W198CDN	Southern	W392VGJ	London	W477XKX	London	WLT901	London
W218CDN	London	W393VGJ	London	W478XKX	London	WLT909	London
W226SNR	Midlands	W394OJC	North West & W	W479XKX	London	WLT916	The Shires
W227SNR	Midlands	W394VGJ	London	W481XKX	London	WLT954	North East
W228SNR	Midlands	W395RBB	North East	W482YGS	The Shires	WSU475	Scotland
W229SNR	Midlands	W395VGJ	London	W483YGS	The Shires	WSU476	Scotland
W231SNR	Midlands	W396RBB	North East	W484YGS	The Shires	X13LUE	North West & W
W232SNR	Midlands	W396VGJ	London	W485YGS	The Shires	X14LUE	North West & W
W233SNR	Midlands	W397RBB	North East	W486YGS	The Shires	X23BLU	North West & W
W234SNR	Midlands	W397VGJ	London	W487YGS	The Shires	X32KON	North West & W
W235SNR	Midlands	W398RBB	North East	W488YGS	The Shires	X143WNL	North East
W236SNR	Midlands	W398VGJ	London	W489YGS	The Shires	X144WNL	North East
W237SNR	Midlands	W399RBB	North East	W491YGS	The Shires	X201ANC	North West & W
W238SNR	Midlands	W399VGJ	London	W492YGS	The Shires	X202ANC	North West & W
W239SNR	Midlands	W401VGJ	London	W493YGS	The Shires	X203ANC	North West & W
W241SNR	Midlands	W402VGJ	London	W494YGS	The Shires	X204ANC	North West & W
W242SNR	Midlands	W403VGJ	London	W495YGS	The Shires	X207ANC	North West & W

Reg	Area	Reg	Area	Reg	Area	Reg	Area
X208ANC	North West & W	X297MBH	The Shires	X508GGO	London	X956DBT	North West & W
X209ANC	North West & W	X415FGP	London	X519GGO	London	XSV691	North East
X209JOF	North West & W	X416AJA	North West & W	X521GGO	London	XYJ427	London
X211ANC	North West & W	X416FGP	London	X522GGO	London	XYJ440	London
X211JOF	North West & W	X417AJA	North West & W	X523GGO	London	Y20BLU	North West & W
X212ANC	North West & W	X417FGP	London	X524GGO	London	Y21BLU	North West & W
X212JOF	North West & W	X418AJA	North West & W	X526GGO	London	Y22CJW	North West & W
X213ANC	North West & W	X418FGP	London	X527GGO	London	Y32TDA	North West & W
X213JOF	North West & W	X419AJA	North West & W	X529GGO	London	Y36KNB	North West & W
X214ANC	North West & W	X419FGP	London	X531GGO	London	Y36TDA	North West & W
X214JOF	North West & W	X421AJA	North West & W	X532GGO	London	Y37KNB	North West & W
X215ANC	North West & W	X421FGP	London	X533GGO	London	Y37TDA	North West & W
X215JOF	North West & W	X422AJA	North West & W	X534GGO	London	Y38KNB	North West & W
X216ANC	North West & W	X422FGP	London	X536GGO	London	Y38TDA	North West & W
X216JOF	North West & W	X423AJA	North West & W	X537GGO	London	Y39TDA	North West & W
X217ANC	North West & W	X423FGP	London	X538GGO	London	Y42HBT	The Shires
X217JOF	North West & W	X424AJA	North West & W	X541GGO	London	Y42TDA	North West & W
X218ANC	North West & W	X424FGP	London	X546GGO	London	Y46ABA	North West & W
X218JOF	North West & W	X425FGP	London	X646WTN	North East	Y46HBT	The Shires
X219ANC	North West & W	X426AJA	North West & W	X647WTN	North East	Y46TDA	North West & W
X221ANC	North West & W	X426FGP	London	X648WTN	North East	Y47ABA	North West & W
X223ANC	North West & W	X427AJA	North West & W	X649WTN	North East	Y47HBT	The Shires
X224ANC	North West & W	X427FGP	London	X651WTN	North East	Y48ABA	North West & W
X226ANC	North West & W	X428FGP	London	X652WTN	North East	Y48HBT	The Shires
X227ANC	North West & W	X428HJA	North West & W	X653WTN	North East	Y49HBT	The Shires
X228ANC	North West & W	X429FGP	London	X654WTN	North East	Y102TGH	London
X229ANC	North West & W	X429HJA	North West & W	X656WTN	North East	Y184TUK	Midlands
X231ANC	North West & W	X431FGP	London	X657WTN	North East	Y189RJU	Midlands
X232ANC	North West & W	X431HJA	North West & W	X675YUG	Yorkshire	Y207RJU	Midlands
X233ANC	North West & W	X432FGP	London	X676YUG	Yorkshire	Y241KBU	North West & W
X234ANC	North West & W	X432HJA	North West & W	X677YUG	Yorkshire	Y242KBU	North West & W
X235ANC	North West & W	X433FGP	London	X678YUG	Yorkshire	Y243KBU	North West & W
X236ANC	North West & W	X433HJA	North West & W	X679YUG	Yorkshire	Y253YBC	Midlands
X237ANC	North West & W	X434FGP	London	X681YUG	Yorkshire	Y254YBC	Midlands
X238ANC	North West & W	X434HJA	North West & W	X682YUG	Yorkshire	Y256YBC	Midlands
X239ANC	North West & W	X435FGP	London	X683YUG	Yorkshire	Y257YBC	Midlands
X239PGT	London	X435HJA	North West & W	X684YUG	Yorkshire	Y258YBC	Midlands
X241ANC	North West & W	X436FGP	London	X685YUG	Yorkshire	Y259YBC	Midlands
X241PGT	London	X436HJA	North West & W	X686YUG	Yorkshire	Y261YBC	Midlands
X242ANC	North West & W	X437FGP	London	X687YUG	Yorkshire	Y262YBC	Midlands
X242PGT	London	X437HJA	North West & W	X688YUG	Yorkshire	Y263YBC	Midlands
X243HJA	North West & W	X438FGP	London	X691YUG	Yorkshire	Y264YBC	Midlands
X243PGT	London	X438HJA	North West & W	X692YUG	Yorkshire	Y265YBC	Midlands
X244HJA	North West & W	X439FGP	London	X693YUG	Yorkshire	Y266YBC	Midlands
X244PGT	London	X439HJA	North West & W	X694YUG	Yorkshire	Y267YBC	Midlands
X246HJA	North West & W	X441FGP	London	X695YUG	Yorkshire	Y291TKJ	Southern
X246PGT	London	X441HJA	North West & W	X696YUG	Yorkshire	Y292TKJ	Southern
X247HJA	North West & W	X442FGP	London	X701DBT	North West & W	Y293TKJ	Southern
X247PGT	London	X442HJA	North West & W	X702DBT	North West & W	Y294TKJ	Southern
X248HJA	North West & W	X443FGP	London	X703DBT	North West & W	Y295TKJ	Southern
X248PGT	London	X443HJA	North West & W	X704DBT	North West & W	Y296TKJ	Southern
X249HJA	North West & W	X445FGP	London	X705DBT	North West & W	Y297TKJ	Southern
X249PGT	London	X445HJA	North West & W	X706DBT	North West & W	Y298TKJ	Southern
X251HJA	North West & W	X446FGP	London	X707DBT	North West & W	Y299TKJ	Southern
X252HBC	Midlands	X446HJA	North West & W	X708DBT	North West & W	Y301TKJ	Southern
X252HJA	North West & W	X447FGP	London	X709DBT	North West & W	Y302TKJ	Southern
X253HJA	North West & W	X447HJA	North West & W	X781NWX	Midlands	Y303TKJ	Southern
X254HJA	North West & W	X448FGP	London	X782NWX	North West & W	Y346UON	Midlands
X256HJA	North West & W	X448HJA	North West & W	X783NWX	Midlands	Y347UON	Midlands
X257HJA	North West & W	X449FGP	London	X801AJA	North West & W	Y348UON	Midlands
X258HJA	North West & W	X449HJA	North West & W	X802AJA	North West & W	Y349UON	Midlands
X259HJA	North West & W	X451FGP	London	X803AJA	North West & W	Y351UON	Midlands
X261OBN	North West & W	X452FGP	London	X804AJA	North West & W	Y352UON	Midlands
X262OBN	North West & W	X453FGP	London	X805AJA	North West & W	Y353UON	Midlands
X263OBN	North West & W	X454FGP	London	X806AJA	North West & W	Y354UON	Midlands
X264OBN	North West & W	X457FGP	London	X807AJA	North West & W	Y356UON	Midlands
X265OBN	North West & W	X458FGP	London	X808AJA	North West & W	Y357UON	Midlands
X266OBN	North West & W	X459FGP	London	X809AJA	North West & W	Y358UON	Midlands
X267OBN	North West & W	X471GGO	London	X811AJA	North West & W	Y361UON	Midlands
X268OBN	North West & W	X475GGO	London	X812AJA	North West & W	Y362UON	Midlands
X269OBN	North West & W	X478GGO	London	X813AJA	North West & W	Y363UON	Midlands
X271OBN	North West & W	X481GGO	London	X814AJA	North West & W	Y364UON	Midlands
X271RFF	North West & W	X485GGO	London	X815AJA	North West & W	Y365UON	Midlands
X272OBN	North West & W	X501GGO	London	X816AJA	North West & W	Y366UON	Midlands
X272RFF	North West & W	X502GGO	London	X817AJA	North West & W	Y367UON	Midlands
X273RFF	North West & W	X503GGO	London	X818AJA	North West & W	Y451KBU	North West & W
X274RFF	North West & W	X504GGO	London	X819AJA	North West & W	Y451UGC	London
X295MBH	The Shires	X506GGO	London	X821AJA	North West & W	Y452KBU	North West & W
X296MBH	The Shires	X507GGO	London	X822AJA	North West & W	Y452UGC	London

Y453KBU	North West & W	Y496UGC	London	Y686EBR	North East	YD02RJO	Yorkshire
Y454KBU	North West & W	Y497UGC	London	Y687EBR	North East	YG52CFA	Yorkshire
Y457KBU	North West & W	Y498UGC	London	Y688EBR	North East	YG52CFD	Yorkshire
Y457KNF	North West & W	Y499UGC	London	Y689EBR	North East	YG52CFE	Yorkshire
Y458KBU	North West & W	Y501UGC	London	Y691EBR	North East	YG52CFF	Yorkshire
Y458KNF	North West & W	Y502UGC	London	Y692EBR	North East	YG52CFJ	Yorkshire
Y459KBU	North West & W	Y503UGC	London	Y693EBR	North East	YG52CFK	Yorkshire
Y461KNF	North West & W	Y504UGC	London	Y694EBR	North East	YG52CFL	Yorkshire
Y461UGC	London	Y506UGC	London	Y701XJF	Midlands	YG52CFM	Yorkshire
Y462KNF	North West & W	Y507UGC	London	Y702XJF	Midlands	YG52CFN	Yorkshire
Y462UGC	London	Y508UGC	London	Y703XJF	Midlands	YG52CFO	Yorkshire
Y463KNF	North West & W	Y509UGC	London	Y704XJF	Midlands	YG52CFP	Yorkshire
Y463UGC	London	Y511UGC	London	Y705XJF	Midlands	YG52CFU	Yorkshire
Y464KNF	North West & W	Y512UGC	London	Y706XJF	Midlands	YG52CFV	Yorkshire
Y464UGC	London	Y513UGC	London	Y707XJF	Midlands	YG52CFX	Yorkshire
Y465KNF	North West & W	Y514UGC	London	Y709XJF	Midlands	YIB2396	The Shires
Y465UGC	London	Y516UGC	London	Y711KNF	North West & W	YIB2397	The Shires
Y466KNF	North West & W	Y517UGC	London	Y712KNF	North West & W	YJ03PFX	Midlands
Y466UGC	London	Y518UGC	London	Y713KNF	North West & W	YJ04BKF	Midlands
Y467KNF	North West & W	Y519UGC	London	Y714KNF	North West & W	YJ04HJC	Yorkshire
Y467UGC	London	Y521UGC	London	Y715KNF	North West & W	YJ04HJD	Yorkshire
Y468KNF	North West & W	Y522UGC	London	Y716KNF	North West & W	YJ04HJE	Yorkshire
Y468UGC	London	Y523UGC	London	Y717KNF	North West & W	YJ04HJF	Yorkshire
Y469KNF	North West & W	Y524UGC	London	Y718KNF	North West & W	YJ04HJG	Yorkshire
Y469UGC	London	Y526UGC	London	Y719KNF	North West & W	YJ05PVT	Midlands
Y471KNF	North West & W	Y527UGC	London	Y721KNF	North West & W	YJ53VFY	Midlands
Y471UGC	London	Y529UGC	London	Y722KNF	North West & W	YJ54CFG	The Shires
Y472KNF	North West & W	Y531UGC	London	Y723KNF	North West & W	YJ54CKE	Midlands
Y472UGC	London	Y532UGC	London	Y724KNF	North West & W	YJ54CKF	Midlands
Y473KNF	North West & W	Y533UGC	London	Y726KNF	North West & W	YJ54CKG	Scotland
Y473UGC	London	Y538VFF	North West & W	Y727KNF	North West & W	YJ54CKK	Scotland
Y474UGC	London	Y539VFF	North West & W	Y728KNF	North West & W	YJ54CPE	Midlands
Y475KNF	North West & W	Y541UGC	London	Y729KNF	North West & W	YJ54CPF	Midlands
Y475UGC	London	Y541UJC	North West & W	Y733KNF	North West & W	YK05CAA	North West & W
Y476UGC	London	Y542UGC	London	Y744KNF	North West & W	YK05CAE	North West & W
Y477UGC	London	Y542UJC	North West & W	Y801DGT	London	YMB512W	North West & W
Y478UGC	London	Y543UGC	London	Y802DGT	London	YN04LXF	The Shires
Y479UGC	London	Y543UJC	North West & W	Y803DGT	London	YN04LXG	The Shires
Y481UGC	London	Y544UGC	London	Y804DGT	London	YN04LXH	The Shires
Y482UGC	London	Y544UJC	North West & W	Y805DGT	London	YN04XZH	North West & W
Y483UGC	London	Y546UGC	London	Y806DGT	London	YN53ELU	Southern
Y484UGC	London	Y546UJC	North West & W	YD02PXW	Yorkshire	YP52JWO	North West & W
Y485UGC	London	Y547UGC	London	YD02PXX	Yorkshire	YP52JWU	North West & W
Y486UGC	London	Y547UJC	North West & W	YD02PXY	Yorkshire	YP52JWW	North West & W
Y487UGC	London	Y548UGC	London	YD02PXZ	Yorkshire	YS02UBX	The Shires
Y488UGC	London	Y548UJC	North West & W	YD02PYU	Yorkshire	YS02UBY	The Shires
Y489UGC	London	Y549UGC	London	YD02PYV	Yorkshire	YSU870	North East
Y491UGC	London	Y549UJC	North West & W	YD02PYW	Yorkshire	YSU871	North East
Y492UGC	London	Y551UJC	North West & W	YD02PYX	Yorkshire		
Y493UGC	London	Y552UJC	North West & W	YD02PYY	Yorkshire		
Y494UGC	London	Y581UGC	London	YD02PYZ	Yorkshire		
Y495UGC	London	Y685EBR	North East	YD02RJJ	Yorkshire		

ISBN 1 904875 25 4

© Published by *British Bus Publishing Ltd*, September 2005
British Bus Publishing Ltd, 16 St Margaret's Drive, Wellington, Telford, TF1 3PH
Telephone: 01952 255669 - Facsimile: 01952 222397

www.britishbuspublishing.co.uk E-mail address: bill@britishbuspublishing.co.uk